HERE'S A LETTER FROM THY DEAR SON

MERCER UNIVERSITY PRESS

Endowed by
TOM WATSON BROWN
and
THE WATSON-BROWN FOUNDATION, INC.

HERE'S A LETTER FROM

THY DEAR SON

*Letters of a Georgia Family During the
Civil War Era*

Edward H. Pulliam, editor

MERCER UNIVERSITY PRESS
Macon, Georgia

MUP/ H1040

© 2024 by Mercer University Press
Published by Mercer University Press
1501 Mercer University Drive
Macon, Georgia 31207
All rights reserved

28 27 26 25 24   5 4 3 2 1

Books published by Mercer University Press are printed on acid-free paper that meets the requirements of the American National Standard for Information Sciences—Permanence of Paper for Printed Library Materials.

Printed and bound in Canada.

This book is set in Adobe Caslon.

Cover/jacket design by Burt&Burt.

ISBN   978-0-88146-911-0
Cataloging-in-Publication Data is available from the Library of Congress

To Lily Alexander Jackson
Olivia Comer Brockmann
Margaret Comer Cavin
Allie Comer Gaither
James Thomas Comer, Jr.
And especially to
Helen Comer Pulliam

They preserved the past.

"Indeed I tremble for my country when I reflect that God is just: that His justice cannot sleep for ever...."
—Thomas Jefferson on Slavery, *Notes on the State of Virginia*, Query XVIII, 1787.

Brian Lamb, "From what you know now and your own political philosophy, if you had a choice and you lived back there [in the South during the Civil War], which side would you have been on?"

Shelby Foote, Civil War historian: "There's absolutely no doubt about it. I'm from Mississippi. I would have been on the Confederate side—right or wrong. I would have fought with my people."
—Brian Lamb Interview with Shelby Foote, C-SPAN Book TV, July 30, 1994 (Rebroadcast on June 1, 2013)

"Come up from the fields father, here's a letter from thy Pete,
And come to the front door mother, here's a letter from thy dear son."
—Walt Whitman, from *Drum-Taps*

Contents

List of Illustrations ix
Genealogical Charts x
Preface xiii

Part 1: Antebellum

1. Simeon David and David Family, 1847–1855	2
2. Pillona White David and Manning Poole Alexander, 1853–1857	37
3. Owen Thomas David, 1855–1859	49
4. Simeon Advances: Simeon David and Francis Harris David, 1855–1859	56
5. Medical School: Pillona Alexander and Manning Poole Alexander, 1858–1859	72
6. War Approaches, June 1859–January 1861	92

Part 2: Civil War

7. Simeon Volunteers, 1861	117
8. Homefront, 1861	124
9. Manning Raises a Company, 1861	131
10. Thomas Goes to Richmond, 1861–1862	136
11. Horatio's First Letters Home, 1862	145
12. Simeon's First Battles, 1861–1862	157
13. Manning Enlists, 1862	180
14. Homefront, 1862–Early 1863	216
15. Simeon and Horatio at Fredericksburg, December 1862–March 1863	224
16. Homefront: Fire, Early 1863	240
17. Horatio David and James Neal at Fredericksburg, 1863	249
18. Chancellorsville: Simeon and Horatio, 1863	261
19. A Hospital and a Journey: Horatio and Thirza, 1863	274
20. Mississippi: Manning, 1863	296
21. Gettysburg: Simeon, May–July 1863	327
22. Homefront, Late 1863–Early 1864	339
23. Manning Returns to the Army, Late 1863–Spring 1864	342
24. Simeon and Horatio Continue the Fight, Early–Middle 1864	363

25. A Wagon Journey: Thirza and Fanny, Mid-July 1864	404
26. Manning Reassigned: Manning and Pillona, Early 1864	408
27. Horatio's Last Battle, July–August 1864	418
28. Manning to Augusta, July–November 1864	431
29. Horatio and Fanny Recovering, January–March 1865	448
30. Sherman Leaves Savannah: Manning and Pillona, January–March 1865	453
31. The War Ends: Manning, Pillona, and Horatio, April–May 1865	468

Part 3: After the War

32. Manning and Pillona, 1865–1880	477
33. Horatio, 1867–1883	505
34. Thirza, James, and Annie David, 1876–1884	512
35. Horatio's Last Years, 1885–1923	519
36. Manning and Pillona, 1881–1915	526
37. Fanny Harris David, 1873	544

Acknowledgments 549
Bibliography 551
Index 579

Illustrations

James and Thirza David
Manning Alexander
Pillona Alexander
Simeon David in his militia uniform
Owen Thomas David
Simeon David in his Confederate uniform
Horatio J. David in his Confederate uniform
Manning Alexander in his Confederate uniform
Manning and Pillona Alexander's family
Robert and Margaret Alexander
Manning's amputation saw
A picnic gathering
Detail from a picnic gathering
Alexander family home
Woman, possibly Emma Savell
Margie Alexander
Older Manning Alexander in his Confederate uniform
Letter from Simeon dated May 9, 1863

Genealogical Charts

Bowen Family Tree
As of 1861
Owen Jones Bowen
(1764–1828)
married 1786
Nancy Ann Jones Bowen
(1762–1848)

Thomas Jones Bowen	Horatio Owen Bowen	Perry Bowen	Hiram Bowen	Thirza Bowen
(1788–1854)	(1792–1860)	(1797–)	(1798–)	(1803–)
m	m	m	m	m
Nancy Yarbrough	Mary Hill	Mary Cox	Charity Blackwell	James H. David
Horatio Yarbrough	Thomas Owen	Reuben Hunter	Amanda	*See David Tree*
Agelina	Abner	Hiram Cox	Owen "Dock"	
Clementina	James Horatio	Malachi "Mac"	Thomas Lindsay	
Elmira	Francis Marion	William Aris	Thirza Ann	
Lavinia	Sarah "Sallie"	Owen	Perry	
Caleb Perry	John Hunter	Teresa Ann	William	
Jonathan Jones		Rhoda Ann	Jesse James	
Andrew Jackson			Nancy Califenny	
			John Hunter	
			Mary Ann Palina	

x

David Family Tree

As of 1861
James Horatio David
(1799)
Married July 31, 1823
Thirza Bowen David
(1803)

Mary Juliette (1826) m Richard Neal	Simeon Bowen (1829) m Frances "Fanny" Harris	Pillina Charity (1831) m Middleton Raymond Bell	Thirza Ann (1833)
James Richard (1843) John Wesley (1845) Ann Olivia (1847) Jesse Horatio (1850)	Eleanora "Ellen" (1856) Thirza Lena (1857) Sarah "Sallie" (1860)	Oscar (1851) Ellen (1854) Walter (1857) William (1859)	

Owen Thomas (1835) m Sue Moon	Pillona "Lona" White (1839) m Manning Poole Alexander *See Alexander Tree*	Horatio James (1842)

xi

Alexander Family Tree

As of 1861
Robert W. Alexander
(1800)
Married c. 1826
Margaret C. Poole
(1806)

William P.	Manning Poole	Samuel H.	Adam O.
(1827)	(1830)	(1832)	(1835)
m	m	m	m
Lou E. Sewell	Pillona White David	Mary E. Gillespie	Susanna Burkhalter
Henry C. (1857)	Nora Linna (1859)		Margaret (1860)
Mary Henrietta (1859)			

James David	Henry C.	Robert C.	John N.
(1839)	(1842–1846)	(1845)	(1848)

xii

Preface

On the night of July 8, 1853, Simeon David sat down to write a letter to his mother. He was twenty-four years old and only recently had become the male head of an extended family of eight—his newly widowed older sister, Mary (age twenty-six), her four small children, one of his own younger sisters, a younger brother, and himself.[1]

Along with Mary, he was responsible for taking care of the small farm in rural Cherokee County, Georgia, that Mary had inherited from her deceased husband. At the same time, he was running the local school. He wrote his mother proudly that they had "the finest crop in the neighborhood" of corn and wheat and that he had taught sixty young "Scholars" in his school, including his niece, nephews, younger sister, and younger brother. He also had prepared for one of his friends the complicated papers for the installment sale of 360 acres.

Simeon clearly was pleased with what he had done so far and confident he could do even more in the future. At the end of his letter, he wrote his mother, "Give my love to all inquiring friends & tell them Simeon's ambition is to be a credit to the 'Day & generation in which he lives.'"

Before long, the thoughts of two other young members of the David family also turned to their futures. Tom, the younger brother who earlier lived with Simeon and Mary, was much less sure than his older brother of what his future would be. At nineteen in 1855 he wrote a friend, "I am at a great a loss to know what I will do next year…I think there is as much probability of my staing [sic] here as anywhere….What I will do and where I will go I have no idea."[2]

A sister also was thinking about her future though in a slightly different way from her older brothers. She had become attracted to the friend to whom her brother Tom had written, and he had become equally attracted to her. They had begun to exchange letters with increasing familiarity.

On March 25, 1856, when she was only sixteen and he was almost twenty-six, she wrote, reminding him of a neighbor's prospective wedding they had talked about when he last visited her and mentioning that the wedding had taken place. So, she continued, had several other local weddings, including one in which, she noted, the wife had been twenty years old and the husband forty.[3]

Although certain, or uncertain, of what they wanted in the future, all three young people believed they would have much control over what that future would be. What they did not know, and did not even imagine, was that waiting for them

---

[1] Simeon Bowen to Mother, July 8, 1853, chapter 1.
[2] O. T. David to friend, August 30, 1855, chapter 3.
[3] Pillona David to Dr. Alexander, March 25, 1856, chapter 2.

only a few years ahead was the wholly life-altering series of events that would affect them and everyone else in their family, and in all of America: the Civil War.

Before the war was over, the young men in the family would serve in the Confederate army. Not all, however, would return home at the war's end. The women of the family stayed home, but there they would face their own challenges. In the following letters, all will tell you themselves what they experienced.

Background

Home

Most of the letters were directed to a farm in rural Georgia, the home of James Horatio David and Thirza Bowen David, the parents of the three young people and the home of their brother and three sisters. For many years it was the center of all their lives.

In 1847, when the letters began, the Davids' farm consisted of approximately one thousand acres of trees, red clay, fields, and fences in North Georgia's Jackson County. It was located, as the crow flies, about sixty miles northeast of Atlanta and about four miles northwest of Maysville, then a hamlet of only a couple of stores, with a post office in one of them.[4]

Early Area History

Years earlier, this part of Georgia had been the land of the Creeks and the Cherokees, yet before the American Revolution, in 1763 and 1773, the Georgia colonial government had entered into treaties with these tribes. Under the treaties, Georgia acquired land along the South Carolina line north and east from what would become Jackson County to accommodate the demands of land speculators and new settlers moving south into Georgia from Pennsylvania, Virginia, and North and South Carolina.[5]

Although the fighting and general turmoil of the Revolution slowed the southern movement of settlers seeking land, after the war that movement regained its momentum and increased. David Hackett Fischer and James C. Kelly in *Away, I'm Bound Away* quote a French visitor to America in 1788: "The active genius of the Americans is always pushing them forward.... After they have spent some time on any piece of land, they move on to another where they hope to do better.... Apparently for Americans a migration to a place several hundred miles away is no more serious than moving from one house to another...."[6]

---

[4] Federal Agricultural Census, Jackson County, Georgia, 1850; Gary, Adams, and staff of *Jackson Herald, Our Time and Place*, 2–15; Elrod, *Historical Notes*, 115.

[5] Coleman, *History of Georgia*, 48–49, 100.

[6] Ibid., 92; Fischer and Kelly, *Away, I'm Bound Away*, 65.

At the southern boundary of that movement was Georgia, and despite the earlier treaties, much of the land the movers might occupy there still belonged to Indians. In 1782, the Cherokees ceded to Georgia land on the fringe of their territory that would become Franklin County (which included territory that later became Jackson County, home of the Davids). A year later, in 1783, a small group of Creeks ceded to Georgia the same land. To Georgians and prospective immigrants, these treaties legally opened up these lands for settlement.[7]

The great majority of the Creeks, however, had not reached an agreement with Georgia about that land and denied the treaties were valid. The following year Indians murdered settlers in the disputed lands, forcing Georgia to activate the militia to protect the new settlers. Throughout the 1780s, Indian attacks on settlers continued. In November 1787 alone, it was reported to Georgia authorities that in the past three months, thirty-one settlers had been killed by Indians and the town and courthouse at Greensboro, Georgia, had been destroyed. Finally, in 1790, the new United States government was able to negotiate an agreement with the disaffected Creeks under which they recognized the cessions of land made in 1783.[8]

This agreement encouraged a new wave of settlers to move into the ceded lands even though it did not completely stop small groups of Indians from harassing and killing settlers there. As a result, the settlers and the governments of South Carolina and Georgia established a series of blockhouses or forts in the ceded lands to which the settlers could come for protection in time of Indian trouble.[9]

Jones and Bowen Families

One of those new settlers was the maternal grandfather of Thirza Bowen David, Malachi Jones III. From a Welsh family, one of whose members had been the first pastor of Abington Presbyterian Church in Abington, Pennsylvania, he had moved from Pennsylvania to the Spartanburg, South Carolina, area before the Revolutionary War. There he joined the 6th South Carolina Infantry Regiment and served as a private for almost four years during the war, from March 1776 to February 1780, very likely participating in a number of the battles fought by that unit.[10]

---

[7] Coleman, *History of Georgia*, 92–93; Coleman, *American Revolution in Georgia*, 238–40; Lane, *Georgia*, 49.

[8] Coleman, *American Revolution in Georgia*, 240–52.

[9] Gary, Adams, and staff of *Jackson Herald*, *Our Time and Place*, 1-6, 1-7; Lane, *Georgia*, 49, 54–65; "Map of the Defensive Plan of the Western Frontier Franklin County 1793," in Acker, *Deeds of Franklin County, Georgia*, 558–59.

[10] Baggs, ed., *History of Abington Presbyterian Church*, 14–16; Severance, "Notes on the Ancestry and Descendants of Horatio Jones," 521–24; Egle, *Proprietary Tax Lists of the County*

Thirza David's future father was Malachi's nephew, Owen Jones Bowen. He was born in Chester County, Pennsylvania, in 1764, one of eight children of Malachi's sister.[11]

When he was in his early twenties, Owen left home and followed his uncle Malachi to Spartanburg. Here about 1886, he married Malachi's daughter, his own first cousin, Nancy Ann Jones. Here also, in 1788, their first child, Thomas Jones Bowen, was born.[12]

Moving on in the tradition of Americans mentioned by the Frenchman quoted earlier, Malachi's son, also named Malachi, was not content to stay in South Carolina with his father. Instead, in the late 1780s, he moved into the risky, Indian-threatened lands of Franklin County, Georgia. Once again following a relative, Owen soon moved to Georgia.[13]

Although by the 1790s most of the Creeks and Cherokees had signed treaties transferring their land to Georgia, some still roamed North Georgia in small bands, looting and killing settlers. A deposition signed in December 1792 by the new settler Owen Bowen gives some indication of the dangers in the country where he and Malachi had chosen to live:

> Owen Bowen of the County of Franklin planter being duly sworn saith that on Thursday Evening last being the twenty ninth when he passed by the house of one Mrs. Crocket a Widow woman in the said County where he saw the said Widow, and advised her to move away into the Fort in the neighborhood as two Indians had been on that Day seen in the Settlement. That the said Mrs. Crocket replied she would move as soon as her son came home. That the next morning the deponent went to the same house, and there he saw the said Mrs. Crocket, together with her son a young man, three young women and three children the youngest about six years old all lying dead, scalped and cruelly mangled & that from every appearance the said murders were committed by Indians by Cherokees as the deponent believes. The deponent further

---

of Chester, 437, 625; "Compiled Service records of Soldiers Who Served in the American Army during the Revolutionary War, 1775–1783," M881, RG 93, roll 0886, vol. 9, pg. 170, NARA; Pruitt, *Abstracts of South Carolina*, 37.

[11] Humphrey, *Pennsylvania Births*, 223, 225; Baggs, ed., *History of Abington Presbyterian Church*, 16; Linn and Egle, eds., *Pennsylvania Marriages*, 363; Martin, *Wills of Chester County*, 39; "Bowen Bible Records," 36.

[12] Martin, *Wills of Chester County*, 39; "Bowen Bible Records," 36, 39; US Census, 1850, Thomas J. Bowen, Jackson County, Georgia; deed from Owen J. Bowen to his son, Thomas J. Bowen, November 21, 1814, Deeds of Jackson County, Georgia, Book F, 10; Pruitt, *Spartanburg County/District South Carolina Deed Abstracts*, 73.

[13] G. G. Smith, *Story of Georgia*, 583; Bowen, Deposition.

saith that there were two War Clubs lying by the dead Bodies and several Arrows sticking in them. This deponent further saith not.[14]

The following year, Owen received a commission as captain of a volunteer troop of horse in the Franklin County militia, whose duty was to guard the settlers from Indian attacks. Apparently, he was an effective soldier because in November some inhabitants of Franklin County complained to the governor of Georgia about the removal of his troop from the frontier. As a result of their complaint, Owen's troop of horses remained until the end of 1794. He was called into service with the dragoons also in 1796 and 1797 to deal with further Indian alarms.[15]

During some of this period, Owen's wife, Nancy Ann Jones Bowen, may have stayed in South Carolina, or at least traveled there for the birth of the couple's second child, another boy, in 1792. In 1796, their third son was born, this time in Jackson County, which had been created out of part of Franklin County that same year. Two years later, in 1798, Owen acquired two tracts of land in Jackson County totaling 862 acres adjoining Shoals Creek, a tributary of the Oconee River, and began farming there. That same year the couple's fourth boy was born.[16]

On June 20, 1803, at their home in Jackson County, the Bowen's first and only daughter, Thirza Bowen, the future addressee of many of these family letters, was born.[17]

David Family

Meanwhile, Isaac David, grandfather of Thirza's future husband James David, moved to Georgia in 1789. He came from Virginia, probably Buckingham County, accompanied by his wife and several children, including their thirteen-year-old daughter, Pillina White David, James's future mother and Thirza's future mother-in-law.[18]

The Davids were descended from a family of Huguenots, French Protestants who fled France for fear of persecution in that predominantly

---

[14] Gary, Adams, and staff of *Jackson Herald, Our Time and Place*, 1-6, 1-7; Lane, *Georgia*, 49, 54–65; Acker, *Deeds of Franklin County, Georgia*, 558–59; Bowen, Deposition.

[15] Kratovil, *Georgia Governors' Journals*, 87, 334; Hays, ed., *Georgia Military Record Book, 1779–1839*, 73; Hays, ed., *Georgia Military Affairs*, 2.1:134, 201; Hays, ed., *Georgia Military Affairs*, 2.2:227, 342a.

[16] Headstones, Clinton United Methodist Church Cemetery, Clinton, Georgia, and Magnolia Plantation Cemetery, Thomas County, Georgia; US Census, 1850, Jones County, Georgia, and Carroll County, Georgia; *Thomasville Weekly*, April 30, 1862; Elrod, *Historical Notes*, 30. Jackson County Deed Book A, 141–43.

[17] David Family Bible; US Census, 1850, Jackson County, Georgia.

[18] Davidson, ed., *Records of Elbert County, Georgia*, 151; Will of Isaac David, Madison County, Georgia, Will Book A, pages 113–14; P. David, genealogical notes.

Catholic country. First, the Davids had gone to England. Then in the early 1700s, they immigrated to a Huguenot colony in Virginia, about twenty miles up the James River from Richmond.[19]

Over several generations, the ancestors of the Georgia Davids moved west in Virginia and married into the English White family. Then Isaac David came south to Georgia.

Isaac was the first David to come to Georgia, but as with Malachi Jones and Owen Bowen in South Carolina, he was followed to Georgia by his nephew Henry David. While living with his uncle's family in this new place, the nephew Henry (again like Owen Bowen earlier) became attracted to his first cousin, Pillina David. On January 10, 1801, Henry and Pillina were married. Henry was twenty years old, and Pillina was twenty-four.[20]

Unlike the Bowens, however, almost seventeen months before Henry and Pillina were married, Pillina gave birth to their first child. He was James Horatio David, Thirza Bowen's future husband.[21]

It is not now clear why the David's marriage followed rather than preceded the birth of their first child. Possibly one or more of Henry or Pillina's parents disapproved of their relationship until a marriage became, in their eyes and perhaps in the eyes of their community, necessary. In the backcountry at this time, however, sexual relations before marriage appeared to be more usual than unusual. A preacher who traveled to the similar Carolina backcountry around this time reported that "94 percent of the brides whom he married in the past year were pregnant on their wedding day."[22]

Whatever the circumstances, this sequence of events did not appear to damage Henry and Pillina's life together. They remained married for forty-five years, until Henry died in 1845. Together they had eleven children.[23]

---

[19] "David Journal," vol. 1, no. 1, 6–7, no. 2, 9–10, no. 3, 2–4; Tinling, *Correspondence of the Three William Byrds*, 184–85; Brock, Documents Chiefly Unpublished Relating to the Huguenot Emigration to Virginia, 77, 97, 106.

[20] Davidson, ed., *Records of Elbert County, Georgia*, 151. Isaac and Peter III were brothers ("David Journal," vol. 1, no. 2, 5; Dorman, "Henry County, Virginia, Will Book I," 181). Isaac married Mildred "Milly" White, and Peter married Mary Elizabeth White (Milly and Mary were sisters). Isaac and Milly had a daughter, Perlina or Pillina (name spelled variously), and Peter and Mary had a son, Henry (Boatman, ed., "Henry White of Buckingham County, Virginia"). Henry and Pillina were married on January 10, 1801. That date and their birth dates are in P. David, genealogical notes.

[21] P. David, genealogical notes.

[22] R. Morgan, *Boone*, 25–26.

[23] P. David, genealogical notes.

PREFACE

In 1804, Henry's uncle Isaac conveyed to Henry 150 acres in Franklin County. The new David family became property owners and began to farm their own land. Slowly they acquired more property in the county.[24]

James H. David and Thirza Bowen

On December 26, 1822, when James was twenty years old, Henry deeded to him 150 acres in Franklin County, the same 150 acres Henry's father had deeded to him. The property was near the border with Jackson County. It also was near where Owen Bowen had his farm and where his daughter Thirza lived.[25]

How Thirza Bowen and James David met is not known for certain, but it may have been at church. In 1810, Owen Bowen was one of four men to whom was deeded on behalf of "the Baptist Church of Candler's Creek" a little over three acres. His home was a mile or less from this site of the future church, about a fifteen-minute horse or wagon ride.[26]

Undoubtedly Owen played an active role in the church, and, when Thirza was seventeen, she became a church member. Very likely even earlier she frequently had attended services and social events at the church.[27]

Young James David, the new owner of property not far from the church, may also have attended church services and social events at Candler's Creek Baptist and may have met Thirza there. In addition to his religious reasons for attending services, he may have attended church gatherings because they were some of the main events in county social life.

However they met, they were married in Jackson County in July 1823, about six months after James became the new owner of his Franklin County property. He was twenty-three and she was twenty.[28]

The Letter Writers and Others in 1847

James H. and Thirza David

In March 1847, when the first of the letters was written, James and Thirza David were forty-seven and forty-four years old and had been married for twenty-four years. They lived on a farm of some one thousand acres on the border of Jackson and Franklin Counties. Of those thousand acres, only 280 were listed in

---

[24] Acker, *Deeds of Franklin County, Georgia*, 183; Poss, *Jackson County, Georgia*, 4; Federal Agricultural Census, Jackson County, Subdivision No. 45, 1850, property of James H. David.

[25] Acker, *Deeds of Franklin County, Georgia*, 435; Owen Bowen from various sellers: Jackson County Deed Books A, 141–43; D, 124; E, 85; I–J, 348; G, 378.

[26] Archibald York to Owen J. Bowen, Ambrose Yarborough, John Hammons, and John Moore for Candlers Creek Baptist Church, Jackson County Deed Book E, 564.

[27] Obituary of Thirza Bowen David, *Jackson Herald*, June 10, 1876.

[28] David Family Bible.

the federal agricultural census of 1850 as "improved." On those improved acres they grew a variety of crops, principally corn, sweet potatoes, and wheat. Their farm also produced wool, pork, butter, and honey.[29]

James, a successful farmer, was a respected member of the community. He had been a Jackson County justice of the peace in 1829. In 1836 he had been one of a volunteer corps of mounted men who were "to be ready at the call of the Governor [of Georgia] to march against the Cherokee in case of difficulties with that tribe." Two years later, the last of the Cherokees were forcibly removed from Georgia. He also was an officer in the Candler's Creek Baptist church.[30]

Thirza, before her marriage, had attended school in Clinton, Georgia, where she lived with her older brother, Horatio, a doctor and farmer. After her marriage, she taught school in Jackson County, riding to her school on horseback. According to family legend, she was at that time the only woman in that part of the county capable of teaching, and she was said to be "very strong physically." She also took special interest in the education and moral training of her own children. It is apparent from the letters that she was the emotional center of the David family.[31]

When the first letter was written in March 1847, James and Thirza's seven children, all of whom wrote or were mentioned in the letters, were as follows:[32]

Mary Juliette David. Known as Mary, she was the oldest David child. In 1847, she was twenty-one years old. She had married Richard Neal five years earlier, just before her sixteenth birthday. The Neals lived in Freemanville, Cherokee County, Georgia, with their two children. A third child would be born shortly after the first letter in the collection was written.

Simeon Bowen David. Known as Simeon or Sim, he was eighteen years old and red-headed. When he wrote to his mother the first letter in the collection, he was living on his own at least part of the year while teaching school in Cherokee County, Georgia. He later became, as will be seen, a member of the Georgia legislature during its important sessions of 1859 and 1860 and still later a captain and company commander in the Confederate army.

---

[29] Ibid.; Federal Agricultural Census, Jackson County, Subdivision No. 45, 1850, property of James H. David.

[30] Elrod, *Historical Notes*, 67, 92–9; Obituary of James David, *Forest News*, March 16, 1878; Coleman, *History of Georgia*, 133–34.

[31] Boone, "Facts gathered by Mrs. G. P. Boone concerning *Mrs. Thirza David*"; Horatio Bowen to his sister, Thirza, August 11, 1857, in chapter 4.

[32] Information concerning the David children is based on the David Family Bible and the letters in the book.

Pillina Charity David. Known as Lina, she was almost sixteen years old and living at home when the first letter was written. Soon she would leave home to be married.

Thirza Ann David. Known as Ann or Annie, she was fourteen years old and living at home in March 1847. She had a twin sister, unnamed, who died at birth. She was the only one of the David children who did not write a letter, at least not one that has survived.

Owen Thomas David. Known as Tom or Toma, he was ten years old and living at home. He would serve as a lieutenant in the Confederate army.

Pillona White David. Called Lona, she was eight years old and living at home. She was the young woman mentioned earlier who wrote to her older male friend. She would be the author of a number of letters in this collection.

Horatio James David. Called Ratio or Rashe, at four years old he was the youngest David child. As will be seen, he later joined his older brother Tom's Confederate regiment as a private.

Davids' Enslaved African Americans.[33] According to the federal Slave Schedule for 1850, the Davids owned ten enslaved African Americans who worked in the fields and about the house. They were a man thirty-eight years old; a woman twenty-nine; four boys aged nineteen, ten, eight, and eight months; and four girls aged fifteen, six, four, and two. The schedule did not list names of enslaved people, but from the letters it appears that the man was Ben; the woman Cinda; three of the boys were Simon, Henry, and Dyse; and probably one the girls was Harriet. Although they would have been a constant presence on the farm, they were mentioned infrequently in the letters.

Manning Poole Alexander. Manning, also known as Elie and MP, was the friend to whom Pillona wrote reminding him about the local weddings. He and Pillona later would marry, and he would be the author of a number of the letters in this collection.

The Alexanders were Scotch-Irish. They came from Ireland to South Carolina, possibly first to the Camden area, as early as 1737.[34]

One hundred years later, in 1839, Robert Alexander, grandson of the first Alexander in America and father of Manning, moved his family from South Carolina to Carnesville, Franklin County, Georgia. Manning was then nine years old.[35]

---

[33] US Census, 1850, Slave Schedule, Jackson County, Georgia, and various letters in the book.

[34] Kirkland and Kennedy, *Historic Camden*, 67–68.

[35] V. Alexander, Elliott, and White, *Pendleton District*, 10; *Michael McGee, applicant, vs. Jane Alexander, Elizabeth Alexander others, defendants,* consent of defendants made a matter of record, Anderson District, South Carolina, Court of Ordinary, August 20, 1849; Lily Alexander Jackson, genealogical notes; letter from Nora Alexander Boone, daughter of Manning

In March 1847, when the first letter in the collection was written, Manning was sixteen years old. He did not enter the life of the David family until several years later. Even later, he would serve as the assistant surgeon of a Confederate regiment.

The Letters

Most of the letters in this book were written to James and Thirza David by members of their family. James and Thirza then gave them to one of their daughters, Pillona David Alexander, who had lived with them during the Civil War and remained living close to them after the war.

Pillona combined those letters with letters she and her husband, Manning Poole Alexander, had exchanged. She passed the collected letters to her youngest daughter, Lily Alexander Jackson, who was their daughter most interested in family history.

Mrs. Jackson had no children. Upon her death, her will specified that the letters go to the five surviving children of an older sister, Margie Alexander Comer. Helen Comer Pulliam, one of those five children, gathered the letters from the other four before her death and gave them to me, her son.

At some time, about a fifth of the original letters that were passed down from Pillona were lost. Those missing letters, however, were transcribed, and the transcriptions notarized in the late 1940s by one of the five Comer children, Olivia Comer Brockmann, and her husband, Charles Brockmann. Charles later co-authored a history of Charlotte, North Carolina.[36] These transcriptions are included in this book.

In making the transcriptions, the Brockmanns corrected the spelling and punctuation of the letters, as can be discovered by a comparison of the transcriptions with the surviving original letters by the same writers. The letters in this book are the corrected transcriptions with little attempt to return them to the original spelling and punctuation.

Also included in the book is another group of original letters donated to Hargrett Library at the University of Georgia by Thirza McDonald Brooks, a granddaughter of one of the Davids' sons, Horatio James David.[37]

Additional letters were discovered in various places. Part of one was discovered online on eBay, part of another that had been printed in an auction catalogue was found at Fredericksburg-Wilderness Battlefield Park by Donald Pfanz and

---

Poole Alexander, October 25, 1946, in my possession; Chaplin, *Riches of Bunyan* (Alexander family copy).

[36] See title page, Blythe and Brockmann, *Hornets' Nest*.
[37] H. David, David Family Papers.

passed on to me, and another was found at Carlisle Barracks, Carlisle, Pennsylvania. A copy of yet another was donated to me by Todd Dorsey of Maysville, Georgia.

As indicated in an old auction catalogue, a few other letters written by the family had survived and been sold, but unfortunately, I have been unable to locate them. Possibly in the future, these letters can be located and added to this volume.

Editorial Method

The following is a story told primarily through letters. Occasionally, relevant newspaper articles, service records, and other documents are added to expand that story.

After each letter or other document are notes that explain unusual terms, identify persons, or clarify difficult passages in the letter. Some notes provide context for material in the letter or otherwise expand upon information in it. Notes also fill in gaps between letters.

Generally, if a person is mentioned only once, that person is not identified in the notes. In addition, not all of the people mentioned in the letters could be identified. The unidentified people, however, likely were friends, fellow soldiers, or in some instances, relatives.

The literacy of the letter writers varied widely. Generally, the misspellings, punctuation, capitalization, and grammar in the letters have been retained in order to give additional insight into the letter writer. Several writers, however, did not use periods or any other form of punctuation to show the end of a sentence. In these cases, at least where it was clear where a sentence ended, I inserted a period for ease of reading.

In addition, in many cases a writer, probably to conserve paper, wrote long discourses covering multiple subjects without using any paragraph breaks. Sometimes an entire letter was written without breaks for paragraphs. To facilitate easier reading, I have divided the letter into paragraphs.

When words obviously were omitted, I have added them and placed brackets around them. Also, when a letter was undated, I inserted a date based on the contents of the letter and on other relevant information and placed the date in brackets.

The Story

The following is the story of the David family as told by their letters and other contemporary documents. In the first letter, the David's oldest son Simeon has left home to begin to make his way in a larger world and is writing home to his mother.

These are real letters, and these were real people.

James and Thirza David, circa 1861.
Courtesy Edward H. Pulliam

Manning Alexander's wedding photograph, 1857.
Courtesy Edward H. Pulliam

Pillona David Alexander's wedding photograph, 1857.
Courtesy Edward H. Pulliam

Simeon David in his militia uniform, 1853.
Courtesy National Park Service, Gettysburg National Military Park

Owen Thomas David, 1861.
Courtesy Edward H. Pulliam

Simeon David in his Confederate uniform, 1861.
Courtesy David Hopper

Horatio J. David in his Confederate uniform, 1861.
Courtesy Library of Congress

Manning Alexander in his Confederate uniform
the day he learned of General Lee's surrender, 1865.
Courtesy Edward H. Pulliam

Manning and Pillona Alexander's family, 1868.
Nora Alexander (standing); Pillona Alexander (seated left)
with Margie Alexander; Manning Alexander (seated right).
Courtesy Edward H. Pulliam

Robert and Margaret (Poole) Alexander, 1861.
Courtesy Edward H. Pulliam

Manning Alexander's saw used in amputations during the war.
Courtesy Edward H. Pulliam

A picnic gathering, possibly a church group, at an unknown location, circa 1872. Manning Alexander (seated far right on stool); Nora Alexander (seated far right on the ground in white dress); Margie Alexander (seated farthest right in black and white dress). All others are unidentified.

Courtesy Edward H. Pulliam

Detail from the picnic photograph, circa 1872.
Courtesy Edward H. Pulliam

Alexander family home in Maysville, Georgia, circa 1883.
Left to right: two unidentified men, possibly the apprentice Emma Savell, Manning Alexander, Pillona Alexander, Lilly Alexander, Mamie Alexander, and Margie Alexander.

Courtesy Edward H. Pulliam

Detail showing woman, possible Emma Savell,
from the Alexander family home photograph, circa 1883.
Courtesy Edward H. Pulliam

Margie Alexander Comer, 1886.
Courtesy Edward H. Pulliam

Manning Alexander in his Confederate uniform, circa 1920.
Courtesy Edward H. Pulliam

Camp 14th Ga Reg't Near Hamilton's
Crossing Va May 9th 1863

My Dear Parents

I embrace the present opportunity of writing to inform you that we have just passed through another battle and through the mercy of God my life has been again spared. Last Saturday Sunday & Monday the Confederates gained one of the greatest victories of this war. We left our camp on Wednesday the 28th of April and marched to a position near Fredericksburg & remained there till Friday morning when it was ascertained that Hooker was trying to flank us on our left about ten miles up the Rappahannock at a place called Chancellorville. Our Brigade took position in line of battle Friday evening about sun set and remained the till about 12 O'clock Saturday when we were remarched out and commenced one of Jackson's world renowned flank movements that has shed so much luster upon our arms. We marched a distance of 12 o 15 miles and gained a position in the enemy's rear about 10 O'clock Saturday night.

First page of a letter from Simeon David dated May 9, 1863, telling of the Battle of Chancellorsville.

Courtesy Edward H. Pulliam

PART 1

ANTEBELLUM

Chapter 1

Simeon David and David Family, 1847–1855

1847

Simeon

Geo. Cherokee county
March 2nd, '47
Dear Mother

    As I promised in the letter I wrote Sister to address you one before long, I have now taken my seat to comply with that promise. I am enjoying very good health with the exception of a severe cold, which I attribute to the changeable weather. There is one case of fever and ague in our neighborhood, though it is not imputed to any local cause. The health of the neighborhood is tolerably good.

    I am very happy to inform you that my school last week was better than it has been before. I had from twenty to twenty-five scholars every day, nearly all girls. I believe that my school will be better all the summer than during the cold weather. Several of my subscribers have small children to send all through the summer who sent none through the winter.

    It would delight you to be at our school-house, Mother, to see twenty-six little girls between the ages of five and thirteen studying their lessons so attentively, and when recess or playtime is announced, of all the merry glee I ever saw they certainly have it. I am learning almost as fast now as when I went to school myself, especially in Grammar and Arithmetic. As I have previously stated, I am very much pleased with school-teaching.

    I was very much pleased indeed to learn that Sister was making arrangements to come home with me when I visit Jackson. Mrs. McAfee and Julia say she must be sure to board with them when she comes.

    I am very thankful to you for the pants sent me by Mr. Neal, though I shall not need them before I come home, if indeed I need them at all. I have worn my brown pants to school every day since I came out here until last week. I expect to wear them some time yet. I have only worn my Kentucky jeans pants one week, and those two pair will last me until June. I have worn my old coat almost every day, and it looks almost as well as when I left home.

    On last Saturday week I visited Sister Mary's (accompanied by Mr. Rasin Bell, who is a whole-souled fellow). I heard the news from modern Palestine, as Green and I call it. I was sorry to hear from you that you had considerable indisposition in the family, though I hope you are all better by this time. Write me immediately after the reception of this that I may know your present condition.

It appears that a great revolution has taken place since I left there. I was both astonished and delighted when I heard that the Red man of the west had gone back to Jackson and built his wigwam. Tell them all the harm I wish them is that they may remain there until I come and will have some fun, for I have got to be an adept in paddling a bateau. Tell the boys not to become smitten with any of the female Indians.

You know it is impossible for me to write home without writing something to Sister Pillina. I will come to close by requesting you to present my love to Grandmother, Father, and the children, the negroes, and all enquiring friends. Receive for yourself the highest esteem and filial love of Your unworthy son,
S. B. David

Most affectionate Sister

Believing as I do that you have some lonesome moments in consequence of my not being there to aggravate you as I was wont to do, I will address you a few lines. In the first place, let me entreat you to be cautious how you labor or you will injure your constitution, for busy as Father is now, he could not have time to stop and dig your tomb.

I tell you yesterday and day before reminded me of old Jackson. It was the last of our singing. On Saturday evening, one other gentleman and myself enjoyed the pleasure of rowing four young ladies half a mile up the pond in the bateau. Sister Pillina, I wish you were here to enjoy it with us. It is splendid fun. We also had the pleasure of escorting them to a temperance lecture at night, where I was very strongly solicited to address the meeting but declined from several causes. On yesterday evening we had a fine crowd to dine with us, among the number the amiable Miss Elizabeth Boring, who as I informed you in my first letter is a chip of the old block.

If this letter is not delayed you will receive it on Friday next, and if Saturday is a good day, I expect to go to Canton with a singing firm. So you may expect that I am there and enjoying myself pretty well. Don't think that I am spending too much of my time bateau riding for it is not the case.

My friends inform me that I am still becoming more popular as a teacher. They express a belief that we'll have fifty scholars after crops are lain by. I am still boarding at Meanses, and am as well pleased as ever. Two months more providence permitting, I'll be home. Write me soon. I subscribe myself,
Very respectfully,
S. B. David

Notes

Simeon David: Simeon had turned eighteen only a month before he wrote this letter.[1]

Thirza Bowen David: Thirza David was Simeon's mother. When Simeon wrote to her, she was forty-three years old and had been married to Simeon's father James Horatio David for twenty-three years. She and her husband were living on a farm in the northwest corner of Jackson County near Maysville, Georgia, the farm where Simeon had been brought up.[2]

Pillina David: Pillina was one of Simeon's sisters. She was living at home with her parents and would be sixteen years old the month after the letter was written.[3]

Cherokee County: Cherokee County now is on the edge of suburban Atlanta, adjoining the city to the north. In 1847, Atlanta was a small town with a population of four hundred, and only that year had changed its name from Marthasville to Atlanta. It was not yet the capital of Georgia (it would not become the state capital until 1868); however, it had good growth potential as the terminus of three rail lines.[4]

The Georgia legislature had established Cherokee County in December 1831, about sixteen years before the letter was written. Then the land still was Cherokee Indian Territory and the location of many Cherokee businesses, farms, and towns. Ultimately, the Cherokees were removed from the territory in the march known as the Trail of Tears, which began in 1838.[5]

The land surface is irregular, hillier in the north where there are a few wooded peaks and flatter in the south where the land was more regularly cultivated. Numerous streams and creeks flow through it, along with the winding Etowa River and its tributaries.[6]

White settlers had begun moving into the Cherokee lands even before the county was established and before the Cherokees were removed. That movement was greatly increased with the discovery of gold at nearby Dahlonega in 1829. The Cherokees' removal, however, and a land lottery the same year sparked a further increase in settlement from outside. Most of the new settlers were of English, Irish, Scottish, Dutch, or German ancestry, and they came from North and South Carolina or from more established Georgia counties, like Franklin and

---

[1] David Family Bible.

[2] Ibid.; Federal Agricultural Census, Jackson County, Subdivision No. 45, 1850.

[3] David Family Bible.

[4] *Georgia Atlas & Gazetteer*, 20; Hepburn, *Georgia History Book*, 71–72; Coleman, *History of Georgia*, 158–59; 208–209.

[5] R. Johnston, *Cherokee County, Georgia*, 10–11, 21–31; Marlin, *History of Cherokee County*, 58–60.

[6] R. Johnston, *Cherokee County, Georgia*, 11–12, 18, 19; Marlin, *History of Cherokee County*, 2, 4.

Jackson. Most became farmers located in the flatter southern part of the county that was well watered by creeks and streams. Their main crop was corn, followed by oats, sweet potatoes, and cotton.[7]

Cherokee County's population in 1834 was 1,342, but by 1840 it had quadrupled to 5,895; by 1850 it had more than doubled to 12,800. It had become a desirable place to live. People came to take advantage of its opportunities—good land for starting farms, improved roads for transportation of goods to market, and growing communities. By 1847, the county contained a nucleus of established families who had built homes of hand-hewn logs, founded churches, constructed flour mills, erected a courthouse, built bridges, and gathered together in villages and communities that contained general stores, churches, and post offices. The village of Etowa, later Canton, of dirt streets and wooden buildings located in the center of the most thickly settled part of the county, had been designated the county seat in 1833. Woodstock had been established as a small community perhaps as early as 1825 and by 1833 had its own post office. Academies to educate the children of the more prosperous citizens were established in Canton, Woodstock, and Hickory Flat. Schools, however, were needed for the now stable farmers and merchants of more modest means.[8]

ague: "An intermittent fever and chills; a fever early thought to be a disease rather than a symptom of one."[9]

Sister: When Simeon wrote "sister" in the first part of the letter, he meant his sister Pillina.

the neighborhood: Simeon does not say in what part of Cherokee County he was living. Judging by the census records for some of the other residents of the county whom he mentions in the letter, he was living in the fifteenth land district or division, which was in the southern middle part of the county around and including Woodstock.[10]

my school: In 1847 there was no effective public education system in Georgia. The Georgia constitution of 1777 provided for the establishment of schools in each county at state expense, but the state failed to vote funds to implement this program. In 1822, the state placed $500,000 in a fund to establish free schools for poor children, but it was distributed in such a manner as to have only limited

---

[7] Marlin, *History of Cherokee County*, 14, 17–18, 39–40, 48, 129; Baldwin and Thomas, *New and Complete Gazetteer*, 225; Coleman, *History of Georgia*, 132.

[8] Marlin, *History of Cherokee County*, 45–46, 48, 57, 103–104; 106; Baldwin and Thomas, *New and Complete Gazetteer*, 226; R. Johnston, *Cherokee County, Georgia*, 19, 25–26, 33–34, 36–47; Cherokee County Historical Society, *Glimpses of Cherokee County*, 45.

[9] Drake, *What Did They Mean by That?*, 5.

[10] Marlin, *History of Cherokee County*, 22, 29–30; US Census, 1850, Cherokee County, Georgia.

effect. As a result, parents who wanted to educate their children had to pay for it themselves.[11]

Well-to-do parents established academies where one or more comparatively well-educated teachers taught pupils in a generally well-made building—all paid for by the parents. Most education, however, was provided in schools known as "field schools," or "tuition" or "subscription" schools. In these schools, students usually were taught by one teacher in a log schoolhouse covered with clapboard that frequently was located in the corner of an old field. It contained the roughest of furniture—log benches to sit on and plank desks for writing.[12]

Generally, the schools were organized annually. A prospective teacher would solicit parents to agree to send their child or children to school and pay for their instruction. If enough parents agreed, the teacher would establish a school. Simeon's school was one of the "field schools." He was paid by pupil, for the days the pupil attended school.[13]

There is no indication that Simeon attended a college or an academy. He probably was educated by his mother, who had stayed with an older brother to attend schools in Eatonton and Clinton, Georgia, where schools were thought to be better than those available in her home in Jackson County. She also taught school herself in Jackson County for several years after she married.[14]

Mrs. McAfee and Julia: Julia may have been Mrs. McAfee's daughter, and Julia and Mrs. McAfee may have been related to Dr. John Miller McAfee, a prosperous doctor, plantation owner, and state senator who lived in the area of Woodstock, Cherokee County.[15]

Mr. Neal: He was Simeon's brother-in-law, Richard Neal, who had married Simeon's oldest sister, Mary Juliette David.[16]

Sister Mary: She is Simeon's oldest sister Mary Juliette David Neal, then twenty years old. She had married Richard Neal five years earlier when she was fifteen and he was twenty.[17]

Raisin Bell: He probably was Rayson Perry Bell, who then was then about nineteen years old.[18]

modern Palestine: Simeon is referring to his parents' home in Jackson County.

---

[11] Coleman, *History of Georgia*, 121; Hepburn, *Georgia History Book*, 151.
[12] H. P. Bell, *Men and Things*, 14–15; Marlin, *History of Cherokee County*, 159–62.
[13] Marlin, *History of Cherokee County*, 161–62.
[14] Boone, "Facts gathered by Mrs. G. P. Boone concerning *Mrs. Thirza David*."
[15] R. Johnston, *Cherokee County, Georgia*, 37.
[16] David Family Bible.
[17] Ibid.; US Census, 1850, Cherokee County, Georgia.
[18] US Census, 1850, Cherokee County, Georgia; US Census, 1870, Acworth, Cobb County, Georgia; grave marker, Wilson Chapel Cemetery, Kaufman County, Texas.

Green: He probably was John Green Lindsay, who in 1853 married one of Simeon's cousins Teresa Ann Bowen. When this letter was written, he was seventeen years old.[19]

bateau: "A lightweight, flat-bottomed riverboat with tapering ends...."[20]

Grandmother: Simeon is referring to the older Pillina David, mother of James H. David. When this letter was written, she was seventy years old.[21]

the children: Simeon was referring to his younger brothers Thomas, age eleven, and Horatio, age four, and his younger sisters, Ann, age thirteen, and Pillona, age seven.[22]

negroes: In the 1850 slave schedule for Jackson County, part of the decennial federal census, Simeon's father is listed as owning ten enslaved people from the ages of thirty-eight years to eight months.

The first person listed was a thirty-eight-year-old man, who was followed immediately by a twenty-nine-year-old woman. They were followed in the listing by eight children: four males, aged nineteen, eleven, eight, and eight months, and four females aged fifteen, six, four, and two.

The schedule lists neither the first or last names of enslaved people. All ten, however, seem to have been one family although at least one of the oldest two children probably was not the child of the older couple.

most affectionate Sister: This addressee was Pillina Charity David.

temperance lecture: The temperance movement regarded alcoholic beverages as harmful to the individual and to society. "Supposedly, drink destroyed families and reputations and brought about poverty, disorder, and crime," one historian explains. At first temperance followers urged people to sign pledges not to drink. Gradually they also became a political movement whose purpose was to enact laws limiting or eliminating the sale of alcoholic beverages.[23]

Miss Elizabeth Boring: She was then twenty years old. In 1850, she married Willis Ballard.[24]

Meanses: A Samuel Means was said to be one of the earliest settlers of Cherokee County.[25]

---

[19] Grave marker, Magnolia Plantation Cemetery, Thomasville, Thomas County, Georgia; marriage was April 4, 1853 (*Jackson County Marriage Book ABC, 1805–1861*, 379).

[20] "Bateau," *Webster's New World College Dictionary*, 123.

[21] US Census, 1850, Jackson County, Georgia; P. David, genealogical notes.

[22] David Family Bible.

[23] Fahey, "Temperance Movement."

[24] Grave marker, Elizabeth Boring Ballard, Ebenezer Methodist Cemetery, Snead, Blount County, Alabama.

[25] Marlin, *History of Cherokee County*, 36–37.

1848

Hall County Boys

Hall Co. Nov. 1848
Mr. Simeon David.
Dear Sir:

    As Christmas is drawing near and we being desirous to have some fun, wish to know if you could project a plan by which we could meet and participate in social enjoyment? If you can propose a plan by which we can meet and associate in, we will attend with the utmost of pleasure, as we think we could enjoy ourselves in the presence of youngsters of Jackson Co. the Ladies especially.

    Our reason for writing is that we generally have a very dull time through Christmas, because there are scarcely any young men and Ladies in this section to associate with. Please inform if you think there is any probability or not of the assemblage. Direct your letter to Clark Thompson, Gainesville, Geo.

    We remain Very respectfully your obedient servants

W. R. Thompson
E. A. Clark
H. J. Thompson
W. I Striblin
O. B. Thompson
A. P. Cowan
A. H. Clark

Notes

Hall County: Hall County adjoined Jackson County to the west.[26]
Gainesville: Gainesville was then and continues to be the county seat of Hall County.[27]

Simeon's Poem

November 12, 1848
Untitled Poem
by Simeon David

    I came to a place where a lone pilgrim lay,
        And pensively stood by his tomb,
    And in a low whisper I heard someone say,
        How sweetly I sleep there below.

---

[26] *Georgia Atlas & Gazetteer*, 21–22.
[27] Dorsey, *History of Hall County*, 12, 16.

The tempest may howl and the loud thunder roar,
    And gathering storms may arise,
Yet calm are my feelings at peace in my soul,
    The tears are all wiped from my eyes.

The cause of my master propelled me from here,
    I bade my companions farewell,
I kissed my dear children who for me now mourn,
    In a far distant region they dwell.

I wandered an alien, a stranger from God,
    No kindred or relative nigh.
I met the contagion, I sunk to the grave,
    My soul fled to mansions on high.

Go tell my companions and children most dear,
    To weep not for me who am gone.
The same hand that led me through scenes most severe,
    Has kindly assisted me home.

Go tell my companions to trust in the Lord,
    To raise up my children for God,
And give my dear children a tender farewell.
    I hope we shall soon meet above.

Written by S. B. David this November 12, 1848.

1850

Simeon

Cherokee Co. Georgia
February 18—'50
Dear Mother

    Since tea this evening Mr. Reed and myself have walked up to the schoolhouse for the purpose of writing some letters on business and to friends. Firstly, I will offer an apology for writing on foolscap paper, that our letter paper is just out, and I conclude as you were anxious to hear from us that I would avail myself of the opportunity.

To relieve you of farther suspense we arrived at home without any accident whatever. On Friday the roads were very bad indeed. We only reached Brown's Ferry, where we got lodging for the night and were hospitably entertained and moderately charged. We left there quite soon and reached Mr. Bell's by Sunday. Yet we passed near Sister Mary's but we had not time to call.

I would have been glad for you to witness the cordial reception with which Sister was received. The Doct was much pleased, as well as myself. He had several professional calls on Saturday night, but deferred paying them until Sunday morning. After breakfast Doct. was compelled to visit some patients, and when Sirus and myself left, Sister was alone except for Mr. Bell's family.

When I bade her goodbye, she looked quite sad and came very near shedding tears. I was very sorry to leave her, but Sirus was anxious to get home and would stay no longer, though I think she will very soon enjoy herself finely. Give yourself no uneasiness about her. I will see her frequently and use every effort within my power to render her comfortable and happy.

I rode with her several miles on Saturday, and she told me to be as I had ever been, not to withhold anything from her now that she was married but to make her my confident as I had ever done. If you receive this letter before next Saturday night, you may think of us all at Mr. Croft's, as Sister and Doct. expect to visit us and go to preaching to Noonday on Sabbath.

Mr. Neal came down and spent the night with us and says that Sister and the children are all well. I sent the portion of cake you gave me to her.

Thomas Croft and William Deal have not reached yet, consequently I have not heard from Uncle William.

In consequence of the rain and snow this morning, our school was quite small today. My school for the year is so near made up that I shall stay here this year.

It is growing late and I have nothing more of particular importance to write. I will come to a close by asking you to write after the reception of this letter and also to pass by all mistakes, as I will not have time to look over and correct it. Whenever you go to Athens, present my best respects to our worthy friend Miss Adaline Sisson. Give my respects to Father, Grandmother, and all the children. Tell Ben I will try to do as he advised me the best I can for myself. Give my love to all the negroes. Accept, dear Mother, the love, veneration, and esteem of

Your red-headed son, S. B. David

Notes

Mr. Reed: He has not been identified, but he probably was a teaching colleague of Simeon's.

foolscap: A sheet of paper approximately thirteen by sixteen or seventeen inches. Foolscap was larger than the stationery Simeon normally used, which was eight by nine and a half inches.[28]

we: Simeon is referring to his sister Pillina and to himself.

Brown's Ferry: This ferry may have been located near where today Brown's Bridge Road (State Road 369) crosses the Chattahoochee River southwest of Gainesville. A bridge was constructed across the river in that location around 1840, but from time to time it was washed out. Possibly a ferry ran from the same place in periods when the bridge was unusable.[29]

Possibly Simeon is referring to Bond's Ferry, which crossed the Chattahoochee River in the lower southeast corner of Hall County as early as 1836. The original of this letter from Simeon is missing, so the accuracy of its transcription cannot be checked.[30]

Sister: Refers to Pillina David. She and Dr. Middleton Raymond Bell were married on February 13, 1850, probably in Jackson County, only five days before this letter was written. She then was eighteen years old.[31]

Doct: Dr. Middleton Raymond Bell lived in Cherokee County, where the newly married couple also would live at the beginning of their marriage. He probably was the brother of Simeon's friend, Rayson Bell. In 1850, M. R. Bell was twenty-five years old.[32]

Sirus was anxious to get home: Sirus was probably Cyrus Dial, then about twenty years old. The Dial family was one of the early families in Woodstock in Cherokee County. Simeon may have been boarding with the Dial family while in the county in 1850.[33]

Noonday: This probably is a reference to a Baptist Church located near Noonday Creek in the Woodstock area. It appears that Simeon attended church there and sang in the choir.[34]

---

[28] "Foolscap," *Webster's New World College Dictionary*, 563; Drake, *What Did They Mean by That?*, 124.

[29] Bramblett, *Forsyth County History Stories*, 45–46; Dorsey, *History of Hall County*, 7, 363; P. Jones, *Annotated Abstracts*, 292, 634.

[30] Dorsey, *History of Hall County*, 362.

[31] David Family Bible.

[32] US Census, 1850, Cherokee County, Georgia; family tree for William Milton Bell, Jr., Ancestry.com.

[33] US Census, 1860, Cherokee County, Georgia; Simeon to parents, November 6, 1850; R. Johnston, *Cherokee County, Georgia*, 38; later letters from Simeon and Pillina.

[34] *Georgia Atlas & Gazetteer*, 20; Letters from Simeon of August 19, 1850, and November 6, 1850.

Uncle William: William David, brother of Simeon's father, James H. David.[35]

Miss Adaline Sisson: Miss Sisson, who lived in Athens, was then eighteen years old.[36]

Ben: Based on subsequent letters, he may have been the thirty-nine-year-old enslaved man held by the David family who was mentioned in a note under the first letter in this collection.

Simeon

Woodstock
August 19th 1850
Dear Mother

I this evening take my seat for the purpose of complying with a promise that I requested Sister to make in her's of last week. My health is quite good at this time and has been for some time except a verry bad cold that I had a few days after Hickory Flat Camp meeting. I feel verry much fatigued this Evening in consequence of a verry long ride on yesterday evening from the Holbrook Camp meeting on the line of Forsythe & Cherokee and in consequence of a great many Scholars to attend to day.

Permit me to boast a little of my fine School. We had on to day 62 Scholars & on last Tuesday we had 65. It would afford you a great deal of pleasure to be here and see my fine School. Ours is a small house & we have the seats arranged like they are at Church several rows across the house. We have from forty to fifty young men and Boys & about twenty day Scholars which is that much extra. I charge 5 cts per day for them and all that are coming now are the children of those who are wealthy[,] consequently my School is now worth between forty five and fifty Dollars per month or from $2.50cts to $2.75cts per day. This I consider verry fair business for a man of my education.

I [have] some half Doz studying Grammer and Geography; ten or fifteen studying Arithmetick and all the rest in the spelling Book. Since the commencement of the School there has been about 100 different Scholars in the School; if they were all to conclude to come at the same time we would have a formidable host sure enough. But notwithstanding all that[,] I am becoming somewhat tired of teaching. I think it quite probable that I shall follow some more active ocupation another year.

---

[35] Letter from P. C. Bell of July 4, 1859, which mentions "Uncle William David"; US Census, 1860, Milton County, Georgia.

[36] US Census, 1850, Athens, Clarke County, Georgia.

I saw Sister & Dr yesterday Evening as I returned home out visiting and found them well. Sister informed me that she had from twenty five to thirty Students daily last week She seems to be well pleased with her new vocation

On last Friday night I went up to Mr Neal's and found them all well except little John who seemed to have something like Cholera Morbus though not dangerously ill. Sister Mary is in quite feeble health as she has never done her house work alone since the birth of her Son. Mr. Neal has erected a Factory and Kiln and has commenced making wares. He thinks [he] can make considerable at it.

I had the pleasure of seeing our venerable old County man Mr Bacon at the camp meeting and hear him say "Yes Yes God send it".

As I am writing entirely by fire light and it is getting late I will stop for to night.
Tuesday morning August 20

I resume my seat this morning to finish writing this letter.

Mr Neal was at Atlanta last week at the fair and saw Cousin Amanda & Thomas Bowen from Carrolls. They were well and Uncle Hiram's Family were all well.

I am verry glad to hear that you are preparing to celebrate the 1st Anniversary of Hurricane Shoals Division in a proper manner. I regretted verry much [not] to get a Banner and have it presented to our Division at our Anniversary. We had a most excellent dinner and every thing passed off finely. If I had time I would give you a detailed account of the proceedings; but a passing notice must suffice. The concourse of persons in attendance were estimated at 2500 but it exceeded that. The Stand was made verry large and beautifully decorated with evergreens and flowers; it was large enough to hold the Speakers the Officers of the G. D. the marshals the Chaplains the Roswell Brass Band and last but not least the Noonday Choir of which I had the honor of being a member.

The Choir consisted of only 9 persons who some say performed their part admirably. At one Oclock the vast assemblage marched to the table to demolish 200 lbs of Pound Cake 100 lbs sweet cakes besides Bread of every quality and kind and meat of every description. Let me tell you how the table was arranged; there was two tables standing close together about 50 feet long upon which the provisions was placed, all around these tables were three ranges of seats upon which the crowd were seated and the viands carried to them by about 50 attendants who were detailed to wait on the table. Every thing passed of finely and the most violent appetites were well pleased.

Mr. Gober told me it was your desire that I live at home next year. It is my intention at present to do so.

I have not written half of what I would like to write but my paper has given out and it is time I was gone to School. Give my respects and love to the Family & all inquiring friends

Your Affectionate Son
Mrs Thirza David   S. B. David
                    [On the back]
Woodstock Ga August 20
Mrs Thirza David
Maysville Jackson Co
            Georgia

Notes

Woodstock: Woodstock is in the south center of Cherokee County. It was once surrounded by excellent agricultural land and located only a few miles from the Kellogg gold mine, all of which contributed to a successful economy. In 1850 it was an unincorporated community but had been the location of a post office since 1833.[37]

Hickory Flat Camp meeting: Hickory Flat is about eight miles northeast of Woodstock. It is one of the oldest communities in Cherokee County and once was considered for the site of the county seat.[38]

Holbrook Camp meeting: The Holbrook camp meeting was established in 1838 and is still active today. In the past, religious services were held by both Baptist and Methodist ministers. The camp meeting was and is located in the corner of Cherokee County near its present-day border with Forsyth and Fulton counties.[39]

Camp meetings: Rev. Lloyd G. Marlin writing in *The History of Cherokee County* describes camp meetings as follows:

> At each camp-ground there was a large, shingle-roofed shed where services were conducted several times a day, and this shed, or "stand," was surrounded on all four sides by a row of small, roughly-constructed [wooden] houses called "tents." When camp-meeting time came around, the owners of the "tents" would move in for the period of the meeting, usually a week; bringing with them a supply of bedding and a generous quantity of food, both raw and ready-cooked. Non-tenters by the scores and hundreds came in wagons and buggies, some going back and forth at night and others camping on the grounds, sleeping as best they could.[40]

Sister: "Sister" is Pillina David Bell.

---

[37] R. Johnston, *Cherokee County, Georgia*, 37–38; Marlin, *History of Cherokee County*, 129–31.
[38] R. Johnston, *Cherokee County, Georgia*, 41–42; Marlin, *History of Cherokee County*, 136–37.
[39] R. Johnston, *Cherokee County, Georgia*, 54; Marlin, *History of Cherokee County*, 176–77; "Welcome to Holbrook Campground," www.holbrookcampground.com; Porter, *Heritage of Cherokee County*, 31.
[40] Marlin, *History of Cherokee County*, 177.

little John: He was John W. Neal, son of Simeon's sister, Mary Juliette Neal, and her husband, Richard Neal. In 1850 he was five years old.[41]

Cholera Morbus: The term's literal Latin meaning is "disease cholera." Cholera is an infection of the small intestines that produces wasting diarrhea that can lead to cramps, vomiting, severe dehydration, and death.[42]

birth of her son: The son referred to was Jesse Horatio Neal, who was born earlier in 1850.[43]

Cousin Amanda and Thomas Bowen from Carrolls: Amanda and Thomas Bowen were children of Hiram Bowen, one of Thirza's brothers, and his wife, Charity. In 1850 they lived with their parents in Carroll County, Georgia. Then Amanda was about thirty and Thomas about twenty-six years old. Letters from Amanda and her future husband John H. Jones appear later in this collection.[44]

Uncle Hiram: Uncle Hiram was Hiram Bowen, one of Thirza's brothers. In 1850 he was fifty-two years old and a farmer in Carroll County, Georgia. Letters from him will appear later in this collection.[45]

Hurricane Shoals Division: The Hurricane Shoals Division was a subordinate division of the Order of the Sons of Temperance, a fraternal society whose members pledged not to "make, buy, sell, or use" alcoholic beverages. They also contributed funds for funeral expenses of brother members, and a more limited amount for their wives' funeral expenses, and for mutual insurance in case of a death or disability. The Georgia Grand Division, or state headquarters, received its charter in late 1846 after its leaders had established five subordinate divisions. By March 1848, there were twenty-five subordinate divisions in Georgia.[46]

Hurricane Shoals is located about three miles south of Maysville and now is the site of a county park.[47]

Officers of the G. D.: These men were the officers of the Georgia Grand Division of the Order of the Sons of Temperance.[48]

viands: "Food of various kinds; esp., choice dishes."[49]

---

[41] US Census, 1850, Cherokee County, Georgia.

[42] D. Simpson, *Cassell's Compact Latin Dictionary*, 143; "Cholera," *Webster's New World College Dictionary*, 264; R. White, *American Ulysses*, 110.

[43] US Census, 1860, Milton County, Georgia.

[44] Will of Owen J. Bowen, Jackson County Will Book A, 118; US Census, 1850, Hiram Bowen, Carroll County, Georgia.

[45] Will of Owen J. Bowen, Jackson County Will Book A, 118; US Census, 1850, Hiram Bowen, Carroll County, Georgia.

[46] Ellis, *History of the Order of the Sons of Temperance*, 177–82; Fahey, "Temperance Movement"; Sons of Temperance, *Constitutions of the Order of the Sons of Temperance*, 11 (quote), 13–14.

[47] See "Hurricane Shoals Park," http://hurricaneshoalspark.org.

[48] Ellis, *History of the Order of the Sons of Temperance*, 177–83.

[49] "Viands," *Webster's New World College Dictionary*, 1609.

Simeon

Woodstock Cherokee County, Ga
November 6th 1850
Dear Parents....

My principle object in writing this letter is to inform you that I expect at the expiration of my School to go to Jackson and live with you next year in order that you (Father) might send any word that you wished me to have and mak any arrangements you thought necessary.

I will tell you some plans that I have been thinking over, one is that you sell or lend me which you please 8 or 10 bushels of wheat and sow it for me this fall as it will not require but little attention. You have land in abundance and you could probably find time to sow it and I could pay you the cash for the wheat and the time spent in sowing or pay you otherwise just [as] you saw proper

If I come home I want to work with the rest, but I want to raise more Cotton than any thing else consequently I shall want a certain number of Acres marked of and have what the ground makes, and the same way with the corn; though I should not want to make any corn for sale.

As regards my horse I scarcely know what to say; I am aiming to get him fat and try to sell him if I can to a good advantage but if I sell I would like very much to buy Dr Bell's Horse for I think he is offering him cheap and as I expect some time in the course of next year to buy a Buggy if I can get one on good terms If I recollect correctly you have five horses at present, and I was counting over to day how many of us there probably would be if I come home next year, to work on the farm and I was of the opinion that four horses could not do the ploughing and milling Etc Etc. I was thinking about this way, that if you could sell Adalaide or Ball that you would then have a use for my horse.

I merely state these things that you might think of them but I do not care anything about knowing precisely what kind of a chance you would give me as I know you would do the best for me that you can. You can talk these things over and when Mother comes out she can tell me the result of your deliberations.

We have some general news of some importance in this County at Present. About the last of August a party of about one Dozen left this County for the California Gold mines. Among the number was Rasin Bell & Mr E Hawall and Son of Forsythe County. Their Friends received a letter from them last week dated the last of Sept stating that they were crossing the isthmus and were attacked by Cholera, and one of the Party Mr. Boger's Son died in half an hour after he was taken. Mr. Bell wrote back to all his Friends whatever they done not to come there as long as they could make ten (10) cents a day here.

Notwithstanding all these reports, William & Cirus Dial Dr John P Boring and Hosea Horton of Jackson started to California last Monday morning. I was at Mr. Dials when they all started and I am certain I have never seen such a parting scene in my life. There were thirty or forty persons in the crowd and every one of them shed tears; it was truly an affecting scene.

DeLaFayette Few of Jackson furnishes Cyrus the money to go to California. He expects to meet them in Opalaka Alabama. Mrs Boger took the death of her Son very hard....

Since writing the first part of this letter yesterday I have come to the conclusion that I would try to get through by Christmas. I will have 35 Days to teach after this week but by using Saturdays I think I can get through, if I possibly can I will.

I want you to be here on the fourth Sabbath in the month and go to Noonday Church with us. I am very thankful to you for the beautiful Pants Pattern you sent me and tell Grandmother I owe her a Debt of gratitude for the hose she sent me. Tell the Children and the Negro's that I expect to be with them next year.

Give my respects to all enquiring Friends and especially to Miss Pillona Sisson. Tell Sister Ann I want to receive a letter from her before I come home to live. I must [close] this letter now therefore I shall not have an opportunity of looking over and correcting. If there is any words left out you will put them in and make sense. Write me before you come out so that I may know precisely when to look

I remain Your affectionate son
To James H. & Thirza David   S. B. David

[Envelope:]
Mrs. Thirza David
By Mr. Joshua Trower

Notes

California Gold mines: Gold was discovered in California early in 1848. In 1849, some eighty thousand fortune hunters went to California.

Georgians in Cherokee County were familiar with the search for gold and the riches gold could yield. In 1828, gold had been discovered at Dahlonega in Lumpkin County, and new settlers rushed into the general area, which included Cherokee County, seeking to make their fortunes. In 1850, panning for gold in Cherokee County creeks and streams still was productive, although not so much as in earlier years. Still, once harvest was finished some farmers would head for the hills, creeks, and streams with their pans. Also in the county, gold was beginning to be mined underground.[50]

---

[50] "California," and "gold rush," *Encyclopedia Britannica*, 3:615, IV:612; R. Johnston, *Cherokee County, Georgia*, 11, 21–22, 33–36.

isthmus: One route to the California gold fields was a voyage by ship to the eastern side of the isthmus of Panama, a trek across land (the isthmus) to the Pacific Ocean, and another ship to California. The isthmus was sixty or so miles of jungle, dark-water rivers, narrow trails, drenching rain, thigh deep mud, and snakes, ants, rats, mosquitos, leeches, alligators, and thieves. Along the way, and in the overcrowded towns on each side of the isthmus, lurked ruinous diseases, such as malaria, yellow fever, typhoid fever, and cholera.[51]

Mr. Boger's son: Peter C. Boger was one of the early settlers of Cherokee County. His son was Franklin Boger, then about twenty-three years old.[52]

Dr. John P. Boring: He was the older brother of Miss Elizabeth Boring mentioned in Simeon's letter of March 2, 1847. He then was twenty-five years old.[53]

Opalaka, Alabama: This probably is a reference to Opelika, Alabama. It is unclear why people heading for California would meet there, except that a rail line from Opelika to Montgomery, Alabama, had recently been completed. Taking the railroad from Opelika to Montgomery would have been faster than proceeding through Alabama by other land transportation. The goal probably would have been Mobile and a ship from there to the Isthmus of Panama.[54]

go to Jackson and live with you next year: Although his friends in Cherokee County, Rayson Bell and Cyrus Dial, left to go to California, Simeon chose not to go with them. He decided instead not to return to Cherokee County.

Pillona Sisson: In 1850 she was twenty-three or twenty-four years old and living in Jackson County. She may have been related to Adaline Sisson mentioned in Simeon's letter of February 18, 1850.[55]

Sister Ann: She was Simeon's sister, Thirza Ann David, then aged seventeen.[56]

Pillina and Dr. M. P. Bell

Cherokee Co. Ga.
Nov. the 11, 1850
Dear parents
    I now seat myself to address you a few lines. We called and saw Mildy a few

---

[51] "California," *Encyclopedia Britannica*, 3:615; Brands, *Age of Gold*, 74–83; Marlin, *History of Cherokee County*, 63.

[52] Marlin, *History of Cherokee County*, 36–37; US Census, 1850, Cherokee County, Georgia; Pillina's letter of Nov. 11, 1850.

[53] Grave marker, Little River Methodist Church Cemetery, Woodstock, Cherokee County, Georgia.

[54] Clark, "Montgomery and West Point Railroad Company," 297–98; Museum of East Alabama, Opelika, https://eastalabama.org, accessed January 31, 2023.

[55] US Census, 1850, Jackson County, Georgia.

[56] David Family Bible.

minutes and drove ahead to Uncle Ab. We reached there about an hour in the night. The next evening we went to Mr. Bell's and spent the night and Friday night we got to Mr. Dials. There we would have spent a very pleasant night, if it had not been for one or two circumstances. The boys were not there. Raisen Bell had just written back melancholy news. Franklin Boger, one of Raisen's company, died on the 27th of Sep near Panama with cholera, and another gentleman from Lumpkin co had also died of cholera.

Mrs. Dial was very much opposed to the boys going to California, in fact, all of their friends requested them to stay. Raisen said tell all of his friends if they could make 10 cents per day by staying at home, do it. The boys started Monday after we got home on Saturday. There was four in company.

Brother came up the night we got home. We spent a pleasant night. He was very thankful for the socks which Grandmother sent him, for he was needing of them. He was well then. I have not seen him since.

Last Tuesday Dr went out to Cass co to Uncle Fain's. He sold his horse to Fain for 92 dollars. I am well pleased with the deal, though we will be much confined at home, but we do not mind that.

While Dr was in Cass co he was called on to know what would cure a case of dropsy. If he would cure her, he would give him 25 dollars. Dr. told him if he would bring her here, he would cure her for 30 dollars. They reached here Saturday night.

If she dies, Dr gets nothing at all. She has been sick about six months. She was taken with the fever and it turned to the Dropsy. There was doctors waiting on her all the time. He spoke of giving Dr the case three months ago but kept waiting to see if the doctors he had employed could not save her. They have given out all hope of her living and would not do any more for her. Saturday night she was very near gone. She could scarcely get enough breath to live on. She is a great deal of trouble. Dr has not slept but very little since she came. I fear she will not live.

Dr is well, with the exception of fatigue. I have a very severe cold caused by exposing myself on Saturday.

I miss Harriet a great deal. Tell her I say howdy. Mother, if you have time to go to see Polly Willis, bring me two breadths of her dress and my dress. Mother, just prepare yours and the children's clothes and come along. Be sure and come. Write just as soon as you get this, and write what night you will be at our house.

I commenced the school this morning a week ago. I had 8 scholars each day last week, and 10 today. I would get out of heart, but others have less than I do.

We have not heard from Sister since we came home. Mother, you must look over the mistakes for the children are fretting me all the time. Brother will be sure to live in Jackson next year and do business in the farm. He says he will. Nancy

Sarton has married one of old man Adams' sons that formerly lived where Mr. Neal lives.

Dr joins me in love to you all. I will close. We remain
                    Your affectionate children
                        Dr. M. R. and P. C. Bell
                            James H. and Thirza David

Notes

Uncle Ab and Uncle Fain: These men have not been identified, but they probably were Dr. Bell's uncles.

Mr. Bell's: Probably M. R. Bell's father, William Milton Bell Jr.[57]

the boys (first time used): Pillina probably is referring here to Cyrus Dial and Simeon. After being out of town and out of communication for several days, she expected to find them at the Dials' house, which probably indicates that Simeon was lodging with the Dials.

the boys (the second and third times used): These were the four referred to in Simeon's letter of a few days earlier who recently had left for the California gold fields, William and Cyrus Dial, John P. Boring, and Hosea Horton.

Cass co: Cass County was renamed Bartow County on December 6, 1861.[58]

dropsy: An abnormal collection of fluid in a part of the body that results in swelling, also called edema. Because of her difficulty in breathing, the woman may have suffered from pulmonary edema or excess fluid in the lungs.[59]

Harriet: Based on 1850 and 1860 census records and subsequent letters in this collection, Harriet probably was the four-year-old girl listed in James H. David's 1850 slave schedule.

1852

Thirza

Freeman Ville May 7 1852
Dear Husband

We arrived here Safely yesterday evening and found Richard expiring thoug he knew us. It is now 1 A M and life is still in the body but entirely unconscious. The disease is now dropsy. if I do not get home Tuesday evening do not be

---

[57] William Milton Bell Jr. family tree, Ancestry.com.
[58] "Bartow County, Georgia," Wikipedia, https://en.wikipedia.org/wiki/Bartow_County,_Georgia, accessed January 31, 2023.
[59] Drake, *What Did They Mean by That?*, 98; "Dropsy," "edema," *Webster's New World College Dictionary*, 447, 462; Berkow, Beers, and Fletcher, eds., *Merck Manual*, 154.

uneasy. One of Cousin Embersons Sons is like to die with Pneumonia. Mary is verry feeble at this with nervous head ache. I will now wait until 6 A M then I Shall be compelld to close this letter to Send it to the [post] office. Richard may be alive till that time but he cannot Survive many hours. I Shall not return till I See the last of him. Your affectionate Wife and Mother

James H David & the children   Thirza David

Now daylight friday morning. Richard is now nomore of earth. precisely at 4 this morning he breathed his last and will be buried this evening. Mary is feeble and I may not be at home Tuesday evening—

T. D.

Notes

Freeman Ville: Freeman Ville, more generally called "Freemanville" or "Freemansville," was where Mary David Neal (Thirza's daughter and Simeon's sister) and Richard Neal's home was located. It was an unincorporated community that then was part of Cherokee County. It was located at the intersection of present-day Freemansville Road and Birmingham Road, about six miles north of Alpharetta in what now is northern Fulton County. In 1906 it had a post office, and it probably had one earlier, although no post office is located there now.[60]

May 7: May 7, 1852, was a Friday.

husband: He was James H. David, then fifty-two years old and living on the David family farm outside Maysville.

the children: These would have been the Davids' children living at home: Thirza Ann David, aged eighteen; Owen Thomas David, aged sixteen; Pillona White David, aged eleven; and Horatio James David, aged nine. The term probably also included Simeon, who seems to have stayed home in Jackson County in 1851 and 1852, as he indicated he might in his last letter in 1850. That may be the reason he apparently wrote no letters during those two years, at least none that have survived.[61]

1853

Simeon

At home [Freemansville] May 19th [1853] 10 o'clock P. M
Dear Mother,

Sister Ann & myself have just returned from Esq Orr's, and have found all the family locked in the sweet embrace of sleep. I found Sister Mary's letter in

---

[60] Candler and Evans, eds., *Georgia*, 85, 595.
[61] David Family Bible.

the envelope but not sealed, I took it out read it over, & found that it contained all the most important news in the country, but there are many things that I want to write.

My School is smaller at this time than for three months—not exceeding twenty five Scholars for a week or two. The children individually and collectively are learning verry fast. Annolivia's illness has prevented her attendance at School for the last two days.

We have just had a verry interesting Union Meeting at Providence. I left Mr Day to teach in my place & went down on Friday, as the Clerk of the Church where the Union meeting is holden has to act as Clerk for the Union meeting. I discharged the duties with entire satisfaction, & since the meeting have copied the preceedings, & have them ready for sending to the Association in August. On Saturday there was a Query introduced as follows. "Is it right for members of the Church to distill & vend ardent spirits if not what course should be pursued towards a brother thus engaged." After considerable discussion it was decided that it was rong by the meeting with one exception

After two sermons bearing on that subject in which one of the preachers asserted that Doggeries were the verry gate to Hell & the road that leads down to the regions of the Damned, the Rev Joseph Gresham the committee man for the county made a regular temperance speech advocating the measure adopted by the Atlanta Convention. He left 2 petitions in my care for me to get subscribers to. Leroy Harris an old sot affixed his name to the petition praying the Legislature to give the people the right to remove the temptation out of his way. Mrs. Hammond took one of the petitions to get female signatures, & she & I are on a race to see who can get the most signatures to our petitions.

On Saturday night two of the delegates to the meeting from Cobb Co spent the night with us. Maj Collins & Capt Austin both excellent men. But to crown the whole there was a young, beautiful, and accomplished young Lady from Forsyth of the name of Street, that came down on Saturday morning, and as her brother is boarding at Mr Devore's teaching School, I enjoyed the pleasure of her company several times to and from Church. Sister Ann & myself spent Sunday evening with them, & Street & myself swaped Sisters. We walked down to Dr Campbell's & Capt Fields's, and passed the evening most delightfully. Mr Street is a young man of unexceptionable morals, and spotless Character. Such evenings are like Angels visits few and far between.

We design making a demand on Father for a horse so soon as crops are laid by. Mr Reavis has sold his mules, & we never borrow but one of Mr Gole['s] consequently one of us has to stay at home. We will have plenty of oats & know a good pasture for the horse to run in, therefore one of your horses had just as well be here as there. We make out any way till August but I think after that we will have to have a horse. Fran paces elegantly & Sister Ann says she would rather ride her than Light foot by far.

I have had me some collars made like the Messrs Hook, & am verry mutch pleased with them. I bout me a pair of black pants from Johnston & Anderson for summer 50 cents per yard.

I hope you will pardon me for not writing the other week for I did not have a thing to write, but I am no more to blame than the rest, but we will not miss another week, but you to be prepared for a disappointment for the letter might be mis sent or otherwise detained.

It is quite late & I shall not have an opportunity of looking over this scrawl, supply the omissions & correct the errors. I feel confident that I shall some day be a useful citizen, at least I desire to be. Give my love to Father, Sister Pillina, Grand Mother if at home, all the children, the Negroes, and all inquiring friends.

Your affectionate

To Mrs. Thirza David   S. B. David

Notes

At home: Simeon was living with his sister Mary in Freemansville.

1853: The original of the letter does not list the year it was written, but when its contents are compared with other letters written by Simeon, it appears to have been written in 1853.

Annolivia: Ann Olivia was the daughter of Mary and Richard Neal. She was six years old when this letter was written.[62]

Providence: Providence was Providence Baptist Church, which still exists on Providence Road north of Alpharetta not far from the former site of Freemansville. The present church site is about a third of a mile from the site in 1853. In 1853, the church was a one-room log building. As the letter mentions, Simeon was a member and had been elected clerk of this congregation.[63]

Union Meeting and *Association*: "Association" refers to a group of Baptist churches in a particular area that have banded together to meet, generally once a year, to consider matters of mutual interest. In 1853, Providence Baptist Church was a member of Hightower Baptist Association. "Union Meeting" refers to a meeting of a smaller group of churches within a Baptist Association. These meetings were held periodically, such as once a month, for worship and consideration of other matters of interest to member churches.[64]

---

[62] US Census, 1860, Milton County, Georgia; grave marker for A [Ann] Olivia [Neal] Lyle, Sunrise Cemetery, Maysville, Banks County, Georgia.

[63] Copsey, "Providence Baptist turns 180 years old."

[64] Burrows, ed., *American Baptist Register for 1852*, 50–54, 61–62; Constitution and Bylaws of the Hightower Baptist Association, http://hightowerbaptist.net/hba-principles/.

Doggery: A cheap saloon, a dive.[65]

temperance measure adopted at the Atlanta Convention: The Temperance Convention met in Atlanta February 22–23, 1853, and adopted a resolution urging the citizens of Georgia to petition the Georgia legislature to allow each county to decide whether "retail traffic in spirituous liquors may be allowed or shall be prohibited" within the county. The petition also should urge the legislature to prohibit such traffic, even in a county that has approved it, unless the trafficker is licensed.[66]

Forsyth: Forsyth County joins Cherokee County to the east.

Street sister and brother: They would be the children of George S. and Mary Street of Forsyth County. The sister would have been either Metilda, then about twenty-six years of age, or Mary, then about twenty-two. The brother would have been Benjamin F., about twenty-eight years old.[67]

Capt. Fields's: He probably was Lawson Fields, who lived nearby and was then about thirty-seven years old. In 1837 during the Second Florida War, he served as a private in the 5th Battalion, Georgia Mounted Volunteers at the age of twenty-one. This war, directed primarily against the Seminole Indians, was carried out by President Van Buren as continuation of President Andrew Jackson's Indian Removal policy. Lawson Field enlisted again in 1863, during the Civil War, at the age of forty-seven as a private in the Georgia Reserves.[68]

Mr. Reavis: Mr. Reavis is John P. Reavis, who in 1853 was about thirty-eight years old, was married, and had four children aged two to eight. He will be mentioned in later letters.[69]

Mr. Gole: He might have been Mr. Gober. Mr. Robert H. Gober lived nearby with his wife and five children. He had married one of Richard Neal's sisters, and thus was Mary Neal's brother-in-law. He then was about forty-two years old.[70]

Simeon

Freemansville Georgia July 8th 1853
Dear Mother

I take my seat to night after returning from the [post] office, & receiving a letter from my Uncle Isaac David giving me the unwelcome news of the drout in

---

[65] "Doggery," *Merriam-Webster Collegiate Dictionary*, 369.
[66] *Southern Banner*, March 10 and April 14, 1853.
[67] US Census, 1850, Forsyth County, Georgia.
[68] US Census, 1850 and 1860, Cherokee County, Georgia; Lawson Fields Enlistment and Service records; Howe, *What Hath God Wrought*, 516–17.
[69] US Census, 1850, Forsyth County, Georgia.
[70] US Census, 1850, Cherokee County, Georgia; Hebron Historical Society, *Hebron Presbyterian Church*, 404.

his neighborhood, to inform you how peculiarly we have been blessed in this verry important respect. On last Saturday evening we had a most excellent rain, a thoroug soaking season. On Monday afternoon we again had a very [fine] rain. Corn & bottom Crops look remarkably well. Wheat is turning out verry well. Our neighbor Willson made 518 shucks that turned out 108 bushels.... .

I am sorry that you insist on the children's coming to the Union meeting [with you]. The children come out for the purpose of going to School, & nothing but a providential circumstance or stern necessity should induce them to change that purpose. If the children go to the Union Meeting first & last it will consume about three weeks of the time that they should be going to School. Well after they returned and went to school about a week the Holbrook camp meeting would come on, & they would have to spoil two weeks again.

I have taught first & last about 60 Scholars already, & there are a great many that have gone now that will go [again] soon, & I think it highly probable the School will be verry large, & if it is I will be compelled to have some assistance....

Our verry worthy neighbor, & estimable friend John P. Reavis has recently sold all his possessions. Dr Joseph Underwood of Habersham County (A Brother of the old [illegible]) came down last week, & on tuesday morning I drew the writings for them & witnessed the signing, reading, & delivery of the papers. Mr. Reavis sold him 9 lots of land containing 360 Acres with four improvements theron, Mill, & Tanyard for twenty five hundred Dollars, Eleven hundred in hand paid, & the remainder in two annual installments.

Underwood is an excellent man, a good Physician, a member of the Baptist Church, & worth about $14000 Dollars. Reavis says if he had his possessions back he would not take 3000 for them.

We have a happy home Mother I assure you. Often do we think & speak of our situation, & the pleasant life that we all live. Often times the whol seven are seated around the fireside reading at one time. you may be sure that is an agreeable sight. Sister Mary & Ann say if they had such Brothers as some girls have they would be miserable in the highest degree.

Dr & Sister arrived last night about the setting of the Sun, left quite early this morning, & Joshua has got back here to night. Our family are all quite well at Present.

The Clock has just told ten, & the crowd are all asleep save myself. Give my love to all inquiring friends, & tell them Simeon's ambition is to be a credit to the "Day & generation in which he lives." Pardon inaccuracies, omissions & carelessness. Give my love to all the Negroes & tell them I want to see them all & shake them by the hand.

Your Affectionate Son S. B. David

Notes

the children: They were Tom, Owen Thomas David, the older of Simeon's two younger brothers, then seventeen years old (later letters and other materials relate much more about him), and Ann, one of Simeon's younger sisters, then age nineteen.[71]

Dr. Joseph Underwood: In 1853, Dr. Underwood was about fifty-three years old. Not long after this letter was written, he moved to Cherokee County to practice medicine and in 1858 became a justice of the county inferior court.[72]

"Day & generation": The original source of this quotation is difficult to determine. The phrase seems to have been in the air at that time Simeon wrote. Earlier, Joseph Smith, the Latter Day Saints' prophet, used the phrase at Kirtland, Ohio, in 1835 when describing a revelation he received. Daniel Webster used it in his address at the completion of the Bunker Hill monument in 1843. Nathaniel Hawthorne's introduction to *The Scarlet Letter*, published in 1850, contains the phrase. Closer to Simeon's home, the phrase appeared from time-to-time in Athens newspapers. For example, it appeared in the *Athenian* in 1829 and the *Southern Banner* in 1840, 1842, 1844, and 1852. Simeon may have picked up the phrase in a newspaper or heard it more than once from a local preacher, politician, or other orator.[73]

Joshua: He possibly is one of the Davids' enslaved males.

Simeon

Freemansville Cherokee County Ga. Sept. 22nd 1853
Dear Mother—

Your verry kind favor of the 12th inst came to hand on Friday last, and found me in the enjoyment of good health. We are all in good health at present with the exception of Sister Mary and she is mutch better. On last Sabbath evening befor Tommy Ann or myself returned from campmeeting, John threw the claw hammer to his sister Anna Olivia to burst open a chestnut burr, and without seeing his mother or she seeing him, he threw it towards the kitchen door, & just at the moment the hammer reached the door Sister walked up to the door, & the hammer struck her just below the left eye, & hurt her eye verry badly.

---

[71] David Family Bible.
[72] US Census, 1850, Habersham County, Georgia; US Census, 1860, Cherokee County, Georgia; Marlin, *History of Cherokee County*, 190.
[73] Boston City Council, *Memorial of the American Patriots*, 244; J. Smith, et al., *Doctrine and Covenants*, 130; Bradley, Beatty, and Long, eds., *American Tradition in Literature*, 557, 563; *Athenian*, August 25, 1829; *Southern Banner*, February 20, 1840, August 19, 1842, April 25, 1844, October 28, 1852.

On Tuesday morning it was verry painful, & verry mutch inflamed, so mutch so that we become somewhat uneasy about it & called in Dr. Hook. He came immediately, & prescribed & her eye has been doing well ever since; in a few days it will be quite well.

I have a verry fine school this week, from thirty five to forty Scholars. I have stoped the children from their Philosophy, & have them devoting all their time to Arithmetic & Grammar. The students are making rapid advancement in their studies, & some of them give indications of superior powers of mind. Ours is a delightful Seminary of learning

Mr Reavis and myself have concluded the trade that I wrote you something about last week. I agreed to give four hundred & twenty five Dollars for the two lots that lie adjoining to me. It is twenty five Dollars more than I intended giving, but I concluded that rather than let any person else get it that I would give it.

I am to give him Mr Gober's note that will be due next christmas & pay him two hundred Dollars. The other hundred will not be due till next christmas year. I did not want to promise but one hundred Dollars next christmas, but I would have had to give twenty-five Dollars more for the place. Six hundred & twenty five Dollars for 120 Acres of land is quite high, but I have no doubt but I can get Eight hundred Dollars for it before twelve months....

Sister Mary & myself have the finest body of land in the neighborhood. There is not [a] hill on the 5 lots but a person might plow up and down. We may at some time wish to sell our places if we do we can sell them mutch better together than we can by themselves. I think taking everything into consideration that I have done well to get off the Gober lots & get this tract. If I should in a year or two wish to sell goods I will have the best stand in the country....

While at the camp ground we made Mrs. Lester's tent our home, & were treated as well as heart could wish. We formed an acquaintance with the Misses Kelogg & also with Miss Anglin, they also stayed at Mrs Lester's tent.

Brother Thomas went down to the Baptist campmeeting in Cobb County, where he had the pleasure of waiting on Capt Field's daughter, Brother Thomas is as popular with the Ladies as any young man in this County. The young Lesters & Mr Henderson were Sister Ann's attendants at the campmeeting.

I have enjoyed this year more than any year since 1848. of course I fly round the girls. I had always forgotten to state anything with regard to Cousin Sarah's death, we received the sad intelligence in due time. Give my love to grand Mother & all inquiring friends

S. B. David

There is a Degarroeau artist stopping now at Freemansville, & if he can take a first-rate likeness I will have mine taken & send it to you. I had forgotten to state that Sister Ann & I came by Mr Dow Harris, on Sunday from the campmeeting & took supper. Sister Ann thinks a great deal of Miss Harris & so does your humble [illegible]

We were somewhat surprised at the news from Fort Gaines. The soil is certainly fertile & the climate salubrious. In this day & age of the world everything any person engages in must be done in a hurry even to having babies. What will the world come to.

We are verry anxious for you to send the waggon by Freeman as the arrangement you have made will suit us precisely the time and all. You must excuse me I have written so mutch since supper that my hand is tired down [illegible]

The children all join in love to you all, or they would if they were awake.

Your Affectionate Son
S. B. David

To Mrs Thirza David
Maysville Georgia

Notes

inst: This abbreviation is short for "instant," and in this case, means that a previous letter was written in the same calendar month as the calendar month in which the current letter is being written. Simeon, however, sometimes seems to mean that the previous letter was written within thirty days before the current letter is being written. He also uses this term to indicate that some other event has taken place or will take place within thirty days of the date of the letter he is writing.[74]

burr: A bur is a sticky seedcase or shell.[75]

Dr. Hook: Dr. Hook was Dr. Jacob Hook, who was listed in the 1860 federal census as a physician living in Freemansville. He was about twenty-nine years old in 1853 and was the brother of Sarah and David Hook, whom Simeon mentioned in an earlier letter.

Four hundred & twenty-five Dollars…Six hundred & twenty-five Dollars: In relating what he paid for the land sold him by Mr. Reavis, Simeon seems to have given two different amounts.

Mr. Gober: This Mr. Gober probably is Robert H. Gober who lived nearby with his wife and five children. He had married one of Richard Neal's sisters, and thus was Mary Neal's brother-in-law. He then was about forty-two years old.[76]

Mrs. Lester and the young Lesters: This family may have been related to Richard Paul Lester who became the captain of Simeon's company in the Civil War,

---

[74] Drake, *What Did They Mean by That?*, 164; "Inst.," *Webster's New World College Dictionary*, 753–54.

[75] "Burr," *Webster's New World College Dictionary*, 199.

[76] US Census, 1850, Cherokee County, Georgia; Hebron Historical Society, *Hebron Presbyterian Church*, 404.

Company E of the 14th Georgia Volunteer Infantry Regiment, also known as the Lester Volunteers.[77]

Capt. Field's daughter: She was Lou (Louisa) Fields.[78]

Cousin Sarah: She is Sarah H. David, a daughter of Uncle Isaac David. She died August 10, 1853, at age eighteen.[79]

Degarroeau artist: Daguerreotype was an early photographic process "by which a picture was made through exposure of a silver surface (made sensitive by iodine) to the vapors of mercury." Simeon found the daguerreotype artist and had his likeness taken in his militia uniform. The likeness shows him wearing an officer's insignia on his shoulders. He had been commissioned a captain in the Jackson County Militia in 1847 and apparently transferred to the Cherokee County militia as an officer. When this letter was written he was twenty-four years old.[80]

Mr. Dow Harris and Miss Harris: Miss Fanny (Frances) Harris soon became Simeon's wife, and Lorenzo Dow Harris his father-in-law. On September 22, 1853, Fanny was about seventeen years old.[81]

News from Fort Gaines: Fort Gaines in Clay County was the home of Simeon's cousin Amanda Bowen, aged about thirty-three in 1853, and her husband and distant cousin, John H. Jones, aged about forty-five. Letters from them are included later in this collection.[82]

Simeon

Freemanville Georgia Dec 1st 1853
Dear and Affectionate Mother,

The ever moving wheels of time have rolled around another Thursday night, and I seat myself beside my little table to respond to your favor of the 20th ult which came to hand by a due course of mail....

Myself and Brother Thomas want the Division to meet while we are there, or at least I want it to meet, and I want to see him initiated while there. Tell Cinda [that] Harriett was well, and growing finely. I must close for I have several

---

[77] Henderson, *Roster of the Confederate Soldiers of Georgia*, 2:366.

[78] US Census, 1850, Cherokee County, Georgia; see Simeon's letter to his brother Thomas, July 20, 1854.

[79] US Census, 1850, Franklin County, Georgia; P. David, genealogical notes; Isaac David Family Cemetery, Erastus, Banks County, Georgia; Chambers, *Cemeteries and Deaths in Banks County*, 79.

[80] Drake, *What Did They Mean by That?*, 83; US Department of Defense, *Georgia Military Records*, 4:48; David Family Bible.

[81] US Census, 1850, L. D. Harris, Forsyth County, Georgia.

[82] US Census, 1850, Hiram Bowen, Carroll County, Georgia; US Census, 1850, John H. Jones, Early County, Georgia.

other letters to write. We all heartily, cheerfully, and joyfully reciprocate the compliments of our friends. As ever

S. B. David

Notes

Ult: Short for "ultimate," this abbreviation refers to something done the month before the month in which the letter was written. In this case, it means that Simeon had received a letter written by his mother on November 20.[83]

Cinda and Harriet: Possibly these are enslaved women, Harriet living with the Raymond Bells and Cinda with the Davids although a record showing that the Bells owned slaves then has not been found.

Harriet was the girl Pillina mentioned missing "a great deal" in her letter of November 11, 1850, and Cinda likely was Harriet's mother, the twenty-nine-year-old woman listed in the slave schedule of 1850 under James H. David. Apparently, Harriet came to live with the Bells after Pillina's earlier letter.

1854

Simeon

Freemansville Georgia July 20th 1854
Dear Brother [Owen Thomas David],

I seat myself to night for the purpose of writing you a few lines to inform you of the passing events of this section of country....

My School is improving somewhat. James & John & Olivia are making fine progress in their studies. They are getting on finely with there Grammar & Geography. James & Ann Olivia can read better than John, but he can study as fast as either of them. I am pleased to see them taking an interest in their studies. James is an exception—every leisure moment that he has he is reading the bible,—he commenced at the book of Genesis and is now in Exodus

Since my hand was sore in the spring James has taken a great deal off of me that I used to do. He most always gets up of a morning and makes fires. He is old enough now to do it, and will have to learn, consequently I let him do it.

I am enjoying this year finely. Sister was too mutch indisposed to go to Providence last Sabbath—I took Miss Lou Underwood down there in my buggy. Next Sabbath Jack Fields & Miss Lou Underwood & Miss Lou Fields and myself are going to Lebanon to preaching. I have never waited on Miss Lou Field any from the fact of your having kept her company some last year. But she thinks that I have a message for her from you, & she is verry anxious to know what it is. I will

---

[83] Drake, *What Did They Mean by That?*, 314–15.

make up some story and tell her if I go with her Sabbath. It is probably several more of the crowd may conclude to go when they learn that we are going....

15 minutes after 10 O'clock—all is still save the snoring of drowsy sleepers, and the constant noise of the Catydid. While I sit in my familiar corner writing to dear and absent Relations, memory takes a backward flight and I live over again all the happy scenes of my childhood. Often times do I think that if we could all be together again how we might enjoy ourselves.

Dear Sister Pillona I have not forgotten her—I hope to morrow's mail will bring me the joyful intelligence that she is nearly well or so far convalescent as to be out of danger. I had not thought to write you that we received Mother's letter last mail. Tell Sister Pillona that I deeply sympathize with her, and if she is likely to die I want to be sent for by all means.

When you commence going to School apply all your powers. Recollect that knowledge is forever. You need never expect to accomplish any thing noble or good without solid information.

Give my respects to Mr Alexander & tell him I wish him great success as a teacher. When you see the widow Garrot give her my best respects—also all the young Ladies of my acquaintance.

Write whether you have any idea of coming out, and if so at what time. One of my students M. C. Underwood of Gordon County went out to Gordon on a visit, and yesterday morning on his way home a parcel of fellows fell upon him and beat him most unmercifully. Myself and the other boys can hardly bear it.

Joseph W Johnston is waiting on Miss Mary Yancy particularly. I expect to go to the Association. Give my love to all inquiring friends. Write at greater length.

O. T. David Your Affectionate Brother S. B. David

Notes

Brother: He was Owen Thomas David, then eighteen years old.

James & John & Olivia: They are Simeon's sister Mary Neal's children. James then was about ten, John about nine, and Ann Olivia about seven. More will be heard about them in later letters.[84]

Jack and Lou Fields: Jack was Richard Jackson Fields, then age about eighteen. Lou Fields was Louisa Fields, then age sixteen. Both were the children of Captain Lawson Fields.[85]

---

[84] US Census, 1860, Milton County, Georgia.
[85] US Census, 1850, Lawson Field, Cherokee County, Georgia; Lawson Fields's Family Tree, Ancestry.com.

Lou Underwood: She was Mary Lou Underwood, a daughter of Dr. Joseph Underwood. In 1854, she was about nineteen years old.[86]

Catydid: A katydid is a long, green insect, the male of which produces "a shrill sound."[87]

Mr. Alexander: Mr. Alexander was Manning Poole Alexander. At the time this letter was written, he was teaching school in Jackson County and both Thomas and Pillona were his pupils. He will play a significant part later in this collection of letters.

Pillina

Woodstock, Cherokee Co. Geo.
Sept. 11th 1854
Dear Father and Mother

I this evening seat myself for the purpose of writing you a few lines. We received a letter from Brother yesterday dated the 3rd, stating that Father and Sister Annie reached home safely and that you were all in good health. Tell Brother when you see him to let this answer in place of one to him as he will see this.

We are all in good health. Our babe is yet without a name. Mother, I wish you could see her pretty blue eyes. They look pert.

Fevers are raging through this county. We term them the Arkansas, Texas, and California fevers. I have never heard of half as many people moving or wanting to move in my life. 3 of the Boarings, James Bell, Howard Bell, Dr. and several others are speaking of starting for California the first of November and perhaps before that time. Some of them are sure to go. Howard says he is bound for the mines if life and health last him.

I know you think it very strange of Dr's notion, but I am not jesting. He is now bent for California, if he can get money enough to get there. Dr says it will not do for us to stay here. He is getting a very good practice, but he says [he's] not getting the money. He has more against the people now than they ever will pay. It is impossible to collect money this year, and if we stay here we will be obliged to have some money. We have about decided to go to Arkansas if Dr. does not go to California. Father says if he goes anywhere, go to California.

I don't know what to say. I feel like I could not leave all my relations, friends, and acquaintances to go to Arkansas, and again I would much rather leave all and go there with Dr than for him to go to California, if he could make half as much.

---

[86] US Census, 1850, Joseph Underwood, Cherokee County, Georgia; Joseph Underwood Family Tree, Ancestry.com.

[87] "Catydid," *Webster's New World College Dictionary*, 794.

Dr thinks I ought to be willing for him to go to California [by himself]. He says it will be the best thing he can do for a living. I say so too, provided he gets back, but there is the risk to run [that he won't]. If I could only know he would get back I would be better satisfied, and if I could not give [in] for Dr to go, I believe he would [give up going].[B]ut for all the boys to go there and make money and I be the cause of his not going would always hurt me, and if we were not to do well [here], I should always blame myself.

I have been trying to give up for him to go some time, and I am much better reconciled now than when he first spoke of going. If he does go I must never give up to my feelings. I must always think of the bright side.

If Dr goes I want to stay with you while he is gone. We have not the money now, but if Dr gets back we will not be an expense to you, and if he does not we can square it anyhow. I don't want to take anything out of the other children's hands.

If you are willing for me to stay with you we would take what clothes we would need, and I reckon our feather-beds, as I would not like to trouble any person to take care of them. We could pack the rest of the things in the clothes-press and leave them at Father Bell's and put everything that won't injure in the house and fasten the doors. I would bring a few of my choice bedclothes.

We doubt whether Dr can get money. He thinks of selling his horse and buggy, wheat, and other things we have to spare. We don't wish you to say anything about Dr's going yet, as it is uncertain. Write soon and let me know whether or not I can stay with you. I am well. Dr joins in love to you all. I remain Your devoted child

P. C. Bell

N. B. There is a great deal of sickness in this neighborhood. Dr has booked about 30 dollars in this month. Brother spoke of our coming to the Camp meeting. It is out of our power to do so. If Cousin Amanda[,] Thomas and T. S. Lucky are there, give them our respects. We are anxious to see them.

To James H and Thriza David

Notes

Brother: Brother is probably Simeon, who appears to have gone to his parents' home in Jackson County for a while or possibly was living there.

our babe: This was a daughter, Ellen E. Bell, who was born June 8, 1854. The Bells already had a son, Oscar R. Bell, then aged about three years old.[88]

---

[88] US Census, 1860, P. C. (Pillina Charity) Bell, Randolph County, Alabama; *Alabama Marriage Index, 1880–1969*, November 7, 1872 (E. E. Bell and A. D. Hunt); grave marker, Ellen E. Hunt, Pine Grove Baptist Church Cemetery, Heflin, Cleburne County, Alabama.

3 of the Boarings: These probably were members of the Isaac Boring family. As mentioned in Simeon's letter of November 6, 1850, Dr. John P. Boring, one of Isaac's sons, already had left for California. Isaac still had three other sons, Francis, age about twenty-four; Julian, age about nineteen; and Alex, age about fourteen.[89]

James and Howard Bell: Howard Bell was probably John Howard Bell, one of Pillina's husband's younger brothers. He also was a brother of Simeon's friend, Rayson Bell, who earlier had gone to California. In 1854 he was about twenty-four years old. James Bell may have been James H. Bell, then twenty-five years old. Possibly he was a distant cousin of Pillina's husband and his brothers.[90]

Dr.: He is Dr. Raymond Bell, Pillina's husband.

clothes-press: An armoire or a chest of drawers fronted by a door within which clothes could be stored flat (pressed).[91]

Cousin Amanda, Thomas, and T. S. Lucky: Cousin Amanda was the daughter of Hiram Bowen, one of Thirza David's brothers, and his wife, Charity Bowen. Thomas was Amanda's brother. T. S. Lucky has not been identified.[92]

1855

Simeon

Freemanville, Georgia
Feb 8—1855
Affectionate Mother

After returning from Mr. Medder's log-rolling, I seat myself to give you some of the passing news of the day....

Last Saturday night my young friend Dr. Cantrell came over to see me. After supper, we walked over to Dr. Underwoods to a negro wedding. We went into the negro house and were greatly amused by seeing the darkies dance. The Dr. came back and remained with us until Sabbath morning.

I then left him and went up to Forsyth to see how all was moving on up there. I found Miss Fanny quite well and in fine spirits. Thursday the first day of March is now the time agreed upon for our wedding if not prevented by some unforeseen event.

---

[89] US Census, 1850, Isaac Boring, Cherokee County, Georgia.

[90] US Census, 1850, William M. Bell, Cherokee County, Georgia; [Bell] Family Tree, Ancestry.com.

[91] Drake, *What Did They Mean by That?*, 60; "Clothes-press," *Webster's New World College Dictionary*, 283.

[92] US Census, 1850, Carroll County, Georgia.

I was very anxious to be there a week sooner, that I might have an opportunity of going to Oconee church. As Saturday will be preaching day and you will all want to go to church, if you would rather we will so arrange it so as not to get there until towards night, but arrange as you like. I am hopeful I will receive your reply to my letter of the 1st inst on tomorrow evening.

I will frankly say to you that since I conversed with Miss Fanny's parents on the subject of our union, and since we have set apart a day for the celebration of our marriage, that I have enjoyed more happiness in the consciousness of having done right than for the same period of time for many months before.

You will have to read this letter to Tom and the girls for I am almost certain that they cannot read it. My fingers are too sore to write.

I would like for you to write to Mr. Alexander to come up at the time I expect to be there, so that we may all be together again. I would like very much for Maj. William T. Millican to be there. I desire to see him very much. But if he were invited, it might be cause for offense.

I am extremely anxious to hear from home again, to hear how Hugh Atkins' disease has terminated.

Old Mr. Harris is not designing to have many at his house the night of the fly-around, only his brothers Archibald and James and their unmarried children. He requested me again to write specially to the children to come. Tell Tom his jeans is plenty good for him to wear. Old Dow says that he looked better at Canton with his jeans than with anything he ever saw him wear.

Miss Mary is only in her fifteenth year, and is very small of her age, but she is becoming quite a favorite among the gentlemen. Bassell Bates is anxious to fly around her, but he will have to shave his forehead before he can shine.

I do not expect Sister or any of the children to accompany me to Jackson this time. They will probably come in the summer. I propose having a new floor put in this house, and a loft put in it soon. Give my love to Grandmother and tell her I concluded to take her advice. Write soon.

Your affectionate son, S. B. David

Notes

log-rolling: A game or contest involving two or more persons, usually men or boys, balancing on a smoothed log floating in a lake or river or an untethered log on the ground. The object is to remain balanced on the log while using the feet to cause the log to turn and the others to lose their balance and fall off into the water or touch the ground.[93]

Mr. Alexander: See the next chapter.

Major William T. Millican: He was a native of Jackson County and later

---

[93] Drake, *What Did They Mean by That?*, 184.

practiced law in Franklin County. In 1853 he was elected brigadier general of the 2nd Brigade, 4th Division of the Georgia Militia. Possibly when Simeon knew him, he was still a major.[94]

Old Mr. Harris and Old Dow: Both of these names refer to Lorenzo Dow Harris, Fanny's father.[95]

Miss Mary: Simeon is referring to Mary E. Harris, Fanny's younger sister.[96]

Bassell Bates: This possibly is Russell Bates, son of Mathia and Susan Bates. If so, he would have been about eighteen years old in 1855.[97]

to fly around her: This phrase probably is a colorful way of saying he would like "to court her."

shave his forehead before he can shine: "Shine" in this connection seems to mean both reflect light and to impress someone favorably. This phrase may be a witticism alluding to Bassell/Russell's needing to get a haircut so the skin underneath can "shine" and he can impress Miss Mary.[98]

Marriage of Simeon B. David and Frances E. Harris[99]
Married

In Forsyth County on the evening of the 1st by Rev. [F.] M. Hawkins[:] Col. S. B. David of Cherokee County to Miss Fanny E Harris of this former place.

Notes

Marriage: Simeon was then twenty-six, and Fanny nineteen.[100]

F. M. Hawkins: Frederick Marshall Hawkins was a prominent Baptist minister in Forsyth County. He was a founder and the first pastor of Friendship Baptist Church and was the pastor of the church at the time of the wedding. He was eulogized as "a man of no ordinary intellect...in mental power, he was the foremost man of his church, in North East Georgia, for half a century."[101]

Col S. B. David: Simeon had been commissioned a colonel in the Cherokee County Militia on February 11, 1854, by Governor Hershel V. Johnson.[102]

---

[94] *Federal Union*, September 27, 1853; G. B. Smith, *History of the Georgia Militia*, 323; US Census, 1860, Franklin County, Georgia; email from Keith Bohannon, April 1, 2015.

[95] Note to Simeon's letter of September 22, 1853, above.

[96] US Census, 1850, Forsyth County, Georgia.

[97] US Census, 1850, Cherokee County, Georgia.

[98] "Shine," *Webster's New World College Dictionary*, 1340.

[99] *Cassville (Georgia) Standard*, March 15, 1855.

[100] David Family Bible; Fanny's grave marker, Old Taylorsville Church Cemetery, Polk County, Georgia; see also Forsyth County Marriage Book C, 40.

[101] Shadburn, ed., *Pioneer History of Forsyth County, Georgia*, 136–37; Boykin, *History of the Baptist Denomination in Georgia*, 256–57; Bagley, *History of Forsyth County, Georgia*, 822–23 (quote).

[102] US Department of Defense, Officers' Commissions, RG 22.01.003, 1849–1558, 120, Georgia Archives, Morrow, Georgia.

Chapter 2

Pillona White David and Manning Poole Alexander, 1853–1857

Introduction

This first letter is slightly out of chronological order in order to introduce the main subjects of this chapter.

Pillona White David (Pillona or Lona), the writer of the letter, was the youngest daughter of Thirza and James David, and Simeon's youngest sister. In 1855, when this letter was written, she was fifteen years old.

Manning Poole Alexander (Manning), the person to whom the letter was written, was then twenty-five years old. A year or so before, he had taught school in the Maysville area. Pillona and her brother Thomas were two of his pupils.

Thus, when Pillona addressed the letter, she referred to him as "Mr. Alexander." At the bottom of the letter, however, she referred to him as "Dr. M. P. Alexander." Apparently, he recently had begun studying medicine and probably also was practicing in a limited way, under an experienced doctor in his home county, Franklin County.

Pillona lived with her mother and father on a farm outside of Maysville in Jackson County. In 1855, Maysville consisted only of a couple of buildings, one of which contained a post office.[1]

1855

Pillona

Maysville July the 5th 1855
Mr Alexander

I seat myself this morning to respond to your letter of the 15th of June which came to hand in due time. I know that ere this time you have been looking for a letter: but I hope that you will not think hard of me when you hear the reason why I have not written. I wrote a letter to you on the fourth sunday but never mailed it because Toma had not the opportunity of writing; then we never thought of the mail route being changed untill it was too late to send a letter last week. The mail now goes down on Friday and comes up on Tuesday. I had almost as soon not have any mail. I will send this whether Toma writes or not.

---

[1] Elrod, *Historical Notes on Jackson County*, 37, 115; Krakow, *Georgia Place Names*, 145.

I was glad to hear that Dr Freeman consented for you to go to his Brothers, as you was anxeous to go; but *verry sorry indeed* that you could not come by as you expected. The time now seems long but it will soon pass of.

We got a letter from Brother last tuesday: some of the children have scarlet fever but are not dangerous as we expect sister Neal in a few weeks. The health of Father's family is verry good except the Whooping cough.

I have enjoyed myself tolerably well since I saw you. On the third Sabbath Annie and I had the company of the Mr Cowens to and from church; I got the oldest one of them. James can talk a "hifalurleton" in stile.

The preachers Hood and Reed were at Candlers Creek on last Sabbath, there is still a great deal of confusion in the church. Dr Mcwhorter has given vacation this week, I suppose he does not intend having an examination, Ratio will commence going to school soon.

There has been a great deal of rain this week, it rained almost all day tuesday, without any cessation.

I expect to have my likness taken some time this summer if I have the opportunity.

You told me to write you a long letter. I have written ever thing that I can think of. When you write tell me how you are pleased with your new home. I will close

I remain as ever your devoted friend

Pellona W. David
Dr M. P. Alexander

Notes

Toma: This is Lona's name for her brother Thomas. Because he also was one of Manning's students, he would have been writing to his former teacher.[2]

Dr. Freeman consented for you to go to his Brothers: This probably is a reference to Dr. Henry Freeman, a native of Jackson County and a noted doctor who had been practicing medicine in Carnesville, Franklin County, Manning's home county, since 1819. He also had represented Franklin County in both houses of the Georgia legislature and had been a justice of the Inferior Court for a number of years. He had several brothers, and it is not clear which brother is referred to in this letter.[3]

Brother: She is referring to Simeon.

---

[2] Lona to M. P. Alexander, June 8, 1857, and Thomas to M. P. Alexander, August 30, 1855, below.

[3] *Southern Banner*, January 21, 1863; Franklin County Historical Society, *History of Franklin County, Georgia*, 782, 784; brothers: email from Laura Mills to FREEMAN-L@rootsweb.com, June 10, 1999, accessed August 6, 2015.

Annie: She is referring to her older sister, Thirza Ann David, then almost twenty-two years old.[4]

the Cowens: The Cowan family was one of the earliest families to settle in the Maysville area. The Cowans mentioned by Pillona are probably James K. Cowan, then about twenty-four years old, and one of his younger brothers, either Edward, then about twenty-two years old, or John, then about twenty.[5]

"hifalurlleton": Pillona probably means "highfalutin," that is "excessively flowery oratorical style."[6]

Candlers Creek: Candlers Creek refers to the Candlers Creek Baptist church, which was located just outside Maysville roughly where Unity Christian Church is now on Unity Church Circle. It was established about 1810, and Pillona's grandfather Owen J. Bowen was one of its first leaders. This was the church attended by the James H. David family. Pillona's parents were long-time members, and Pillona's father was an officer of the church.[7]

Dr. Mcwhorther: He has not been identified, but it appears he is someone with authority at Pillona's school and has given the school a vacation.

Ratio: She is referring to Horatio James David, her younger brother, then twelve years old. He was the author of many letters that appear later in this book.

new home: It is unclear where this was.

1853

Mary Jane George
April 17, 1853
Dear Cousin [Manning Poole Alexander]

I now take the present opportunity of writing you a few lines to let you know that we are all well excepting Mother. she has been very sick but she is better than she was. I hope when these few lines reach you they will find you enjoying good health.

I received your letter the other week and was glad to here from you but I have not had the time to answer it untill the present for every night I have to study very hard. there are a great many young ladies in this village now agoing to school. there are 90 schollars in one school and 80 in the other. I think you ought to come here and see them for some of them are verry pretty.

---

[4] David Family Bible.
[5] US Census, 1850, Jackson County, Georgia; Dorsey, *History of Hall County*, 16.
[6] "Highfalutin," *Webster's New World College Dictionary*, 684.
[7] Conversation with Danny Elrod and other members of Unity Christian Church at Unity Church, July 29, 2012; Jackson County Deed Book E, 564; *Forest News*, June 10, 1876; *Forest News*, March 16, 1878.

It will not be but about 3 weeks untill the cars will arrive at rocky river. they are in nine miles of the place. I expect it will be a great day when they arrive in Anderson.

That Man Hutchison is to be hung in Anderson the first friday in May and that time will soon be here.

Granmother was better the last time I heard from her. Uncle Billy is not Married yet and I expect you will have to come and put him in the notion for I have tried to get him to Marry but all I have said is in vain.

There are 6 young ladies in our school that will Graduate the last week in June. I wish you could be here then.

I want you to send me the name of that young man that sent me his best respects in your next letter for I want to know who it was and when I find out I will send him my best respects.

so I have nothing more to write that would interest you so nothing more but remain your most affectionated Cousin untill Death

M J George

Answer my letter as soon as you get these few lines. write often and I will do the same. Good bye

Mary Jane George your devoted Cousin

Notes

Manning Poole Alexander: He was born in Anderson County, South Carolina on April 26, 1830, and was known as Elie, Manning, or M. P. When he was ten years old, he moved with his family to Georgia. They lived on a farm about five miles east of Carnesville in Franklin County. Manning had one older brother, five younger brothers, and no sisters.

His parents were Scotch-Irish and Presbyterian. His grandfather, Manning Poole, owned part of the land on which Anderson, South Carolina, was built. According to family lore, his mother, Margaret Poole Alexander, was such a strict observer of the Sabbath that on Saturday she always baked enough loaves of salt-rising bread to last until Monday. She did not even wash dishes on Sundays. She was a great reader, however, and spent most of Sunday reading.[8]

---

[8] Chaplin, *Riches of Bunyan* (Alexander family copy); Jackson and Teeples, *South Carolina 1830 Census Index*, 1; Jackson and Teeples, *South Carolina 1840 Census Index*, 1; US Census, 1850, Franklin County, Georgia; handwritten and undated genealogical notes of Lily Alexander Jackson, youngest daughter of M. P. Alexander, in my possession (cited hereafter as Lily Alexander Jackson, genealogical notes); Nora Alexander Boone (M. P. Alexander's oldest daughter) to Olivia Comer Brockmann (daughter of Nora's younger sister Margie Alexander Comer), October 25, 1946, in my possession; Vandiver, *Traditions and History of Anderson County*, 10–11, 22.

When this letter was written, Manning was studying at the Starrsville Academy in Starrsville, Newton County, Georgia.⁹

Mary Jane George and Mother: Mary Jane George was Manning Poole Alexander's first cousin. She was the daughter of Elizabeth Poole George, a sister of Manning's mother, Margaret Poole Alexander. Her father was Ezekiel George, a cabinet maker and furniture dealer. She later married George Frederick Tolly, a Prussian immigrant who was an apprentice with her father. Her husband later became mayor of Anderson, and Mary Jane was known affectionately as "Mrs. Mayor Tolly."¹⁰

Anderson: She is referring to Anderson, South Carolina, in the southwest part of South Carolina.

the cars will arrive at rocky river: Rocky River is located east of Anderson. It flows from north to south and empties into the Savannah River. The cars were railroad cars.

Two rail lines were being built in the Anderson area in the late 1840s and the early 1850s. One was to go from Anderson to Knoxville, Tennessee, and was called the Blue Ridge Railway. The other was to run between Columbia, South Carolina, and Greenville, South Carolina, and was called the Greenville and Columbia Railroad. The rail line Mary Jane is writing about probably was a spur of the Greenville and Columbia that was being built to go from the G and C depot at Belton, South Carolina, to Anderson to link that line with the Blue Ridge Railway.¹¹

Hutchison: He has not been identified.

Granmother: She probably was Mary Jane and Manning's grandmother, Mary Poole, who in 1853 would have been about seventy-six years old.¹²

Uncle Billy: Uncle Billy probably was William H. Poole, Manning and Mary Jane George's mother's brother. In 1853, he would have been about forty-two years old.¹³

---

⁹ See immediately following letter.

¹⁰ Lily Alexander Jackson, M.P. Alexander's youngest daughter, to Olivia Comer Brockmann, daughter one of Lily's older sisters, Margie Alexander Comer, August 8, 1946, in my possession; Vandiver, *Traditions and History of Anderson County*, 24–25.

¹¹ Rand McNally, "South Carolina State Map"; "Rocky River (South Carolina)," Wikipedia, https://en.wikipedia.org/wiki/Rocky_River_(South_Carolina), accessed February 1, 2023; "Greenville & Columbia RR," South Carolina roadside marker no. 4-36, Belton, South Carolina; Vandiver, *Traditions and History of Anderson County*, 180–81, 194; *Abbeville Banner*, May 12, 1853.

¹² US Census, 1850, Anderson, South Carolina; Administration of Manning Poole Estate, 1845, Anderson County Will Book 1, 303.

¹³ US Census, 1850, Anderson County, South Carolina; Olivia Brockmann to Lily Alexander Jackson, March 13, 1949, in my possession.

Morgan H. Looney

To those whom it may concern.

The bearer of this, Mr. M. P. Alexander, has been under my charge, as a Student, the whole of the present year, and was with me a portion of last year in the same capacity. I can cheerfully recommend him as a young man of excellent moral character, as one honorable, upright, and highminded in an eminent degree.—I can also recommend him as being well qualified to teach any of the branches ordinarily taught in country schools. He is moreover an excellent Algebraist both in simple and quadratic Equations; can teach Chemistry, Geometry, Mental Philosophy; Physiology, etc.

I unhesitatingly commend him then to the favorable notice of any neighborhood wanting a school, and to the liberal patronage of his fellow citizens.

Starrsville, Geo. Oct. 31st., 1853
M. H. Looney
Prin. of Starrsville Academy

Notes

Morgan H. Looney: Professor Looney grew up in Carnesville, Franklin County, Manning Alexander's hometown. Looney was about three years older than Manning.

At the age of fourteen, Morgan Looney became a teacher and taught for the following fifty-five years in schools in Georgia, Florida, Mississippi, Alabama, and Texas. In 1853 he was about twenty-six years old and teaching at Starrsville Academy. In 1854, Alexander H. Stephens, later vice president of the Confederacy, said of Looney, "As an educator [he] has no equal in the South."[14]

Starrsville Academy: This school was established in Starrsville, Newton County, Georgia, in 1837.[15]

1854

G. C. Looney

At home
Dec. 8th 1854
Dear Elie [Manning Poole Alexander]:

---

[14] Loyd, "Morgan H. Looney," 20; *Atlanta Constitution*, May 10, 1908; US Census, 1850, Coweta County, Georgia; National Register of Historic Places Registration Form for the Starrsville Historic District, United States Department of the Interior, National Park Service, 1998 (quote).

[15] National Register of Historic Places Registration Form for the Starrsville Historic District, United States Department of the Interior, National Park Service, 1998.

I fondly hope these lines will find you well as I am not only well but enjoy myself first-rate. I suppose William Elie has brought his better half with him home. I wish you could have been here with me and Jack and Lewis Gaines. We would have had so much fun. They both have stayed all night with me. I reckon you will be here by next Friday or Saturday night If you will write to me what night you will be here I'll let Jack and Lewis know and we will have a good time. Also Morgan wrote to me yesterday to come on to Palmetto as soon as I could and I'll be obliged to wait until I collect the money that is owing to him as he needs it worse than ever.

I am as ever your confidant and faithful friend

To M. P. A

G. C. Looney

[On the back of an advertisement for Palmetto Academy in Palmetto, Georgia, which apparently was sent with this letter, is written: "Read this and see if you can not come out here next year! G. C. L."]

Notes

G. C. Looney: He was George C. Looney, one of Morgan H. Looney's younger brothers. In 1854, he was about eighteen years old. See notes on the previous document for Morgan H. Looney.[16]

William Elie: This was William P. Alexander, Manning's older brother, who in 1854 was twenty-seven years old. In September 1854, about three months earlier, he had married Lou E. Sewell.[17]

Palmetto Academy: This was a new school to be located in Palmetto, Carroll County, Georgia, that Morgan Looney was in the process of establishing. It was a school for both young men and women.[18]

1856

Pillona

Maysville Ga March the 25th 1856
Dr. Alexander

I take my seat this evening to respond to your letter of the 8th Inst which came to hand by a due course of mail. I think from what you wrote you must have had a good practice since you were home else you charge pretty high: I hope your efforts will be crowned with success.

---

[16] US Census, 1850, Noah Looney, Franklin County, Georgia.
[17] Chaplin, *Riches of Bunyan* (Alexander family copy); US Census, 1850, Robert Alexander, Franklin County, Georgia.
[18] Palmetto Academy advertisement dated September 27, 1854, in my possession.

The wedding that we were speaking of when you were here that of Miss Sallie Wells and Mr. Miller came of on the 6th of this month. I think John has got a good wife; Hugh Atkins and Miss Ange Miller were the attendants. About two weeks ago Miss Mary Brooks and a Mr. Rennolds were joined together in holy bonds of matrimony She was twenty years old, and he an old Widower of forty On the same night Miss Wather and a Mr Stevenson living near Comersville were married.

Brother Thomas came home a week or two after you were here and spent two weeks with us, while Father and Annie went to Cheroke. They were all enjoying good health.

If Mother goes to Cherokee I expect to go with her but it is entirely owing to sercumstances whether she goes or not, if we go we will start the last of this week or next.

They had rather a sudden death in the neighborhood of Phidelta week before last. Mr James Jones died of enflamation of the brain, he was taken on tuesday night and died Friday morning. Brother Thomas Annie and I went to the burying on Sunday; he was buried with Masonic honors, there was the most people there I ever saw at a burying

That evening we took dinner at Mr Harpers. his Sister in-law Miss Molly Harkrep is staying with them.

Yesterday evening the fire got out between Deral Andersons and James Ellersons. nearly all of our folks and several of the neighbors went to stop the fire. when they got the fire stoped, they went to cutting down trees. while cutting down a burning tree it fell before they thought it would and fell on Mr. Andersons old dave. he lived till about ten o clock last night. They think it also brushed Father as it fell

I must tell you of some of my work since I saw you: I have woven one of the prettiest coverlets ever you saw I suppose.

We are all enjoying good health now but Mother. she has the same irregular beeting of the heart but not so bad as it used to be

I weigh *110 lbs* the most I ever did.

Dr Thillyo says when I go to baking—send for him and he will toat bark for me: do you not think I had better send for him the 1st day of April: As ever your affectionate friend

   Dr. M. P. Alexander   Pillona W. David

"Forget me not I only ask this simple boon of thee
And may it be an easy task sometimes to think of me"

Notes

Hugh Atkins: He probably was the Hugh Atkins who in March 1856 was twenty-one years old. He is mentioned again in following letters.[19]

She was twenty years old, and he an old Widower of forty: When Pillona wrote this letter, she was sixteen years old, and Manning was almost twenty-six.[20]

toat bark for me: "Toat" probably is a mistaken spelling of "tote," meaning "carry." Maybe Dr. Thillyo is offering to carry bark for Pillona to use when making a fire over which to bake breads or cakes. The reference to April 1st may mean that if she does ask "Dr. Thillyo" to tote bark for her, it will be only as a joke.[21]

boon: A welcome benefit.[22]

Pillona

Maysville Ga
July 15th 1856
Dr. Alexander:

I seat myself this evening to write in response to your letter of the 1rst inst. which came to hand in due time.

I was verry happy to hear of your good practice and also of your being in such fine spirits, but I fear you have had the blues since then: I have not had the blues *much* since I saw you.

I think I am enjoying as good or better health than I have in a year only I am now taking a *verry bad* cold: the family are all in good health; Dyer is lying yet in the same position you saw him, we cannot tell whether the bone is knitting or not.

On the next saturday night after you were here Sister Ann and I spent the night at Mr Atkins and went to sabbbath School next day; and enjoyed ourselves tolerably well. On the first saturday and Sabbath we went to Sandlers [Candlers?] creek and had a verry good metting.

Last Sabbath we went to Pleasant hill and took dinner at Mr. S. Cowens: that night Miss Sallie Candler and Hugh Atkins staid with us.

Uncle Franklin and Wife came up to day. they are all in the rom talking and I hardly know what I am writing but you know you told me to not wait for something to write but to set down and write something, for it would do you but I almost *know* that this will not *interest* you.

---

[19] US Census, 1850, Jackson County, Georgia; grave marker, Sunrise Cemetery, Maysville, Banks County, Georgia.
[20] David Family Bible; Chaplin, *Riches of Bunyan* (Alexander family copy).
[21] "Tote," *Webster's New World College Dictionary*, 1530.
[22] "Boon," ibid., 171.

Oh I must tell you of the presents that I am going to have when I get to be neighbor to Aunt David, she says she will give me two *Shanghai chickens*. dont you think that will be some inducement.

You wrote me that you expected to pay me a visit about the fourth Sunday: I am sorry to say that you will have to postpone your visit 2 or 3 weeks: Brother Thomas expects to start to Cherokee next monday or Tuesday morning; he expects to be there about 3 weeks I think it will be the best opportunity and probably the only one that I will have to go directly. We expect to be at a baptist Camp meeting at bethlahem the first Sabbath in august and an association at Providence the second Sabbath.

I would be so glad if you could get this letter in time to come up before we start, but I fear you will not I think you had best not come after monday night; for we think to start Tuesday morning.

If you cant come before; I want you to come the sooner after I get back. I will say that I will be back by the third Sabbath in august or probably a day or two before. I do think this is the most unconnected scawl that I have ever written; the only favor I ask of you is to burn this as soon as you read it.

But if you knew my condition you would not look for anything better, for my head and nose has been paining me verry much.

I have written every thing that I think will interest you so no more only I remain as ever your most devoted friend.

Pleasant dreams to you good night
Pillona W. David
Dr. M. P. Alexander

Notes

Dyer: Because Pillona uses only one name and no title when referring to him and because he is mentioned in connection with the family, he probably is an enslaved man owned by the David family.

Mr. Atkins, Hugh Atkins: Hugh Atkins probably is the Hugh Atkins mentioned in the letter of March 25. Mr. Atkins likely is his father, Abram Atkins.

Uncle Franklin and Wife: They may have been Henry Franklin David and wife, Mary, who lived in nearby Franklin County. Henry was a younger brother of James H. David.[23]

I hardly know what I am writing: At a number of different places in the letter, Pillona has crossed out words. At other places, she has added letters to words or inserted words above the line.

Aunt David: She probably was Mary David, Uncle Franklin's wife.

---

[23] P. David, genealogical notes; US Census, 1850, Franklin County, Georgia.

Shanghai chickens: This breed, also referred to as Cochins, was imported from China to England and America in the mid to late 1840s. They were unusually large and thought to be extremely good layers. At one time they were something of a sensation and were so much in demand that a "Cochin craze" or boom developed around them. Gradually, however, their popularity waned, as it had somewhat by the time this letter was written.[24]

1857

Pillona

Maysville Ga
June 8th 1857
Dr. Alexander—

It is with the greatest pleasure, that I seat myself this evening to respond to your letter of the 31st May which came to hand on Tuesday last. I assure you the perusal of the contents afforded me much pleasure. I fear you will be looking for a letter before you get this. Toma is going to town in a day or two. I will git him to mail it there. (*you know why*)

Pardon me if I fail to interest this time but you know you told me to write whether I had anything to write or not and I will comply with your requst. Dr Bell and family left on wednesday after dinner: I regreted parting with sister and the children worse than I ever did before, all was so lonely and still after they had gone; I had something very much like the blues all that week.

Yesterday I went to Candlerscreek. had a fine singing in the morning and pretty good congregation. Oh! you ought to have been here friday evening to have gone strawbury hunting, I eat so many then and so much *strawbury tart* saturday that it nearly made me sick.

Brother Thomas expects to be at a weding in Jefferson thursday night. little Sue Randolph (about 14 years old) & Mr Mccory are to be married. Toma is boarding there.

When you write tell me whether Dr Starr is boarding with you or not and also if Drayton Cunningham is in Coledge. Some advice Be careful to not to take the *blues* & get to want to see your *Mama* to bad & also to not *smoke the pipe* or chew tobacco & be sure to go to preaching as often as you can. It is getting late and I have to attend to the Culinary affairs so good-bye to night.

Tuesday morn. June 9th

I take up my pen to finish my letter. Well if what I dreamed last night was true I would not write any more; I dreamed that I was writing to you and saw you

---

[24] Bennett, *Poultry Book*, 31–39; "Our Book Table," 25; L. Salmon and Hawkins, "Cochins."

coming. I put down my pen an was talking with you: *but oh*! how we are deceived sometimes by imagination; for when I awoke I found that it was only *in the land of dreams that I saw you.*

I have been reading a verry interesting little book (the title is) Gleanings from memory or stories of my childhood. Oh! if I could only recall 10 or 8 years I feel now that I would be perfectly happy, for then I would know so little of this false world & would be looked upon only [as] a child: but we pass our *happiest moments* and never know it. The health of the family is good. Nothing more at present. *Yours most truly.*

Write soon.

Dr. M. P. Alexander   Lona W. David

N. B. I will send you some poetry about *Telling the secret*, but probably you have seen, heard or *known something about it before*

Notes

Toma: Pillona is referring to her brother Thomas.

Jefferson: Jefferson was and is the county seat of Jackson County.

Coledge: There were over forty institutions that styled themselves "colleges" in Georgia by 1860. Some were actually no more than secondary schools. It is unclear to which one Pillona was referring.[25]

Gleanings from Memory: This book was written by "A Mother" and published in 1853 by the American Sunday School Union. It consists of ninety pages of what are described as "moral tales."

poetry about Telling the secret: This poetry has not been identified.

Married

At the residence of James H. David, Esq. of Jackson county, on Tuesday, 20th Oct., by Rev. Wm. P. Reid, Dr. M. P. Alexander of Franklin county, and Miss Pillona W. David.[26]

Notes

Rev. Wm. P. Reid: He was a minister at Candler's Creek Baptist Church.[27]

Manning and Pillona: Manning was then twenty-seven years old, and Pillona had just turned eighteen.

---

[25] Coleman, *History of Georgia*, 176.
[26] *Southern Banner*, October 29, 1857, 3.
[27] US Census, 1850, Hall County, Georgia; See Pillona's letter of July 5, 1855, the first document in this chapter (although there, she spells his name "Reed").

Chapter 3

Owen Thomas David, 1855–1859

Introduction

Owen Thomas David, the subject of this chapter, was the middle son of James H. and Thirza David. In August 1855 he was twenty years old. Simeon mentioned him occasionally in his letters in chapter 1, and Pillona refers to him in her letters in chapter 2 as "Toma." Earlier he had been one of Manning's students.[1]

1855

John H. Jones and Amanda M. Jones

Fort Gaines   Ap'l 22 1855
Dr Cousin Thomas
 In reply to yours of last month we will in the first place say that it affords us much pleasure to hear that you are all well & in the second place please give our sincere congratulations to Cousin Simeon & his lady.
 We are verry glad to learn that you comtemplate paying us a visit next fall and hope you will not disappoint us as all the rest of our relations do & have done heretofore. we had hoped that you and cousin Ann would have come to see us last winter but as always heretofore in such expectations we have been disappointed....
 You have no doubt learned from our letter to your Mother that Owen is married. he married a young lady by the name of Amanda A. Whitehurst. We have quite a surplus of fine looking young ladies here and if you will come and see us Amanda says we will show you all the ropes and almost insure you success with some of the *tip topest kind of gals*....
 Don't fail to write to us soon again and give us all the news You must excuse our delay in replying to yours as our courts in three or four county round are just over and I have not had time to devote to any thing but them until now. Give our respects and love to all and believe us your Cousin truly
 A. M. Jones
 Jno H. Jones
 Cousin Thomas

---

[1] David Family Bible.

I enclose you the half of a hundred dollar bill which I wish you to deliver to Madison Strickland the first opertunity. He gave me $200 to buy hides with for him. I have purchased about $100 worth for him and have them ready to ship to him as soon as the river rises so I can, and find it next to imposible to get more. I have [already] enclosed the other half to him and when you give him this half get him to credit my receipt with $100 retired.

Amanda says if you will come down she will give you some *dots* that will please you. But you must write and give us all the news

Your cousin *Jno H. Jones*

Notes

John H. Jones and Amanda M. Jones: John and Amanda were husband and wife. Also, John and Amanda both were Thomas's cousins. Amanda was the daughter of one of Thirza's brothers, and John was the son of one of Thirza's uncles. That relationship also meant that John and Amanda were cousins to each other, first cousins once removed.

Both were older than Thomas. Amanda was about thirty-one years old, and John was about forty-three. They had married relatively late in life, on November 14, 1852. Another of their letters appears later in this collection. John was a lawyer and farmer. He was admitted to practice before the Georgia Supreme Court in 1846.[2]

Fort Gaines: Fort Gaines was and is located in the southwest part of Georgia just across the Chattahoochee River from Alabama. It was incorporated by the Georgia legislature in 1842. John H. Jones was one of the first commissioners of the new town.

In 1853, Fort Gaines was part of Early County. The following year, however, Clay County was created, and Fort Gaines was made its county seat.[3]

our congratulations to Simeon and his lady: Simeon was married in March 1855.[4]

Ann: She was one of Thomas's sisters.

Owen: He was Owen Bulow Bowen, one of Amanda's brothers, who married Amanda Ann Rebecca Whitehurst on January 18, 1855.[5]

---

[2] US Census, 1850, Hiram Bowen, Carroll County, Georgia; US Census, 1850, John H. Jones, Early County, Georgia; *Georgia Marriage Records from Select Counties, 1828–1978*, 378; Kelly, *Reports of Cases in Law and Equity*, ix, xx.

[3] State of Georgia, *Acts of the General Assembly of the State of Georgia, 1842*, 99; L. Morgan, "Fort Gaines"; roadside marker, "Clay County," Fort Gaines, Georgia.

[4] See chapter 1.

[5] US Census, 1850, Carroll County, Georgia; Alabama, Ancestry.com, *Compiled Marriages from Selected Counties, 1809–1920*, Henry County, Alabama.

our courts: John H. Jones was a lawyer.[6]
the river: the Chattahoochee River
the half of a hundred dollar bill: Today if someone presents both halves of a bill, the bill can be redeemed at full value. If a person presents only half of a bill, however, it could be redeemed at full value only if the person presents sufficient evidence to demonstrate that the other half has been destroyed.[7]

In 1855, it's likely the same rules would have applied. The procedure of mailing two halves of a note separately was an effort to lessen the chance that the money would be stolen.

dots: This word possibly is a joking reference to the definition of "dot" as "a woman's marriage dowry," that is, "the property that a woman brings to her husband at marriage." Amanda may be telling Thomas that if he comes for a visit, she will introduce him to some eligible girls he might like and possibly marry.[8]

Thomas

Maysville   Aug the 30th 1855
Dear Friend [Manning]

I seat myself to inform you that I am well and have been enjoying verry good health for a considerable length of time. The family are all well with the acception of colds. The neighbors are jenerally well.

Manning you must excuse me for not writing sooner for it has been for want of an oppertunity. I have just returned from cherokee where I spent som verry pleasent moments.[Even] if my old sweet heart is married cherokee has not lost its charms. The ladies are verry good looking an there are sum of the first and second quality and large number of the 3rd 4th and last qualities.

The people generally in that county are healthy.

Please supply where words and letters are wanting.

Manning our crop is verry good and in traveling I find crops to be verry fine. it is thought that corn can be bought at 25 cts per bushel. I hardly think it can be bought that cheap but I think it will sell 35 or 40 cts from the heap.

Manning I am at as great a loss to know what I will do next year as I was last, but I think there is as much probability of my staing here as any where. Dr. Bell has just been to see us and he proffers to give me as much good bottom land as I can tend. you know that I cant get that here. S. H. Jones Esq has made me some splendid propositions. What I will do and where I will go I have no idea.

Manning when I write again I will take more tim and try to write better. write soon and give me all the news your Devited Friend

---

[6] US Census, 1850, Early County, Georgia.
[7] US Bureau of Engraving and Printing, "Redeemed Mutilated Currency."
[8] "Dowry," "Dots," *Webster's New World College Dictionary*, 437, 441.

O. T. David
M. P. A.

Notes

from the heap: Apparently the reference is to selling corn from a pile of loose ears of different sizes that had not been sorted.

S. H. Jones, Esq.: He has not been identified.

1856

Simeon

[Part of letter dated April 29, 1856, from Forsyth County]
Dear Brother [Thomas], ...

When you write another April fool try to ascertain the middle name of the Lady you direct it too. The one wrote out here was claimed by two or more person. Mary M. J. & Mary E. D. both claimed it. Mary J took it out of the office and kept it awhile but I believe Mary D. has it now. I was appealed too, to know which one I thought it was sent too, of course I would not say. Sometime when you are writing to me write Mary D a pretty little letter and inclose it in mine and sign your name to it. Then you can shine as bright as you please when you come out.

I want you to be certain to be here by the 1st Sabbath in August to be at Campmeeting if not sooner. I think you can get a good deal of work to do in this neighborhood when you come out.

Give Dr Eaton my fraternal compliments & tell him to come with you if he can leave his sweetheart long enough. Write me a great long letter immediately, and give me all the news

Your Affectionate Brother,
Dr. O. T. DavidS. B. David

Notes

Part of a Letter: The rest of the letter is in chapter 5.

Dr. Eaton: Doctor William Eaton was a dentist in Thomasville, Thomas County, Georgia, home of Perry and Polly Bowen, Thirza David's brother and his wife. Thomasville is near the Georgia-Florida line.[9]

---

[9] MacIntyre, *History of Thomas County, Georgia*, 35; Perry Bowen to James David, June 23, 1856, in chapter 4; *Georgia Atlas & Gazetteer*, 66.

Dr. O. T. David: Simeon refers to his brother as "Dr." O. T. David. Thomas had started practicing dentistry, probably in the office of Dr. Eaton.[10]

1858

David Family Bible

Owen Thomas David was married to Susan C. Moon Dec 9th 1858

Note

Susan C. Moon: She was Susan Catherine Moon, who in 1858 was about eighteen years old. Owen Thomas David would have been twenty-three years old.[11]

1859

Thomas and Sue Moon David

Monroe March the 12 1859
Dear Mother

I know you have been expecting a letter from me and not oly that but expected to see me last Sabbath. I am sorry that I could not get [hole in letter]. we fully intended to go but the day we intended to start was a verry wet one and we could not go. we started friday and went to Cpt Moon's and I then would have 20 miles to go on saturday and I was compelled to go home Monday. I am verry sorry that I could not go.

We are getting on finely at our home and are awl well. Mr Moon has two hand working with me. he gave us a girl 13 years old at nine hundred Dollars. She is a very likely girl. he also gave us a good horse at 100 Dollars. he offers me or Bob the place [at] 1500 Dollars I dont know which will take it. he will give me land some where if I dont take this.

I went to work as soon as we [hole in letter] and have been going it all the time. I am verry much behind with my work especially plowing for it has rained every week since we moved. if I was not so behind we would come next first sabbath, but it is out of my power to do so, but I hope you will come to see us if we cant do the same. You must let Ratio bring Annie down and stay with us a month or two for Sue is lonely when I am at work and would be pleased to have her company.

---

[10] Perry and Polly Bowen to James David, April 24, 1859, in my possession; US Census, 1860, Jackson County, Georgia.

[11] US Census, 1850, Jackson County, Georgia; David Family Bible.

I must say to you that I like farming better than dentistry. I can eat more sleep sweeter and am more contented than I ever have been. I think I will plant 15 or 20 acres in cotton and I hope I will make a good crop as I am verry needy. Mr Moon gets half that is made and is at all the expense with the acception that we find our groceries

We have been to town to meeting today and had a fine sermon. we [hole in letter] with old friend Pattildo and spent the evening in town. Mr and Mrs Pattildo are our Father & Mother in Walton [County]. they treat us verry well.

You thought Sue was to tender to work but I tell you she is the girl. she can make pots and ovens get [illegible] any thing that is necessary to be done she good at it.

I must close as Sue wants room on this sheat to write to Lona about that monky. give my respects to all and regard me as ever your son

O. T. David

Dear Lona

I must write Something to you about the monkey. Lona I expect you think to much of it I wish I could see the little monkey. I know it is a fine looking chap but the dear little Creatures [page torn] dont want them. I think Tom & I can do well with out such propity or at least I think so. [page torn] will ask you for your little monkey when I see you. I don't have any idie of getting it.

We should like to come soon but all so bussy I do not know when we will See you. we shall look for you all to come to See us this Spring. tell Annie she will enjoy herself if she will come and Stay with us awhile. I must [page torn].

write soon give my love to all I remain your Sister

Sue David

Notes

Monroe: Monroe, Georgia, is in Walton County, east of Atlanta.

Mr. Moon: He was Sue's father, Robert Moon, a prosperous Jackson County farmer, who in 1859 would have been about fifty-eight years old. Sue was one of seven children in the family.[12]

Bob: This probably is Sue's older brother, Robert B. Moon, who in 1859 would have been twenty-one years old.[13]

I like farming better than dentistry: Apparently Thomas later changed his mind about going full time into farming. He also turned down the Walton County property, or it was taken by his brother-in-law, who was listed in the 1860 census as living in Walton County. In the 1860 census, Thomas's profession was listed as dentist, and he was recorded as living in Jackson County.

---

[12] US Census, 1850 and 1860, Jackson County, Georgia.

[13] US Census, 1850, Jackson County, Georgia; US Census, 1860, Walton County, Georgia.

Walton: Walton County, Georgia, is located east of Atlanta.

monkey: This possibly is a reference to Nora Alexander, who was born to Pillona and Manning Alexander on January 17, 1859, about two months before this letter was written. A mischievous child sometimes is referred to as a "monkey."[14]

When the letter was written, Manning was attending medical school in Cincinnati, Ohio (see chapter 5). Pillona may have been staying with her mother while her husband was away.

---

[14] "Monkey," *Webster's New World College Dictionary*, 945. For more about Nora, see letters in chapter 5 and other chapters.

Chapter 4

Simeon Advances: Simeon David and Francis Harris David, 1855–1859

1855

Simeon

Freemansville Georgia April 5th 1855
Dear Mother
    I seat myself this morning to inform you of the few passing events of any interest in this community. We are all in the enjoyment of good health at the present; and our neighborhood is unusually healthy, more so than at any previous period for months even years.
    Myself and the boys are driving on finely with our crops. We are about done breaking our land but have not planted any in consiquence of the extreme coldness of the spring.
    On last Saturday morning there being a fair prospect of rain[,] I and the boys set a great many log-heaps [on fire] and kept them mended up till about 3 P M when the wind rose to such an alarming height that our little cabins were in imminent danger of being burned up as the sparks wer blown in the precise direction of the houses. The boys and myself worked at it with the occasional assistance of Sister and Fanny till 10 O'clock at night. Sunday morning Mrs Gober's Bill and myself cut down and watered out a great many trees lest they might do mischief.
    We enjoy life splendidly—all get along finely. I have had more real enjoyment since I was married than I had had for many months previous. Fanny and myself go to Father Harris as often as convenient where they always seem verry anxious to see us. They are verry kind to us, making us some present of something almost every time we go there.
    Mr Posey Reavis and Dr Hook have aplied for letters of administration on Mr Gober's Estate. I do not know how Mrs Gober will get along. Bill or the place one or the other will have to be sold to pay the debts. From the best information we can get we think Mr Gober was owing to the amount of twelve hundred Dollars. Mr Gober is owing me to the amount of 250 Dollars and I will be obliged to have it for I am not able to loose it.

Mrs Gober is verry much opposed to selling the place and I believe would rather sell Bill than the Place. Bill is verry anxious to be sold to persons living in the neighborhood.

There is a beautiful rain falling now though we are not needing rain much for we had a fine rain on last Tuesday.

I went to the Lodge last Monday night and remained at Town till Tuesday evening. The Temperance party in this county have been soliciting me to be a candidate on that ticket for the Legislature, but I told them that I did not want to be a candidate of any Party.

The Temperance Candidate B. H. Overby Esq will get a great many votes in this section of the State. If there are three parties in Georgia Overby will get the highest number of votes. The opinion prevails in this section of the country that there will be no election by the people.

Mr Gober informed me that you expected to be here in May. We want you to be certain and come. Fanny Sister and the children send their love to you all. Give mine to Grandmother & all write soon

Your affectionate S. B. David

Notes

Freemansville: This was an unincorporated community in Cherokee County. When this letter was written, Simeon and his new wife, Fanny, were living there with his older sister Mary David Neal, widow of Richard Neal, and her four children.

the boys: They were Simeon's nephews, the oldest children of Mary and Richard Neal. When the letter was written, James was about eleven years old, and John was about ten. The Neals also had a third child, Jesse, but he then was only five and may not have helped in the work described.[1]

Sister: She was Mary David Neal.

Mrs. Gober's Bill: He was an enslaved man owned by the Gobers.

Mr. and Mrs. Gober: They probably were Robert H. and Frances Gober. In 1855, they would have been about forty-three and thirty-nine respectively. Robert Gober had married one of Richard Neal's sisters, and thus was Mary Neal's brother-in-law.[2]

The Gobers, Posey Reavis, and Dr. Hook all were mentioned in letters and notes in chapter 1.

---

[1] See letters in chapter 1; US Census, 1850, Cherokee County, Georgia.
[2] US Census, 1850, Robert H. Gober, Cherokee County, Georgia; Ancestry.com, *Georgia Marriages, 1699–1944*, Franklin County.

Father Harris: He was Fanny's father, Lorenzo Dow Harris.[3]

the Lodge: Simeon was a member of the Masons.[4]

Temperance Party: According to resolutions the party adopted in its state convention in Atlanta on February 22, 1855, the Temperance Party promoted "the prohibition of the traffic in ardent spirits as a beverage" and considered that goal as "paramount to all discussions now under discussion in this State."[5]

Simeon rejected this invitation to be a candidate. Later, however, as will be seen, when he received an offer from another party, he accepted.

Basil H. Overby: He was a lawyer and sometimes Methodist minister who was candidate for governor of Georgia in 1855. He had started out as a lawyer in Jefferson, Georgia, the county seat of Jackson County, before moving to Atlanta. Simeon seems to have been wrong about the number of votes Overby would get in his area. Among the three candidates for governor, Overby got only eleven percent of the votes cast in Jackson County and the same percentage of votes cast in Simeon's home county of Cherokee. Overby received only six percent of the vote statewide.[6]

no election by the people: The Georgia Constitution provides that if none of the candidates in the election for governor received a majority of the votes cast, the state legislature could elect the governor by a joint vote of both houses.[7]

Children: Beside the three boys mentioned above, Mary Neal's children included Ann Olivia Neal, age about eight in 1855.[8]

Grandmother: She was James H. David's mother, Pillina David. In 1855 she was about seventy-eight years old and living with James and Thirza.[9]

1856

Simeon

At Home Forsyth Co., Ga. Apr. 29th 1856
Dear Brother [Owen Thomas David]

It has been such a great while since there have been any letters passed between us that I have forgotten which wrote last. But of one thing I am certain, I have not written since the birth of the Princess Mary Elenora, which grand event

---

[3] See letters and notes in chapter 1.
[4] *Southern Banner*, March 15, 1865.
[5] *Augusta Chronicle*, March 2, 1855.
[6] Fahey, "Temperance Movement"; *Federal Union*, October 8, 1855, extra edition; D. Richardson, *Others*, 184–88.
[7] McElreath, *Treatise on the Constitution of Georgia*, 108–109.
[8] US Census, 1850, Mary J. Neal, Milton County, Georgia.
[9] US Census, 1850, James H. David, Jackson County, Georgia; P. David, genealogical notes.

that was celebrated by bonfires and illuminations occurred on the 6th inst. She grows finely and bills fair to soon be flirting with beaux. Fanny is quite well.

I am not quite done planting yet, have bottoms [to] plant, then I will be done. I was on the grand jury court week and lost the whole week and got a little behind with my farm. I "extinguished" myself during court week. I was a stranger at first, but I soon got the hang of it and the most of them looking up to me. It was resolved to elect a committee of three to examine into the financial condition of the county between this and the next sitting of the court. William Rogers, Thomas W. Mayfield, and myself were that committee. We will enter upon the discharge of our duties about the middle of July and will receive two Dollars per day for our services. Do you not think that is doing pretty well for my short residence in the county[?]

Some of the clergy have been playing the wild of late. A few days ago the Rev Drury Hutchins took the stage at Cummings in company with a Lady and went to parts unknown. The Lady has always stood as fair as any lady in Forsyth or any other county. Her Husband is gone to California and sent her at one time 800 Dollars in gold, at another time 100 Dollars. But Hutchins has been visiting her for some time, having her do all his fine sowing for two years.

Not long since[,] his wife & Son found a letter that she had written him imploring him to take her off or she was a ruined woman. She lived in the neighborhood of Cellogg's and Hutchins gave the hack-driver from Dalonegah to Cummng twenty Dollars to bring her down to Cumming. They managed so as not to let her be recognized. When she got there Hutchins met her there and they left immediately.

Hutchins was gone several days and came back without her. No one knows where she is. She is the wife of Mr Francis Kane, Daughter of Mr. George Bell who is related to the Jack Bell of Jefferson, and Cousin to the Lawyer H. P. Bell. I have no doubt but Hutchins [is] out to have his head cut smooth off. My opinion is he has been acting this way for years, he is now a ruined man.

The other Preacher alluded to is Henry P Pitchford of Cotoosa County. [All] I know about that is a woman swore a child to him, & he was stopped awhile from preaching, but has gone to preaching again. You know we always thought he was a snake in the grass.... .

Your Affectionate Brother,
Dr. O. T. David   S. B. David

Notes

At Home, Forsyth County: Simeon no longer lived with his sister Mary Neal and her family in Freemansville but had moved to the Vickery's Creek area of Forsyth County, which was only five or six miles west of Freemansville.

Forsyth County had been created out of Cherokee County in December 1832. Farmers were attracted to the new county by its dark, sandy soil that was particularly good for growing corn, wheat, and cotton. Certainly another early attraction to settlers was the county's location between two gold belts: The Dahlonega Gold Belt running through the northwest corner of the county and the Hall County Gold Belt through the east part of the entire county. As a result, several small scale but profitable mining operations were established in the county.[10]

Princess Mary Eleanora: She later was known more informally as Ellen.

Cumming: Cumming was established as the county seat of Forsyth County in 1834. It is in roughly the middle of the county. In 1849 it had a population of about four hundred, two churches, two hotels, two schools, five stores, a masonic lodge (of which Simeon later was a member), and assorted other buildings. In 1854, a brick courthouse was constructed in Cumming to replace a frame one. It was here that Simeon likely met as part of the grand jury during court week.[11]

Rev. Drury Hutchens and Mrs. Kane: At a meeting of the members of the American Party in Forsyth County held in 1855, Rev. D. Hutchins was the losing candidate in an election to determine who would represent the party in the race for the Forsyth County seat in the Georgia House of Representatives.[12]

On May 15, 1856, the following article appeared on page 2 of the *Southern Watchman*:

A Bad Egg!

The *Marietta Georgian* announces that the Rev. Mr. Hutchins, of Forsyth County (about 65 years of age and a Baptist minister for the last 25 years), passed through that place lately on his way to "furrin parts," in company with a "grass widow" whose husband is in California, and leaving at home his own wife and children—under the pretence that he was in search of a new location out west. The fallen old man took letters of dismission and recommendation, from the church, for himself and *wife*.

hack-driver: A "hack" was horse-drawn vehicle, such as a carriage, coach, or wagon, for hire and a "hack-driver" was a person who drove such a vehicle.[13]

Dahlonega: Was a town about thirty miles northeast of Cumming.[14]

---

[10] Bagley, *History of Forsyth County, Georgia*, 230, 279–90; Shadburn, ed., *Pioneer History of Forsyth County, Georgia*, 30, 65; Bramblett, *Forsyth County History Stories*, 88.

[11] Bagley, *History of Forsyth County, Georgia*, 354–55, 370; Shadburn, ed., *Pioneer History of Forsyth County, Georgia*, 37, 65; Bramblett, *Forsyth County History Stories*, 51.

[12] *Southern Watchman*, August 30, 1855.

[13] *Webster's New World College Dictionary*, 651.

[14] *Georgia Atlas & Gazetteer*, 20, 21, 15.

Jefferson: Jefferson was and is the county seat of Jackson County.[15]

Omitted part of letter: The omitted part of the letter is in chapter 3 concerning Owen Thomas David and the April Fool's joke.

Simeon

Forsyth Co, Georgia   Oct. 16, 1856
Dear Parents

I seat myself to night to reply to Mother's letter that was received by due course of Mail. I am sorry that I have not written sooner, but first one thing and then another has prevented me. I have no [illegible] that is large enough to send to the office and frequently have not the time to spare. But I want the following to be the understanding between us; that Silence is always to mean good health and reasonable prosperity.

Although there is a great deal of sickness and a good many deaths in this section of country, we are still blessed with good health except that our little pratler is complaining of thrash, but I think will be well in a day or two. She grows finely and can sit alone & begin to crawl a little. You have no idea of the amount of satisfaction she is to us.

There are chills and fever and ague & fever all round us. There have been several deaths, mostly children in this neighborhood. Cobb's Mill Pond just below us has caused sickness all around it, & my opinion is that nothing but a considerable extent of thick woods had saved us. I have a piece of bottom corn near the head of the pond that I am afraid to gather until the weather gets cool.

There are distressing times in Sister Mary's neighborhood. Mr. Maddus has lost two grown daughters, Jane and Mary. Old Mrs Yancey has recently died, & Mr Lewis Tucker (Soloman Peek's father-in-law) got drunk at Sol's & left there for home verry early one morning last week, & in attempting to cross the creek on his way home fell from his horse, face foremost into the water and was drowned. The Coroner was sent for and an inquest held over the body. The verdict of the jury was that he came to his death by being drowned with water.

The grocery at the crossroads near Sol Peek's that has caused so mutch suffering and desolation and woe is about to go down since Tucker's sad end. Civil, respectable persons have been afraid to pass the grocery all this year.

Sister Mary sent up the boys last week to assist me in hauling up my corn so that she could get my wagon & oxen to haul hers this week. My upland turned out better than I expected. We shucked Tuesday night last, & I think there were some thirty five or 40 Barrels. I had 13 wagon loads of the upland & I think the

---

[15] Elrod, *Historical Notes on Jackson County*, 41.

bottom will pay the rent and make me three or four more. I will not lack much of having my [corn] crib full.

My potatoes are tolerably good, some of them fine considering the drought. Peas were mostly killed by the early frosts, and cotton materially injured.

I had expected to start this morning to the great mass meeting at Atlanta, but the unlikelyness of the weather prevented. I saw Dr Bell's brother James at Cumming last Sab day. He tells me that Dr. Bell is making a fortune practicing medicine, that he gets all that he can do. He says Dr. has been offered 1200 Dollars for his tract of land that only cost him 600, but refuses to take less than 1500 Dollars.

Mr Harris and family treat me with a great deal of friendship and respect, more than they ever have since I have been married. They send Mary off with me to Town or to Campmeetings to stay two or three days ten times sooner than they would with either of her Brothers. They find that I am as unyielding in my principles as Gibraltar itself. They now respect me for it. Neither of you need ever have any uneasiness about me, for if I an't get my rights by fair means, I will by foul.

Rogers, Mayfield, & Myself closed our labors after thirty five days work, and found that the county had been defrauded by its officers of near two thousand Dollars. The county will pay us two dollars each per day for our services. I must close.

your affectionate Son S. B. David
J. H. & Thirza David

Notes

thrash: This probably is a reference to "thrush," which is an infection causing sores in the mouth.[16]

ague: This means an intermittent fever and chills. At the time Simeon wrote, a fever was thought to be a disease rather than a symptom of a disease.[17]

great mass meeting in Atlanta: This was a large, state-wide Democratic Party campaign rally; 1856 was a presidential election year, and the Democratic Party candidates were James Buchanan for president and John C. Breckinridge for vice president.[18]

sent Mary off with me: Mary was Mary Harris, Fanny's younger sister. In 1858 she was about seventeen years old.

---

[16] Drake, *What Did They Mean by That?*, 305; Dunglison, *Dictionary of Medical Science*, 70, 1034.

[17] Drake, *What Did They Mean by That?*, 5; Dunglison, *Dictionary of Medical Science*, 27.

[18] *Southern Banner*, October 16, 1856.

Rogers, Mayfield, & Myself: As indicated in Simeon's letter of April 29, 1856, the three men had been appointed to examine the financial condition of the county.

Simeon

Vickerys Creek Ga   Nov 25th 1856
Dear Mother

Your affectionate letter of the 18th inst was duly received & we are truly sorry, indeed grieved, that you have heard nothing from Tommy or rather that you have passed so many uneasy hours about him. I hope long ere this letter reaches you, you will have heard all about him. I was to meet him in Canton Wednesday after he left, by promise but my mule became lame & I was disappointed in going. The fifth of this month, or wednesday after the Presidential election, he addressed me a lengthy letter from Dr Bell's, giving me a full description of his travels from Canton to Alabama, his ride on the "Iron horse"—his examination of the Steam Boats at Rome,—the amount of work he did at Harlan's, etc etc. He also stated that he expected to come through Forsyth on his way home, & I have been looking for him for the last ten days: But as he has not come I am inclined to think that he has gone by way of Fort Gains. I have no doubt he wrote you but his letter was mismailed somehow or other. This is all I know about him

After reading your letter, I thought we would try to visit you before Christmas, But under the circumstances I don't think we can conveniently. In the first place, if we were to go, Fanny would want a new dress & I a new overcoat & some other things that would amount to some ten or fifteen Dollars. by staying at home we [hole in letter] do without all that. 2ndly our fattening hogs, cattle, & out hogs would all have to be left in the care of other people & lastly I cannot spare the time, for I promised Uncle Isaac that when we visited you again we would go to see him [too].

I am verry thankful for the pants pattern, but as I have a wife to make pants for me I will relinquish all claim to them & you can give them to Tommy. Keep the china cup till I see you & I will then take care of it as long as I live.

I will give a history of how I am getting on. My corn crop was considerably better than I expected, from the No of loads & the size of the crib I think I made about 50 Barrels of corn, 15 bushels of potatoes, 61½ bushels of wheat 300 doz of oats & ten Dollars worth of cotton. I have received twenty Dollars & expect forty more for my services at Cummings—the interest of what little money I have will be forty Dollars.

I am fattening 7 verry pretty shoats that I design to make weigh 1000 pounds. I sowed 6 Bushels of wheat, have had 6 ground into flour & sold 6 1/2 at $1.00 per Bushel. I design selling 25 or 30 Bushels more wheat, also oats, Potatoes, corn & pork or Bacon. I hope I shall have enough of the above named commodities to sell to bring upwards of 150 Dollars. I owe nothing at all, except for a cow that I bought last week at $11.50 cts. My Oxen have grown greatly since last spring & are worth fifty Dollars. My mule is the finest in the country of her age & is worth 175 Dollars.

I am not making these statements in any boastful spirit, but merely to let you know how I am getting along in the world in pecuniary point of view. I desire to feel thankful to Heaven that my labors temporally, have been so signally blessed under all the circumstances.

It is not our calculation at present to stay here more than another year. We expect to move on a place that Father Harris has recently bought lying on the Frog Town road just above the Baptist Camp Ground. The tract contains 144 Acres, 25 or thirty of which is excellent bottom, lying about half mile above the ford between Dupree's & Arch Harris. It cost one thousand Dollars and is the best bargain that has been bought in this country in years. The former owner Shepherd Jenkins pays Seventy Dollars, the interest on 1000, rent, next year. I think by another fall I can sell this place [where I now live] for 500 Dollars. if I do it will only require 400 more to pay for the Jenkins place.

This place has a court ground & store house upon it & we purpose having Vickery's Creek post office moved there as soon as congress meets again. The only objection I have to [the] place is its being to close to the camp ground & Church, it is just five miles from Cumming. It has a double house, with a chimney in the middle, one end used as a dwelling, the other as a Kitchen, good stables and other out buildings on it. Col Elizur Newton of Athens owns a lot lying near it with 25 or 30 Acres of bottom on it that I want to buy. I have written him respecting it but have received no answer. I forgot to state the bottom on this place was nearly all fresh, some of it with the first crop on it the remainder with the second, all of it well ditched & drained

Enough about my affairs. Sister Mary is doing wonderfully. She has made verry nearly or quite as mutch corn as she did last year & has cotton, wheat, oats, potatoes, & probably pork or Bacon to sell, in short Sister Mary & the Boys are making money. She is making arrangements to refund to Father this winter. But I am sorry to tell you that poor little Ann Olivia's health is failing. I want you if there is any passing to let her go to your house & stay till spring, I think she needs recreation & rest.

Well Mother I have written four pages & am not done yet, but will finish. To Sisters Ann & Lona Give Dear old grand Mother our best warmest love & respects. Tell her I verry mutch want her to see our little Darling Ellen

Your Affectionate Son S. B. David

Notes

fattening hogs and out hogs: Fattening hogs were probably hogs kept confined in an enclosure where they could be fed plentifully in preparation for being slaughtered for meat. Out hogs likely were those less confined in a place where they can forage for themselves.

Uncle Isaac: He was Isaac M. David, a younger brother of James H. David. In October 1856, he was forty-seven years old and living in Franklin County with his wife and children.[19]

shoats: A shoat is "a young, weaned pig."[20]

Frog Town: This was a community in northwestern Forsyth County also known as Hightower.[21]

1857

Mary Juliette Neal

[Freemansville April 6, 1857]
Dear Father and Mother [James H. and Thirza David]

I received your kind letter of the 10th of March by Brother Thomas. I was thankful to hear that you were all enjoying common health. When Brother Thomas told me you had expected to come with him, I was so anxious to see you, but I was almost sorry for a few hours that I had written anything to cause you to wait longer. I have had but little opportunity since then to write to you, as it is not very long now until the time you set to come. It may be almost useless but for fear you are expecting a letter, I will write a few lines.

We are all well. James' foot has healed entirely. For some weeks after ploughing all day he often complains of his ankle paining him.

We commenced planting corn last week. It will take one day yet to finish the eight-acre piece we have commenced. It has been very dry for the season, until yesterday there was light showers during the day. Last night was quite wet and considerable hail. Today is cold and windy. What little vegetation has put out was injured by the cold and hail last night. I have not hired but one day's work in the field this year, though I have assisted more than I did last spring.

I bought from Mr. Griffin a small house that stood in the yard where Esq Orr lived, also a plank floor and rock chimney where Massey lived. I had the plank floor put in the house, our old kitchen moved out for a shuck-house, the other house put up in the same place, for a kitchen. I had new sills put under it

---

[19] US Census, 1850, Franklin County, Georgia; P. David, genealogical notes.
[20] "Shoat," *Webster's New World College Dictionary*, 1341.
[21] Bramblett, *Forsyth County History Stories*, 52.

and new boards to cover it, with a rock chimney. The work is all done, and I have been using the kitchen one week. It has cost me, beside our own labor, $17 seventeen-dollars, which is all paid except four dollars.

I paid all that I was owing in Cherokee the commencement of this year. I have only sixteen dollars at this time, with the ten that Uncle William paid me before he went to Franklin. I have not seen him since he returned. I have twelve dollars owing me in good hands, that I have no doubt of getting when I call for it.

As Jan. is idle, and I have been housed from the wind and not much tired, I expect to go to Mr Revis' tonight to get him to assist me to value the things as you requested and make a return of it when he does his.

Dear parents, perhaps I have written more than was necessary about my temporal matters but thinking I could not abridge it satisfactorily and believing it would be acceptable to you, I have been tedious. It is our great privilege amid toil and fatigue to cast all our care upon the Lord and enjoy a cheerful, resigned, and happy frame of mind.

Tell Ann Olivia her brothers often speak of her. They think if Sissy is as anxious to come home as they are for her to come, she thinks long of the time. I want [either] Sister Ann or Lona to be sure to come with Father. Give my love to Grandmother, Sisters, and all the family. I remain

Your devoted daughter
M. J. Neal

Notes

Freemansville April 6, 1857: This letter is a transcription of an original letter that has been lost. Apparently, there was no place or date in the original, but someone has written "April 6, 1857" on the transcription. That seems a reasonable date. Freemansville is the likely place.

Uncle William: He was William A. David, a younger brother of James H. David. In April 1857 he was fifty-five years old.[22]

1858

Simeon

Vickerys Creek Ga   Jan 10th 1858
    Dear Brother [Owen Thomas David]
    I have long delayed writing you for the reason that I have not gone about it. We are all well except that Fanny has a verry severe cold.

---

[22] See letter from P. C. Bell of July 4, 1859, in chapter 4, which mentions "Uncle William David"; US Census, 1860, Milton County, Georgia; P. David, genealogical notes.

I suppose you have heard long since that we have another daughter, born on the third of Dec last, we have not named her as yet. She is a verry pretty, promising, thriving child.

Elenora enjoys excellent health, is as fat as a pig and as funny as a cricket. She can talk almost right plain, says Mas Simeon & Miss Frances. Sings I can "tarry but a night" and cuts a great many extras,

At James Harris Sale I purchased the thrash, fan, running gear & all the apparatus belonging there to[,] with the entire controll of the house and lot as long as I saw proper to let it stay there[,] for the sum of Ninety-two Dollars. I also bought 30 bushels of wheat at 80 cts per Bush & nearly 1000 lbs of seed cotton at $2.80 cts per hund. for speculation. from present indications the cotton speculation will be over [to the] left but I am determined not to sell till I can make something by the operation

I am determined to make the thrash pay for itself this year. My arrangements are all made to commence thrashing oats on tomorrow morning. I have swopped off my Oxen for a beautiful fine mule 2 years old last fall and work mules now entirely, it cost me about 110 Dollars, Kit has grown & fattened a great deal since you saw her & is now the finest mule in all the country. I have hired Lewis Burgess (one that used to live with Posey Reavis) to live with me this year at 8 Dollars per month and he board[s] himself.

I have torn down my old kitchen and moved it and put it up on the road between me and Lummus. I have 25 Acres sown in what that will make if wheat is as good as last year 150 bushels. it is verry promising at present. I have killed two of my fattening hogs and have 7 yet to kill that will average 175 pounds. I have worked along and just about made a living as long as I am going to. I am determined to make something now or break one or the other.

Willson Harris is making arrangements to go to California when the old man Harral goes back which will be towards the last of this month. Newton Harral asked the old folks for Mary last week & they will marry either just before or just after the old man Harral starts. You & Ann will be invited to the wedding and must come.

I believe from all the indications that Mary Jim & Landrum Delany will marry. She will drive her ducks to a bad market certain. There is a little Dr. Nichols a vermonter that located in Cumming last Summer that is flying round Mat some. Mat will marry him if she can get him. Jasper Pool & Anderson Smith's daughter married not long since, Davis from Polk County came out this Christmas to take Mary Dow home with him & because she would not go it liked to have killed him.

The Harris Negroes were sold the 1st Tuesday inst. All brought 1104 Dollars. Bill Dinsmore bought him, & P. Reavis [bought] John at 1000 Dollars.

I have scratched al this on my knee by fire light and thinks you will excuse me if I quit. Fanny sends love to you, & your sweet heart. Hand & Ansel Harrel and Dr Bogle & wife are going to California.

Write soon. Your Brother S. B. David

Notes

another daughter: She later was named Lena.

"tarry but a night": This is part of the first line of a hymn, "I'm a Pilgrim," by Mary Dana Shindler. The first verse:

I'm a pilgrim, and I'm a stranger,
I can tarry, I can tarry but a night;
Do not detain me, for I am going
To where the fountains are ever flowing:
I'm a pilgrim, and I'm a stranger,
I can tarry, I can tarry but a night.[23]

cuts a great many extras: This phrase probably means that Eleanora sings other songs or maybe does other things, such as dance about.

James Harris: This was one of Fanny Harris David's older brothers, who in 1858 was about twenty-eight years old.[24]

cotton speculation over the left: This phrase means that the price of cotton will be in the debit column, which under accounting practices is on the left side of a ledger. Simeon probably means that he has spent more money raising cotton than he can make by selling it then.[25]

I am determined to make something now or break one or the other: Apparently Simeon is determined either to be successful or to go bankrupt.

Willson Harris: This was another of Fanny's older brothers, who in 1858 was about twenty-four years old.[26]

Mary and Newton Harall: Mary was Fanny's younger sister, who in 1858 was about nineteen years old. She did marry Newton Harrell a month later.[27]

Ann: This was Simeon and Thomas's sister.

Davis from Polk County: He possibly was a brother of Van William Davis from Polk County. Van William Davis will appear in this narrative after the Civil War.

---

[23] "I'm a Pilgrim, and I'm a stranger," Hymnary.org, https://hymnary.org/text/im_a_pilgrim_and_im_a_stranger_i_can_tar, accessed October 7, 2020.

[24] US Census, 1850, L. D. Harris, Forsyth County, Georgia.

[25] "Debit," *Webster's New World College Dictionary*, 381.

[26] US Census, 1850, L. D. Harris, Forsyth County, Georgia.

[27] Ibid.; *Forsyth County Record of Marriages, Book C, 1853–1858*, 120.

1859

Democratic Meeting in Forsyth County[28]
Cumming, Ga., May 3d, 1859

Pursuant to previous notice a respectable portion of the Democratic party of Forsyth county assembled in the court house to-day for the purpose of appointing delegates to the Gubernatorial and Congressional Conventions.

On motion, the meeting was organized by calling A. G. Hutchins, Esq., to the chair and requesting Col. S. B. David to act as Secretary... .

Delegates to the Gainsville Convention

Col. S. B. David, A. G. Hutchins, Esq., Dr. J. L. Hugs, Dr. M. W. Sutton....

Notes

Col. S. B. David to act as Secretary: Colonel was Simeon's militia rank. Simeon had been commissioned a colonel in the Cherokee County Militia on February 11, 1854, by Governor Hershel V. Johnson. He likely retained his rank in the Forsyth County militia. This meeting is not the first time that Simeon had been asked to be the secretary of a Democratic Party meeting in Forsyth County. Two years earlier he had served as secretary at such a meeting, and there may have been other occasions.[29]

Gainsville Convention: This convention was a meeting of the Democratic Party of the 6th Congressional District and was held in Gainesville on July 13, 1859. Although elected as a delegate to the convention, Simeon was not listed as having attended.[30]

ELECTION RETURNS—1859[31]
MEMBERS OF THE LEGISLATURE...

Forsyth—Hutchins, Davi[d], Bruton

Notes

The first named was elected to the Senate, the next two were elected to the House of Representatives.

The election was held on the first Monday in October, October 3, 1859. Simeon had been nominated to run for one of Forsyth County's two seats in the Georgia House of Representatives at a meeting of the Forsyth County

---

[28] *Atlanta Weekly Intelligencer*, May 19, 1859, 2.
[29] Military Commissions microfilm, Georgia Archives, Morrow, Georgia; *Atlanta Daily Intelligencer and Examiner*, November 12, 1857.
[30] *Southern Banner*, July 21, 1859.
[31] Southern Watchman, October 13, 1859, 2.

Democratic Party earlier in 1859. That meeting seems not to have been reported in the local papers, or possibly it was reported in an issue of the relevant paper that has not survived.[32]

Each county had one or two seats in the House and one in the Senate. Forsyth County had two seats in the House: A. Bruton was the other House member for Forsyth, and A. G. Hutchins was the Senate member for Forsyth. Both, like Simeon, were Democrats. Those elected in 1859 served in the General Assembly for two annual sessions, those of 1859 and 1860.[33]

During the 1859 session, the speaker of the house appointed Simeon to two standing committees, the committee on public education and the committee on enrollment. Simeon actually was appointed chairman of the committee on enrollment.[34]

It was unusual for a freshman representative attending his first session of the General Assembly to be appointed chairman of a standing committee. The duties of the committee on enrollment, however, were primarily clerical. They included preparing an error-free, official final copy of each bill passed by the House. Once the committee chairman was satisfied with the copy, he proceeded to the House floor and formally presented the final copy to the speaker of the house for the speaker's signature. Being chairman of the enrollment committee once was described as "a most onerous and responsible position." Possibly it was not a position that was widely sought after. However, it did allow Simeon to be recognized and speak on the House floor, even if briefly and formally, and receive some visibility.[35]

The 1859 session began on November 2, 1859. One of the first items the House adopted on its first full day of business was a resolution condemning John Brown's raid at Harper's Ferry, which had occurred October 16–18, less than a month earlier: "We regard the effort to excite the slaves of the South to a servile insurrection with the most intense indignation, and trust the parties to this insane and treasonable plot, may meet with the most prompt and signal punishment."

---

[32] *Southern Watchman*, September 22, 1859; see *Federal Union*, August 9, 1859, and September 13, 1859, for examples of meetings of county Democratic Parties that nominated candidates for the legislature.

[33] *Daily Federal Union*, November 11, 1859; Georgia House of Representatives, Journal of the House of Representatives, 1859, 5.

[34] Georgia House of Representatives, Journal of the House of Representatives, 1859, 52–53.

[35] Ibid., 73, 151; Battey & Co., *Biographical Souvenir*, 159; "Enroll," *Webster's New World College Dictionary*, 484; "How a Bill Is Passed in the Georgia Legislature," ACCG, http://www.accg.org/library/how_a_bill_becomes_law.pdf, accessed September 18, 2023.

The resolution also supported "the prompt and energetic action of Governor Wise, of Virginia, and of President Buchanan in suppressing the outbreak."[36]

The session adjourned on December 16. On December 10, however, Simeon was excused from attendance for the remainder of the session "on account of sickness in his family." Who was sick and the nature of that illness, unfortunately, are not known.[37]

The 1860 session began on November 7, 1860, only a day after Abraham Lincoln was elected president. Events of that session are addressed in chapter 6.

---

[36] "John Brown's raid on Harper's Ferry," Wikipedia, https://en.wikipedia.org/wiki/John_Brown%27s_raid_on_Harpers_Ferry, accessed October 8, 2020; Georgia House of Representatives, *Journal of the House of Representatives, 1859*, 3, 9:357–58, 516.

[37] Georgia House of Representatives, *Journal of the House of Representatives, 1859*, 9:357–58, 516.

Chapter 5

Medical School: Pillona Alexander and Manning Poole Alexander, 1858–1859

1858

H. L. Steele

Tunnel Hill S. C.
Apr 19th 1858
Dr. Alexander
    As I moved from Clarksville soon after I wrote you I did not receive your letter until yesterday. my object for writing you was simply to sell my medicine to prevent the trouble of moving them. I would not have left Clarksville if it had not been that I got a good offer here. I think I got while at Clarksville (11 months) near eight (800) hundred dollars worth of practice I think I have & will get about ($700) seven hundred of it. My practice increased gradually from the time I went there until I left.
    If you go there you will find Dr Rush a complete gentleman. [He] will take no under handed turn on you at all. If you go there H L Smith can tell you more about my practice than any one else as I left the asset in his hand for collection He knows more about them than I do myself.
    I have not a doubt but that you could do well when you get there.
I remain your best wisher
H L Steele
Dr M P Alexander

Notes

Clarkesville: Clarksville is in Habersham County in the northeast part of Georgia. A small part of it shares a border with South Carolina. Manning did not move his practice there.[1]

***

A. O. Alexander

Cass Co Ga
Oct the 11th 1858

---

[1] *Georgia Atlas & Gazetteer*, 16.

Dear brother[Manning Poole Alexander] I will drp you a few lines to let you no how I am. I can not say to you that I am well at this time as I have a pain in my hip which dis able me to travel at this time to some exten. you must not think that I am not able to walk but I can not ride to do any good. it paines me to set in a chair long at a time.

I am at uncle John Millwee & have bin hear a bout 4 weeks. I came up here with the intention of teach[ing] school at Adairsville but failed in getting a school sufficient to Justify me in teaching.

As soon as I get able to ride goin back to Polk [County] to see my wheat & then I shall come home.

being dis able to ride is the reasen tha I have not written to you before now. So nothing more.

Yours most truly A. O. Alexander
direct yours to Rome

Notes

A. O. Alexander: He was Adam O. Alexander, a younger brother of Manning. When the letter was written he was twenty-three years old. Information about his service during the war appears below.[2]

uncle John Millwee: According to family lore, Manning's grandmother on his mother's side was Mary Millwee. She had a brother named John who probably was this Uncle John.[3]

Cass County and Adairsville: Adairsville was located in Cass County, which later became Bartow County, in the northwest part of Georgia around sixty miles south of Chattanooga, Tennessee. During the Civil War, Manning himself stayed with his uncle John for about three weeks on leave from the Confederate army to recuperate from a reoccurring medical problem (see chapter 23).[4]

Polk: Polk County is in northwest Georgia adjoining Alabama. To the northeast, it also borders Bartow County.[5]

Rome: Rome, Georgia, is in Floyd County in northwest Georgia. The county shares a border with Polk County to the south and Alabama to the west.[6]

1859

---

[2] Chaplin, *Riches of Bunyan* (Alexander family copy).

[3] Draft application for membership in the Daughters of the American Revolution, in my possession.

[4] *Georgia Atlas & Gazetteer*, 19; "Bartow County, Georgia," Wikipedia, https://en.wikipedia.org/wiki/Bartow_County,_Georgia, accessed March 10, 2016.

[5] *Georgia Atlas & Gazetteer*, 18–19.

[6] *Georgia Atlas & Gazetteer*, 18.

Manning Poole Alexander

Cincinnati Ohio
March 19th 1859

Well Dear [Pillona David Alexander] my week's work is dun and the first thing on hand is to write letters and of course your's stands at the head of the list. I hope you have received boath my other communications ear [ere] thas time and I furthermore hope to receive something from you *soon*. I have been going to the Postoffice for the last week hoping every time to get something that I wanted most of all things, but I have been disappointed every time yet I think though I will here from you in a few days

Well dear, I have just eat a harty supper and again resume my pen. I am getting on finly taking all things into consideration. If you and Linna were here I would "be in town" sure. I think you say I am in town anyhow, well its true I am in "some considerable." But you know we use the expression when we [want] to be understood to mean that we are *well* situated.

I expect to remain where I am as long as I stay in the City. I would not exchange it for any place in the City. Our landlady is very kind and obliging. She dose her coocking more like the country people than any where that I have seen. But you need not infer from what I have said that we have such fair as we have in the country though it is beter than I expected. we have a plenty and that, that is tolrebly good.

You know dear how much I believe in "*longing*," but I will acknowledg that I almost long for some of that turnip salid, jole, corn bread and butter-milk you had for dinner to-day. I toled Mrs Edwards that I was a perfect "cow-brute" after turnip greens so she went to market this morning and got some, but dear she did not coock it to right, she boiled it in cold, no clear, water and put butter on it. You see they have no jole. Well it done better than you would have thought. I prased it highly of course and eat of it hartily telling her at the same time how my better half served it up which was my way so I think next time it will come "right side up with care"

My health is *very* good now I can eat as hartily as I ever did in my life. I was sick about a week as I wrote you when I first came to the city; but that just set me strate. Well I am a little like the Indians tree [—] I am a little over strate about, or just before meal time I lean over a little when I start to the dining room.

I am well pleased so far with the college. If they will just give me a sheape skin when I get redy to start home they will do me a favor. I tell them that is what I came for and I am going to have it.

I am discecting now and have been for a week. We will get through [dissecting] the insuing week. I take great interest in it. it is the only means of acquiring a knowledg of Anatemy.

We have had fine wether ever since we came. very plesent indeed untill a day or two since. It rained thursday and until yesterday evening when it turned colder and commenced snowing—to-day has been very March like—windy and cold. I think there will be some ice in the morning.

I am geting some what acustumed to the continual rattle of drays, carriages, omnibuses, bells, the whistle of Railroad and Steamboat engins. There are fires almost every day but I have neve been out yet to see the engines play. I should like to see them but I am not going out at night. it is not altogether safe.

Well dear I must close. Write me soon. Write me when you expect to go to Father's. Dont work to hard. Our commencement will come of between 15th and 20th of May, so if I have luck I will be down to see you and Nora by 1st June.

Your Affectionate Husband

M. P. Alexander

Direct—

Dr M. P. Alexander Care of

J. G. Henshall No. 110

Sixth Street

Cincinnati

Ohio.

[Envelope]

3 cents stamp

Cincinnati 20 postmark

Mrs. M. P. Alexander

Maysville

Georgia

Notes

Cincinnati, Ohio: The original settlement of Cincinnati on the Ohio River began in 1788, and the town was incorporated in 1802. By midcentury, it had grown to be the sixth largest city in the United States. During 1852 reportedly "over 8,000 steamboats arrived and departed from Cincinnati's Public Landing." The federal census of 1860 listed its population as 161,044.[7]

Manning was in Cincinnati attending the Eclectic Medical Institute of Cincinnati. The Institute was chartered in 1845 and taught a combination of traditional and nontraditional medicine, relying principally on the nontraditional. A later study of the school summarized it as "a school based on plant medicines, maintenance of the body's vital force, avoidance of depletive remedies and the dual concepts of specific diagnosis and specific medication." It strongly opposed

---

[7] Hessler, *Cincinnati*, 7, 13; Greve, *Centennial History of Cincinnati*, 686; Haller, *Alternative Medicine*, 1.

the indiscriminate use of mineral medicines, such as mercury and arsenic, and to such harsh practices of traditional medicine as bleeding, leeching, blistering, purging (using strong laxatives), and vomiting. There were several schools in the United States that taught eclectic medicine, but the Institute of Cincinnati was known affectionately as the "mother institute."[8]

In order to obtain a diploma from the institute, a student had to pass "a thorough, critical, and impartial examination" given by the faculty. To qualify to take the examination, he or she—the institute trained and graduated women—had to meet one of several alternative criteria, one of which was that the student had been "for four years next preceding engaged in a constant and reputable practice of medicine" and had "attended one full course of medical lectures in this Institute."[9]

Manning had been practicing for the required four years and had enrolled in the institute on February 24, 1859, for its spring term, a sixteen-week course, which included the study of anatomy, physiology, chemistry, pharmacology, toxicology, theory and practice of medicine, surgery, obstetrics, medical jurisprudence, and clinical medicine. He was on his way to qualify for a diploma.[10]

Manning's medical education was somewhat typical of medical education at that time. "By the 1850s the typical medical practitioner had attended one set of lectures for five or six months, perhaps less," Freemon writes in *Gangrene and Glory*, "and then the following year he heard the same lectures again. He might have worked with a practicing doctor, a remnant of the old medical tradition, but he might have had no apprenticeship at all."[11]

His surgery course likely would have included the treatment of gunshot wounds, although in spring 1859, Manning would not have predicted how important this aspect of his studies would soon become to him and to many of his professors and fellow students.[12]

Linna and Nora: Both these names refer to Nora Alexander, who was born January 17, 1859, only two months before this letter was written. Some documents refer to her as Nora L. Alexander. Thus, Linna may be her middle name,

---

[8] "Eclectic Medical Institute of Cincinnati Matriculation Records," 2; Felter, *History of the Eclectic Medical Institute*, 22–23, 92; Haller, *Alternative Medicine*, xi–xii, 7, 11 (quotes).

[9] Felter, *History of the Eclectic Medical Institute*, 22–23 (quotes); Haller, *Alternative Medicine*, 97–98, 167.

[10] "Eclectic Medical Institute of Cincinnati Matriculation Records," 2; Felter, *History of the Eclectic Medical Institute*, 79–80; Haller, *Alternative Medicine*, 25.

[11] Freemon, *Gangrene and Glory*, 24.

[12] Paine, *Epitome of the American Eclectic Practice of Medicine*, 495–96.

and perhaps the Alexanders had not yet decided whether to call her Linna or Nora.[13]

jole: Was a common way of writing "jowl." As used in this letter, it refers to the cheek of a pig. Hog jole and turnip greens was a popular dish in the South.[14]

cow-brute: Euphemism for "bull." Others were "male cow" and "gentleman cow."[15]

Indians tree: This phrase appears to be a reference to an old simile that likens something to the Indian's tree that stood so straight it leaned the other way.[16]

sheape skin: Sheepskin refers to the use of sheepskin to make parchment that was used for diplomas, and thus means a diploma.[17]

Father's: Manning is referring to Pillona's father, James H. David.

Manning Poole Alexander

Cincinnati Ohio
March 27th 1859
Dear,

Having just finished a good breakfiast of fish and chees I feel just like siting down and having [a] long chat with you.

Yours of 11, 14th was received and red. I need not tell you with the greatest pleasure. I had grown exceedingly anxious to here from you and "the babe." Yours came to hand on Monday after it was writen—6 days coming. You need not be uneasy if you dont get letters regularly becaus they do not always go directly throug. Sometimes the mail-packets do not make connections owing to dense fogs that rise on the rivers at night making it so dark that they cannot pilot the boats.

Well dear, you said for me to write just as soon as I received yours. You will pardon me for not doing so as I had just started a letter the day before I received yours. You request me to write all the news. Now you know my disposition with regard [to] complying with your requests, but you will pleas pardon me *this* time. It would fill the Watchman or Banner. I guess I will have a "fine squad of it" when I get home. You recollect I told you last saturday-night that we had turnip greens for dinner boiled in clear water and buttered, and what [I] said to Mrs Edwards. Well, sure enough on Monday the "greens" came up "all right." Now

---

[13] Grave marker for Nora Alexander Boone, Sunrise Cemetery, Maysville, Georgia; marriage record for George P. Boone and Nora L. Alexander, December 5, 1876 (*Jackson County Marriages Book F*, 1873–1884, 169).

[14] De Vere, *Americanisms*, 496.

[15] Keyes, *Euphemania*, 29.

[16] *Charlotte News*, December 4, 1900.

[17] "Sheepskin," *Webster's New World College Dictionary*, 1337.

what do you think I did. You can guess the very first time. Well I did. Just forked them under my shirt "some considerable."

Now maybe you would like to know what we have to eat and whether we have enough or not. We have a plenty and quite a variety. Some articles we have all the time other things are varied. We have biusquit and loaf bred for breakfast and supper[,] corn bred for dinner. Stewed fruit preserves and molasses all the time. We have beef pork ham and chicken generally and *fish* about twice a week. Desert at dinner—a variety of other articles too tedious to mention.

So you see we live pr*eety* well. I have every reason to believe that our coocking is done in a desent manner from the fact that the lady dose it all herself. I have been in the kitchen department a time or two and every thing looks neet. You see I hapened in there on purpose to loock round.

So much for the eating department. Now I must tell you something about our room and sleeping apartment. Our room is about15 feet *long* and 18 *wide*. Fuirniture—good *feather* bed, fine stid. wash stand chairs bookcase scenter-table etc etc. So you see we are prety well fixed.

Well let us change the subject a little. I am yet well pleased with the faculty. The Prof of Practice & Matesa-Medicas is rather tedious and old fashioned. Prof Newton is a great one. he is a man of my own hart. The other professers are comparatively you [young?]. the Prof of Physiology, "pro tem," is a Georgia Heart. You may find his name in the graduating class of that announcement that I got of Dr. Lattner. He is a talented little fellow and as I am a Georgian too we are becoming some what intimate.

The Prof of Chemistry is very talented. He is through. he has lectured 2 hours a day in order to get through and go home. He lives in Iowa. He examined the graduating class before he started [home]. I'll tell you dear he rubed me close. I am afraid he has black-balled me. But I don't think he ought to because I did not here much of his lectures. He gave me to understand that allowances would be mad in as much as it was not my fault. I believe him to be a gentleman in the true sence of the word.

The class held a meeting for the purpose of expressing their thanks and approbation to Prof Garrison for the able and gentlemanly manner in which he has filled his chair—Chemistry—The meeting was called to order by appointing Dr. Brady of Ala. to preside. On motion of Dr. Duncan of Iowa, Dr. Beechum of S. C. was appointed Secretary. The object of the meeting was explained by the President. On motion of—well—let me see—Oh! a Georgian a committy of 3 was appointed to prepare a preamble and resolution for the action of the meeting, Whereapon the president appointed Dr. Duncan Henshall, (son of secretary) and, that same Georgian [as] the com. Meeting then adjourned until 8 o clock next morning. [Then] the preamble and resolution were red and adopted. It was then moovd that the secretary present a copy of the resolution to Prof Garrison and another to Editer [of the] E. M. Journal with request to publish. Meeting then adjourned.

The Prof was highly pleased with the testimonials of the class. After he had closed his fairwell address myself and severel of the students went into the antiroom to take our leave of him. He was trying to straten a copper wire. I proposed to assist him. I raped one end of it round a shuvel handle, he raped the other end around a round bar of iron. We then tryed our strength. Our Demonstrater of Anatemy Dr. E. Freeman,—who by the way is a clever joviel littel fellow—caught Prof Garrison around the wast and Dr. Beechem caught me likewise. We pulled and tuged and laughed. We wer about matched. After we got the wire stratened I toled the Prof that I supposed that would be the last "pulle" *I* would get at *him* which created quite a laugh. We then took our leave.

I am through dissecting. And I don't regret it either not because I dislike it but our subject had become so horibly disorganized that little was to be learned. We have students from almost every State in the union. We have none from Mexico. However there is a part of a Mexican here, but not as a student. it stays in the show case. The specimen is the foot and leg of Gen. Santa-Anna.

Oh! Yes Dear. I must tell you. I and our crowd went to the Musium last night. Admitance 25 cts. I don't think I have ever spent a quarter to more advantage in all my life. Dear I wished for you so much. If you was here one week you could see more than you ever saw in your life. Dont think I am going to get extravigent. I shall spend nothing but what I think that I am geting value received for but more about the mussuim.

I saw many things that was very interesting. All kinds of anamals birds snakes fish shells of every variety relics of annisent architecture [illegible] instruments of ware thousands of years old and all the great battles—and a great variety of collections that would be impossable for me to mention here. Among which was a representation of the "Infernal Regions" which is the most awful sight I ever beheld. The widest stretch of the immagination could not such a seen. I will tell you about it when I have the happiness to see you

I am hapy to learn that you and the babe are getting on and so well. I expect you and babe will fly round on a high string while I'm gone. well that's all right. I have not flew round any yet. you see I have not "learned the ropes" yet,

I am coming down some of these sundays to see you fix up babe to go to meeting. If I get through my work in time I will be down maybe by 1st June. But you must not be disapointed if I don't get there by that time. We will have a jolly crowd as we come. 6 or 8 of the students will go as far as Atlanta. But I need not be talking of leaving here yet.

My health is very good. all I have to gard against is my apetite.

The wethe has been very pleasant ever since I have been here. There was one or two days last week that was rather march like but it is very pleasent now. It is quite pleasent to-day. I see a peach tree in the lot below our place that is beginning to bloom. I am told that veagatation is later in the country.

Well Dear I must close. I could write all day. I must save some news for next time. Kiss babe for me. I feel very well to day. I had my hair cut yesterday-evening and well shampooned which has improoved my loocks and feelings very much.

Write often. every week.

   Your Affectionate Husband

Notes

mail packets: These were ships or boats "that carried passengers, mail, or goods on a regular schedule." A "packet" was a paper envelope, but gradually the word also grew to refer to a ship that carried the mail from port to port.[18]

Watchman or Banner: *Southern Watchman* and *Southern Banner* were the newspapers in Athens, Georgia, at the time the letter was written.

Just forked them under my shirt: Manning likely was not being literal. He probably meant simply that he had gotten them into his stomach the usual way.

Materia & Medica: This term refers to "the study of the tools with which the practitioner has to work in the cure of disease." It could be defined as the study of the different types of agents (medicines), what parts of the body they affect, and how they affect those parts.[19]

Prof of Practice and Materia & Medica: In 1859 the professor of this subject was Dr. Lorenzo Elbridge Jones, fifty years old, originally from Massachusetts.[20]

Prof Newton: He was the Ohioan Dr. Robert Stafford Newton, professor of clinical medicine and surgery, editor and publisher of the *Eclectic Medical Journal*, and dean of the faculty, then forty-one.[21]

Prof of Physiology: Dr. Charles Thomas Hart professor of physiology and medical jurisprudence was born in Sunbury, Georgia, and graduated from the University of Georgia. In 1859 he was twenty-four years old, five years younger than M. P., who was twenty-nine.[22]

pro tem: For the time being, temporarily.[23]

---

[18] Drake, *What Did They Mean by That?*, 214 (quote); Lepore, *Book of Ages*, 112.
[19] Dunglison, *Dictionary of Medical Science*, 629–30.
[20] Felter, *History of the Eclectic Medical Institute*, 46, 92–93.
[21] Ibid., 46, 79, 106–107.
[22] Ibid., 46, 124–25.
[23] "Pro-tem," *Webster's New World College Dictionary*, 1169.

Dr. Lattner: Dr. Joseph Travis Lattner of Fairview, Georgia, graduated from the Eclectic Medical Institute in 1853. He was four years older than Manning and probably was the person who interested Manning in the Institute.[24]

Prof of Chemistry: This was Dr. Herod Daily Garrison, who held the chair for chemistry, pharmacy, and toxicology. He hailed originally from Indiana, and in 1859, he was twenty-six years old. A colleague wrote of Dr. Garrison:

> As a teacher, Professor Garrison had remarkable power to interest those under his instruction. He was never dry nor dull. He could infuse interest into subjects which to most are uninviting or even forbidding. His clearness of apprehension coupled with equal clearness of statement, his power of apt illustration and his unconventional modes of expression, lightened here and there by bursts of humor which were as natural as they were fascinating, enchained his pupils' attention and enabled him to make strong and lasting impressions upon their minds.[25]

Dr. Henshall (son of the secretary): J. G. Henshall was a member of the board of trustees of the institute and secretary of the board from 1856 to 1868.[26]

Demonstrater of Anatemy Dr. E. Freeman: Dr. Edwin Freeman was professor of general, special, and pathological anatomy. Originally from Nova Scotia, in 1859 he was twenty-five years old. He served with the Union Army in Kentucky near Cincinnati when units of the Confederate army, including the regiment in which Manning was the assistant surgeon, threatened the city. He also later served with the Union army in Virginia, Tennessee, and Mississippi.[27]

last pulle I would get at him: Manning seems to be using "pull" to imply, jokingly, that as this is the last time he will tug the professor toward him, it also is the last time he will have some special influence (pull) with the professor.[28]

foot and leg of Gen. Santa-Anna: General Antonio Lopez de Santa Anna was the leader of the Mexican forces that captured the Alamo in 1836 during the Texas revolution against Mexico. Later, in 1838, he lost his left leg in a skirmish with the French at Vera Cruz. He got an artificial leg and later buried his real leg with full military honors.

Then during the Mexican-American War in 1847, he made such a hasty retreat from advancing US forces that he left his false leg behind in camp. It was captured by a unit from Illinois, and the Illini brought it back to a museum in

---

[24] "Eclectic Medical Institute of Cincinnati Matriculation Records," 83; Lattner, *Lattner Story*, 25.

[25] Felter, *History of the Eclectic Medical Institute*, 46, 122–24.

[26] Ibid., 40, 70.

[27] Ibid., 46, 120–22.

[28] "Pull," *Webster's New World College Dictionary*, 1177–178.

their home state. It went on tour for a time, and it may have been on tour in Cincinnati when Manning wrote about it.[29]

Musium: This museum was the Western Academy of Natural Sciences. A few years before Manning visited, it had incorporated the collections of an earlier Cincinnati museum, the Western Museum. It is known today as the Museum of Natural History & Science and is part of Cincinnati Museum Center.[30]

Pillona and Nora Alexander

Maysville Ga   April 3rd 1859

Well Dear [Manning Poole Alexander] as we cannot go to preaching today I think I can spend my time more *pleasantly* in writing to you than any other way. I received yours of the 19 ult last Monday. I was not looking for a letter then but it was a *verry agreeable* surprise: I was glad to hear that you was well and getting on so well.

I hope ere this that you have received both my other letters. Dear I know it seemed a *long time* to you before you got our first letter for the time got to seem long to me before I got your first: *Dearest* I would have replied the next mail after the reception of your last letter but we have no envelopes till friday and then I was making our little darling a little white dress of the one [I wore when] you used to fly round me to wear to preaching to day, but it rained verry hard all day yesterday & until this morning when the creek was to full to cross: and you see sweet couldn't wear its new dress. Father, Mother and I went to Mrs. Mintz's last sunday and spent the evening.

Well dearest I have just eaten a hearty dinner of the turnip greens that you *longed* for; it seems to me to if you only could have eaten dinner with us to day it would have afforded me more *pleasure* than any thing I now know of. Dearest if I could only be there to coock turnip greens and everything else the way you love it

The time will soon come when you will visit us and I do hope it will be a *continued visit* then.

I have just been nursing our dear little babae (a privalige that you cannot have now): she will li in my lap or the cradle and laugh and hollow out till we can hear her from one room to the other. Pa she causes me to pass pleasantly all that would be my loansome moments. she is very healthy and grows fast weighed 12 pounds this morning and can nearly sit alone. Pa you know she must be a good babe for I can spin 10 cnts [counts] of wool and take care of her.

---

[29] Galehouse, "Texas Fighting for Santa Anna's Leg."
[30] See Museum of Natural History & Science, https://www.cincymuseum.org/sciencemuseum/.

My health generally is very good. I can eat as hearty as I did last fall (*when you fed me potatoes*). I am taking a cold and have a slight toothache today and therefore dont feel much like writing. It is raining again this evening.

I received a letter from your Father & Mother last Monday. they are all well had got one letter from you. they wrote for me to come down and stay with them a while and if I couldnt come to write to them. I am going to write to them this evening; I think it is almost impossible for me to go: there has been so much rain. they can't spare a horse only when it is too wet to plow and then you know the waters are too high: it wont be verry long till you will go and I would rather wait and go with you.

Mrs. A Killgore had a son born yesterday morning. we heard it weighed 7¾ lbs. I want to see *who* it favors. Mother has given me 7 lbs. of wool which will make about 20 yds. I want to spin and weave that and weave some bed-covers if I can and also do some quilting.

I believe I have written all I can think of now. don't study too hard. write me often and write me long letters like your last was. write just as soon as you get this. As ever your Affectionate Wife,

M. P. Alexander   N. L. and P. W. Alexander

Notes

Weighed 12 pounds: At the top of the second page of the letter, Manning had added in pencil: "Nora weighed 12 pounds at 2½ months old."

"*spin 10 cnts [counts] of wool.... 7 lbs. of wool which will make about 20 yds.*": Lona is writing about making (spinning) yarn from fibers of wool, probably using a spinning wheel. One count is a specific length of yarn spun.[31]

Manning Poole Alexander

[Printed across the top of the stationery Manning used is a woodblock print, a view of Cincinnati from the Kentucky side of the Ohio River, that was published originally by Block & Co., No. 32 West Sixth Street.]

VIEW OF CINCINNATI
Cincinnati Ohio
Apr. 3d/59
Dear

I have been strolling about the greater portion of the day—the clock is just now striking seven—I guess you think I spend most of my idle time that way and

---

[31] "Spinning," *Webster's New World College Dictionary*, 659, 1400.

some that I should spend otherwise Well you know dear when I listen to seven lectures a day for 6 days in the week—it is enough or as much as I should impose upon my nervous system, and then there is much to be seen here and you know I don't have the opportunity of visiting such a place often.

I was out to see the court-house this evening. It is said to be one of the finest—in fact it is *the* finest court-house in the United States. It is the most magnificent building I ever saw.

You may think strange of my writing oftener than I spoke of when I left home. Well dear you can account for that in this way: I want to here from you and the babe oftener than once in two weeks and reasoning from analogy I presume that one a week is not oftener than you wish to here from your humble servent. I can take the time to write you one a week without interfering with my studies. But don't infer from this remark that I will write every week for I have my theosis to prepare now soon and that, you know will consume some time and again you may not get all the letters I write may not com to hand.

But I will advert a little. while I was strolling over the City in company with 4 or 5 lively fellow students you are mistaken if you think that I never thought where you and babe were. I toled some of the boys that I new where my "sweet hart" was. I could see you—not as I see this paper exactly, but nearly so—that is if you are well which I hop you are. If I mistake not you was at Candler's Creek to-day. Well you and babe had better make good use of your tim and fly round on the upper *ten* for I am coming "down South" next summer some time and then "dad" will watch for himself.

You know I toled you last week that the Prof of Chemistry had closed his course and that I was fearfull he had "black-balled" me, but I have learned enough since to know that all is right. So much for that. I hope I will return to Geo right side up.

Don't get gloomy nor anything of the kind. There was a great many April fools played off. Some of the boys wrote an April fool and laid it on the Prof. Desk. it created quite a laugh. I played a little one on the boarders at our house. I got into the dining room by a private dore and rang the dinner bell. The boys ran down stares and into the dining room, but they found nothing on the table neither did they find me.

Well dear you will have to pardon me for not "crouding" this sheat. The wether has been very fine. we have some frosts these morning. we had quite a heavy rain last night. to day was fine[,] that is[,] it was plesent on the streets with one's over coat buttoned up.

I guess you and Mother and (I had like to have forgotten) Ellen have been planting beans last week. Well make them grow fast, have a mess of them coocked—well I cant say exactly when but I would say along about 1st or 5th

June. Tell Ellen that I have got her and aunt Ann a sweet heart picked out but I don't know wether they will come home with me or not.

Write me just as oftin as you possibly can. I am well except cold and I am geting better of that. I will write you soon again. Good Night

Your Affectionate Husband
M. P. Alexander

Notes

fly round on the upper ten: Manning was referring, facetiously, to circulating among the upper crust of society. The phrase "upper ten" is taken from an article and book written in 1852 by Charles Astor Bristed titled *The Upper Ten Thousand: Sketches of American Society* about the activities of members of the top society of New York.[32]

Ellen: She may have been Eleanora "Ellen" David, Simeon and Fanny's daughter, who then was a few days short of turning three years old. Pillona may have written to Manning earlier that Ellen was visiting.

aunt Ann: She probably was Ann David, Pillona's older sister, then twenty-five.

Pillona Alexander

Maysville Ga   April 18th/59
Dearest

I take my seat this morning to reply to yours of the 3rd ult which came to hand last Wednesday. Dear when I spoke of writing this morning some of them said they did not think it was necessary to write so often but I think I know best how glad it makes *pa* to hear from his *gal* and *baby*. Dear I am busy but I know I *can* take time to write to the one that is *dearer* to me than all others.

Pa I was glad to hear that you was well and getting on so well with your studies. I hope that you will come home "rite [illegible]" sure enough. Dear you ought to have been here yesterday to have gone to meeting to the grove with babe and I. you would not have been ashamed to have seen it by the side of the other little babes: I dont say it because it is ours but I do think it was the "*best whitest looking* crow" of the bunch.

We had frost again last night no ice I fear the wheat & corn is injured this time and perhaps the remaining fruit. it is cold this morning; we have had verry warm weather.

---

[32] Bristed, *The Upper Ten Thousand: Sketches of American Society by A New Yorker* (London: John W. Parker and Son, 1852); see, for example, *Southern Banner*, April 23, 1857; *Southern Watchman*, April 2, 1857.

I got a letter from Billy and Lou last week. they and Father Alie are well. he wrote that Sam had been sick all this spring[,] the first that I had heard of it: She said they intended to have come to seen us last week but got their buggy broke all to pieces & cant come now. Billy says theirs is a fat babe, Lou says it is pretty. he says it is ugly. Never mind we'l show them a pretty one or at least a good one. our babe hardly cries any. she is getting rude but I think she will be good natured. Pa I wish you could have seen her trying to get holt of those green grass flowers that are in my bonnet yesterday.

Well pa babe has just got up and I have dressed her & am ready to write again while sweet is lying here in the cradle laughing & playing by herself: She was just three months old yesterday. Dear you thought you loved her when you started but if you dont love her better now than you did then I love her the best for she gets dearer to me every day. Pa if you think I write too much about the babe you must tell me so for I judge you by myself. I would want to know all about it but those letters are intended only for Dear Pa to look at.

Dearest you said I must not get gloomy. dont be uneasy about that. I am getting along just as well as you could wish me to. I had no idea I could pass the time half so well when you started.

Annie says tell you the widower Chandler is married but he has got a brother that is "more samer."

Oh! yes you have got some more kinsfolk now. guess who it is. well if you haint heard I bet you cant guess. Billy said Adam wrote to him he was going to marry a miss Susanah Burkhater about the middle of march. Adam didn't wait as long as you and Billy did. if he is married I hope he has done well.

Dr & Nina expect to be here in about two weeks and mayby Toma & Sue. now you come down and we'll have a fine time of it

Dear I am getting as slim & "little" as I used to be. I can wear the most of my dresses again. I must write to Billy and Lou to day if I have time and I believe I have written all to you that will interest you. Pa babe kisses all of your letters or puts them in her little mouth. I will let her kiss and wad up this one so you can see some of the work of her little hands. No more this time. please write as often as you can. As ever your *affectionate* wife

M. P. AlexanderP. W. Alexander

Notes

the *"best whitest looking crow" of the bunch*: *A Dictionary of American Proverbs* includes the following as one of its proverbs: "Every mother crow thinks hers is the whitest." The proverb thus equates black with undesirable, white with desirable. The *Dictionary* defines proverbs generally as "concise statements of apparent truths that have common currency."[33]

Billy and Lou: They were Manning's older brother William P. Alexander and his wife, Lou Sewell Alexander. They were married October 11, 1854, when Billy was twenty-seven years old and Lou was twenty-one.[34]

Father Alie: He is Manning's father, Robert W. Alexander.[35]

Sam: He was one of Manning's younger brothers. At the time the letter was written, he was twenty-six years old.[36]

Billy and Lou's fat, ugly or pretty babe: He was Henry C. Alexander. When the letter was written, he was one or two years old.[37]

Adam and Susan Burhater: Adam was another of Manning's younger brothers. He married Susan Burkhalter on March 23, 1859, when he was twenty-six years old. A letter from Adam appears earlier in this chapter and more will be learned about him later.[38]

Dr. and Nina: They are Dr. Middleton Raymond Bell and his wife Pillina David Bell, one of Pillona's older sisters.[39]

Toma and Sue: Pillona is referring to her brother Owen Thomas David and his wife Sue.[40]

Manning Poole Alexander

Cincinnati Ohio
April 18th /59
My Dearest:

I am hapy to inform that yours of the 11th inst is before me. It came to hand this morning I supose it came in last night on board the packet Telegraph No. 3 or Jacob Strader, they always bring my news.

Dear it is so much pleasure to receive a letter from you I must insist upon your writing every week sure. But dear, you must pardon me for not writing a long letter to day for I am buisily ingaged with my thesis this week. I must get it ready to hand in by Saturday at furthest. My petition for graduation has been

---

[33] Mieder, Kingsbury, and Harder, *Dictionary of American Proverbs*, xii, 163.

[34] Chaplin, *Riches of Bunyan* (Alexander family copy); grave marker for Lou E. Alexander, Hudson River Baptist Church Cemetery, Carnesville, Georgia; Ancestry.com, *Georgia Marriages, 1699–1944*.

[35] US Census, 1850, Franklin County, Georgia; Chaplin, *Riches of Bunyan* (Alexander family copy).

[36] Chaplin, *Riches of Bunyan* (Alexander family copy).

[37] US Census, 1860, Madison County, Georgia.

[38] Chaplin, *Riches of Bunyan* (Alexander family copy).

[39] See chapter 1.

[40] See chapter 3.

received. Our Prof of Physiology has been puting in 2 hours a day and to-day he has finished his course. He quised us an hour. I missed but *one* question, so you see my chance in a [illegible] is pretty good for his vote. The time goes off very slow in deed. I feel like a caged bird here. I am compeled as you know to stay till "the last day in the evening."

Dear you don't know how I sit of evenings and imagin I see you as you glid from one room to another to the kitchen and back and around. then when you pass the *cradle* where that blessed little creature lies sucking its thumbs and turning its head when it hears your footsteps[,] now laughing crowing now streatching out its hands[,] how plainly I see all those movements, but they are all imaginary of course. then again I can here the sound of your Geo-Piano. it drones of that tune of 12 cnts a day. I would love to here the sound of that instrument, but there is so much fuss here I cant quite catch the sound really. They just rattle along the streets with their amnibuses drays etc just like they diden't care a scent whether I here anything or not. Don't you think they are very impolite?

But dear I don't say that you play too many tunes on your Piano but I am very fearful you play too long. Don't work so hard Dear. If I could only spend some of those evenings with you and our dear darling I would be so hapy but I cannot yet a while. Then there are those rosted potatoes, why I have not seen one since I have been in the City. Yes and those fried ones and that sliced pie. Oh! I cant stand [it]. And there is the butter-milk too—well I am not going to stay here always, no sir.

I should be very glad if Dr. Bell and famely would not come to georgia. Dear you sugjest that I had better write you when and where you had better meet me. Well dear I cant tell yet when I will get off from here and then I don't know how long it will take me to come. I will leave here I think between 20 and 25th of May. If I can learn I will write. If it would be as conveneant it would cost less to meet me at the Circle. When I find out I will write as near the tim as I can. You write where it would be the most convenant for [you] then to meet me. I can come in a day of the tim

I think you need not think that our fair is the best in the world though it is as good as the City offres. There the bell has rang and I must go to dinner.

Well dear I have just finished dinner and a prety harty one you may be sure. I must hurry and close. it will soon be college time.

The wether has been cooler so far during this month than it was last. We had quite a snow storm yesterday. I am sorry to here that the fruit is killed. Write me often Dear. I neve spend any time half so plesenly as when reading your dear letters. I have not bought mee any clothing. Tomorrow will be two months since I lef you dear. The time is more than half out, ain't you glad.

Kiss the *Babe* for me. Write every thing you can think of. Give my love to all the family. Good-by dearest for another week. Pardon the bad scribling for I have done it.

Yours Devotedly
M. P. Alexander
[Envelope]
Mrs. M. P. Alexander
   Maysville
   Georgia

Notes

Prof of Physiology: He was George Thomas Hart from Georgia. See note to the letter from Manning of March 27, 1859, above.

Geo-Piano: Apparently this was a type of piano, but Manning really is referring to Pillona's spinning wheel. See note to Pillona's letter of April 3 about the amount of wool she can spin.

the Circle: This is a reference to Social Circle, Georgia, which was a railroad stop on the rail line running from Atlanta to Augusta.[41]

Manning Poole Alexander

Cincinnati Ohio May 8th 1859
My Dear—
Yours of 2d inst is at hand. It was hapily received and *more* happily red this afternoon.

I was so happy to learn that you was well and that dear *babe* was better. But dear this is one time that I have not *much* of interest to write. of course I know every thing I write is of interest but I mean I have no special news this time. I am in good health at present and have been since my last.

The most pleasent thing is that we have but ONE more week to stay in Cincinnati. Arn't you glad? I hear you say YES. That is our course will be out next tuesday, one day *sooner* than I wrote you last week. Now my *Dear* I was not disagreeably disappointed when we were informed that our commencement would come of on tusday night 17th inst. The degrees will be conferred between 8 and 9 oclock tusday-night. I will leave here at 12 oclock wednesday.

Dearest by the tim you get this inteligents I will be "Sailing down the River on the Ohio." I design taking a Boat to Louisville. Then by Rail Road and Stage to Nashville. then by railroad. Now with regard to meeting me. You state that they can meet me at Monroe or at Athens. Well Dear I will say meet me at Monroe. I can get home as soon if not sooner and with 3 or 4 dollars less cost.

---

[41] Coleman, *History of Georgia*, 159–60; Lloyd, "Lloyd's map of the southern states."

I think that I will be able to reach the circle by Sunday at farthest. I may get there by the night train on Saturday. It may be *posiable* that I can reach the Circle by the day train on Saturday—but you need not make any calculations opon that. From all that I can learn about the railroad connection I think Sunday is as soon as I can reach the Circle. I will say then meet me at Monroe Sunday 22d inst. or if it is not conveineant to meet me there[,] meet me at Athens on Monday following. I would have to stop over at Union Point until Monday morning.

You don't know how restless and anxious we are all geting especially those who have somthing interesting at home. Every hour is counted. We don't know who will graduate yet. the examination will come off this week—There the supper bell has rang—

Well now I have finished my supper and now I'll proceed. don't be uneasy if I don't get home as soon as I have stated for there is so many connections to make that I might miss and then it would throw me back 24 hours.

My dear I could have fully appreciated the occasion you refur to with all our connections. My cup would have been filled to overflowing. I regret that I could not have been there. I will look for another letter from you about the last of this week.

Well dear here I am on the 4th page and I thought when I began to write that I could not fill two pages. Dr. Osmint and another young man from Georgia started home last Saturday. I went down to the Boat to see them off. Now dear I tell you I felt like I ought to be going [with them]. But there was something else that [said] stay. Now what do you suppose it was? I trust it was a *sheep-skin*, I have some fears that it was not.

Well My dear, next time I write or the next letter I write I will come and bring it to you. that will be clever won't it?

Good Night my dearest.

M. P. Alexander.

Notes

"*Sailing Down the River on the Ohio*": Manning is quoting a line from a minstrel song written by Daniel Decatur Emmett (who generally is credited with writing "Dixie") known as "Dance, Boatman, Dance."[42]

the Circle: Social Circle, Georgia. See the note to Manning's letter of April 18, 1859.

Railroad and Monroe, Social Circle, Union Point, and Athens: A rail line ran from Atlanta to Social Circle and continued further east to Augusta. Manning could have left the train at Social Circle, but there was no rail line to take him

---

[42] Waltz, ed., *Minnesota Heritage Songbook,*" 25, 27.

from there to Monroe, which was about ten miles north of Social Circle. It is unclear how Manning planned to get to Monroe.

As an alternative, he could continue on the line from Atlanta to the next rail station, Union Point. There was a branch line from Union Point to Athens that he then could have taken.[43]

Eclectic Medical Institute

Cincinnati, Ohio
Chartered, March 10th 1845
Know all men by these presents that
Manning Poole Alexander
Has sustained an honorable examination before the Faculty of this Institute on all the departments of Medical Science, and has been found duly qualified to discharge all the highly responsible, important and complicated duties attached to the office of **Physician, Surgeon** AND **Accoucheur**, wherefore, we, the Board of Trustees and Faculty of the **Eclectic Medical Institute of Cincinnati** by the authority vested in us by the Legislature of the State of Ohio, do confer on him the degree of *Doctor of Medicine* with all the honors, privileges and immunities thereunto belonging, both in this country and among all nations.

In testimony whereof the Seal of this Institute has been affixed and the President, the Vice President and Secretary of the Board of Trustees and the Members of the Faculty have subscribed their names at the City of Cincinnati this 17th day of May AD 1859.

[Following were the signatures of the president, vice president, secretary, and all the professors of the Eclectic Medical Institute.]

Notes

Accoucheur: Obstetrician.[44]

---

[43] Lloyd, "Lloyd's map of the southern states"; *Georgia Atlas & Gazetteer*, 27.
[44] "Accoucheur," *Webster's New World College Dictionary*, 9.

Chapter 6

War Approaches, June 1859–January 1861

1859

A Lunatic at Large[1]

By a letter from Dr. M. P Alexander, we learn that a man calling himself Sylvanus Stokes, went to the house of Mr. J. H. Powers, in the neighborhood of Mossy Creek camp ground, in White county, on the 8th inst., and after entering the yard proceeded to divest himself of his clothing, whereupon the women who were in the house ran in a field where a neighbor was at work. He hastened to their house, and found it enveloped in flames, but Stokes was gone. He lay in the woods until the night of the 9th inst. when he was arrested and committed to Habersham jail.

Stokes says he was directed to set fire to the house by the spirit of God. He professes to be a phrenologist—says he was born in McMinn county, Tennessee—removed to Alabama when 10 years old, and afterwards to Mississippi, where he joined the Baptist church and was permitted to preach.

Since that time, it would appear from his own statements, he has been roaming about, in various sections of the country mostly in the Northwest.

He is about 20 years of age—5 feet 9 inches high—weighs about 150 lbs.—light hair, light goatee, fair complexion, large grays eyes, full face.

When he first came to the neighborhood he called himself Joseph Burriss; he now calls himself Sylvanus Stokes, and the poor creature is evidently partially insane.

Notes

Mossy Creek campground: The Mossy Creek area of White County is about twenty-five or thirty miles north of Maysville.[2]

phrenologist: A practitioner of phrenology, "a system, popular esp. in the 19th century, based on the assumption that an analysis of character can be made by a study of the shape and protuberances of the skull."[3]

---

[1] *Southern Watchman*, June 16, 1859.
[2] *Georgia Atlas & Gazetteer*, 15, 21, 22.
[3] "Phrenology," *Webster's New World College Dictionary*, 1100.

1860

Simeon

At Home Thursday June 14th 1860

Dear Parents—Your joint favor was received by due course of mail. we were sorry to hear of the disease and deaths among your cattle. Our family are all in the enjoyment of good health....

There never has been a time since the first settling of this country that corn was as scarce as at present. I sold 260 bushels at $1.00 per Bushel & could have sold 1000 bushels if I had had it. Corn is worth or will bring all you ask for it but I believe the sellers are only asking $1.10. It is thought by a great many that wheat will be worth $2.00 per Bushel.

Write me pretty soon whether you are expecting a traveler through your section. I have declined the trip to Alabama for several reasons. My thrashing trip will consume some of the time that I designed to employ preparing to go to Alabama. Our Superior Court commences the 3rd Monday in August and I am one of the grand jury. If we have an ordinary amount of rain I will have some cribs to build. I have more that ought to be done before I start to Milledgeville than I can accomplish without going to Alabama.

I want Mother to take her trip to Alabama. From present indications I think there will be no Camp meeting at Bethlehem this year. We have just had our house painted on the outside, a job that cost us fifty Dollars.

I wrote to Tomy to day at twelve & have scribbled this on my knee since supper by fire light. I believe I have written all that I can think of.

Sister Mary James & Jesse were here last Friday night after School. Mary's employers continued her School for the balance of the year and are wonderfully pleased with her as a Teacher. They have had some corn to buy but not much.

Your Affectionate
Son   S. B. David

Friday June 15th

P. S. The rain is falling beautifully this morning with a prospect of continuing through the day. We need a ground soaker to make oats.

As to the political troubles in the land, I attribute them more to the envy of aspiring men than to any difference of opinion. The secession movement at Charleston was the result of a combination of some of the Southern Senators to defeat Douglas' nomination. Dont suffer yourself to be deceived by the congressional protection humbug. it is an ignis faterres that lures but to destroy. I commend to your careful consideration the letters of Stephens, & Gov Johnson, to the Macon Committee. They contain the true doctrine & the course they advise will be pursued by all the Southern States, Cobb, & Tombs, to the contrary notwithstanding. I intend to support the nominee of the Baltimore convention, with the Cincinatta platform & the "Dred Scott" decision annexed. Let us reflect dispassionately before we commit ourselves.

S. B. D.

Notes

cribs: Simeon is referring to corn cribs, a structure for storing corn.[4]

Milledgeville: Milledgeville was the capital of Georgia from 1807 to 1868. It is where the state legislature met. In 1859, Simeon had been elected to a two-year term in the Georgia House of Representatives as one of the two members from Forsyth County.[5]

The legislature session for 1860 began on November 7. When Simeon wrote about starting to Milledgeville, he was looking ahead to the fall when he would go there to serve in the legislature.[6]

Charleston: The Democratic National Convention met in Charleston, South Carolina, from April 23, 1860, through May 2, 1860, to choose the nominee of the party and the issues that the party would support in the presidential campaign of 1860. As the convention wore on, the issues that would be in the party's platform gradually became the primary thrust of the delegates' deliberations, and the main issue, as it had been for decades, was whether a new western territory would be admitted into the Union as a free or slave state and who would make that decision.[7]

When the Democrats met in their national convention in Cincinnati in 1856, they adopted a platform that declared that Congress should not interfere with slavery in the territories, either for or against. The platform also indicated who would decide whether slavery should be permitted or prohibited in the territories. In an effort to hold the party together for the election, this part of the platform was purposely ambiguous. It endorsed the concept known as "popular sovereignty," which generally permitted the residents of a territory to determine whether to allow or prohibit slavery within its boundaries, but the platform did not define this concept with precision. The strategy worked. It helped the party

---

[4] "Crib," *Webster's New World College Dictionary*, 350.

[5] Coleman, *History of Georgia*, 208–209; Georgia House of Representatives, *Journal of the House of Representatives, 1859*, 5.

[6] Georgia House of Representatives, Journal of the House of Representatives, 1860, 1.

[7] Nevins, *Ordeal of the Union*, 4:200–28.

remain sufficiently united so that the Democratic Party nominee, James Buchanan, was elected president in November.[8]

At the Charleston Convention, however, disagreement between Northern and Southern delegates could not be papered over. Delegates favoring Senator Stephen A. Douglas as the Democratic nominee for president, who were mainly from the North, passed a platform that essentially repeated the Cincinnati platform on slavery—for noninterference by Congress with slavery in the territories and for popular sovereignty.

This year, though, convention delegates from the South strongly objected to this platform. They referred to "popular sovereignty" as "squatter sovereignty," implying that the North would pack any territorial vote on slavery with men brought into the territory for the sole purpose of voting to prohibit slavery. If slavery were prohibited, no slave holder would move there, and the territory would eventually become a free state. If many territories were admitted to the Union as free states, antislavery interests would dominate Congress, which likely would pass anti-slavery legislation.[9]

The Southern delegates demanded that the platform drop popular sovereignty and that it instead advocate explicit congressional protection for the right to bring slaves into the territories. Some Southern delegates even hoped that insistence on this position would split the Democratic Party and give them the dominant power in a new party and perhaps eventually in a new nation.[10]

When the Douglas/Northern platform was adopted, most of the Southern delegates, including a majority of the Georgia delegates, promptly walked out of the convention, assembled elsewhere in Charleston, and talked of secession. They did little, however, other than deciding to adjourn to meet again in Richmond on June 11.[11]

The delegates who remained in the convention were unable to agree on a nominee and instead voted to reconvene the convention in Baltimore on June 18, three days after Simeon wrote the postscript to this letter. When the Southern delegates who walked out of the Charleston Convention met in Richmond on

---

[8] *Portraits and Sketches*, 15–19; Nevins, *Ordeal of the Union*, 2:512–13; Nicolay and Hay, *Abraham Lincoln*, 39–40; Potter and Fehrenbacher, *Impending Crisis*, 262; Greeman, "Democratic Convention of 1860," 225–26.

[9] Encyclopaedia Britannica, *Annals of America*, 9:190–91; McPherson, *Battle Cry of Freedom*, 213–15; Greeman, "Democratic Convention of 1860," 226, 231–32; Nevins, *Ordeal of the Union*, 4:214–20.

[10] Nevins, *Ordeal of the Union*, 4:202, 206–207, 211, 215–20; McPherson, *Battle Cry of Freedom*, 213–15; W. C. Davis, *Look Away!*, 22–23.

[11] Nevins, *Ordeal of the Union*, 4:220–21; Greeman, "Democratic Convention of 1860," 226, 232–35, 243; Coleman, *History of Georgia*, 148.

June 11, they decided to send to the Baltimore Convention virtually the same delegates who had walked out at Charleston.[12]

Simeon reviewed the results of the Charleston Convention and seemed to think that the actions by the delegates who left the convention really did not constitute a serious movement toward secession but were simply a move to prevent Douglas from being nominated and an attempt to promote themselves for the future.

"congressional protection humbug": The reference to "congressional protection" is to the demand by the Southern delegates to the Charleston Democratic Convention for Congress to pass legislation to protect slavery. Simeon thought it was "humbug" because it was an "ignis faterres that lures but to destroy."

"Ignis faterres": This term probably was meant to be *ignis fatuus*, Latin for "foolish light" (*ignis*, fire, beacon; *fatuus*, foolish). Charlotte Brontë uses this term in her 1847 novel *Jane Eyre*: "it is madness in all women to let a secret love kindle within them, which, if unreturned and unknown, must devour the life that feeds it; and, if discovered and responded to, must lead, *ignis-fatuus*-like, into miry wilds whence there is no extrication." A note in a modern version of that novel defines "*ignis-fatuus*-like": "Like Will o' th Wisp, a flitting light on marshy land, receding only to recur elsewhere, drawing a traveler to his death."[13]

Simeon also may be alluding to the legendary practice of wreckers along a sea coast who, during a storm at sea when visibility was poor, would light a bonfire or place a lantern on a dangerous part of the shore so that it appeared to a ship at sea that another ship had found safe anchorage there. Then when the ship sailed in from the sea toward the light and apparent safety, it would wreck on a rocky shore, and the wreckers would rush aboard to salvage its cargo.[14]

Simeon's point is that the secessionists demand for congressional protection is only a way for "aspiring men" to lure Southerners away from the Democratic Party, thus splintering and destroying it so they might control the resulting Southern faction.

Macon Committee: On May 5, 1860, after the failure of the Charleston Convention and before Georgia selected delegates to the Baltimore Convention, thirteen men from Macon, alarmed that the proceedings of the Charleston Convention threatened "the integrity and overthrow of the Democratic Party," wrote to several prominent Georgia Democrats for their counsel. What should the Georgia delegates to the Baltimore Convention do?[15]

---

[12] Nevins, *Ordeal of the Union*, 4:221–22, 266–68; Greeman, "Democratic Convention of 1860," 234–35, 242–43.

[13] D. Simpson, *Cassell's Compact Latin Dictionary*, 90, 108; Brontë, *Jane Eyre*, 186–87, 552; H. W. Fowler and F. G. Fowler, *Concise Oxford Dictionary*, 590.

[14] Bathurst, *Lighthouse Stevensons*, 28–29.

[15] *Southern Banner*, May 17, 1860.

The four men Simeon mentions—Stephens, Johnson, Toombs, and Cobb—all had been leaders in state and national politics and been speaking, writing, and acting in regard to the slavery issue throughout the 1850s and longer. All responded to the letter from the Macon Committee, and their responses or summaries of them were printed in various Georgia newspapers. A summary of their responses follows:

Stephens

Alexander Hamilton Stephens was forty-eight years old when he responded to the Macon Committee. He had represented Georgia in the US House of Representatives from October 1843 to March 1859. He had participated in the major debates on issues surrounding admission of territories, including debates on the Missouri Compromise, Kansas-Nebraska Act, and the constitution for the Kansas Territory.

In his response to the Macon Committee, he viewed the main question to be settled at the Baltimore Convention as "whether the doctrine of non-intervention by Congress with slavery in the Territories ought to be adhered to or abandoned by the South." He argued that Southerners should stay with the traditional Southern position of noninterference. By noninterference he meant that Congress should not pass any law on the subject of slavery in the territories, either for or against. Congress should not interfere in that issue at all. That was the position Democratic Party delegates from both the North and the South took in the platform adopted by the Democratic Convention in Cincinnati in 1856.

He disagreed with the delegates at Charleston who demanded that Congress protect slavery in the territories as a condition of the Southern states' remaining in the Union, and when the party refused to agree with them, walked out of the convention. He thought that position dangerous and unnecessary.

It was dangerous:

> shall we stand by our principles, or shall we, cutting loose from our moorings where we have been safely anchored so many years, launch out again into unknown seas, upon new and perilous adventures, under the guide and pilotage of those who prove themselves to have no more fixedness of purpose or stability as to objects or policy than the shifting winds by which we shall be driven.

It was unnecessary. Traditionally the party had relied on the courts rather than Congress to decide whether a territory could allow or prohibit slavery. The Supreme Court had supported the South in its decision in the *Dred Scott* case. That case held that Black people were not citizens within the meaning of the Constitution, and that Congress had no authority to exclude slavery from the territories because slaves were private property and their ownership was protected by the Constitution as ownership of other property was protected.

In addition, Stephens argued that under the traditional doctrine, Southerners retained the unrestricted right to extend slavery into the territories wherever the people want it, as was done in Arkansas, Tennessee, Kentucky, and other states. Moreover, the institution of slavery "rests upon great truths, which can never be successfully assailed by reason or argument," and it will prevail.

Finally, he urged the party to send delegates to the Baltimore Convention to advocate adoption of the traditional doctrine as the best way to hold the party and the country together. If that were done, he was confident that a person then would be nominated acceptable to all sections of the party. Yet if this approach failed, it would be the North's fault and the South's hands would be "clear of all blame."[16]

Johnson

Herschel Vespasian Johnson was forty-seven years old when he responded to the Macon letter. He had been a US senator in 1848 and 1849 and a two-term governor of Georgia from 1853 to 1857.

In his letter in response to the Macon Committee, Johnson took roughly the same position as Stephens. He wrote that the South should not demand that Congress intervene to protect slavery in the territories. In the past the South had asked only that Congress *not* intervene at all on that issue. Democrats should leave the question of slavery in a territory to the people of the territory, subject to the Constitution, which provides ample protection of slavery. Continuing to demand Congress act to protect slavery would only antagonize the North, lead to disruption within the Democratic Party, and tend to disrupt the Union. "I have no blind devotion to the Union, but in my judgment there is no existing cause to justify dissolution," he wrote. In order to preserve the integrity of the national Democratic Party and defeat its opponents, Georgia should send delegates to the Baltimore Convention who would provide calmness, prudence, and high statesmanship with these views in mind.[17]

The Baltimore Convention selected Johnson as the vice presidential candidate to campaign with presidential candidate Stephen A. Douglas as part of the Democratic Party that remained after delegates from the Southern states again bolted the convention and the party.[18]

---

[16] R. M. Johnston and Browne, *Life of Alexander Stephens*, 20, 172–75, 346–48, 357–64, 385; "Alexander H. Stephens," Wikipedia, https://en.wikipedia.org/wiki/Alexander_H._Stephens, accessed February 11, 2015.

[17] *Weekly Georgia Telegraph*, May 18, 1860; Flippin, *Herschel V. Johnson of Georgia*, xiii, 1, 7, 94–101.

[18] Nevins, *Ordeal of the Union*, 271.

Cobb

Howell Cobb was forty-four years old when he responded to the Macon Committee letter. He had served in Congress from 1843 to 1851, and he was speaker of the US House of Representatives from 1849 to 1851, governor of Georgia from 1851 to 1853, and secretary of the treasury under President James Buchanan from 1857 to 1860.[19]

In his response to the Macon letter, Cobb expressed concern about the threat to the South and the Union but disagreed with Stephens and Johnson in that he expressly favored the action of the Southern delegates in walking out of the Charleston convention.

He wrote, "It cannot be disguised that both the safety of the South and the integrity of the Union are seriously threatened.... I have looked to the national Democratic party as the only political organization in which the sound constitutional elements of the whole country could be brought into united and cordial cooperation." The actions of the Charleston Convention, however, seriously threatened the ability of the party to achieve this cooperation.

Cobb pointed out that at the Charleston convention a majority of *delegates* (in sixteen primarily Northern states) pushed through a platform and favored a candidate that a majority of the *states* (seventeen—all fifteen Southern states plus Oregon and California) opposed. (This result was possible because the winning sixteen states had more delegates at the convention than the losing seventeen states, and the platform vote was determined by majority of delegates rather than a majority of states.)

Cobb continued that the platform supported by the losing delegates, mainly from Southern states, only recognized that the citizens of Southern states have the same right under the Constitution to take their "property" into the territories as any other United States citizens have to take their property there, "nothing more—nothing less." The adopted platform, however, would not guarantee them that right, and the principal supporter of that platform, Senator Stephen Douglas, did not support their having that right.

He argued further that in such a closely divided convention, it was unprecedented and unjust for one faction to force a platform and a nominee on another faction and then expect the losing faction to surrender and to campaign and elect the other faction's candidate. Thus, the Southern states were justified in walking out of the convention.

It also was not for the good of the party when the losing faction was composed of states that were certain to vote with the party, whereas states in the wining faction were less certain to do so.

---

[19] H. Montgomery, *Howell Cobb's Confederate Career*, 13–18; Boykin, ed., *Memorial Volume of the Hon. Howell Cobb*, 13, 19–31.

He urged that a convention of Georgia Democrats be assembled and that the convention "give the action of our delegates at Charleston their cordial approval and authorize them in cooperation with the delegates of those States with whom they acted at Charleston to renew at Baltimore their efforts for a settlement of the difficulties which led to a disruption at Charleston." He continued that the endorsement of the actions of the Georgia delegates at Charleston would be "the best instruction for their future conduct" at Baltimore. If the delegates are firm and true to this course, their "true friends at the North" will not "force upon you terms of humiliation."[20]

Cobb later became the first president of the Provisional Confederate States Congress from February 1861 to February 1862. While still president, Cobb recruited a regiment that became the 16th Georgia Volunteer Infantry Regiment. Both of Simeon's younger brothers, Thomas and Horatio, would become part of this regiment.

When Cobb resigned his position as president of the Confederate Congress, he was promoted and became the commander of a brigade (which included the 16th Georgia, Thomas and Horatio's regiment) as a brigadier general. He held that position until October 1862.[21]

Toombs

Robert Toombs was forty-nine years old when he responded to the Macon letter. He had served in the US House of Representatives from 1845 to 1853 and had been a US senator since 1853.[22]

In his response to the Macon Committee he wrote that the policy of non-intervention by Congress must be continued. With this stance, he was much like Stephens and Johnson. He believed, however, that the doctrine of popular sovereignty in the platform adopted by the delegates who stayed at the convention at Charleston could lead to allowing territories to vote to prohibit slavery within their boundaries. He asserted that nothing would induce him to agree that "there is any rightful power *anywhere*, to exclude slave property from any portion of the public domain (open for settlement to others [e.g., a territory]), except within the limits of a sovereign State and by her authority" [emphasis original]. He strongly implied that this belief was supported by the Constitution.

He understood, however, that after the Southern delegates left the convention, delegates from New York made a proposition that might lead to a satisfactory resolution of the differences of the factions. Thus, he believed that the

---

[20] *Southern Banner*, May 17, 1860; Nevins, *Ordeal of the Union*, 4:214–22.
[21] H. Montgomery, *Howell Cobb's Confederate Career*, 23–77.
[22] Stovall, *Robert Toombs*, 4, 56, 107, 205–208.

seceding delegates should attend the Baltimore Convention, and then if their principles are not treated satisfactorily, they could convene separately.

He continued, "I do not concur in the opinion that the danger to the Union is even one of our greatest perils. *Our greatest danger today is that the Union will survive the Constitution.* The great body of your enemies in the north, who hate the Constitution, and daily trample it under their feet, profess an ardent attachment to the Union; and, I doubt not, feel such attachment for a Union unrestrained by the Constitution" [emphasis original]. He, however, felt no attachment to a Union "unrestrained by the Constitution."[23]

Baltimore Convention: As described in a note above, at the earlier Democratic Party's convention in Charleston, the party was unable to nominate a candidate for the presidency. The delegates to that convention who had not walked out decided to reconvene in Baltimore on June 18 (three days after Simeon wrote the postscript to this letter). Then they would attempt again, as a united party, to adopt a platform and nominate a candidate.

At the Democratic Party convention in Baltimore in June, the party again split into two factions when the Southern delegates again walked out. The regular delegates who stayed nominated Stephen A. Douglas for president and Alabamian Benjamin Fitzpatrick as vice president. Later, when Fitzpatrick declined the nomination, Herschel V. Johnson, a former Georgia governor and US senator, was chosen to replace him. The convention also stayed with the Cincinnati platform that the party remnant had adopted in Charleston.[24]

"*Cincinatta platform*": As mentioned in a note above, this was the platform adopted by the Democratic Party when it met in Cincinnati in 1856.

Dred Scott *decision*: This is a reference to a decision of the Supreme Court handed down in 1857 in *Dred Scott v. Sandford*. The case was brought by Scott, a slave, who sued for his freedom based on his having lived with his master, an army doctor, for several years in a free state and a free territory before he returned to the slave state of Missouri.

The case ruled that both enslaved and free Black people, were not citizens within the meaning of the Constitution, and thus Scott had no standing to sue. Further, Congress had no authority to exclude slavery from the territories because slaves were private property and protected by the Constitution as other property was protected.[25]

---

[23] *Augusta Chronicle*, May 19, 1860; Stovall, *Robert Toombs*, 179–81.

[24] Nevins, *Ordeal of the Union*, 4:268–71; Greeman, "Democratic Convention of 1860," 244–52.

[25] Encyclopaedia Britannica, *Annals of America*, 8:440–51; McPherson, *Battle Cry of Freedom*, 170–76.

Simeon's position: As he wrote, Simeon generally adopted the stance advocated by Alexander Stephens and Herschel Johnson. He supported the ambiguity of the Cincinnati Platform as the best way to keep the Democratic Party unified. He regarded as divisive the position of the renegade faction at Charleston that favored congressional legislation requiring that slavery be allowed in the territories. He apparently believed that the *Dred Scott* decision made such legislation unnecessary because that case held that under the Constitution, Congress could not prevent slavery within the boundaries of a territory.

John H. Jones

Fort Gaines Ga Nov 15 1860
Mrs Thirza David
Dr Cousin

After a long silence I have concluded to try to revive our correspondence. I hardly know whose fault it is that we have not kept it up but suppose it is negligence in both parties

In the first place I will say to you that we are all in pretty good health but rather low in spirits on account of a heavy loss we have recently sustained. On the night of the election (6th inst) some scamp sot fire to & burned out a whole block of buildings in our place amongst which was my Office.

The building was partly mine[;] my interest in it was worth $1000 or $1200 dollars. the whole building was worth about $3000—My law library was worth about $1000. Then any furniture & other things I had in it was worth near $1000 more. all was destroyed. I had an Iron Safe in it in which I had most of my most valuable papers and as fortune would have it saved them in a damaged condition. I considder my clear loss not less than $2000—we had a little insurance on the house not enough to do much towards rebuilding.

the house was occupied on the lower story as a dry Goods store & Printing office. not an article of either was saved—It burned out a Dry Goods Store a large wholesale Grocery a Drug Store Masonic Hall one Dwelling & furniture & one grog shop Three Law offices a Watch shop Degaurian office Printing office Bank office & other out buildings. The whole loss not less than $40,000—Insurance about one half.

The loss at this time falls pretty heavy on some of us. It does seam like we have bad luck. I have laboured all my life until I am beginning to be an old man and have had to struggle through misfortune after misfortune & had gotten along to when I was getting comfortable in life and still misfortune follows me. I however would not murmur if it had been an accident. But having no doubt that it was the work of some vile scamp now in our midst who is now seeking an oportunity to set some other person on fire or burn up some of our dwellings[,] I do feel vexed and would try to kill the rascal if I could find him.

Our family connexion are all in good health and nothing new or important amongst us.

Our Crops are verry sorry both corn & cotton. Corn was almost a failure. provisions are going to be scarce & high.

Our people are much excited about our Government and speak strongly in favour of secession. I fear a storm will soon burst over our heads such a one as has not been seen since the American revolution. I think every Christian Patriott ought to supplicate the throne of the Almighty to guide us in the right path. God allmighty himself can only see the end—I dread it.

Our babe now about 20 months old is running all about and beginning to talk. he is through his teething and is a fine little mischievous boy a consolation to our hearts above all other earthly pleasures. We have never given him a name yet only Pony. Amanda is in pretty good health & spirits considering our misfortunes. her mother & father both well

You must excuse this confused letter as I have not got settled down in my mind since the fire to any steady business. I have taken an other office have 3 or 4 law Books left & am not going to be discouraged. I hope I have enough left to still be comfortable

You must write soon & give us all the news and do come & see us if you can. the Rail Road runs through to our place. 'Manda sends all her love to you all & a thousand other little sayings if I had room to write it. Remember me to Cousin James and all friends & Connexion

Your Cousin

Jno. H. Jones

The envelope of this letter was in my safe & a large two story building burnt down over it.

Notes

John H. Jones: John H. Jones was married to his cousin Amanda Bowen Jones. Amanda was the daughter of Thirza's youngest brother, Hiram. John H. Jones was the son of one of Hiram's and Thirza's uncles on their mother's side. Thus, Amanda Bowen Jones and John H. Jones were first cousins once removed.[26] Additional letters from John and Amanda are in chapters 3 and 19.

Fort Gaines: Fort Gaines was and is located in Clay County in the southwest part of Georgia just across the Chattahoochee River from Alabama.[27]

---

[26] US Census, 1850, Hiram Bowen, Carroll County, Georgia; US Census, 1850, John H. Jones, Early County, Georgia; *Georgia Marriage Records from Select Counties, 1828–1978*, 378.

[27] *Georgia Atlas & Gazetteer*, 48.

the night of the election: This was the presidential election on November 6, 1860, when Abraham Lincoln was elected.

Degaurian office: John H. Jones probably is referring to the office of someone who made pictures called daguerreotypes, an early type of photographs produced using a chemically treated metal plate.[28]

I am beginning to be an old man: At the time this letter was written, John H. Jones was about fifty-two years old.[29]

Our Babe: He was another John Jones.[30]

the Rail Road: This was the Southwestern Railroad, which was chartered in 1845. By 1860 it had run a line from Macon to Albany with a branch line to Fort Gaines. At Macon it connected with other rail lines that went into other parts of the state.[31]

1861

Georgia's Ordinance of Secession[32]

GEORGIA STATE CONVENTION—ORDINANCE OF SECESSION PASSES

Milledgeville, Jan. 19…The Ordinance of Secession was adopted by the Convention at 2 o'clock by a vote of 208 ayes to 89 nays. The majority was 119.[33]

THE ORDINANCE OF SECESSION

The following is the ordinance of secession by which the State of Georgia was taken out of the Union:

An Ordinance to dissolve the Union between the State of Georgia and the other States, united with her, under the compact of Government entitled the Constitution of the United States:

We, the people of Georgia, in Convention assembled do declare, and ordain, and it is hereby declared and ordained, that the ordinance adopted by the people of the State of Georgia, in the Convention of 1788, whereby the Constitution of the United States was ratified and adopted, and also all acts, and parts of acts of

---

[28] "Daguerreotype," *Webster's New World College Dictionary*, 372, Drake, *What Did They Mean by That?*, 83.

[29] US Census, 1860, Clay County, Georgia.

[30] Ibid.

[31] Coleman, *History of Georgia*, 159–60.

[32] *Southern Watchman*, January 23, 1861.

[33] The vote taken by the Convention a day earlier on a resolution proposing immediate secession signaled the outcome of the vote on the official ordinance. The resolution passed 166 to 130 (Carey and Justice, "Secession," 37–38).

the General Assembly, ratifying and adopting amendments to the said constitution, are hereby repealed, rescinded and abrogated.

We do further declare and ordain that the Union now subsisting between the State of Georgia and the other States, under the title of the United States of America is hereby dissolved, and that the State of Georgia is in the full possession and exercise of all those rights of Sovereignty which belong and appertain to a free and independent State.

Simeon and Fanny

Vickerys Creek Ga Jan 23rd 1861
My Dear Father & Mother—

I seat myself this morning to respond to your kind and affectionate letter of the 24th ult and also to the information brought us by Mr Bynum. I have delayed writing from the fact that I have had no general news to communicate.

I supposed that some of the members of the Legislature from your section of the State had told you that I was a zealous secessionist. The glorious news reached us on yesterday that Georgia had passed the ordnance of Secession by a majority [of] 119. There has been no time within the last forty years that I would as soon have been in the Legislature as 59 & 60. I consider the calling [of] a convention by the Legislature to carry the State out of the union one of the most glorious acts that ever could have been passed.

You need have no apprehensions of war. I have never believed there would be any war of consequence. It will be a bloodless revolution for the hand of Providence is in it all.

We have learned that Isaac David was a candidate for the convention in Banks county on the Union sensation. if so I am glad he was beaten. We have a large majority of Submissionists and a good many Abolitionists in this county, but we managed to get H Strickland a secessionist in the convention by running one on each side and making no fight.

We are all well and getting on well. Every thing went on well while I was gone. I have hired a man of the name of Martin, a big stout fellow at 10 Dollars per month. He is a good shoe maker, and a tolerably good mechanic.

Sister Mary and the two younger children were up here Saturday night till Sunday evening. They are all well and getting along well. Sister Mary has a fine School. Milton county only paid 50 cts in the Dollar of the public School fund.

it seemes to be a long time till the Association. But I am aiming to repair my houses this spring and summer, and probably cant come till then. Write soon and give me all the news.

Your affectionate children S. B. & F. E. David

Notes

Legislature in 59 and 60: The Georgia General Assembly convened for the start of its 1860 session on November 7, 1860, only a day after Abraham Lincoln was elected president, defeating three other candidates.

Background

As noted earlier, at the Democratic Party convention in Baltimore in June, the party again had split into two factions when the Southern delegates walked out. The regular delegates who stayed nominated Stephen A. Douglas for president and former Georgia governor Herschel V. Johnson as vice president. They then adopted a platform that allowed territories to vote whether to be slave or free.

The faction that walked out of the convention nominated John C. Breckenridge for president on a platform that favored extending slavery to the territories.

The third candidate was that of a new party, the Constitutional Union party, which favored standing by the Constitution and opposed secession. Its nominee for president was John C. Bell.

In Georgia, the vote for president was Breckinridge, 51,893 (49 percent); Bell, 42,886 (40 percent); and Douglas, 11,580 (11 percent). Lincoln was not on the Georgia ballot.[34]

Abraham Lincoln was viewed in Georgia as being antislavery and anti-South, and the legislators arrived in Milledgeville for their annual session very nervous and agitated about his election. More subtle options had been abandoned, and the principal discussion was whether Georgia should secede immediately or should wait to see what action the new administration and the other Southern states would take before deciding whether to secede. The secede-now group became known as "secessionists" to its supporters and "precipitators" to its foes. On the other hand, the wait-and-see group became known as "cooperationists," to its supporters and as "submissionists" to its detractors.

By November 9, two days into the session, Georgia legislators knew that South Carolina and Alabama were very likely to hold conventions to consider seceding from the Union. In addition, Georgia had a larger population than any other state in the lower South, and it stood between and separated South Carolina and Florida on one hand and Alabama and Mississippi on the other. All four of those latter states seemed likely to secede. People in Georgia and throughout the South probably realized that if Georgia did not secede, any new, deep-South nation was likely to be severely compromised.[35]

That day, November 9, a legislator said he did not want to submit "to the rule of Abolitionists, free negroes, and Black Republicans" and introduced a resolution calling for the Southern states to convene in Atlanta to consider "what

---

[34] Coleman, *History of Georgia*, 149; Osborn, "Sectional Crisis," 33.
[35] Freehling and Simpson, *Secession Debated*, ix–x.

course is best to be pursued under present circumstances, and under Republican menace and rule." Another legislator who did not want to wait introduced a resolution calling for immediate secession.[36]

In this heated atmosphere, on November 12, 13, and 14, some of the leading men of Georgia addressed the legislators on the all-consuming issue. Simeon was there to listen. Three of them spoke as follows:

Thomas R. R. Cobb

First, speaking on November 12 was one of the most passionate of the secede-now group, the thirty-seven-year-old lawyer and sometimes revival preacher Thomas R. R. Cobb, younger brother of Howell Cobb. His speech, packed with warnings and exhortations, was on the theme "Disunion or Dishonor."

He asserted first that Lincoln's election violated both the letter and spirit of the Constitution, and it represented a severe threat to the vital institutions of the South. He proclaimed that "this Constitution was made for white men...for the happiness and protection of their race." Yet, "our slaves are first stolen from our midst on underground Railroads and then voted at Northern ballot boxes to select rulers for you and me." And the rulers they have selected were the worst of men, the abolitionists with their "fanatical ravings." Observe the "mottled ranks" of their followers: "free negroes and boot-blacks, coachmen and domestics, infidels and free-lovers, spiritual rappers and every other shade of mania and folly."

"Is this situation temporary?" he asked. He answered,

> All history speaks but one voice. Tell me when and where the craving appetite of fanaticism was ever gorged with victims; when and where its bloody hands were ever stayed by the consciousness of satiety; when and where its deaf ears ever listened to reason or argument or persuasion or selfishness; when and where it ever died from fatigue or yielded except in blood.

He continued: "What then is our remedy? Shall it be the boy's redress of recrimination, the bully's redress of braggadocio, or the manly freeman's redress of Independence?"

That independence must come now. Don't be fooled, he exhorted.

> The suggestion for delay comes from various quarters.... My friends, there is danger in delay. The North, flush with victory, construes and will construe every indication of hesitancy into a dastardly fear—every voice for delay into the quakings of cowardice.... Let Georgia speak now, and a Northern

---

[36] *Daily Federal Union*, November 9 and 11, 1860 (quotes); Coleman, *History of Georgia*, 149–50; *Southern Watchman*, December 6 and 19, 1860; Nevins, *Ordeal of the Union*, 4:287–89; Carey and Justice, "Secession," 37–38.

Regiment will never cross the border line. Let Georgia delay, and they will make scourges to whip the cowards to obedience.

"Come, then, legislators," he concluded,

> selected as you are to represent the wisdom and intelligence of Georgia; wait not till the grog shops and crossroads shall send up a discordant word from a divided people but act as leaders in guiding and forming public opinion. Speak no uncertain words, but let your united voice go forth to be resounded from every mountain top and echoed from every gaping valley; let it be written in the rainbow which spans our Falls; and read upon the crest of every wave upon our ocean shores until it shall put a tongue in every bleeding wound of Georgia's mangled honor which shall cry in Heaven for "Liberty or Death."

Thomas R. R. Cobb later became a brigadier general in the Army of Northern Virginia and was killed at the Battle of Fredericksburg.[37]

Robert Toombs

The next day, T. R. R. Cobb was followed by Senator Robert Toombs, another secede-now proponent, who was something of a brawler. He had been a troublemaker at the University of Georgia, had been suspended once, and was later expelled. At the time of his speech, he had a strong voice and weighed over two hundred pounds.

Toombs argued that in 1788, "sovereign and independent states" had banded together under the Constitution for the mutual protection of their common interests. Since then, however, the South had been treated unequally. Northerners had received from Congress "bounties under the name of protection [tariffs] for every trade, craft and calling they pursue," with no similar provision for Southerners. Not satisfied, the North's "Anti-slavery or Abolitionist party of the North" had sought in Congress to limit the ability of Southerners to take their slaves with them into the new territories. Southerners, however, had sought only "equality in the common territories—equal enjoyment of them with their property, to that [enjoyment] extended to Northern citizens and their property—nothing more."

Moreover, in federal laws enacted both in 1797 and 1850, the North agreed to deliver to their rightful owners all slaves who fled to Northern states. Since then, however, thirteen Northern states had passed laws nullifying those laws within their boundaries.

---

[37] *Southern Watchman*, December 6, 1860; Freehling and Simpson, *Secession Debated*, 3–30; Warner, *Generals in Gray*, 56.

Once the new president was sworn in on March 4, Toombs continued, Northern abolitionists would control the federal executive including its army, navy, and treasury. Then they could achieve their main purpose: "final and total abolition of slavery" wherever it was found.

Toombs then addressed all Georgians directly: "Strike while it is yet time.... Withdraw yourself from such a confederacy; it is your right to do so; your duty to do so."[38]

Toombs later became secretary of state in the Confederate government and still later a brigadier general in the Confederacy's Army of Northern Virginia. In Toombs's final speech to the Senate when he resigned in January 1861, he emphatically addressed its Northern members: "We want no negro equality, no negro citizenship; we want no mongrel race to degrade our own; and as one man [we] would meet you upon the border with the sword in one hand and the torch in the other."[39]

Alexander Stephens

On November 14, Alexander Stephens, answering Cobb and Toombs, advocated for the wait-and-see position. Unlike Toombs he was slight, weighing only ninety-five pounds, and "had the hairless face of a boy and the higher-pitched tones of a woman." He was forty-eight years old.[40]

The vote in Georgia for the moderate presidential candidate Bell gave some indication that the wait-and-see position had considerable support in the state. On the night of Stephens's speech, Athens's *Southern Watchman* newspaper, which supported the more moderate position on secession, reported, "The Hall of Representatives was crowded to suffocation.... The galleries and aisles were thronged with ladies, and every available spot was occupied. The desks, chairs, aisles and windows were unable to accommodate the vast multitude, and hundreds left [the Hall], unable to get an opportunity to hear." As Stephens made his way, with difficulty, through the crowd to the podium, "for five minutes the buildings shook beneath the cheers and screams from the audience."[41]

Once the crowd quieted, Stephens began to speak: "My object is not to stir up strife, but to allay it; not to appeal to your passions, but to your reason...if after hearing you disagree, let us agree to disagree, and part as we met, friends." He continued, "Before looking to extreme measures, let us first see, as Georgians,

---

[38] *Georgia Weekly Telegraph*, November 13, 1860; Freehling and Simpson, *Secession Debated*, 31–51.
[39] Stovall, *Robert Toombs*, 221, 235; Barnhart, "Apostles of the Lost Cause," 386.
[40] Freehling and Simpson, *Secession Debated*, 51.
[41] *Southern Watchman*, November 22, 1860.

that everything that can be done to preserve our rights, our interests and our honor, as well as the peace of the country in the Union, be first done."

"First....In my judgment the election of no man, constitutionally chosen to that high office the presidency, is sufficient cause for any state to separate from the Union....Let us not anticipate a threatened evil. If he [Lincoln] violates the Constitution then will come our time to act." Meanwhile, "this Government of our fathers, with all its defects, comes nearer the objects of all good Governments than any other on the face of the earth, is my settled conviction." Have we not in both the North and South "grown great, prosperous and happy" under the federal government's operation?

However, he admitted that "great danger may come from the election I have spoken of. If the policies of Mr. Lincoln and his Republicans and states should be carried out or attempted to be carried out, no man in Georgia will be more willing than myself to defend our rights, interest and honor at every hazard and in the last extremities."

But this had not happened yet. "If his policy shall be carried out in repealing or modifying the Fugitive Slave Law [requiring Northern states to return escaped slaves to their owners] so as to weaken its efficacy, Georgia has declared that she will in the last resort disrupt the ties of the Union, and I say so too." If this took place, or if the Northern states attempted to ban expansion of slavery into new territories and states, it would be considered "an act of aggression." However, "I would wait for an act of aggression."

In the meantime, what should the legislature do?

> My recommendation to you would be this:...let a Convention of the people of Georgia be called to which [these questions] may be all referred....the Legislature is not the proper body to sever our federal relations....You must refer this question to the people and you must wait to hear from the crossroads and even the groceries; for the people in this country, whether at the crossroads or groceries [for some reason, not exactly using T. R. R. Cobb's "grog shops and crossroads" phrase]; whether in the cottages or the palaces, are all equal, and they are the sovereigns in this country....The Legislature were not elected for such a purpose. They came here to do their duty as Legislators. They have sworn to support the Constitution of the United States. They did not come here to disrupt this government.

Then "Should Georgia determine to go out of the Union, I speak for one, though my views might not agree with them, whatever the result may be, I shall bow to the will of her people. Their cause is my cause, and their destiny is my destiny, and I trust this will be the ultimate course of all."

Also, all Southern states should gather in conference "so that if the evil has got beyond our control, which God, in his mercy, grant may not be the case, let us not be divided among ourselves."

In summary, Stephens concluded, "My position is for the maintenance of the honor, the rights, the equality, the security, and the glory of my native State in the Union if possible; but if these cannot be maintained in the Union, then I am for their maintenance at all hazards out of it."[42]

Stephens soon became vice president of the Confederacy. In Savannah on March 21, 1861, as vice president, he made a speech explaining the new constitution of the Confederacy to the people of Georgia, a speech that later became known as the "Cornerstone Speech." In it he said, "Our new government['s]…foundations are laid, its corner stone rests upon the great truth that the negro is not equal to the white man—that slavery, subordination to the superior race, is his natural and normal condition." In the same speech, he also stated that "African slavery as it exists among us—[is] the proper status of the Negro in our form of civilization. This was the immediate cause of the late rupture and present revolution."[43]

Legislature Votes

On November 19, the Senate passed unanimously a bill to require the governor to call a convention of Georgians to meet on January 16, 1861, to determine whether Georgia should secede. On January 2, each county would select delegates to the convention.

The next day, the House took up the bill. Before its vote was taken, Simeon, on the floor of the House, called for a recorded vote of the yeas and nays "in order to make the record solemn and imposing." The House then passed the bill unanimously with each representative recording his yea vote.

The following day, the governor issued a proclamation calling for the convention.[44]

Isaac David: He was Simeon's uncle, one of James H. David's younger brothers. In January 1861, he would have been fifty-one years old and was living in Banks County.[45]

Submissionists: The derogatory name the secessionists called those people, such as Alexander Stephens, who at the time favored staying in the Union at least long enough to see what would happen next.

H. Strickland: "H. Strickland" was Hardy Strickland Jr., forty-two, who with his brother Henry operated a gold mine in Forsyth County. He had been in the Georgia House of Representatives from 1847 to 1850 and the Georgia Senate

---

[42] *Southern Watchman*, November 29, 1860; Freehling and Simpson, *Secession Debated*, 51–79.
[43] Hebert, *Cornerstone of the Confederacy*, 222–23.
[44] *Southern Recorder*, November 27, 1860; *Southern Banner*, November 29, 1860; *Daily Federal Union*, November 27, 1860; Carey and Justice, "Secession," 35–38.
[45] US Census, 1860, Banks County, Georgia; P. David, genealogical notes.

from 1853 to 1858. In August 1860, he was selected as a presidential elector for John C. Breckinridge and made public speeches on behalf of Breckinridge in several Georgia counties before the election.[46]

"*we managed to get H Strickland a secessionist [selected] in the convention by running one on each side and making no fight*": Although the actual election for delegates to the state convention to consider secession was held on January 2, 1862, in Forsyth County the effective selection was made at a county-wide convention of five to six hundred Forsyth County citizens of all parties and factions held in Cumming on December 4.[47]

At the Forsyth convention, Hardy Strickland and Hiram Parks Bell were unanimously selected as delegates. H. P. Bell (age thirty-three) was a successful lawyer who had been selected as a presidential elector for John Bell of the Constitutional Union party. Before the presidential election, he appeared on behalf of Bell at public meetings in several Georgia counties, frequently speaking with Hardy Strickland and in opposition to him.[48]

Simeon probably meant that before the convention, a deal was arranged that provided for a person on each side of the controversial secession issue be nominated so that each side would be represented at the state convention and a bitter fight within the county avoided. Thus, Strickland (for secession) and Bell (against) were nominated.

One of the people who had a prominent role in the Forsyth County meeting was Josiah Blair Patterson. Patterson introduced and moved the adoption of the platform that the county delegates adopted unanimously. At age forty-four, Patterson was a teacher at Cumming Academy, and as fellow teachers in the county, he and Simeon probably knew each other. Before long, in the Confederate army their acquaintance would become much closer.[49]

On January 2, Strickland and Bell were officially elected as delegates to the state convention.[50]

---

[46] *Southern Banner*, August 16, 1860, September 27, 1860; Shadburn, ed., *Pioneer History of Forsyth County, Georgia*, 58–59, 385; Bagley, *History of Forsyth County, Georgia*, 287, 289; Fortson, *Georgia Official and Statistical Register*, 1250, 1467.

[47] *Southern Banner*, December 20, 1860.

[48] *Southern Banner*, September 27, 1860, December 20, 1860; *Southern Watchman*, August 16, 1860; September 27, November 7, 1860, December 19, 1860; Shadburn, ed., *Pioneer History of Forsyth County, Georgia*, 161, 199–200.

[49] *Southern Banner*, December 20, 1860; *Pioneer History*, 52, 338.

[50] *Southern Watchman*, January 23, 1861.

At the state convention, on January 19, 1861, the delegates voted for secession 208 to 89. As planned, Strickland voted for secession while Bell voted against it. Both, however, signed the formal ordinance of secession five days later.[51]

H. P. Bell would have a further role to play in the story of the David family.

Milton County: Milton County was created out of parts of Cherokee, Forsyth, and Cobb counties in 1857. It merged with Fulton County in 1932.[52]

public School fund: A general elementary school fund was created by state legislation in 1858 and funded by the annual net earnings of the Western and Atlantic Railroad, which was owned by the state. "Each county was authorized to use these funds for instruction of children in 'the elementary branches of education' as it might see fit," wrote professor William H. Kilpatrick of Teachers college, Columbia University."[53]

the Association: This term referred to a number of Baptist churches that had banded together to meet, generally once a year, to consider matters of mutual interest.[54]

---

[51] Shadburn, ed., *Pioneer History of Forsyth County, Georgia*, 200; W. Miller and Pohanka, *Illustrated History of the Civil War*, 47; Carey and Justice, "Secession," 38.

[52] Dilman, "Milton County."

[53] Kilpatrick, "Beginnings of the Public School System in Georgia," 14–16; Coleman, *History of Georgia*, 137, 142.

[54] Burrows, ed., *American Baptist Register for 1852*, 50–54, 61–62.

PART 2

CIVIL WAR

1861–1865

Chapter 7

Simeon Volunteers, 1861

Simeon

Huntersville Pocahontas Co Va Aug 9th 1861
My Dear Father & Mother

    I seat myself this morning after several weeks delay to perform the pleasing duty of writing you a history of our travels in Virginia. Knowing the deep interest you feel in your soldier boys I am reprehensible for keeping you in suspense so long. But I have had so much work to do that I have only found time to write to Fanny.

    We rendezvoused at Atlanta on the 15th and left the 17th July Wednesday night, and reached Lynchburg Va the following Sunday morning. We went into camps there and remained one week, leaving Lynchburg on Monday the 29 & arriving at Staunton in Augusta County Tuesday the 30th July. We then left the Rail Road and took up the line of march for this point a distance of 82 miles and reached here in 6 days.

    The Gentleman that received the appointment of Qarter Master not having come on the Col appointed me at Staunton to perform the duties of Quarter Master till he comes on. I am discharging its arduous and responsible duties to the best of my ability, and giving general satisfaction. From Staunton, to Monterey, a distance of 46 miles I performed its duties on feet. At that point I was furnished a splendid horse and have got along finely ever since.

    Virginia west of the Allegheny mountains is a mountainous, sterile, cold, dreary, desolate waste—totally unfit for the habitations of men. But for the principle of giving up a portion of the "Mother of States and Statesmen" to the enemy this part of the State is not worth the life of a single human being.

    A feeling of desolation overpowers me and bears upon me like an incubus. The productions of the country are grass, buckwheat, a little Rye, and a little wheat, with an occasional patch of corn. No kind of fruit meets the eye but a few green apples. The inhabitants instead of being generous, warm hearted and chivalric, are cold blooded, inhospitable and distant. The whole appearance of the country and its inhabitants is forbidding in the extreme. But for all that we have to do our duty.

    I have not heard a word from Tommy, & Ratio, more than they were in Richmond. I have heard that Howell Cobb's Regiment is coming to this part of Virginia. I do not know whether it is true. I would like to be with the boys but I am satisfied that Eastern Va is much more pleasant than this dreary waste.

The "Troup Artillery" from Athens Ga have been in company with us ever since we left Staunton and are encamped here now. Two of Judge Lumpkin's sons—one of Howel Cobb's—one of John H. Newton's and representatives from all the first families in Athens are in the company. They are a set of noble fellows and I love them like Brothers. I forgot to mention that Dr. Reese's son one of the editors of the Southern banner is also along.

My health has been pretty good all the time though I am a little unwell with Diarrhoea. If I get killed or die here I want to be carried to Ga and be buried. I see no reason why a mans morals should be injured in the army. If we meet no more on earth I hope we will meet where sorrows never come and parting is no more. I will not ask you to write me till I write you again.

Your Affectionate Son S. B. David

Notes

Huntersville, Pocahontas County, Virginia: Huntersville and Pocahontas County were part of Virginia when Simeon wrote this letter. Along with several other counties in western Virginia, however, Pocahontas County would become part of the new state of West Virginia on June 20, 1863.[1]

"We rendezvoused in Atlanta": Simeon joined the Lester Volunteers, a company raised on July 4, 1861, in Forsyth County by Richard Paul Lester, a local attorney. On that day Lester was elected captain. The same day Simeon was elected first lieutenant, the second in command of the company. In the early days of the Civil War, company officers were elected by the men in their company. This practice was a continuation of a citizen-soldier tradition that persisted in America since at least the time of the French and Indian War.[2]

The Lester Volunteers were the first company to leave Cumming in Forsyth County. It was reported that "They marched around the courthouse square and as they approached David Walker's Store on the north side of the square, they paused while he sang a song for them." They then proceeded to Atlanta, where on July 17, 1861, they became company E of the 14th Georgia Regiment and signed on to serve for three years or the duration of the war.[3]

The Confederate army was organized generally as follows:

The maximum number of a *company* was one hundred men. It was commanded by a captain and three lieutenants as commissioned officers, plus sergeants and corporals as noncommissioned officers.

A *regiment* was composed of ten companies, one thousand men. As the war progressed, there frequently were fewer men in a regiment, sometimes as few as

---

[1] Snell, *West Virginia and the Civil War*, 82–84.
[2] Bagley, *History of Forsyth County, Georgia*, 428; Bledsoe, *Citizen-Officers*, 13–15, 28–29.
[3] Bagley, *History of Forsyth County, Georgia*, 389; Folsom, *Heroes and Martyrs*, 144.

two or three hundred. Regimental field officers were a colonel, lieutenant colonel, and major.

Two or more regiments composed a *brigade* although there generally were four or five regiments to a brigade. The brigade was commanded by a brigadier general.

Generally four brigades composed a *division*, commanded by a major general, and generally three divisions composed a *corps*, commanded by a lieutenant general.[4]

Earlier, on April 12, 1861, a Confederate force had fired on United States soldiers at Fort Sumter, an island in Charleston's harbor. On April 15, President Lincoln issued a proclamation calling for states that had not seceded, then including Virginia, to furnish 75,000 militia troops to "suppress said combinations [of seceded states] and to cause the laws to be duly executed."[5]

Two days later, on April 17, the Virginia convention voted to secede. The secession vote was ratified by voters throughout the state on May 23, 1861. Early the following morning, United States soldiers crossed the Potomac River and seized portions of Virginia. During the seizure, a Northern soldier and a Virginia civilian were killed.[6]

For many Georgians, and Southerners throughout the Confederacy, war with the Northern states began on the day Union soldiers crossed into Virginia. They considered the Northern action of May 24 an invasion of their homeland and a clear indication that the North would not allow the Southern states to leave the United States and go their own way. There would be no "bloodless revolution" as Simeon had prophesized in his letter of January 23, 1861, in chapter 6. Instead, Southerners now believed they would have to fight to defend their homes. One new Georgia regiment expressed the prevailing sentiment in an ad placed in an Atlanta newspaper, which read in part, "The war in Virginia is our war, and the defense of the homes of her citizens is the defense of our homes; their success is our success."[7]

Already existing infantry units from Georgia and other Southern states rushed to Virginia to aid in her defense. In addition, states and communities

---

[4] Casler, *Four Years in the Stonewall Brigade*, 18.

[5] McPherson, *Battle Cry of Freedom*, 263, 273–75; Guernsey and Alden, *Harpers Pictorial History*, 65.

[6] Edward H. House, "The Taking of Alexandria: Full Details of the Movement, Tearing down the Rebel Flag, the Murder of Co. Ellsworth, Minute and Accurate Account," *New York Tribune*, May 14, 1861; Heineman, et al., *Old Dominion, New Commonwealth*, 219, 223.

[7] B. Simpson, Sears, and Sheehan-Dean, *Civil War*, 401–403; *Southern Confederacy* (Atlanta), May 29 and June 9, 1861; *Milledgeville Southern Federal Union*, May 28, 1861; *Augusta Chronicle*, May 28, 1861; *Southern Watchman*, May 29 and June 5, 1861.

throughout the Confederacy raised additional regiments, including Simeon's 14th Georgia Volunteers, to fight the Union army.[8]

the duties of Quartermaster: Generally a quartermaster was in charge of providing soldiers with all supplies except ordinance (an ordinance officer's concern) and food (concern of a commissary officer). Within a quartermaster's province were things such as clothing, shoes, tents, knapsacks, wagons, horses, and forage for horses.[9]

"Mother of States and Statesmen": This phrase refers to Virginia.[10]

Tommy and Ratio: They are Simeon's two younger brothers. Both were in the 16th Georgia Volunteer Infantry Regiment. Letters from them are included in some of the following chapters.

Howell Cobb's Regiment: Howell Cobb was the former governor of Georgia, longtime member of the United States House of Representatives, speaker of the house, and secretary of the treasury who had responded to the Macon Committee letter as indicated in a note to Simeon's letter of June 14, 1860, in chapter 6. He was also the commander of the 16th Georgia when it was first organized. His regiment did not go to western Virginia as Simeon had heard they might, but instead was ordered to Richmond, Virginia, and then to near Yorktown, Virginia.[11]

Southern banner: This was one of two newspapers published in Athens, Georgia, at the time Simeon was writing.[12]

Simeon

Sept. 2, 1861
Marlin Bottom, near Huntersville, Pocohontas Co. Va.
My dear Father and Mother:

I have not heard one word from you, but hope you are well. I feel it to be my duty although I cannot hear from you to keep you advised of the condition of my health and my whereabouts.

Since I wrote you before, I have had a severe attack of measles that confined me to the room and bed about a week. I was taken two weeks ago today, but did

---

[8] Derry, *Confederate Military History: Georgia*, 64; Hattaway and Jones, *How the North Won*, 27; Gallagher et al., *Civil War*, 40; Foote, *Civil War*, 1:56; McPherson, *Battle Cry of Freedom*, 310–11.

[9] R. E. L. Krick, *Staff Officers in Gray*, 28; Bohannon, "Dirty, Ragged, and Ill-Provided For," 106–108, 121, 126–28; Garrison, *Encyclopedia of Civil War Usage*, 202.

[10] *Southern Banner*, July 26, 1860, and February 13, 1861.

[11] Rigdon, *Georgia 16th Infantry Regiment*, 71, 95, 100; H. Montgomery, *Howell Cobb's Confederate Career*, 9–23, 33–39.

[12] See North Georgia, Georgia Historic Newspapers, Digital Library of Georgia, https://gahistoricnewspapers.galileo.usg.edu/regions/north/.

not know that I had measles till Wednesday, when upon getting up, I was broken out all over with them.

I had the good fortune to get into the house of a very clever old man named McGlaughlin, who has an excellent wife and everything that was necessary to make me comfortable. I have been here now twelve days, and expect to stay a week or ten days longer before I join the regt. I would have asked for a furlough to go home and spend a few weeks, but we are expecting an engagement with the Federal Army under Rosencrantz inside of three weeks, and I want to be here and be in the fight if I am able.

There is and has been a great deal of sickness in our regt. mostly measles and mumps with some cases of typhoid fever, pneumonia, rheumatism, etc. We have had several deaths in the regiment, though the health is now rapidly improving from the fact that nearly all have the measles that never had them.

We are all much better satisfied with the people and country now than we were a month ago. Our regiment, all of them that were able, moved up four miles further in the direction of the Big Springs, being now 8 miles from Huntersville on the Big Springs road.

I have not heard one word from brothers Thomas or Horatio since I left home. I hope when I hear from you I will hear something from them.

I have not had a word from Fanny and only one short letter from Mr. Harris. I learned from Mr. Harris' letter that John Neal was doing no good. He is putting up a workshop with a view of making furniture. I told him before I left that he might have the third of all he and Charity could make on my place after this year. But he is determined to be of no account and will never be anything but a disgrace to his relations. I have entirely given him up.

I want you to write to Fanny and enclose a letter to him and implore him to abandon his wild notions and try to be somebody. If you or Father, one or both, could spare the time to go out to my house this fall, I would be truly glad, if you could only stay a day or two, and try to get John started right. If he turns out to do no good, I do not know what Fanny will do. If he does so badly that Fanny has to drive him off, if you can spare Sister Anna to go and stay with her I will give her whatever is right, and will pay you ten dollar per month for Simon if you can spare him to go there and wait on them.

If Fanny has to break up housekeeping, it will nearly break me up. I am of the opinion that the war will close this side of twelve months, and we will all return to the bosom of our families.

My dear mother, if you have not written me, do write when you get this letter, and write whether you have written or not, for I am exceedingly anxious to hear from you. My love to the negroes and all enquiring friends.

                    Your affectionate son,
                          S. B. David

P. S. When you write, send that prescription Dr. Bell gave you in Alabama for running off the bowels. I have not been troubled much so far. My landlady was taken violently ill last night and we are fearful she will die.

S. B. D.

Notes

measles: Later in his letter, Simeon adds, "There is and has been a great deal of sickness in our regt. mostly measles and mumps with some cases of typhoid fever, pneumonia, rheumatism, etc." This experience of Simeon's regiment was not at all unusual. It has been estimated that only one-fourth of the deaths in the Confederate forces were attributed to battle causes, whereas three-fourths of deaths were caused by disease. During the war a Confederate doctor wrote, "I trust we will be exposed to no greater danger in the future than the bullets, for they do not compare in destructiveness with disease."

Part of the problem was that many men in Confederate units were from rural areas, as was Simeon, and unlike soldiers from urban areas, they had never been exposed to many communicable diseases. Those diseases, even the primarily children's diseases, could prove fatal. One authority reports, "it is a matter of record that more havoc was caused by measles, an extremely infectious disease, during the early months of the war than by any other ailment." Although few soldiers died of measles alone, a body weakened by measles then was more susceptible to more serious diseases.[13]

an engagement with the Federal army under Rosencrantz: On July 22, General George B. McClellan, who had been in command of the Union forces in western Virginia, was ordered to Washington to take over what would become the Army of the Potomac. General William S. Rosecrans replaced him as the head of the western Virginia Union forces.[14]

Western Virginia was important for both political and strategic reasons. Politically, in June the region's inhabitants had met in convention at Wheeling, passed an ordinance creating a new state government loyal to the United States, and elected a governor for this "Restored Government of Virginia." The Union wanted to protect this new government, which would become the new state of West Virginia, while the Confederacy wanted to destroy it.

Strategically, if the Confederacy controlled the area, it could sever the Baltimore and Ohio Railroad, which was a key route for sending Union supplies and soldiers from the west to the battlefields in the east. If the Union controlled the

---

[13] H. H. Cunningham, *Doctors in Gray*, 5, 164, 188–90 (first quote); Meier, *Nature's Civil War*, 35–36; Welch, *Confederate Surgeon's Letters to His Wife*, 45 (second quote).

[14] Wagner, *Timeline of the Civil War*, 31–32; Guernsey and Alden, *Harpers Pictorial History*, 142; Cox, "McClellan in West Virginia," 142.

area, however, it would be in position to threaten the Shenandoah Valley and the flank of the Confederate army in Virginia.[15]

The engagement with General Rosecrans that Simeon expected took place on September 10 on the Gauley River at Carnifex Ferry in Nicholas County about thirty-five or forty miles southeast of Charleston. Union forces under General Rosecrans attacked Confederate forces under General John B. Floyd, a former governor of Virginia, who were entrenched in the heights above the river and the ferry with their backs to the river. The attack convinced Floyd that his position was untenable with the forces under his command, and during the night of September 10–11, he crossed the Gauley River and continued to march away from Rosecrans's Union army.[16]

Simeon's 14th Georgia was to be part of Floyd's command, but because sickness had severely weakened the regiment and because of the distance and poor quality of the roads, they did not join Floyd's forces at the engagement. Estimates of the number of the regiment who were sick and incapacitated varied from 25 to 84 percent.[17]

John Neal: He was Simeon's nephew, then sixteen old. On October 6, 1861, a month after this letter was written, he enlisted in the 38th Georgia Volunteer Infantry.[18]

Charity: It is unclear who she was. There appears to be no record of John Neal marrying until after the Civil War.

Simon: He probably was one of Thirza and James's enslaved men.

Dr. Bell in Alabama: He was Simeon's brother-in-law, husband of his sister Pillina.

---

[15] Snell, *West Virginia and the Civil War*, 26–27, 46–48; Foote, *Civil War*, 1:128; Cox, "McClellan in West Virginia," 126; Roland, *American Iliad*, 54.

[16] Cox, "McClellan in West Virginia," 1:143–46; *OR*, ser. 1, vol. 5, 128–29, 146–48; Guernsey and Alden, *Harpers Pictorial History*, 144.

[17] *OR*, ser. 1, vol. 5, 147, 164; Dewberry, *History of the 14th Georgia*, 8–9; Josiah Blair Patterson to Mary Patterson and children, October 4, 1861; Folsom, *Heroes and Martyrs*, 145.

[18] US Census, 1860, Milton County, Georgia; Bagley, *History of Forsyth County, Georgia*, 439.

Chapter 8

Homefront, 1861

Pillina Bell

Chulafinnee Ala July the 16th, 1961
Dear Mother,

We received yours of the 19th abt better then a week ago. I would have started a letter to you last Friday but from some cause unknown to me the mail did not come. Your letter was a long time coming. We were thankful to hear you were all in common health....

I must say something to you respecting the volunteers that have left our county for I can't put war out of my mind these days. Four companies have left our county, the last left last Thursday. It was quite a serious time with us here that day. There was one hundred and twenty in that company. I will mention the names of some that I think you are acquainted with. Dr. Ghent, Dr. Pitman, Dr. Shepard of Arbachoocha, Dr. Kemp of Wedowee. All them have lived in our place. Ihon Floid Smith, John McClintic, Coon Caldwell. I do not know that any of you are acquainted with any more that have gone.

Brother Horatio [,] I cannot get to feel willing for you to go. I fear you will not be able to stand the hardships you would have to undergo. Oscar can't talk about his uncle ratio going to war. If you do go have your amberty taken for me and I will pay for it. Dear ratio I would beg you not to go if I thought it would do any good. I think brother Simeon and Brother Thomas could stand it much better than you and then it does not look fare for all of one family to go. Write as soon as you receive this. Let me know when the boys start....

As ever your daughter Pillina C. Bell.

Notes

Source of this letter part: This part of a family letter was found quoted on eBay, the internet auction site.

Chulafinnee, Ala.: A settlement on Chulafinee Creek now in Cleburne County, Alabama.[1]

Oscar: He was Pillina's son, then about ten years old.[2]

ratio: He was Horatio, one of Simeon's younger brothers, then twenty years old. Several letters from him are contained below.[3]

---

[1] Read, *Indian Place Names in Alabama*, 20.
[2] US Census, 1860, Northern Division, Randolph County, Alabama.
[3] David Family Bible.

amberty: Pillina is referring to an ambrotype picture, "an early kind of photograph, consisting of a glass negative backed by a dark surface so as to appear positive."[4]

Thirza

[early September 1861, Maysville, Georgia]
Dear Children [Pillina and M. R. Bell]

Your kind favr of 20 ult was recd last wednesday and gave joy to more than Father Annie & I. on the night before 27 Mary & Fannie and all their families arrived on a short visit rather unexpectedly, and to make our happiness more complete the enclosed letter from our dear Simeon came with yours the first we had rec'd from him but Fannie had rec'd some whitch she brought with her.

On wednesday we sent James Neal after Pillona but Chatahoochie was so full she could not get here. on the same day we sent Dise after Sue and she could not get here till friday on account of high water. yesterday morning Mary and Fanny started home and this morning Sue left for her home. Miss Blalock came with Sue but her Bro George lives with her and would have come but he was unwell.

Yesterday we rec'd a letter from Tommy & Ratio whitch I will enclose. It will be a source of comfort to you and the dear little children. I would send one of Ratios letters written by him but it would make this too heavy. Say to Dear little Oscar when Uncle Ratio gets home Grand Ma and him will come to Alabama to see you all

Dear Pillina if you were here now to assist me we could make cloth to keep many a poor soldier warm. I have furnished brown Janes for 11 pair of pants and I will not have but 50 cts per yard though I could [get] allmost any price. Dr Alexander has a company allmost made and he has sent me word to make all the Gray Janes I possibly can for uniform coats and brown for pants. I am goin to prepare 30 yds white worp No 4 tomorrow. I have the wool allready spun mixed in the proportion 2/3 black and 1/3 white. it is for Tommy Ratio Dr Alx John Neal and Simeon coats. Fanny took the spun yarn home with her to [illegible word] Simeons [illegible word] and brown for pants and wool to make him shirts and drawers. they will freeze in that northern climate without a great deal of [illegible]. [Most of the last two sentences were written wrapped around the margin of the writing paper.]

John Neal has volunteered and James wanted to but would not without his mothers consent. Mary came in part to get our advice. We advised James to stay with his mother and he consented to do so. I gave Mary one of my fine new

---

[4] "Ambrotype," *Webster's New World College Dictionary*, 44.

blankets to make John flannel. We have urged him to go in Drs company and I think he will. Dr and Lony wants him to.

I will say we are all well except bad colds, but Simon cut his foot and done nothing for 3 weeks. Henry has a rising under the ball of his foot that he has not been able to sit up for two weeks. it is running now but I have no idea he will be able to work in two wks more.

I have furnished wool for 14 pair of heavy woollen socks and have had the most of them knit. that is entirely gratis. I will not wait for you to reply but will write often to let you hear from your Bro

[last line cut off, apparently to fit envelope]

[The letter was rotated ninety degrees, and the following lines were written across the previous lines.]

We had a severe shock of an earth quake here yesterday morning about daylight. Dear Pillina preserve these letters and when you write send them back one at a time.

Horatio had his Ambrotype taken in Richmond it is so mutch like him I want to look at it all the time. Simeon is in the 14th Regiment Brumley is the Colonel. I dread to hear from him for it [is] reported they have had a bad winter in Virginia.

Notes

Letter date and place: This letter contained no date or place. However, it was written on the last page of Simeon's letter of August 9, 1861, from Huntersville, Pocahontas County. That, plus the contents, would date it as early September 1861.

Dise: He probably was one of the Davids' enslaved men.

I have furnished brown Janes: "Janes" were jeans.

White worp No. 4: She probably means "warp" instead of "worp." In weaving the warps are "the set of threads running lengthwise in the loom and crossed by the weft."[5]

John Neal has volunteered.... We have urged him to go to Drs company: John W. Neal did join Dr. Alexander's company, the Bell Volunteers of Hall County. See chapter 9.

James: When this letter was written, James Neal was about a month short of his eighteenth birthday. He did enlist in Company B of the 38th Georgia Volunteer Infantry Regiment, on February 27, 1862.[6]

---

[5] "Warp," *Webster's New World College Dictionary*, 1630.
[6] Bagley, *History of Forsyth County, Georgia*, 439.

Simon and Henry: These probably are two of the Davids' enslaved men.
gratis: Free.[7]

Hiram Bowen

Henry City, Ala. Sunday November 18—1861
Dear Brother & Sister [James H. and Thirza David]

As it has been sometime since I have heard any news from you…[I] address you at present….

Some 2 months past Cousin John recd a letter from Thomas O. David. I saw [from] the letter he wrote that him & his youngest Brother wer both at Richmond, Va I think & that Simeon was also in the army, tho he did not know whear. he wishit to know if any of our family was in the camps and if so whear at. Cousin John answered him immediately that Jessy J. Bowen was at manasa station & had been ever since the first or midle of May. he left hoame the 11th of May & was there during all the main fighting tho at the time of the two principal battles Bull Run & Manassas he was confined to the hospital sick & continued down before and after better than 2 months tho now for the last 2 or 3 months is quite healthy and some 30 lbs heavier than when he left hoame & in fine spirits. he is under Captain A. C. Gorden of the abbeville greys, Alabama 6th Redgment, Colonel Sieble.

write me on receibt of this & tell me all the matter. I heard from Cousin Wiliam's letter that one of Isaac Davids sons was sent home dead also.

Dear Brother and family. I have no news that would interest you now. All is gloom with us all in consequence of the war…tho I feare not our Yankey foes as I feal that Justice is on our side & I see the simpathys of all the foreign powers are on our side & I doubt not that God is with us & I feal confident of success. Recognisance of our independance is not far distant by England and france & when that is done they will Raise the blockade tho as you see they Yankeys are swarming round our Southern borders by thousands at Savannah tho we have as many Bold Bunker hill farmers on our Southern borders & they have a many double-barrelled shooters and Bowie knives [illegible] that will slay thousands of Yankeys when they land on our shores as they are now doing. So much for the war.

Our familys are all in tolerable health at this time & have been this season with the exception of Owens little boy sum 12 months old died the 8th of October with inflamation of the bowels from teathing[,] within 3 hours of the same age of his little girl that died 2 years past in the same way. Owen is geting a large practice, him and copardner sum for a thousand dollars.

---

[7] "Gratis," *Webster's New World College Dictionary*, 633.

Cousin Johns family and all are in fine health. there little boy is a perfect Blackeye pea. I have not had a letter from Perry since July 60 nor one from Thomas Bowen since January. he settled in Panola County Eastern Texas & males his letters from Pine hill, Rusk Cty.

I rec'd a letter from my son Wiliam in Hot spring Cty, Arkansas Recently stating that he had ben sick with Bilious fever and not able to doo any work ever since the last of July & just geting about tho he had made a plentyfull crop & that 2 of his Brother in laws had just returned from the Mazaori army & had been in the Springfield battle tho escapet unhurt. I am acquanted with them. he said the enemy keld some 6 hundred of our men & that our men whipd them and kild them nearly all & after they started to retreat the Texas wrangers persued them & slew them with their swords and Boaa knives for ten miles. Wiliam Harp said the enemy fierd on them whilst they was at breakfast & a cannonball went plum through his tent.

Cally has been in Thomas Cty nearly 12 months tho for the last 2 months has been at hoame. She had a letter lately from Roady Ann Bowen. She stated all well thare & that Hiram & Owen & Green Linsey was all gone to the Army.

I am stil living on part of the land I first bought in Alabama—192 akers with about 30 cleared. My youngest son John H. is with me & we mak a plenty full living & are getting along hapily as moast of people in the world. fine crops in our county corn & cotton especially. corn only worth from 50 to 75 cts. per bushel. the poark cannot be bought at any price. beef worth from 6 to 7 cts by the quarter & scarce at that. I am this weak engaged in boiling my surup and sugar sum 1½ or 2 barrels. [I] have built a mill of my own.

I have the chance of purchasing the land back from the man I soald [it] to for what is due me on his notes 1250 Dollars tho there is another man waiting if I doo not take it to pay the money for it at the same price. I am not determined but what I shall take the money and strike for Southern Texas say Galveston and be a shepherd, the best business on earth superior to Brother's vineyard of Jones Cty.

[written down one side of the letter] Jessy is now at Union Mills near fairfax station, 6th Alabama Regiment, Col. Seibles.

for the want of more paper I Fare you wel.
Hiram Bowen

Notes

Hiram Bowen: He was a brother of Thirza Bowen David. At the time the letter was written, he was about sixty-three years old.[8]

Missing parts of letter: The missing parts of this letter appear in chapter 10.

---

[8] US Census, 1850, Division 11, Carroll County, Georgia.

Cousin John: He is John H. Jones. A letter from him is in chapter 6.

T. O. David and Thomas O. David: Refers to Owen Thomas David. Hiram is uncertain of his name and confuses it.

Jessy J. Bowen: He was Hiram's youngest son.[9]

Two principal battles Bull Run and Manassas: At this time there had been only one battle. It was called Bull Run by the Union and Manassas by the Confederates. A second Battle of Bull Run or Battle of Manassas was fought in late August 1862.[10]

One of Isaac David's sons: Isaac M. David was a younger brother of James H. David. His son, William H. David, was a member of the 24th Georgia Regiment and died on October 27, 1861, at the age of twenty-two. He probably died of disease because the 24th was not involved in fighting at that time.[11]

Yankeys...at Savannah: In early November 1861, Union Navy and ground forces captured Port Royal Sound, Beaufort, South Carolina, and the adjacent area, located only about thirty or thirty-five miles north of Savannah. Georgia Infantry, artillery, and navy units were part of Port Royal's unsuccessful defense.[12]

Owen: He was Owen B. Bowen, another of Hiram's sons, who was a doctor living in Alabama.

Perry: He was Hiram's older brother.

Thomas Bowen: He was another of Hiram's sons.[13]

Springfield Battle: The battle took place at Wilson's Creek, ten miles from Springfield, Missouri. The Union forces under Brigadier General Nathan Lyon attacked Confederate forces, whose command was split between Major General Sterling Price leading the Missouri militia and Brigadier General Ben McCullough leading units from Louisiana, Texas, and Arkansas.

The Union forces attacked both the front and the back of the Confederate forces, but the Confederate forces outnumbered the Union two to one. Both attacking Union forces broke and fled, most running all the way back to Springfield and some further.[14]

Cally: She was one of Hiram's daughters.[15]

Roady Ann Bowen: Brother Perry's youngest daughter.[16]

---

[9] Ibid.

[10] Gallagher et al., *Civil War*, 44–47, 61–62.

[11] Service records; Derry, *Confederate Military History: Georgia*, 76–77; *Southern Banner*, December 4, 1861.

[12] Nevins, *Ordeal of the Union*, 1:372–74; Ammen, "Du Pont and the Port Royal Expedition," 1:671–91; Derry, *Confederate Military History: Georgia*, 56–59.

[13] US Census, 1850, Division 11, Carroll County, Georgia.

[14] Foote, *Civil War*, 1:90–95.

[15] US Census, 1850, Division 11, Carroll County, Georgia.

[16] US Census, 1850, Subdivision 45, Jackson County, Georgia.

Hiram and Owen and Green Linsey: These were two of Perry's sons and his son-in-law.[17]

Brother's vineyard: This brother was Horatio Bowen who lived in Jones County.[18]

fairfax station: Fairfax Station is in northern Virginia about sixteen miles southwest of Washington.[19]

---

[17] Ibid.; US Census, 1860, Thomas County, Georgia.
[18] US Census, 1860, Jones County, Georgia.
[19] *Virginia Atlas & Gazetteer*, 76–77; P. Jones, *Annotated Abstracts*, vii, 636.

Chapter 9

Manning Raises a Company, 1861

A Patriotic Bachelor[1]

Dear Watchman: Aaron Bell, Esq., of Polksville, uniforms Capt. Alexander's company, which is now organized for the war, at that place. This shows the true patriot in our friend Bell, and is a fine example for his brother bachelors. We do think that he does not deserve to be a *bachelor*, but deserves the hand and heart of a *belle* as clever and patriotic as he is.

He has given freely to other companies and has also made Rev. Mr. Harben a present of his fine rifle. Long may he live to do such noble deeds and enjoy life.

Capt. Alexander's company unanimously voted to name the company "Bell Volunteers," in honor of Mr. Bell. That was just and right.

Respectfully,
M. P. CALDWELL

Notes

Polksville: Polksville was located in Hall County near its northern border, probably roughly where highways 283 and 52 intersect today.[2]

Rev. Mr. Harben: In the first five days of September, a Methodist preacher, Rev. T. B. Harben of Lexington, Oglethorpe County, addressed people at towns in Banks, Jackson, and Hall counties about his raising a regiment to fight for the Confederacy. The regiment was to be armed with rifles donated by the people of Georgia. He asked "everybody who wants to go to the war, and has a gun, to come along, and bring his gun; and everybody who has a gun, and is not going, to contribute his gun, which will be put in the hands of someone, who will go." Governor Brown agreed to modify the rifles at the expense of the state to make them suitable for use by the regiment.[3]

Propelled perhaps in part by an account of the Confederate victory at the Battle of First Manassas, reported on the front page *Southern Watchman* of September 4, Manning was able quickly to raise his company, which was to be a part of Rev. Harben's regiment. It was the fifth company raised in Hall County.[4]

---

[1] *Southern Watchman*, September 11, 1861.

[2] Dorsey, *History of Hall County*, iv; Johnson, "Johnson's Georgia and Alabama."

[3] *Southern Banner*, August 21, 1861, September 11, 1861; *Southern Watchman*, September 4, 1861, September 11, 1861.

[4] *Southern Watchman*, September 4 and 11, 1861.

Bell Volunteers: An undated muster roll of the Bell Volunteers in the handwriting of Manning Alexander is in my possession. It contains eighty-four names and is more complete than a roll of the company found in the *Southern Watchman* for October 30, 1861.

Member number twenty on the roll is M. P. Alexander's nephew John W. Neal, a son of Mary David Neal. Member number one on the roll is J. D. Alexander, one of Manning's younger brothers.[5]

Manning Poole Alexander's Commission as Captain, Bell Volunteers

EXECUTIVE DEPARTMENT,
ADJUTANT GENERAL'S OFFICE,
Milledgeville, Ga.,
September 23rd 1861

Capt M. P. Alexander
Bell Vols Gainesville Hall Co
SIR:
      Herewith you have the commission of yourself as

Captain and of John E. Waters and Taylor Armer as 1st and 2nd Lieuts
And of S. C. Falkner as Ensign Of Bell Vols—

You will please state in writing, directed to this office immediately,
Whether you accept the commission, and if so, whether
You have taken and subscribed the oath thereto attached

Very respectfully,
Your obedient servant,
Sept 14, 1861   Henry C. Wayne
                ADJUTANT GENERAL

STATE OF GEORGIA

By his Excellency, Joseph E. Brown, Governor and Commander in Chief of the Army and Navy of this State, and the Militia thereof:
To M. P. Alexander
Greeting:

---

[5] Thirza David to Pillina and M. R. Bell, September 1861, in chapter 9; Chaplin, *Riches of Bunyan* (Alexander family copy).

WE, reposing especial trust and confidence in your patriotism, valor, conduct, and fidelity, do, by these presents, constitute and appoint you Captain of the Bell Vols. of the Militia formed for the defence of the State, and for repelling every hostile invasion thereof. You are, therefore, carefully and diligently to discharge the duty of Captain as aforesaid, by doing and performing all manner of things thereunto belonging. And we do strictly charge and require all Officers and Privates under your command, to be obedient to your orders as such. And you are to observe and follow such orders and directions, from time to time, as you shall receive from me, or a future Governor and Commander-in-Chief of this State for the time being, or any other of your superior Officers, in pursuance of the trust reposed in you. This Commission to continue in force during your usual residence within the county to which you belong, unless removed by sentence of a Court Martial, or by the Governor, on the address of two-thirds of each branch of the General Assembly.

GIVEN under my Hand and the Seal of the Executive Department at the Capitol in Milledgeville, this the Fourteenth day of September in the year of our Lord one thousand eight hundred and sixty-one, and of the Independence of the State of Georgia the eighty-fifth.

By the Governor.

—*Henry C. Wayne*
Adjutant General

I do solemnly swear that I will bear true faith and allegiance to the State of Georgia, and to the utmost of my power and ability, observe, conform to, support and defend the Constitution thereof, without any reservation or equivocation whatsoever, and the Constitution of the Confederate States.

Sworn to and subscribed before me, this the day of 186_

[The latter document was signed vertically on the left side "Joseph E Brown."]

Notes

Commission from the governor: In at least the early days of the Civil War, the governor of Georgia's granting a commission to a company grade officer was primarily a formality. He generally ratified a company election that already had taken place.[6]

Bell Volunteers: The story of the next steps in what was to be the short life of Manning's Bell Volunteers, plus that of three other volunteer companies from the

---

[6] Bledsoe, *Citizen-Officers*, 36.

Hall County area that were to be part of the Harben Regiment, is told primarily by letters to the *Southern Banner* and the *Southern Watchman* written by members of the other companies. For some reason, Manning did not write letters home during this period, or, if he did, they have not survived.

In mid-October 1861, Captain Alexander and the Bell Volunteers received orders to rendezvous in Savannah on October 24 with the other elements of Reverend Harben's regiment. The company was to enlist for twelve months and to be employed the coming winter in defense of the Georgia coast.[7]

The Bell Volunteers marched from Hall County to Athens where, on October 22, after an "eloquent address" by a Colonel John Billups, they boarded a train for Savannah accompanied by a company from Jackson County. At Augusta they were provided with "an excellent supper, served up by the ladies of the city, to which we did full justice, and returned our hardy thanks." They then changed trains for Savannah.

When they arrived in Savannah, they found the city suffering from yellow fever. As a result, they were ordered to proceed to Camp Harrison, about seventy miles southwest of Savannah in Wayne County, near Screven. There they were to be mustered into service as part of the Confederate army and begin training.[8]

Camp Harrison was under the command of General George P. Harrison, who in early September had been appointed by Georgia governor Brown to form and arm a brigade of Georgia state troops. He was in the process of doing so, and his new brigade of state troops also was gathering at Camp Harrison.

General Harrison was not greatly concerned with Georgians who were to be mustered into service in the Confederate Army, such as the Bell Volunteers, rather than mustered into the Georgia state forces. Thus, when the Bell Volunteers and the three other companies of Harben's unit reached Harrison's camp, they found that General Harrison had few tents, cooking utensils, provisions, or other military items to supply these future Confederate companies.[9]

The next few days were somewhat confusing. Rev. Harben, who had been elected major of the four companies that temporarily formed a new battalion; Captain Mintz, commander of the company from Jackson County; and others traveled to and from Milledgeville to see about supplies and further instructions from the governor.

In the meantime, a captain of one of the state companies was having trouble retaining his men. To compensate, he began to bribe men who were to become part of the Confederate army to join his now short-handed company. He was not

---

[7] *Southern Watchman*, October 16, 1861, and December 4, 1861.

[8] *Southern Watchman*, October 23, October 30, and November 13, 1861; *Southern Banner*, December 4, 1861; Smedlund, *Camp Fires of Georgia Troops*, 147–48.

[9] Derry, *Confederate Military History: Georgia*, 55; *Southern Watchman*, November 13, 1861.

shy about pointing out that his state troops had enlisted for only six months, rather than the full year expected of Confederate troops.[10]

The Bell Volunteers and other men in Harben's Battalion had not yet been mustered into Confederate service and were growing more disgusted each day with the delay and their lack of supplies. Also, many of Manning's men preferred the shorter enlistment term. As a result, a number of men in his company, plus men from the other companies, agreed to switch to the state company.

To remove Harben's men from the influence of the state troops, it was arranged for them to go back to Savannah by train, yet when the train for Savannah arrived on the appointed day, the waiting men found it lacked cars to carry them. They had no choice but to return to camp.

There the men found not only that the state troops had used their few tent poles for firewood but also that they would be served supper only after the state troops were served theirs. As a result, they were not fed until late into the night and then were served only the poorest quality of beef and cornmeal.[11]

The following day the men of the battalion finally made it to Savannah. By then, however, most were "perfectly worn out by broken promises and disappointments" and voted not to be mustered into service at all but to return home. Those who were willing to stay were insufficient to form a battalion, and their companies were disbanded. Thus, Captain Alexander and his remaining men traveled back to Hall County, presumably without being cheered and fed along the way.[12]

---

[10] *Southern Watchman*, November 13, 1861; *Southern Banner*, December 4, 1861.
[11] *Southern Watchman*, November 13, 1861; *Southern Banner*, December 4, 1861.
[12] *Southern Banner*, December 4, 1861; *Southern Watchman*, November 6, 1861.

Chapter 10

Thomas Goes to Richmond, 1861–1862

1861

Flag Presentation at Centre-Hill Jackson County and Response
by Lieutenant Owen Thomas David

On Saturday, the 13th inst., the ladies in the vicinity of Centre-Hill, Jackson county [*sic*], assembled at that place for the purpose of presenting a flag to the Centre-Hill Guards. Mrs. D. R. Lyle having been chosen on the part of the ladies, in presenting the flag said:

Gentlemen of the Centre-Hill Guards

I appear before you on the present occasion, with mingled emotions of joy and sorrow, of pain and pleasure. Pain, that the circumstances which surround us, and the dangers with which our country is threatened, demands your military service; and pleasure, that you have so nobly and so bravely volunteered your services in its defense. And as an evidence of our high appreciation of you, I, on behalf of the ladies in the vicinity of Centre Hill, present to you this banner; and in presenting it we feel assured, yes, we know, that as long as one man remains of the Centre-Hill Guards, its folds will never trail in the dust, nor be trodden under foot by a Black Republican.

A few months since, and the people of the once United States, were the most prosperous and happy nation upon the face of the Globe, and but for Abolition demagogues, and Black Republican tyranny, we would to-day, have been in our primitive glory. But a dark cloud has obscured our clear sky, at least, for a season. Thus, however, we believe to be only a prelude to a brighter day than has ever dawned upon the Southern country. We are not unmindful of the great sacrifice you are making in this cause.—You are leaving the comforts of home, kind friends, and some of you beloved wives and darling children, to undergo the hardships and privations of the soldier's life. But in all this, you have our warmest sympathy. We feel proud of this brave company; yes, language is inadequate to express the high regard we entertain for you. The departure of the Centre-Hill Guards from our midst, will bring forth many a sigh, many a tear, and cause many a heart to bleed as it never did before. But I assure you that you carry with you our best wishes and our prayers, and we verily believe, that ere six months has passed away, our own Confederate flag will be floating over the Capitol at Washington City, proclaiming to the world that its halls are no longer contaminated with Black Republicanism. We hope, and ardently desire, that you may every one to a man, be permitted to return with this banner, to your pleasant homes and the dear ones you are now soon to leave; and we pray that you may come back with not even a scar made by a Northern foe. But should any of you fall a victim at the hands of our enemies, we earnestly pray God, that you may fall with the armor of the christian [sic], as well as that of a soldier, on, and be granted a happy admittance into the blissful abode of the Redeemer, where no war is known, no tears are ever shed, and no farewells are ever said.

At the conclusion of her remarks, Lieut. O. T. David, on the part of the Guards, responded as follows:

Ladies of the vicinity of Centre-Hill:

I appear before you, in behalf of this company, to receive from you this beautiful flag, as a token of the high regard you have for us as soldiers; and while we feel that in this act we have been highly honored, we feel bound by all the ties that bind us to our mothers, wives and sisters, and bind us to this once happy country, to preserve these colors under all circumstances. Yes, fair ones, rest assured, that amidst the roar of cannon and the rattle of musketry, we pledge you our words, our sacred honor, and our lives that these colors shall be firmly planted and kept unfurled to the breeze, as long as there is a strong arm, or a brave heart left to defend it. The folds of this beautiful flag may trail in the dust, but not till the arm that bears it, falls palsied to its position, or the body to its mother dust; and then to remain no longer than it would take to hoist it by other hands, equally brave and patriotic. We go not as many have done for a year, but we go to stay as long as Northern rebels threaten you with destruction. We may return soon and find you all as we leave you, but many of those fair forms may be slumbering in the dust, and the finger of time may carve wrinkles on the faces of these brave boys, and the older members of our company may grow gray, and many of both, old and young, may fall on the field of battle; but, if there is one left when peace is restored to this distracted country, this flag shall be returned, and you shall have the pleasure of looking upon it again, if it be in shreds, or as a seine; it will but tell where your boys have been; where perhaps, your friends have fallen.

Ladies, you have given us the Confederate colors, representing the eleven seceded States, and where one of these Stars call us, we will go—from the Potomac to the Gulf—and from the Atlantic to the Rio Grande, making war upon the foul invaders of our common country. It is true, that we prefer a clime approximating as near this as possible, but we go expecting nothing but hardships and privations, as all good soldiers do, when they are striking for liberty. Yes, we love liberty better than our lives, and we are willing, if needs be, [to] fall in the cause of our beloved land.

We receive this flag with mixed emotions of sorrow and joy; sorrow—for when we behold it, it tells us that we must bid farewell to those fair forms and lovely faces; joy—when we recollect that it is the greatest boon you can bestow upon us. We gladly receive it, and bear it to the battle-fields of Virginia, trusting in your prayers to Almighty God, and valor as soldiers, for its success, hoping that it may soon wave over the Federal Capitol; that it may be recognized by all nations, and that it "may ever wave, over the land of the free, and the home of the brave."

The proceedings were witnessed by a large crowd of persons of both sexes. The spirit of devotion to the South, evinced on the occasion, was most gratifying. If the same spirit prevails in other sections, our triumph is certain. The ladies of the vicinity have been particularly zealous in making uniforms, and doing other things for the comfort of the volunteers.[1]

Notes

Centre Hill vicinity: This area was between Hoschton in southern Jackson County and Winder in northern Barrow County. Before and during the Civil War, Winder and the surrounding area were in Jackson County. The name of the area is said to be derived from the positioning of three hills, one in the north near Hoschton, one in the south near Winder, and the one in the middle, located between the two, was called "Centre Hill." It is believed that the company was composed largely of members of the Rockwell Lodge of the Free and Accepted Masons located near Winder on the Rockwell Church Road. Thomas was a Mason as was the captain of the Centre Hill Guards, Abner M. Reynolds.[2]

Lt. O. T. David and Private Horatio David: When the Centre Hill Guards was formed, Thomas David was living in, or just outside, Monroe, Georgia, about fifteen miles south of Winder. He was married and twenty-five years old. His brother Horatio also joined the Centre Hill Guards but as a private. At that time, he was eighteen years old and living at home near Maysville.[3]

---

[1] *Southern Banner*, July 24, 1861.

[2] Elrod, *Historical Notes*, 37–38; Rigdon, *Georgia 16th Infantry Regiment*, 94; "Rockwell Lodge, No 191, of Free and Accepted Masons," *Southern Watchman*, February 11, 1858; conversation with regional historian and Confederate re-enactor Mark Pentcost in Jefferson, Georgia, January 17, 2016; Barrow County historical marker, "Rockwell Universalist Church," located on Georgia Road 53 north of Winder.

[3] Chapter 3, letter from Thomas, March 15, 1859; *Southern Banner*, July 24, 1861.

Thomas

Camp Cobb Richmond Va. Aug. the 23 61
Dear Father & Mother

I dont thinnk you have heard from us often enough though I have been particular carful to tel Ratio to write to you. for fear he has not written full enough for your satisfaction I will spent a portion of this Sabbath in writing to you.

I am glad to say to you that we are boath verry well and well pleased. Horatio had a severe cold a few days ago. he was on guard one day when the weather was quite inclement but he is verry well now.

We git plenty to eat and we can cook it so it eats finely. we have as fine beef as you ever saw and we mak splenddid hash. I think it will compare finely with Sudy's or your cooking. The officers have to furnish their own provision. the officers have ther friends ten in number in their tents. the ten privates draw their rations which make the substantials and we furnish something a little better. we then put it all on one table and by this means we have verry good fair, we frequently have vegetables.

We have measels in the camp plenty and Ratio and myself had had every opportunity to get them and have not as yet. I think it doubtful whether we take them or not. if we do I want to take them while we are here.

There has not been but one death in the regiment and I dont think it would have occurred if it had been properly treated. we had no surgeon at the time to see properly to the sick.

The drum is now sounding for preaching and Sergeant is bedding us fallin. I wl write when I come back.

Well I have got back from preaching and heard a splendid talk to soldiers urging them to do cheerfully all things that are enjoned upon [them and] to endurr hardship as good soliers.

we cant tel you where we will go to but think likely to yorktown which is on the James some distance below this place. from what I can gather it is tolerabl healthy and we will get plenty of fish to eat.

Dear Parents we have been thinking we might obtain furlows to come home and see you all, but I now think it verry uncertain as we all have to be here to drill so that we may know how to compete with the enemy on the field of battle. Sue is verry desierous that I should come home but she will have to learn to be content with her lot making the best of it she can.

I [am] well pleased with the life of soldier and I am better pleased with my ofice than I expected. I rank with the 2and Lieut drawing the sam pay which is $80.00 per month. it may appear to you that I ougt to save som money. I may save a little but it want be much for my expenses are heavy.

I dont know for sertain where Brother Simeon is. I am trying to get som clu at his whereabouts today. I want you to be sertain and write me all you know about him so that I can have the pleasure of corresponding with him. I have written a letter to Sister Mary but have not received any answer & I here from Sue about once a week and I assure you that it gives me much pleasure.

we received the gloves and comforts you sent us and I am verry thankful for them and if it is possible Brother shall have one of them.

Father I hope you will quit laboring so hard for I fear it will cill you. Set about and see that the negros work. I want you to give all the negrows my respects. tell Old Ben that we are in Old Virgin that plase that I have herd him talk about so much.

Mother I want you [and] Father to remember in your daily pettitions asking you to preserve us thru this campain and that we may be permitted to return to you. I must close. Give my love to all.

Your Son O. T. David

[Postscript in pencil]

Father: I want you to get yarbro to make me a pair of boots, tell him not to make them to heavy. if they are i cant march.

The reason i want boots, is that there is a great deal of snow here in the winter. I can't get a pair of shoes here for less than 3$.

Send them with the uniform. I will send the measure.

Notes

Camp Cobb Richmond Va: The Centre Hill Guards left Athens by train on July 18. They arrived in Richmond shortly afterward. In Richmond they became Company B of the 16th Georgia Volunteer Infantry Regiment, a regiment that the Confederate government had authorized Howell Cobb (the former congressman, speaker of the US House of Representatives, governor of Georgia, and secretary of treasury) to raise.

On August 15, the regiment elected Cobb as their colonel and commanding officer by acclamation, and its campground was named after him. The camp was located at Richmond's Fair Grounds, about a mile from the State Capitol building.[4]

Sudy: She probably the young woman listed in the 1860 slave schedule as twenty-six years old and belonging to James H. David.

measles in the camp regular: The situation became worse. A short article in the *Richmond Whig* on September 10, 1861, listed, by name fifteen soldiers of the 16th Georgia Regiment who had died during the week ending on Sunday,

---

[4] *Southern Banner*, July 24, 1861; H. Montgomery, *Howell Cobb's Confederate Career*, 14–17, 32–34; Byrd, *Confederate Sharpshooter*, 14, 17; Smedlund, *Camp Fires of Georgia Troops*, 92–93.

September 8. At least one of them was from Thomas's Company B. The article further reported, "Sickness prevails in this Regiment to such an extent, that it hardly musters half of its members on parade."[5]

Sue: She was his wife. See chapter 3.

negros: The 1860 federal slave schedule listed James H. David as owning ten enslaved people ranging in age from one to forty-nine.

Old Ben: He probably was the slave listed under James H. David's name in the 1860 slave schedule as being forty-nine years old.

yarbro: This may have been one of the Davids' slaves, although Thomas's uncle, Thomas Jones Bowen, married a Nancy Yarbrough, and this "yarbro" maybe a brother or other relative of hers.[6]

Owen Thomas David's Obituary

Tribute of Respect

Departed this life, in Richmond, Va., on Saturday, 5th Oct., 1861, Dr. O. T. David, (aged 26 years and 1 month) 2d Lieutenant of the Center-Hill Guards, known as Company B, 16th Regiment, Ga. Volunteers. He died of Typhoid fever, after an illness of 5 weeks. His body was brought to Georgia and interred in the graveyard, near his residence, in Jackson county. The burial was performed by the Masonic Fraternity, of Rockwell, with the usual honors. Thus cut down in the prime of life, the Confederate Government has lost a firm and valiant officer—Jackson county has been deprived of one of her best and most useful citizens—the Masonic Lodge, of a worthy and consistent member. He was a kind and affectionate husband. He embraced religion in his 16th year, attached himself to the Baptist Church, and was a consistent member until his death. He not only expressed an entire resignation to the holy will of God, but a trusting willingness to go, fearing no evil, as he trusted for salvation and eternal life in the merits of the Lord Jesus Christ, alone, by whose precious blood he felt that he had been delivered from sin and its fearful condemnation. For several days and nights, previous to his dissolution, the violence of his disease prevented the possibility of communicating views and experiences to his wife and friends, who surrounded his bed, yet they have no lingering doubt of his safe passage to the better world above. We deeply deplore his loss. We know that we have lost a worthy brother, but our loss is his eternal gain. We deeply sympathize with his bereaved wife, and tender to her our heartfelt sympathy. Therefore,

---

[5] *Southern Banner*, August 28, 1861; Roberson, *In Care of Yellow River*, 24.
[6] War of 1812, Widow's Pension, No. 18, 280, February 27, 1879, NARA.

Resolved, That our Lodge be draped in mourning for the usual length of time.

"I want to live a Christian here,
I want to die a shouting;
I want to feel my Jesus near
When soul and body's parting."
    M. A Patman
    S. G. Hunter
    H. C. White
     Committee[7]

Notes

5th Oct, 1861: This date was confirmed when Thomas's wife filed for pay due him at the time of his death. As part of the file, Thomas's company commander wrote that Thomas died on October 5, 1861, and his wife received his pay only until October 5.[8]

Dr. O. T. David: This title apparently referred to O. T.'s time as a dentist as indicated in notes in chapter 3.

He died of typhoid fever: It was remembered in the family that he died of measles. Possibly he contracted both diseases. A body weakened by measles was then more susceptible to more serious diseases, such as typhoid fever.[9]

"I want to live a Christian here, I want to die a shouting": These are the opening lines of "New Harmony," a hymn from a shape-note singing tradition called the Sacred Heart. The lines appear to have been developed from an old song sung on plantations by enslaved African Americans.[10]

Hiram Bowen

Henry City, Ala. Sunday November 18—1861
Dear Brother & Sister [James H. and Thirza David]
  As it has been sometime since I have heard any news from you & last eavning hearing the melancholy news by a Recent letter from Cousin Wiliam Jones to his brother John of the death of your son T. O. David, induce me to address you at present—Dear Brother & Sister if it was possible to say any thing

---

[7] *Southern Watchman*, December 11, 1861.
[8] File on the Application for Pay Due filed by Mrs. Susan C. David on November 4, 1961, part of Owen T. David's Service records.
[9] Undated reminiscences of Thomas's niece, Nora Alexander Boone, in my possession; H. H. Cunningham, *Doctors in Gray*, 188–90.
[10] B. White and King, *Sacred Harp*, 406; "Sacred Harp," Wikipedia, https://en.wikipedia.org/wiki/Sacred_Harp, accessed February 6, 2023; Barton, *Old Plantation Hymns*, 12.

to you that would console a broken heart it would gratify me to do so tho alas—we must all submit to the will of him that put us hear a little while to stay. from dust we sprang & to dust we must return & if God be for us hoe [who] can be against us. he has a design in all things....

Hiram Bowen

Notes

Hiram Bowen: He was a brother of Thirza Bowen David. The remainder of this letter is in chapter 8.

Cousin John: He is John H. Jones. Letters from him are in chapters 3 and 6.

T. O. David and Thomas O. David: Refers to Owen Thomas David. Hiram is uncertain of his name and confuses it.

1862

Sue David

Mulberry, March 12, 1862
Dear Mother, [Thirza]

I received your letter last Sunday, saying something about Tommy's funeral being at your house. When I talked to Mr. Davis at Bethabra the 2nd Sabbath in last Feb. he said he would some rather preach it at Bethabra. he said that was the propper place to have it preached, being near where he [Tommy] lived and in the church there, and volunteered and went of [off to war] here, and was buried here

I told him you wanted it preached up at your church. He then asked me which I had rather. I told him I was going to have it preached at bethabra untill you come down and mentioned about having it up there. then I had studied about it.

I sent him word I wanted him to preach it, but did not say where at. he thought it would be at Bethabra. I have had it given out to be at Bethabra several times not knowing you was givin it out up there. he said he would get Mr Reed to come down here at that time.

I suppose he give it out again last Sunday at Bethabra to be the fifth Sunday. I have had it given out four or five times since the second Sunday in Febuary. I heard somebody say that Mr Kelly give it out at ceder creek on the third Sunday in last mounth, to be at bethabra. I do not know who told him to give it out, but he did so some one told me that heard him.

I am sorry you will be disappointed. I hope [you] will not think hard of me for it was immaterial with me, but as Mr. Davis has given it out so often and I no [know] I want you all to come down the fifth Sunday. Come down on Saturday.

You said something about going to see Sim & Fannie. I would like to go but I will have so much work to do for Tobe and George I cant go. we are all well. hope this will find you the same. I remain

Yours as ever   S. C. David

Notes

Mulberry: Mulberry was the nearest post office to Thomas and Sue's home. It was located north of Winder in Barrow County, then Jackson County, near where State Route 53 crosses the Mulberry River, not far from present-day Mulberry Road.[11]

Tobe and George: These were two of Sue's brothers, Robert B. "Tobe" Moon, then about twenty-four, and George M. Moon, then about eighteen.[12]

Sue David's marriage: Sue later married W. J. Collins (sometimes referred to as J. W. Collins) on October 20, 1867, in Jackson County.[13]

---

[11] Owen Thomas and Sue David's entry in US Census, 1860, Jackson County; Elrod, *Historical Notes*, 114.

[12] US Census, 1850, Jackson County; Thirza David to Pillina and M. R. Bell in chapter 8; Mays Family Tree for Robert B. "Tobe" Moon, http://person.ancestry.com/tree/16440175/person/28016531191/facts, accessed on March 29, 2016.

[13] Marriage Certificate, State of Georgia, Jackson County, October 20, 1867.

Chapter 11

Horatio's First Letters Home, 1862

Horatio

Yorktown, Va.
Feb. the 22, 1862
Dear Mother

    I seat myself to answer your kind letter. I was happy to hear that you were all in common health. I have been pestered with the jaundice right bad, but I am well of them now. While sick, I had nothing that I could eat, and you may suppose that I thought of your table a 1000 times.

    Mother, I have no news of interest to write you. You hear more truth about the war than I do. We have all been wishing that we could go where fighting was going on, but I think we will get a taste of it before long.

    Mother, I will never forget Brother Tom. I miss him now as though he died yesterday. Every time I go in the officers house there is one gone that ought to be there.

    Mother, if the South whips the North I expect to see you on this earth, but if the reverse, I can't meet you this side of the grave. I will try to be prepared to meet you there.

    Tell Tom Henderson that I would have written to him more, but this is all the paper I have at present. I remain

                      Your son, more affectionate than ever,
                              Horatio J. David

Notes

Yorktown, Va.: Yorktown is on the York River about twenty miles upriver from the Chesapeake Bay. Horatio was camped less than two miles from Yorktown on the Yorktown-Williamsburg Road. Yorktown is located on a roughly eighty-mile-long peninsula that stretches from the Chesapeake Bay west between the York and James Rivers to Richmond, then the capital of the Confederacy.

    The peninsula was strategically important as a route to Richmond, a key objective of Union forces throughout the war. A Union army that landed on the eastern tip of the peninsula would have a straight shot overland to Richmond. In late-March 1862, a large Union force under General George B. McClellan began making such a landing.

Earlier a Confederate army had fortified a twelve-mile long line running across the peninsula from Yorktown, on the York River, south to the James River. On April 4, McClellan's army began moving toward that Confederate line. Shortly afterward, a series of battles known as the Peninsula Campaign began.[1]

jaundice: "[A] condition in which the eyeballs, the skin, and the urine become abnormally yellowish as a result of increased amounts of bile pigments in the blood."[2]

Pillona Alexander

[This is part of a letter; for the full letter, see chapter 13.]
Gillsville Hall Co Ga May 4th
1862
Dear husband [Manning Poole Alexander]
....Mother got a letter from S. B. David last Wednesday. he has gone to Yorktown and camped in 3 miles of Ratios reg. he hunted up Ratio & found him well & hearty. he was in the battle of the 16th and came out unscathed. he stood in water thigh deep during the fight. Sim says he is a brave looking boy. Brother did not get there till after the fight....
Pillona W. Alexander

Notes

Mother got a letter from S. B. David last Wednesday: S. B. David was Simeon, and "last Wednesday" would have been April 30, 1862. That letter apparently has not survived. Simeon's regiment arrived in Yorktown in mid-April and left on May 5 for the Richmond vicinity.[3]

battle of the 16th: On April 16, the Union army under General McClellan attacked roughly the center of the Confederate line.

That line stretched from Yorktown south about twelve miles across the peninsula between the York and the James Rivers. A large stream known as the Warwick River extended most of the way between the York and the James, and the Confederates under General John Bankhead Magruder were positioned in a line behind the Warwick, between that river and Richmond.

In the part of the line not protected by the Warwick, the Confederates were behind land made naturally boggy by a number of small streams, tributaries of the Warwick, that wandered through it. Magruder increased the swampy character

---

[1] Simmons, *Concise Encyclopedia*, 160; Dowdey, *Seven Days*, 38–39, 42; Quarstein and Moore, *Yorktown's Civil War Siege*, 15, 16; Woodworth, "Confederate Military Leadership," 127; Smedlund, *Camp Fires of Georgia Troops*, 181.

[2] "Jaundice," *Webster's New World College Dictionary*, 778.

[3] Folsom, *Heroes and Martyrs*, 147.

of this part of the line by building dams on the Warwick that channeled water from the river and further inundated the land to his front.

Two dams already existed on the Warwick, and at roughly the center of the line, where the Union army attacked, was Dam No. 1. The attack and ensuing battle there became known as the Battle of Dam No. 1 or the Battle of Lee's Mill.[4]

Although the 16th Georgia Regiment had been in a few skirmishes, this was its first real battle. It also was the first battle of the Peninsula Campaign. Horatio did not write about this battle, at least not in a letter that has survived and made public, but he was in it, as Simeon indicated.[5]

Only a few days before Horatio wrote his first letter, Howell Cobb, the commander of Horatio's regiment, was promoted to brigadier general and became the head of the 2nd Brigade, part of the Confederate Department of the Peninsula, whose overall commander was General Magruder. The 2nd Brigade included the 16th Georgia.[6]

Early in the battle, a Union force managed to cross the Warwick River, overwhelm a North Carolina unit, and occupy its trenches as the Carolinians made a disorderly retreat. The 16th, along with other units in General Cobb's brigade, was ordered from about a half a mile away to advance in double-quick time to support the fleeing North Carolinians. As one soldier in the 16th wrote, "We just run in and shot when we had the chance and never formed no line. If a man could get behind a tree it was alright." Horatio apparently got into a stream or pond where "he stood in water thigh deep during the fight," and that, too, turned out also to be "alright."

The advance of the 16th and other regiments turned the Union tide. As General Cobb wrote in his after action report, "[T]he enemy were twice successfully repulsed, and finally driven across the stream [the Warwick] and beyond the range of our fire in great confusion and with severe loss."

In the battle the Union suffered approximately 165 casualties; the Confederates approximately 75. The 16th was reported to have lost two killed and six or seven wounded.[7]

---

[4] Quarstein and Moore, *Yorktown's Civil War Siege*, 82–84, 104–105; Burton, *Peninsula & Seven Days*, 19–21; H. Montgomery, *Howell Cobb's Confederate Career*, 54–55; Dowdey, *Seven Days*, 42.

[5] Byrd, *Confederate Sharpshooter*, 27, H. Montgomery, *Howell Cobb's Confederate Career*, 56; Sears, *To the Gates of Richmond*, 55.

[6] Byrd, *Confederate Sharpshooter*, 25.

[7] Quarstein and Moore, *Yorktown's Civil War Siege*, 106–10, 159; Roberson, *In Care of Yellow River*, 73–74 (1st quote); H. Montgomery, *Howell Cobb's Confederate Career*, 56–57; *OR*, ser. 1, vol. 11, pt. 2, 416–18, 419–20; Byrd, *Confederate Sharpshooter*, 27–28.

Horatio

[late May 1862 from a hospital in Richmond]
Mother

I was in greate suspense for you when I got this letter. I received one from cousin Helen Winters. she sayd that you had not received one from me since the fight. Mother Do not think hard of me for I have written many letters to you since the fight. the first I wrote was on the 8th may and have written evry 3 days since that time when I could get paper.

I would like very much to be at home with you all, but duty calls me here, so I can stay content. give my love to, Hero[?], John, and the family and howdy to the negroes. The scarf you send me is very nice. I would like to see you weaving them this sumer.

pleas send me a shirt and drawers with the coat and pants. 2 shirts will not be to much. if you were to see me now you would not know me. Im sun burnt so badly.

H. J. David

Notes

Date and place: Although no date is given for this letter, information in the letter indicates it was written sometime after May 8. When it is compared with other letters in this collection, it is apparent that the year was 1862.

It probably was written from a hospital in Richmond. Horatio's service records in the National Archives indicate that Horatio was admitted to Chimborazo Hospital No. 3 in Richmond on May 14, 1862, with acute diarrhea and transferred on May 22 to Camp Winder.

Chimborazo was a huge hospital complex on Chimborazo Hill on the east side of Richmond consisting of about 150 one-story wooden pavilions, each one hundred feet long and thirty feet wide.

Camp Winder had been established as a hospital only a month before Horatio was transferred there on 125 acres near present-day Winder Street. In time it grew to be a hospital complex three times the size of Chimborazo. In early May 1862, it "housed approximately 2,500 sick soldiers," but there were only seven surgeons to care for them all.[8]

---

[8] Freemon, *Gangrene and Glory*, 77–78; Waitt, *Confederate Military Hospitals in Richmond*, 21–22; Coles, "Richmond, the Confederate Hospital City," 79; Calcutt, *Richmond's Wartime Hospitals*, 58.

the fight: The fight Horatio refers to may have been the Battle of Williamsburg, fought on May 5, 1862. Although the battle was widely reported in the Athens newspapers, the 16th Georgia took no part in it.[9]

Instead, Horatio may have been referring to the Battle of Dam #1 on April 16 that Pillona mentioned in her letter of May 4 and is explained in the note to that letter above.

Hero and John: It is not clear who they were. From the rest of the sentence, it seems they were not family members or enslaved people owned by the family. Possibly they were two of Horatio's friends, or maybe they were the family dogs.

Simeon [excerpt]

Near Drewry's Bluff
[July 1862]
My Dear Parents….

Horatio and I met on Tuesday [illegible] for the first time after the fighting. I felt very grateful that [illegible] Gen. Cobb's Brigade was in the dreadful fight of Tuesday but Horatio came through unhurt, as I afterwards learned though I have not seen him since that day. I tried to prevail on him to take some money, but he said he did not need it.

Notes

Simeon's Letter: For the full letter see chapter 12.

Date of letter: The letter is undated, but from the events the full letter describes, it would have been sent in July 1862.

Drewry's Bluff: Drewry's Bluff is located on a bend of the James River about seven miles below Richmond.[10]

Horatio and I met on Tuesday [illegible] for the first time after the fighting. I felt very grateful that [illegible] Gen. Cobb's Brigade was in the dreadful fight of Tuesday, but Horatio came through unhurt, as I afterwards learned though I have not seen him since that day: The Tuesday Simeon refers to is apparently Tuesday, July 1, the day of the Battle of Malvern Hill. It was one of a series of battles called the Seven Days that were fought east of Richmond on the peninsula between the James and York rivers June 25–July 1, 1862. These battles were fought between General Robert E. Lee's Army of Northern Virginia and General George B. McClellan's

---

[9] McPherson, *Battle Cry of Freedom*, 427; Foote, *Civil War*, 1:410–11; H. Montgomery, *Howell Cobb's Confederate Career*, 58; *Southern Watchman*, May 14, 1862; *Southern Banner*, May 14, 1862.

[10] Sears, *To the Gates of Richmond*, 93.

Army of the Potomac. Cobb's Brigade, including the 16th Georgia, was one of two brigades that were part of General John B. Magruder's division.[11]

Simeon apparently met Horatio in the morning of Tuesday, July 1, before the battle began. When he wrote this letter, he had not seen him after the battle but had heard he survived it, which he did.

dreadful fight of Tuesday (Battle of Malvern Hill): The 16th was engaged during only one of the first six days of the Seven Days Battles, and then only slightly. Around four o'clock in the afternoon on July 1, the seventh day, however, Cobb's Brigade arrived in front of Malvern Hill where a battle had been ongoing since about eleven thirty that morning. When they looked at the battleground, they saw that the Union forces held an extremely strong defensive position. The Union soldiers were on top of the 150-foot high plateau. The approach to the hill was bordered on each side by small streams or swamps that funneled the Confederate advance across open fields straight to the base of the hill. On top of the hill were some one hundred cannons and twenty-five thousand to thirty thousand Union soldiers.[12]

The artillery had been pounding the Confederate forces on and around the open fields all afternoon. Cobb's Brigade was on the Confederate right, and not long after it arrived, its men and other nearby Confederate forces were ordered to charge the hill. Cobb's Brigade moved forward with three of its four regiments, while the 16th was ordered to remain behind in a ravine in reserve. The charging troops made determined efforts over and over again to break the enemy line without success. Before long, the 16th joined the charge.[13]

One soldier of the 16th described their efforts:

> The first command given was to fix bayonets and charge the battery which the gallant men in great heroism did but we had to charge through an open field for about a half mile under the open and well directed fire of a heavy battery well supported with infantry. The grapeshot and bombs cut our lines down so rapidly our officers found it could not be taken. We were ordered back to reform and tried it again but did not succeed and retired the second time.[14]

Confederate forces on the Confederate left, opposite Cobb's Brigade, fared no better. The battle finally ceased about nine o'clock that evening, with Union forces still in control of the hill. Estimates of Confederates losses were about fifty-

---

[11] McPherson, *Battle Cry of Freedom*, 465; Roland, *American Iliad*, 74; Boatner, *Civil War Dictionary*, 731; Sears, *To the Gates of Richmond*, 389.

[12] Byrd, *Confederate Sharpshooter*, 31–35; H. Montgomery, *Howell Cobb's Confederate Career*, 61–62; Porter, "The Battle of Malvern Hill," 2:409; McPherson, *Battle Cry of Freedom*, 469; Foote, *Civil War*, 1:510.

[13] Byrd, *Confederate Sharpshooter*, 31–35.

[14] Roberson, *In Care of Yellow River*, 86.

five hundred men and the Union about half as many. The 16th Georgia had lost sixty-three men killed, wounded, or missing. At least two of those killed were in Horatio's company.[15]

The next chapter tells about Simeon and the Seven Days Battles.

Horatio

Richmond, Va.
Sept. the 6th, 1862
Dear Mother

    I seat myself to inform you that I am alive and doing well at present.

    I am in McLaws division hospital 2 miles from Richmond. Our fare here is tolerably good. We get a plenty of beef and bread. we get black tea for supper and good coffee for breakfast. For dinner we get beef and chicken-soup. I am well of the dyspepsia and I cured it by eating nothing but bread and water and three small drams of whisky a day. The chronic diarrhea is still working on me and if you know of any cure for it I want you to tell me what it is.

    I have not heard from Brother Sim since he left here to go to the Valley of Virginia. His brigade was in the fight at Manassas Junction, but I do not know whether he was in it or not.

    Mother, I want you to make me an over shirt. I want you to make it just like the one you made me last winter only I want the tail made longer and I want it of a gray color and 2 pockets in the breast. Make my uniform coat a short roundabout coat like you used to make when I was about 12 years old. Make my pants smaller than the last ones you sent me. They were too large every way and I want both coat and pants trimmed with very narrow green tape. I want you to make me some underclothing, some socks, 2 undershirts, and a comfort. Do not send these clothes until you get a good chance for I don't want them lost. Send the things that I wrote for in the other letter as soon as you get the chance. Write as soon as you can for I have not heard from you since the last of July.

    Direction. Direct your letter to
H. J. David
McLaws Division Hospital
Richmond, Va.
In care of Dr. Todd

Notes

McLaws Division hospital: "McLaws" was Brigadier General Lafayette McLaws. On July 26, after the Seven Days Battles, the Army of Northern Virginia was reorganized again, and Cobb's Brigade, including the 16th Georgia,

---

[15] Byrd, *Confederate Sharpshooter*, 34–35 and note 22; McPherson, *Battle Cry of Freedom*, 470.

became part of McLaws's Division. McLaws was a West Point graduate, and like the men of the 16th, was a Georgia native.[16]

dyspepsia: "A state of the stomach, in which its functions are disturbed, without the presence of other diseases, or when, if other diseases are present, they are of but minor importance."[17]

the fight at Manassas Junction: This is a reference to the Battle of Second Manassas or Second Bull Run, which took place in late August 1862. Simeon's regiment, the 14th Georgia, was then part of Thomas's Brigade, named after its commander Colonel (later Brigadier General) Edward L. Thomas, Hill's Division, Jackson's Corps. As Horatio indicated, the brigade, and Simeon's regiment, took part in the battle. It is not clear whether Simeon was with the regiment then, although he probably was. He was part of the regiment only two weeks earlier when he wrote home. He did not write about taking part in the battle, although possibly a letter he wrote has not survived.[18]

comfort: Although a "comfort" or "comforter" usually referred to bed coverings that frequently were quilted, "comforter" also may refer to a woolen scarf. As Horatio mentions in the next letter, in this instance he was writing about the latter.[19]

Horatio

McLaws Division Hospital near Richmond, Va.
Sept. the 24—1862
Dear Mother

The reception of your kind letter which I received today overjoyed me for I have not received a letter from you since I came to this place. It was dated Sept. the 14, 1862.

I was glad to hear that you were all tolerably well. I was sorry to hear of the accident that James Neal happened to. I was also sorry to hear of Cousin Tom Henderson's illness.

Mother I have some bad news to tell you. Our brigade is almost ruined. Cousin James David of the 16th regt. was killed. Capt. Thompson and a great many others that I have not time to mention. I have heard nothing from our company but I know half of them are killed and taken prisoner. When our brigade came out of the fight there were not enough men to make one regiment (5 regt.

---

[16] Byrd, *Confederate Sharpshooter*, 36–37; Oeffinger, *Soldier's General*, 4–5.

[17] Dunglison, *Dictionary of Medical Science*, 334.

[18] Gallagher et al., *Civil War*, 61–62; Folsom, *Heroes and Martyrs*, 115–18; letter from Simeon of August 15, 1862, in chapter 12.

[19] Drake, *What Did They Mean by That?*, 65; "Comfort," and "Comforter," *Websters New World College Dictionary*, 298.

in a brig.) There were 600 conscripts sent from town yesterday to fill out our brigade.

Dear Mother I am going to the relief of our dear boys soon. I will leave this place in the morning and go to the remainder of my regiment if I can but do not expect the Dr. will let me go though I do very well at present.

Mother it makes me so mad to think of the way that our regiment has been cut up that I can hardly write.

Mother tell Sister Lony that I am glad she has a husband that is able and willing to fight for his glorious country.

Mother I am quite young yet and it is probable that I will be able to fight a long time yet, and I now can give revenge to our dear boys that have fallen in the late battles in Maryland. I rather than 50 fortunes to have been there to help them.

Mother our lovely land may be subjugated but never while a heart beats in my body.

Mother I want to see you all badly but I am afraid for you to start here. There is no telling one day where we will be the next.

Tell the negroes that I want to see them very badly. Tell them that I have been in two hard-fought battles and many dangerous pickett and skirmish fights and am yet alive and will be home to see them again. Tell them to do all they can to make a living while we are driving the Yankees from our land and if I ever get home they shall be treated well as long as I live. Tell them it is not because I hate the Yankees that I am fighting them but because I love the land in which we live. Tell Simon I wish I had him here tonight. I think he would make a good soldier.

I have not heard from Brother Sim since he left here. Please write me whether Dr. Bell is in service or not. Do not send any clothes until you know where I am. It was to tie around my neck that I wanted the comforter.

Before I would desert, I would cut my own throat. I wish I could hear of those deserters being shot, and if they belonged to this part of the army they would be.

Write immediately. I can't put in enough love. Tell Cousin Bell hurrah for her. She is the right kind of a girl for the war. I hope I will get home to see her some time. I want to see her because you say she is so much like me. Give my love to Cousin Minta Henderson and all the rest of the connection. Farewell, dear father, mother, sisters, and negroes.

H. J. David

Notes

The accident that James Neal happened to: The service records of James Neal, Horatio's cousin, who was a member of the 38th Georgia Volunteer Infantry Regiment, indicate that he was hospitalized in Farmville, Virginia, from July 22 to October 16, 1862. They also record that the hospitalization was necessary because of a "Contusion from R Road," apparently sustained while traveling on a railroad.

Cousin James David: He was James M. David, a sergeant in the 16th Georgia Volunteer Infantry Regiment. His service records indicate he was killed in the Battle of Crampton's Gap, September 14, 1862. He was about thirty-eight years old. See the next note for information about the battle.[20]

our dear boys that have fallen in the late battles in Maryland: Horatio is referring both to the Battle of Crampton's Gap, fought on September 14, 1862, and the Battle of Sharpsburg, as it was known in the South, or Battle of Antietam, as it was known in the North, fought on September 17, 1862.[21]

These battles came about when General Lee decided, for several reasons, to invade Maryland. His goal was "to supply his hungry troops, attempt to bring the state into the Confederacy, and possibly obtain foreign recognition of Confederate independence." Yet when he crossed the Potomac River and moved into western Maryland on September 5, the cool reception he and his men received disappointed him and caused him to change plans. He determined to head for Harrisburg, Pennsylvania, capture it (an important rail center), sever Union communications between the eastern seaboard states and states to the northwest, seize rich farmlands in Pennsylvania to feed his soldiers, and threaten Washington, Baltimore, and Philadelphia. During this movement North, his army would march to the west of a long line of mountains in Maryland called generally South Mountain. These mountains would separate him from federal armies to the east.[22]

While Lee marched most of his army north along South Mountain toward Pennsylvania, he boldly directed a significant part of it under General Thomas J. "Stonewall" Jackson, including Simeon's 14th Georgia, to return south and seize Harper's Ferry at the mouth of the Potomac in order to protect his line of communications to the south. Jackson was successful in capturing Harper's Ferry; however, General McClellan, again in charge of the Army of the Potomac and located several miles east of South Mountain, moved faster toward South Mountain and the rest of Lee's army than Lee anticipated.[23]

South Mountain itself was not a solid shield against an attack from the east. Several passes through the mountain existed. McClellan sent armies to the two major ones with orders to march through them in order to do several things: separate Jackson's army at Harper's Ferry from the remainder of Lee's army to the

---

[20] US Census, 1860, Madison County.
[21] Byrd, *Confederate Sharpshooter*, 38–47.
[22] Roland, *American Iliad*, 77–79.
[23] Ibid., 79.

north (then near Hagerstown, Maryland); possibly prevent Jackson from taking Harper's Ferry; and defeat Lee while Jackson was away.[24]

Lee soon learned of McClellan's move and warned Major General Lafayaette McLaws, the Jackson subordinate at Harper's Ferry who was the most exposed to a Union attack from the north, to watch his rear. Meanwhile, three Confederate regiments already had been posted to guard one of the mountain passes, Crampton's Gap. They soon were augmented by another regiment of infantry, two regiments of cavalry, and a battery of artillery. Based on Lee's information, McLaws also ordered Cobb's Brigade, including the 16th Georgia, to join the forces at the gap. His order to Cobb was to "hold it [the gap] if need be at the cost of every man in his command."[25]

The Confederates had fewer than one thousand men at Crampton's Gap when the Union attacked on September 14. When they were joined later by Cobb's Brigade of an additional twelve hundred men, the total was still only twenty-two hundred. Against them was a Union force of some 12,300. Not surprisingly, the Union troops drove Cobb's Brigade and the other Confederates out of the pass. Although they did not hold the gap as McLaws ordered, the Confederates were somewhat successful in that the Union stopped at the western head of the pass and neglected to move aggressively from there down into the valley to cut the Confederate army in two.[26]

The cost, however, as Horatio's letter indicates, was high. The 16th Georgia had entered the battle with a total of 368 officers and men. When the battle was over, 187 either were killed, wounded, taken prisoner, or missing, a loss of slightly over 50 percent. Of the twenty-four in the regiment listed as killed, seven were from Horatio's company, including its commander, Captain Abner M. Reynolds. At least sixteen more from Company B were captured.[27]

General Cobb was temporarily too ill and exhausted to continue in command. The remaining members of his brigade were placed under Lieutenant Colonel C. C. Sanders of the 24th Georgia. They now were down to only 357 officers and men in the entire brigade. In one company of the 16th Georgia, Company H, only five men were capable of fighting.[28]

Then on September 17, only three days after the Battle of Crampton's Gap, this severely depleted brigade fought in the Battle of Antietam, first under

---

[24] Ibid., 80; Sears, *Landscape Turned Red*, 127–32; *Southern Watchman*, October 1, 1862.

[25] Sears, *Landscape Turned Red*, 138–40, 159–62; Byrd, *Confederate Sharpshooter*, 39; *OR*, ser. 1, vol. 19, pt. 1, 870; *Southern Watchman*, October 1, 1862 (quote).

[26] Sears, *Landscape Turned Red*, 161–64, 172–73; Byrd, *Confederate Sharpshooter*, 39; *OR*, ser. 1, vol. 19, pt. 1, 870.

[27] *OR*, ser. 1, vol. 19, pt. 1, 861; Byrd, *Confederate Sharpshooter*, 39–42; *Southern Watchman*, October 29, 1862; Rigdon, *Georgia 16th Infantry Regiment*, 94–114.

[28] Byrd, *Confederate Sharpshooter*, 44–45; Roberson, *In Care of Yellow River*, 12, 97.

Lieutenant Colonel Sanders and then under Lieutenant Colonel William McRae of the 15th North Carolina. They defended the notorious Sunken Road (also known as Bloody Lane) until they ran out of ammunition and retired. At the end of that day, the brigade had lost an additional 156 officers and men killed, wounded, or missing, almost 45 percent of those who had begun the day. The 16th lost an additional twenty-six officers and men.[29]

In the two battles, Horatio's brigade indeed was "almost ruined," and Horatio's regiment had lost 60 percent of its officers and men.

Tell the negroes....: The following sentences may have been prompted by President Lincoln's issuance of a preliminary Emancipation Proclamation two days earlier, on September 22. That preliminary proclamation stated that on January 1, 1863, the president would issue a formal proclamation declaring all slaves in Georgia and the other rebellious Southern states to be free.[30]

Simon: He probably was one of the enslaved men owned by the Davids, possibly one close to Horatio's age. He is mentioned also in Simeon's letter of September 2, 1861, in chapter 7, Thirza's letter of early September in chapter 8, and other letters.

---

[29] *OR*, ser. 1, vol. 19, pt. 1, 862, 871–72; Byrd, *Confederate Sharpshooter*, 44–47; Sears, *Landscape Turned Red*, 261, 274–80.

[30] Encyclopaedia Britannica, *Annals of America*, 9:398–99.

Chapter 12

Simeon's First Battles, 1861–1862

1861

Josiah B. Patterson to Cornelia Patterson

Manassas Junction Va. Decr. 12th. 1861
My Dear Daughter
....I would not have you suppose that our situation is at all uncomfortable. we have fire places in our tents and the weather is not very cold. We have bedsteads made by driving down forks in the ground and spreading plank and covering them with hay or straw. I have been very fortunate in regard to supplying myself with bed clothes. I have the two quilts that I brought from home and six good heavy blankets. S. B. David my bedfellow is not so well supplied but will be when Lieut. H. Paxton returns as he sent to his wife for a supply. We then can bid defiance to the weather even at 80. north Lat.... .
Your unworthy father
J B Patterson

Notes

Josiah B. Patterson: He was 2nd Lieutenant Josiah B. Patterson, then forty-two years old. Before the war he was, like Simeon, a schoolteacher in Forsyth County. When Simeon was the first lieutenant of Company E, Patterson was one of the two second lieutenants in the company.[1]

Patterson also played a prominent role at the Forsyth County convention that chose delegates for the Georgia secessionist convention, as mentioned in a note to Simeon's letter of January 23, 1861, found in chapter 6.

Manassas Junction Va: Located about twenty-five miles southwest of Washington, D. C., this was the scene of the First Battle of Manassas or First Bull Run fought July 21, 1861.[2]

Simeon's last letter in chapter 7 was from Huntersville, Virginia (now West Virginia). The 14th Georgia left Huntersville in late October and marched to

---

[1] US Census, 1860, Forsyth County; Henderson, *Roster of the Confederate Soldiers of Georgia*, 2:366; Patterson, "The Incomplete Correspondence of Lieut. Josiah Blair Patterson," letter of December 12, 1861.

[2] Gallagher et al., *Civil War*, 43–47.

Millboro, Virginia, where it boarded railroad cars that took them to Manassas, arriving there around November 19.[3]

Simeon

Manassas Junction
Dec. 24, 1861
My dear Mother

Your affecting and affectionate letter of the [illegible]th inst. came to hand Sunday week, and your letter of the 11th Nov. directed to Huntersville and forwarded from that point and received this morning.

Be assured, dear Mother, that our letters were treasured as precious jewels. I had long been anxious to hear the sad particulars of my dear brother's death. Both of your letters were satisfactory on that point. While death has visited many families, he had passed ours, and it remained for my dear brother to die the most glorious of all deaths, the death of a soldier fighting under freedom's banner for the Sunny South. Let us hope, as we have good reason to do, that the loss of our brother and son is his eternal gain. May we all so live by the grace of God that when the summons comes we may be also ready, and that we may have a re-union beyond the skies.

I received a letter from Brother Ratio in reply to one that I wrote him, stating that he was well, and well pleased with the treatment he received from his officers, and was utterly opposed to a transfer, saying at the same time that theirs was the best regiment in the Confederate service.

We have had an order from Gen. Beauregard that after Christmas there would be furloughs granted (to seven commissioned officers, 2 Capts. and 5 lieutenants, and one hundred privates from each regiment, ten from each company), until all have the opportunity of going home that desired to go or that are able to go pecuniarily. The capt. and the 2nd lieutenant of the company are both absent at home, and will not return till some time in January. Lieut. Patterson and myself are expecting to go in what is called the 2nd set of seven commissioned officers, and will leave here about the first of February next. I wrote to Fanny yesterday that she might look for me about the 7th of February and to make her arrangements to go to your house, so as to be there the 3rd Sabbath in Feb.

I will write you again between now and then, and if I find there will be no doubt of my coming, I want Dr. Alex. and Lona and poor Sue to be there that I may see them too. Life is sweet and I would like to live, if it be the will of Heaven, to a good old age, but if I could see my own family and all of you once more (a thing that I never expected to do when I left home) I could die better satisfied.

---

[3] Folsom, *Heroes and Martyrs*, 146; Patterson, "The Incomplete Correspondence of Lieut. Josiah Blair Patterson," letter of November 19, 1861.

I wrote to and received a very affectionate letter from my dear sister Pillina since I wrote to you before. All were well. She was suffering great uneasiness about her brothers in the service. She was anxious to know whether I have plenty of clothing and bed-clothing to make me comfortable, to which I reply that I have an abundance of both.

I never was in better health, and am getting as fat as a bear, weighing this morning 171 pounds. We put up last week the walls of our winter quarters of oak poles, ½ mile from Manassas. I worked regularly from Monday morning till Friday night. There is some doubt of our getting into them on account of the difficulty of getting something to cover them, board timber being out of the question and the demand for planks being so great that it cannot be furnished.

Last night the wind blew a perfect hurricane all night. Our tents hopped and flopped all night, keeping the most of us awake. We have previously had a beautiful spell of weather for three or four weeks.

Fanny writes me that they have got their corn all up and shucked, making 65 wagon loads, their hogs fat, waiting for weather to kill, and everything going on prosperously. I have sent home out of my pay three hundred and fifty dollars, that annoys some of my neighbors very much. They say I am making a fortune out of the war. I will swap places with any of them that thinks so. Write soon, giving me all the news.

Your affectionate son,
S. B. David

Notes

my dear brother's death: He was Owen Thomas David. For details about his death, see chapter 10.

Gen. Beauregard: He was General Pierre Gustave Toutant Beauregard. At the time this letter was written, he commanded I Corps of the Army of the Potomac (later renamed by General Robert E. Lee as the Army of Northern Virginia) under General Joseph E. Johnston. A month after this letter was written, Beauregard was reassigned to Kentucky.[4]

Leave with the "2nd set of commissioned officers": Although it is not recorded when Simeon got the leave mentioned in the letter, Lt. Patterson was granted leave on January 13, 1862, according to his service records. Presumably, Simeon was granted leave on the same day.

Simeon may have done some recruiting for his company while at home. His service records contain an undated receipt signed by "S. B. David 1st Lieut & Recruiting Officer Co. 'E' 14th Regt Ga Vols" for a check for $239.15 drawn on

---

[4] Dowdey, *Seven Days*, 131; Boatner, *Civil War Dictionary*, 178; Folsom, *Heroes and Martyrs*, 146; Freeman, *Lee's Lieutenants*, 1:109.

the Farmers Bank of Virginia "for recruiting purposes." This was the only known time when he was a first lieutenant that he received leave to return home from Virginia.[5]

"my pay of three hundred and fifty dollars: As a first lieutenant, Simeon made $90 a month.[6]

Simeon

near Drewry's Bluff
My dear parents[7]

I have delayed writing to you much longer than I intended, but we have had such exciting times for more than two weeks that I have not felt like writing.

I will commence by saying that I was in three of the late battles and under fire in the fourth one, the explosion of the enemy's shells killing one and wounding seven of our men, though we never fired a gun. The captain of the company being sick, the command devolved on me, through all the series of battles. We commenced on Thursday evening the 26th of June having a dreadful fight, in which two of our company were killed dead, four others severely wounded, one of whom has certainly since died, and we fear two others. Myself and one other man [were] lightly wounded.

While marching forward at the head of my company, across a bottom that the enemy had thrown the water upon by damming the creek, a bolt struck me with tremendous force in the lower part of my stomach, striking the buckle of my pistol-belt and glancing [illegible] my vest and coat [illegible] right shoulder. The ball cut a [illegible] shirt and pants, and grazed the [illegible] to bleed me considerably. By the next morning, all my abdomen was perfectly black and very much swollen, and so painful that I could not bear my drawers or pants buttoned, but I determined to go as long as I could walk. When the ball struck me, I fell to the ground, and it was some fifteen minutes before I entirely recovered.

On the next evening, Friday, we overtook the enemy again, and fought by far the most tremendous battle of the whole war. Our Brigade and regiment were engaged again on Friday evening, but did not suffer so severely as on the previous evening. I had two men wounded, one only a scratch over the right eye.

Other divisions of the army engaged the enemy on Saturday and Sunday, our Brigade was engaged again on Monday evening but did not suffer very

---

[5] Patterson's service records; Simeon's service records, in "Compiled Service Records of Confederate Soldiers Who Served in Organizations from the State of Georgia" (all service records hereafter cited as "service records").

[6] Pay vouchers in Simeon's service records.

[7] This letter is undated, but from the events it describes, it probably was written in mid-late July 1862.

severely. I had one man wounded in that fight. We bivouacked that night as well as every preceding night, on the field of battle.

During the night we received large re-inforcements consisting of Magruder's and Euger's divisions, among whom was General Howell Cobb. Horatio and I met on Tuesday [illegible] for the first time after the fighting. I felt very grateful that [illegible] Gen. Cobb's Brigade was in the dreadful fight of Tuesday, but Horatio came through unhurt, as I afterwards learned though I have not seen him since that day. I tried to prevail on him to take some money, but he said he did not need it.

The regiment to which James Neal belongs was in the fight and his Capt. McClosky was seriously wounded. After diligent inquiry I have not been able to ascertain whether James Neal was in the fight or was hurt. I hear that McClosky's company suffered severely, but I have heard no names but himself.

It is not necessary for me to inform you, for you already know that we achieved brilliant victories in all of these hereafter world-renowned battles. But oh, the anguish and riven hearts that these six days of fighting made in Georgia alone, to say nothing of the other states. No regiment fought more gallantly than the 18th Georgia. Levi McCulloch was said to be horribly mangled with shell. Lieut. Selman took command of the company, and was soon wounded when the [command fell?] on Lieut. Calahan. [illegible] being absent, said to be sick, however, I saw him in Richmond a week [illegible] when he told me he was about well, and expected to join his company in a day or so. Some of Capt. Reynold's men think he is off feigning sick for fear of lead. We have had a great many officers absent in the last battles that ought to be exposed.

I put on clean shirt yesterday evening for the first time in nineteen days, and I am the only commissioned officer in the regiment (field or company) that has remained with the regiment all the time, never having left it an hour. I am not disposed to boast of my bravery, but I feel that my conduct has been such that my friends need not be ashamed of me. I have been in four severe battles and under fire in the fifth one, and had an abiding confidence in my own breast that I have done my duty on every occasion. I have always been anxious to know whether I was a brave man or not, or whether I would act bravely in battle. I feel perfectly cool and am not in the least excited.

Tell the girls that I will copy and send "The Soldier's Dream" for them in my next letter. I received your last letter in due time, and destroy them all before going into these battles. Write soon

      Your affectionate son,

          S. B. David

Notes

Drewry's Bluff: Drewry's Bluff overlooks a bend of the James River about nine miles below Richmond.[8]

I was in three of the late battles and under fire in the fourth one: Simeon is referring to a series of battles on the peninsula between the James and York Rivers known as the Seven Days Battles. They consisted of the major battles of Mechanicsville or Beaver Dam Creek on Thursday, June 26; Gaine's Mill on Friday, June 27; Savage's Station on Sunday, June 29; Frayser's Farm or Glendale on Monday, June 30; and Malvern Hill on Tuesday, July 1; plus a smaller battle on June 25 known as Oak Grove.

When Simeon's brigade began this series of battles, it had the effective strength (the number of men it actually could put into a battle) of about 1,750 men. When these battles were over, it had lost 563 men killed or wounded, almost a third of its strength.[9]

Just before these battles, Federal General George McClellan continued to move his strong Union army from Yorktown slowly west up the Peninsula (formed by the York River to the north and the James River to the south) toward Richmond. In front of him, General Joseph Johnston, commander of the Confederate army on the Peninsula, continued to retreat also in the direction of Richmond.

On May 31, McClellan had reached within about eight miles of Richmond when Johnston launched a poorly coordinated attack. The attack stopped the Union army's advance, but during the battle, known as Seven Pines or Fair Oaks, Johnston was severely wounded. The shot that wounded Johnston was called by a Northern journalist "the saddest shot fired during the war" because, as a result, command of the Confederate army on the Peninsula was given to General Robert E. Lee, and things began to change.[10]

Thursday evening the 26th of June: The battle Simeon describes on this day is the opening major battle of the Seven Days, the Battle of Mechanicsville or Battle of Beaver Dam Creek.

A few miles north of Richmond, the Chickahominy River flows generally from northwest to southeast down roughly the middle of the Peninsula until, about halfway down, it curves south to the James River. On June 26, General McClellan had about one third of his army on the north side of the

---

[8] Simmons, *Concise Encyclopedia*, 75.

[9] Boatner, *Civil War Dictionary*, 731–32; Folsom, *Heroes and Martyrs*, 115; Crenshaw, *Richmond Shall Not Be Given Up*, 26.

[10] Johnson and Ward, *Johnson's Map of the Vicinity of Richmond and Peninsular Campaign in Virginia*; Gallagher et al., *Civil War, Civil War*, 52; Hattaway and Jones, *How the North Won*, 187–89; Sears, *To the Gates of Richmond*, 117–45; Dowdey, *Seven Days*, 3, 126–27 (quote).

Chickahominy and about two thirds on the south side, both facing west toward Richmond. General Johnston had massed his Confederate army around Richmond to the south of the Chickahominy.[11]

General Lee, in his first action as commander of the Confederate army on the Peninsula, planned to hold the Union army to the south of the Chickahominy with about one third of his army, while the other part of the Confederate army around Richmond would cross to the north side of the river and attack the Union army there. In addition, General Stonewall Jackson's command was to march south from the Shenandoah Valley to aid the Confederate forces north of the Chickahominy by flanking the Union forces there. With the addition of Jackson's force, Lee would have two-thirds of his command north of the Chickahominy and one-third south of it, thus reversing the strength of the Confederate and Union armies facing each other on each side of the river.[12]

Simeon's 14th Georgia Regiment was part of Joseph R. Anderson's brigade composed of four Georgia regiments and one Louisiana battalion. Anderson's was one of the six brigades in General Ambrose Powell Hill's "Light Division."[13]

Lee's somewhat complicated plan was for General Stonewall Jackson's command, marching south from the Shenandoah Valley, to attack the right flank of the Union army north of the Chickahominy in and near the hamlet of Mechanicsville. Once Hill knew that Jackson was approaching, he was to direct his division to cross to the north side of the Chickahominy. Once across, Hill and his men were to march eastward to drive the light force of the Union army out of Mechanicsville. They then would continue attacking east to strike the right and front of the main Union force north of the Chickahominy, which was well-fortified behind Beaver Dam Creek about a mile east of Mechanicsville. Moreover, once Hill's eastward advance from Mechanicsville had cleared a bridge across the Chickahominy of Union men defending it, two more divisions, General James Longstreet's and General David Harvey Hill's, would march across the bridge onto the north side of the river and also strike the Federals. Longstreet's Division would attack the left part of the Federals' line in general support of A. P. Hill, and D. H. Hill's division would support Jackson's attack on the Union right.[14]

That was the overall plan. The battle would start when the 14th Regiment and the rest of Hill's Division crossed the Chickahominy and attacked Union forces at Mechanicsville. They were not supposed to cross, however, until it was

---

[11] Johnson and Ward, *Johnson's Map of the Vicinity of Richmond and Peninsular Campaign in Virginia*; Gallagher et al., *Civil War*, 53; Sears, *To the Gates of Richmond*, 117–19.
[12] Hattaway and Jones, *How the North Won*, 192–96; Gallagher et al., *Civil War*, 53.
[13] *OR*, ser. 1, vol. 11, pt. 2, 487, 877.
[14] Robertson, *General A. P. Hill*, 66–68, 71; *OR*, ser. 1, vol. 11, pt. 2, 491, 498–99.

clear that Jackson was moving to attack from the north. Jackson was to be in place about seven o'clock in the morning on the 26th.

By three o'clock in the afternoon, however, Jackson had yet to appear. Hill, impatient, decided not to wait longer but to cross the river immediately and attack.[15]

As planned, his men quickly cleared the light Union force from Mechanicsville and moved eastward to attack the main Federal position behind Beaver Dam Creek. General Anderson's brigade was on the extreme left of Hill's Division as it marched. The 14th Georgia and the 35th Georgia (along with a Louisiana battalion) were on the left of the brigade as it advanced and were the first of the brigade to strike the Federals at the creek. (The brigade's other two regiments were held in reserve.)[16]

It was when the 14th Georgia was wading through the marshy, flooded ground approaching the creek that Simeon was struck on his belt buckle. While he gradually recovered from the blow, the 35th Georgia and some of the 14th managed to cross the creek. Along with the Louisiana Battalion, they pushed back the Federal soldiers but not back far enough to break the Union line. They then held their ground against a counterattack until nightfall stopped the fighting.[17]

For various, still-controversial reasons, Jackson never did join the battle that day. Other Confederate units attacked to the right of Anderson's Brigade, but they were even less successful than Anderson's men in dislodging the Federals from their position. At the end of the day, the Confederate advance had stalled, and almost all the Confederates were still west of the creek and just west of the Union force.[18]

On the next evening, Friday, we overtook the enemy again, and fought by far the most tremendous battle of the whole war. This was June 27th and the Battle of Gaines Mill.

During the night after the Battle of Mechanicsville, Union General McClellan learned that Jackson finally had arrived and taken a position from which he easily could attack his right flank north of the Chickahominy. Feeling vulnerable, McClellan ordered his men to withdraw further east four miles to the Gaines Mill area. They did so without the Confederates being aware of their leaving. After retreating, they deployed at another strong defensive position—on the

---

[15] Robertson, *General A. P. Hill*, 66–70; *OR*, ser. 1, vol. 11, pt. 2, 491, 498–99, 835.

[16] *OR*, ser. 1, vol. 11, pt. 2, 835–36, 877–78; Patterson, "The Incomplete Correspondence of Lieut. Josiah Blair Patterson," letter of July 12, 1862.

[17] *OR*, ser. 1, vol. 11, pt. 2, 835–36, 877–78; Patterson, "The Incomplete Correspondence of Lieut. Josiah Blair Patterson," letter of July 12, 1862.

[18] Robertson, *Stonewall Jackson*, 467–74.

banks of and atop a hill behind another creek, Boatswain's Creek, sometimes known as Boatswain's Swamp.[19]

Meanwhile, Lee, unaware that McClellan had changed positions, planned to keep the pressure on by attacking his earlier position on Beaver Dam Creek again the following morning. When morning came, Simeon's regiment deployed and, as a soldier later recorded, "everyone present rushed forward with locked bayonets at the signal of our artillery's halt. No one was there."[20]

Realizing the Federals had withdrawn, Lee adjusted his plan. He ordered the Confederates to continue their advance with A. P. Hill in the center, Longstreet on his right, and D. H. Hill on his left along with Jackson, who now had only an easy march to join the other Confederates.

As Simeon's regiment continued advancing, it found the hastily retreating Union army had left behind "many wagon loads of dead and wounded Yankee bodies, discarded tents, haversacks, knapsacks, blankets, overcoats, canteens, and wagons of every size." One soldier observed that "bottles of champagne lay like quail in the grass." Not until around noon did A. P. Hill's men meet serious resistance. By then they had discovered the Federals behind Boatswain's Creek and halted as Lee reviewed this new Union position.[21]

Lee looked out over primarily open fields that sloped down to the creek. On the other side of the creek, wooded land sloped steeply upward to a plateau. Although he may not have seen them clearly, among the trees on the far side of the creek, the Federals had dug three lines of trenches one above the other up the hill like terraces, and they had placed cannon on the plateau at the hill's top.[22]

After examining the position, Lee consulted with his generals and decided they should attack in unison across the entire front. As the Confederates began to move forward, however, Longstreet, on A. P. Hill's right, was delayed when his men received heavy fire from Union artillery on the hilltop while they struggled across creeks and swamps. Also, Jackson, on Hill's left, was delayed once again when he took a wrong road and lost time retracing his steps. D. H. Hill,

---

[19] Sears, *To the Gates of Richmond*, 210–15; Crenshaw, *Richmond Shall Not Be Given Up*, 39–41; Burton, *Extraordinary Circumstances*, 79–81.

[20] Dewberry, *History of the 14th Georgia*, 19; Sears, *To the Gates of Richmond*, 212–13; Burton, *Extraordinary Circumstances*, 82–84.

[21] Dewberry, *History of the 14th Georgia*, 19 (1st quote); Sears, *To the Gates of Richmond*, 217–23; Hattaway and Jones, *How the North Won*, 197 (2nd quote).

[22] Sears, *To the Gates of Richmond*, 213–15, 222–23; R. K. Krick, "Men Who Carried This Position," 189; Robertson, *General A. P. Hill*, 82; McElfresh, "The Battlefield of Cold Harbor" (map).

who was to support Jackson on the left, had run into stiffer resistance than expected and decided to wait for Jackson.[23]

Because of the delays on his right and on his left, A. P. Hill attacked first, again as a lone division, hitting primarily the middle of the Union line, its strongest part. The Union commander at the battle observed the results: "brigade after brigade [of Hill's Division] seemed almost to melt away before the concentrated fire of our artillery and infantry." A. P. Hill's biographer James A. Robertson Jr. wrote: "the Light Division was slowly being destroyed for lack of support."[24]

Anderson's Brigade, including Simeon's 14th Georgia, was the third of Hill's six brigades to become engaged. As Anderson's men came to a crest of the first hill, they found themselves faced with the ravine and creek that separated them from the enemy on the hill beyond. "Here," General Anderson reported, "the brigade encountered a very hot fire, both of musketry and shell, which brought us to a halt from the double-quick in which I had commenced the charge."

Anderson's Brigade finally made three charges against the far Union line on the hill above the creek without success. After these efforts to reach the enemy and experiencing "some wavering in the center" of his own line, Anderson ordered his men to lie down and hold their position at the crest of the hill where they had started. Soon, A. P. Hill himself realized his brigade needed support to succeed and ordered all of his command to halt.[25]

Around 7 p.m., Jackson and Longstreet caught up with Hill. At last Lee had all of his major units together. Only about an hour and half of daylight remained, but Lee ordered one last charge. It was a disjointed rush over fields; through swamp, creek, and woods; and up the hill. With fits and starts and separate battles between units and even individuals, the Confederates finally broke the Union line. The Federals retreated, some in an orderly manner, and some, a reporter for the *New York Tribune* wrote, "broken, disordered, routed."[26]

Although Hill's Division had suffered casualties of roughly 20 percent, Lee had included it in the final coordinated attack that drove the Union forces from their position. This time, however, it was not the lead division.[27]

---

[23] Sears, *To the Gates of Richmond*, 217–26; Robertson, *General A. P. Hill*, 82–86; Crenshaw, *Richmond Shall Not Be Given Up*, 38, 45.

[24] Robertson, *General A. P. Hill*, 82–86 (1st and 2nd quotes); Sears, *To the Gates of Richmond*, 213–26.

[25] *OR*, ser. 1, vol. 11, pt. 2, 836–37, 878–81; Robertson, *General A. P. Hill*, 83–85.

[26] Robertson, *General A. P. Hill*, 85–86; *OR*, ser. 1, vol. 11, pt. 2, 837, 879; Sears, *To the Gates of Richmond*, 237–48 (quote); E. P. Alexander, "Seven Days Begin," 256; R. K. Krick, "Men Who Carried This Position," 181–216.

[27] Robertson, *General A. P. Hill*, 85–86; *OR*, ser. 1, vol. 11, pt. 2, 837.

Other divisions of the army engaged the enemy on Saturday and Sunday: The next day, Saturday, June 28, Hill's Division "rested, attended to the wounded, buried the dead, and confiscated supplies" that the fleeing Union army had discarded. On Sunday, June 29, Hill and the rest of the Confederate army north of the Chickahominy crossed the river and followed the retreating Federals south toward the James River.[28]

our Brigade was engaged again on Monday evening but did not suffer very severely: This engagement was the Battle of Frayser's Farm or Battle of Glendale on June 30.

Now south of the Chickahominy, part of the Union army halted to protect the retreat of their slow-moving wagon train and the rest of the army. Lee attacked with Longstreet's Division, going in late in the day without expected support from other Confederate units. The Federals had at least twice the number of men as the Confederates. Longstreet met with initial success, but soon the numerous Union troops began to move toward both his flanks. Lee then ordered Hill's Division into the fight. Hill sent five of his six brigades forward, holding Anderson's Brigade, including Simeon's regiment, in reserve.[29]

Still the Union army advanced. Finally, as it began to grow dark, Hill ordered Anderson's Brigade forward, directing them "to advance cautiously and be careful not to fire on our friends" in front of them. Anderson aligned the 14th Georgia and the Louisiana Battalion on one side of a road and his three other regiments on the other, and his men began moving toward the enemy. "Obeying my instructions to the letter," Hill observed, "[they] received the fire of the enemy at 70 paces before engaging themselves." Some wavering South Carolinians were reformed and also sent into the fight, and "in less than five minutes," Hill reported, "all firing ceased and the enemy retired." The Federals, however, had held on long enough to allow the wagon train and the remainder of the army to continue retreating unharmed.[30]

under fire in the fourth one, the explosion of the enemy's shells killing one and wounding seven of our men, though we never fired a gun: This fourth battle was the Battle of Malvern Hill on July 1.

Hill's Division did not take an active part in it. As Simeon reported, fresh regiments had arrived earlier at the Confederate camp (Magruder's and Euger's divisions—Horatio's 16th Georgia was part of Magruder's Division, as mentioned in an earlier note). Hill's men were given much needed rest.

---

[28] Robertson, *General A. P. Hill*, 86–87.

[29] Ibid., 87–89; *OR*, ser. 1, vol. 11, pt. 2, 837–38; Crenshaw, *Battle of Glendale*, 53–62, 66–110.

[30] Robertson, *General A. P. Hill*, 89–93; *OR*, ser. 1, vol. 11, pt. 2, 838–39 (quotes); 879–80; Crenshaw, *Battle of Glendale*, 110–22; Hall, *Diary of George Washington Hall*, 1:10–11. (Hall mistakenly records that what he describes took place on the 29th, rather than the 30th.)

Toward the end of the day, however, Hill sent Anderson's and another brigade forward when it appeared that their assistance might be needed. They waited in a forward position and were under fire, but, as Simeon wrote, they were never sent into battle and never exchanged a shot with the enemy.[31]

Horatio: For further information, see the note to this portion of the letter that appears in chapter 11.

The regiment in which James Neal belongs was in the fight....: James Neal, Simeon's young cousin, was in the 38th Georgia Volunteer Infantry Regiment. The 38th was part of General A. R. Lawton's brigade in Stonewall Jackson's Corps. From scattered documents in James's service record, it appears that he was in "the fight" (Malvern Hill), and it is clear that he did survive it. As Horatio's letter of September 24, 1862 (in chapter 11), indicates, James was injured in a railroad accident about a month later.[32]

Capt. McClosky: George W. McCleskey was the commander of James's Company, Company B. He was wounded at the Battle of Gaines Mill and died about three weeks later. Casualties in the 38th in the battles of Gaines Mill were two officers killed and four wounded, fifty-two enlisted men killed and 114 wounded.[33]

No regiment fought more gallantly than the 18th Georgia: The 18th Georgia Volunteer Infantry Regiment was the only non-Texas regiment in General John B. Hood's brigade in Stonewall Jackson's corps. Hood reported that in the Battle of Gaines Mill, the regiment lost sixteen killed, 126 wounded, and three missing. Hood's Brigade, including the 18th Georgia, had been a key part of the Confederate success in that battle.[34]

Lieutenants McCulloch, Selman, and Callahan: All three of these men were in Company C of the 18th, the "Jackson County Volunteers," which was composed of men from the David family's home county.

The "horribly mangled" Lieutenant Levi McCullough was even a distant David family relative. Two of his sisters had married two of Simeon's cousins, both sons of Uncle Perry Bowen. Levi did not survive the Battle of Gaines Mill.

Second Lieutenant J. B. Sillman, who took command of the company after McCullough was wounded, was promoted to first lieutenant on the day of the battle and was himself wounded that day but survived the battle.

---

[31] For more on this battle, see chapter 11 and the note to the excerpt of this letter that concerns Horatio's role in the battle. See also, Robertson, *General A. P. Hill*, 93–94; *OR*, ser. 1, vol. 11, pt. 2, 839; Hall, *Diary of George Washington Hall*, 1:11.

[32] Henderson, *Roster of the Confederate Soldiers of Georgia*, 4:141; *OR*, ser. 1, vol. 11, pt. 2, 484.

[33] Henderson, *Roster of the Confederate Soldiers of Georgia*, 4:134; service records; *OR*, ser. 1, vol. 11, pt. 2, 597, 836.

[34] *OR* ser. 1, vol. 11, pt. 2, 483, 569; R. K. Krick, "Men Who Carried This Position," 181–216.

Second Lieutenant Callahan apparently took over when Lieutenant Sillman was wounded. He survived the battle but was killed near Sayler's Creek, Virginia, on April 6, 1865, almost at the end of the war.[35]

[illegible] being absent, said to be sick: This possibly was a reference to the C Company commander at the time of the Seven Days battles, Captain D. L. Jarrett. His service records do not indicate where he was during that time. Two months later, on August 30, 1862, he was wounded in the Second Battle of Manassas and died of his wounds a week later.[36]

Capt. Reynolds: Captain Abner M. Reynolds was commander of Company B, 16th Georgia, Horatio's company. According to his service records, he was listed as "sick in Richmond" on June 1. He was killed about three months later at the Battle of Crampton's Gap.[37]

I have been in four severe battles: The fourth severe battle Simeon was in was not one of the Seven Days battles but one fought almost a month earlier, Seven Pines or Fair Oaks, the battle of May 31 in which General Johnston was severely wounded.

In that battle, Simeon's regiment was not under General A. P. Hill but in General Wade Hampton's brigade, General W. H. C. Whiting's division, part of Johnston's left wing under General Gustavus W. Smith. Hampton's Brigade was thrust into battle late in the day. It advanced across some eight hundred yards of open fields, a patch of woods, and a bit of swampy ground against a heavily fortified and manned Union position. When the men got within fifty paces of the enemy's line "the batteries of the enemy belched forth their thunders, showering a perfect hail storm of canister and grape into our lines, while a withering force of musketry was poured upon us," a survivor of the regiment later wrote. Most of the brigade retreated in disorder. Simeon's regiment suffered ten killed and twenty-eight wounded.[38]

"The Soldier's Dream": This poem was written by British poet Thomas Campbell (1777–1844).[39]

The Soldier's Dream
Our bugles sang truce—for the night-cloud had lowered,
And the sentinel stars set their watch in the sky;

---

[35] US Census, 1850 and 1860, Jackson County, Georgia; Henderson, *Roster of the Confederate Soldiers of Georgia*, 2:636; Gallagher et al., *Civil War*, 224–25.

[36] Henderson, *Roster of the Confederate Soldiers of Georgia*, 2:636.

[37] Service records.

[38] Folsom, *Heroes and Martyrs*, 147–48; Sears, *To the Gates of Richmond*, 134–40, 374; Dowdey, *Seven Days*, 119–22; Hall, *Diary of George Washington Hall*, [1:6–7; Patterson, "The Incomplete Correspondence of Lieut. Josiah Blair Patterson," letters of June 5 and 13, 1862.

[39] Campbell, *Complete Poetical Works*, 8, 28, 160–61.

And thousands had sunk on the ground overpowered,
The weary to sleep, and the wounded to die.

When reposing that night on my pallet of straw,
By the wolf-scaring fagot that guarded the slain;
At the dead of the night a sweet vision I saw,
And thrice ere the morning I dreamed it again.

Methought from the battle-field's dreadful array,
Far, far I had roamed on a desolate track:
'Twas Autumn,—and sunshine arose on the way
To the home of my fathers, that welcomed me back.

I flew to the pleasant fields traversed so oft
In life's morning march, when my bosom was young;
I heard my own mountain-goats bleating aloft,
And knew the sweet strain that the corn-reapers sung.

Then pledged we the wine-cup, and fondly I swore,
From my home and my weeping friends never to part;
My little ones kissed me a thousand times o'er,
And my wife sobbed aloud in her fullness of heart.

Stay, stay with us,—rest, thou art weary and worn;
And fain was their war-broken soldier to stay:—
But sorrow returned with the dawning of the morn,
And the voice in my dreaming ear melted away.

The *Southern Confederacy* (an Atlanta newspaper) on October 3, 1862, published a poem by the same name written by a M. Louise Rogers. This poem expressed the same sentiments as Caldwell's poem and even had a similar first verse:

The battle is o'er and the stars glimmer down
On the white, ghastly dead that are strewed on the ground.
The deep cannon hushed; and the war-steed's shrill neigh
Is now silenced by death, who has feasted this day;
And a soldier too weary to watch or to weep,
Wraps his mantle about him and sinks down to sleep.

It may be possible that Simeon was writing about Rogers's poem rather than Caldwell's. Although that poem was not printed in the Atlanta paper until after

Simeon wrote this letter, it may have been printed in another newspaper that Simeon had seen.

I received your last letter in due time, and destroy them all before going into these battles: It is not clear why Simeon wanted to destroy letters from home before going into battle. Probably he was concerned that he might be killed, and some Union soldier searching his body would find them and read them.

1862

Simeon

Gordonsville, Va. August 15th, 1862
My Dear Mother

I wrote you from Richmond about the end of last month that our Division was going to join the forces of Stonewall Jackson. We were marched from our camp last Wednesday week and attacked the armies of the federal Gen'l *Pope* last Saturday about 5 miles from Culpepper Court house in Culpepper County at 4 O'clock in the evening and in 4 hours they were the worst whipped army that I ever saw.

Gen. Jackson is certainly one of the most consummate Generals that I ever saw. Our Regiment has been in several battles heretofore and while suffering greatly itself I do not know that we inflicted much injury upon the enemy. But in this battle we suffered very little ourselves and inflicted dreadful injury upon the enemy. Col Thomas who is commanding our Brigade says he has no doubt that our Regt killed and wounded one man for every man we carried into the field. The Regiment had none killed, 16 wounded none mortally, our company did not have a man hurt.

When we first marched into the battlefield the 47th and 48th Alabama Regts had got into confusion and came running right into our Regt. They confused us so much that we lost sight of the other Regts. of our Brigade and the Lieut Col of the Regt. seized the colors of the Regt and rushed to the front several of us by his side. The Regt. soon formed upon him and the panic stricken Alabamians got over their fright and returned to the charge when we soon had the enemy flying in the utmost confusion. After they commenced retreating they seemed to become perfectly panic stricken and overshot us entirely. Our boys poured a deadly fire into them and their dead covered the ground like the leaves of autumn.

After driving them about half a mile a large number of our forces got into a lane and the Yankee cavalry attempted to charge them. Our column was so solid they could not break it and they were compelled to turn to the right and they ran at full speed the whole length of our line about 75 yards from us our men pouring a tremendous fire into them all the way, twenty horses were left dead upon the field and many more riders. I emptied three barrels of my pistol at them while they were passing, with what effect I cannot tell.

We charged across the field immediately over which they had charged and in passing a wounded Yankee he asked me for a drink of water. You remember when I was elected militia captain that I bought a sword of Mike Willson that he got from Uncle Thomas Bowen. I still have that sword and have carried it in my hand in six battles and I know that Uncle Thomas Bowen never disgraced it and I don't intend to. When the Yankee asked me for water I laid down my sword to give him some from my canteen. I also turned his head up the hill and in the hurry of leaving I forgot my sword.

I soon thought of it and ran back to get it, but it was gone. I never regretted the loss of anything so much in my life. I told the Yankee I had lost my sword waiting on him, he told me to take his sword and I unbuckled his scabbard from his saddle and went on with a heavy heart. But fortunately one of my Regt picked it up and I got it the next day. No amount of money could get that sword from me now, and if I live to come home I intend to bring that old *damascus blade* with me.

We killed more than 500 Yankees and wounded from 2 to 3000 besides capturing from 5 to 800 prisoners. Our loss in killed and wounded did not exceed 500. We drove the enemy entirely from the battlefield and slept upon it that night. We held it on Sunday, and on Monday permitted the enemy to bury his dead under a flag of truce.

[The letter ends here; back page is blank.]

Notes

our Division was going to join the forces of Stonewall Jackson: On July 26, General Lee ordered A. P. Hill to join Stonewall Jackson's forces then at Gordonsville, Virginia, the site of a railroad junction that connected Richmond with its corn, wheat, and other supplies in the Shenandoah Valley.

A few days earlier, General Anderson had resigned as the commander of Simeon's brigade, and Colonel Edward L. Thomas, who had been commander of the 35th Georgia regiment within the brigade, became the brigade's new commander.[40]

we attacked the armies of federal Gen'l Pope: This attack was the Battle of Cedar Mountain (Battle of Slaughter Mountain or Battle of Cedar Run), between Stonewall Jackson and Union generals Nathaniel P. Banks and John Pope, fought on Saturday, August 9, 1862.

---

[40] Robertson, *General A. P. Hill*, 98; Dowdey and Manarin, *Wartime Papers of R. E. Lee*, 239–40; Folsom, *Heroes and Martyrs*, 45–46, 148–49; Foote, *Civil War*, 1:588–89.

Before the battle, Lincoln had reorganized the Union army. Even before the Seven Days Battles, Lincoln had been losing confidence in General McClellan and had demoted him from general-in-chief of the US Army to commander of only part of the army, the Department of the Potomac. McClellan's disappointing performance in the Seven Days did not motivate Lincoln to reappoint him general-in-chief. Instead, on July 11, Lincoln appointed Major General Henry W. Halleck to be overall commander of the Union army.[41]

As part of the reorganization, Lincoln earlier had decided to combine the three separate Union armies in the Washington area that had been assigned "to protect Washington, control the Shenandoah Valley, and draw Confederate troops from Richmond" into one army called the Army of Virginia. He appointed Major General John Pope commander of this new army. In one of his first actions, Pope began concentrating his three armies in the neighborhood of Culpeper, Virginia, about seventy miles southwest of Washington. His ultimate objective was to move against Richmond.[42]

Meanwhile, Lincoln had ordered McClellan to move his army from the Peninsula back to the Washington area. McClellan, however, delayed. Lee noticed this delay and saw a possible opportunity. He ordered Jackson to move north, "observe the enemy's movements closely," and "avail himself of any opportunity to attack that might arise." As Simeon wrote, to support Jackson, Lee ordered A. P. Hill's division, and thus Simeon, to join him.[43]

On August 9, Pope had not yet pulled together all his scattered forces. Jackson with his force of roughly twenty-four thousand men, which now consisted of divisions led by Major General Richard S. Ewell, Brigadier General C. S. Winder, and General A. P. Hill, was advancing from Orange Courthouse toward Culpeper planning to pick off one of Pope's isolated segments. About six miles south of Culpeper, his leading elements ran into a Federal force led by General Nathaniel P. Banks. Pope had ordered Banks south from Culpeper to delay Jackson's advance while he consolidated the remainder of his forces.[44]

August 9 was an exceedingly hot day. Men who were there remembered the "intense heat" and "the hottest sun you ever saw." One wrote that the air "was as hot as a bake oven." A Tennessean remembered "the big men continually falling

---

[41] Stackpole, *From Second Bull Run to Gettysburg*, 2–7; Hattaway and Jones, *How the North Won*, 208–209, *Virginia Atlas & Gazetteer*, 69, 75–76.

[42] Stackpole, *From Second Bull Run to Gettysburg*, 7–15; Hennessy, "Second Bull Run Campaign," 120–21, 126–27; *Virginia Atlas & Gazetteer*, 69, 75–76.

[43] R. K. Krick, *Stonewall Jackson at Cedar Creek*, 7 (quote); Hennessy, "Second Bull Run Campaign," 126–27; Stackpole, *From Second Bull Run to Gettysburg*, 13–15.

[44] Stackpole, *From Second Bull Run to Gettysburg*, 25–33; R. K. Krick, *Stonewall Jackson at Cedar Creek*, 7; *OR*, ser. 1, vol. 12, pt. 2, 215. On the number of Jackson's men, see Allan, *Stonewall Jackson*, 1:165, but compare R. K. Krick, *Stonewall Jackson at Cedar Creek*, 45.

by the wayside, worn out by fatigue and oppressive heat." By two in the afternoon, the temperature in Washington, D. C., not far away, was 98 degrees and the heat index there was later calculated to be 109 degrees. The temperature later was thought to be "the highest recorded on the day of battle for any major action in the Virginia theater."[45]

Early in the day, Jackson's command was marching north on the hot, dusty road toward Culpeper. Ahead of them on the road's right side was a lane that led back from the road about 1,250 yards to a farmhouse owned by the Crittenden family, which gave the lane its name, Crittenden Lane. Going down the lane toward the Crittenden house, the lane's right side was all woods and the lane's left side was bordered by a rectangular field, the first half of which was cleared land and the second half, tall corn. The Federals were somewhere in woods on the far side of this cornfield. After its intersection with the lane, the main road continued toward Culpeper. On its right it passed the cleared land and cornfield. On its left, woods ran for about a quarter mile from the intersection then opened out to a rectangular-shaped wheat field, then woods again. On this side of the road also, the Federals were in the far woods.[46]

This area along the main road to Culpeper and along the Crittenden Lane would become the focus of the battle.

In the lead of the advancing Confederate column was Ewell's Division, followed by Winder's, with Hill's far behind. Upon learning in the early afternoon that a federal force was before him near Crittenden Lane, Jackson ordered Ewell to position two of his three brigades and his artillery at Cedar Mountain, located some distance away from and to the right of the Culpeper Road and past the Crittenden farmhouse. He ordered Ewell's third brigade, under General Jubal A. Early, plus one regiment from one of Ewell's other brigades, to advance up Culpepper Road as soon as Winder's division came even with him (Early).

About 2:15 p.m., when Early saw Winder approaching, he immediately led his men forward, drove a small force of Union cavalry away from the Crittenden Lane area, and took a position along the lane to the right of the Culpeper main road, facing the cornfield.[47]

When Winder's Division came up the road to Crittenden Lane, two of its four brigades were stationed to the left of the road in the woods facing the wheat field. One, that commanded by General William B. Taliaferro, less one regiment, was positioned facing the cornfield on Crittenden Lane just to the left of Early's

---

[45] R. K. Krick, *Stonewall Jackson at Cedar Creek*, 34–35 (1st quote), 48–49 (3rd quote), 63–65 (4th quote), 135 (2nd quote); R. K. Krick, *Civil War Weather in Virginia*, 66–68 (5th quote); Dewberry, *History of the 14th Georgia*, 24; Harding, "Death by Dewpoint," 55.

[46] McElfresh, "Cedar Mountain Battlefield" (map); Allan, *Stonewall Jackson*, 2:169; R. K. Krick, *Stonewall Jackson at Cedar Mountain*, 47, 73–75.

[47] R. K. Krick, *Stonewall Jackson at Cedar Mountain*, 39–42, 47–61.

Brigade. Soon additional Confederate artillery moved into the area.[48]

Union artillery and infantry had settled for the moment behind the cornfield to the right of the main road and in the woods facing the wheat field on the left of the main road. From four o'clock to a quarter to six, the Union and Confederate artillery fired back and forth with minimal infantry action. About a quarter to six, however, Union infantry began to attack across both the cornfield and the wheat field.[49]

Earlier, Jackson had realized there was a gap along Crittenden Lane between Early's right and the Crittenden's farmhouse. Fortunately for the Confederates, Hill's "Light Division" had begun arriving onto Crittenden Lane. Three regiments of Thomas's Brigade of Georgians were in the lead. Jackson immediately sent these three regiments down along the lane to Early and the far right of the Confederate line. Early had just begun filling in the gap there with Thomas's men when the Union struck through the cornfield.[50]

Thomas's fourth regiment, Simeon's 14th Georgia, had been at the end of the brigade's formation when Thomas's Brigade started advancing into woods to the right of the Culpeper Road, woods that led ultimately to the Crittenden Lane. However, the 14th had been delayed and fell behind the rest of the brigade. In fact, it still was in the woods when the rest of the brigade emerged onto Crittenden Lane and was positioned by Early to the far right of the Confederate line on the lane.[51]

When we first marched into the battlefield the 47th and 48th Alabama Regts. had got into confusion and came running right at our Regt.: The Federals had attacked on both sides of the main road to Culpeper—through the wheat field on the left and through the cornfield on the right. To the right at Crittenden Lane, Early's line was holding. There the Union advance had been stopped.[52]

Things were different, however, on the other side of the main road at the wheat field. The Confederates had been poorly positioned in the woods at the front edge of the field, exactly where the Federals were headed. The charging Union soldiers quickly took advantage of the weak alignment, routed the Confederates, and were beginning to pour across the main road, firing and yelling, headed directly toward the left flank of the Confederate line on Crittenden Lane.[53]

The left flank of the Confederate line on the lane was manned by four regiments of Taliaferro's Brigade, two from Alabama and two from Virginia. The

---

[48] Ibid., 62–64, 67–85, 112–16.
[49] Ibid., 68–103, 117, 120–22, 142–46.
[50] Ibid., 108–109, 116.
[51] Ibid., 255.
[52] Ibid., 117–41, 142–49, 187, 251–54.
[53] Ibid., 142–90.

two Alabama regiments, the 47th and the 48th, were fresh troops never before exposed to combat. They were positioned along the lane on either side of the brigade with the two Virginia regiments between them.[54]

The inexperienced Alabamans had held their ground against the Federals charging their front through the cornfield. Then, however, they saw bursting forth on their left a horde of Union soldiers heading directly across the main road toward them. The left-most regiment, 47th Alabama, disintegrated as its men turned and fled across Crittenden Lane to the comparative comfort of the woods there. Its brother unit, the 48th, soon joined them.[55]

As Simeon wrote, it was now that the 14th Georgia stepped out of those woods onto Crittenden Lane and into the "confusion" of the fleeing Alabamans.

Earlier, as the 14th passed through the trees, gaps had developed in its original line of battle formation. When the men of the 14th reached Crittenden Lane and began to reform, the fleeing Alabamians plowed into them. A member of the 14th later wrote that the Alabamans "retreated in wild disorder across the road [lane], breaking through our ranks." In addition, "by their exaggerated and panic stricken reports," they also were "spreading dismay among our scattered men, who involuntarily began also to give back."[56]

At this critical moment, the writer continued (and as Simeon also wrote), Lieutenant Colonel Folsom, now commander of the regiment when the normal commander was wounded earlier in the battle, "seized the colors, sprang to the front, and waving on high the glorious battle flag of the Confederacy, called on the 14th...'Boys, are you going to leave your Colonel?'" The call had its desired effect. "[W]ith a tremendous shout of: 'We'll stand by you, Colonel, to the last!'" the men of the 14th rallied to him.[57]

Although many of the Alabamans continued to flee, some did not but rallied with the 14th. Now numbering some eight hundred to nine hundred men, the combined regiments formed a line of battle along the lane and leveled "a terrific, well-aimed and destructive fire" upon the advancing Federals, who broke and fled back to the woods on the other side of the Culpeper road.[58]

Then Colonel Folsom led the Georgians and Alabamans some three hundred yards across the cornfield to the edge of the main road to Culpeper, "banner in his left hand, and his pistol in his right," while staying "constantly thirty to fifty yards in advance of the line, a most conspicuous mark for the Yankee sharp

---

[54] Ibid., 33, 34, 85, 187–89.

[55] Ibid., 187–91.

[56] Ibid., 255; *Savannah Republican*, August 26, 1862.

[57] *Savannah Republican*, August 26, 1862. Lieutenant Colonel Folsom had become commander of the regiment when its normal commander, Colonel Felix Price, was wounded in the hand by a shell fragment as the regiment passed through the woods.

[58] Ibid.

shooters."[59]

a large number of our forces got into a lane and the Yankee cavalry attempted to charge them: At this point in the battle, the charge of the 14th Georgia and a scattering of Alabamans had taken them up to the Culpeper Road (the "lane" Simeon mentioned) across from the wheat field, where they halted. Then, as General Hill reported, the enemy "made an attempt to retrieve his fortunes" by a charge of his own, a cavalry charge by the First Battalion of the First Pennsylvania Cavalry under Major R. I. Falls.[60]

By then other Confederates had joined the men of the 14th on the road. The first these men knew that something new was happening was when they heard a thundering noise coming from the woods behind the wheat field on the opposite side of the road. In the next instant they saw Union cavalry "with their sabers drawn" riding hard from the woods, angling across the wheat field, heading straight toward them. As the Federals rode onward, Colonel Folsom told his men to hold their fire until he gave the word. A waiting member of the 14th later described the pell-mell approach of the horsemen as "magnificent," another as "splendid." As the cavalry got closer, the men of the 14th could feel the earth "fairly trembling" from the pounding of the horses' hooves.[61]

When the cavalry was about sixty yards from the Confederates, Colonel Folsom gave the order to fire, and a member of the 14th recorded what happened next: "down went horses and riders in one confused undistinguishable mass" as the front row of horses and riders were hit and fell in front of those following, many of whom stumbled into them and also went down.[62]

As Simeon wrote, this confused, falling mass of Union cavalrymen failed to break the Confederates' solid line, and, abandoning their direct charge, swerved to their (the Confederates') right, and "ran at full speed" parallel to the Culpeper Road "the whole length of our line," presenting their flank to the 14th and other Confederates who poured "a tremendous fire into them all the way, twenty horses were left dead upon the field and many more riders" before the cavalry could reach

---

[59] Ibid.; Folsom, *Heroes and Martyrs*, 149; R. K. Krick, *Stonewall Jackson at Cedar Mountain*, 257.

[60] R. K. Krick, *Stonewall Jackson at Cedar Mountain*, 257; *OR*, ser. 1, vol. 12, pt. 2, 93, 140–42, 216 (quote).

[61] R. K. Krick, *Stonewall Jackson at Cedar Mountain*, 232–37, 259–62 (2nd, 3rd, 4th quotes); Grimsley, *Battles in Culpeper County*, 30–31; *Savannah Republican*, August 26, 1862 (1st quote); *Southern Confederacy*, August 21, 1862; Dewberry, *History of the 14th Georgia*, 24.

[62] *OR*, ser. 1, vol. 12, pt. 2, 126; *Savannah Republican*, August 26, 1862 (quote); Goldsmith, "Cavalry versus Infantry," 219.

the woods from which they had come.[63]

Before the charge, the First Battalion of the First Pennsylvania Cavalry consisted of 164 officers and men. When it returned to the Union lines, it consisted of 71. It had lost 43 percent of its men.[64]

We charged across the field immediately over which they [the Union cavalry] had charged: It was now growing dark. On the left of the main road, the Confederates, led by Jackson personally, had driven the Federals out of the woods, across the wheat field, and beyond. Jackson ordered Hill to pursue the now fleeing, terrified Union soldiers. In response, Hill ordered his brigades that had been more lightly engaged in the earlier fighting than Thomas's to lead the way.[65]

The 14th still was part of the pursuit, and it was then that Simeon lost his sword. Close to 11 p.m., Jackson received word that the enemy was being reinforced by troops moving south from Culpeper and ordered the pursuers to halt.[66]

In his after-action report of the battle, General Hill summed up the activities of the 14th: "The Fourteenth Georgia, under the gallant Colonel Folsom, having become separated from the rest of the brigade by our fugitives, charged the advancing enemy with brilliant success."[67]

Uncle Thomas Bowen: He was Thirza's oldest brother, who had died in 1854. He had served from November 1814 to May 1815 as a private and later a "storekeeper" in Captain N. Garrison's company of the Georgia militia during the War of 1812. He probably was not in combat during his service, although it is not clear that Simeon was aware of that.[68]

We killed more than 500 Yankees: The official casualty report for the Union at the Battle of Cedar Mountain was 314 killed, 1,445 wounded, and 622 missing or captured for a total loss of 2,381 men. The Confederate loss in killed and wounded was 1,276.[69]

As for the 14th Georgia, Simeon wrote, "The Regiment had none killed, 16 wounded none mortally." Another source indicated that the 14th actually lost one man killed and nine wounded. Either way, as Simeon wrote, the regiment "suffered very little."[70]

---

[63] *Savannah Republican*, August 26, 1862; *Southern Confederacy* (Atlanta), August 21, 1862; R. K. Krick, *Stonewall Jackson at Cedar Mountain*, 259–60; Goldsmith, "Cavalry versus Infantry," 219.

[64] *OR*, ser. 1, vol. 12, pt. 2, 92–93, 140–42.

[65] Ibid., 216, 219–20, 232; R. K. Krick, *Stonewall Jackson at Cedar Mountain*, 202–31, 264–76; Robertson, *General A. P. Hill*, 107–108; *Southern Confederacy*, August 21, 1862.

[66] Robertson, *General A. P. Hill*, 107–108.

[67] *OR*, ser. 1, vol. 12, pt. 2, 216.

[68] Thomas Bowen's widow's pension application; Coleman, *History of Georgia*, 102–104.

[69] *OR*, ser. 1, vol. 12, pt. 2, 139, 180.

[70] Folsom, *Heroes and Martyrs*, 149.

Service Record of Simeon David

S. B. David
Capt. Co. E. 14th Regt Ga.
Appears on a
Register
Containing Rosters of Commissioned Officers, Pro-
Visional Army Confederate States
Date of appointment _____ Nov. 8, 1862

Notes

Capt. Co. E. 14th Regt Ga.: Simeon was appointed captain of Company E on November 8, 1862, after Captain Lester was appointed major (the third in command of the regiment) following a series of resignations and promotions in October and November 1862 among the regiment's field officers.[71]

These resignations included the resignation of its regimental commander, Colonel Felix Price, two months after he was wounded in the hand and dropped out of the Battle of Cedar Mountain to be replaced by Lieutenant Colonel Folsom. It is unlikely that the men of the 14th were sorry to see him go. Private William Edward Rogers of Simeon's company wrote home earlier that Price was a "miserable contemptable low flung, low life vagabond" who was once so drunk he fell off his horse. Lieutenant Josiah Patterson, Simeon's tent mate in Manassas, wrote his wife in December 1861 that Price had been "Court martialed for drunkenness and improper conduct toward a Lady" resulting in his being "publicly reprimanded in General Orders." He had been elected originally, according to Patterson, through "trickery intrigue and chicanery."[72]

After the Battle of Cedar Run, the subject of Simeon's last letter, and before Simeon's promotion, the regiment, and presumably Simeon, fought in the 2nd Battle of Manassas (August 28–30, 1862) although no letters from Simeon have survived indicating that he took part in the fight. The 14th also fought at Harper's Ferry on September 15 but stayed there to guard the town and missed the Battle of Antietam two days later.[73]

---

[71] Service records of Felix L. Price, Robert W. Folsom, William A. Harris, James M. Fielder, and Richard P. Lester, 14th Georgia Infantry Regiment, National Archives; CSA War Department, *Regulations for the Army of the Confederate States, 1863*, 5–7.

[72] Shadburn and Brooke, *Crimson and Sabres*, 23; R. K. Krick, *Lee's Colonels*, 310; Patterson, "Incomplete Correspondence," letter to his wife, December 10, 1861.

[73] Robertson, *General A. P. Hill*, 115–26, 133–41; Gallagher et al., *Civil War*, 64–66.

Chapter 13

Manning Enlists, 1862

Manning and Pillona Alexander

Gillsville Apr 1st 1862
Dear husband

I seat myself this morning to write you a few lines. I have heard that Jo Story has come home and that he and James Elison will start back in the morning; I heard that you would not leave there till next Saturday, but I think verry probable that you have left there before this time, but I want to write and send some little things to you and if you are gone Jo Story can take them on anyhow. I will send James knife and cap and will send you a little butter.

I have not got your drawers ready yet and I think I had better not send them till your others are nearer worn out. you might get them all lost. I will make them and when you think you need them let me know and I will send them the first chance. I want you to write to me along what kind of clothes you will need. I don't think we can make grey cotton mixed unless they can card it at the factory. we will enquire about it.

My *Dear* we dont know what to do about your boots. Father went to see Yarbrough yesterday. he is gone to big shanty. he has quit work and gone to farming. Jo Tomson sent me a pair of boots to look at but they are to small for you. he has not got any leather to make any more. Father has got some leather that he thinks will do to fix your boots or make some shoes though he will need it next fall. I am afraid that Thomson will not make a good boot and one that will fit you. Dear if you can I think maybe it would be the best and least trouble to git your boots yourself and then they would fit you. but if you cant get any we will try to have them fixed somehow.

Dearest I wrote you a letter the other day from Sister Mary's about my shoes. I dont know whether you got it or not. I left my new Sunday shoes in Mrs Harise's trunk the day I went down to the camp and forgot to take them out. I dont know blackstocks given name. maybe you can find it out. I want you to get them and send them home by Mr Ellison

Dear we got on to Sister's safely that day about 2 hours by sun and John got there before sundown with light-foot. We started next morning with her and came home in the 2 days and never drove out of a walk. we walked up every hill of any size and down some of them. it was about an hour in the night when we got home.

Brother Thomas's funeral was preached last sunday by Mr Reed. Mr. Willison and Billy were both there. There was a large congregation a good many ladies and a few men. he preached a good sermon. I wish you could have been there. Dear I want you to go to preaching as often as possible and read your bible too. I don't have any idea that you will curse and swear and get into disipation as some of them do. Dear if I did think so it would trouble me a great deal but I have no fears.

We are all well. I have the headache a little and am taking a cold. Nora is well. the little thing cried right hard that day after we left you. *Dear it was worse* than the first parting to me. I asked Nora just now what she wanted me to write to pa. she said tell pa I want *to kiss him and fight him like a bear; maybe mama wouldn't care* if she could *do the same.*

Dear if you dont get the place as surgeon try to content yourself anyhow for money and this worlds goods are not much now. I will close this time. I remain as ever your *affectionate and loving wife.*

Pellona W. Alexander

M. P. Alexander

Tell Neut Austin I am verry much obliged to him for doctoring our horse. give all the boys that enquire about me my respects and best wishes. Our horse buck was verry sick on sunday while I was gone. they think it was a gravel. it looked like he would die; he seemed entirely well next morning. Cousin John Jones wanted to get him to plough. I was afraid as he had been sick to let him go for fear he would get down poor again and I think we had better sell him if we can; write me what you think about it.

Notes

Gillsville: Gillsville was and is a village in the northeastern part of Georgia. In the 1860s, it was in Hall County just across the line between Hall and Jackson Counties and a little southwest of the Banks County line. Later, when Banks County was extended around 1870, Gillsville became partly in Banks County and partly in Hall County, as it is today.

It was and is only about five miles from Maysville. At one time Gillsville was known as Stonethrow, possibly to indicate how close it was to the county line. It was about four and a half miles from the David family farm.

Gillsville had a post office as early as 1833 and had a Confederate post office in 1862. It is unclear whether the Alexanders lived in Gillsville or outside it, but it seems Gillsville was the closest post office to their home.[1]

---

[1] Elrod, *Historical Notes*, 37; Krakow, *Georgia Place Names*, 93; Dorsey, *History of Hall County*, 1–2, 97, 371–72.

Dear husband: When this letter was written, Manning was about three weeks shy of his thirty-second birthday, and Pillona was twenty-three years old. Their daughter Nora was three years old.

Jo Story and James Ellison: Jo Story was Joseph M. Storey, who when the letter was written was Captain and Company Commander of Company G of the 43rd Georgia, a company raised in Jackson County. James Ellison may have been the James Ellison who was a private in Company B of the 43rd Georgia, a company raised in Cherokee County, or it may have been his father.[2]

I heard you will not leave there until next saturday: The "there" Pillona referred to is Camp McDonald, which was located seven miles northwest of Marietta on the Western and Atlantic Railroad at Big Shanty (present day Kennesaw, Georgia). It was located on the grounds of the Georgia Military Institute and was the largest of Georgia's camps for instruction of new troops.[3]

On March 4, 1862, Manning had enlisted as a private in a company formed in Hall County known as Brown's Boys, possibly named after Georgia's then-governor Joseph E. Brown. Shortly afterward, the company arrived at Big Shanty and on March 20 was organized as Company K of the 43rd Georgia Volunteer Infantry Regiment.[4]

On March 28, General Robert E. Lee ordered the 43rd Georgia to become part of the Department of East Tennessee under Major General Kirby Smith. General Smith then ordered the regiment to leave Big Shanty and to report to Camp Harris near Chattanooga, Tennessee. It is unclear when the regiment actually left. The "next saturday" when Pillona thought the regiment would leave would have been April 5, and possibly it left then. Whatever the case, it had arrived at Camp Harris by April 10.[5]

Manning may not have left with the regiment. From the following letters and an envelope for one of them, it appears Manning was ill and remained at Big Shanty, although in a private home rather than a military hospital.

grey cotton…card it: Carding is the process of taking clumps of raw cotton and using machines or handheld paddles with metal spikes to brush, clean, and disentangle the short cotton fibers into strands to prepare it for spinning.[6]

---

[2] Service records; Rigdon, *Georgia 43rd Infantry Regiment*, 83, 165.

[3] *Southern Banner*, February 19, 1862; March 26, 1862; and April 23, 1862; Coleman, *History of Georgia*, 158; Inscoe, *Civil War in Georgia*, 6; Roberts and Clark, *Atlanta's Fighting Forty-Second*, 16; Smedlund, *Camp Fires of Georgia Troops*, 201–205.

[4] Service Record; *Southern Banner*, March 26, 1862; Sifakis, *Compendium of the Confederate Armies*, 255.

[5] J. W. Bell, *43rd Georgia Infantry Regiment*, 8–9; Goodson, *Georgia Confederate 7,000*, 1:17, 2:21; *OR*, ser. 1, vol. 10, pt. 2, 409.

[6] "Carding," *Webster's New World College Dictionary*, 225; Wikipedia "Carding," https://en.wikipedia.org/wiki/Carding, accessed May 24, 2016.

Yarbrough: Pillona's aunt, the wife of Uncle Thomas Jones Bowen, was Nancy Yarbrough. The Yarbrough Pillona referred to is probably one of Aunt Nancy's relatives.[7]

light-foot: This is probably the name of a horse.

John: He probably was sister Mary Neal's son John Neal.

Brother Thomas's funeral: For more details about the death of Owen Thomas David, see chapter 10.

Mr. Reed: He was Rev. Wm. P. Reid, the minister at Candler's Creek Baptist Church.[8]

if you don't get the place as surgeon: Manning had applied to be a surgeon in the regiment. Each regiment had a surgeon and an assistant surgeon. Entering a unit as a private was a way of becoming a surgeon in that unit.[9]

Neut Austin: He probably was Jacob Newton Austin, a private in Company K.[10]

Our horse buck was verry sick...they think it was a gravel: "A gravel" that can make a horse sick may have been "a deposit of small concretions that form in the kidneys or gallbladder and that may be retained, passed on to the urinary bladder, or passed out of the body." Buck was not sold and will appear later in the letters. "Gravel" in reference to a horse also means an abscess in a horse's hoof caused by gravel or other foreign matter. The foreign matter penetrates the hoof, bringing bacteria with it that causes the abscess and makes the horse appear lame.[11]

Pillona

Gillsville Hall Co Ga   April 10th 1862
Dear husband

I seat myself to night to respond to your verry welcome letters of the 1st and 7enth inst which came to hand in due time; the first I got sunday morning that you sent by Yarborough.

Arnold Ellison got home saturday evening. Annie Nora and I went to see him on Sunday. the letter money and shoes were all right. Arnold did not sit up but verry little that day but I hear that he is mending slowly.

Dear it does me a great deal of good to hear from you and get letters from you so often thouh I cant see you. I was going to write to you this evening when I heard that Wallace had come home. I went to see him this evening and got the

---

[7] Thomas J. Bowen pension records; Smith, "Bowen Bible Records," 39.
[8] See chapter 2.
[9] Freemon, *Gangrene and Glory*, 28, 41.
[10] Service records.
[11] "Gravel," *Webster's New World College Dictionary*, 633; "Prevent Painful Horse Hoof Abscesses, horses-and-horses-in-formation.com.

letter and money you sent me. that makes $38 I have received. I want to go up in Hall the last of this week to see about the pay for the Cow and Corn and settle of that note. I want us to pay up our debts as fast as we can though we cant collect what is owing us.

I will bring down several of your books and if you want any but the dictionary write me & I will send them by Mintz. I will send some little things to you by Ansel if he can take them if not I will send them by Mintz.

My Dear I dont think we can make any cotton & wool mixed. they cant card it at the factory. We can make you some woolen pants without lining but I think you had better try to buy you a black sumer coat if you can get it at a reasonable price. a thick one will be so warm especially if you get the assistant surgeons place which I hope you will. All the men that come home are well pleased with you as surgeon. Ansel said you done all for Jerry that could be done. I think they are satisfied that you done all you could.

Poor Lizzie she took it verry hard. It was a sad sight to see her and her little orphan children. I could not help but think who would have it to bear next. is it I[?] I hope not but it may be. Dear how could I bear it.

Dear husband I want you to try to prepare for death. we know not when it is coming. you may die sudenly as poor Jerry did. go to preaching often as you can. My prayer is that if we never meet again in this world that we may meet in that bright land where parting and sorrows are known no more.

We ought to be submissive to the will of God. are we not willing to give up every thing for our country[?] you *have given* up all & left me and little Nora and the pleasures of home to die if needs be in defence of your country. is not that enough for anyone to give[?] I am willing to give up every thing in this world but you. I dont feel that I *can give* you up for what would any thing be to me without you.

Let us cheer up. we have gained a great victory in Tenesee in the past week. report says our forses killed and took prisoner the whole federal army. I hope it is so.

We have not heard from H. J. D. in 3 weeks. we heard they are at Golesborough. We have not heard from Sim since he left the shanty.

I think you had better write to Uncle Adam Poole and know whether Mrs Horton will pay. she is to pay that money or not. I dont know the [post] office [address]. Also write to John Sewill again.

John Desvois of Hall Co is dead. I have heard that you all have sent after Obe Tomson & Allen Bell. write me whether is it is or not.

I asked Nora to day what I must write to pa. she said tell him I hugged you for him. she says she wants to see you badly. she fatting and grows fast and is as rude as ever. if you need any little thing write me and I will send it by Capt Mintz.

I reckon you are in Knoxville to night. a long ways of. Good night. I must go to bed.

[The following was written in pencil and is badly faded.]

Friday morning [April 11] we are all well this morning. I will not send any clothes this time. I send all by Mintz. I send you [several words illegible] any other that you want send for. Yarbrough will [illegible] your shoes. I will send them by Mintz. I must close. write often. I want to hear from you if I cant see you. Nora says howdy. As ever your loving wife P. W. Alexander

[The following was written in the same ink as was used in the letter written before the part written in pencil.] Write often be certain; and write me all the news. tell Tom Henderson his Ma was here yesterday. they are all well. Mr Whites folks are all well.

Notes

Arnold Ellison: He may have been William A. Ellison, a private in Company G of the 43rd Georgia, which was formed in Jackson County with Michael M. Mintz as captain. He possibly was a brother of the James Ellison mentioned in the previous letter.[12]

Wallace: There were several soldiers with the last name Wallace or Wallis in the 43rd regiment, including a Private Bolin D. Wallis in Company G.[13]

Mintz: He was Michael M. Mintz, then age forty-four. Mintz was elected captain of Company G of the 43rd from Jackson County when the company was formed, but he resigned as medically disabled on July 5, 1862, about three months after Pillona wrote this letter. Like Manning, he earlier had raised a company that was disbanded, as related in chapter 9.[14]

Ansel: He was Private Ansel M. Culpepper of Company G of the 43rd Georgia.[15]

Jerry and Lizzie: Jerry was Private Jerry Sanders, who died at Camp McDonald on April 2, 1862, of "brain fever" (inflammation of the brain) after an illness of two days. He was about twenty-six years old. Lizzie was Elizabeth Sanders, his wife, also about twenty-six years old. They might have had only one child, a daughter, about four years old, rather than the "children" Lona thought.[16]

a great victory in Tenesee: This "victory" was the Battle of Shiloh fought April 6–7, 1862. The South was victorious on the first day of the battle, but on the

---

[12] Service records; US Census, 1850, Cherokee County, Georgia.

[13] Service records.

[14] Ibid.; Rigdon, *Georgia 43rd Infantry Regiment*, 163.

[15] Service records.

[16] Ibid.; Rigdon, *Georgia 43rd Infantry Regiment*, 174; US Census, 1860, Jackson County; Dunglison, *Dictionary of Medical Science*, 790–91.

second day General Grant counterattacked, forcing the Confederates to withdraw and yield the ground they had won the day before.

When this letter was written, the Athens papers, which would have been, at least indirectly, the source of Pillona's information, had printed only the results of the first day (under such headlines as "Glorious News from the West"). Apparently, what happened on the first day was the only information the papers had received before going to press.[17]

H. J. D. at Golesborough: Horatio James David and the 16th Georgia were stationed at Goldsboro, North Carolina, from March 22 to early April.[18]

Sim: As Simeon indicated in his letter of December 24, 1861, in chapter 12, he planned to be home on leave in early 1862. He must have gone home around then and returned to his unit by train leaving from Big Shanty.

Uncle Adam Poole: He was Manning's mother's brother.[19]

I reckon you are in Knoxville to night: The 43rd was actually at a camp near Chattanooga, although Manning, ill, probably remained at Big Shanty.[20]

Pillona

[This letter was written on the last page of the immediately previous letter.]
Monday night April the 14th 1862
Dear husband

I will write you a few lines more tonight. I carried this letter up to Mr Whites friday morning to send by A. Culpepper but he has not gone yet and we have heard that he has the Measles so I sent for the letter and thought I would send it by mail

Now dont think hard of me for not writing sooner as I thought you would have got the letter before this time; I will do better after this. Dear write to us often as you can. Sometimes I take the Blues a little and then a letter does me a great deal of good.

Capt. Mintz got home last Friday. I got your letter that evening. was glad to hear you were well. Dont trouble yourself about not getting the assistant Surgeons place. it is risking too much money on uncertainty to go to Richmond. I think we can get along someway anyhow. I will make all your clothes that I can & when you need anything Just write to me.

Dear I dream about you nearly every night. I dreamed last Friday night that you had gone perfectly beside yourself and they had brought you home. I thought

---

[17] Gallagher et al., *Civil War*, 114–18; *Southern Banner* and *Southern Watchman*, April 9, 1862.
[18] Byrd, *Confederate Sharpshooter*, 25–26; H. Montgomery, *Howell Cobb's Confederate Career*, 53–55.
[19] Will of Manning Poole, filed in 1845, Anderson County, South Carolina Will Book, 1:303.
[20] See note to the April 1, 1862, letter from Pillona in this chapter.

you would not speak to me. I thought all you wanted to do was to fill up the roads with logs and brush so that Lincolns Army could not pass though the country. it pestered me worse than any dream I ever dreamed before but I hope there is nothing of it.

Dear I am verry fraid you will have brain fever or billous Colic. Tell the boys all about how to wait on you if you should take it. tell them I want them to wait on you just as good as they can and I never will get done thanking them for it. tell them they all have my best wishes.

It rained yesterday all last night and all day today. I am afraid there will be a fresh.

Mother & I have got our potatoes planted. We will send your shoes by Mintz and any other little thing that I want to send. I will send Cokers note by Mintz. Mother said it did not make any difference about the bucket & box. I wish you could come this cold rainy night and sleep on the bed with me and little Nora.

It is late. I must close. I remain your wife more affectionate than ever, to M. P. Alexander Norah L & P. W. Alexander

[Written on upper left side of letter]

Nora is asleep & cant [tell me what to] write this time. she talks a great deal about wanting to see you and to hug & kiss you. I don't think she would ever forget you. good bye tonight pa.

"When shall we meet again"

Notes

Culpepper: He was Private Ansel M. Culpepper of Company G of the 43rd Georgia.[21]

it is risking too much money on uncertainty to go to Richmond: Apparently Manning was considering going to Richmond to try to obtain the assistant surgeon position.

brain fever: Inflammation of part of the brain. An example is meningitis, which is inflammation to the lining of the brain. It can be caused by a virus or by bacteria.[22]

bilious colic: A pain in the abdomen caused by accumulation of bile that results in vomiting and pain, soreness, or tenderness in the abdomen.[23]

fresh: Probably short for "freshet," "a sudden overflowing of a stream because of melting snow or heavy rain."[24]

---

[21] Service records.

[22] Dunglison, *Dictionary of Medical Science*, 790–91; Berkow, Beers, and Fletcher, eds., *Merck Manual*, 372–73.

[23] Dunglison, *Dictionary of Medical Science*, 234; Comfort, *Practice of Medicine*, 169–71.

[24] "Freshet," *Webster's New World College Dictionary*, 579.

"*When shall we meet again*": This is the first line of the first stanza of a popular hymn. The complete first stanza is as follows:

When shall we meet again,
Meet ne'er to sever;
When shall peace wreathe her chain
Round us forever?
Our hearts will ne'er repose,
Safe from each blast that blows,
In this dark vale of woes,
Never, no, never![25]

Pillona

Gillsville Hall Co Ga   Apr 26th 1862
Dear husband:

your letter of the 21st came to hand this evening which I was verry glad to receive but was verry sorry to hear of your illness which I hoped was not so bad as we had heard; but I know you are verry low or you could have written yourself; I am so glad to hear that you are at a private house where you can have a good bed & every necessary comfort, instead of being in a dirty hospital and lying on a pallet of st[r]aw. I hope you are a great deal better now than when the letter was written.

Give my thanks to Mr Latners family for their kindness and attention to you in your sickness away from *loved* ones and friends. It would be a source of greater pleasure to me than any thing in the world to wait on you in your sickness. if you dont get any better write me and I will come to see you let it cost what it will. If you had have written for me to come I would start with Capt Mintz in the morning; As soon as you get well enough to travil and can get any person to come with you I want you to come home and recruit your health *be sure to*.

There is a good deal of sickness here; old Mrs. Billy Turk died with Pneumonia. old Mr. Hogan is dead. We are well but our little Norah she only has a bad cold and hoarsenes. she wants to see her pa verry badly.

I sent to you by Dr Litle a bed-tick and pillow 2 pillow cases 1 towel 2 pair pants a pair of shoes an bottle of wine and some litle sweet cakes. I hope you have got them before this time.

If you need any money let me know and I will send you some by the next one passing. please write to me every day or two until you get well. It is late. I cant write any more too night, The Family all join me in love to you

---

[25] Baptist Trustees, *Psalms and Hymns*, 604.

I remain as [e]ver your affectionate Wife.
Pillona W. Alexander
To Dr. M. P. Alexander
[Envelope:]
M P Alexander
Care of Capt [illegible]
Col Harris 43 regiment Ga Vol
Big Shanty Cobb Co Ga.

Notes

Dr. Litle: He probably was Dr. Atiller F. W. Little, who was originally from Pennsylvania and had married Elizabeth Sisson of Jackson County.[26]

bed-tick: This was a homemade mattress—a bag made of heavy cloth filled with straw, feathers or rags.[27]

Pillona Alexander and Thirza David

Gillsville Hall Co Ga May 4th
1862
Dear husband

I seat myself this sabbath morning to respond to yours of the 25 and 27 of April which came to hand in due time the first on wednesday and the other last night. It is useless for me to say to you that I was *glad* to receive them for of course you know that. Dear you dont know how much good it does me to get a letter from you so often especially when you are sick for my whole existence and being are bound up with your and little Noras and if you were gone I dont think I would want to live any longer. Dear we *cant* be thankful enough to the good one for your recovery while so many poor soldiers are dying far away from home and loved ones every day. Dear I sometimes ask the question to myself why was your life spared; was it in answer to the prayers of a fond wife and Mother[?] perhaps [it was] that you might live longer to prepare for death. if it was Dear dont misuse the golden opportunity. "Put your trust in God."

I am verry sorry that you did not get the wine. it would have strengthened you so, I am afraid it was not broken accidentally but we cant tell.

John Sisson wrote to Litle to come on. he thought there was a good chance for him to get in as Dr Wills was reported for drunkiness and Dr Alexander was dangerously sick and that the sick had no attention at all. I reckon he thought you would die and wanted Litle there to take your place but maybe he is disapointed.

---

[26] US Census, 1860, Jackson County, Georgia.
[27] Drake, *What Did They Mean by That?*, 18, 305.

Mother got a letter from S. B. David last Wednesday. he has gone to Yorktown and camped in 3 miles of Ratios reg. he hunted up Ratio & found him well & hearty. he was in the battle of the 16th and came out unscathed. he stood in water thigh deep during the fight Sim says he is a brave looking boy. Brother did not get there till after the fight.

We got a letter from James neal at Savanah. he is tolerable well. they are expecting a fight there all the time. he wanted to know your address.

Brother said Ratio spoke of getting a transfer over to your reg. I expect to send this letter by the Culpeper boys. I wish you and Ratio were together. then you could wait on each other when sick. Mother says dont say anything about what Sisson wrote. We are all well I am stouter than I have been in a long time. I wove 4¼ yds. of Janes the other day.

I will write to your Father & Mother this evening. there is plenty of fruit. Nora says you must come home and get plums & peaches. The rust is in the wheat pretty bad. our potatoes are coming up. our shoats grow very pretty.

Dear you are right about not going on duty to soon. money is nothing to your health. I am afraid you did not kip money enough. write to me if you haint and I will try to send you some. write me if your shoes will do. I must quit and go to meeting. I will write more next time. Ma & Nora wants to see pa verry badly. Mother & Nora sends you a bunch of flowers. as ever you loving wife & daughter. good bye.

Dr. M. P. Alexander   Pillona W. Alexander

P. S. Write often. Lony forgot to mention it. I wish you could See Nora Struting about this morning ready for church. The prospect for a crop is gloomy. the wather is so wet and cold. the bugs and worms seem bent to destroy enything they can. If we were all prepared I think death would be a relief. Conqured we must not be. annihilated is preferable. We will do all we can to cheer Lony but She gets melancholy Sometimes. We all think of you often. Your Mother

Thirza David

[in Thirza's handwriting] Lony will Send a note

Notes

John Sisson: He was a private in Company G. of the 43rd Georgia and Dr. Little's brother-in-law.[28]

Dr. Wills: Dr. John Wills of Gainesville, Hall County, Georgia, was appointed surgeon in the Confederate States Army on July 12, 1862, to take rank from March 20, 1862. He was assigned to the 43rd Georgia Regiment to be its surgeon. He is mentioned in later letters also.[29]

---

[28] US Census, 1850, Jackson County.
[29] Service records.

S. B. David and Ratio: S. B. David was Simeon Bowen David and Ratio was Horatio David. For more information on this part of Pillona's letter, see chapter 11.

James Neal at savannah: James R. Neal, Pillona's sister Mary's son, was in Company B, 38th Georgia Infantry Regiment.[30] His letter to Thirza from Savannah that Pillona refers to is apparently lost. Part of a letter he wrote to Thirza soon after that missing letter follows:

> May 7, 1862
> Camp Mercer Savannah, Ga.
> Dear Grandma
> I seat myself to try to drop a few lines in the way of an answer to your kind letter of the second. I was sorry to hear of Uncle Dr.'s illness. It is reported here that there is a great deal more sickness among the army of the west [next few lines illegible because of the fold of the paper] The company so far has lost only one man by death. [Ink spilled over a large part of the remaining page making it illegible] I will write as soon as I have the chance to both of my uncles, but I would a great deal rather see them than write either of them, if it was so that I could.
>
> Grandma, it is a trying time for the people of the Confederate States, now to have to bear arms, and the prospect is gloomy for the usual crops, and the enemy seems to be gaining every point that is important to our people. Tell Auntie that it is tolerable hard for the boys to have to stand guard every other day. We all saw an easy time until we were taken away, but the thirty boys [James and his friends] were in the front edge of our Legion, and picketed all round the town.
>
> I received a letter this week from home. Mother wrote that Jesse had the whooping-cough for three or four weeks. She said that he had no life at all, he would cough and cry and [The letter breaks off at the bottom of the page, and the next page is gone. There is no signature, but it probably was written by James Neal. Jesse was James Neal's younger brother.]

Culpepper boys: They were Ansel M., Caleb C., and William H. Culpepper, all of Company G, although all three likely were not home at the same time.[31]

Janes: Jeans.

rust in the wheat: Rust is a plant disease characterized by reddish brown spots.[32]

---

[30] Ibid.
[31] Service records.
[32] "Rust," *Webster's New World College Dictionary*, 1274.

shoats: A "shoat" is "a young, weaned pig."³³

I seat myself this sabbath morning to respond to yours of the 25 and 27 April.... Dear you are right about not going on duty too soon: From these sentences and other parts of the letter, it seems that by April 27 Manning had recovered from his illness and may have reached Chattanooga. The 43rd Georgia had been stationed at Camp Harris, about a mile down the Tennessee River from Chattanooga, since early April. It also seems that by the 27th, he still had not reported for duty.

However, he may not have delayed reporting for duty very long. In late April, a private in the regiment wrote home that there was much sickness in the regiment—"some of them vary bad of"—and that five or six had died. The second in command of the regiment wrote in his memoirs that in the 43rd's camp near Chattanooga, "Measles, flux, dysentery and brain fever attacked the troops; some died and nearly all, were more or less, sick." Even though Manning still had not joined his regiment, he probably was assigned, or soon would be assigned, to help treat the numerous sick men of the regiment at Chattanooga. Manning had not yet been appointed regimental assistant surgeon permanently, but his service records indicate that he had been appointed assistant surgeon provisionally on March 20.³⁴

In addition, on April 29, the regiment was under fire for the first time and for the first time suffered casualties.

Shortly before April 29, the 43rd Georgia and the 39th Georgia, both under the command of Brigadier General Danville Leadbetter, were ordered to defend two bridges, a main bridge and a railroad bridge, that crossed the Tennessee River from Alabama about thirty miles west of Chattanooga. Union forces on the Alabama side of the river near Stevenson were reported to be advancing toward the bridges. The Georgia troops' mission was to prevent them from crossing the bridges and marching on to Chattanooga. However, if they could not defend the bridges, they were to destroy them.

Unfortunately, the Georgians were unable to defend them. In addition, although they successfully destroyed the railroad bridge, the main bridge still remained intact, and the Federals streamed across it. General Leadbetter, regarding his position as "untenable," as he later reported, ordered the Georgians to retreat back to camp near Chattanooga. Later, the Confederates moved forward to defend the route to the Chattanooga, but the Federals chose not to advance but to cross back over the bridge to Alabama instead, destroying it in their wake.³⁵

---

[33] "Shoat," ibid., 1341.

[34] Hitt, "David M. Hitt Letters," April 25, 1862 (quote), and May 2, 1862; H. P. Bell, *Men and Things*, 83 (quote); Smedlund, *Camp Fires of Georgia Troops*, 146–47.

[35] H. P. Bell, *Men and Things*, 83–84; *Southern Watchman*, May 7, 1862; Storey, "Joseph M. Storey Collection," Storey to his wife, Eliza (Lizzie) Storey, May 2, 1862; Hitt, "David M. Hitt

It is unclear exactly how many wounded the surgeons, possibly including Manning, needed to treat after the engagement. At least one member of the 43rd Georgia was killed that day. Two others died at a hospital in Chattanooga on the day of the battle, possibly succumbing to wounds received during the fighting. At least several others were reported as wounded.[36]

Margaret Poole Alexander

Franklin Co ga May the 18 1862
dear son [Manning P. Alexander]
    it [is] with pleasure I set myself to drop you a few lines to let you know that we are all well at present hoping this may come to hand and find you injoying the same blessing. we receivd yours of the 10 and was glad [to] hear you had got wel. we had heard you ware sick in the hospital.
    we recived a leter from AO dated the 3 of may which gave great satisfaction. he was well and had marcht three days to reinforce General Jackson. he had crost the mountains and was in three miles of him reday [ready] to respond to him whenever he cald. I se in the papers that they have bin fiting. his post office is gordensvill va. he wants to hear from you all. he has ben in bicket [picket] fiting [fighting].
    we heard from sam last wek. he was well. he & EY has got a fine daughter. james [is] well of the messls [measles] and gone to noxvill when we heard last. i hope you will all have your health now and i pray the lord will screne you from the bullts.
    it is dishartning. it looks lik there could not be anuf [crops] made to do the people. wheat is generly sorry tho i think we will have good crop. it lookes well now and is in the [illegible]. the rust is confind to the blade.
    i am in hops you will have good luck have your heath and get home agane and want you to try your best to gane the good will of the people and not do as they say some dose. [They do] not care what becomes of them so [long as they] get the pay. if you shold have th good luck to get a good name and get home aliv it will [be] an honer to you as long as you live.
    i have not heard from lona since you left home. we got a letter from sussana a few days [ago]. shee was well and had a fine daughter. I want to see you all once more. i pray that the lord will bring you all back home agane. wright often and

---

Letters," Hitt to his wife, Jane A. Hitt, May 2, 1862; *OR*, ser. 1, vol. 10, pt. 1, 655–59 (quote); Parks, *General Edmund Kirby Smith*, 178.

[36] Rigdon, *Georgia 43rd Infantry Regiment*, 65, 167, 175; service records for John Carrol of Company A; H. P. Bell, *Men and Things*, 83; *OR*, ser. 1, vol. 10, pt. 1, 657; Storey, "Joseph M. Storey Collection," Storey to his wife, Eliza (Lizzie) W. Storey, May 2, 1862.

let me know how you are as it is all the satisfaction we have. so no more at presant but [I] remans your kind mother till death, Margaret Alexander

direct your letters to belton as bob keeps the ofice

Notes

Margaret Poole Alexander: She was Manning's mother. When the letter was written, she was fifty-five years old and living with her husband outside Carnesville, Franklin County, Georgia.[37]

AO: This was Adam O. Alexander, one of Manning's younger brothers. Manning had one older brother and five younger brothers. He had no sisters. Adam was a private in Company D of the 21st Georgia Volunteer Infantry.[38]

reinforce General Jackson: AO's 21st Georgia was part of Major General Richard Ewell's division. On May 3, when AO wrote his letter, Ewell's men were in Elk Run Valley near Virginia's Shenandoah Valley. General Jackson was not far away making his way to Staunton, Virginia, at the beginning of what would become known as the Valley Campaign of 1862.[39]

Sam and EY: Sam was Samuel H. Alexander, another of Manning's younger brothers. His wife was Mary E. Gillespie (called EY), and their daughter, born in 1862, was Buena E. Alexander. When this letter was written, Sam was serving as a private with the 29th Georgia Infantry Regiment. There are letters from him below.[40]

James: James D. Alexander was another of Manning's younger brothers. He was 1st sergeant in the 9th Battalion Georgia Infantry.[41]

sussana: She was Susanna Burkhalter Alexander, Adam Alexander's wife.[42]

belton: Belton was, and is, Belton, South Carolina, in Anderson County.[43]

bob keeps the ofice: Bob probably was a brother of Manning's mother or a relative of Manning's father. Both his father and mother had lived in Anderson County, South Carolina before moving to Georgia. The "office" probably was the post office in Belton.[44]

---

[37] US Census, 1860, Franklin County, Georgia; Chaplin, *Riches of Bunyan* (Alexander family copy).

[38] Service records; Chaplin, *Riches of Bunyan* (Alexander family copy).

[39] Burton, *Extraordinary Circumstances*, 415; Farwell, *Stonewall*, 250–51, 253–57; Gallagher et al., *Civil War*, 50–53.

[40] US Census, 1870, Franklin County; Chaplin, *Riches of Bunyan* (Alexander family copy); service records.

[41] Chaplin, *Riches of Bunyan* (Alexander family copy); service records for J. D. Alexander listed under J. A. Alexander.

[42] Chaplin, *Riches of Bunyan* (Alexander family copy).

[43] *Rand McNally 2019 Road Atlas*, 92.

[44] Jackson and Teeples, *South Carolina 1830 Census Index*, 14.

Secretary of War to Manning

Confederate States of America

WAR DEPARTMENT
Richmond July 12th 1862

You are hereby informed that the President has appointed you
Assistant Surgeon
Forty third Georgia Regiment
In the Provisional Army in the service of the Confederate States: to rank as such from the twentieth-day of March one thousand eight hundred and sixty two. Should the Senate, at their next session, advise and consent thereto, you will be commissioned accordingly.

Immediately on receipt hereof, please to communicate to this Department, through the Adjutant and Inspector General's Office, your acceptance or non-acceptance of said appointment; and with your letter of acceptance, return to the Adjutant and Inspector General the OATH, herewith enclosed, properly filled up, SUBSCRIBED and ATTESTED, reporting at the same time your AGE, RESIDENCE when appointed, and the STATE in which you were BORN.

Should you accept, you will report for duty to Col Harris

Geo W. Randolph
Secretary of War.

Dr. M. P. Alexander
Asst Surgeon 43rd Ga. Regt

Notes

rank as such from the twentieth-day of March one thousand eight hundred and sixty two: This date was almost four months before the day (July 12) this notice was sent to Manning. His service records indicate that Manning was appointed provisionally at the regimental level on March 20, and undoubtedly began serving as assistant surgeon on that date, if not earlier.

Geo W. Randolph: George Wythe Randolph, Confederate secretary of war, was President Thomas Jefferson's grandson.[45]

Manning

McMillan Station Tenn
July 26th 1862
My Dear,

---

[45] Boatner, *Civil War Dictionary*, 678–79.

As I promised in the short note I droped you when I first arrived here–to write you again soon, I now seat myself to redeem the promise. I went from here to the regt. and returned last night to this point.

Well dear–I stayed all night at uncle Adams the night after I left you. the next night I stayed at a Mr Byrdens one mile from Decature. he would not charge me a cent for lodging. I would have gon to Atlanta that night but I broke down in my legs and thighs. I was not at all fateagued but my legs felt like every musle was strained but I slept it all off that night.

Next morning I put out for Atlanta. got there at 8 oclock [and] got transportation–left at 10. got to Dalton at 1 [and] had Bucks car put on the East Tenn and Geo R R track. I went into a passenger car and went to sleep till 2 oclock when we left for Knoxville[,] where we arrived–I mean I and Buck—next day at 12 all safe and sound. The whole trip cost me but 2 dollars

I found our brigade wagons in Knoxville and went out with them I went Monday up to camp. I found but a few there. the brigad had moved out to Cedar ford 6 miles west of the camp where I left them.

Capt Rieves had just come in with severel recruits. Maj Boyeds boys ware among them–I tell you dear I was glad to see them have to come out at last.

I went out to the regt tusday and returned here last night I am in fine health have been improving evey day—you know I was quite well for severel days before I left home. If I can continue in as good health as I am now I will injoy myself very well taking *all* things into consideration

I do not know yet whether I will remain here but a day or two or not. I may go back to regt to-morrow. Robt White is here yet and very sick but I think his condition is better than it was last Monday. Tell Mrs. White I think he will get well. Thomas Henderson and William White are as well as I ever saw them. all the boys in the neighborhood are well.

Dr. Wills would have resigned while I was gon if I had been here and I would have been appointed principle surgeon sure[,] but Col Harris received a petition from Jackson Co. signed by over 40 men asking Dr. Wills to resign[,] which he will not now do under any sircumstac whatever. I have not seen the petition but I judg Dr. Anderson (if I should know him or rather polute the title with his name) is at the bottom of it. The request had the effect to prevent Wills from resigning and consequently me from being appointed principle surgeon, but I am very well satisfied. Maj Kellogg has been to Richmond. He brought my communication so the thing is safe now.

he saw Simeon. he was well. I saw Rev Masborn yesterday–Chaplin of Wrights Legion. He says James Neal came through the fight unhurt and was well a few day ago. Mrs Mashburn is just from the Legion. I have not been able to learn any thing more from Adam yet. I heard from Jim a few days ago. he was well. I saw a man yesterday going to the Brigade. he said he would go to see Jim last night.

Tell Mrs Loggans to go to the clerk of the Court and proseed just as though Mr Loggans had been mustared into service. she can get the bounty and wages boath. Maj Kellogg says he will send Capt Story the instructions how to proceed but she can get that from any lawyer. The claim should be sent to Richmond.

We have not drawn any money yet We think we will get some in 10 or 15 days. I think it uncertain. I have not had Buck valued yet. I want him to fill up a little.

There is but little prospect for a fight yet. Dont take the blues dear—dont be so gloomy—look on the bright side awhile. My mouth has got well. I can eat any thing now and a fine chance of it too. I got a fine drink of cider as I came out from Knoxville. I drank 5 large glasses!!! I never felt it. Fruit is beginning to ripen here now. You know I will have my share. There is a very fine prospect for corn here—rain a plenty.

Rev Mashburn says Gen. Stonewall Jackson is an Elder of the Presbyterian Church and a very pious man. So that settles the question as to the Gen Jackson's religious principles. When Mother learns that she will think more of him than ever.

Write me long letters Dear—direct to Knoxville Write soon
Yours most Affectionatly
M. P. Alexander

Notes

McMillan Station Tennessee: McMillan Station was a station on the East Tennessee and Virginia Railroad about thirteen miles northeast of Knoxville.[46]

uncle Adams: He probably was Manning's mother's brother, Adam Poole of Gwinnett County, Georgia.[47]

Buck: Manning's horse.

our brigade: At the time the letter was written, the 43rd regiment was assigned to the 4th Brigade under Colonel A. W. Reynolds. That brigade was part of the 1st Division under Brigadier General Carter L. Stevenson in the Department of East Tennessee, Major General E. Kirby Smith, commanding.[48]

Stevenson's command had been holding Cumberland Gap, the primary path through the Cumberland Mountains into Kentucky from East Tennessee, but had evacuated the Gap on June 18. General Smith was consolidating his forces to defend Chattanooga, a vital location in the supply route from Georgia west. A

---

[46] *OR*, ser. 1, vol. 16, pt. 2, 701; *Knoxville News Sentinel*, June 23, 2013.
[47] US Census, 1860, Gwinnett County.
[48] *OR*, ser. 1, vol. 16, pt. 2, 715, 719.

Union army quickly took Stevenson's place in the Gap while Stevenson determined to make a stand at Clinch Mountain, a range of mountains between Cumberland Gap and Knoxville.[49]

Cedar Ford: This is the old name of present-day Luttrell, Tennessee, in Union County. It was located near the southwest end of the Clinch Mountain range where Stevenson planned to make a stand against any Union force marching south from Cumberland Gap.[50]

Capt. Reives: He was captain of Company K of the 43rd Georgia Regiment.[51]

Maj Boyeds boys: There was no Major Boyd in the 43rd Georgia Regiment. However, C. Hopson Boyd of Hall County had four sons who served as privates in Company K of the 43rd Georgia. In later years, C. H. Boyd was known as Colonel Boyd. He had served as sheriff of Hall County before the Civil War and after the war as a member of the Georgia legislature. He might have been known as Major Boyd when this letter was written, which may have been a militia title or a courtesy title.[52]

Dr. Wills: Dr. John Wills of Gainesville, Hall County, Georgia, was appointed surgeon in the Confederate States Army on July 12, 1862, to take rank from March 20, 1862. He was assigned to the 43rd Georgia Regiment to be its surgeon. He was paid from March 10, 1862, to January 3, 1863, and no further record of his service was found.[53]

Col. Harris: He was Colonel Alpheus Skidmore Harris, commander of the 43rd Georgia.[54]

Dr. Anderson: He has not been identified.

Maj Kellog: He was Major Henry C. Kellogg, third in command of the regiment when this letter was written.[55]

Maj Kellogg has been to Richmond. He brought my communication so the thing is safe now: This must have been Manning's acceptance of the assistant surgeon position and his oath mentioned in the secretary of war's appointment letter that is immediately above.

James Neal came through the fight unhurt: The fight was really the Seven Days Battles. Rev. Mashborn, who was said by Simeon to be the chaplain of Wright's Legion, knew about James because Wright's Legion had been combined with the

---

[49] Parks, *General Edmund Kirby Smith*, 186–89; *Rand McNally 2019 Road Atlas*, 95.

[50] "Luttrell, Tennessee," Wikipedia, https://en.wikipedia.org/wiki/Luttrell,_Tennessee, accessed June 28, 2016; Parks, *General Edmund Kirby Smith*, 189.

[51] Service records.

[52] Service records; *Gainesville Eagle*, July 30, 1880.

[53] Service records; US Census, 1850, Hall County, Georgia (listed under "C. H. Bard.")

[54] Rigdon, *Georgia 43rd Infantry Regiment*, 55–57.

[55] Ibid.

25th Georgia to form the 38th Georgia, James's regiment. For more on James Neal and the Seven Days Battles, see the note concerning him under Simeon's letter of early July 1862 in chapter 12.[56]

Adam: This was Adam O. Alexander, one of Manning's younger brothers. See note in immediately previous letter.

Jim: He was Manning's younger brother James D. Alexander. His 9th Georgia Battalion was in a different brigade from the one Manning was in, but his brigade was also in General Stevenson's division.[57]

Mrs. Loggans: She was Amanda M. Loggins, widow of Private Samuel T. Loggins of Company G of the 43rd Georgia. Private Loggins had died in Atlanta on June 23, 1862.[58]

Manning

Head Quarters Near Barbersville Ky
Aug 27st 1862
My Dear:

You will be surprised when I tell you that we are in Kentucky. And my dear you must pardon me if I don't write you a long letter this time. I have meateiral enough to writ a half doz pages but I have not time to write as it is night.

We are now on our way to Barbersville Ky—we ware ordered from Cumberland Gap last Saturday night. we marched all night—reached Rogers Gap sunday morning and since that time we have been marching over the roughest country I ever saw. we have had to pull the artillery and wagons over the mountes by hand.

Gen. Smith crossed Rogers Gap last week and got in the rear of the yanks at cumberland gap and cut of their supplies and we are going to rein[force] him at Barbersville, Ky. we will reach there to morrow we have got them compledly surrounded.

I am geting along *first rate* I never got your letter of 12st intill last friday. I was truly *glad* to here from you and dear little nora.

Gen Smith made a fine hall when he cut the yanks off. He got 110 wagons and teams all loaded with commissay stores My opinion is that we are going to push the campaighn right into the interior of Ky.

Dear dont be uneasy about me if you dont here from me regularly for it is all together uncertain when I have the chance to write you again.

Dear—you will please have my winter clothing made but don't send them to me unless you *know* they will come through. make them as heavy as you can.

---

[56] Derry, *Confederate Military History: Georgia*, 116.
[57] *OR*, ser. 1, vol. 16, pt. 2, 715, 719.
[58] Service records.

make me 2 pair flannel drawers. Make my bed clothing as hevy as you can for I can have it hauled as long as any thing goes. Also have me a pair of boots put up of the best quality no matter what they cost. this country will be so muddy in the winter that I cant get along without boots. Have them mad broad or large No 8s.

We are about 75 miles north of Knoxville Ten. So you see my dear that we are geting out into "deep water." Give your self no uneasiness. I am geting along very easily since I have got buck to ride. he is fatter than you ever saw him. I had him valued the other day—He was put at 200 dollars.

I get some milk now and as much fruit as any boddy, but tell dear little Norah that pa has not seen but one watermelon this year, but he will make it all up when he gets home.

Dear direct your letters to Knoxville. I may get them and I may not. I will write you again the first chance.

I think Simeon had better have Ratio discharged. It is as easy to get a discharge as a furlough. I fear he will not have any more health, while he remains in the army.

I must close my dear. we go to Barbersville in the morning and from there I know not.

Kiss Norah for me Write soon. Yours most truly,
M. P. Alexander
[Written vertically on the envelope:]
M. P. Alexander
Asst Surgeon
43rd Geo. Regt.
      D U E 10 [postmark]
      Mrs. M. P. Alexander
      Wall Street
      Georgia

Notes

Barbersville Ky: In late March 1861, President Abraham Lincoln wrote about Kentucky in a letter to a senator from Illinois marked "Private & confidential": "I think to lose Kentucky is nearly the same as to lose the whole game."[59]

Although leaders of the Confederacy would not have been familiar with Lincoln's statement, they were familiar with the idea behind it—that if Kentucky were to secede, Missouri and probably Maryland would soon follow, making the Union's position very precarious. With that thought in mind, plus other considerations, such as Kentucky's strategic location militarily, the South determined to

---

[59] Fehrenbacher, *Abraham Lincoln*, 268–70, 737–38.

invade and conquer the state, replace its current governor with a governor friendly to the South, and secure its secession.[60]

The plan to move into Kentucky gradually evolved beginning on July 31 when General Kirby Smith met in Chattanooga with Major General Braxton Bragg. Bragg in mid-June had assumed command of the entire Confederate Western Department and outranked Smith. Together they agreed that Smith would seize Cumberland Gap while Bragg concentrated his forces around Chattanooga. If Smith was successful, both forces were to move into middle Tennessee to cut off a Union force there.

About ten days later, however, at Smith's urging, they modified the plan. Smith would not capture Cumberland Gap, but hold the Union forces there with part of his army while the other part maneuvered around the Gap and marched into Kentucky, going first to Barbourville.[61]

As the crow flies, Barbourville is about twenty-five miles northwest of Cumberland Gap, longer by road. An officer with General Smith described it as "a dilapidated village," but still "the metropolis of this mountain region."[62]

we ware ordered from Cumberland Gap last Saturday night: Before getting to Barbourville, some of Smith's men were directed to Cumberland Gap. Smith had one cavalry regiment and four infantry divisions under his command. Each of the four infantry divisions was commanded by a brigadier general: Stevenson, Heth, Churchill, and Cleburne.[63]

The 43rd was part of Reynolds's Brigade, which was part of Stevenson's Division. Stevenson's Division was ordered to Cumberland Gap to confront the Union forces there.[64]

On August 4, the division left camp heading toward Cumberland Gap. Two days later, the division reached Tazewell, Tennessee, about a dozen miles southeast of the Gap, and found elements of the Union army already in the town. The Confederates attacked. There were two brigades marching in front of Reynolds's Brigade, and they did the major fighting for the Confederates. They forced the Union troops out of Tazewell, and, overnight, the Federals retreated to

---

[60] Lambert, *When the Ripe Pears Fell*, 2–4.

[61] *OR*, ser. 1, vol. 17, pt. 2, 606; *OR*, ser. 1, vol. 16, pt. 2, 741, 748–49; Foote, *Civil War*, 1:575–77.

[62] Hammond, "Campaign of General E. Kirby Smith," 9:247; *Kentucky Atlas & Gazetteer*, 87.

[63] Lambert, *When the Ripe Pears Fell*, 229–30; *OR*, ser. 1, vol. 16, pt. 2, 777–78; Hammond, "Campaign of General E. Kirby Smith," 9:247.

[64] *OR*, ser. 1, vol. 16, pt. 2, 719, 737, 738–39, 741, 746.

Cumberland Gap. The 43rd apparently took no part in the fighting and suffered no losses.[65]

Stevenson's whole division then camped a few miles east of Tazewell until August 16 when it again began its march toward Cumberland Gap. The next day the division was within three miles of the Gap when the Union forces at the Gap opened fire on the division's leading elements. There the division halted.[66]

Meanwhile, on August 18, General Smith and two of his other divisions, having bypassed Cumberland Gap, arrived in Barbourville. Four days later, Smith's third division under General Henry Heth arrived in Barbourville. The same day, Smith ordered General Stevenson to send a brigade from his division to join Smith in Barbourville and there become part of Heth's Division. Stevenson chose Reynolds's Brigade, including Manning's 43rd Georgia, to join Smith. As Manning reported in his letter, the brigade left the following night, Saturday, August 23, for Barbourville.[67]

Rogers Gap: Rogers Gap was an alternative to Cumberland Gap as a way to proceed through the Cumberland Mountains from east Tennessee toward Kentucky. It is about fifteen miles southwest of Cumberland Gap near the present-day town of Speedwell, Tennessee. Smith took the Rogers Gap Route to Barbourville.[68]

Gen. Smith made a fine hall: In his report to General Bragg, Smith recorded that he had captured "some 50 prisoners, including the sick (no supplies) and a few wagons." In a later letter to Richmond, he expanded his haul to "some 50 prisoners, a train of near 50 wagons, and a few stores."[69]

My opinion is that we are going to push the campaighn right into the interior of Ky: Manning was right. On August 20, Smith informed Bragg that he was advancing further into Kentucky and heading for Lexington. On August 24, Bragg agreed to Smith's advance.[70]

General Cleburne's division left Barbourville on the 25th, followed shortly by General Churchill's. Smith stayed until the 27th, and Heth's Division, which was to guard and transport the supply train, stayed until around August 29, when that division, including the 43rd, left Barbourville for the interior of Kentucky.[71]

---

[65] *Southern Banner*, August 13, 1862; *OR*, ser. 1, vol. 16, pt. 2, 301, 341, 747, 752; W. H. H. Rogers, *Bible Records*, 7; Goodson, *Georgia Confederate 7,000*, 114; Clemmer, "Some Reminiscences of the Firing Line," 59–61.

[66] Clemmer, "Some Reminiscences of the Firing Line," 60–61.

[67] *OR*, ser. 1, vol. 16, pt. 2, 755, 766–67, 769, 777–78.

[68] *OR*, ser. 1, vol. 10, pt. 1, 58; *OR*, ser. 1, vol. 16, pt. 2, 755; *Kentucky Atlas & Gazetteer*, 87.

[69] *OR*, ser. 1, vol. 16, pt. 2, 766; 777.

[70] Ibid., 766–67, 775.

[71] *OR*, ser. 1, vol. 16, pt. 2, 775, 778, 782; Heth, *Memoirs*, 165; Hammond, "Campaign of General E. Kirby Smith," 9:248–49.

Dear dont be uneasy about me if you dont here from me regularly: Again Manning was correct. General Smith wrote General Bragg on August 24 that once he left Barbourville, "my communication with East Tennessee will be lost," which meant that communication between his forces and Georgia would also be lost. Lona did not receive a letter from Manning again until two months later when the 43rd returned to Tennessee (the next letter).[72]

Manning

Camp Hatton Tenn.
Oct 26th 1862
My Dear Lona:

How thankful I am to be permitted to rite you once more. you will be surprised [no] doubt when you here that we are back here again. When I write you last I thought we were going to fight but we ware only preparing to leave Kentucky. whad a glorious time going into Ky but as *in*glorious a one coming out. the retreat from that state setles the fate not only of Kentucky—I fear—but of our government. We had a very hard time on our retreat. All our wagons ware ordered forward and the troops left to march 85 miles through a dry baren and mountainous country. But Dear I will not try to give you the details till I am better situated.

It has been snowing here all day and I am siting under an old wagon sheat propped up on some sticks so the chance [is] very bad for writing. we lost all our tents when we started on our retreat.

After we started back I heard that Jim was 15 miles back sick. I resolved that he should not be left to fall into the hands of the enemy, so I went back and found him at uncle Bronston's unable to walk from Rheumatism of the knee and hip. I put him on my horse and mad for the command but I had to walk so fast and not being used to it I soon broke down. I bought a young horse 4 years old and saddle for 80 dollars by which I was able to reach the command and get jim through all safe which I would have done had I had to have stolen the best horse in Ky.

I have got him here and have sent him to a hous there to stay till he gets well. I gave 8 dollars for a comfort and fine blanket. I can do now tolrebly well. I don't know whether you will have the chance to send me any clothing or not. if you do, send one pair pants 2 pair woolen drawers one pair socks a pair gloves and two shirts. I do not know whare we will go to from here. My opinion is we will go to Va. or middle Tenn.

My Dear I never wanted to here from you half so badly in my life. please write immediately. direct to Knoxville and it will be forwarded. I dred to here from Simeon & Ratio. I learn boath commands ware cut to pieces. My Dear you

---

[72] *OR*, ser. 1, vol. 16, pt. 2, 775.

must pardon me for not writing more at length but it is so cold and disagreeable that I must close. I have just heard the baneful news of the death of John D. Miller. Kiss dear little Nora for me. pa thinks of *big* dear and *little* dear evey hour.

Yours most Truly
M P Alexander

Notes

Camp Hatton, Tennessee: Camp Hatton was near Blaine's Crossroad, now the town of Blaine, about a dozen miles northeast of Knoxville.[73]

whad a glorious time going into Kentucky but as inglorious a one coming out: As mentioned in a note to the previous letter, Manning left Barbourville, Kentucky, for the interior of the state around August 29 along with the rest of the 43rd Georgia. They were part of Heth's Division, one of four divisions of General Kirby Smith's newly renamed Army of Kentucky. Two of Smith's divisions had left Barbourville a few days earlier, and Heth's Division followed them with the army's supply train. Its mission was not only to protect the supplies but to cover the rear of the army as it advanced. Smith's fourth division under General Stevenson stayed at Cumberland Gap to contain there a Union force under General Morgan.[74]

Smith and Manning March into Kentucky

At first the army marched around and over barren mountains where water was scarce and the locals unfriendly. When, however, they reached the end of this stretch and entered the rolling land of central Kentucky "the cheery songs of the men told that they were in the best of spirits, and ready for any adventure that might betide them in the 'Blue Grass,'" one of them wrote several years later.[75]

On August 29, just as Heth's Division, including the 43rd, was leaving Barbourville, Confederate cavalry screening Smith's two advance divisions ran into a Union force just short of Richmond, Kentucky, about thirty miles south of Lexington. There was a brief skirmish, which turned out to be a preliminary engagement for the full scale battle the next day.

For most of August 30, the Confederate and Union troops fought in and around Richmond until finally the Confederates completely routed the Union

---

[73] Ritter, "Sketch of the Third Battery of Maryland Artillery," 331; *Rand McNally 2019 Road Atlas*, 95; Smedlund, *Camp Fires of Georgia Troops*, 149–50.

[74] *OR*, ser. 1, vol. 16, pt. 2, 775; 777, 780; Hammond, "Campaign of General E. Kirby Smith," 9:248–49, 291; Vieux Seconde, "Notes on General E. Kirby Smith's Kentucky Campaign," 198.

[75] Foote, *Civil War*, 1:650–51; Vieux Seconde, "Notes on General E. Kirby Smith's Kentucky Campaign," 199 (quote); Hammond, "Campaign of General E. Kirby Smith," 9:249.

forces, capturing around forty-three hundred prisoners, plentiful stores, and numerous small arms.[76]

Two days later, Heth's Division caught up with the two leading divisions. Too late to participate in the battle, men of the division spent that day and much of the next paroling prisoners, while the division's surgeons, including Manning, helped treat the wounded from the Richmond battle. On September 2, General Kirby Smith and his three divisions entered Lexington without opposition and were gloriously received by many of the townspeople.[77]

Smith temporarily made Lexington his headquarters.

What to do next? The Confederates believed that the path to Covington, Kentucky, about seventy miles north of Lexington and just across the Ohio River from Cincinnati, Ohio, was poorly defended, as was Cincinnati itself. Thus, around September 3, Smith ordered Heth to make a demonstration of Confederate strength at Cincinnati.

Heth left immediately with two of his brigades, one of which was Reynolds's, which included the 43rd. By September 6, Heth, Reynolds, and their men were on the outskirts of Covington. The 43rd was in the vanguard, and Reynolds ordered its commander to throw out pickets just in front of the Union lines.

Manning must have had mixed feelings standing with a hostile army just across the river from the city where he had spent several challenging months studying medicine, study that soon would prove useful if the Confederates attacked. Whatever Manning may have thought, however, Reynolds was reported to have been supremely confident of his men and to have said "his Georgians would storm Gibraltar with barlow-knives."

He did not get a chance to test them. Heth wrote years later that he was about to order Reynolds and the other men under his command to attack when he received a message from Smith ordering him not to attack but withdraw a few miles back toward Lexington and wait for further orders.[78]

Braxton Bragg Enters Kentucky

Meanwhile, the vanguard of Bragg's army had entered Kentucky around September 10 by way of Tompkinsville, a little over one hundred miles west of

---

[76] Lambert, *When the Ripe Pears Fell*, 44–45 and following; Foote, *Civil War*, 1:650–53; Boatner, *Civil War Dictionary*, 697–98.

[77] Hammond, "Campaign of General E. Kirby Smith," 9:289–92; Heth, *Memoirs*, 165; Foote, *Civil War*, 653; Kolakowski, *Civil War at Perryville*, 38; Lambert, *When the Ripe Pears Fell*, 180; Walker, *Hell's Broke Loose in Georgia*, 41.

[78] Heth, *Memoirs*, 165–66; *OR*, ser. 1, vol. 16, pt. 2, 807, 812; H. P. Bell, *Men and Things*, 86; Lambert, *When the Ripe Pears Fell*, 180; Collins, *History of Kentucky*, 111; *OR*, ser. 1, vol. 16, pt. 2, 812, 830.

Cumberland Gap. By September 14, General Bragg and his army had reached Glasgow, Kentucky, still over one hundred miles, as the crow flies, southwest of Lexington and Smith's army.[79]

In the meantime, under Major General Don Carlos Buell, the largest Union army in Tennessee had followed Bragg into Kentucky. Its plan was to reinforce a small force at Louisville and prevent that city from being seized by the Confederates. Bragg, however, was between Buell and Louisville and could move either onward to seize Louisville or turn around and attack Buell. However, in a controversial decision, Bragg did neither. Instead, he moved east to Bardstown, leaving the way clear for Buell to march unmolested to Louisville, which Buell promptly did.[80]

For several days the Confederates did little. Bragg stayed in Bardstown and Smith stayed in Lexington. While they were in their separate places, word reached Smith that the Union force at Cumberland Gap had left there on September 17, heading north toward Mount Sterling, about twenty-five miles east of Lexington. General Stevenson, whose division Smith had left to guard Cumberland Gap, was pursuing him.[81]

This information produced a flurry of activity. On September 21, Smith countermanded his earlier order to Heth to move part of his army further south. Instead, he was to keep it where he was. Two days later, he ordered Heth to move all of his command to Frankfort, located west of Lexington, between Lexington and Louisville. Here Heth could aid Bragg if he should attack Buell.

Then the next day, Smith again changed his mind and ordered Heth to "move by forced marches to Mount Sterling," east of Lexington, even "marching at night if necessary," to confront the Union force moving there from the Cumberland Gap. Heth arrived at Mount Sterling with most of his division on September 25.[82]

Once in Mount Sterling, Heth stayed for a few days awaiting the Union troops from the Gap. The Federals, however, bypassed Mount Sterling and went instead into Ohio by a route further east. That threat eliminated, Bragg ordered Smith to concentrate his forces, including Heth's Division, in Frankfort, the capital of Kentucky. There on October 4 Bragg planned to celebrate the inauguration a new governor of Kentucky sympathetic to the South.

---

[79] *OR*, ser. 1, vol. 16, pt. 2, 808, 815; Horn, *Army of Tennessee*, 167; *Kentucky Atlas & Gazetteer*, 1.
[80] Horn, *Army of Tennessee*, 166, 168–72; Foote, *Civil War*, 1:656–61.
[81] *OR*, ser. 1, vol. 16, pt. 2, 844, 847, 850.
[82] Ibid., 860, 866–67, 869–73.

On October 2 in Frankfort, Bragg and Smith finally met in Kentucky for the first time. The same day, Heth's Division also reached Frankfort, but as seemed to be a pattern, it would not stay there long.[83]

In the meantime, on October 1 Buell's Federal force in Louisville had begun leaving the city in two wings. One wing moved east toward the Confederates in Frankfort, and the larger wing moved southeast toward Bardstown. The first wing reached the outskirts of Frankfort on October 4, and the unsettling boom of Union guns could be heard in Frankfort during the new governor's inauguration. This development surprised and rattled Bragg, who ordered the city evacuated in what one of his men called "an immediate and rapid retreat" and General Smith called a "skedaddle."

Under his orders his men marched toward Harrodsburg, about thirty miles south of Frankfort, just as Union troops entered the abandoned capital. The new governor also evacuated Frankfort, having lasted only a few hours in his capital city. As one soldier in Smith's army later wrote, the new governor had not stayed long enough "to warm his seat."[84]

Bragg Fights Buell While Heth and Manning March To and Fro

Bragg was greatly concerned with the Union force that had taken Frankfort, believing it to be Buell's main force and that it threatened his own army, although Buell's main force actually was headed further west and south toward Bardstown. As a result of Bragg's misplaced concern, for much of the next five days Heth's Division marched back and forth within an area between Frankfort and Harrodsburg, about thirty miles south of Frankfort, seeking a Union army to confront.

At first they were sent to Versailles to participate in a battle that never took place because the enemy was not there. Then they were to meet the enemy at Lawrenceburg, but when they got there, again the enemy was elsewhere. In the process, the division crossed the Kentucky River from east to west, then retraced its steps and crossed it from west to east, then again crossed the river back from east to west.[85]

While the division was going to and fro, on October 8, a part of Bragg's army fought the Union's actual main force at Perryville, a village about ten miles southeast of Harrodsburg in Central Kentucky. This probably was the most significant battle of the Kentucky campaign. When it took place, however, Heth's

---

[83] Parks, *General Edmund Kirby Smith*, 232; *OR*, ser. 1, vol. 16, pt. 2, 898, 901, 903; Kolakowski, *Civil War at Perryville*, 82–83.

[84] Kolakowski, *Civil War at Perryville*, 77; 82–84; *OR*, ser. 1, vol. 16, pt. 2, 905; Hammond, "Campaign of General E. Kirby Smith," 9:459; Collins, *History of Kentucky*, 113; N. Fowler, "Johnny Reb's Impressions of Kentucky," 207–208.

[85] Horn, *Army of Tennessee*, 176–80; *OR*, ser. 1, vol. 16, pt. 2, 905, 915–21, 924–27.

Division, the 43rd, and other parts of Smith's army were in the vicinity of Lawrenceburg, about thirty miles north of Perryville, and did not participate in the battle at all.[86]

Even though the Battle of Perryville was generally considered a Confederate victory, the day after it was over, Bragg ordered his army there to withdraw to the Harrodsburg area where Smith's forces would join him. It was anticipated that once Bragg had all his forces together another battle with Buell would commence.[87]

Bragg Returns to Tennessee

However, in another controversial decision, Bragg decided not to fight. Instead, on October 13, he ordered all the Confederates back to Tennessee.

To get to Tennessee, Bragg's and Smith's armies would march together southeast to Lancaster, Kentucky. Then they would split. Smith's army was to return toward Tennessee the way they had come, by Berea and Big Hill, while Bragg's own army was to take a more southern route, through Crab Orchard and Mt. Vernon. Their paths would cross near London, Kentucky, and both would return through Barbourville and Cumberland Gap.

Bragg's army had the more direct and easier route and reached London before Smith's. This meant that Smith would bring up the rear all the way to Barbourville and Cumberland Gap. Of Smith's army, General Stevenson's division, which had rejoined Smith after abandoning the pursuit of the retreating Union force it had followed from Cumberland Gap, and a cavalry unit would be the rear guard for the entire army. Just in front of them would be Heth's Division with the supply train for both armies. Meanwhile, the Union army was in pursuit.[88]

The main part of Smith's army struggled past Big Hill on October 15–17. As Manning indicated, the army's mood was much less enthusiastic leaving Kentucky than it had been entering the state. General Smith reported that his men were "broken down and exhausted, having been taxed by six days' and nights' forced marches and hard work." His command had toiled "day and night" pulling his and Bragg's supply trains up Big Hill, which was some eighteen miles across. One of Smith's officers later wrote that all fifteen hundred men of Heth's Division made up a working party: "The soldiers lined the road on either side from the foot to the summit of this immense and rugged hill, and as the starved and

---

[86] *OR*, ser. 1, vol. 16, pt. 2, 926–28; Kolakowski, *Civil War at Perryville*, 87–136, 138; Hammond, "Campaign of General E. Kirby Smith," 10:70–71.

[87] Horn, *Army of Tennessee*, 185–87.

[88] Horn, *Army of Tennessee*, 187–89; *OR*, ser. 1, vol. 16, pt. 2, 939–44, 949, 959; Kolakowski, *Civil War at Perryville*, 138–41; Parks, *General Edmund Kirby Smith*, 237–41; Hammond, "Campaign of General E. Kirby Smith," 10:71–76.

tired mules faltered and fell, seized the wagons and lifted them by sheer force over the worst places." Fortunately for them, the Union's pursuit was being delayed by Confederate cavalry.[89]

Heth's Division finally made it past London, probably on the 18th, while days earlier Bragg's army had passed London and moved on ahead. The division passed through Barbourville and reached Flat Lick, Kentucky, about fifteen miles southeast of Barbourville on the 21st. General Smith reported that his command had traveled on "the worst road I have ever traveled; in some places impassable, so that a new one has to be made. My command from exhaustion in drawing the wagons and artillery up the hills and not having had sleep for some nights, are very much scattered along the road." His troops also suffered from a severe shortage of water in a drought that had lasted in the area since about August 15. The Confederates got a break, however, when the Union forces stopped their pursuit just south of London.[90]

On the 22nd, the head of Smith's army finally reached Cumberland Gap only to discover that most of the provisions Smith hoped to find there for his men already had been consumed or carried away by Bragg's army, which had preceded him there by three days and then moved on.

To make matters worse, Smith received a request from Bragg to send men to him in Knoxville to be part of his newly planned operations in Middle Tennessee. To this Smith responded bluntly, "The condition of my command now is such as to render any immediate operations with it impossible. The men are worn down from exposure and want of food. They are much in want of shoes, clothing, and blankets. There cannot now be more than 6,000 effective men left in my whole force." Earlier Smith had written, "My men have suffered on this march everything excepting actual starvation. There must be not less than 10,000 of them scattered through the country [along the entire march route] trying to find something upon which to live."[91]

On October 25, Smith ordered Heth to move his men to Lenoir Station in Tennessee, southwest of Knoxville. Camp Hatton, Tennessee, from which Manning wrote this letter on October 26, was on the way there.[92]

---

[89] *OR*, ser. 1, vol. 16, pt. 2, 940, 943, 949, 958, 959, 960; Hammond, "Campaign of General E. Kirby Smith," 10:75–76; *Kentucky Atlas & Gazetteer*, 52, 69; Walker, *Hell's Broke Loose in Georgia*, 49; Palencia, *On Rising Ground*, 69.

[90] *OR*, ser. 1, vol. 16, pt. 2, 967, 974–75; Hammond, "Campaign of General E. Kirby Smith," 10:75–76; N. Fowler, "Johnny Reb's Impressions of Kentucky," 213–14 (note 44); *Kentucky Atlas & Gazetteer*, 87.

[91] *OR*, ser. 1, vol. 16, pt. 2, 970, 974, 975; Parks, *General Edmund Kirby Smith*, 241–42; Hammond, "Campaign of General E. Kirby Smith," 10:72.

[92] *OR*, ser. 1, vol. 16, pt. 2, 978. Camp Hatton was near Blaine's Crossroad, now the town of Blaine, about a dozen miles northeast of Knoxville.

A sergeant in the 43rd described his impression of the march in a letter home on October 25, 1862, also written from Camp Hatton: "we have had the hardest time I reckon of any army in the Confederacy[.] we marched 800 miles or more through heat and dust with the worst water ever was drunk[,] part of the time on half rations and sometimes not time to cook it[.] we frequently marched nearly all night but we got here today."[93]

Notes

I heard that Jim was 15 miles back: Jim was one of Manning's younger brothers, James D. Alexander. According to Jim's service records, at the time the letter was written, he was a sergeant in Company C of the 9th Battalion Georgia Infantry. That unit was part of Stevenson's 1st Division and Barton's 3rd Brigade. Also, according to Jim's service records, on November 1, 1862, about a week after Manning wrote this letter, Jim enlisted as a private in Company K of the 43rd Georgia.[94]

It has been snowing here all day: A weather report for October 25, the day before Manning wrote this letter: "Heavy snow, from 4 to 12 inches deep, all over the state, heaviest in the mountain region of south-eastern Ky." This probably is a reasonably good description of the snow in northeastern Tennessee also.[95]

Uncle Bronstons: He has not been identified.

I dred to here from Simeon & Ratio. I learn boath commands ware cut to pieces: Manning is referring to the Battle of Antietam or Sharpsburg, which took place on September 17, 1862. Simeon's unit had helped capture Harper's Ferry two days earlier and afterward remained there on guard duty. It did not participate in the battle. Horatio's unit suffered badly at the Battle of Crampton's Gap on September 14 and at Antietam, but Horatio was not with it. He was sick and had remained in a hospital in Richmond.[96]

John D. Miller: He probably was the John D. Miller who was a farmer near Polksville in Hall County in 1860 and possibly the J. D. Miller who in Polksville in 1861 had enlisted in Manning's ill-fated company, the Bell Volunteers. If so, he left a wife and nine-year-old daughter.[97]

---

[93] Sergeant Lewis Stovall to his wife, Grace G. Stovall, October 25, 1862 (Roberts and Clark, *Atlanta's Fighting Forty-Second*, 43; General Barton & Stovall History/Heritage Association, https://www.generalbartonandstovall.com, members only section, accessed April 24, 2020.

[94] *OR*, ser. 1, vol. 16, pt. 2, 719, 984.

[95] Collins, *History of Kentucky*, 115.

[96] See note to Simeon's service record entry of November 8, 1862, in chapter 12 and note to Horatio's letter of September 24, 1862, in chapter 11; Robertson, *General A. P. Hill*, 133–41; Gallagher et al., *Civil War*, 64–66.

[97] US Census, 1860, Hall County; see chapter 9.

Manning

Lenor's Station Tenn.
November 1, 1862
My Dear Lona,

    I presume, dear, you have learned before *now* that I am among the living. I have written two letters but I suppose the first one was lost on the way as Mr White tell me you have not received any intelligence from me since I crossed the mountins. Dear I regret that you have suffered so much uneasyness for me but you see circumstances ware such that it could not be otherwise. I hope such a thing will not occur again.

    Dear, I will not attempt to give you a description of Kentucky nor a history of our march as I have alredy done so befor to a limited extent. We ware on the march for more than two months and marched over 700 miles. But we are again back in East Tenn but whare our destiny for the winter campaign will be is not yet known. I think we will stay here som 8 or 10 days—the brigades are being reorganized. After which time I suppose we will be sent out to our winter quarters. Dear I would have been so happy if you had known I was here and had come up with him [Mr. White].

    When we get stationed I am going to write you and [you] must come to see me.

    I am partly supplied with clothing Mr. White toled me you had som clothing—you also wrote you had my overcoat cut. I have a very good Yankey overcoat but I will need a dress coat. Now if you have had my overcoat cut so as to button the cape on so that it can be taken off and the coat worn as a dress coat, make it and send it for I can sell my overcoat that I have here for twice what it cost me. My gray coat is a little thin though there is no brake in it yet. I could put it away till next spring and it would answer the purpose then. I will ned one pair of pants two shirts two pair flannel drawers a pair of socks and a pair of gloves. I have 2 pair of cotton flannel drawers that I got in Lexington that will last me all winter. I have a pair of very good boots but you may send those that you have had made. I am glad you got them so cheap—such boots cannot be bought for less than $30.00 in Knoxville. Those I have will last me through the great part of the winter and the others will do me all the spring and summer. there will be a detail sent home from each company to get up clothing and I will get whoever goes home from Capt Stories Company to bring mine. I want a heavy comfort or 2 blankets. I soled the blanket I got in Kentucky for $10.00—2.00 dollars more than I gave for the comfort and blanket boath. It was too fine for such use as this.

    We will draw some money in a few days and I will send you some home—enough to pay our debts if I draw that much also to buy some salt. Brother Jim is with me yet but this transfer is not signed up yet. he is not fit for duty yet.

Write me dear all about how you are geting along. we have plenty of fine beef but I miss that fine butter milk and sweet potatoes very much. Oh, how I could injoy a dinner of corn bread potatoes and butter milk. Well may be this acussed war will not last always. Under the late exemtion act I would [be] exempt ware I not in service. Very sure I would avail my self of that act ware I out of service. Don't think I am dissatisfied but if I was at home I have had experience enough not to try it again. Write me all about how our hogs are doing and all the *little* things we have any claim to.

Tell *Little* dear to write pa howdy again. I have got 2 letter from you since 12 Aug. If we should be stationed any whare on the rail road I very highly appreciate a sack of diced peaches or apples and would not at all object to a sack of potatoes. And if we [are] station[ed] any whare that you can get to us by rail road you must come and bring me a *mess of chicken*

Well dear I will stop. Write me soon. Direct to Knoxville and they will be sent to me. I will write just as soon as we move.

Yours Most Affectionately
M. P. Alexander

Notes

Lenor's Station Tenn.: Lenoir's Station was a station on the East Tennessee and Georgia Railroad between Chattanooga and Knoxville. It was located about twenty miles southwest of Knoxville and now is known as Lenoir City.[98]

Stationery: The stationery on which Manning wrote this letter has "US" surrounded by a wreath embossed in its upper left corner. Possibly he took it from some Union Army source in his march through Kentucky.

Mr White: There were several soldiers whose last name was White in Company G of the 43rd, the company that was raised in Jackson County. This Mr. White probably was the father of one or more of them.[99]

We ware on the march for more than two months and marched over 700 miles: It is difficult to arrive at an accurate estimate of the number of miles Manning and Heth's Division marched on their invasion of Kentucky. Another member of the 43rd estimated that the unit marched eight hundred miles.[100]

As the crow flies, it is a about 180 miles from Cumberland Gap to Covington, Kentucky, which would mean a round trip of more than 360 miles. On the ground, however, with all that route's twists and turns, particularly through the mountains, the actual distance marched would be longer than that, possibly

---

[98] Coleman, *History of Georgia*, 158; Rand McNally, "Tennessee State Road Map."
[99] Rigdon, *Georgia 43rd Infantry Regiment*, 176.
[100] Sergeant Lewis Stovall to his wife, Grace G. Stovall, October 25, 1862 (Roberts and Clark, *Atlanta's Fighting Forty-Second*, 43; General Barton & Stovall History/Heritage Association, https://www.generalbartonandstovall.com, members only section, accessed April 24, 2020).

considerably longer. In addition, the 43rd marched to several different places within the area between Frankfort and Harrodsburg, and occasionally retraced its steps. Probably five hundred miles would be a conservative estimate, and seven hundred miles might not be far wrong. They marched all that distance without once coming close enough to the enemy to fight him.[101]

Capt. Stories Company: He was Joseph M. Storey, company commander of Company G of the 43rd Georgia from Jackson County.[102]

late exemption act: The Confederate Congress passed on October 11, 1862, an act that exempted from military service in the Confederate army men in a number of occupations and offices deemed otherwise vital to the war effort. Among those exempted occupations were physicians who had been practicing medicine for at least five years before passage of the act. Manning would have qualified for this exemption, but apparently it did not apply to those already serving in the Confederate army.[103]

Manning

Camp 43rd Geo Regt. Near
Lenrs Station Tenn Nov 12th 1862
My Dear

    I will send you a few lines by Mr Jesse Carter who is going home after clothing etc for Capt Stories Company. I will send you ($350) three hundred and fifty dollars by him. I want you dear to pay every cent we ow just as soon as you get it. Hire some one to take the money and go round and pay all the debts. It is more than I can ask your Pa to do. I do not know the exact amount I am owing in Augusta; but I think it is about $22 or $23 dollars. if you have any oportunity of sending it do so. It is an account with Spears & Hight, Drugist. My note with the Longs in Athens is about 18 dollars, Lattne's note is about 25 dollars, Abe Atkins, about 15 dollars, from 15 to 25 dollars to Bagwell and others about Carnesville. You can go down to fathers and get him to settle that as there is a settlement between father and Morris & me about those cows. Then the note John Henderson holds is about the amount. Be careful, if any one should refuse to take Confederate money, to have a witness, for it is a lawful tender and if they don't take it I will never pay them.

    If there is any left you can dispose of it as you think best. Father spoke to me least summer about some money. you can let him have it if you think best. I would have been extreamly glad to have come home, but I cant get off. I applied for a leave of absence but through the rascality of a certan Doctor in this regt, I

---

[101] See notes for the previous letter; *Kentucky Atlas & Gazetteer*, 1.
[102] Rigdon, *Georgia 43rd Infantry Regiment*, 165.
[103] Matthews, *Public Laws of the Confederate States*, 77–79.

have failed to get it. It may come to-night if so I will be home before you get this. Say nothing about this though. My foot is geting better.

Dear, send my clothing by Mr Carter. Send me one pair pants 2 shirts one pair socks one pair gloves 2 pair flannel drawers and the over coat. I will sell the one I now have to jim. He is transferred to this regt. now. Also send me some dried fruit if you can. send me as much as you can also some butter. I have a good mess chest with all the equipments necessary so I am fixing up to live.

You need not sent my boots now as I have a good pair. Oil them well and put them away. I could not get such a pair now for 30 dollars. Send me som potatoes if you can stick them in some corner. I forgot to mention the beding. Send me one comfort or two blankets.

Dear Mr. Carter is about redy to start I must close Tell dea little Nora that Pa is very well and thinks of "little dear" evey day. I would be vey glad to be with you to night and drink some new butter milk and eat potatoes and fresh butter. I must close. Write often

Yours most
Affectionatly
M. P. Alexander

Notes

Jesse Carter: He might have been Jesse Carter from Hall County, who would have been about forty-eight in 1862 and had two sons of military age.[104]

Carnesville: Carnesville was in Franklin County, Manning's family home. Manning lived there from the age of about ten, his age when the family moved there from South Carolina, until he left home.[105]

Manning Examines a Captain

Manchester Tenn Dec 6th, 1862

Captain John F. Rives Co K of the 43rd Regiment Geo Volunteers having applied for a certificate on which to ground his Resignation I do hereby certify that I have carefully examined this officer and find him affected with deafness of the left ear and partial deafness of the right ear and that in consequence thereof, he is in my opinion unfit for duty. I further declare my belief that he is wholy unable to discharge the duties of his office and will not be during the present war.

I therefore recommend that his Resignation be accepted.
M P Alexander Assistant
Surgeon 43rd Regt.

---

[104] US Census, 1860, Hall County.
[105] See introduction.

Notes

Manchester, Tennessee: Manchester is about sixty miles southeast of Nashville.[106]

Captain John F. Rives: He was the company commander of Company K. His resignation was approved later in December.[107]

Mississipi: Two weeks later, the 43rd, reorganized into a new brigade, boarded a train for Vicksburg, Mississippi.

---

[106] Rand McNally, "Tennessee State Road Map."
[107] Service records.

Chapter 14

Homefront, 1862–Early 1863

1862

Reuben H. Bowen

Thomas County Georgia
Aprile the 27th 1862

    Dear Uncle and Aunt [James and Thirza David] it becomes my painful duty to inform you of the death of Father who died last Wednesday the 23rd inst with Dropsy of the chest after a long a[nd] painful sickness, his funeral was preached the day he was buried.

    this leaves the balance of the family well Hiram[,] Malachi[,] Owen[,] and J. G. Lindsey are all in the army, Owen an[d] Green ware at home when Father died, on a sick furlow. Owen starts back to his post tomorrow morning. Green is not yet able to go back.

    I shall not go in the army as the conscript law does not reach me and it is verry well it is so for I do not see how it would be possible for me to leave home now. you must pardon my short letter this time as I am not in a proper frame of mind for writing, write us soon

    R H Bowen

Notes

Reuben H. Bowen: Reuben Hunter Bowen was the son of Thirza's brother, Perry Bowen, and his wife Mary Cox Bowen. When this letter was written, he was about thirty-six years old.[1]

Father: He was Thirza's brother Perry Bowen, who died April 23, 1862, at the age of sixty-three.[2]

Dropsy of the chest: Dropsy, or edema, is an excess of fluid in a body cavity, the chest in this case, that results in swelling.[3]

Hiram Malachi Owen and J. G. Lindsey: Hiram, Malachi, and Owen were Reuben's brothers. J. G. Lindsey was Reuben's brother-in-law.[4]

---

[1] US Census, 1860, Thomas County.
[2] Tombstone, Magnolia Plantation Cemetery, Thomas County, Georgia.
[3] "Dropsy," "Edema," *Webster's New World College Dictionary*, 447, 462.
[4] US Census, 1850, Thomas County; *Jackson County Marriage Book A B C, 1805–1860*, 379.

Green: This was John Green Lindsey, the husband of Reuben's sister Teresa Ann.[5]

conscript law: On April 16, 1862, President Davis signed into law a bill that authorized him to place into military service all white males between the ages of eighteen and thirty-five. At the time the letter was written, Reuben was thirty-six years old.[6]

Pillina and Milton Raymond Bell

Chulafinnee, Ala.
August the 15—1862
Dear parents and sisters [James, Thirza, and Annie David and Pillona Alexander]

I have seated myself to answer your very kind letters. Lony's dated July 20th, Mother's August the 3rd.

We were very glad to hear from you and oh, how thankful I do feel that Brothers S. B. and Ratio and James Neal got through the battle at Richmond without being killed. I was very sorry to hear that dear brother Ratio was in bad health. It is bad enough to be in camps when they are well. I hope he will succeed in getting a furlough or a discharge. We would be so glad to see him once more. All the children want to see him. If he does come home and you think he would be able to stand the trip, we would be glad for you to come and see us, though I do not want him to injure himself.

We regretted very much to hear of your suffering so much with your arm and shoulder, but thankful to hear in your last letter that you were well again. Dear Lony I am so glad that you got to see Dr. Alexander one time more, and we are proud that he is surgeon of the regt. and do hope that he will get back home and you will again be happy together.

There is a battalion of cavalry camped at Oxford Cal County. The conscript officers of the city are still holding on giving the people a chance to enlist, yet John started off to the army last Monday morning. He has gone to the company that Largus Bell is in. Myrtalas is going back to her father's to live. I am very sorry she is going to leave our neighborhood. She is a good-hearted thing. She has two children. I have decided for Dr. not to go to the war until he is obliged to go. The men in this county are nearly all gone now.

We understand there is factory thread in Widowee at four dollars per bunch. We will try to get what we need, and spin it up. We are much obliged to you for the offer of your thread, but I know you need it yourself and we do not see how

---

[5] Ibid.
[6] McPherson, *Embattled Rebel*, 70–72; Matthews, *Public Laws of the Confederate States*, 29; tombstone, Magnolia Plantation Cemetery, Thomas County, Georgia.

we could go to see you all this year. We want you all to come to see us when you can.

Dear Lony, don't weave so as to injure your health. We are all well. Mother, wool and thread are so high that you ought to ask a good price for your jeans.

Write often, give us all the news from brothers S. B. & Ratio, Dr. Alex, and James Neal. As ever, your devoted children,

M. R. & P. C. Bell

The children are telling me to write something for them, but I must mail this letter. I am very thankful to you for the envelopes you have sent me, but we have bought some at last.

P. C. Bell

Notes

Chulafinnee, Ala.: A settlement on Chulafinee Creek now in Cleburne County, Alabama.[7]

Dear parents and sisters: It seems that Lona Alexander has gone to live with her parents while Manning was away in the army.[8]

the battle at Richmond: This probably is a reference to the Seven Days Battles of June 25–July 1, 1862.[9]

Oxford Cal County: This is a reference to the town of Oxford in Calhoun County, Alabama.[10]

Dear Lony I am so glad that you got to see Dr. Alexander one time more, and we are proud that he is surgeon of the regt.: Manning Alexander had been appointed assistant surgeon of the 43rd and had been home on leave.[11]

The conscript officers of the city: These probably were officials appointed to implement the Confederate conscript act.

John: He was John H. Bell, brother of Dr. M. R. Bell, Pillina's husband.[12]

Largus Bell: He was Largus R. Bell, a brother of M. R. Bell.[13]

Myrtalas: She was Myrtalas X. Bell, a sister of M. R. Bell. She had married John P. Barker a couple of years earlier. At the time the letter was written, he had just enlisted in the Confederate army, and she apparently decided to return to her father in Georgia.[14]

---

[7] Read, *Indian Place Names in Alabama*, 20.
[8] See below in this chapter, Pillina Bell to the Davids, January 16, 1863.
[9] Boatner, *Civil War Dictionary*, 731–32; see also note to the letter from Simion of late July 1862 in chapter 12.
[10] *Rand McNally 2019 Road Atlas*, 4.
[11] See chapter 13.
[12] US Census, 1850, Cherokee County, Georgia.
[13] Ibid.
[14] Ibid., service records.

Widowee: This reference probably is to the town of Wedowee, or the area around it, in Randolph County, Alabama, a county adjoining Cleburne County to the south.[15]

Margaret Alexander

Franklin Co ga september the 25 1862

Dear daughter [Pillona] I set my self to respond to youre very kind letter. we ware truly glad to heare that you ware all blest with good health which is the gratest of all blessings and was glad to [k]now that you sympeside [sympathize] with us in our sore distress which semes to be all that we can bare. to have a deare son shot down in the b[l]oom of lif on the battle field and leve a wife and two little children to suffer want of many of the comforts of life is truly distresing but ther is a ray of com fort. he died an onerbe [honorable] death. died in the defence of the cappitel of his cntry and I hope has gone to rest.

from what sussanna wrote to me you wanted to [k]now how sam was. well he has bin at home about a month and started back last tusday. he never has bin very well since June. he got a furlow for ten days and was taken very sick on the rode home and was very bad for about ten days. he has got about and gone back but I feare he will relaps agane as he is very weak and lookes bad.

lizzy has had a very bad spell of newralgy in the fase but is geting better. the baby has had a bad spell of croope and cold but is well now. the rest of the famely is all well.

we recievd a letter from brother William O Alexander about the death of his son. he was wounded on the 27 of june in three places. he was shot thro the hips while liiing on the battle field. he said he went to richmond to him as soon as he got the word and found him in a bad fix but he had him cleend and [put] on a cleene bed and he apperd to to be a geting better for about a weak and took the fever and died in two days. he said that he was perfectly resind [resigned] to dy.

james lewis is not dead as was reported. bery got them all home and they are all well now and I exspect they are gone back. we have not heard from M P in a good while. we heard from james last weke. he was well then but I dred to hear from them for fear I hear something bad. you wrote to me tha M P had sent me som coffy which I thank him kindly for but I dont [k]now when I will get it as I dont [k]now when I will get th chance to come and see you and get it. we want to see you and little nora very bad. tell nora that grndma thinks about her evry day an wold give any thing to see her. granpa and robert and john wants to see her very bad. we want you to come down if you possile can and see us. we feele

---

[15] *Rand McNally 2019 Road Atlas*, 4.

very lonsum and it wold be a cosolation for you to come and stay a few days if [illegible].

I have all jameses close reddy to send to him so no mor at present. the famly all joines in giveng our love to you and all the famly. wright as son as you get this and let us [k]now how you are. I send you a pese of my dress [no signature]

Notes

dear son shot down in the b[l]oom of lif: He was Adam, one of Manning's younger brothers, a private in Company D of the 21st Georgia Volunteer Infantry. (Manning's mother refers to Manning as M. P. in this letter.) Adam was killed in Virginia at the Battle of Gaines Mill, one of the Seven Days battles, on June 27, 1862, at the age of twenty-six.[16]

two little children: These were Adam's daughters, Margaret, about two years old, and Nancy, less than a year.[17]

Sussanna: Adam's wife.[18]

Sam: Sam was Samuel H. Alexander, another of Manning's younger brothers. He was serving as a private with the 29th Georgia Infantry Regiment. See letters from him later.[19]

lizzy: This probably was Sam's wife, Mary E. Alexander. Her middle initial probably stands for Elizabeth.[20]

newralgy: Neuralgia in 1874 was defined as "A generic name for a number of diseases, the chief symptom of which is a very acute pain, exacerbating or intermitting, which follows the course of a nervous branch, extends to it ramifications, and seems, therefore, to be seated in the nerve."[21]

the baby: She was Sam and Lizzy's daughter, Buena, who was born in 1862.[22]

croope: Croup is "a condition resulting from any obstruction of the larynx, esp. an inflammation of the respiratory passages, with labored breathing, sharp and abrupt coughing, and laryngeal spasm."[23]

William O. Alexander and son: William O. Alexander was Manning's uncle. His son was James P. Alexander, about twenty years old, who was a private in Company K of the 1st Regiment of Rifles, South Carolina Volunteers. He died

---

[16] Service records; Chaplin, *Riches of Bunyan* (Alexander family copy).

[17] US Census, 1870, Franklin County, Georgia.

[18] Alexander family records in Chaplin, *Riches of Bunyan*.

[19] Alexander family records in Chaplin, *Riches of Bunyan*; US Census, 1870, Franklin County, Georgia; service records.

[20] US Census, 1870, Franklin County, Georgia.

[21] Dunglison, *Dictionary of Medical Science*, 698.

[22] US Census, 1870, Franklin County, Georgia.

[23] "Croup," *Webster's New World Dictionary*, 355.

on July 10, 1862, of wounds received on June 27 in the Battle of Gaines Mill, the same battle in which Adam Alexander was killed.[24]

James Lewis and bery: He was James W. Lewis who lived in Carrollton, Georgia, when he enlisted as a private in Company F., Cobbs Legion. His father was Elisha Berry Lewis, and his mother was Martha Poole Lewis, who was Margaret Alexander's sister. They lived in Anderson County, South Carolina. Beside James, Berry and Martha Lewis had two other sons who were old enough to serve in the army.[25]

James: James D. Alexander was another of Manning's younger brothers. He was 1st sergeant in the 9th Battalion Georgia Infantry until Manning brought him back from Kentucky. He then enlisted in the 43rd Georgia with Manning.[26]

grandpa and robert and john: Grandpa was Manning's father, Robert Alexander, and Robert and John were two more of Manning's younger brothers.[27]

1863

Pillina Bell

Chulafinnee, Alabama
January the 16, 1863
Dear Mother

Yours of the 22 December is now before me, though it was a long time on the road. We were getting uneasy about you. We were very thankful that you reached home safe, found all well and doing well.

We were glad to hear that dear little Ratio was fortunate enough to go through another battle without getting hurt, though he must have suffered a great deal with cold. It grieves me to think that we cannot hear from Brother Simeon and James Neal. I can't tell what to think of you for not getting letters from them, though I hope you have heard before this time.

Dear sister Lonie, I was very sorry indeed to hear of Dr. passing through Atlanta and you not having the chance to see him. But Lona, cheer up and be as happy as you possibly can under the circumstances. I do hope the day is not far distant when you will again be happy together. I know you are at Father's and they will all try to make you happy, but still that will not fill a husband's place. I

---

[24] Service records; *Michael McGee applicant vs. Jane Alexander, Elizabeth Alexander & others*, Court of Ordinary Records, Anderson District, South Carolina, August 20, 1849.

[25] US Census, 1860, Anderson County, South Carolina; service records.

[26] See chapter 14, Alexander family records in Chaplin, *Riches of Bunyan*; service records for J. D. Alexander listed under J. A. Alexander.

[27] Alexander family records in Chaplin, *Riches of Bunyan*.

will write to Dr. without fail. I would have written to him before, but I feared I could not interest him.

This has been the coldest day we have had this winter. We had some snow last night. I know Bear has suffered with cold today, and tomorrow will be colder than today. The poor soldiers in the army will be obliged to suffer the cold [in] this kind of weather.

We are all enjoying good health. Harriet never had any bad luck. She is as well as ever. Her babe grows finely.

Some of our soldiers have got home that were wounded in the Murfreesboro battle. They were in the 22nd Alabama regiment.

Write as soon as you receive this. Give all the news from the boys. Dr. and the children join me in love to you all. I remain Your devoted daughter until death.

Pillina C. Bell

Notes

Horatio...through another battle: This battle was the Battle of Fredericksburg, which was fought on December 13, 1862. In chapter 11, Horatio was ill in the hospital, but he had rejoined his regiment in time to fight in the Battle of Fredericksburg. He survived. More about this battle and Horatio's and Simeon's roles in it is in the next chapter.[28]

we cannot hear from Brother Simeon and James Neal: Both also survived the Battle of Fredericksburg.[29]

Dr. passing through Atlanta: Dr. M. P. Alexander passed through Atlanta around December 20 with the 43rd on his way by train to Vicksburg, Mississippi.[30]

Bear: This possibly was a reference to a horse or maybe a dog owned by the Bells.

Harriet and her babe: She probably is the girl whom Pillina referred to in chapter 1 in the letters of November 11, 1850, and December 1, 1853. Moreover, she may have been the Davids' enslaved girl who was listed as being four years old in the listing for James H. David in the 1850 federal slave schedule but who was missing from his listing in the 1860 slave schedule.

According to Pillina in her 1850 letter, she missed Harriet very much, and according to her 1853 letter, Harriet was living then with Pillina and Pillina's husband. Probably Harriet came from the Davids to live with Pillina sometime

---

[28] Boatner, *Civil War Dictionary*, 311–13; note to Simeon's letter, December 5, 1862, in chapter 14.

[29] Note to Simeon's letter, December 5, 1862, in chapter 15.

[30] Note to Manning's letter, April 24, 1863, in chapter 20.

between 1850 and 1853. If so, Harriet would have been about sixteen when this letter was written. It is unclear who is the father of her baby.

Murfreesboro battle: This battle is usually referred to as the Battle of Stones River. Stones River was near Murfreesboro, Tennessee, and the battle took place December 31, 1862–January 3, 1863.[31]

---

[31] Gallagher et al., *Civil War*, 130–32; Boatner, *Civil War Dictionary*, 803–808.

Chapter 15

Simeon and Horatio at Fredericksburg, December 1862–March 1863

1862

Simeon

Fredericksburg, Va.
Dec. 5—1862
My dear parents

After a considerable lapse of time, I seat myself this morning to devote a leisure moment in writing you. Let me say in the outset that I was never in better health than at present, nor have I been in the least unwell for several months. I used to be somewhat troubled with my bowels, had to be careful about my diet, but now my bowels are just right, and have not been out of order for months.

Our division left the Valley of Virginia on the 22 ult. and marched continuously for 12 days, a distance of 170 miles, through the most beautiful country and over the most delightful roads on earth. I think the Valley of Virginia is the eden of the whole earth, and its population before the war the happiest on earth. There is wheat enough in the Valley now to feed the Confederate army twelve months. Though 100 miles from railroad transportation, we were anxious to spend the winter in the Valley.

We marched up the Valley pike in the direction of Staunton 50 miles. We then turned in a southeastern direction across the Blue Ridge mountains, there being two principal ranges. It required one whole day to cross the main range, being fifteen mile from the foot of the mountains on one side to the foot of the mountains on the other.

The scenery was beautiful and grand beyond description. Although the mountain was very high, the road was so scientifically engineered that it was only a gentle slope. We could march all the time without fatigue. The road would frequently wind half a mile and go back within 30 yards of the road below.

Our Brigade was in front, and we were four hours in getting to the top. When we reached the summit, I imagined myself on the top of Fame's temple, and looking back on the army below forcibly reminded me of the toiling thousands who are struggling to reach the summit of that far-famed eminence. Some were nearly up and echoed back our triumphant shout with a shout of hope, some were two-thirds up, some half-way, and would stop by the wayside, as it were, to gather strength for another effort. Others were just starting on the toilsome journey. I stood and gazed at the beauties of nature until my soul was filled with a strange rapture, and I was forcibly reminded of the beautiful message that was indited by a young lady and transmitted to the magnetic wire for the first time after its completion in the United States—"What God hath wrought."

We continued our route by way of Madison and Orange courthouses to this point. The Confederates have a large force in this vicinity, confronting, no doubt, a still larger force of the enemy on the opposite side of the Rappahannock river. We may have a battle soon. No-one can tell. I understand the 16th Ga. Regt. is somewhere in this vicinity but I have not had an opportunity of hunting it up. I have not heard a word from Ratio or James Neal for several weeks.

I thought two months and even six weeks ago that I would be certain to get to go home and be with Fanny in her confinement. But I have learned that a man need make no calculation on anything with any degree of certainty while in the army. I hope it was convenient to you to go to Forsyth and be with her in her confinement. After I found that I could not get off, I thought it would be better to not inform Fanny that I was not coming, but let her still be looking for me up to the time of her confinement. I am extremely anxious to hear from you and from Fanny. I intend to come home as soon as I can possibly get off, but I cannot tell when that will be. I would not leave now till I see whether we will have a fight here if I could.

When you write me, give me all the news. Give me the news from Dr. Alexander, also from Dr. Bell and Sister Pillina. When you see Sue, tell her that a cousin of hers, Jesse Eaves, son of the preacher that married the old widow Thurmond, is a member of Co. K from Cass county, of our regiment. He is as gallant and brave young man as I ever saw. Previous to the battle of "Cedar Run," he was Corporal. On account of his gallantry, he was promoted the 2nd Sergt. of his company. After the battle of Manassas, Shantello, Harper's Ferry, and Shepherdstown, he was promoted by a vote of his co. to 3rd Lieut. his opponent only receiving 5 votes. On one occasion he came very near shooting some cowardly Virginians who were running out of a fight.

I have heard that Col William Williams of the 15th Ga. was killed at the battle of Sharpsburg, but do not know that it is positively true. When you write, give me the names of all my friends who have been killed in the late battle. For a month after the battle, we saw no papers, therefore we know nothing of who was killed except from hearsay.

I have extended this letter to a very great length. hope to hear from you soon. My love to Anna, Lona, the negroes, and all enquiring friends. Believe me as every your affectionate son S. B. David

Notes

marched continuously for 12 days, a distance of 170 miles: Another soldier on the same march estimated that they had marched 175 miles in twelve days.[1]

across the Blue Ridge mountains, there being two principal ranges: The two principal ranges were the Massanutten Mountain to the west and the Blue Ridge Mountain to the east. Simeon's brigade, part of A. P. Hill's Light Division in Stonewall Jackson's corps, marched across these two ranges by the Blue Ridge Turnpike, which extended some fifty-six miles from near New Market to Gordonsville. It had been completed about nine years earlier at a cost of $176,000, financed by selling shares of stock to individuals and the Commonwealth of Virginia.

The turnpike crossed the main range, the Blue Ridge Mountain, at Fishers Gap. Its route proceeded through what now is Shenandoah National Park, winding up the west side of the Blue Ridge Mountain, as Simeon described, along roughly the route of present-day Red Gate Fire Road to today's Skyline Drive. It then proceeded down the east side along approximately the present-day Rose River Fire Road, State Route 670, and State Route 231 to Madison, Virginia.[2]

Fame's temple: This may be a reference to the poem "The Temple of Fame: A Vision" by Alexander Pope. A line near the beginning reads: "I stood, methought, betwixt Earth, Seas, and Skies; / The whole Creation open to my Eyes ..."[3]

"What God hath wrought": This phrase is from Numbers 23:23, which reads in part, "it shall be said of Jacob and of Israel, What hath God wrought!" It was the first message Samuel F. B. Morse sent and received over a telegraph wire on May 24, 1844. The message was suggested by Nancy Goodrich Ellsworth, who passed it on to her daughter Annie Ellsworth (with whom Morse was in love), who passed it on to Morse.[4]

We may have a battle soon.... I understand the 16th Georgia is somewhere in the vicinity: Both Simeon's prediction and understanding turned out to be accurate. The Battle of Fredericksburg was fought on December 13, 1862, and both Simeon and the 14th Georgia and Horatio and the 16th Georgia were part of it.

In December 1862, the principal goal of the Union army was still to capture Richmond. Fredericksburg was on the most direct overland route from

---

[1] Welch, *Confederate Surgeon's Letters to His Wife*, 36.

[2] *Virginia Gazetteer & Atlas*, 68, 73–74, Robertson, *General A. P. Hill*, 158; Dewberry, *History of the 14th Georgia*, 40; "Map 10, Appalachian Trail and Other Trails in Shenandoah National Park Central District"; Virginia Highway marker JE7, "Blue Ridge Turnpike"; Woodward, *For Home and Honor*, 60–61; Gottfried, *Maps of Fredericksburg*, 261–62.

[3] See Early English Books Online Text Creation Partnership, http://name.umdl.umich.edu/004809333.0001.000.

[4] Howe, *What Hath God Wrought*, 1–3.

Washington to Richmond, as it still is today. (Today Interstate 95, the major east coast interstate highway from Maine to Richmond and further south, passes along the edge of Fredericksburg.) A modern historian has written, "A direct approach to Richmond [in 1862] was desirable because it would require a short and more easily defensible line of communications while shielding Washington."[5]

Replacing McClellan, Major General Ambrose E. Burnside had just become commanding general of the Army of the Potomac. By late November 1862, he had amassed 120,000 to 130,000 men on the opposite side of the Rappahannock River from Fredericksburg. Unfortunately for him, the pontoon bridges he needed to cross the river and attack Lee's Confederates on the other side had not yet arrived. While Burnside and the Union army waited for them, Lee received reinforcements, including Stonewall Jackson's Corps containing Simeon and the 14th Georgia, and skillfully arranged and strongly fortified his position.[6]

After the pontoons finally got to Fredericksburg, Burnside planned to attack the Confederates at two main places: the Confederate right flank located downriver south of Fredericksburg and the middle of the Confederate line at Fredericksburg itself. The goal was for the attacking force downriver to cave in the Confederates' right flank, then pursue it upriver to attack the Confederates in and around Fredericksburg itself. Meanwhile a second Union force was to attack Fredericksburg head-on, go through the town, and attack the Confederates on the town's other side. The combined Union forces thus would meet at Fredericksburg and compel the entire Confederate force to withdraw in shambles.[7]

At the opening of the battle, Lee's forces numbered some seventy-five thousand men, about fifty thousand fewer than Burnside's Army of the Potomac. Jackson's Corps was stationed on the right of the Confederate line with Hill's Division on the far right. Unfortunately for the Confederates, Hill positioned his men in such a way as to leave a gap of "scraggly woods, dense underbrush, and swampy ground" some six hundred yards wide between two of his front line brigades facing the Union army. Just behind one of these front line brigades were Simeon and the 14th Georgia in Brigadier General Edward L. Thomas's brigade, all Georgians.[8]

By the morning of the 13th, Union forces had received the pontoons and crossed the Rappahannock River to the Confederates' side—they both occupied

---

[5] Gottfried, *Maps of Fredericksburg*, 20; O'Reilly, *Fredericksburg Campaign*, 21.

[6] Gallagher et al., *Civil War*, 68–69; O'Reilly, *Fredericksburg Campaign*, 23–27, 32, 45–48; Gottfried, *Maps of Fredericksburg*, 80–81; Allan, *Stonewall Jackson*, 2:463.

[7] Gallagher et al., *Civil War*, 69; O'Reilly, *Fredericksburg Campaign*, 53–54; Rable, *Fredericksburg! Fredericksburg!*, 144, 149, 185.

[8] Robertson, *General A. P. Hill*, 160–61 (quote); O'Reilly, *Fredericksburg Campaign*, 128–32; Gottfried, *Maps of Fredericksburg*, 76–77, 80–81; Allan, *Stonewall Jackson*, 2:468–69, 477–79; Rable, *Fredericksburg! Fredericksburg!*, 148, 193–94.

Fredericksburg itself and held the ground across the river in front of the Confederate right flank. Now the Federals were ready to attack.[9]

The Downriver Attack

Downriver, around eight thirty to nine in the morning on December 13, elements of Burnside's Union army, who already had crossed the Rappahannock, began marching in the direction of Jackson's Confederate line. Initially they were delayed by Confederate artillery. After one o'clock, however, some Union units forced their way through the boggy gap in Jackson and Hill's line, flanking and scattering men of the front line brigades on either side. In response to a request for help, Thomas advanced his brigade, the 14th Georgia (Simeon commanding his company) and the 49th Georgia leading, against the Union forces that had broken through.[10]

These two lead regiments met the Union soldiers, stopped them, and forced them to retreat. The 14th Georgia and Simeon then followed the fleeing Federals through a patch of woods to the edge of a field. There Colonel Folsom, the regiment's commander, ordered his men to kneel behind a line of trees, keep quiet, and wait.[11]

As they were getting settled, the men of the 14th saw, emerging from trees on the other side of the field, several lines of Union soldiers advancing "in a splendid line of battle." Folsom told his men to wait until the Federals got within fifty yards before opening fire. However, "a gaily dressed mounted officer" prancing before the Union men and encouraging them onward, proved too attractive a target. First one Confederate, then others, took a shot at him. The officer fell, the Federals halted, and Folsom ordered his men to fire, which they did with a deadly volley.[12]

In response, the first Union line fired once, then, caught in an open field, quickly turned and fled. The second line advanced and stood and fired for ten to fifteen minutes before they, too, fled. A third line advanced, lasted a short while, then "panic-stricken" and "casting away their guns and blankets so as to expedite their flight," they joined the others in a rush to the rear. At last, the three other

---

[9] Gallagher et al., *Civil War*, 71; Gottfried, *Maps of Fredericksburg*, 84–85.
[10] Robertson, *General A. P. Hill*, 161–66; O'Reilly, *Fredericksburg Campaign*, 137–211; Gottfried, *Maps of Fredericksburg*, 88–124; Rable, *Fredericksburg! Fredericksburg!*, 194–217, 244; Allan, *Stonewall Jackson*, 2:482–89; *Southern Recorder*, January 6, 1863.
[11] O'Reilly, *Fredericksburg Campaign*, 210–12; *Weekly Constitutionalist* (Augusta), January 21, 1863; Allan, *Stonewall Jackson*, 2:489.
[12] O'Reilly, *Fredericksburg Campaign*, 210–12; *Weekly Constitutionalist* (Augusta), January 21, 1863 (quotes); Allan, *Stonewall Jackson*, 2:489.

regiments of Thomas's Brigade, which had been near the 14th but unobserved because of a dense thicket, joined the 14th.[13]

The brigade was united just in time. Federals in greater force attacked for their fourth try. In the fight that followed, the brigade held, but some Federal troops managed to maneuver around the 14th's flank on the right of the entire brigade line. As the Federals advanced toward the exposed flank, Colonel Folsom saw them and promptly ordered an attack with fixed bayonets, much like the attack he led at Cedar Mountain. The regiment "with a mighty cheer" charged the Union force. Only then did the Federals pull back from the flank and retreat.[14]

About the same time, Burnside's army withdrew all along Jackson's front. By three o'clock that afternoon, the major fighting on the downriver front to the south of Fredericksburg was over. The Union army had failed to achieve its objective of routing the Confederates.[15]

In that fighting, the 14th Georgia had lost about a third of its men. A Milledgeville, Georgia, newspaper listed losses for Company E "Lt S B David com'ding" as nineteen wounded, including "Sergt L H Hope, thigh severely; Corpl J L Bennett, abdomen, slight; J L Light, arm and thigh, severely...."[16]

The Town Attack

At Fredericksburg itself, the Union attack began at roughly eleven o'clock on the morning of the 13th. Federal forces had gathered at the city's western-most line of buildings. (They also had crossed the Rappahannock earlier while being heavily contested.) A few hundred yards beyond, across an open field that sloped slightly upward, Confederate infantry and artillery awaited them.

The Southerners' infantry stood at a well-traveled sunken road in a ditch behind a stone wall four feet high and four hundred yards long. A modern historian wrote that the stone wall was "just the right height for a rifleman to rest his gun barrel, and more than high enough to protect him as he sank down to reload." The Confederate artillery was arranged just behind the wall and the sunken road on two hills known as Marye's Heights. Like the infantry, the artillery also faced the open field over which the Union troops must advance.[17]

As Simeon thought, the 16th Georgia and Simeon's brother Horatio were in fact in the vicinity. The 16th was part of Brigadier General Thomas R. R.

---

[13] O'Reilly, *Fredericksburg Campaign*, 210–12; *Central Georgian* (Sandersville), January 7, 1862; Folsom, *Heroes and Martyrs*, 151.

[14] O'Reilly, *Fredericksburg Campaign*, 212 (quote).

[15] Allan, *Stonewall Jackson*, 2:491; Gottfried, *Maps of Fredericksburg*, 136.

[16] *Southern Recorder*, January 6, 1863; Folsom, *Heroes and Martyrs*, 151.

[17] Allan, *Stonewall Jackson*, 2:468, 492–94; O'Reilly, *Fredericksburg Campaign*, 246–51; Gottfried, *Maps of Fredericksburg*, 238–139; Matteson, *A Worse Place than Hell*, 229 (quote).

Cobb's brigade in Major General Lafayette McLaws's division of Lieutenant General James Longstreet's Corps. It was Cobb's Brigade, along with a regiment from North Carolina, who on the 13th stood with their muskets in the sunken road behind the stone wall awaiting an attack.[18]

At first that day, the 16th Georgia Regiment was not with the rest of Cobb's Brigade. About noon on December 11, two days earlier, the 16th, along with another regiment, had been ordered to take up a position on the river just south of Fredericksburg to help a Mississippi regiment defend against a Federal crossing of the river there. Despite the presence of the three regiments, however, federal infantry succeeded in crossing the river, and with Union artillery firing from high ground across the river, forced the Confederate regiments to retreat to a secondary position. There they spent the night.[19]

The next morning, December 12, the 16th rejoined its brigade at Marye's Heights, but by then, General Cobb had positioned the rest of the brigade on the sunken road. He decided not to have the 16th join them. Instead, he placed them in reserve on the other side of the Heights from the sunken road.[20]

On the 13th as the Federals advanced across the open field toward the stone wall, the Confederates behind it waited until the Union men were close enough that they could "count the buttons" on the Federals' blouses. Then, as a Confederate later wrote, we "rose to our feet & poured volley after volley into their ranks which told a most deadening effect…another column & another & still another came to their support. But our well-aimed shots were more than they could stand." An artillery officer on Marye's Heights observed, "the Georgians in the road below us rose up, and, glancing an instant along their rifle barrels, let loose a storm of lead into the faces of the advance brigade. This was too much; the column hesitated, and then, turning, took refuge behind the [nearby] bank.[21]

By mid-afternoon, the Confederates had repulsed several strong Union attacks. Then other regiments, including the 16th Georgia and Horatio, were advanced to reinforce those already behind the stone wall. The 16th took its position at the far right part of the wall.[22]

---

[18] *OR*, ser. 1, vol. 21, 579–80, 1070; *Central Georgian*, January 7, 1863.

[19] *OR*, ser. 1, vol. 21, 579, 599; *Central Georgian*, January 7, 1863; Byrd, *Confederate Sharpshooter*, 53; J. W. Woods, "History of Service," 110; *Southern Banner*, December 24, 1862, January 7, 1863.

[20] Byrd, *Confederate Sharpshooter*, 53–54; O'Reilly, *Fredericksburg Campaign*, 103.

[21] S. A. Cunningham, ed., *Confederate Veteran*, 7:309 (1st quote); Gallagher et al., *Civil War*, 72–73 (2nd quote); Owen, "The Yankees Attack Marye's Heights," 237 (3rd quote); J. W. Woods, "History of Service," 111; *OR*, ser. 1, vol. 21, 608; O'Reilly, *Fredericksburg Campaign*, 246–354.

[22] *OR*, ser. 1, vol. 21, 580, 608; Allan, *Stonewall Jackson*, 2:499, 502–503; Byrd, *Confederate Sharpshooter*, 54–56.

The soldiers behind the wall were now four deep. As General McLaws later described, once the Federals got close enough, "The front rank, firing, stepped back, and the next in rear took its place and, after firing, was replaced by the next, and so on in rotation. In this way the volley firing was made nearly continuous and…very destructive." A North Carolinian later described the results on the Union attacks: "They came up by acres and our boys fired into the dense masses without fear of missing and with a fair prospect of cutting down two at a time." One Union soldier was riveted by a particularly eerie effect of that continuous firing: "the corpses that covered the ground in our front seemed to be kept constantly in motion from the kick of the rebel bullets striking them."[23]

Along with other infantry units behind the stone wall and the artillery on Marye's Heights, the 16th helped turn away several more Union assaults. A modern historian has likened the successive charges and repulses to "successive waves of a surf dashing against a shore, breaking up, receding, leaving a thin line [of dead] on the sand to mark their farthest reach." More succinctly, one Union general observed that the area in front of the sunken road "was a great slaughter pen."[24]

As it began to get dark, the Union finally stopped sending its men forward. The field in front of the stone wall was covered with dead soldiers in blue. As a Confederate soldier wrote, "a man could not walk along without stepping on dead bodies." In the fighting before and immediately around the stone wall, there were eight Union casualties for every one Confederate casualty. One Georgia Confederate wrote home to his wife immediately after the battle of its effect on the Union: "many good and true women that could say 'Husband' last Saturday morning when they rose were widows when the sun set and many children that could say 'Father' were orphans."[25]

Cobb's Brigade was not unscathed. Its most prominent loss was its commander, Brigadier General Thomas R. R. Cobb, the same man Simeon heard address the Georgia legislature passionately back in 1860 (see a note to Simeon's letter of January 23, 1861, in chapter 6). He was killed by an exploding Union shell shortly after the first Union assault. The 16th itself had four killed, sixty-

---

[23] McLaws, "The Confederate Left at Fredericksburg," 3:93 (1st quote); Walkup, *Writings of a Rebel Colonel*, 81 (2nd quote); Reardon, "The Forlorn Hope," 92 (3rd quote).

[24] Stackpole, *Battle of Fredericksburg*, 38 (1st quote); Gallagher et al., *Civil War*, 72–73 (2nd quote).

[25] O'Reilly, *Fredericksburg Campaign*, 458 (1st quote); Lane, ed., *"Dear Mother: Don't Grieve about me,"* 199 (2nd quote); Allan, *Stonewall Jackson*, 2:506–507; O'Reilly, *Fredericksburg Campaign*, 363ff, 499.

two wounded, and four missing. Company B, Horatio's company, had three men wounded.[26]

The Union Retreats across the Rappahannock

Two days later, on December 15, the Union army retreated back across the river. General Burnside did not renew an attack, and the fighting in Virginia had ended for 1862. In late January, Burnside was replaced by General Joseph Hooker. Both Simeon and Horatio had survived.[27]

be with Fanny in her confinement: Fanny had become pregnant during Simeon's last leave. A girl, Virginia Frances "Jennie" David, was born in November or December 1862. Family tradition holds that Simeon wanted her named for the state of Virginia.[28]

1863

Simeon David as Recorder of a Court of Inquiry

January 3, 1863
Confederate States of America

To Lt S. B. David Co 'E' 14th Regt Ga Vols. as Recorder of Court of Inquiry convened by order of Gen A. P. Hill at Gen Thomas, Head Quarters on the 3rd of Jan 1863 for the trial of Lt. J. Morris Co 'E' 35th Regt Ga Vols,

[F]or (8) eight days service as Recorder $1.25 per Diem $10.00
Jan 3rd 1863   Approved
                     [s] RH Gray, Lt. Col 22d N. C.
                     Presdt Court of Inquiry.

Received of R T Taylor [illegible] $10.00

Ten Dollars in full of (8) Eight days service as Recorder of court of Inquiry in the trial of Lt. Morris Co 'E' 35th Regt Ga Vols held at Gen Thomas, Head Quarters and convened by order of Gen A. P. HIll

                     S. B. David 1st Lt Co 'E'
                     14th Regt Ga Vols and Recorder of
                     Court of inquiry

---

[26] Byrd, *Confederate Sharpshooter*, 56–58; *OR*, ser. 1, vol. 21, 584; *Southern Banner*, December 24, 1862, and January 14, 1863.

[27] Byrd, *Confederate Sharpshooter*, 58–60; Gottfried, *Maps of Fredericksburg*, 240, 250.

[28] Note to Simeon's letter of December 21, 1861, in chapter 12; letter in this chapter from Simeon dated January 21, 1863; email from David Hopper, a Simeon descendant, dated November 3, 2016.

Notes

Recorder of Court of Inquiry: Courts of inquiry were convened "to examine into the nature of any transaction, accusation, or imputation against any officer or soldier." A court of inquiry was an investigative body whose duty was only to provide information to a commander. Unless required to do so, it was prohibited from giving an opinion on the merits of the matter being investigated.

A court of inquiry could be used to determine whether a court martial should be brought against an officer or soldier. A court of inquiry also could be requested by a soldier or officer to clear his name from some adverse imputation.

The specific job of the recorder was "to reduce the proceedings and evidence to writing" and to administer oaths to members of the court.[29]

Simeon was one of three officers, who, on December 10, 1862, were ordered to assemble "on the 13th December 1862 or as soon thereafter as practicable to investigate the circumstances leading to the order issued from the Head Quarters of Maj. Genl. A. P. Hill's division Sept. 24th 62, and subject to the approval of the Secretary of War, dropping him [Lt. Morris] from the rolls of his company."[30]

J. Morris: He was 2nd Lieutenant John F. Morris of Company E, 35th Georgia Voluntary Infantry Regiment. On September 24, 1862, General A. P. Hill's headquarters ordered him "dropped from the rolls of his company," that is, he was cashiered or dismissed. What precisely Morris was charged with doing or not doing that led to his dismissal has not been discovered. After this order was issued, Lieutenant Morris requested General Lee to order a court of inquiry to examine the reasons for the order, and General Lee did so.[31]

The court of inquiry, of course, was not held on December 13, the date of the Battle of Fredericksburg. On December 30, it was postponed still further when one of the three officers on the court was replaced because he was absent on sick leave. According to Simeon's payment records above, the court convened on January 3, 1863, and was in session for eight days.[32]

A record of the court proceedings and their results has not been found. Lieutenant Morris's service records, however, do not contain any entries after

---

[29] Bunch, *Military Justice*, 23, 152–53.

[30] Special Order 267, paragraph XVI, September 24, 1862, M921, "Orders and Circulars Issued by the Army of the Potomac and the Army and Department of Northern Virginia C.S.A. 1861–1866," roll 2:253, NARA.

[31] Special Order 267, paragraph XVI, September 24, 1862, M921, "Orders and Circulars Issued by the Army of the Potomac and the Army and Department of Northern Virginia C.S.A. 1861–1866," roll 2:253, NARA; Morris Service records.

[32] Special Order 282, paragraph XVI, December 30, 1862, M921, "Orders and Circulars Issued by the Army of the Potomac and the Army and Department of Northern Virginia C.S.A. 1861–1866," roll 2:6–7, NARA; Service records of Lieutenant Colonel Thomas Ruffin, 13th Regiment North Carolina Infantry (state troops).

September 30, 1862. Yet an Atlanta newspaper listed the casualties among the brigade staff of General William T. Wofford, a native Georgian, at the Battle of Chancellorsville (fought in May 1863). The list included a "Lieut J Morris" who was "wounded in the side seriously."

This J. Morris may or may not have been the same J. Morris of the court of inquiry. Possibly J. Morris of the 35th was exonerated by the court of inquiry and was allowed back in the army. Further, it may be that Morris found his way back into the army in some way despite being dismissed earlier. A position on a senior officer's staff was not an elected position but was made by appointment by the senior officer. General Wofford could have appointed Morris to his staff regardless of his past record.[33]

Simeon

Vickery's Crossing
Jan. 21—1863
My affectionate parents

I avail myself of the opportunity offered this morning of writing to inform you that I reached home last Friday night and found Fanny and the children all well. We have concluded to try to visit you to embrace the 1st Sunday in Feb. Our intention now is to leave home tomorrow week, the 29th, and reach your house Friday the 30th, and stay till Monday morning. I reckon we will bring none of the children but the babe. I think the babe is about the prettiest child we have ever had.

Sister Mary Neal came up on Monday night and stayed with us till yesterday. All well. James sent her $80 by me.

I have not determined yet whether I will make an effort to extend my furlough. I hardly think I will. I do not want to be away from the army long.

I have not seen Horatio for several weeks before I left the camp. Suppose he is well.

I believe I think of nothing else that would interest you. Fanny and the children join in love to you all. I remain Your affectionate son, S. B. David

P. S. I have just written to Sue to meet us at your house, that will obviate the trouble of your writing or sending. S. B. D.

Notes

Vickery's Crossing: A few miles southwest of Cumming, this was the location of Fanny and Simeon's home in Forsyth County. Apparently Simeon was home on leave.

---

[33] *Southern Confederacy* (Atlanta), May 18, 1863; Bledsoe, *Citizen-Officers*, 50.

I reckon we will bring none of the children but the babe: Simeon and Fanny's children then were Mary Eleanora "Ellen," age six; Thirza Lena, age five; Sarah B. "Sallie," age three; and Virginia Frances "Jennie," only about a month or six weeks old.[34]

James: He was James R. Neal, Mary David Neal's son and Simeon's nephew. He was in Company B, 38th Georgia Volunteer Infantry.[35]

Sue: She was Sue Moon David, widow of Simeon's brother Owen Thomas David.[36]

Simeon

Camp Gregg near Fredericksburg, Va.
March 12—1863
My dear parents

I will avail myself of an opportunity afforded this morning of writing you to inform you of my continued good health and spirits. I left home Feb the 10th Tuesday and reached Richmond on the following Saturday. I stopped over there one week having some claims collected for the families of deceased soldiers. I reached the regt. on the 21st of Feb. in the best of health and found our noble company all well.

On Sunday the 22nd of February the biggest snow fell that I ever saw, being on an average one foot in depth. It lay on the ground several days during which the regt. and brigades had some of the finest sport snowballing I ever saw. The weather for the past ten days has been very changeable though we have had a good deal of good weather.

Everything is quiet on both sides of the Rappahannock, except that the Yankees fired a few artillery shots on yesterday morning. We have had no explanation yet.

Our regiment is still in winter quarters and would be doing finely if we could get a little more beef to eat. The men have eaten beef till they like it so much better than bacon. A beef's liver is a very rare dish. Officers have to pay very high now for their commissaries, 40 cts per pound for bacon, 20 cts for beef, 8cts for flour. The Government is issuing plenty of sugar now, but we have done without until we do not care much about it.

---

[34] US Census, 1870, Polk County, Georgia; headstone for Ella David Hagan Trippe, Old Taylorsville Church Cemetery, Polk County, Georgia; headstone for Lenna David Pittman, Lime Branch Cemetery, Polk County, Georgia; headstone for Sallie B. Lowry, Rose Hill Cemetery Rockmart, Polk County, Georgia; letter from Simeon dated December 5, 1862, above.

[35] See notes on James Neal in earlier chapters.

[36] See chapters 3 and 10.

General Lee has just detailed a general court-martial for our Brigade for the trial of commissioned officers and capital offences of which I am appointed Judge Advocate. The court is to be a permanent one for the trial [of] offences already committed. Our captain Lester is under arrest under charges preferred by myself and will probably be tried by that court.

We are all looking with a great deal of anxiety to Charleston and Savannah. I am glad that Gov. Brown has called out his militia officers who have been skulking behind their little commissions to keep out of the service of their country. If there is a fight, I hope they will get in it.

I have not seen Horatio or heard one word from him since my return to the regiment and with all the inquiries that I have made, I do not know if McLaws's division has left the vicinity of Fredericksburg. I have understood from some that it had, from others that it had not. There was a young lieut. down here from the 16th Ga Regt. a few days before I reached here that told the boys that Horatio was quite well.

At the urgent request of Mr. George Kellogg, I made an application for a furlough of 8 days to go under flag of truce to Manassas battleground to look for remains of his son Freeman, but Gen Hill said it was unsafe to go now, the enemy being in possession of the country.

Our regt. goes on picket every twelfth day and will have to go tomorrow. I have not heard from Fanny since I left home. I had your jeans made into a beautiful suit that is the admiration of the whole regiment. When I sit down to our little side bacon, bread and wheat coffee, I think of the splendid fare under which your table literally groaned when I was there. Write soon. Love to all. Your affectionate son,

S. B. David

Notes

Camp Gregg: This camp was located about eight miles below (downriver) Fredericksburg.[37]

Judge Advocate: the judge advocate was "the most important person on a military court or court martial" in the Confederate Army. He performed many, in some cases all, of the duties that in a civilian criminal trial today would be performed by the clerk of court, court reporter, prosecutor, and judge. It was his duty, among other things, to take the defendant's plea, swear in witnesses, and record the court proceedings, including the testimony of all witnesses. He also was the prosecutor although he could deputize someone else to prosecute in his place. In this role he examined and cross-examined witnesses and even could give evidence

---

[37] Robertson, *General A. P. Hill*, 169; Folsom, *Heroes and Martyrs*, 151; Smedlund, *Camp Fires of Georgia Troops*, 141.

at the trial. In addition, he advised other members of the court "on points of law, custom, and form, and invites its attention to every deviation therefrom." Moreover, if the defendant was accompanied by someone as counsel, that person could not ask questions of witnesses directly but had to submit questions to the judge advocate in writing, and the judge advocate would put the questions to the witness.

The members of the court, a minimum of five officers, acted as a jury, making a determination of guilty or not guilty and passing sentence. Court members also could question witnesses.

Overall, as a manual on the duties of a judge advocate indicated, "Justice is the object for which the court is convened and the Judge Advocate appointed; to this aim all their inquiries and attention ought to be directed."

The judge advocate was required to submit a record of the proceedings to the commander-in-chief who ordered the court martial. The commander-in-chief could sign and approve the verdict and sentence or remand the case for reconsideration by the same court that heard the case originally.[38]

Capt Lester is under arrest: Richard P. Lester was the original commander of Company E of the 14th, Simeon's company. He assumed the duties of the major of the regiment on November 8, 1862, four months before this letter was written, when that office became vacant because of the promotion of the officer who had held that position. On the same date, Simeon assumed the duties of the position vacated by Lester, commander of Company E.[39]

Lester faced four charges: conduct unbecoming an officer and gentleman, disgraceful conduct in the presence of the enemy, drunkenness, and absence without leave. A general court martial was appointed on March 7, 1863, to try Lester on those charges. His and Simeon's regimental commander Colonel R. W. Folsom was appointed president (senior officer) of the court martial. Lester's trial began approximately a month later.[40]

Lieutenant Josiah Patterson, also in Company E, wrote home about Lester's court martial: "Capt. Lesters trial ceases this evening [April 21, 1863]. It will be sometime before the finding of the court is known as Genl Lee must review and approve the sentence before it is made public. But my impression is that the sentence will not exceed a reprimand of the Brigadeer Genl or Col of our Regt. It

---

[38] Gilchrist, *Duties of a Judge Advocate*, 2, 10–12 (2nd quote), 16–21, 37–40 (quote); Young, "Instructions for the guidance of Courts Martial and Judges Advocates," 2, 6–7, 9; Bunch, *Military Justice*, 2–3, 6–7 (1st quote), 15–20, 35–36, 149–50, 152.

[39] See note in chapter 12.

[40] General Order No. 34, paragraph II, Headquarters of the Army of Northern Virginia, March 7, 1863, and General Order No. 66, paragraph XV, Headquarters of the Army of Northern Virginia, May 25, 1853, M921, "Orders and Circulars Issued by the Army of the Potomac and the Army and Department of the Army of Northern Virginia C. S. A. 1861–1866," roll 1, NARA.

may not amount to that." (Patterson also mentioned in his letter of April 21, 1863: "Lieut David is on Court Martial.")[41]

Patterson was correct that the outcome would not damage Lester seriously. Lester was found not guilty on all four charges, but he was found guilty of "on the evening of the 1st of September 1862, act[ing] imprudently in the presence of the common foe, by exclaiming, 'Men, take care of yourselves, we are flanked,' at and near the battle field of Chantilly." (The Battle of Chantilly was fought on September 1, 1862, as Jackson pursued the retreating Union General Pope after Pope's loss at Second Manassas, August 29–30.)

The court, however, explained that "considering the circumstances, we attach no further criminality thereto." The court also found that Lester "Did leave his regiment without proper authority, and did report himself immediately at a hospital in Richmond." This latter incident took place in October 1862. These were considered minor infractions, and for them the court sentenced Lester to be reprimanded by the president of the court martial (his then commanding officer) in the presence of the members of the court only.[42]

On review of the sentence of the court, General Lee approved the court's findings and sentence and continued, "but inasmuch as to an officer of true military spirit, the censure of his peers, without regard to the words by which this is conveyed, is as severe as it can be made—so much of the sentence as require the reprimand to be administered by the president of the court is remitted. He will be relieved from arrest and resume his sword."[43]

As noted above, Lester had assumed the duties of major in the regiment, the third highest ranking officer in the regiment's chain of command, *after* the incidents for which he was charged took place and before the court martial was held. That factor probably was taken into account in his sentence. He later was promoted to lieutenant colonel and in September 1864 became colonel and commander of the regiment. Simeon took Lester's place as company commander when Lester was promoted to major.[44]

Both Simeon and Patterson refer to Lester as "Capt. Lester," and the court martial records refer to him in that rank also. Yet as mentioned, Lester had been promoted to major several months earlier, on November 8, 1862. What seems likely to have happened was that Simeon and Lester, as ordered, undertook the duties of a higher office because of a vacancy in that office. Later, when they were promoted officially to the rank appropriate to that office, the promotion was

---

[41] Patterson, letter of April 21, 1863.
[42] General Order No. 66; Lester service records; Wagner, *Timeline of the Civil War*, 89.
[43] General Order No. 66.
[44] Lester's and Simeon's Service records and see chapter 12.

backdated to the date they actually assumed the duties of that office. Before the official promotion, however, they retained the rank they had earlier.

Although Simeon brought the charges against Lester and probably also testified against him, that seems not to have hurt Simeon. He received his official promotion to captain about two months after the court martial ended although, as noted above, the promotion apparently was backdated to November of the year before.[45]

Charleston and Savannah: The Union navy had established a blockade of both Charleston and Savannah, but it was not completely successful in preventing blockade runners from entering those ports.

At Charleston, Union forces earlier had attempted to capture the city by land but had been unsuccessful. Then on the last day of January, Confederate ships took the offensive. They confronted the blockaders outside the harbor and extensively damaged two of them. This action, however, did not lift the blockade for any length of time. Around the time of Simeon's letter, the Confederate commander in Charleston was reporting, "Already six monitors [as in the *Monitor* and the *Merrimac*]…are in the waters of my department…and transports with troops are still arriving from the North." He did not believe an attack would be delayed for long, and it was not. On April 7, Charleston harbor was attacked by fully nine new Union ironclads. The Confederates, however, were able to repulse them.[46]

Savannah was protected from the south by Fort McAllister on the Ogeechee River. On January 27, a Union ironclad and several wooden gunboats vigorously shelled the fort for most of the day with little results. Union ships also bombarded the Fort on February 1, 27, and 28 and on March 3, with the same minimal results. Despite the Union's lack of success, these continued attacks on Savannah's principal defense were unsettling.[47]

---

[45] Simeon's Service records.
[46] Foote, *Civil War*, 2:221–32.
[47] Welborn and Houston, "Union Blockade and Coastal Occupation," 54–55.

Chapter 16

Homefront: Fire, Early 1863

A. Adams to Thirza David

Mch 19—63
Mrs David
    My Dear friend I sent you yesterday by Manda Hogan[,] as use[d] to be[,] some paper and 1 Botte of ink and we suckseded in getting one Bolt of cloth which we send to you, thinking it will help you a little as you have lost all of your clothes.

    I would like to send you something else, but you know thair is nuthing here in the way of dress goods. I am rather affraid to send the cloth by the Hack, but will risk it anyway as you may need it rite way. I Could not get it yesterday as I would have sent it with the paper and please dont let any one know anything about us sending it to you. I will tell you why when I see you.

    Write me as soon as you get the cloth as I shall be anxious to know if it reaches you,
    In haste your true friend
    A. Adams
    March 19th 1863

Notes

as you have lost all of your clothes: Thirza and James David had a fire that destroyed a part of their home and outbuildings. At the time, Pillona and her daughter Nora were living with the Davids, as was the Davids' daughter, Anna. (See following letters.) Although they also lost a great portion of their belongings, too, among the things they saved were the earlier letters that are in this volume.

Hack: Horse or wagon for hire.[1]

A Adams: She or he has not been identified.

Pillona and Milton Raymond Bell

Chulafinne, Ala.
March 21—1863
Dear parents and sisters [James, Thirza, and Annie David and Pillona Alexander]
    We received your kind favor of the 18th this evening. We were very glad indeed to hear from you, and thankful that you were all alive and well, but grieved

---

[1] Drake, *What Did They Mean by That?*, 144.

to hear of your house being nearly all burnt up. Your loss is great. what you have worked for all your lifetime was consumed in a few minutes, and you were so well fixed with outbuildings. It grieves me to think of your not having clothes enough to wear. It is almost impossible to buy clothes of any kind now.

I have been watching the office for a letter from you [for] two weeks. I was expecting to hear bad news. I feared it would inform me of the death of some of you. No-one need not tell me that there is nothing in my dreams, for I never expect to believe [such a person]. Wednesday night before your house was burnt or Thursday night after it burnt, I dreamed a dream that I could not get off my mind. I think it was Thursday night. Dr. says it was Wednesday night. I called to Dr. and told him my dream, and next morning I asked him what he thought of my dream. He said he had forgotten what it was. I told him again, he said it was nothing but a dream and never think of it any more, but I told him to remember it, for we would hear something that would remind us of my dream. When I see you I will tell you my dream.

Mother, I never could think to write to you about your leaving your sack here, but I will take care of it, also John's shirt-collar. Anna, I have a calico dress-pattern—10 yds—You shall have it, if you will accept a dress of it. I will bring it to you.

P. C. Bell

If we get off to Georgia at all it will be some time in May, the last, I expect. We cannot stay at your house longer than three days.

I have got lengths of coarse white muslin I will send you a scrap of it. It is a yard wide if you think you can wear it and get a dress of it. I will send a scrap of it in this letter.

You never said in your letter whether you saved your crockery or not. Dr. says if you have to buy anything and have not money enough on hand to pay, to get it on credit and write to him immediately and he will send you money by mail. Dr. says he has got five hundred dollars on hand that he can't use to any advantage. If you want it you can have it immediately.

I hardly know what to say about visiting you. It is difficult for any person to travel in this country that is under 40 years of age. Dr. Says he can get the Probate Judge to assign his tax papers, and he thinks that would carry him safe, provided the Exemption law is not repealed. It would be a hard case if he were conscripted, all of us so far from home, something of this kind is all we know of now, but will hinder us from going.

Write to us, what it is that you have not got or can't get in the way of clothing, and if I have got it, I will divide with you when I come.

Lony, I wrote to Dr. Alexander some time since, but have not received an answer yet. Write to us if you have factory thread on hand or whether you can get it or not. Wilson has quit taking Confederate money awhile. He sells thread for provisions. He gives one bunch of thread for ten lbs. of bacon. I am going to get me some that way. I know you will need a great deal of thread.

I have Mr. Jones' harness that you gave me. If I come, I will bring them to you if you want them. I have never used them.

Mother, perhaps you will need all of your wool this year as you have lost so many of your things. I do not want it if you need it for the family use. If not, I will be glad to get some. Do not try to color it. I want to help you in place of your helping me. Write as soon as you get this.

M. R. and P. C. Bell

Notes

John: He probably was John Neal, Thirza's grandson and Pillina's nephew, and he accompanied Thirza on her visit. The series of letters immediately following this letter indicate that he was not in the army when Thirza made her visit, although he had enlisted in Company B of the 38th Georgia Volunteer Infantry in 1861 at the age of sixteen. At the time this letter was written, he was seventeen years old.[2]

Anna: She was Pillina's sister, who was living at home with her parents.

Exemption law: The Confederate Congress passed on October 11, 1862, an act that exempted a number of occupations and offices deemed vital to the war effort from military service in the Confederate army. Among those occupations exempted were physicians who had been practicing medicine for at least five years before passage of the act.[3]

Mary Juliette Neal

March 22—1863

Dear parents and sister [James and Thirza David and Pillona Alexander[4]

I have taken my seat this lovely quiet Sabbath evening to write to you. We are all in the enjoyment of common health for which we should or ought to be very thankful.

Ann Olivia received a letter from Brother Horatio near two weeks ago. He directed that to Alpharetta. He wrote that he had written to John but had received no answer. John's letter is at Hickory Flat, I suppose. I think we will get it this evening. Ann Olivia wrote to him the same week she received his. I intend writing to him this week.

---

[2] Service records; US Census, 1860, Milton County, Georgia.
[3] Matthews, *Public Laws of the Confederate States of America*, 77–79.
[4] The letter does not indicate where it was from, but a following letter indicates it was from Freemanville, Georgia.

HOMEFRONT: FIRE, EARLY 1863

I received a lengthy letter from James Friday night. They are within 4 or 5 miles of Fredericksburg, half mile of the railroad, one mile of the ground they occupied at the Fredericksburg battle.

March 25

We received Sister Pillona's and Mother's joint letters this morning. I was shocked at the reading of the first few lines. It grieved me to know that the clothes you needed to wear, the lard and flour that you could have eaten were destroyed by the flames. Of course the old homestead will hardly look natural and much that you have both made by years of toil was lost in a few minutes but how small indeed the loss compared to one of the family. After reflecting a few minutes my heart is filled with gratitude and thankfulness that it was only the house and property and not one of my dear parents. Surely our Heavenly Father has dealt mercifully with us in not requiring a greater sacrifice.

I thought at first of trying to visit you immediately, but it is such a busy time in the farm to take the mules away. I know it will cost you a great deal to buy what you will be compelled to have. It would be a pleasure to me to assist you in any way that I can. The muslin dress is not altered, nor the blue worsted one. It has only been worn a few times. The straw bonnet is still the same. Ann Olivia has been talking of using the ribbon. I have between 60 and 70 yards of white cloth not made up. I expected to make it all up, but I can do without some of it. I want Father to have a vest off of one of short cloth. I want to know whether you can buy lard or not. There has been a great many goods in Marietta heretofore. I do not know how it has been since the beginning of the new year.

March 27—1863

I will try to finish my letter. I have just got back from Roswell. I carried 24 yds. of check cloth and they let me have 3 bunches and ¼. I was very sorry to hear of your misfortune. Times are so hard, to buy is almost impossible. If it is not too much trouble, please send me the cloth shoe patterns in a letter. Mrs. Leiter's patterns.

I scribbled night before last by firelight expecting to send the letter to Roswell the next morning but failed to send it. I fear you will never [see] it.

Some excitement among the neighbors about thread and salt. It is getting too high. The soldiers' families have been to Alpharetta after corn this week, but I did not suppose I was going to get any. Mrs. Wilson sent me word to go quick or it would be all gone. I shall go to see him this morning though it is fast day. I have not eaten though there was no [church] meeting near to go to.

The flannel shirts I cut out for James are not made. I have no doubt but Father needs them. I wish he had them. I hardly can give up to go to Jackson, but the plowing is needed so much [illegible].

I think Mother[,] Lona or Annie could come with me. I want to assist you in some way. Let me ask you all not to try to work harder than you did heretofore to make up your loss nor give away to despair, nor do nothing that will injure your minds, health, or religious enjoyment. If you do not come, write immediately. I think of trying to buy back the 30 yards of cloth I sold Lewis Hook. If I do, there will be about 10 yards I would like for some of you to have. The children join in love to you all.

M. J. Neal

Ann Olivia Neal to Thirza David and Pillona Alexander

Freemanville, Milton Co. Ga
March 24—'63
Dear Grandma

I this night avail myself of the precious privilege of writing to you. I would have written sooner but I did not have anything of importance to write. Mother is not at home, and John and Jesse are gone to bed, and I thought I would write if I could keep awake long enough.

We received a letter from Jamie last mail. He was very well. They have moved in 4 or 5 miles of Fredericksburg and a half mile of the railway. They have plenty to eat with what they can buy. They draw flour, bacon, sugar, and rice. I have received a letter from Uncle Ratio since I came home. John received a letter from Uncle H. J. this morning that was written the 24th January. He directed it to Hickory Flat. That is the reason it was so long coming.

We are getting on very well with our crops considering the weather. I have ploughed some. Our logs are rolled and we are burning them now. You were some troubled about John and Cousin Sarah liking each other too much. Well, you need not be uneasy. You may think they have had some hard feelings some way though they have not. Cousin is staying at Uncle Williams now

Dear Aunt Pillona

I have been looking for a letter from you every mail for two weeks. You said you would write as soon as you received a letter from Dr. I hope you have heard from him before now. If you have not bought Nora a hat yet, and she can wait until there is some passing, I will give her a Confederate hat. I think they are much prettier than the Northern ones. They are made of rye straw.

[Ann Olivia Neal]

Notes

Letters' arrangement: These letters were written to the senior Davids and to Lona David Alexander by two different people, Mary Neal and her daughter Ann

Oliva Neal. The originals of the letters are missing, but from the old (1940s) transcriptions and the notes on them, it seems Mary and Ann Olivia were writing at different times, and apparently, one occasionally wrote on the back of an earlier letter from the other person.

It is somewhat difficult to tell from the transcriptions exactly how these different letters appeared on the original stationery because the notes on the transcriptions are unclear. It seemed best, particularly for ease in reading, to group the letters from Mary and those from Ann Olivia separately, regardless of where they may have appeared on the original stationery.

Freemanville, Marietta, Roswell, Alpharetta, Hickory Flat: Freemanville was where Mary Neal's home was located. It was an unincorporated community that then was part of Milton County, a county that no longer exists. It was located at the intersection of present-day Freemansville Road and Birmingham Road, about six miles north of Alpharetta in what now is northern Fulton County. Roswell was about six miles southwest of Alpharetta, and Marietta about eleven miles southwest of Roswell. Both now are part of greater Atlanta. Hickory Flat was an unincorporated community with a post office in Cherokee County a few miles west of Freemanville.[5]

Ann Olivia: She was the daughter of Mary Neal. When the letter was written she was fifteen years old.[6]

Horatio or H. J.: Mary Neal's youngest brother. For letters concerning Horatio and Fredericksburg, see chapters 15 and 17.

John: He was Mary's middle son and one of Ann Olivia's brothers, John W. Neal. Apparently he was at home and no longer in the Confederate army. He was seventeen years old when this letter was written.

James or Jamie: He was Mary's oldest son and one of Ann Olivia's older brothers, James R. Neal. He was a private in Company B of the 38th Georgia Infantry Regiment.[7]

Jesse: He was Jesse Horatio Neal, Mary's youngest son and Ann Olivia's youngest brother. When the letter was written, he was about thirteen years old.[8]

Cousin Sarah and Uncle William: Uncle William was William David, brother of James H. David. Cousin Sarah may have been Sarah Elizabeth David,

---

[5] *Georgia Atlas & Gazetteer*, 20; Marlin, *History of Cherokee County*, 134–37.

[6] US Census, 1860, Milton County, Georgia; tombstone, Sunrise Cemetery, Maysville, Georgia.

[7] Service records.

[8] US Census, 1860, Milton County, Georgia.

daughter of Morrisett David, a distant cousin. She would have been about twenty years old when this letter was written.[9]

Simeon [excerpt]

Camp Gregg near Fredericksburg
March 31, 1863
My dear Mother

Your very extraordinary letter of the 22nd inst. came to hand yesterday evening. I never shall be able to tell you how I felt, and I was at a loss to know which affected me the most, the loss of the dear old homestead where the happiest days of my life have been spent, or the unconscious resignation evinced by the tone of your letter. I undertook to read such portions of the letter as referred to the burning to my friends and broke down and took a good hearty cry which relieved me very much. But I do feel thankful to our Heavenly Father that it is no worse than it is. While it is bad enough, it might have been much worse. I felt so thankful that your corn and bacon was saved, your thread and looms, and most of the farming utensils. Your seven feather beds was a very heavy item and so was your bedclothes and wearing apparel. I feel so sorry that poor little Lona sustained such heavy loss, just starting as she is in the world.

I went to the Quartermaster of the Regt this morning and drew $90 on my pay for the month of March, and I will enclose $50 to you to dispose of as you see proper. I want you to distinctly understand that the money is sent to be used in buying whatever articles or things you may most need. There is some risk in sending it by mail, but I will try it, as there is no express office this side of Richmond.

I would not undertake to build a better house while the war lasts, but to make out with that one. I was glad to hear that the neighbors had assisted you in fixing a place to stay in with some comfort. I thought when I was there that it was the prettiest and most conveniently fixed place I ever saw.

As soon as you receive this letter, write me what you think was your actual loss in dollars and cents besides the house. I hope you will not sacrifice any property but wait awhile and see what is your actual condition. Tell the Negroes I want them all to see how much they can work and how much they can make with God's blessing. Pray to our Heavenly Father to avert any other calamity or disaster....

S. B. David

---

[9] Letter of July 4, 1859, from P. C. Bell, which mentions "Uncle William David"; US Census, 1860, Milton County, Georgia; US Census, 1850, Madison County, Georgia; R. Jones, *War Comes to Broad River*, 317–19, 321.

My excellent friend Patterson who was at home wounded last fall when Father passed through Cummin asked me to tender to Father his sincere condolence and best compliments.

Notes

Partial letter: The latter part of this letter is in chapter 17.

Patterson: He is Josiah Blair Patterson, a lieutenant in Simeon's Company. He was from Forsyth County, and when Simeon's letter was written was about forty-four years old.[10]

Henry D. Carson

Carters Depot E St Tenn
April the 25 1863
Dear Uncl & Aunt [James and Thirza David]

it is with much pleasure I seat my Self this morning to attemt to write you a letter. I am in good health & have been so all the time since I was with you when I was at home. my desire is those lines may come to hand in due time & find you all in the enjoyment of lifes Blessings.

I was very sorry to heare of the serious assident that you have happened to since I was there but am happy to learn it is not as bad as I first heard it was. I first learnt you lost all your corn & meat but have since learnt you saved your corne & meat & some things in the house. it must be a trying time [illegible] in such times & more at this Season of the year.

I have no news to write in the line of war news. our Bat is now Station at thee two Bridges thee Yankies burnt some time ago. thee Bridges are compleated again or as near as they will be untill the war ends. I think we will stay heare sometime. thee Bridges are very well fortified. we are makeing all preparations for thee Yankies. Shoud they ever attemt to Burn the Bridges again they will meat a warm reception

Aunt I wish to know whether or not you can make some janes for mee this Summer provided the war lasts & I live. I will have to Buy janes or wool[,] one or thee other. it seames like you will be in a peculiar situation to make janes for sale & I had determind to apply to [you] to make Some janes for mee from thee first you told mee you had been makeing Janes for sale. So if you can make some for me please let me know it so if you cant that I muz make arrangements with some other person. if you can make it I will want enough to make a cote vest & pare of pants. if you can make it write what you can afford to make it at per yds. [I] will want a light gray color.

---

[10] Patterson's service records; US Census, 1860, Forsyth County, Georgia.

I must close for the present. I want you to write to me when you receive thes lines. I will be glad for you to write to me as often as you can. it is a grate pleasure to mee to receive a letter from any of my connections or acquaintance. no more but remains your Nephew untill Death Farewell

Henry D. Carson

To
Mr. & Mrs. James David
PS Direct your letter to Carters Depot [illegible] & in care of Cap [illegible] at 16 Ga Bat

Notes

Carter's Depot: This depot was a fuel and water stop on the East Tennessee and Virginia Railroad. It was located on a high plateau overlooking the Watauga River on the outskirts of present-day Watauga, Tennessee, in the state's northeast corner. Its importance was due to its being "on the north end of a wooden trestle, sixty feet high and four hundred feet long, which bridged the Watauga River." The railroad was a key transportation route linking Georgia, Tennessee, and Virginia.[11]

Uncl and Aunt: In 1860, Henry D. Carson had married Lois M. David, the daughter of James David's brother Henry. At the time the letter was written, Henry Carson was about twenty-six years old, and Lois was about twenty-one. Henry was then a corporal in Company E of the 1st Regiment Georgia Partisan Rangers, which soon became part of the 16th Battalion Georgia Cavalry.[12]

Bridges: This is a reference to the railroad trestle or possibly trestles across the Watauga River.[13]

---

[11] Piston, *Carter's Raid*, 51.
[12] Service records; US Census, 1850, Franklin County, Georgia; *Georgia Marriage Records, 1699–1944*; Pillina David David's notebook.
[13] Piston, *Carter's Raid*, 51.

Chapter 17

Horatio David and James Neal at Fredericksburg, 1863

Horatio

March the 12th, 1863
Camp 16th Ga Regt
Fredericksburg, Va
Dear Mother

The reason i have not written to you sooner is that i have been waiting for Lt. Cox to come back, but he has not returned. his time was out yesterday.

Mother i have some good news to write you, there is a large revival going on in town; i was there last sunday night. there was at the church about 700 persons 50 of which were ladys. there was over 100 men begging the forgiveness of their sins. all of them were soldiers and i saw among them our colonel; it does me good to see the work going on although i am not a Christian myself.

There is a large number of citizens [illegible] removing back to town, but i think they will have to leave there soon for we think the yankees will try us again soon at the same place; but if they do we will give them fits. our boys do not dread them here at all. they have been keen to fight them ever since our general was killed; as for my self i would rather fight them here than any where else for our position is very good and you know the position is half the battle. I was elected 2 second sergeant of our company on the 3rd day of February. there was six boys running and i was elected by 5 votes mejority. it is a very small office but it will keep me from some hard duty such as building fortification and Regimental guard duty.

Capt Venable and my self have been making a [illegible] potato pie today; we are good hands.

John Deverel is in tolerable good health and fine spirits. my health is very good. i weigh 147 lbs. my back is weak. i suppose it was caused by a shell bursting close to me at some time.

you need not look for peace in 12 months in my opinion.

Mother i am very thankful to you for your kindness to me

Your son
H. J. David

remember me to all of the family white and black

I would like to come home to see you the best in the world but i will not get to come home till all of the men go that have ever been, carrying Brother Thomas home counts as a furlough for me

Notes

Lt. Cox: He probably was Lt. H. J. Cox in Horatio's Company B.[1]

Capt. Venable: He was John Mooreman Venable from Jackson County. He was elected captain of Company B after Captain Reynolds was killed at the Battle of Crampton's Gap in September 1862. At the time the letter was written, he was about thirty-eight years old.[2]

John Deverel: He was a friend of Horatio's from Jackson County who now was a private in Horatio's company. John was about six months younger than Horatio.[3]

carrying Brother Thomas home: See chapter 10.

Horatio

March [18 or 19], 1863
Fredericksburg, Va.
Dear Mother

I went to see Sim last Tuesday and stayed all night with him. He was in good health. I learned more about home than if I had been there myself.

The young lady that you all think—you are all mistaken about my writing to any young lady that is in Georgia. I have not written but 2 letters to young ladies at home except connections.

I received a letter from Ann Olivia Neal just now. They are all well. I have not seen James Neal yet. He is far off now. I will go to see him soon.

I believe I wrote to you about being 3rd sergeant. I hope I will have some better news to write you next time.

The things you sent by Lieutenant Cox came safe. Cpt. Venable has been very sick, but he is getting better. I weigh 147 lbs. as fat as a coon in persimmon time. Write soon.

H. J. David

Notes

I learned more about home than if I had been there myself: Simeon had returned to his regiment from the leave he wrote about in chapter 15.

connections: Relatives.[4]

---

[1] Service records; Rigdon, *Georgia 16th Infantry Regiment*, 96.

[2] Service records; Rigdon, *Georgia 16th Infantry Regiment*, 95; US Census, 1860, Jackson County, Georgia; T. Harris, *Portraits of a Southern Place*, 23.

[3] Service records; Rigdon, *Georgia 16th Infantry Regiment*, 101; US Census, 1850, Jackson County, Georgia; tombstone, Mount Pleasant Cemetery, Whitfield County, Georgia.

[4] *Webster's New World College Dictionary*, 315–16.

Ann Olivia Neal: She was his cousin, daughter of Mary Neal and sister of James R. Neal. When the letter was written she was fifteen years old.[5]

Horatio

March the 25 1863
Camp near Fredericksburg
Dear mother

I received your letter of the 15th which afforded me great sorrow. i never did hear any thing that shook me so much as that but i thank god that none of you were burned in it; as to the enfield gun and other things of mine it makes no difference so dont grieve your self a bout that. The prospects are fair for me to get an office that will pay me 80$ per month. if i do happen to get the place i can help you to build another house.

you wrote to me about clothing. i have plenty of clothing to do me this summer. if i nead any more clothes i can get them from the government.

James Neal came to see me last Saturday. he was in good health. John Deverel is getting on finely.

Mother i was elected 3 third Lieutenant on the 19th day of march; but i will have to be examined by a board consisted of 5 of the best officers in the brigade; please do not say any thing about it for fear that i am rejected. Give my love to Father sisters Nora and all of the negroes.

The people that you are acquainted with here all send their respects to you. capt Venable's health is no better

As ever your son
Horatio J. David
PS
Write to me in the next letter, howe many dollars worth of property you suppose you lost
Be lively and chearful

Notes

Nora: She was M. P. and Pillona Alexander's young daughter. Apparently, Pillona, Nora, and the senior Davids continued living together after the fire.

i will have to be examined by a board: In 1862, the Confederate Army issued two General Orders that "granted generals the authority to convene boards of examination to scrutinize newly promoted officers," including newly elected

---

[5] US Census, 1860, Milton County, Georgia; Tombstone, Sunrise Cemetery, Maysville, Georgia.

officers, to determine whether they were able to instruct and control their commands and generally were efficient and sober.[6]

James R. Neal

Camp Near Fredericksburg, Va
March 28th 1863
Dear Grandma [Thirza David]:
    I seat myself to write a few lines to let you know that I am still among the land of the living;
    I recd a letter from mother yesterday evening she said that they wair all well an doing well, Grandma I have more money at this time than I realy kneed; an I will send you the mony that I borrowed of you last summer while at the Hospital;
    you may think strainge of my sending the money to you after your writing to me to keep the mony untill you ast me for it; Grandma I may be without mony some other time and want to borrow again;
    I will send the $6 dollars to you in this letter; so if I should ever want any that I would not feal at a lost to send to you again. I will send the money and then if I kneed any I will send again to you; I find it is a good ideah to keep on the good side of all friends;
    If I keep the money I may spent it foolishly and sometime kneed it worse than I will when I spent it [now, which I would] if I wair to keep it;
    Grandma sister Ana wrote to me that you advised me to leave off writing to some of our relations mor again; I wrote one letter in answer to one that I had recd, an waited some time and did not get an answer; an I wrote again, to know whether Hellen had written to me or not; I did not know but what she had written a letter an I had never received it. I have never written but four or five letters their and I expect what I have written to sufice untill I know mor about what is the matter;
    I went to see Uncle Ratio the other day. he was injoying himself finely;
    I am in for very good health; the General health is tolerable good at this time;
    I will close for this time. we had a very fine day yesterday hear. it has been raining all this morning hear ;
    I remain your unworthy Grand son until death; write soon for I am anxious to hear from you all;
    J. R. Neal

---

[6] Bledsoe, *Citizen-Officers, 47–48*; See also Horatio's letter of April 7, below.

Notes

Hellen: She has not been identified. She may have been one of James's relatives on his father's side.

Simeon

Camp Gregg near Fredericksburg
March 31, 1863
My dear Mother...

Horatio was down to see me about two weeks ago looking better than I ever saw him. He was weighing 150 lbs. and very handsome and as dignified in manner and deportment as any young man I ever saw of his age. He is 2nd lieut. of his company, a very pretty position. I have not seen James Neal since I wrote you before, but have heard that he is well.

We are making preparations for an active spring campaign, sending off all our surplus baggage. Our Regt has been in its present quarters since the 16th Dec., longer than we have been in one place since the commencement of the war.

There seems to be a great deal of interest manifested in our camp on the subject of religion. A member of our regiment was baptized a few days ago that professed to have been converted and converted since Christmas. Rev. Mr. Bennett, Chaplain of the 45th Ga. Regt, baptized Capt. Tuggle of Hall County last Sunday. Mr. Bennett's father resides near Athens. Every night till bedtime is spent by the men singing hymns and songs.

I received a letter from Fanny a day or two ago. All well. My own health is very good. My love to all. Your affectionate son,

S. B. David

Note

Omission: The earlier part of this letter is in chapter 16.

Horatio

April the 3rd 1863
Camp 16th Ga. Regt
Near Fredericksburg, Va.
Dear Mother

I seat my self this pleasant morning to inform you that i am well and getting on finely. i was examined to day by the board of examiners of this brigade. i stood a very good examination; so you may Direct your letters to Lt. H. J. David of Co. B, 16th Ga.

I have no news of interest to write i do not now whether the yankies will attack us here again or not; they have been making some threats for the last 2 or 3 days.

i am as fat and hearty as i want to be. John Deverel is well and lively.

i will not have time to write any more fore the drum is beating for us to make ready for general revile.

[H. J. David]

Notes

Signature: This letter has no signature, but the handwriting and contents indicate it is from Horatio.

revilee: Reveille was the first assembly of the day for a military unit.[7]

James R. Neal

Near Hamilton's Crossing
Camp 38 Regt Ga Vols
April 6th 1863
Dear Aunt [Pillona Alexander]

I with an ansious heart perused your letter which caim through in due time; I was truly sory to hear of your misfortune; I know that you hardly feal like you wair at hoam sinse the burning.

Aunt I have nothing of importance to relate to you this morning; I wrote a letter to grandma the first of last week; I put six dollars in that letter that I borrowed from her while I was in the Hospital last summer;

I went to see Uncle Ratio two or three weeks sinse. he was well when I saw him; he had been to see Uncle Simeon a week or such a matter before I saw him.

Aunt you mentioned something concerning the soldiers at Vicksburg seeing a heard time; we have a heard time hear but I would not near swap places with the soldiers at Vicksburg; I have been on the coast a while and tried that sufficiently to be satisfyed; we have heard fighting hear and sickness plenty; but I think from what I can learn that their is more sickness in the western Army than their is hear in the virginnia Army.

Their is some talk of the yankey Army moving to their right; that is up the Rappahannock; I donot know whether to believe any such reports or not; I am not suffering any uneasiness about fighting yet;

The health of the Army generally is tolerably good as far as I know; the camp in which I am a member; has but little sickness; I have injoyed very good health excepting diareah a few times this winter; I am enjoying the best of health now; I would like to see you very much but it is imposible now; when you write to

---

[7] "Reveille," *Webster's New World College Dictionary*, 1243.

Uncle Dr. Alex give him my love and respects; I do not know his address; I will cloas as I have nothing more to write; I remain your nephew,

J R Neal

[on a separate scrap of paper]

Grandma [Thirza David] I have nothing of interest to write to you this morning. I mentioned the mony that I [illegible] to you in my last letter; if you recd it let me know;

I got to reflecting after the post and I thought it best to send that to you, an all [the other money] that I did not kneed to mother so that if I wair to get without again I could send again to mother or your self and not be at any trouble. grandma then if I wair to get killed or to dy I had rather that mother had my mony than any soldier; I kept what I thought I would kneed an sent the balance hoam. if I should kneed any more mony I can but send for it; keep the mony that I sent untill I call upon you for it; I will call for it when I kneed it if I ever kneed it; I will cloas; write soon; I remain your grandson;

T David   J. R. Neal

Notes

Hamilton's Crossing: Hamilton's Crossing was southeast of Fredericksburg where the Richmond, Fredericksburg & Potomac Railroad crossed Mine Road, Military Road, and a road leading to the Rappahannock River that now is state road 608. During the Battle of Fredericksburg, it was the location of the right of the Confederate infantry's line.[8]

Vicksburg: Manning Alexander was stationed in the Vicksburg, Mississippi area (see chapter 20).

Horatio

April the 7th, 1863
Camp 16th Ga. Regt.
near Fredericksburg, Va.
Dear Mother and Sister [Thirza David and Pillona Alexander]

I received your kind letters today. Of course they afforded me great pleasure. I was happy to hear that you had your little house furnished and fixed up so comfortable.

I was very sorry to hear of the misfortune of my friend Ellison. I hope he will come clear. I will not say anything about it at any rate.

As I wrote to you in my last letter about the examination that I had to undergo I will now explain it to you. General Lee will not allow a man to have office in his army without he is examined to see whether he is competent to fulfill it. I

---

[8] Stackpole, *Battle of Fredericksburg*, 18; Eastern National, "The Battle of Fredericksburg, 1.

was examined on the 3rd of this month and went through without missing but one question that was asked me, and since that time I have been drilling the recruits and conscripts.

Sister, tell Dr. Alex. to write to me. I have written to him but I guess he has not received it. He has not answered it anyway. I wrote to you in one of my letters about visiting brother Sim.

Mr John Millican and Jasper Daily [Davis?] has just now come in. They are both well. I will have to close my letter in order to receive them.

Give my love to Father and Anna and all of my relatives. Tell the negroes all howdy for me. John Deveril is quite well. I am in fine health.

H. J. David

Notes

Ellison: There are several Ellisons mentioned in a letter from Manning Alexander in chapter 13 as being in the 43rd Georgia with him, particularly Arnold Ellison from Jackson County. The Ellison Horatio is writing about may have been one of them.

John Millican and Jasper Dailey: They have not been identified.

Horatio

April the 13th 1863
Camp Anna 16th Ga. Regt.
near F'kburg
Dear Mother

I cannot get letters from you regular, but I know it is not your fault. I think it is the fault of the postmaster at Richmond.

We had a good meeting at our camp yesterday. A gentleman from Alabama preached to us. He was a noble preacher. The whole regiment turned out to hear him, and there was right smart revival.

The Yankees are still lying in front of us, and I do not know whether we will have another fight here or not. I hardly think we will. The Yankees dread crossing the river, and it will be to their interest to stay on the other side.

I received a letter from Sim a few days ago. He was well. Our regt is in fine health. At present, I am not keen to fight, but if we have to do it, I want to do it now, so that we can make another march.

I was glad to hear by your last that you were fixed so well in your little house. I wish I was there with you just one day or two. I could enjoy myself so well with you all if I could go and stay one week. Then I could come back and stay content as long as the war lasted, but I can do that anyhow. We must not get tired of serving our country. To look at our Congress now, it is rather discouraging but we can have a better one when our smart men get home from the army.

John Deverell is well and lively as a cricket. Tell little Sarah that Uncle Rashe being an officer will not help him to get home very much. Those that go home so much do very little good when they are here.

Give my love to Father and sisters, tell all the negroes howdy for me. Tell Simon I want him to write to me about his new wife, whether she is a good one or not, how many children he has got, etc. I am as ever,

H. J. David

P. S. Mother, Capt. Venable wants you to weave him a nice bit of gray jeans, and I want you to make me one also. I will tell you more about it in my next letter. Make the coat a frock one, double-breasted, short waist and long tails, sleeves large and roomy. The pants I want them made just like the ones you sent me all except the legs. Make them longer, but very little. Put a stripe on them one-quarter of an inch wide, striping the front part of the leg. Make them a little larger around the waist. I do not want my boys to be ashamed of me. The last clothes you sent me were good enough but they are worn and dirty. Please have these made very nice. I will pay the expense if I have good luck. Make them light. I want them for summer wear. Get nice military buttons, bright ones. They cost a large price, but I will pay for them.

Notes

Camp Anna: This camp was located six miles from Fredericksburg in Spotsylvania County.[9]

little Sarah: She was Simeon's daughter Sarah or Sallie, then age three.[10]

Simon: He probably was one of the Davids' enslaved people.

frock coat: A "double-breasted dress coat with a full skirt reaching to the knees."[11]

Horatio

April the 17th, '63
Camp 16th Ga. Regt near Fredericksburg, Va.
Dear parents

I have been looking for a letter from you several days, but I have not received any as yet. But I will write to you so that you may not be uneasy about me.

- [9] Smedlund, *Camp Fires of Georgia Troops*, 50.
- [10] US Census, 1860, Forsyth County, Georgia; tombstone, Rose Hill Cemetery, Rockmart, Polk County, Georgia.
- [11] "Frock coat," *Webster's New World College Dictionary*, 581.

I have no news to write except that we have a good meeting going on here. It has been going on 2 weeks and there has not been but two sermons preached the whole time, yet there is great interest taken in it. The members of the church of all branches have formed a church called the Christian Soldiers Association. It is working well. There is no dispute about denominations. They do well together. The Association meets every night just after roll-call. They do not have any preaching. Our preacher has gone home. They pray and sing. There is a good many coming every night.

I have not seen or heard of Brother and James since I wrote to you last.

The health of our regiment is very good now. The men are all in fine spirits. I think they would fight well now if they had the chance. I do not know anything about the movements of the enemy, but they are moving some way. I expect we will have to fight them here again.

We drill 2 times every day and 2 hours each drill, and between drills we amuse ourselves by playing town-ball, cat, baste, bull-pen, etc. I will have to drill more. I have just come in from drill. I am tired but I will finish my letter.

I heard while on drill that Davis Bradley was here, and I must close and go to see him. John Deverall is well, and one of the peartest and most lively boys we have in our company. I am in fine health myself.

As I wrote to you in my last letter, Capt. Palmer McKennally wants you to make him some nice gray jeans as soon as you can. I want you to make me a suit of gray jeans (the coat) make it frock coat, short waist and long tails, sleeves large and roomy, double breasted. Trim the collars and cuffs with blue cloth. Please get bright buttons if you can. I will pay you for it if I have good luck. The pants, make them as you did the last you sent me except that waist 1 inch larger, the legs somewhat larger with a black welt in the outside seams, line the inside of them with thin cotton cloth. Get Mr. Thomas to make me a nice pair of shoes size 5, don't make them larger than No. 5. All you have sent were too large.

Don't think strange of me telling you so precise how to make them. I do it so you will know how to make them to my notions.

Mother, I want these things as soon as possible. My old ones (clothes) are getting worn smartly, and I don't want the boys that elected me to be ashamed of me. I would have bought me a uniform here, but it will cost me $200. That is too much to pay for clothes when I can get good ones without it.

H. J. David

Notes

town-ball, cat, baste, bull-pen: These games were basically children's games. Town-ball and cat or cat-ball were played with a bat and ball and were precursors of baseball.[12]

Baste was a game of two teams and a home base for each team. Each of the teams tried to capture members of the other team while they were away from the safety of their home base.[13]

Bull-pen or corner ball probably was played something like versions of dodgeball are played today. One team was inside a square or circle and the other team was outside. As it was generally played, members of the team outside would throw a ball at the ones inside, trying to hit them one by one or force them outside the enclosure and thus eliminate them. If, however, the ball was caught by a person inside the enclosure, the thrower was eliminated.[14]

Davis Bradley: He has not been identified.

Horatio

Camp Anna—16th Ga Regt
April the 22—'63
Dear Mother

I received your kind letter yesterday which afforded me great pleasure. I was glad also to hear from Dr. Alexander. We are glad to hear that wheat crops look so well. I was sorry to hear of the oats being killed.

I wish I could get home one more time to see you. If I could stay one week with you, then I could come back and stay satisfied till the war ends but we must not suffer ourselves to think about it in such a manner for it is our duty to stay here, therefore we must content ourselves to stay away from home, parents, and friends.

Mother, I have no news to write that would interest you. We think the Yankees are leaving in small squads so small that they think we do not know it but if they don't watch out we will have our eyes open.

Capt. Venable is trying to get special furlough to go home. If he gets it he will go home in 2 weeks. If you please, send my clothes by him. Tell my sister Ann I want her to make me two nice colored shirts if she will. Mother, send me

---

[12] Drake, *What Did They Mean by That?*, 132; "Town ball," Wikipedia, https://en.wikipedia.org/wiki/Town_ball, and "Old Cat," Wikipedia, https://en.wikipedia.org/wiki/Old_cat accessed January 12, 2017.

[13] Scott, *Complete History of Fairfield County, Ohio*, 251–52.

[14] Ibid.; Dickson, *Dickson Baseball Dictionary*, 145–46; Beard, "How to Play Corner Ball," http://www.inquiry.net/outdoor/summer/ball/cornerball.htm (accessed September 19, 2023).

some drawers and socks at the same time, for it will be all the chance this summer. If he goes, I will write to you in time.

Tell Miss Ann Deveral that her present was received and that John and I feasted on them finely. John Deveral is well, sends his respects to all of the family.

There is brigade guard mounting in front of the tent this morning. The brass band is performing beautifully. That is the advantage we have of you. we can hear fine music every day and everything else that keeps us finely all the time.

I am very well. I will not forget this time to sign my name. Your affectionate son, H. J. David

Notes

We think the Yankees are leaving in small squads: Some federal troops were leaving the immediate Fredericksburg area and marching west in preparation for crossing the Rappahannock and Rapidan rivers upstream and attacking the Confederates in Fredericksburg from that direction. It was a maneuver that very soon would lead to the Battle of Chancellorsville.

Miss Ann Deveral: She was John Deverell's sister and was about eighteen years old when this letter was written.[15]

---

[15] US Census, 1850, Jackson County, Georgia.

Chapter 18

Chancellorsville: Simeon and Horatio, 1863

Simeon

Camp 14th Ga. Regt. Near Hamilton's Crossing Va. May 9th 1863
My Dear Parents

I embrace the present opportunity of writing to inform you that we have just passed through another battle and through the mercy of God my life has been again spared.

Last Saturday Sunday & Monday the Confederates gained one of the greatest victories of this war. We left our camp on Wednesday the 28th of April and marched to a position near Fredericksburg & remained there till Friday morning when it was ascertained that Hooker was trying to flank us on our left about ten miles up the Rappab hannock at a place called Chancellorsville. Our Brigade took position in line of battle Friday evening about sunset and remained there till about 12 O'clock Saturday when we were marched out and commenced one of Jackson's world renowned flank movements that have shed so much luster upon our arms.

We marched a distance of 12 or 15 miles and gained a position in the enemy's rear about 10 O'clock Saturday night. D. H. Hill's division was in front of ours & engaged the enemy in their rear about an hour by sun driving them before them. During the fight on Saturday evening, Gen. Lane's North Carolina Brigade got into confusion mistook Genls Jackson & Hill and their respective staffs for Yankee cavalry and fired upon and wounded them both. Gen. Jackson in the left arm so as to render amputation necessary, and a ball through the right hand. Gen Hill slightly. Gen. J. E. B. Stewart commanded Jackson's corps on Sunday and Gen Pender commanded A. P. Hill's division.

Our Brigade got into position of battle about midnight Saturday night and lay upon their arms without sleeping the balance of the night. The enemy were building a breastwork about two hundred yards in front of us all night Saturday night and at Sun rise our pickets were ordered to advance and open the fight. After half an hours skirmishing on the part of the pickets our whole line of battle was ordered to advance, which they did in beautiful Style, with a tremendous shout that almost made the earth tremble and in fifteen minutes the enemy's whole line had broken and fled in the wildest confusion our boys scaling the breastworks and rushing on with the impetuosity of an avalanche.

Our Regt as usual suffered severely mostly on account of being the first one to scale the works. We had one Capt. Killed, another mortally wounded, 1 Lieut mortally wounded, and two others severely wounded. Lieut Col James M Fielder of our Regt had his leg broken and had to be amputated. He married the daughter of Adam Williamson formerly of Jackson County. We carried 208 men into action—77 killed and wounded—8 of whom were killed dead.

I received a slight wound on the left arm between the shoulder and elbow, breaking the skin & bruising the arm considerably. I never looked at it till the fight was over.

After we drove the enemy back on the left we had nothing to do but watch them till they were driven back on the right which was not done till about 10 O'clock.

While a portion of the army were fighting them at Chancellorsville, another portion was fighting them at Fredericksburg. On Monday and Tuesday night the whole of Hooker's grand Army recrossed to the Rappahannock most awfully thrashed. Our loss considering the magnitude of the job, was very small, especially in killed.

On Thursday before the battle I saw Ratio and James. They were both well. I have not seen either of them since the fight but have reason to believe that neither of them are hurt. Horatio is discharging the duties of Lieut with credit to himself and to the entire satisfaction of his officers. On Sunday evening after the battle in the morning I saw John Bowen, of the 12th Ga and Jesse Bowen of the 6th Alabama, neither of them were hurt. John told me that he had received a letter conveying the sad intelligence of Cousin Abner's death.

I was truly sorry to learn from your letter that your loss was so heavy. I had hoped it was not so mutch. I am glad that you are so resigned, and can say with the Psalmist "the Lord giveth and the Lord taketh away blessed be the name of the Lord."

I received a long and affectionate letter from Fanny this evening, all well. My kit mule kicked Janis on the legs very nearly breaking them both, but Mr Harris took my crop in with his and they are getting along finely.

My health is very good. Let me hear from you soon. Your Affectionate Son
S. B. David

Notes

Near Hamilton's Crossing: Hamilton's Crossing was where the Richmond, Fredericksburg & Potomac Railroad crossed both Old Mine Road and Military Road about four miles south of Fredericksburg.[1]

We have just passed through another battle: This was the long, complicated Battle of Chancellorsville fought May 1–4, 1863.

The Union Marches, and the Confederates Respond

---

[1] Rable, *Fredericksburg! Fredericksburg!*, xvi.

In late April, just before the battle, the Union and Confederate forces occupied roughly the same positions they had occupied at the end of the Battle of Fredericksburg. The Union forces under General Joseph "Fighting Joe" Hooker, who had replaced Burnside, numbered approximately 134,000. The Confederates under Lee numbered less than half that number, approximately sixty-one thousand.[2]

The Union objective in this new fighting season was still to capture Richmond. Hooker's plan to accomplish this goal was similar to Burnside's—part of his troops would remain in front of Fredericksburg while another part would attempt to flank Lee. The differences were that the troops in front of Fredericksburg, some forty thousand men, were to hold Lee in place rather than try to capture the city, and Hooker's flanking movement, composed of another forty thousand men, would cross the Rappahannock and then the Rapidan Rivers at places several miles northwest and upriver from Fredericksburg, rather than a short distance southeast and downriver of the town. The remainder of Hooker's troops would be held in reserve to reinforce one or both of the other forces, except for Union cavalry, which would ride toward Richmond to cut off Confederate communications with Fredericksburg and block Lee should he retreat from Fredericksburg.[3]

By Thursday, April 30, Hooker and much of his flanking force had crossed the rivers successfully and lead elements had reached Chancellorsville, a large house and former tavern at a crossroad about ten to eleven miles west of Fredericksburg. Lee, however, did not wait for Hooker to come to him. Leaving only ten thousand troops in Fredericksburg, he marched around fifty thousand men upriver toward Hooker. Lee's First Corps, including Horatio's 16th Georgia, part of Wofford's Brigade, McLaws's Division, was among the fifty thousand that left Fredericksburg. Most of Jackson's 2nd Corps, which included Simeon's 14th Georgia of Thomas's Brigade of Hill's Division, also was part of the Confederate force heading toward Hooker.[4]

May 1st: The Armies Meet

The Confederate and Union upriver armies met on Friday, May 1, about three and a half miles east of Chancellorsville. After a short clash, Hooker, surprisingly, ordered a withdrawal back west toward Chancellorsville, surrendering the initiative to Lee.[5]

---

[2] Furguson, *Chancellorsville 1863*, 88; Boatner, *Civil War Dictionary*, 136–37.

[3] Furguson, *Chancellorsville 1863*, 63–68, Boatner, *Civil War Dictionary*, 136–37; Sears, *Chancellorsville*, 131–45.

[4] Furguson, *Chancellorsville 1863*, 88, 105–15, 120; Sears, *Chancellorsville*, 175–81, 187–89, 191–92; Gallagher et al., *Civil War*, 75–77; *OR*, ser. 1, vol. 25, pt. 1, 789, 791.

[5] Furguson, *Chancellorsville 1863*, 123–32; Sears, *Chancellorsville*, 196–213, 219–24; Gallagher et al., *Civil War*, 77.

May 2nd: Lee Takes the Initiative

The next day, May 2, Lee took the initiative. He divided his army again, keeping fourteen thousand men in front of Hooker, including Horatio's 16th Georgia and Wofford's Brigade, and sending most of the remainder of his men, including Simeon's 14th Georgia and Thomas's Brigade, with General Jackson on a flanking movement of his own around Hooker's right flank.[6]

Late in the afternoon of May 2, Jackson, having marched more than twelve miles, was in position. He attacked and overran the Union corps on Hooker's right, stopping only when darkness fell. Simeon's brigade, however, was not part of this action. Along with another brigade, it had turned back to confront Union soldiers harassing the rear of Jackson's column and had not been able to join the main force when the attack started.[7]

Meanwhile, Lee ordered his troops facing Hooker's army on the Union left to hold Hooker's troops opposite in position. As part of this holding action, once Lee's men learned that Jackson had attacked, they were also to attack, but not "seriously." (Although as it turned out, when Horatio and the rest of Wofford's Brigade attacked, they became more heavily engaged than intended. As General McLaws later wrote, "Wofford became so seriously engaged [with Federal reinforced skirmishers] that I directed him to withdraw, which was done in good order, his men in good spirits, after driving the enemy to their intrenchments.")[8]

In a major blow to the Confederate cause, that evening after the attack generals Jackson and Hill were wounded by North Carolina soldiers as Simeon described. At the same time, as Simeon also mentioned, the Federals opposite Jackson expected the Confederates to renew their attack the next morning and had begun frantically to build breastworks to protect their new position.[9]

May 3rd: Charges and Counter-charges

The following morning (Sunday, May 3), Jackson's men (now under General J. E. B. Stuart) on the Confederate left, including A. P. Hill's old division (now under General Henry Heth, the same man Manning had served under in Kentucky, not General Pender as Simeon wrote), together with Lee on the Confederate right, attacked with the goal of uniting the two wings of the Confederate

---

[6] Furguson, *Chancellorsville 1863*, 138–47; Sears, *Chancellorsville*, 230–35; Gallagher et al., *Civil War*, 77.

[7] Furguson, *Chancellorsville 1863*, 151–56, 162–84, 189–211; Sears, *Chancellorsville*, 238–45, 254–92, 300–302; Dewberry, *History of the 14th Georgia*, 52–53; Bigelow, *Campaign of Chancellorsville*, 281–84, 292.

[8] Furguson, *Chancellorsville 1863*, 185; Sears, *Chancellorsville*, 282–83; Gallagher et al., *Civil War*, 77; *OR*, ser. 1, vol. 25, pt. 1, 826 (quotes).

[9] Furguson, *Chancellorsville 1863*, 199–207, 212–16; Sears, *Chancellorsville*, 292–300; Dewberry, *History of the 14th Georgia*, 53–53; R. K. Krick, "The Smoothbore Volley," 107–42.

army and pushing Hooker back toward the Rappahannock River. The successful attack that day on the Union breastworks that Simeon took part in and described was part of this action on the Confederate left.[10]

The attack began about five thirty in the morning. Simeon's regiment was the end regiment on the left of the Confederate line. As the line advanced, "The enemy vanished like snow in the sunshine," a member of Simeon's brigade reported later.[11]

A few Union soldiers, however, did not flee. A captain in Simeon's regiment, one of the first men across the Union breastworks, experienced his first hand-to-hand combat:

> A young Federal soldier came at me with fixed bayonet. With sword in my right hand, I knocked up his musket, and grabbed it with my left hand. The tussle was a fearful one; but George Kelly, a sergeant of Company D, shot and broke the Federal's thigh. The poor fellow fell, but continued to fight game. I could have cleaved his head with my sword, and Kelly started to brain him with his clubbed musket; but I forbade it, and called on my brave enemy to surrender, or I would have him shot, which he did in broken English. He was a German and a brave fellow.[12]

Stuart's attack overran the first two lines of breastworks on the Union right, as Simeon described, but the Federals had several lines of defense and troops available to counterattack. In fact, on attacking the third line, Simeon's brigade found itself unsupported on either side or the rear by other Confederates, subjected to heavy artillery fire, and running low on ammunition. In that dire situation, fresh Union troops counterattacked, forcing the brigade to retreat to the first Federal line of breastworks. They continued the fight from there.[13]

Other Confederate actions that followed on the Confederate left were chaotic. A modern historian wrote, "The exact sequence in which Stuart's brigades advanced, retreated, then advanced again was impossible for the officers involved to sort out, even immediately after the battle," and their reports reflected their confusion. Apparently, however, much the same thing happened to other units in the Confederate attack as happened to Simeon's brigade, that is, they first advanced and then to some extent retreated.[14]

---

[10] Furguson, *Chancellorsville 1863*, 206–12, 215; Sears, *Chancellorsville*, 313–16.

[11] Furguson, *Chancellorsville 1863*, 217–18, 220–25; Sears, *Chancellorsville*, 317, 323–27; O'Reilly "Chancellorsville," 16–17, 20 (quote).

[12] Goldsmith, "'Stonewall' Jackson's Last Grand Blow," 519–20.

[13] Furguson, *Chancellorsville 1863*, 217, 225–27, 229; Sears, *Chancellorsville*, 325–27; Dewberry, *History of the 14th Georgia*, 53; Bigelow, *Campaign of Chancellorsville*, 352–53.

[14] Furguson, *Chancellorsville 1863*, 222 (quote), 229–39; Sears, *Chancellorsville*, 317–23, 327–36.

As best that can be determined, soon after Simeon's brigade established itself behind the old Federal breastworks, a wave of fresh Confederate units swept past it toward the Federal lines, but it was not long before they too were repulsed with considerable losses and joined Simeon's brigade and others behind Union breastworks. The same thing happened again to a third wave of attacking Confederates. In between Confederate attacks, the Federals counterattacked, and the survivors of Simeon's brigade and of the units in succeeding waves repulsed them in turn.[15]

Late in the morning, things changed when Stuart's men on the Confederate left linked up with Lee's men on the Confederate right, who too had been energetically attacking. Together they attacked once more. The two Confederate forces caught the Union army between them and drove the fleeing Federals through Chancellorsville toward the Rappahannock River. A member of the 14th Georgia described the battlefield after the Union soldiers fled as "litterally covered with knapsacks, haver sacks, Blankets, oilcloths, frying pans, over-coats and clothing of various kinds." The Union forces, however, regrouped and began to fortify a new position shaped like a horseshoe with its two ends located on the river and its curved head roughly three miles from the river.[16]

Meanwhile, on the same day back at Fredericksburg, the Federals opposite the town had attacked. By early afternoon, they had overcome most of the small force of Confederates there. They then turned and began advancing west toward Lee's position east of Chancellorsville.[17]

To halt this new threat, Lee divided his army once again, sending about half his troops from opposite Hooker at Chancellorsville on the Confederate right (including Horatio's 16th Georgia) to confront the Union troops moving from Fredericksburg. Later that afternoon, along with remaining men of Confederate units that had been defending Fredericksburg, they met the Union advance and stopped it.[18]

May 4: Little Change

On Monday, May 4, convinced that Hooker would remain on the defensive around Chancellorsville, Lee took additional troops away from there to aid in attacking the Union force near Fredericksburg. (Simeon's regiment was not part of this contingent and remained facing Hooker.) The armies opposing each other

---

[15] Furguson, *Chancellorsville 1863*, 222 (quote), 229–39; Sears, *Chancellorsville*, 317–23, 327–36.

[16] Furguson, *Chancellorsville 1863*, 243–53, 270; Sears, *Chancellorsville*, 339–66, 372–73; Hall, *Diary of George Washington Hall*, [vol?]40 (quote).

[17] Furguson, *Chancellorsville 1863*, 254–67, 271–71; Sears, *Chancellorsville*, 347–57, 371–72.

[18] Furguson, *Chancellorsville 1863*, 268, 273–80; Sears, *Chancellorsville*, 372, 373–86; O'Reilly "Chancellorsville," 15–17.

near Chancellorsville remained inactive, while near Fredericksburg, Lee's attack against the Union troops there developed slowly, and once begun, was inconclusive. As it began to grow dark, the Union still remained on the south side of the Rappahannock.[19]

May 5–6: The Union Army Departs

At the end of May 4, Hooker had two groups of Union soldiers on the south side of the Rappahannock about five miles apart, one near Chancellorsville and one near Fredericksburg. Both had their backs to the river, and both faced Confederate forces. The night of May 4–5, the Fredericksburg group retreated across the river. The night of May 5–6, the Chancellorsville group did the same. The Battle of Chancellorsville was over.[20]

Simeon's 14th Georgia lost eight killed and sixty-seven wounded, much as Simeon wrote. It was the highest number of casualties of any regiment in his brigade.[21]

Wednesday the 28th April: Simeon is mistaken as to the date. In 1863, the 28th was on a Tuesday. Wednesday the 29th is the correct date for the movement Simeon described.[22]

line of battle: To form a line of battle in preparation for an attack, a regiment, for example, would form a long line facing the enemy. Usually, the line would be two ranks (or two lines) deep, one rank behind the other.[23]

D. H. Hill's Division was in front of ours: D. H. Hill was not in command of his division at Chancellorsville. He had been sent to his native North Carolina, and his old division was commanded during the battle by Brig. Gen. Robert E. Rodes.[24]

General Jackson wounded: Jackson had been hit by three bullets. One hit his right hand, a second his lower left arm, and the third shattered a bone in his upper left arm near his shoulder. At about two in the morning on May 3, around five hours after he was wounded, General Jackson's left arm was amputated two inches below the shoulder. He died a week later of pneumonia that developed because of his weakened condition caused by the wounds and the amputation.[25]

Gen Pender commanded A. P. Hill's Division: Simeon was wrong. As mentioned in a previous note, after A. P. Hill was wounded, General Heth

---

[19] Furguson, *Chancellorsville 1863*, 293–99; Sears, *Chancellorsville*, 393–407, 410–20.

[20] Furguson, *Chancellorsville 1863*, 292, 299–305, 309–18; Sears, *Chancellorsville*, 412–13, 418–30.

[21] Sears, *Chancellorsville*, 496.

[22] Ibid., 148–49, 159; *Southern Watchman*, January 14, 1863 (1863 calendar).

[23] Garrison, *Encyclopedia of Civil War Usage*, 147; Griffith, *Battle Tactics*, 60, 99–101.

[24] Sears, *Chancellorsville*, 50, 278.

[25] Ibid., 292–97, 306–307, 446–48; R. K. Krick, "The Smoothbore Volley," 107–42.

commanded the division through the remainder of the battle. Pender did command the division after Lee reorganized his army on May 30, 1863, when Hill was promoted to command the 3rd Corps.[26]

We [14th Georgia] carried 208 men into action—77 killed and wounded—8 of whom were killed dead: The official casualty report for the 14th Georgia report eight killed and sixty-seven wounded.[27]

John Bowen and Jesse Bowen: John Bowen was 1st Lieutenant John H. Bowen, a son of Thirza's brother Horatio. When the letter was written, he was about twenty-one years old. He was later killed in the Spotsylvania Campaign in May 1864.[28]

Jesse Bowen was Sergeant Jesse J. Bowen, son of Hiram, another of Thirza's brothers. He was wounded and taken prisoner at Gettysburg and survived the war. At the time the letter was written, he was about twenty-six years old.[29]

Cousin Abner: He was Abner H. Bowen, son of Thirza's brother Horatio and brother of Lieutenant John H. Bowen. According to family tradition, he died on April 13 or 14, 1863. The cause of his death is not known. He is reported to have served as an assistant surgeon in the 12th Georgia.[30]

Janis (who was kicked by a mule): She may have been the enslaved girl listed under Simeon's name on the 1860 federal census slave schedule for Forsyth County, the only slave listed under his name. In 1860 she was twelve years old, and in May 1863, she would have been about fifteen.

Horatio: Horatio's 16th Georgia was in Wofford's Brigade, McLaws's Division. Horatio and his brigade were part of Lee's force that marched from Fredericksburg to Chancellorsville on May 1, and they ended up fighting in all four days of the Battle of Chancellorsville.

Near Chancellorsville on May 1, they were assaulted by Union artillery and infantry and assaulted the enemy in return. On May 2, the brigade attacked Hooker on the Union left more "seriously" than intended while Jackson made his flanking movement and attacked the Union right.

Early the next day, May 3, at the same time Simeon and others of Jackson's, now Jeb Stuart's, men began their attack against the Union right, Horatio's brigade attacked Hooker's left again. Then later that same day Lee ordered it to turn back east to confront the new threat emerging from Fredericksburg after the Union had captured the town.

---

[26] *OR*, ser. 1, vol. 25, pt. 1, 889–92; *OR*, ser. 1, vol. 25, pt. 2, 840.
[27] *OR*, ser. 1, vol. 25, pt. 1, 807.
[28] Service records; US Census, 1860, Jones County, Georgia.
[29] Service records; US Census, 1850, Carroll County, Georgia.
[30] US Census, 1860, Jones County, Georgia.

Finally, the late evening and night of the following day, May 4, Horatio's brigade and another brigade advanced against the Federals near Fredericksburg and drove the enemy before them. Thus, the 16th Georgia fought on all four days of the Battle of Chancellorsville.[31]

Horatio's Brigade on May 3rd

Early on May 3, while Simeon and others attacked the Union right, Horatio and his regiment engaged in what for them was probably the most hazardous fighting of the four-days battle at Chancellorsville. This was when their brigade and other Confederate brigades attacked Hooker's left wing about a half mile southeast of Chancellorsville.

That morning not long after sunrise, Horatio's and other Confederate brigades were stationed in a stand of thick woods separated from the Union line by an open field they would have to cross to reach the Federal position. The attack began when the brigades' skirmishers were ordered to advance.

As the skirmishers moved across the field toward the Union line, they saw before them breastworks built in a crooked line in a dense wood. The works had been constructed of fallen trees and brush, which had been piled thickly together to form a wall. A ditch had been dug in front, and dirt from the ditch was thrown against the works for added protection. In addition, ends of large tree branches had been sharpened and placed in the wall pointed outward toward the advancing skirmishers.[32]

As ordered, the Confederate skirmishers began to run forward (with "their peculiar yell" a Union soldier wrote) in a loose line that stretched across the field from side to side. When they approached the enemy, they began firing at will, sometimes from a kneeling and sometimes from a prone position, but they kept their general alignment while continuing to move forward. They fought for about half an hour, principally to gauge the enemy's strength, then retired back into the thick woods where Horatio's and other Confederate brigades were assembling.[33]

Once assembled, Horatio and his fellow Confederates started out from the woods across the open field toward the enemy. At first they probably moved slowly in textbook fashion, shoulder-to-shoulder, elbows touching elbows, in two lines, one close behind the other. Their two lines, like those of the skirmishers earlier, stretched across the field from side to side. As they advanced, they took heavy fire from both Federal muskets and Federal artillery. When gaps opened in

---

[31] Byrd, *Confederate Sharpshooter*, 67–73.

[32] *Southern Confederacy* (Atlanta), May 19, 1863; *OR*, ser. 1, vol. 25, pt. 1, 342–44; Garrison, *Encyclopedia of Civil War Usage*, 3, 35.

[33] *OR*, ser. 1, vol. 25, pt. 1, 343 (quote); *Southern Watchman*, May 27, 1863; W. C. Davis, *Rebels and Yankees*, 44; McPherson, *Battle Cry of Freedom*, 474; Griffith, *Battle Tactics*, 99–10, 154–56; Sherman, *Memoirs*, 885–87.

the lines, the command was to "close up," and the men moved sideways as best they could and continued their shoulder-to-shoulder advance.[34]

Upon command, they stopped and fired, some kneeling, some standing. They continued firing without command and continued to advance, attempting to stay in line and close together as much as possible. Every so often, individuals or groups stopped again and fired. Some may have done as Alabama soldiers did in the Seven Days Battles: they would fire a shot, "roll over on our backs, place our guns between our feet and load as quick as possible, roll over on the other side and shoot."

One of these, a soldier in the 16th, a veteran of several battles, wrote home describing how he felt during an advance. As his company moved forward, he saw a friend near him get shot. His friend begged for help, but the soldier recorded, "I had no time to lose. It was everyman for himself for they was falling on my right and left and my disposition inclined to try to return the fire with as much injury as possible."[35]

The Confederates got within eighty to one hundred feet of the Union breastworks, slugging it out face-to-face with the Federals before being stopped. Then, "after an hour's hard fighting," a Union officer wrote, "the enemy gave way and retired in confusion, followed by the cheers of our men."[36]

In the woods, the Confederates regrouped, reforming their lines and reuniting with friends and comrades. Again, the brigades attacked, with again the same results.

For a third time the Confederates regrouped in the woods. This time they slowly advanced in two closely massed columns. Rather than stretched across the field, they moved forward in several shorter lines stacked one behind the other with a narrower front. As these two massed columns approached the crooked line of the enemy breastworks, the 16th Georgia was near the center of a column, its battle flag clearly visible to the Federals.[37]

By now the Confederates had discovered a weak point in the Union line, and the 16th headed straight for it. In the Union breastworks a place had been left relatively open so skirmishers could hurry back in. Although filled with logs,

---

[34] *OR*, ser. 1, vol. 25, pt. 1, 343; McPherson, *Battle Cry of Freedom*, 473, 475–76; Bledsoe, *Citizen-Officers*, 201, 203–204; Garrison, *Encyclopedia of Civil War Usage*, 51; Detzer, *Donnybrook*, 43–44; Hess, *Union Soldier in Battle*, 115; Stoker and Elam, "Strategy, Operations, and Tactics," 86–87.

[35] Griffith, *Battle Tactics*, 89, 112–13; 154–55; Stoker and Elam, "Strategy, Operations, and Tactics," 86–87; LeVan, *Great War of Destruction*, 106 (1st quote); Roberson, *In Care of Yellow River*, 123 (2nd quote).

[36] *OR*, ser. 1, vol. 25, pt. 1, 343 (quote); Griffith, *Battle Tactics*, 138–40.

[37] *OR*, ser. 1, vol. 25, pt. 1, 343–44; Hess, *Union Soldier in Battle*, 115, 152–54; Griffith, *Battle Tactics*, 150–54; Detzer, *Donnybrook*, 43.

this spot had no ditch in front and no dirt thrown against the logs to allow the logs there to be moved fairly quickly to let in the skirmishers. In addition, no men had been positioned behind those logs.[38]

The Union officer in command saw the men of the 16th, their flag clearly visible, heading toward the vulnerable spot and quickly ordered his men placed on either side to defend it. Some of those men, running short of ammunition, loaded and fired buckshot at the oncoming 16th. At first undeterred, Horatio and his men continued their attack. The regiment's flagbearer had gotten within thirty-five feet of the breastworks when the Federals singled him out and shot him. Another member of the regiment picked up the flag, and he too was shot.[39]

Ultimately, the sweeping Union fire had its effect. The Confederates, standing largely unprotected in the field, were again checked. Soon the 16th and the other units fell back across the clearing and into the woods.

There Horatio's brigade began to reassemble once again. Observing the enemy line, General Wofford, the brigade's commander, noticed that the Federals appeared to be preparing to retreat. He urged his men to form quickly for another attack. Then, one of his brigade reported, "The order was given to fix bayonets and move out of the timber." This time it would not be a slow advance but a rapid charge with no firing as they dashed forward.

What Wofford had observed was the Union regiment defending the breastworks beginning to pull back for lack of ammunition and being replaced by another regiment. At this fortuitous disruption in the Union ranks, his brigade rushed forward, the men cheering and Wofford yelling, "Charge them with a will! Give them some steel!"

In the Union men's resulting confusion, the brigade's charge carried the breastworks, the Federals pulled back, and "a considerable body" of Union soldiers surrendered.[40]

Although the way forward seemed relatively clear, the brigade did not pursue the Federals all the way to Chancellorsville. Before they had that chance, Lee ordered Horatio's brigade and others under General McLaws's command to turn around and go back toward Fredericksburg to help stop the Union force advancing from there.

During the four-day Battle of Chancellorsville, the 16th suffered a total of 133 casualties—18 killed and 115 wounded. It has been estimated that the average strength of a Confederate regiment then that had seen much action, as had the 16th, would have been around four hundred men. If that were the case, during

---

[38] *OR*, ser. 1, vol. 25, pt. 1, 344.
[39] Ibid.
[40] Byrd, *Confederate Sharpshooter*, 70 (1st and 2nd quotes); G. J. Smith, *"One of the Most Daring of Men,"* 69, 72, 192n26; *OR*, ser. 1, vol. 25, pt. 1, 176, 331–35, 826 (3rd quote), 834–35.

the Battle of Chancellorsville the 16th sustained casualties amounting to about a third of its strength.

One member of the 16th wrote home right after the battle, "our regiment lost more men than we ever have in arry fight yet." He continued, "Our company looks like a platoon. We have only 36 men present in the company." (A company's full designated strength was roughly one hundred men and officers.)[41]

Horatio's Role

Apparently, no letters from Horatio have survived to tell precisely what he did during the Battle of Chancellorsville, particularly on the dangerous day of May 3. Considering the usual duties of a lieutenant in combat, however, it may be possible to reconstruct what he likely did that day.

Horatio had just been promoted to lieutenant, and Chancellorsville was his first battle with that rank. He was twenty years old. As a lieutenant, in combat his overall duties were, in the words of one Civil War lieutenant, "to cheer and encourage the men, and aid the company commander in managing the company." A lieutenant did this in a variety of ways, according to a modern historian, such as transmitting and executing orders, "maintaining a conspicuous presence along the firing line," and demonstrating a "willingness to ignore danger." He also was expected to "maintain fire discipline, preserve alignments, [and] keep order in the ranks."

The textbook position of a lieutenant whose company was advancing in line of battle, as Horatio's was in the early assaults on May 3, was two paces behind the line. In this position, a lieutenant could not always accomplish his different duties effectively, particularly when the firing on both sides began. Instead, in the noise and smoke of battle he might find it necessary to move among his men transmitting and issuing orders, encouraging their actions, and demonstrating to them courage, calmness, and command under fire.

At times in combat, it was necessary for an officer to use coercion as a form of encouragement. From his position two paces behind a line of battle particularly, a lieutenant could serve as a file closer, whose role was to keep the men maintaining their places in line, closed up, and obeying orders. In performing this duty, he could threaten punishment, or even shoot someone who failed to comply.[42]

---

[41] *OR*, ser. 1, vol. 25, pt. 1, 806, 826–27; *Southern Confederacy* (Atlanta), May 19, 1863; Roberson, *In Care of Yellow River*, 122–24 (quote, 124); Sears, *Chancellorsville*, 372–86, 400–403; Griffith, *Battle Tactics*, 92; Bledsoe, *Citizen-Officers*, 62–63; Furguson, *Chancellorsville 1863*, 88; Detzer, *Donnybrook*, 112–13; G. J. Smith, *"One of the Most Daring of Men,"* 72–76, 192.

[42] Bledsoe, *Citizen-Officers*, 162–75.

Horatio likely performed some of these duties during the Chancellorsville battle. Wherever he was precisely and whatever he did, he also likely was eager to perform well in his first battle as an officer and to demonstrate his bravery.

A. S. C. Williams to James H. David

Gen Hosp No Richmond va
May the 7 1863
Mr. J. H. David Dir Sir

I By the Request of your sone seat My self to drop you a few linnes to let you noe how he is. he is Wounded in the Small of the Back. it is a flesh Wound. he told Mee to rite to you and say to you that hee thout that hee wad Bee able for Duty sune for it is Jest a flesh Wound and sed tell you that you must Not Bee oneesy for hee Wad Bee where hee cald Write him sel sune. I left him at the horse Pittle 15 Miles from the Rale rode and hee cood not walk. I cant tell when hee will get to Richmond. Soe I will close. excuse My Bad Writing and speling for My bely herts soe Bad I cant set up well.

    A. S. C. Williams
    16 Rig Ga vol co (F)
    Captain McRae co

Notes

your sone: He was writing about Horatio.

A. S. C. Williams: At the time he wrote this letter A. S. C. Williams was a corporal in Company F of the 16th Georgia. He was listed as seriously wounded in the thigh.[43]

---

[43] Service records; *Southern Confederacy* (Atlanta), May 18, 1863.

Chapter 19

A Hospital and a Journey: Horatio and Thirza, 1863

Horatio

Richmond Va Gen. Hospital No. 10
May __ 1863
Dear Mother

    I take this opportunity to write you once more. I have not heard from you. This makes the third letter I have written you since I have been wounded and have not received any reply yet.

    My wound is no better than it was when I first came here. I am yet very weak. I am at a hospital where I get tolerable good fare. I have very good attention but I am very tired of staying here. I hope as soon as I get better I will be able to get a furlough and come home but they are not giving any now to any one.

    Dear Mother, write to me soon as you receive this for I am very anxious to hear from you. Direct your letter to Gen Hospital No. 10
Richmond City, Va
Nothing more at present. Your aft. Son

                                        H. J. David

Notes

Date: This version of the letter is taken from a transcription of the original, the original having been lost. The transcription lists the date as April 20, 1863. Because Horatio was not wounded until early May, the date is obviously wrong. The correct date must be sometime between May 7, when Corporal A. S. C. Williams reported that Horatio had not yet reached Richmond, and May 20, the date of Horatio's next letter, his first correctly dated letter from the hospital where he was taken.

Gen. Hospital No. 10: This hospital was located at the southwest corner of Main and 19th streets in Richmond, fronting on Main Street. Its capacity was more than three hundred patients. Earlier it was known as the Union Hotel.[1]

List of Casualties in Wofford's Brigade

McLaws' Division, in the Engagements
Near Chancellorsville, Va.[2]

---

[1] Waitt, *Confederate Military Hospitals in Richmond*, 13.
[2] *Southern Confederacy* (Atlanta), May 18, 1863, 1.

16th GEORGIA REGIMENT

....

Company B, Capt J M Venable Commanding, Killed, privates J. E. Lyle, E. O. Collins Wounded, Lt. H J David, hip seriously....

Note

Capt J M Venable Commanding: He was Captain John Mooreman Venable from Jackson County. He was elected captain of Company B after Captain Reynolds was killed at the Battle of Crampton's Gap in September 1862. At the time the letter was written, he was about thirty-eight years old.[3]

J. M. Venable

Camp Anna May 18th, 1863
Lt. H. J. David
Dear Sir [Horatio]

I received your note yesterday and was glad to hear that you was getting some better. I hope you will soon recover from your wound. I send you some pay Rolls with my certificate. get someone to fill out [letter torn] and there will be no difficulty in getting your money.

[torn] boys is ginerally well.

Your Obedient
Servant
J. M. Venable

Horatio

May 20, '63
Gen. Hospital # 10
Room 50
Dear Mother

I received your kind letter of the 15th this morning. I was happy to hear you were all well.

Mother, I will state to you the exact condition of myself. The ball struck me on the hipbone in front where it joins the backbone and then it glanced and struck the backbone and ranged up the backbone 2 inches and stopped. Therefore it passed [through] 4 inches in the flesh.

---

[3] Service records; Rigdon, *Georgia 16th Infantry Regiment*, 95; US Census, 1860, Jackson County, Georgia; T. Harris, *Portraits of a Southern Place*, 23.

the hipbone is slightly fractured. I can't walk [but] a few steps at the time. I can sit up at a table long enough to write by bearing the weight of my body on my arm. My wound runs a great deal. I have but little use of my back and hips. I do not think it is dangerous. I think it will take a long time to get well, 4 months maybe.

I have stated the case to you as well as I can. You can do as you think best. Of course I would like to see you though I will not ask you to come. My board is $2 a day.

I have not heard from James. I was slightly wounded in the arm. The last time I saw John Deveral he was standing in the front rank shooting as fast as he could load.

Your son,
H. J. David

Notes

My wound runs a great deal: Draining of a wound is part of the normal healing process, but prolonged draining may be a sign of infection.[4]

James: He is James Neal, and he survived the battle.
John Deveral: He survived the battle.[5]

Simeon

Camp Gregg, near Guinea's Station
Va May 25, 1863
My affectionate Mother

Your short but very affecting favor of the 15th inst. came to hand a few days ago and found me alive and in tolerably good health. I have not been entirely well since the late tremendous battles, but I have been on duty all the time.

I learned of Horatio's being wounded a few days after I wrote you, from a member of our regiment down there with our Lieut. Col. Fielder who died at the same hospital where Horatio is staying. He sent me word by this gentleman that he was out of money and did not know that he could draw on Richmond and wanted me to send him some money and go to him myself if possible. I saw the authorities and learned that it would be impossible to get off but sent him thirty dollars by a young man of my company that was going to the hospital.

The quartermaster of our regiment, Capt. E. A. Higgins, came up from Richmond yesterday and informed me that he called to see Ratio and that he was doing very well, that he had drawn more than one hundred dollars of his own

---

[4] Fletcher, "Managing Wound Exudate," 51.
[5] Service records.

besides the thirty I sent him. Ratio told him that he would be able to walk in a few days.

Capt. Higgins also saw Col. Thomas of Ratio's regiment who has a wounded son in the same room with Ratio and says that Thomas spoke of Ratio in the highest terms as an excellent young officer brave as Julius Caesar and that he would certainly make his mark if the war continued long. Higgins did not think there would be much chance for Horatio to go home.

So soon as I heard he was wounded I wrote to my friend Mrs. Barber where he was and told her if possible to go to the hospital and hunt him up and do all she could for him. I have not heard whether she has been to see him. His situation has caused me a great deal of anxiety but I shall not rest easy.

There seems to be an impression that Gen. Lee will make a forward movement soon though we can't tell anything about it. We are in delightful camps and enjoying ourselves very much, very little to do. There is a very general revival of religion going on in our Brigade at this time, baptizing every day. There are several churches in the surrounding country that our men go to every Sabbath.

I have not heard from Fanny in more than two weeks. I can't help feeling a little uneasy.

Our prospects seem a little gloomy in the west, but I hope they will work out right. From all accounts, the wheat crop bids to be fair, to be very good in the Southern states.

I forgot to mention that my arm that was slightly wounded in the last battle is about well. With my humble prayers for you all, I remain as ever,

Your affectionate son,
S. B. David

Notes

our Lieut. Col. Fielder: Lt. Colonel Fielder was the regimental commander of the 14th Georgia. He was wounded at Chancellorsville on May 3, when, according to Simeon's letter of May 9, 1863, in chapter 18, he had his leg broken. It had to be amputated, and as Simeon mentions he died of his wounds. Although Simeon does not mention the date of his death, his service records indicate it was May 10.[6]

Col. Thomas of Horatio's regiment and wounded son: The colonel was Lieutenant Colonel Henry P. Thomas, second in command of the 16th Georgia. His son was Captain E. B. Thomas of the 24th Georgia. Lt. Col. Thomas was killed at Knoxville on November 29, 1863.[7]

---

[6] Henderson, *Roster of the Confederate Soldiers of Georgia*, 2:360; service records.
[7] Derry, *Confederate Military History: Georgia*, 38–39; Henderson, *Roster of the Confederate Soldiers of Georgia*, 2:480; service records.

Mrs. Barber: Mrs. Barber (Barbour?) has not been identified.

impression that Gen. Lee will make a forward movement soon: Lee did. See chapter 21.

Our prospects are a little gloomy in the west: This perhaps was an understatement. By May 25, 1863, when Simeon wrote this letter, the Union army occupied most of Tennessee and much of Mississippi. In addition, the key railroad junction of Chattanooga in East Tennessee was being threatened.

The Union also had captured New Orleans and controlled the Mississippi River except the areas around Port Hudson, Louisiana, and Vicksburg, Mississippi. Yet those latter two areas also were poised to fall to the Union. In particular, Grant had a large Confederate army contained in Vicksburg. Manning Alexander was with the Confederates inside Vicksburg, and more about that campaign will be related in the next chapter.[8]

Thirza

Richmond Va
May 28 1863
Dear husband and children and neighbors

I am now sitting by Ratio's bedside. I find him comfortably situated and doing well. I found him sitting up writing a letter to someone in his regiment. Chronic diorrhea pesters him some.

I went with two men from Clarke Co. in whose care I came on. I had the misfortune to have my shawl snatched off my arm in going from the Car to the Omnibus in Augusta, but I done very well. We missed the connection at Branchville and had to lie over till next day 12 oclock. We travelled in crowded cars, refugees from Miss.

I have been sleeping a nap on the bed of the General of the hospital. I feel much refreshed. I have not had an opportunity of lying down since I took the cars Monday morning.

I am as well as I ever was. I design to get a room here in the hospital where I can attend to him. I think I shall succeed.

When I arrived in the city, I put myself and baggage on an omnibus and ordered him to drive to Mrs. Susan N. Barbers. I told her I came there on the request of my son Lieut. David. She received me in such a manner I felt almost like I was at home.

The gentleman who came with me is named Fullylove. I have not seen him since I parted with him at the depot. He had not seen his nephew and friends when I parted with him.

---

[8] Gallagher et al., *Civil War*, 120–43.

Do not be uneasy about me. I intend to bring him with me, if I keep well. I will do the best I can to save money. I only spent 25 cts for something to eat till I got here. I will send you the amounts I spent coming but I am with my child.

$5.75 fare from Athens to Augusta
$5.50 fare Augusta to Kingsville
$10.00 from Kingsville to Wilmington
$5 from Wilmington to Weldon—1/2 fare
$1.00 omnibus fare at Petersburg
$1.20—1/2 fare from Petersburg to Richmond
$2.00 from Weldon to Petersburg
$2.00 omnibus fare in Richmond
$33.20 total expense

I am now going up to [Mrs. Barbers?] to stay all night. I have not seen the ward nurse and can't tell yet whether I can get a room or not.

I fear I shall not get to see Simeon. Ratio says to feed the chickens good and have plenty against he gets home.

Ratio's soldier friends are coming in so I can't write.

Your own wife and mother

Give my love to all the neighbors

Thirza David

Notes

I am now sitting by Ratio's bedside: Thirza possibly made the journey to Ratio in part because in 1863, as a Confederate reported, "when a soldier was sent to a hospital he was expected to die." When she began the journey, she was less than a month away from her sixtieth birthday.[9]

Branchville: Branchville is a small town in the southern part of South Carolina about midway between Augusta and Charleston.[10]

bowels, diorrea: "[D]iarrhea was the most common sickness of Civil War soldiers. With a mortality rate of around ten percent, bowel complaints would prove the number-one killer by the war's end."[11]

Clarke Co.: Athens, where Thirza began her train journey, is in Clarke County.[12]

the Car and cars: Thirza means a railroad car or railroad cars.

Omnibus: An enclosed vehicle frequently mounted on springs that transported passengers and their luggage along city streets. It was drawn by a horse or

---

[9] Welch, *Confederate Surgeon's Letters to His Wife*, 74–75; David Family Bible.
[10] *Rand McNally 2019 Road Atlas*, 92.
[11] Meier, *Nature's Civil War*, 59.
[12] *Georgia Atlas & Gazetteer*, 22.

horses, and the driver rode outside the vehicle, usually on a seat in front of and above the cabin carrying the passengers.[13]

since I took to the cars Monday morning: Thirza started her journey on the morning of Monday, May 25 and did not arrive in Richmond until about three days later, sometime on Thursday, May 28, the day she wrote the letter.

Mr. Fullylove: This gentleman may have been Henry M. Fullilove, who in May 1863 lived in Clarke County and was about forty-four years old. If he was the man who accompanied Thirza to Richmond, not long after he returned to Georgia he enlisted as a private in Company G of the 9th Georgia Infantry (State Guards), perhaps motivated, in part, by his experiences in Richmond.[14]

$33.20 total expense: It appears that Thirza's addition is incorrect. The total of the amounts listed is $32.45 rather than $33.20. The original of this letter, however, has been lost, and what remains is a transcription. It is possible that the transcriber missed an entry or maybe two. The transcribed copy includes no cost for the omnibus in Augusta to which she was transferring when she lost her scarf and does not include the twenty-five cents she says she spent for food.

Thirza's itinerary: Civil War rail lines in the South had been constructed by different railroad companies. This inefficient arrangement meant someone traveling long distances frequently had to get off one train and board another run by a different rail line in order to arrive at the final destination. To get from Athens to Richmond, Thirza likely would have made at least five train changes.

Georgia: Thirza began her train journey at Athens, about twenty-five miles from her home. She traveled on the Georgia Railroad from Athens to Augusta.

South Carolina: From Augusta, she crossed the Savannah River to Hamburg, South Carolina. From there she traveled on the South Carolina Railroad to Branchville and then on to Kingsville, South Carolina, in the middle of the state.

South and North Carolina: From Kingsville she traveled by the Wilmington and Manchester Railroad to Wilmington, North Carolina. From Wilmington she rode on the Wilmington & Weldon line to Weldon, North Carolina, near the border between North Carolina and Virginia.

North Carolina and Virginia: From Weldon to Petersburg, Virginia, she rode on the Petersburg Railroad, and from Petersburg to Richmond she was on the Richmond and Petersburg Railroad.[15]

---

[13] Drake, *What Did They Mean by That?*, 211; "Horsebus," Wikipedia, https://en.wikipedia.org/wiki/Horsebus , accessed January 19, 2017.

[14] US Census, 1860, Clarke County, Georgia; service records.

[15] Coleman, *History of Georgia*, 156–59; Black, *Railroads of the Confederacy*, 6; Hotchkiss, "Railroad Map of South Carolina."

A HOSPITAL AND A JOURNEY: HORATIO AND THIRZA, 1863

Thirza

Richmond June 2nd 1863
Dear Husband and family

I now divote a few minutes to letting you know how we are doing. I am in good health. Ratio is improving evry way. The wound is doing as well as could be desired. it discharges a great deal of Matter not less than 4 or 5 table spoonfulls evry day. I dress it my self 4 times a day. I am with him alone in a room where I am as private as if I were at home when I please to bolt the door.

When I came to him his bowels were a greater source of affiction than the wound. both together was making him very fast. I waited till he was moved out of the room to where we were alone. I commenced using remedies for his Bowels. I am vry happy to say his bowels are allmost natural.

I have no idea yet when we shall be able to start home. The head Dr has promised to try to get him a Furlough as soon as he thinks him able to travel.

Ratios skin when I came looked dead and sallow. allmost a skeleton. his skin is getting a healthy collor. His flesh gaining fast. his strenght increasing but he cant bend his back, can crook at the hips but has to keep his back perfectly stright. I hope it will not allwas remain so.

The fan is only tolerable good but not so bad but what it might be worse.

Ratio recd a letter from Pillina and Dr Bell this morning written since they recd mine giving them information of his being wounded. Pillina wants to know when he thinks he will be at home so they can meet him there. I wrote to them and to Mary and you all last saturday. I want to know whether James Neal is wounded or not. We have just recd a letter from Simeon written since he recd the one I wrote Saturday before I started. he says there is no chance for him to get off to come to see me.

Columbus Harwell is in the city wounded. One of Ratio's company came in yesterday right from him. he is about a mile from here in Chomboragoo Hospital. he is wounded in the Hip. a flesh wound. [He] is going about on crutches. will soon be well I hope. I cant go to see him because I have no company.

I never expect to regret coming. I never intend to leav him (Ratio) till he is able to come with me if he could get the chance. If they will not let him come, I can come home feeling that I have done my duty.

Dear Nora grand mother went out this morning on the Dock and got you a pretty stone to bring home. Ratio sends love to White and black. he is very anxious to come home with me and the Dr has promised he shall as soon as he gets able to travel if he can get him a Furlough.

be not uneasy about me. I have found many good friends. But to my Friend above I try [to] look for aid and guidance.

Capt Fletcher Parks son of Rev William Parks, is here Sick with Inflammation. I dont think him dangerous though he suffers a good deal.

Now this is the way I am gitting along. I have ham and Butter plenty Honey Syrup Sugar and Coffee. I can buy a loaf of Bakers bread for 20 cts that do me 3 days at last. The wash pan in this room was so rusty I went out yesterday and gave 3 dollars for one. I also gave 1 ¾ dollar for a pound of sugar. it was very nice. I gave 50 cts for a small bottle of Ink. I shall not be at my expens for Board. nursing my son makes up for my using the bed. I shall not have mutch washing done.

Your Wife and Mother
[Written perpendicular across script]
Direct to
Liet H. J. David
General Hospital,
No 10
Richmond Va
James H. David
And Childrn   T. David

Notes

Columbus Harwell: He was a twenty-three-year old private in Horatio's regiment from Jackson County. He survived the war.[16]

Chomboragoo Hospital: This was the Chimborazo Hospital, a gigantic hospital complex covering forty acres located on a hill that then was to the east of Richmond. Its normal occupancy rate was said to be three thousand.[17]

Capt. Fletcher Parks, Rev. William Parks: Rev. William J. Parks was a Methodist minister from Franklin County. His son was Captain W. F. Parks of the 24th Georgia Infantry. Captain Parks survived the war.[18]

Thirza

Richmond June 4 1863
Dear Husband and children

I will write you a few lines for I know how long it would seem to me if I were at home and any of you had to wait a week at a time without hearing.

---

[16] Service records; US Census, 1850, Jackson County, Georgia; tombstone, Lebanon United Methodist Church Cemetery, Gillsville, Georgia.

[17] Freemon, *Gangrene and Glory*, 77–78; Waitt, *Confederate Military Hospitals in Richmond*, 19; Bollet, *Civil War Medicine*, 223.

[18] Service records; US Census, 1850, Franklin County, Georgia.

A HOSPITAL AND A JOURNEY: HORATIO AND THIRZA, 1863

I am quite well. Horatio is mending slowly. I think I could bring him home without injury but the Dr. says it would not do yet. I believe he is keeping him here to get the 2 dollars a day and if it was not for what I brought he would weaken instead of strengthening. The constant drain from the wound gives him a good appetite. Ratio's breakfast is a small piece of baker's bread, could be squeezed to the size of a hen egg, a small bit of veal or mutton fried, the blood at the center, without the name of gravy, one boiled egg without salt or pepper. Dinner some kind of slop called soup made of the scraps of raw meat that the men could not eat at breakfast. Supper tough bread only not well baked, some syrup, and small bowl of sweet milk. I forgot to say he had a little fish boiled 2 or three times.

Be not uneasy. I brought the provisions as good luck ordered it. What they lack I made up. He has fattened as fast as a pig since I first came. I believe and so does he if I had not come when I did he perhaps would not have survived long.

I have no idea of getting a furlough from Genl. Lee. If we got anything it will be a transfer to some other hospital, Atlanta or Macon. Augusta we think will be the most convenient place to have him transferred to. Ratio is very afraid he don't intend to let him go anywhere. I don't intend to leave him. If I can't get him off I intend to wait [here] some time yet. He can't bear the idea of my leaving him till he can knock about in town. I have to watch his bowels. I am afraid to leave him here anyhow.

If he was able to go to his regiment I could leave him with a light heart. I am coming [could come?] home without company. You need not be uneasy. I have learned how to travel. He has to pay two dollars per day for my bed. I eat my own food and my nursing him would pay for my bed. My time is precious and more so is the life of my child.

We are as comfortably situated as can be. The water tank is in the passage not more than 50 feet from our room door. The wound runs a great deal but don't smell much bad now. He can get up off of his bed and lie down without help and walk carefully across the room several times if he wishes without resting.

Mr. Callihan and Mrs. Morgan and Mr. Whitehead are all going in a few days. We could have company if we could get him off. I have some hope that maybe we can do something yet in a few days.

He is now having the second copious passage today. The drain of the wound and his bowels with what he gets here to nourish him would exhaust him in a few weeks— yes, days. I am now going to burn some spirits for his wound. Remember me to all my kind neighbors and you and them pray for us.

T. David

Notes

Mr. Callihan, Mrs. Morgan, and Mr. Whitehead: Mr. Whitehead probably was Elridge Whitehead, age about fifty-three, of Jackson County who had two sons, John C. and Marcus J. Whitehead in Horatio's regiment. Mr. Callihan and Mrs. Morgan are partially identified in the immediately following letter.[19]

burn some spirits for his wound: Although alcohol and spirits ("strong alcoholic liquid") themselves might qualify for use as antiseptics, they apparently were not used often for this purpose during the Civil War. It is unclear, however, why burning spirits would be beneficial for wounds, although one early author did recommend it for producing a vapor that reduced fever.[20]

Thirza

[June 4 or June 5 (?), Richmond]

Now near the dinner-hour. Ratio's trip downstairs and back has fatigued him considerably but has not caused any pain.

Ratio has now eat dinner but not what was furnished here. I found a place day before yesterday where they gave me the flour, and I found butter to shorten them and made him some good biscuit. He eats them and I eat the tough baker's bread. His bowels have mended ever since I got the biscuit.

I never will leave him here while I can use my own provisions. Ratio eats my ham except today and occasionally they bring him a piece of boiled ham. I can get more biscuit when these give out. The soup they bring him he can't eat, nor I either but [you all] keep it dark. It might get back here.

Mrs. William Morgan and Callihan of Jefferson left for home yesterday, not this hospital, but not far off. Blake Morgan is wounded but not able to travel.

Mrs. Morgan had to pay 5 dollars a day board. I had the luck. Bringing my provisions was a good streak.

If I can keep the right side of those in authority about the home as I think I have now got it, I am not much afraid. I think he will get a transfer when the doctor thinks him able to travel. My time is a great loss but not to be compared with the life of my child

I must go and mail this letter. Your mother.

Ratio sends love to everybody.

---

[19] Service records; US Census, 1850, Jackson County, Georgia.
[20] "Spirits," *Webster's New World College Dictionary*, 1400; Schroeder-Lein, *Encyclopedia of Civil War Medicine*, 26–27; Jennings, "A plain elementary Explanation," 369–72.

Notes

Date and place: This scrap of a letter contained no date or place. It appears, however, to have been part of the June 4 letter, or possibly was written the next day, June 5.

not this hospital, but not far off: The meaning of this phrase is unclear, but possibly it refers to the location of the relative or relatives whom Mrs. Morgan and Mr. Callihan were visiting.

Thirza

Richmond, Va June 6, 1863
Dear Husband childrin and Neighbors

I am hapy to inform you I am enjoying the best of health. Ratio I think is mending fast. the Dr said to a friend of Ratios who was speaking to him on the subject of recommending a transfer for him that he certainly would as soon as he thought him able to travel without endangering his life and said in a week or 10 days he thought he could go.

Ratio fined up yesterday and went down on the lower Ward where I found him when I came. Ratio had improved so in his looks they were surprised. One of them observed that was the fruits of having a Mother to nurse him.

He was to have his pants open behind and his coat is so short behind I went out yesterday and bought him a sack coat cost 19 dollars. It is part worsted dark very good, all the cotton coats were too light a cotton, I have to look about today for some guilt lace to put on this coat and the new uniform suit we will make him.

Now breakfast over[,] Ratio has washed, and his bed up, put on his New coat and has gone down and is siting in or outside the front door. With a staff in one hand and the other on the Ballustrade he can go down and up stairs alone. There are sevral here that the leg was shirred and amputated that are going any where they please on crutches. Ratios was a serfice wound as I believed. Mutch longer getting well if he ever gets well than a leg or arm amputated.

I have not had a word from you yet. I have heard nothing yet from James Neal wether he was hurt or not. Ratio got a letter written by Simeon after he had recd mine written the day before I started. Simeon Said nothing would give him more pleasure than to meet me at his sick rom but it was utterly out of his power to come. [The following was written upside down between lines.] I will keep Pillina posted about coming. [The normal letter is resumed.] I wrote to him again after I got heir but have recd no reply yet.

He said to Ratio if he did not think his wound dangerous he ought to have advised me not to come. I am rejoiced that I did come and always expect to be. He believes now and so do I that he would have died if I had not come. his general health was failing fast when I got here. It is now improving as fast. The diet was not nourishing enough to counteract the drain from the wound on the system and his bowel sinking him at the same time. If I live to get home and a Kind Providence Blesses me with health I will make it up. if I never do I shall not spend a great fortune.

You have no idea how the dear child wants to see his native land again. It would be a great satisfaction to even see the dogs at home. If he gets a transfer to Augusta I may have to leave him there a short time but my intention is to bring him with me if possible.

Don't be uneasy about me. my homespun dress does me no harm. Dear Lony be of good cheer. Vicksburg still holds out. I want to hear from home if you have had rain or not and how you all are. Pray for us. May Kind Heaven bless you all

T. David

Notes

sack coat: "[A] man's loose-fitting, straight-backed coat." It usually fell straight from the shoulders.[21]

worsted: "[A] fabric, usually of high quality, made entirely from wool or wool yarn."[22]

Ballustrade: A balustrade is a railing along a stairway supported by small posts called balusters.[23]

shirred: Thirza was familiar with sewing procedures but not with amputation methods. Thus she used the sewing term "shirred" to describe what appeared to her to have been done during an amputation.

"Shirring" in sewing terms means "a gathering made in cloth by drawing the material up on parallel rows of short running stitches." During the Civil War there were two main methods of amputation, circular and flap. As described in the *Encyclopedia of Civil War Medicine*, "In a circular amputation the tissue and skin were rolled up like a sleeve or cuff. After the muscle and bone were cut, the cuff was rolled down and sown closed to from the sump. The flap amputation involved cutting the skin and tissue in such a way as to leave two long flaps that would be folded and sewn back over the end of the bone." Thirza would have referred to one of these methods as "shirred."[24]

Vicksburg still holds out: Union General Grant had surrounded Vicksburg since mid-May 1863. On the day this letter was written, Vicksburg still had not

---

[21] "Sack coat," *Webster's New World College Dictionary*, 1277.
[22] Drake, *What Did They Mean by That?*, 330.
[23] "Ballustrade," *Webster's New World College Dictionary*, 113.
[24] "Shirring," *Webster's New World College Dictionary*, 1341; Schroeder-Lein, *Encyclopedia of Civil War Medicine*, 16.

surrendered. Dr. M. P. Alexander was in Vicksburg at this time. The next chapter describes the experience there.[25]

Thirza

Richmond June 9, 1863
Dear family

    This morning at sunrise after having dressed Ratio's wound, [we] sit down to infor[m] how we were agreeably surprised last night when we were in our room at our little table eating supper, some[one] gently tapped at the door. I opend and to [my] inexpressible joy my own Simeon stood before. [Written upside down between lines: "Simeon has a furlough of 5 days."]

    it is not worth while to say I was glad. It seems to me I ought to be one of the most thank full person on earth. I have been blessd beyond my expectation all the time. My health could be no better. Ratio is improving fast in his general health. the wound also is doing as well as desirable but it is as I thought at first a severe and could soon be made a dangerous wound.

    I buy flour and have buiscit baked for him to eat entirely. I eat the other bread when I can, corn bread we don't get one particle. I boil some of my rice allmost evy day. I boil ham every morning give it to him. I eat what is brought to him if I can. I have not used more than half of my butter yet.

    We are just as comfortably situated as I could desire with regard to situation perfectly private when we wish to be. our door opens into a passage 100 feet long rooms on each side containing wounded officers. One capt wounded at 7 pines. seval wounded at time Ratio was with an arm or leg amputated are well enough and gone home.

    I have no idea now if I had not come that he evr would have recoverd. I shall allwas be thankfull that I was so impressed to come and that you all consented for me to come. Ratio is now beginning to look like himself. the wound discharges a great deal of matter. Makes it the more important to nourish him evry way I can.

    I have no idea certain when we will get of. I [illegible] hope we will before Simeon leaves so that he can assist us. I have no thought he could sit up all the way nor mutch of the way but I could make him pallets of our blankets. I think we could get to Augusta and then rest a while. don't be uneasy about me. I feel that I cant be half thankfull enough for the great success I have had so far.

    It is quite cool here now. unpleasantly so. I have not been too warm but a few times since I left home.

    Ratio is in fine spirits. he sends love to Father Sister and Nora also to all the connection and neighbors. Ratio sends howdy to all the blacks at home and to

---

[25] Wagner, *Timeline of the Civil War*, 131–32, 143.

those of the Neighbors. says to ours tend the Watermellon vines well for he wants to have a pull at a many a one. He wants particular care taken of his Horse.

dont be uneasy about us. I am getting very impatient to hear from home. I have not heard one word yet. I fear you have not had rain.

I must close. Receive assurance of tenderest regard for you all, Husband Daughters, Sweet little Nora too, Blacks. also tell little John and Juddy howdy.

J. H. David   T. David

Notes

Simeon has a furlough of five days: Simeon's regiment, the 14th Georgia, was under General A. P. Hill. It did not begin leaving Fredericksburg and marching toward Pennsylvania until June 14 or shortly afterward. This time was well after most of the rest of Lee's army already was on its way north. In fact, the 14th was one of the last units to begin the march.

Assuming Simeon's five-day pass was granted on June 8, the day before he arrived at Horatio's room, he would have been back with his regiment in time for the march.[26]

7 pines: The Battle of Seven Pines (or Battle of Fair Oaks) was fought on the peninsula between the James and York rivers east of Richmond May 31–June 1, 1862, more than a year before this letter was written.[27]

John and Juddy: It is unclear who they were. Possibly they were young enslaved African American children owned by the Davids. The 1860 federal slave schedule lists James H. David as owning a one-year-old boy, who may have been John. A girl may have been born during the three or so years after the schedule was completed, and she may have been Juddy.

Thirza

Augusta Ga June 16 1863
Dear Husband and Children

I will drop you a few lines. I wrote to you on sunday in the evening. we left Richmond last friday 12 inst and made connection evry time. Ratio was allmost exhausted when we got here Sunday morning. he was compelled to travel in a sitting posture from 10 oclock Saturday night till we got here.

The abscess that I wrote about in my last letter broke into the wound yesterday and ran a great deal. The swelling and inflammation has subsided and it is allmost free from pain when he is still. I keep a plaster of Salve on the hole and apply cold clothes changed every 10 minutes all over the small of the back and

---

[26] Dewberry, *History of the 14th Georgia*, 60; Robertson, *General A. P. Hill*, 198–200.
[27] Wagner, *Timeline of the Civil War*, 74–75.

hip, right hip. he has to lie on his left side entirely. only when he occasionally turns on his bowels he sits up but very little on the side of the bed. his Bowels are mutch better Since he arrived here but not well yet.

Ratios general health is now improving. he is in high spirits. now thinks he will get home but has no idea he ever would have seen home again if I had not gone to him.

I am informed they are about forming a medical board here when they will be able to grant Furloughs. Ratio will get one as soon as it can be arranged.

We are just as comfortably situated as we wish to be, a good room. we are on the third floor where the air can circulate freely. plenty to eat as good as we want. Ratio will have to pay one dollar per day my board and washing gratis. I wash all the cloths I use in dressing his wound. I bought a new wash pan in Richmond to use on the road for whitch I paid 3 dollars. We have one furnished us here to use, and a bucket and pitcher to hold water. If we were at home it would take all my time to wait on him any way.

Mr Thornton has just been in and says he is aiming to get him leave of absence before the board is formed. I hope he will succeed. it is uncertain when he will get it, we may have to let him rest at Union Point. When we get to Athens we will let you know when to send for us.

I have never had better health in my life. I never can be thankfull enough for my good health and blessings any way.

I have just heard to day of a great excitement here and up the country of an expected Yankee raid. I fear it was so where you live also. I have not heard one word from home Since I left but I will not be uneasy for it will do no good.

We may get off to morrow and we may not for some days. We are doing verry well here. Ratio is improving and gaining strength. I hardly think it worth while to write for I hope we shall leave here befor a letter would come now.

Grandma has got a little rock for Nora from Drurrys Bluf and one from James River also. Remember us to all enquiring friends. be not uneasy about us. we will get along some of these days we hope.

Your Own Wife and mother

T David

[Written upside down and between the lines]

Well now dinner [is] over. Ratio and I think we had better stay. we fair so mutch better than we possibly can do at home. I must tell you what we had for dinner. white headed cabbage squash bacon and beef boiled onion sauce yam potatoes sweet milk good corn bread and loaf wheat bread. I hope we have not hurt our selves but let us sure greatly tempted to be intemperate.

Notes

Mr. Thornton: He has not been identified.

Union Point: Union Point, Georgia, was where the Georgia Railroad coming from Augusta divided, one branch going to Atlanta and the other on to Athens.[28]

an expected Yankee raid: The headline on page 1 of the *Augusta Chronicle* of June 11, five days before Thirza wrote the letter, read, "To Arms! To Arms." The first sentence immediately following read, "The town was thrown into intense excitement this morning by the report that a party of Yankee raiders (what number is not known) were approaching this city from Lincoln County, where it is said they are now."

In response, the colonel commanding the city's defenses sounded the alarm and declared martial law. Some twelve hundred men in six infantry companies, a cavalry troop, and an artillery battery rapidly assembled in front of City Hall where arms and ammunition were distributed. They remained on alert for several hours. Then late in the afternoon, most were dismissed while one infantry company, the cavalry troop, and a section of artillery stayed on guard overnight.

The expected raid turned out to be a rumor. The result, however, was that Augusta was thoroughly aroused. The *Chronicle* urged that the rumor should "excite our alarm and stimulate us to redouble our exertions in the cause of self-defense." The mayor proclaimed, "It is indispensable that our vigilance should not be allowed to relax." He also set out specific actions for city defense, such as requesting all businesses to shut down at five o'clock each day so that their employees capable of bearing arms could drill and prepare themselves "for usefulness when the final crisis shall come."

In addition, on June 22, Governor Brown issued a proclamation stating that the enemy was "making preparations to send raids of mounted men through Georgia…leaving our country now the home of a happy people, little better than a desolate waste behind them." Like the Augusta mayor, he followed this announcement with detailed actions to be taken for the state's defense.[29]

Thirza

[Augusta, June 16, 1863]

Mr. Thornton has just been in and informs us that he has talked with Dr. Ford and he informed him that the board will sit tomorrow and if it does and he gets a Furlough we will go up to Athens on Thursday if Ratio is able to travel. I will write when we get to Athens where A or Dire [is] to come, the trunk will have to be carried up on the Hack. The little Waggon must come and plenty of straw and two more Pillows. I already have one pillow.

---

[28] Black, *Railroads of the Confederacy*, xxix.
[29] *Augusta Chronicle*, June 11, 12, 13, 24, 1863.

Notes

Date and place: This note was written, in Thirza's handwriting, on a scrap of paper. She did not indicate the date or place, but it probably was written on June 16, the same day as the letter immediately above. It also probably was sent home in the same envelope as that letter.

Dr. Ford: He was Dr. Lewis D. Ford. At the time Thirza wrote this note, he was about sixty-two years old and in charge of a Confederate hospital in Augusta connected with the Medical College of Georgia.[30]

Thursday: The next Thursday was June 18.

A or Dire: They likely were two of the Davids' enslaved people.

Hack: A "hack" was horse-drawn vehicle (such as a carriage, coach, or wagon) for hire.[31]

Thirza

Augusta [Wednesday] June 17 1863
Dear Family

I am happy to inform I am in good health and Ratio's general health is better than when we got here last Sunday morning.

There has been efforts making all the week to get Ratio leave of absence to go home without effect. The Matron Mrs. Crumpton advised me to go myself to Dr Ford. I done so and in as humble a manner as possible requested him to permit me to carry my son home stating the length of time I had been from home that I had not heard word from home since I left. The Dr wrote out a permit for him to go home and await a Furlough. You cant immagine how thankfull I was. We are just as happily situated here as heart could desire but it is not home.

In the morning at 6 oclock we will start for Athens. I hope [to] get there tomorrow. I shall not mail this till we get to Athens.

Send Dire down Saturday. he can do as well as you can James.

we may not get all the way home in one day. if I find he gets very mutch fatigued I shall stop half way.

Put in a strawbed and two sheets one light one to put over him. that old checked counterpain would be best to throw over him. two pillows at least also a chamber pot so that he would not have to get out of the waggon if his bowels were trouble some, his bowels are better now. Let Dire bring a good baked hen for us to come home on. I want you to make some egg bread baked in cakes like

---

[30] "Confederate Applications for Presidential Pardons, 1865–1867," RG 94, Records of the Adjutant General's Office, 1780–1917, M1003, application dated August 5, 1865, NARA; US Census, 1860, Augusta, Georgia.

[31] "Hack," *Webster's New World College Dictionary*, 651.

fritters. dont make a biscuit. we dont want them. We shall have to drive in a walk all the way home, I hav no idea he can bear a trot.

[The following note written on the same page as the letter above.]

June Thursday 18 1863

Dear Family I have just landed at Mr Newton. Ratio is fatigued but stood the journey today better than we expected. I want Dire to bring down the little Waggon Saturday. I have not heard one word from home since I left. My health is very good. friday and Saturday will be two long days. I will close. Our love to all. we shall try to get home on Sunday. your Wife and Mother

Thirza David

Notes

counterpain: A counterpane is a coverlet or bedspread. It formerly was sewn in squares like windowpanes, but in the period when this letter was written, it might be of any pattern.[32]

Mr. Newton: He may have been John H. Newton, sixty-two, a merchant and farmer who lived in Athens when the letter was written.[33]

we shall try to get home on Sunday: Thirza and Horatio did arrive home, and Horatio did recover. Additional letters from him and more information about him are in some of the following chapters.

A. M. and John H. Jones

Fort Gaines, Ga.
June 21, 1863
Dear Cousin Thirza:

Yours dated Richmond, Va. of the 8th inst. was duly received, by which we were glad to hear that you were well, but sorry to hear that Horatio had been wounded, and we hope that before this you and he are both safe at home.

Poor little Rashe. he has seen some pretty hard times as well as many others. I do think this war has no parallel in history for cruelty and unjustifiable rascality on the part of the enemies. I sometimes think can it be possible that we are fighting a civilized race of human beings. They surely act more like savages than civilized beings. Surely our great Heavenly Father will avenge our wrongs by pouring down his wrath on their deserving heads. When I look around and see our poor boys killed, wounded, and maimed, our country, towns, and villages laid in ruins, our fields laid waste, our property pillaged and carried off, our altars desecrated, and the persons of our fair daughters violated, I ask myself what is our

---

[32] "Counterpane," *Webster's New World College Dictionary*, 339; Drake, *What Did They Mean by That?*, 73.

[33] US Census, 1860, Athens, Georgia; gravestone, Oconee Hill Cemetery, Athens, Georgia.

crime and why are we thus treated. Surely the great God will take vengeance on such a race of vandals for thus treating a people whose only crime is that they wish to govern themselves in their own way.

Cousin Thirza, I look for this war to close under the black flag, and could we be to blame, all things considered, to make it a war of extermination? But enough of this subject now.

This leaves us all in perfectly good health and with but little news of importance of a private nature. The crops in this country are generally good and are now about laid by. We are having an abundance of rain, I fear enough to injure them some. Corn is in silk tassels and our fruit beginning to ripen. Our wheat crop, though small, is generally very good. Our people are generally preparing to live within themselves. The spinning-wheel can be heard in almost every house in the country, and ladies who used to go in silks and muslins are now satisfied to go clad in homespun. Our planters are seeking to raise bountifully of provisions to the neglect of cotton.

The young and middle-aged men are with few exceptions in the army. Willie is at Vicksburg, Jesse and John at Fredericksburg, Va. Jesse went through the hottest of the fight at Chancellorsville, and came out unhurt. Last year he was badly wounded at Seven Pines. He came home and got able to go back time enough to go into the great battle of Sharpsburg, and has been in every battle fought by Genl Lee since then, and has never been touched. John has never been in battle except a few skirmishes. Willie has been in several battles and has never been hurt so far as we know.

My brother David Jones oldest son John has been in the army over two years and is now at Vicksburg or near ther under Genl Breckinridge. Caleb Bowen and his two brothers are all at Vicksburg. Also Cousin Perry Bowen's sons. We had a letter from Caleb dated 8th inst. He was well, but complained some of the hardships they had to undergo which no doubt were heavy. Cousin Hiram and family are well, as also Owen and family.

We would all like to see you very much and hope to see this cruel war close so that we may meet again our friends who are both in and out of the army. Though we have not corresponded for some time, you have not been forgotten by us. We have talked of you and wished to see you, and many a time have spoken of poor little Rashe, and wondered how he came on in the army. We had not heard of his being wounded till we got your letter. We hope he is well by this time.

We had heard of your misfortune by fire some time since, and regretted your loss very much. From having experienced heavy losses by fire ourselves, we will know how to sympathize with you, and with us, it is our lot to have to live [as] a neighbor to the scamp who we believe was the instigator of the fire. We sustained a loss of between 3 & 4000 dollars, and have to stand it and look every day at the scamp who we believe caused it.

We hope that the great Father of all will yet let us live to see this war close out honorably to us, and that we may see our friends all return home and that we may still be happy.

We have two little children living, a little boy going on 5 and a little girl going on two years old, which if we are permitted to keep, ought to be sufficient to make us happy in this life. Our little girl is named Jessie, and Amanda says she looks like Cousin Pelona looked when she was small, or more properly speaking, like old Grandmother Bowen. Our little boy, though going on 5 years old, is still without a name except a little nickname—"Pony." He is a fine boy, and says when he gets to be a man, he is going to have a pretty name and go to the war to help kill Yankees.

Manda says aside from your loss she is grieved because the old house, the home of her grandfather and grandmother and her mother was burned. With her it was rather a sacred place, being first her grandfather's residence then the residence of her favorite aunt and a place where she herself had spent many of the happiest days of life. Amanda says how glad she would be to see you and talk with you, and that she hopes she may yet be permitted to visit you at the old place in Jackson.

She says Caleb told her that you was in Campbell, and that you stopped and saw her sister Thirza's grave, and that she is rejoiced to think you stopped and saw it. Thirza's children are with us going to school and learning well. The oldest will soon be grown. Caleb stopped a few days with us as he was on his way to Mississippi. He was sick and stopped a few days to get well.

Little Pony has gathered some little flowers which he sends to his little Cousin Linna. Amanda Helena says tell you she and Mary are taking music lessons, and their teacher says they are learning very fast. She sends Cousin Anna some geraniums with Pony's flowers. Hoping to hear from you soon, we close by subscribing ourselves

        Your affectionate cousins,
A. M. Jones
Jno. H. Jones

Notes

A. M. and John H. Jones: They were first cousins once removed to each other and were husband and wife. A. M. Jones was Amanda M. Bowen Jones, daughter of Thirza's youngest brother, Hiram Bowen. John H. Jones was the son of one of Hiram and Thirza's uncles on their mother's side, the Jones side. Another letters from them is in chapter 6.

we hope that before this you and he are both safe at home: Thirza and Horatio did arrive home, and Horatio did recover. Additional letters from him and more information about him are in some of the following chapters.

I look for this war to close under the black flag: A black flag in the Civil War era meant that those flying it would take no prisoners, in effect, show no mercy to their captives.[34]

Willie, Jesse, and John Bowen: They are all Amanda's brothers, and thus Thirza's nephews. All three survived the war.[35]

Caleb Bowen and his two brothers: They were all sons of Thirza's deceased brother Thomas. In addition, Caleb had married Amanda Jones's sister Thirza.[36]

Losses by fire: For Thirza's loss, see chapter 16. For the Jones's loss, see chapter 6.

Pony: He is listed in the 1860 census as "John."[37]

the old house, the home of her grandfather and grandmother and her mother was burned: At the time of the fire described in chapter 16, Thirza and her family apparently were living in a house in Jackson County that had belonged to Amanda's grandfather and grandmother, Jesse and Mary Blackwell. Amanda's mother Charity Blackwell Bowen would have lived there with her parents and possibly also later with her husband and her daughter Amanda.[38]

Jesse Blackwell deeded property on the Grove River in Jackson County to James H. David on January 18, 1831, and this land probably contained the Davids' house that burned.[39]

sister Thirza's grave: Sister Thirza was Amanda's sister and the wife of Caleb Bowen, as mentioned in a note above. She died on November 7, 1862.[40]

Cousin Linna: She may have been one of Simeon's daughters, Thirza Lena David, who would have been six years old when this letter was written.[41]

Amanda Helena and Mary: Amanda Helena Bowen was the daughter of Caleb and Thirza Bowen, and thus Amanda Jones's niece.[42]

Mary was Mary Ann Palina Bowen, Amanda Jones's youngest sister. She was recorded in the 1860 census for Clay County, Georgia, as living with John H. and Amanda.[43]

---

[34] Garrison, *Encyclopedia of Civil War Usage*, 27.
[35] Service records, US Census, 1850, Carroll County, Georgia.
[36] US Census, 1860, Campbell, Georgia; "Bowen Bible Records," 36.
[37] US Census, 1860, Clay County, Georgia.
[38] "Bowen Bible Records," 36, 38, 39; US Census, 1850, Carroll County, Georgia.
[39] Jackson County Deed Book I–J, 178.
[40] Gravestone, Bowen Family Cemetery, Douglas County, Georgia.
[41] Gravestone, Lime Branch Cemetery, Polk County, Georgia.
[42] US Census, 1860, Campbell County, Georgia.
[43] See also US Census, 1850, Carroll County Georgia, entry for Hiram Bowen.

Chapter 20

Mississippi: Manning, 1863

Pillina Bell

Chulafinnee, Alabama
January the 16, 1863
Dear Mother

Yours of the 22 December is now before me, though it was a long time on the road....

Dear sister Lonie, I was very sorry indeed to hear of Dr. passing through Atlanta and you not having the chance to see him. But Lona, cheer up and be as happy as you possibly can under the circumstances. I do hope the day is not far distant when you will again be happy together. I know you are at Father's and they will all try to make you happy, but still that will not fill a husband's place. I will write to Dr. without fail. I would have written to him before, but I feared I could not interest him..... .

P. C. Bell

Notes

Letter omissions: This entire letter appears in chapter 14.

Dr. passing through Atlanta: At the end of chapter 13, Dr. M. P. Alexander and the 43rd Georgia had returned to Tennessee from an expedition into Kentucky, and on December 6, 1862, they were camped in Manchester, about sixty miles southeast of Nashville. They still were under General Kirby Smith's command but now as part of the newly organized and newly named Army of Tennessee under the overall command of General Bragg.[1]

Several days later, the 43rd was combined with four other Georgia regiments (the 40th, 41st, 42nd, and 52nd) to form a Georgia brigade under Brigadier General Seth M. Barton. Barton's Brigade was assigned to General Carter Stevenson's division, which still was part of Bragg's Army of Tennessee. That soon changed.[2]

Journey

On December 15, President Davis, in Chattanooga to inspect the western army, ordered Bragg to prepare Stevenson's Division to travel to Mississippi. There it was to join General John C. Pemberton's command centered on Vicksburg. Thus on December 19, the 43rd boarded a train for Mississippi.[3]

---

[1] *OR*, ser. 1, vol. 20, pt. 2, 411–13.
[2] *OR*, ser. 1, vol. 17, pt. 2, 824, 831.
[3] Connelly, *Autumn of Glory*, 30–41; H. P. Bell, *Men and Things*, 89.

The train hurriedly passed through Chattanooga, Tennessee; Atlanta and West Point, Georgia; and Montgomery, Alabama. At Tensaw Wharf south of Montgomery, the soldiers left the train and boarded steamboats that took them down the Tensaw River to Mobile. From Mobile they continued their train journey, rolling through Meridian, Mississippi, to Jackson and arriving finally at Vicksburg the evening of December 27. (Part of this journey would have been along the same rail line over which Simeon's friends traveled to the California gold fields in 1850 as noted in chapter 1.) Manning probably did not have time to write a letter to Lona to tell her to meet him at Atlanta. He even may not have known where he was going until it was too late.[4]

The reason for the hurry quickly became clear as soon as train reached Vicksburg that evening. There the men of the 43rd and three other regiments of Barton's Brigade disembarked from the train, formed up, and marched immediately to Chickasaw Bayou north of Vicksburg where they joined the skirmishers and men in trenches at the center of a Confederate line that during the day had been defending Vicksburg from an attack from the north. In fact, a Federal force already had attacked this line earlier that day, and Barton's Brigade arrived just in time to meet a renewed attack at four thirty the following morning just after they arrived.[5]

Preliminaries to the Attack on Vicksburg

The Union was focusing on Vicksburg as part of its national strategic plan that included controlling the Mississippi River in order to split the Confederacy in two and halt the transfer of supplies and men between the Confederate states in the East and Confederate states and battleground areas west of the Mississippi. Control of the Mississippi also would offer the Union a marvelous waterway from which to launch invasions of Southern territory.[6]

The Union had occupied New Orleans earlier, in April, and Memphis in June 1862. By November, the South held only two river ports that seriously hindered Federal movement on the Mississippi: Port Hudson, Louisiana, and Vicksburg. That month, General Ulysses S. Grant, commander of the Union forces in West Tennessee, decided to capture Vicksburg.[7]

Headquartered in Grand Junction, Tennessee, fifty miles east of Memphis and 250 miles northeast of Vicksburg, Grant planned to attack in two wings. He

---

[4] Goodson, *Georgia Confederate 7,000*, 2:41–42; Black, *Railroads of the Confederacy*, xxiv, 6; Connor, *Confederate Diary*, 17–19; Roberts and Clark, *Atlanta's Fighting Forty-second*, 62–63; note to Simeon's letter of November 6, 1850, in chapter 1; Palencia, *On Rising Ground*, 94.

[5] *OR*, ser. 1, vol. 17, pt. 1, 666, 677–78.

[6] Gallagher et al., *Civil War*, 41–42; W. C. Davis, "Military Affairs in the West, 1861–1865," 63–64.

[7] Ballard, *Vicksburg*, 29; Gallagher et al., *Civil War*, 123, 133–34; Foote, *Civil War*, 2:60–61.

would lead an overland invasion south through the middle of Mississippi and then turn west to Vicksburg. General William Tecumseh Sherman would command a river assault down the Mississippi and the Yazoo rivers from Memphis to Vicksburg.

Grant began moving south in early November. He established a large supply base at Holly Springs, Mississippi, about twenty miles south of the Tennessee-Mississippi border, and continued marching south. Then on December 5, his forward elements were stopped by the Confederates under General Pemberton near Coffeeville, Mississippi, still about 150 miles from Vicksburg. Grant decided he would keep Pemberton's Confederates occupied there while Sherman moved his amphibious force downriver to attack the Confederate force at Vicksburg, which Pemberton depleted when he took part of it to attack Grant. If Pemberton retreated, Grant would follow him to join Sherman at Vicksburg.[8]

Events took place, however, that made Grant change his mind. On December 20, Confederate General Earl Van Dorn carried out a lightning raid on Grant's supply depot at Holly Springs "destroying Grant's reserve supplies of food, forage, and munitions" and capturing fifteen hundred Union soldiers. Van Dorn continued through parts of North Mississippi and southern Tennessee, ripping up railroad tracks. At the same time, Nathan Bedford Forrest was raiding along the railroad in West Tennessee. As historian Shelby Foote wrote about Grant's predicament, "Van Dorn having destroyed his supplies on hand and Forrest having made it impossible for him to bring up more, he could neither move forward nor stand still. There was no way he could go but back, and this he proceeded to do...."[9]

Meanwhile, Sherman already had left Memphis headed down the Mississippi River with a fleet of about sixty-four transports ships (loaded with some 32,500 soldiers), ironclads, more lightly armored "tinclads," wooden gunboats, and rams. Unfortunately, communications between Grant and Sherman had been disrupted, with the result that Grant was unable to alert Sherman that he was retreating, could not join him at Vicksburg, and was even unable hold all Pemberton's men at Coffeeville.[10]

Sherman arrived at the mouth of the Yazoo River, north of Vicksburg, on December 25. His plan was to proceed from there up the Yazoo, land on its southern bank near an area called Chickasaw Bayou, and then march his troops overland to Vicksburg.

Between the banks of the Yazoo and Vicksburg, however, were the bayou and a line of bluffs called Walnut Hills. Grant and Sherman thought neither

---

[8] Foote, *Civil War*, 2:60–65.
[9] Ibid., 2:69–73 (quotes, 72).
[10] Ibid., 73–74 (quote, 74).

would present much of a problem in the advance to Vicksburg. They apparently were unaware of the nature of Chickasaw Bayou that Sherman would need to cross—two and a half to three miles of flat bottom land covered by a daunting morass of swamps, bayous, creeks, lakes, and marshy ground "brooded over by cypresses and water oaks with long gray beards of Spanish moss." They also did not seem to appreciate that the bayou led to the base of Walnut Hills, which brooded over the swampy Bayou as surely as the cypresses and oaks.[11]

Before Sherman's men reached Chickasaw Bayou, the Confederates had fortified the hills beyond the swampy ground. At their base, they had dug trenches and rifle pits and constructed earthworks. Along their sides, they had dug more trenches, and on their tops, artillery had been strategically placed to cover the probable Union approaches. There the Confederates waited for the Union army to appear.[12]

The Battle of Chickasaw Bayou

The Union men arrived, and skirmishing began on December 26. Sherman's first major assault on the hills took place the following day. The Confederates checked his advance, but they did so without the aid of Barton's Brigade, which had yet to arrive.[13]

Barton's Brigade, less one regiment, finally arrived on the night of December 27 and was placed in the center of the Confederate line. After action reports do not record where Manning and the 43rd Georgia were stationed. They seem to have been held in reserve and probably were positioned close to the center of Barton's area and a little to the rear so the regiment could be moved to the left or the right as needed.[14]

Wherever it was exactly, its men and those of Barton's other regiments were subject to shelling by Union guns and bullets from Union sharpshooters beginning at four thirty on the morning of December 28 and continuing, as General Barton reported, "with increased force and vigor until night-fall." Fighting continued along the Confederate line for the following two days. Barton reported that on December 29, "The enemy made five efforts to take the breastworks by storm...but on every occasion was repulsed with heavy loss." The next day, "the attack was renewed but with less vigor." Finally on January 2, Sherman gave up, re-embarked his forces, and left.

Barton expanded on the Federals' heavy losses: "Near by, nine large grave-trenches, of capacity of 75 men each, were left filled. Hundreds [earlier] were

---

[11] Ibid., 63, 75–77 (quote, 75); Ballard, *Vicksburg*, 130–33; Carter, *Final Fortress*, 99–100; *OR*, ser. 1, vol. 17, pt. 1, 672, 681; Esposito, *West Point Atlas*, 104.

[12] *OR*, ser. 1, vol. 17, pt. 1, 666, 672; Ballard, *Vicksburg*, 132–33.

[13] *OR*, ser. 1, vol. 17, pt. 1, 666, 681.

[14] Ibid., 666–68; 677–78; Ballard, *Vicksburg*, 135–36, 139, 141.

permitted to be carried off, and the ground for 150 yards in front of the breastworks gave frightful evidence of the great slaughter committed there."[15]

Apparently, the 43rd was not actively engaged in the fighting, although the other Barton regiments were very much so. The other regiments suffered a number of casualties, but the only person in the 43rd who was wounded was its commander, Lieutenant Colonel Hiram P. Bell, the same man who Simeon reported in chapter 6 was elected to the Secession Convention from Forsyth County in January 1861. A Union sharpshooter shot Bell in the left leg between the knee and ankle at sunrise on the December 29 as he was moving among his men instructing them to change their positions. Manning probably treated him initially, but the wound was serious enough that he had to be removed to a hospital in Vicksburg itself. He then was moved to a private home where he eventually recovered but not sufficiently to rejoin the regiment.[16]

Shortly after the end of the battle, Manning and the 43rd, amidst almost continuous rain or snow, settled in to defend Vicksburg.[17]

Manning, Acting Head Regimental Surgeon

It is probable that for the first more than three months that the 43rd Georgia was at Vicksburg, Manning was the sole medical officer for the regiment.

Each regiment had a surgeon and an assistant surgeon. John Wills had been appointed regimental surgeon of the 43rd Georgia in July 1862. The last entry in Wills's service records indicates that he was paid on January 2, 1863, for services with the regiment from November 1, 1862, through January 1, 1863. The person making the payment has not been identified with any regiment in the Confederate army and particularly not with the 43rd Georgia.

Moreover, around the last of February or early March 1863, the commander of the 43rd recommended that a new doctor be appointed the head surgeon of the regiment, implying that Dr. Wills had left the regiment.

It seems probable that while the regiment was in Tennessee, Dr. Wills had made plans to leave it. Thus, when the 43rd's train got to Atlanta, then an important medical center for the Confederacy, he disembarked before going all the way to Mississippi. It was in Atlanta that the unidentified official paid him for his last services with the regiment.

Merinus Henry Van Dyke, the new head surgeon, did not arrive in Vicksburg until around March 20, 1863. Thus, from late December until March 20,

---

[15] *OR*, ser. 1, vol. 17, pt. 1, 667–68, 673–78 (quotes, 677–78).

[16] *OR*, ser. 1, vol. 17, pt. 1, 671, 678; Rogers, *Bible Records*, 106; H. P. Bell, *Men and Things*, 89–90; Bell's service records.

[17] Goodson, *Georgia Confederate 7,000*, 2:46–49, 3:137.

Manning was the only medical officer for the seven or eight hundred men of the 43rd.[18]

Manning

Vicksburg Miss
April 24th 1863
My Dear,

This pleasant sunday morning [I] will spend in responding to your much esteeamed favor of 13th inst. which came to hand last Sunday 6 days after date. As ever I was much gratified to here from you and I was the better pleased because it was more lengthy than usual. That is the way I want you to write. Write all about every thing.

I could write a great deal about the movements of the army but I suppose you can get all I know and much more from the papers. We received some news here of a raid by the Yankees upon the Southern Rail-road—which is in our rear. it cuts off all communications at present. I don't know when you will get this for there is no mail going now at all. The report is that they destroyed or tore up about 12 miles of track and burned two stations and one train of cars loaded with sugar. If this be true—which I believe [it] to be—it will take severel days to repair it. I hop it will benefit this Department in the end—they will be more watchful.

I am a little fearful the enemy are going to make another strong effort to get in our rear from below. They came down last tuesday night with five transports and one gun boat. we sunk one of the boats and damaged 2 more so that they floated down with the current. Two of the crew of the boat that was sunk jumped overboard and by means of life preservers swam to the shore and gave themselves up; but I have not heard what they said. My fears are that they will land a force below here and try to make their way through the county to the rail road and cut us off. If they attempt that we will have to give them an open field fight. I have no fears but what we can whip them. my only fear is that we have not sufficient force to meet them in that direction and hold this place too. I am fully satisfied that they will never attac this place by direct assalt.

Our Brigade went out yesterday for review and are out to-day for review and inspection. I was out yesterday. I declined going to-day. I have written to Dr Bell but I don't know whether they have got my letter or not. I would be most happy to come home but it seems that I am the last one to get off.

I was fearful that, that place could not be got or that it was not so good as Tanner represented it. You are write about Tanner not being right. He is partially

---

[18] John Wills, surgeon, service records; M. H. Van Dyke, surgeon, service records, particularly letter from Kellogg to Cooper, August 29, 1863; Rigdon, *Georgia 43rd Infantry Regiment*, 60; H. H. Cunningham, *Doctors in Gray*, 61.

insane. I wish I could get to come home and look round. I think I could find a little place some whare that we could do well on.

Find out whare Mr Whites land is, how much bottom there is and what he will take for it. I would *much* prefur a place with some bottom on it. What land is the Harril land? dose it join your pas and how much is there of it? I would give your pa a good price for the Duncan place, but I coulde'nt ask him to sell that. The only objection to it is [that it is] out of the way I intend to settle as near our relations as I can if I live to get home. Your pas and ma have always been so good to us I feel under obligation to them. I wrote to father to look about fir a place that would suit us, but I would rather live somewhere in the vicinity of *your* pas as you could get along better although there are some in that neighborhood that I could not have any dealings with.

Dear, I am not able to decid what we had better do with what money we have. You[r] pa has always been so kind to us. I would regret very much to loose an oportunity to do him a favor but I believe I will suggest that we keep it a month or two. may be by that time we can see further. I don't know when I will get to send any more home. When I do I want it funded [invested] in whateve persent [percent] it will bring.

We cant get any flour here now but we get bolted meal which dose very well. I am making arrangements to get milk and a few vegetable. I find that I can live cheaper and far better and agreeably by so doing Jim is gone now after 2 gal. milk. I don't know yet exactly what it will cost. I will tell you next time. There is scarcly anything in Vickburg and very high what is there. There is no Turkey-red. I have sold the saddle I got in Kentuckey for 15.00 dollars. It was so flat it hurt bucks back. I will have to buy me an other as my old one is about "plaid out". My health was never better. Billy White and Herndon are well. I am glad to here that Ratio has got a position. It will be so much easier on him.

I would expect a letter from you to-day had it not been for the Yankee raid. Hug and kiss Nor for me—Give my love to all the family—Most Truly

M. P. Alexander

Notes

a raid by the Yankees upon the Southern Rail-road: Manning is referring to a Union cavalry raid through the heart of Mississippi of some seventeen hundred men led by Colonel Benjamin H. Grierson. The raid's purpose was to distract Pemberton from Grant's other activities and cause him to send men to counter the raid, men who otherwise might have been used to defend Vicksburg.

The raid started in La Grange in southwestern Tennessee on April 17, ended in Baton Rouge, Louisiana, on May 2, and covered some six hundred miles. By April 24, when Manning wrote his letter, Grierson was at a railroad station in Mississippi between Jackson and the large town of Meridian near the

Mississippi-Alabama border. There he was busy tearing up tracks on the Southern Railroad of Mississippi that connected Vicksburg and Jackson with points east in the Confederacy.[19]

I am a little fearful the enemy are going to make another strong effort to get in our rear from below. They came down last tuesday night with five transports and one gun boat. Manning was right to be fearful. The enemy in fact was going "to get in our rear from below." Sending transports and a gunboat south was one of the first moves in Grant's ultimately successful operation to capture Vicksburg.

Union Difficulties with Vicksburg

Vicksburg, because of its geographic position, was very difficult to attack. The Mississippi flowed generally south from Memphis, but just before reaching Vicksburg, it bent and began flowing to the northeast. This northeasterly flow continued for about three and a half miles. Then the river made a dramatically sharp turn of almost 180 degrees and began flowing in the opposite direction, to the southwest. As it continued this southwesterly flow, it passed Vicksburg sitting on its left (east) bank atop a high bluff, two hundred feet above. Flowing past the city, its strong current washed against the base of the bluff. With Confederate cannons mounted on top of the bluff, it was thought impossible to assault the city from the river.[20]

Grant and most of his men were located in Tennessee up the Mississippi north of Vicksburg. Yet it also was difficult to approach the city from the north by land because of the swampy ground and the line of hills that Sherman encountered unsuccessfully in the Battle of Chickasaw Bayou. However, to approach the city from the south, it was thought that Union forces would have to do one of two things: They either would have to pass the guns on the bluffs in ships heavily loaded with troops, unlikely without heavy casualties, or march through or around the swampy ground in Louisiana on the west side of the Mississippi, also unlikely, or at least difficult.

Also, if they took the second approach and if they marched successfully through the Louisiana swamps, they then somehow would have to make their way across the river to the Mississippi side south of Vicksburg. Once there, they then must march to Vicksburg with only the food and forage they could find along the way, something which Grant already had discovered to be difficult when he came south from Tennessee through Holly Springs in December.[21]

---

[19] T. Smith, *Champion Hill*, 29–30; Ballard, *Vicksburg*, 207–208; Wagner, *Timeline of the Civil War*, 118.

[20] Morgan, "The Assault on Chickasaw Bluffs," 3:465; Everhart, *Vicksburg*, 8–11; Foote, *Civil War*, 2:62; T. Smith, *Champion Hill*, 3.

[21] Foote, *Civil War*, 2:58–61, Everhart, *Vicksburg*, 8–11.

Grant's Initial Efforts

Still, during January, February, March, and early April, the area's rainy season, Grant attempted to find some way for men and supplies to be moved to dry land east of Vicksburg, ready to attack the city, without having them pass directly under the cannons on the bluffs.

To do this, he attempted to build canals or other waterways through the swamps, bayous, lakes, and flooded ground on the west side of the river, the opposite side from Vicksburg. He also tried to clear waterways to allow men and supplies to move through the same type of terrain on the east side of the river, north of Vicksburg. Coming from this direction, when they reached dry land, the men and supplies then could be moved rapidly to the east of Vicksburg itself, ready to attack. All these efforts, however, either failed or were abandoned.[22]

Manning and the 43rd Georgia

During this time, the 43rd Georgia built rifle pits and breastworks and waited for another attack. Manning probably split his time, spending most of it with the 43rd at its post outside town and part in the several hospitals in Vicksburg where sick members of the regiment were taken. It is clear that at least as late as early February and probably earlier, as indicated in an earlier note, Manning was the only surgeon for the 43rd. A new head surgeon, Merinus Henry Van Dyke, did not arrive in Vicksburg until around March 20.[23]

The regiment also was involved marginally in one of Grant's last forays from north of Vicksburg, an adventure known informally as the Deer Creek Expedition. The expedition began in early April when Grant landed troops at Greenville, Mississippi, on the east side of the Mississippi River about ninety miles north of Vicksburg. Their objectives were to march overland south from there along Deer Creek, clear the area of guerrillas and Confederate soldiers who had been firing on Union boats as they sailed down the Mississippi toward Vicksburg, and seize cattle, corn, hogs, and other products planters in the area had been sending to the Confederates in Vicksburg.

The Confederates successfully halted this expedition after the Federals were still short of their objective by about twenty-five miles. After a brief fight, the Union men retreated to Greenville, seizing or destroying everything in their path.

Before Confederate commanders in Vicksburg learned of the retreat, however, they ordered the 43rd to board boats and travel up several waterways to reinforce the Confederate troops in front of the Union force. Manning and the

---

[22] Boatner, *Civil War Dictionary*, 871–73; Gallagher et al., *Civil War*, 134–36; Everhart, *Vicksburg*, 10–16; Foote, *Civil War*, 2:189–95, 201–20.

[23] Fowler, Washington A, Co. B, 43rd Georgia, "Letters," March 4 and March 10, 1863; Shankle letter, February 13, 1863; Van Dyke service records.

new head regimental surgeon would have sailed with them. By the time the 43rd arrived, they found no Union troops there. ("The Yankees had gone into a hole, and taken the hole in after them," one member of the 43rd wrote to the *Southern Watchman*.) Instead of confronting the Federals, they spent four days disgustedly wading through mud and water waiting to see if the Federals would return. Once again, as in Kentucky, the 43rd had marched but had not fought. They then returned to Vicksburg the way they had come.[24]

Grant's Final Effort

Grant finally decided to attack Vicksburg by marching his army south on the Louisiana side of the river to a point on the Mississippi south of Vicksburg and then ferrying them across by transports the Union navy brought south on the river past Vicksburg. His army already had begun its march south when the first of the navy's transports passed Vicksburg on April 16. More vessels, including ones carrying ammunition and supplies, sailed past on April 22, as Manning recorded. Both times they suffered only insignificant losses. Thus Grant's "strong effort to get in our rear from below," as Manning feared, had begun. Soon the 43rd would be part of the "open field fight" that Manning predicted.[25]

Tanner: He has not been identified. Possibly, he was someone in Jackson County whom Lona had consulted about land she and Manning might purchase.

bottom: This word refers to bottom land, which is low-lying land along a river or stream that usually is particularly fertile because the river or stream has sometimes overflowed its banks and deposited extra nutrients onto the land.[26]

bolted meal: This phrase refers to an edible grain that has been sifted to separate fine from coarse particles, rather than grain that has not been sifted and then been coarsely ground.[27]

Turkey-red: This term refers to a bright red coloring used to dye cotton cloth.[28]

Manning

Camp Magnolia
9 miles below V Burg

---

[24] *OR*, ser. 1, vol. 24, pt. 1, 501–11; *OR*, ser. 1, vol. 24, pt. 3, 158, 186–87, 201–202, 208, 710–12, 715–19, 724, 729–30, 735; *Southern Watchman*, May 13, 1863, letter from J. C. M. (probably 1st Lieutenant Jerome C. Mathews of Company H. 43rd Infantry); Fowler, Washington A, Co. B, 43rd Georgia, "Letters," April 17, 1863.

[25] Ballard, *Vicksburg*, 191–92, 194, 198; T. Smith, *Champion Hill*, 14–15, 26–28.

[26] "Bottom," *Webster's New World College Dictionary*, 175.

[27] "Bolt," ibid, 168; "Meal," ibid., 905; "sift," ibid., 1350.

[28] "Turkey red," ibid., 1561; Wikipedia, "Turkey red," https://en.wikipedia.org/wiki/Turkey_red, accessed March 2, 2017.

May 7th 1863
My Dear,

    Just after I had finished my last letter we received orders to break up camp and go below. The regt as I told you then was gon. So now we are camped in a beautiful magnolia grove hence the name of the camp.

    We had an ingagement with the enemy near fort Gibbson last week. We only had 2 brigades and the Yanks had four divisions consequently we ware driven back.

    The enemy are estimated at 60,000. There will be a general engagement some whare in this section before a great while I think but I cant tell when. It may be in a few days but I am of opinion that [it]will be some weeks or longer. I have no fears of the result when it dose come. We have a fine army here now.
[Written on the margin of the letter] I have paper plenty free & draw paper every month

    Dear—why is it you cant [get] letters from me regularly? I write every week. I think it probable that the Yankees intercepted them. But now dear you must not be uneasy about me now if you don't get letters regularly for we have taken the field for active operations and I may not always be able to write every week. While we stay here we will get the mail as regularly as we did at Vicksburg.

    My Dear I received your very kind letter of 29th ult. yesterday. I regret very much that you cant here from me but don't take the blues if you can help it. I shall not keep any thing consealed in regard to my health. I am very well at this time except my eyes are a little sore.

    I don't suppose I can send any sugar now as we have left the City. I am very sorry I cant on all you[r] account and peticularly for Nora. I know how she would jump around and smack her hands if she could see a sack of sugar come. There are any amount of black berries in this county. If I can get some sugar and flour and *milk* when they get ripe I will live fat awhile.

    I forgot to mention that I also received yours of 23rd ult. in due time. I am about as fat as usual. May be it would be best for you to wait till I come home to *fatten*. I heard not long since of a couple marrying by telegraph. I can't say that I fancy that way of marrying much. I don't know whether you could *fatten* that way or not. at least I am a little like the old lady—*the old way is good enough for me.*

    This move has broke into all my milk arrangements, but if we stay here long I think I will get it up again.

    You have done right with the money. May be you had better keep it a while and look about. If I could only get to come hom I think I could find a little farm.

    I am sorry to tell you that Buck has strayed off. I turned him out about a week ago to graze as I had been in the habit of doing as well as every body else. But he didn't come back at night. I hunted 3 days for him but never could here a word of him. We ware then ordered off. I have offered a reward of 25 dollars but have no idea of getting him. I think I am born to bad luck. But dear I am not like I use to be in that respect. I just let it go. I am riding one of the quartermasters horses. I shall not buy any other horse.

I will not need any shirts before next winter if then. I will need some pants and drawers next fall probabily by the last of Sept. I will keep you posted about my clothing.

We have just received news of another fight and victory in Va. Also of the capture of 1600 federals in 20 miles of Rome Geo. Our batteries set a boat on fire as she attempted to run by the other night. She had on board 25 feds and 10 days rations for 60,000 troops which was all burned.

James Armor was kiled Monday night from a limb falling on him while he was asleep under a tree. He lived till tusday night. he suffered a great deal.

The wether is very cool here now. I fear there will be frost in the up country.

Yours most Truly
M P Alexander

Notes

Camp Magnolia: The location of this camp probably was near Redbone Church, south of Vicksburg on the road from Warrenton to Harkinson's Ferry at the Big Black River. Around the time this letter was written, Barton's Brigade and other Confederate units were guarding the approaches to Vicksburg from the south. General Pemberton had become convinced that Grant's major strike against Vicksburg would come from the south (see the next note).[29]

We had an ingagement with the enemy near fort Gibbson last week: On April 30, Grant began landing his troops on the Mississippi side of the river at Bruinsburg, about thirty miles south of Vicksburg. Immediately Grant's leading XIII Corps under Major General John A. McClernand began marching toward Port Gibson ten miles inland. Port Gibson was "an important hub of roads leading to Vicksburg, Grand Gulf [an important river port], and inland to Jackson." In addition, in the area were key bridges that crossed Bayou Pierre.

Before reaching the town, he was met on May 1 by an assortment of quickly assembled forces under the general command of Confederate General John S. Bowen. In the ensuing battle, Bowen's force of about eight thousand men were not able to stop McClernand's Corps, consisting of four divisions of about seventeen thousand men. McClernand continued onward to occupy Port Gibson and Grand Gulf.[30]

---

[29] Esposito, *West Point Atlas*, 104; Bearss, *Campaign for Vicksburg*, 445–46, 452–55; Palencia, *On Rising Ground*, 110.

[30] T. Smith, *Champion Hill*, 34–35, 38–59 (quote, 39–40); Everhart, *Vicksburg*, 21.

There will be a general engagement some whare in this section before a great while I think: Manning was correct. By May 7, Grant had all of his men across the river, and his force now numbered about forty-five thousand men. On that day, he began moving the bulk of his men northeasterly toward the railroad between Vicksburg and Jackson, the state's capital.

On their way, Grant's men fought two significant battles beside the one at Port Gibson: one at Raymond, "a cross-road village 15 miles from Jackson," on May 12 and the other at Jackson itself. At Raymond, again an outnumbered Confederate force was unable to block the Union advance. Then on May 14, Grant captured Jackson after overwhelming a light Confederate force covering the city's evacuation.

At daylight the following morning, May 15, Grant began moving part of his army west from Jackson toward Vicksburg while the part of his army still at Raymond, southwest of Jackson, began moving north to join Grant. On their way to Vicksburg, they met Confederate forces under General John C. Pemberton, coming east from the Vicksburg area.

Pemberton originally had planned to attack Grant in the rear while the Confederates in Jackson under General Joseph E. Johnston, now recovered from his wound on the Virginia peninsula and now Pemberton's superior, held Grant in place at Jackson. On May 14, however, Pemberton, then about halfway between Vicksburg and Jackson, held a council of war with his generals and decided to move southeast to attack Grant's supply lines instead. Pemberton thus began moving his army south.

However, the next morning, Pemberton learned that Jackson had fallen and Johnston had retreated to the northeast, away from Vicksburg and away from him. Moreover, Johnston now wanted Pemberton to meet him at a town north of where Pemberton was, which meant that Pemberton needed to turn his whole command around and head back the way he had just come. In addition, Pemberton was unaware that Grant was marching toward him. Just as Pemberton began the complicated task of turning his army, Grant struck.

Then ensued the "general engagement" that Manning had predicted, and the 43rd Georgia had a part in it.[31]

The Battle

The battle, known as Champion Hill to the Federals and Baker's Creek to the Confederates, was fought on May 16, 1863, at a place equal distance between Vicksburg and Jackson (about twenty-two miles each way). The Federals had seven divisions, about thirty-two thousand men, under Grant, and they heavily

---

[31] Everhart, *Vicksburg*, 21–26 (quote, 25); T. Smith, *Champion Hill*, 61–107, 125, 141–45; Roberts and Clark, *Atlanta's Fighting Forty-second*, 77–81; *Southern Banner*, May 20, 1863.

outnumbered the Confederates' three divisions (Stevenson's, Bowen's, and Loring's), roughly sixteen or seventeen thousand men, under Pemberton.[32]

About half past noon, roughly midway through the battle, Barton's Brigade, including the 43rd Georgia, part of Stevenson's Division, was helping to hold the middle of the Confederate line. (This battle was the first large, open field battle Manning's regiment had participated in since it was organized over a year earlier.) Meanwhile, two other brigades of Stevenson's Division were attempting to hold the extreme left of the line, but they were being opposed by a much superior Union force and were in danger of being enveloped by the Federals. If that happened, the Federals could have gone around the Confederate left and been able to attack the Confederate line from the rear with devastating consequences.[33]

To counter the Federals, Stevenson ordered Barton's Brigade to march to the aid of Stevenson's other two brigades. It was to take a position to the left of those brigades and thus extend the Confederate line to keep it from being turned. This move would place Barton and the 43rd at the left end of the entire Confederate army.[34]

Barton marched his brigade toward its new position at "double-quick" time—about a mile and a half over fences and through fields, thickets, and clumps of woods. Once there, just north of the Jackson Road (which led from Jackson to Vicksburg, the part of the road today called "Billy Fields Road"), the brigade began forming a line of battle. In front of him Barton saw open pasture that led to a line of dense woods about three hundred yards away. He also saw that a strong force of Federals had attacked the Confederate brigade immediately to his right, and as the men of that brigade began falling back toward him, he realized that the left of the Confederate line was collapsing. What would be his best move now?[35]

Manning and Other Medical Personnel

It is unclear where Manning and other men of the 43rd's medical support contingent were located at this point in this very fluid battle. The textbook plan for the assistant surgeon in the field was for him to travel with the regiment. When the troops deployed for action, he was to move a short distance to the rear of the battle line, just out of reach of the enemy's musket shot, and establish a primary treatment or first aid station. Ideally, he would locate it in a place as sheltered from shot and shell as available, such as a nearby house or barn or simply in a deep gully.

---

[32] T. Smith, *Champion Hill*, 103–106, 115–16, 130.
[33] Ibid., 179–88, 192–214; J. Johnston, "Joseph W. Anderson, B. L.," 396.
[34] T. Smith, *Champion Hill*, 214–15; *OR*, ser. 1, vol. 24, pt. 2, 94–95, 100.
[35] T. Smith, *Champion Hill*, 214–23; Bearss, *Campaign for Vicksburg*, 598–99; *OR*, ser. 1, vol. 24, pt. 2, 100 (quote); Roberts and Clark, *Atlanta's Fighting Forty-second*, 82–87.

With him would have been a group of litter bearers who were unarmed and wore special badges to identify them as different from fighting troops. As the fighting troops advanced to meet the enemy, the bearers followed them. When men were wounded, the bearers carried them back to the first aid station where the assistant surgeon "bandaged wounds, stopped bleeding, splintered broken bones, and gave opiates or whiskey to dull the pain." He then saw that the wounded were promptly carried to the rear, either by ambulance (horse or mule drawn), or by the litter bearers.[36]

At the first aid station, "no elaborate surgical procedure was undertaken unless there was urgent necessity for it." The elaborate medical procedures, such as amputations, would take place further to the rear where the 43rd's regimental surgeon, M. H. Van Dyke, along with surgeons from other regiments in the brigade, would have established a field infirmary or hospital where the severely wounded would be brought by the ambulances and treated. The field hospital would have been located in a house or other structure if one were available. A Union soldier, however, reported visiting a Confederate field hospital after the battle that was located in a cornfield where the wounded "were laying around between the corn rows" with no shelter from the sun.[37]

Because this was the regiment's first big battle, Manning likely would have proceeded in accordance with this textbook plan. He would have established a first aid station to the rear of the regiment behind its new line, probably a short distance south of the Jackson Road while the regiment was to the north of the road. There he might have planted a red flag to direct the walking wounded and litter bearers to his position and show Union artillery his benevolent mission. He would have opened his instrument case and gotten from aides pails of water, wash basins, and a knapsack filled with bandages and anesthetics. He generally would have prepared to receive wounded men.[38]

General Barton Decides

Meanwhile, Barton had made his decision. He immediately ordered three of his regiments, including the 43rd, to advance quickly to meet the enemy that

---

[36] Schroeder-Lein, *Encyclopedia of Civil War Medicine*, 151–53, 296; (quote, 152); P. Ward, *Simon Baruch*, 32–33; H. H. Cunningham, *Doctors in Gray*, 114–16; Gindlesperger, *Bullets & Bandages*, 15.

[37] H. H. Cunningham, *Doctors in Gray*, 114–16 (1st quote, 115); P. Ward, *Simon Baruch*, 32–33; Chisolm, *Manual of Military Surgery*, 139–43; Schroeder-Lein, *Encyclopedia of Civil War Medicine*, 151–53, 296; Howell, *Hill of Death*, 19 (2nd quote); Welch, *Confederate Surgeon's Letters to His Wife*, 25–26; J. Johnston, "Joseph W. Anderson, B. L.," 398; Cotton, *Vicksburg*, 13.

[38] T. Brown, "Gaines's Mill, June 27, 1862," 145; Dalton, "They Did Not Seem to Respect It Much," https://www.civilwarmed.org/surgeons-call/medical-evacuation-insignia, accessed August 12, 2021.

had turned the Confederates' left flank and was now directly in front of him. Upon hearing the order, the 43rd's commander, Colonel Skidmore Harris, called to his regiment, "Boys never give up the conflict! If I am shot down, press on and gain the victory!" Then, with Harris in the lead, they charged.

Barton later reported that "with impetuous gallantry...[the three regiments] dashed upon the enemy's line, broke it, and drove it back about 300 yards."[39]

Manning likely would have watched the advance of the three regiments and would have sent litter bearers to follow them as he heard the crackle of musket fire from the other side of the road.

The triumph of the three regiments in pushing back the enemy, however, was only temporary. When their charge ended, they found that, although they had pushed back a part of the Union force to their front, other Union soldiers were pressuring them from each side. Two Confederate brigades on Barton's right had retreated so far that they had left Barton's regiments' right side exposed. At the same time, not only were there Federals to their right and in front of them but an entire Federal brigade had maneuvered around the regiments' unsupported left flank. Barton's three regiments were in danger of being completely surrounded, and the 43rd, the furthest left of the three, was the most exposed.[40]

By then the leadership ranks of the 43rd had been depleted. The regimental commander, Colonel Harris, had been shot in the head and soon was dead. (Later he was buried near where he fell by Federal soldiers from Illinois.) Two company commanders, three other company officers, and six sergeants had been wounded. Another company commander, two more lieutenants, and eleven more sergeants were being surrounded and soon would be captured.

Facing envelopment and losing its leaders, the 43rd, along with the other two brigade regiments, retreated in disorder. Many men in the 43rd, however,

---

[39] *OR*, ser. 1, vol. 24, pt. 2, 100 (2nd quote); T. Smith, *Champion Hill*, 223–26, 413 (1st quote, 26).

[40] *OR*, ser. 1, vol. 24, pt. 2, 94–95, 100; T. Smith, *Champion Hill*, 223–32, 382–83; J. Johnston, "Joseph W. Anderson, B. L.," 395–96. In *Champion Hill*, Smith was mistaken when he placed the 43rd as the far right regiment of the three that Barton ordered to charge the advancing Federals (223). He apparently assumed that when Barton listed in his report the three regiments he ordered forward, he listed them on the page in the same order they appeared on the ground—that is, from left to right. If this were the case, the 43rd would have been the farthest on the right on the ground as it was the farthest right on the page (*OR*, ser. 1, vol. 24, pt. 2, 100). However, Johnston, in his article on Anderson, quotes Barton as writing in a letter that the *40th Georgia* was the far right regiment (396). Thus, in the *OR*, Barton was listing the regiments on the page in a different order (from right to left) than they had been on the ground, making the 43rd the farthest to the left. See also Stevenson's report (*OR*, ser. 1, vol. 24, pt. 2, 94–95), which list the regiments in his division in order that goes from right to left.

did not retreat fast enough and were captured by the quickly enveloping Union troops.[41]

The Confederates were not finished, however. Bowen's Division, which earlier had been to the right of Stevenson's Division in the middle of the Confederate line, rushed forward in a counterattack. Bowen's attack was immediately successful, driving the Union forces back. Meanwhile, Stevenson had managed to reform remnants of his division, including some men from Barton's Brigade, and joined the counterattack.[42]

Ultimately, however, both efforts were overcome by the overwhelming weight of the Federal forces facing the Confederates. Around five that afternoon, Pemberton realized he was in danger of losing much of his army and ordered his men to retreat.

Earlier, Barton himself and some men from his regiments had managed to cross Baker's Creek, a deep, muddy stream that separated the site of the battle from Vicksburg, at the upper of two available crossing points. Once on the Vicksburg side of the creek, they held the creek crossing open for a time before retreating further toward Vicksburg. Some scattered members of Barton's Brigade also made their way toward Vicksburg across Baker's Creek at the lower crossing further south.[43]

Manning, the Head Surgeon, and the Wounded Men of the 43rd

After the battle, the 43rd's head surgeon Van Dyke and at least three hospital stewards stayed with a field hospital treating wounded. There they and the wounded were captured. In addition, other wounded men of the 43rd apparently were captured on the battlefield before they had a chance to reach the field hospital or even reach Manning at his temporary aid station. When lists of men lost in the battle that appeared in two Athens newspapers are compared with service records and other sources, it appears that at least 280 men of the 43rd were captured during the battle. Of those approximately ninety (32 percent) were wounded.[44]

At his first aid station, Manning likely would have treated at least some of the wounded before sending them back to the field hospital for further treatment. There they later were captured.

---

[41] T. Smith, *Champion Hill*, 230–31, 368; J. W. Bell, *43rd Georgia Infantry*, 18; *Southern Watchman*, June 17, 1863.

[42] T. Smith, *Champion Hill*, 233–85.

[43] Ibid., 128, 231–32, 287–336, 352–54; Roberts and Clark, *Atlanta's Fighting Forty-Second*, 86–87; *OR*, ser. 1, vol. 24, pt. 1, 264–65.

[44] *Southern Watchman*, June 10, 1863; *Southern Banner*, July 8, 1863; service records for Calip G. Baker, James C. Arrowood, and Richard Martin.

Manning, however, was not captured. When the scattered remnants of the 43rd retreated across Bakers Creek along with others of Barton's Brigade, Manning accompanied them. Some of the 43rd retreating were wounded who had managed to escape capture, and Manning would have treated their wounds, to the extent he could, during the retreat.[45]

The two surgeons of the 43rd may have consulted about this division of duties beforehand, Van Dyke staying with the wounded in the field hospital and Manning retreating to Vicksburg with the mobile wounded and the remainder of the regiment. More likely, this division came about because of their different locations and the flow of battle.

With available information it is impossible to tell who treated which of the captured and wounded men on the day of the battle, Manning at the first aid station or Van Dyke at the field hospital. Possibly both treated the same man at their different locations.

The two surgeons, however, would have been dealing with such wounds as that suffered by Private Andrew P. Moore of Company I, a gunshot wound that began in the right arm: "the ball entered the arm about two inches below the shoulder joint fracturing the Humerous & passing inwards and upwards making its exit just above the sternum, in its course fracturing the clavicle." Also, Private William A. Fowler of Company E was wounded in the upper left arm, requiring his arm to be amputated "about half way between the elbow and shoulder joints." Private Lucius C. Bradley of Company L's wound was described as "upper lobe of right lung transfixed by con [cannon?] ball." Private Bradley died in a Union hospital on June 2. Manning might have patched up one or more of these men as well as he could and sent him to Van Dyke at the field hospital.[46]

Overall, the 43rd had been severely weakened. As it went into battle it had approximately seven hundred men. In the battle it lost about 320 men killed, wounded, and captured—roughly 46 percent. Only about 380 of the men who began the battle made their way back to Vicksburg.[47]

---

[45] Notes later in this chapter report the names of some members of the 43rd who were wounded and made it back to Vicksburg.

[46] Service records of Moore, Fowler, and Bradley; *Southern Banner*, July 8, 1863.

[47] *OR*, ser. 1, vol. 24, pt. 2, 100; *OR*, ser. 1, vol. 24, pt. 3, 702–703; "List of Confederates Captured at Vicksburg, Mississippi, July 4, 1863," NARA; *Southern Watchman*, June 10, 1863; *Southern Banner*, July 8, 1863. *Southern Watchman* contains the names of officers and men killed, wounded, and captured in the Battle of Champion Hill. *Southern Banner* contains a list dated June 23 prepared by head regimental surgeon Van Dyke that records the names of the killed and wounded. It also indicates who died of their wounds. When the two lists are compared with service records and other sources, it seems both contain discrepancies regarding specific soldiers, but they appear to yield a reliable overall number of losses. However, Roberts and Clark estimate the 43rd's losses were much greater than 46 percent, probably closer to 60 percent (*Atlanta's Fighting Forty-Second*, 87).

The Retreat to Vicksburg

Very late the night of the battle, the remaining men of Stevenson's Division were sent across the Big Black River, the last obstacle to the Union advance on Vicksburg. A modern historian wrote that the men of the division "had borne the brunt of the early fighting at Champion Hill" and were exhausted. As soon as they arrived at the other side of the river, "they fell on the ground and slept."[48]

The division had been so depleted and disorganized that following morning Pemberton ordered it back to Vicksburg. Later that day, part of Pemberton's force tried to stop the Federals at the Big Black River, but that effort failed. The way was open for Grant and his Union army to move on to Vicksburg. Soon Grant began his siege of the city that would last for forty-seven days.[49]

Another fight and victory in Va.: This fight and victory was the Battle of Chancellorsville (see chapter 18).

Also of the capture of 1600 federals in 20 miles of Rome Geo: Manning is referring to Confederate General Nathan Bedford Forrest's capture on May 3, 1863, between Gadsden, Alabama, and Rome, Georgia, of a large body of Union cavalry under Colonel Abel D. Streight.[50]

James Armor: James F. Armor (Armour or Armer) was a private from Hall County in Company K of the 43rd Georgia. At the time the letter was written, he was about nineteen years old.[51]

Lily Alexander Jackson to Allie Comer Gaither (c. 1965)

...Manning Poole Alexander M. D. was in the siege of Vicksburg during the war. There, he had a terrible experience. The enemy surrounded the Southern forces for 40 days & they could not get food or mail or any thing else. Papa did not, but many men had to eat mule meat. My mother, then about 22 or 23 yrs old was almost worried sick for she knew where Papa was but could get no word at all from him....

Notes

Lily Alexander Jackson: She was Manning's fourth and youngest daughter. She was born December 6, 1877, when her father was forty-seven years old and

---

[48] *OR*, ser. 1, vol. 24, pt. 1, 266; *OR*, ser. 1, vol. 24, pt. 2, 97; Korn, *War on the Mississippi*, 122 (quote).

[49] *OR*, ser. 1, vol. 24, pt. 2, 97; T. Smith, *Champion Hill*, 389–96; Ballard, *Vicksburg*, 310–18.

[50] Horn, *Army of Tennessee*, 234.

[51] US Census, 1860, Hall County, Georgia; service records.

her mother was thirty-eight. At the time this letter likely was written, she was around eighty-eight years old.[52]

Allie Comer Gaither: She was Lily Jackson's niece, daughter of Lily's sister, Margie Alexander Comer.

My mother was 22 or 23 years old: She actually was twenty-four years old during the siege of Vicksburg.[53]

siege of Vicksburg: The siege lasted for forty-seven days, from May 18 to July 4, 1863.[54]

Confederates Return to Vicksburg

On May 17 and continuing into early the 18th, Manning and other survivors of the 43rd returned to Vicksburg, along with other men of Pemberton's army who fought at Champion Hill and still were able to return. A woman living in Vicksburg described the scene:

> From 12 o'clock until late in the night the streets and roads were jammed with wagons, cannons, horses, men, mules, stock, sheep, everything you can imagine that appertains to an army—being brought hurriedly within the entrenchments. Nothing like order prevailed, of course, as divisions, brigades and regiments were broken and separated.[55]

The men themselves presented "[a] woeful sight," another woman wrote, "a beaten, demoralized army that came rushing back—humanity in the last throes of endurance. Wan, hollow-eyed, ragged, foot-sore, bloody, the men limped along."[56]

These defeated men joined the two fresh divisions Pemberton had left behind at Vicksburg to guard the city. Altogether, Pemberton had approximately thirty thousand men with which to defend Vicksburg.[57]

As rapidly as possible, the units were reorganized and assigned to man different segments of the defensive works. That line of works stretched eight to nine miles along the crest of a ridge from the Mississippi River north of the city around the city in a rough half circle back to the Mississippi south of the city. Men of the 43rd Georgia and those of other Confederate units worked to reinforce and repair their line, digging trenches and rifle pits and reinforcing breastworks, battery emplacements, and forts of timber and earthwork that continued throughout the siege. Doing this work, the men began to recover their spirit. Morale also may

---

[52] US Census, 1880, Jackson County, Georgia; Lily Jackson's grave marker, Oconee Hill Cemetery, Athens, Georgia.
[53] David Family Bible.
[54] D. Miller, *Vicksburg*, 418.
[55] Hoehling, *Vicksburg*, 20.
[56] Cotton, *Vicksburg*, 18.
[57] Korn, *War on the Mississippi*, 126; Everhart, *Vicksburg*, 34; Ballard, *Vicksburg*, 319, 398.

have been helped when they understood they were completing a line fortified with nine major forts built with earthen walls up to twenty feet thick and connected by deep trenches and rifle pits, the whole behind a deep ravine.[58]

The remnants of Stevenson's Division were placed overlooking the Mississippi to the south of town at the right wing of the Confederate line defending Vicksburg, with Barton's severely weakened brigade at the far right end of the line. (Barton reported that over 42 percent of his brigade had been lost.) Pemberton thought Grant would attack the center of the Confederate line and wanted Stevenson's depleted and disorganized division placed at a relatively remote location where they would have time to regroup and revive.[59]

When he arrived in Vicksburg, Manning likely ensured that the wounded men of the 43rd who needed further treatment were sent to one of the several hospitals for the wounded in Vicksburg. He then made his way to the south of the Vicksburg where the 43rd was stationed.

Grant to Vicksburg

Following close behind the Confederates, Grant's army reached Vicksburg on May 18. At that time Grant had about forty-five thousand troops compared to the approximately thirty-thousand troops with Pemberton inside the Confederate lines. By mid-June, however, Grant's army had swelled to seventy-seven thousand, more than double Pemberton's.[60]

On May 19, Grant attacked the Confederate left and center but made little progress. On May 22, he attacked again, again with little progress. During these attacks the Federals made only tentative and unsuccessful efforts against Barton's Brigade.

After these attacks failed, Grant resolved to begin a siege. He had the Confederates completely surrounded, cut off from resupply of food, ammunition, medicine, and manpower. They also were cut off from any communication with the world beyond their own lines, except for the rare occasion when a brave courier made his way through or around Grant's lines. They would remain that way for forty-seven days.[61]

---

[58] *OR*, ser. 1, vol. 24, pt. 1, 271, 273; *OR*, ser. 1, vol. 24, pt. 3, 926–27; Hoehling, *Vicksburg*, 25, 68, 90; Ballard, *Vicksburg*, 321–24; D. Miller, *Vicksburg*, 419; interpretive marker no. 4, "Siege and Defense Lines," Vicksburg Battlefield Museum; Everhart, *Vicksburg*, 33–34.

[59] *OR*, ser. 1, vol. 24, pt. 1, 271, 273; *OR*, ser. 1, vol. 24, pt. 2, 100, 343–44, 355; *OR*, ser. 1, vol. 24, pt. 3, 926–27; Ballard, *Vicksburg*, 320–22; Walker, *Hell's Broke Loose in Georgia*, 86; Palencia, *On Rising Ground*, 142.

[60] Carter, *Final Fortress*, 239; Korn, *War on the Mississippi*, 126; D. Miller, *Vicksburg*, 415; Walker, *Hell's Broke Loose in Georgia*, 86.

[61] Ballard, *Vicksburg*, 326–51; D. Miller, *Vicksburg*, 443.

Manning in Charge

Once again, as early in the year, Manning was the only remaining medical officer with the 43rd. As soon as possible after arriving back in Vicksburg, he would have established a field hospital or infirmary near where the regiment was holding its part of the Confederate defenses. This facility probably was a hospital tent erected in as safe a place as possible, such as in a gully or ravine that provided some shelter from enemy fire. A hospital tent was "fourteen by fifteen feet with eleven foot ceilings and oil cloth or canvas floors. Each tent could accommodate eight to ten patients." The patients lay on cots, sacks filled with straw, or on the floor.

The field hospital may have been located in a house, barn, or other more solid structure if one were near the regiment's position. Such buildings, however, may have been scarce because the extreme right of the line where the regiment was located was roughly two miles from the city.

Wherever the field hospital was located, there Manning would have held daily sick calls and given first aid to the wounded throughout the forty-seven days of the siege.[62]

Because of the losses at Champion Hill, Manning would have had fewer men to care for now than he had earlier in Vicksburg before the arrival of Dr. Van Dyke. Still, there would have been about 380 men under his sole care, and the likelihood they would need care was now much greater for several reasons.

Sickness: Exposed, Debilitated, Ill-Nourished, and Wet

The constant threat of Federal attack required the Confederates to man their line continuously, always on guard. Yet because of the length of the line and the limited number of Confederates to man it, soldiers were rotated in and out of the trenches only rarely, if at all. One member of the garrison reported, "Whole companies would lie back of the breastworks for three weeks without leaving the lines for a moment." They stayed there and stood watch and repaired defensive works in rain, hail, and mud or in the broiling Mississippi sun that brought temperatures near one hundred degrees with a minimum of shade or shelter. If a rain came pouring down, drenching them, they still had to remain at their post in their wet clothes until the hot sun dried them.[63]

In addition, they suffered a gradually diminishing supply of food. The soldiers were completely cut off from the outside world. Delivery of adequate food

---

[62] CSA War Department, *Regulations of the Army of the Confederate States, 1863*, 282; Mitchell, "Improvisation, Adaptation and Innovation," 114–15 (quote); Stover, "Civil War Canvas Tents"; Schroeder-Lein, *Encyclopedia of Civil War Medicine*, 151–53.

[63] Everhart, *Vicksburg*, 41; *Southern Watchman*, July 29, 1863 (quote, 2); *Southern Banner*, August 5, 1863; Hoehling, *Vicksburg*, 60, 114; Bollet, *Civil War Medicine*, 25.

was impossible. A soldier in Vicksburg later reported, "For about four days after the siege commenced, the troops were allowed full rations. At the expiration of that time, they were gradually reduced to the following amount of food: 2 oz flour, 4 oz bacon, 1½ oz rice 2 oz peas (the latter not eatable) and 4 oz sugar—making a total of 14½ oz [sic] of food per day."[64]

Dogs and cats were no longer seen prowling around town. It was reported that "rats are hanging dressed in the market for sale." A boy avowed that fried rat had a taste "fully equal to that of squirrels."[65]

Early in the siege, a large number of mules and horses, but not all, had been driven out of the Confederate lines to the Union because the Confederates lacked fodder to feed them. Before long, however, some in Vicksburg were wishing more had been retained. As mentioned in the part of the letter quoted earlier, Manning later told his family that he never ate mule meat but that many men in Vicksburg did. One Vicksburg inhabitant reported, "A certain number of mules are killed each day by the commissaries, and are issued to the men, all of whom prefer the fresh meat, though it be of mule, to the bacon and salt rations that they have eaten for so long a time without change." Still, not all mules were eaten. One soldier noted that "the stench from dead mules and horses (killed by shell) is intolerable."[66]

A concoction that was devised as part of the Confederate soldier's diet was something called "pea bread." Supplied as a substitute for the usual bread, it was composed of cornmeal and ground "cow peas," small beans that normally were fed to livestock. When water was added to this mixture and the whole placed into a pan, camp cooks baked it over a fire, producing "a nauseous composition, as the corn-meal cooked in half the time the peas-meal did, so this stuff was half raw." The result was hard on the outside, "so hard, that one might have knocked down a full-grown steer with a chunk of it," and sickish, raw pea-meal in the center. A modern historian summarized, "Its effect on the digestive systems of the Confederate soldiers was possibly the equivalent of a secret Yankee weapon."[67]

The quality of the water soldiers drank also led to illness. Men had to haul it from the river, sometimes a great distance, making it extremely warm. It also

---

[64] Hoehling, *Vicksburg*, 60; G. Ward, Burns, and Burns, *Civil War*, 238–39; *Southern Watchman*, July 29, 1863 (quote, 1).

[65] Hoehling, *Vicksburg*, 40–41; "A Union Woman Suffers through the Siege," 667 (1st quote); Gallagher et al., *Civil War*, 140; G. Ward, Burns, and Burns, *Civil War*, 239 (2nd quote).

[66] Hoehling, *Vicksburg*, 52; Gallagher et al., *Civil War*, 140; Loughborough, *My Cave Life in Vicksburg*, 116–17 (1st quote, 116); *OR*, ser. 1, vol. 24, pt. 1, 274; M. Smith, *Smell of Battle*, 109 (2nd quote).

[67] Everhart, *Vicksburg*, 41–42 (1st and 3rd quotes); Hoehling, *Vicksburg*, 82–83 (2nd quote).

was muddy, frequently contaminated, and generally disagreeable. Disease and intestinal disorders were the results.[68]

Whatever they ate and drank, it was not enough, or of good enough quality, to keep them healthy, particularly given their long exposure to all weathers in the trenches. One modern historian has written, "By late June, almost half the Confederates were on the sick list or in the hospital."[69]

Wounds: Enemy Shells and Sharpshooters

As if these factors were not enough to plague the Confederates and place them in hospitals or worse, there also were the continual threat of sharpshooters and almost continuous shelling from large mortars and cannons of many sizes.

Describing the Union sharpshooters, General Grant later wrote: "our sharpshooters...were always on the alert and ready to fire at a head whenever it showed itself above the rebel works." A Confederate described the danger: "The enemy's sharpshooters were all splendid shots, and after the first few days of the siege it was a very dangerous thing for any one to look over the breast works. So accurately did they aim, and such numbers were they that a hat placed on a stick and held above the fort for two minutes was pierced by 15 minnie balls." A newspaperman in Vicksburg reported, "the minie balls swept the line of entrenchments night and day, making it almost certain death for any of the men to show their bodies above the parapet of our works."[70]

One Confederate officer found out later why Federal sharpshooters became so accurate. He noted that the Confederates, whose breastworks generally were on the tops of ridges, were higher than the Federals lower down. That meant when a Confederate rose above the breastworks or "poked a rifle through a firing port," he was silhouetted against the sky, making him an easier target. Moreover, once the Federals got the range of a Confederate gun port, they would lash a gun in such a way as to preserve its aim. Then "when a hole was darkeneded by a Confederate head, the trigger was pulled and a bullet was put through it with unfailing accuracy."[71]

Possibly worse was the almost continuous shelling day and night, from one side of the city by gunboats and huge naval mortars on rafts in the river and from the other side by some 220 cannons in the Federal lines. Missiles—solid shot, grape shot (canisters loaded with small balls), and cannon and mortar shells—

---

[68] Gregory, "Vicksburg during the Siege," 120; Loughborough, *My Cave Life in Vicksburg*, 104, Everhart, *Vicksburg*, 40; D. Miller, *Vicksburg*, 467–68; Smith, *Siege of Vicksburg*, 212.

[69] G. Ward, Burns, and Burns, *Civil War*, 240 (quote), Everhart, *Vicksburg*, 49; Hoehling, *Vicksburg*, 130.

[70] Grant, *Memoirs and Selected Letters*, 360 (1st quote); *Southern Watchman*, July 29, 1863 (2nd quote); Hoehling, *Vicksburg*, 59.

[71] Barr, *Civil War Captain and His Lady*, 226.

landed on the city itself, on the defensive works some distance from the city, and on the inhabited land in between. They were immensely destructive not only when they struck someone directly, resulting in terrible wounds and death, but also when some dropped and exploded, sending deadly fragments in every direction. Moreover, while flying through the air toward and into the city they produced terrifying sounds that made it difficult to sleep and rattled the nerves of both soldiers and civilians.[72]

A woman in Vicksburg described the effect of cannon fire:

> My heart stood still as we would hear the reports from the guns and the rushing and fearful sound of the shell as it came toward us. As it neared, the noise became more deafening; the air was full of the rushing sound; pains darted through my temples; my ears were full of the confusing noise; and as it exploded, the report flashed through my head like an electric shock...and, with a low, singing sound, the fragments sped on in their work of death.[73]

The mortars with their high arcs, presented an awesome sight, particularly at night. As one observer wrote, from the river they soared upward "rising steadily and shiningly in great parabolic curves, descending in ever increasing swiftness, and falling with deafening shriek and explosion, hurling in many a radius their ponderous fragments."[74]

City Hospitals

While Manning would have held daily sick calls and given first aid to the wounded at the 43rd's field hospital, he would have transferred the severely ill and the badly wounded to hospitals in the city and from time to time might have gone there to visit them.

Amidst the shelling, hunger, sickness, and wounding, he would have found the city hospitals severely overcrowded. An army doctor recorded that "some poor fellows are compelled to lay out in the open air and get attention from any Dr. who happens to pass that way." An army chaplain described a similar scene: "The wounded were placed in tents on either side [of the hospital] in deep hollows. As I entered one of these valleys, a most horrid spectacle greeted my eyes. Every tent was filled with the wounded and dying. There they lay, poor, helpless sufferers; some groaning from excessive pain, others pale and silent through weakness and

---

[72] Grant, *Personal Memoirs*, 363; Loughborough, *My Cave Life in Vicksburg*, 56–57, 125; Hoehling, *Vicksburg*, 21, 40, 89; *Southern Watchman*, July 29, 1863; Gregory, "Vicksburg during the Siege," 116–17; *OR*, ser. 1, vol. 24, pt. 3, 926, 958.

[73] Loughborough, *My Cave Life in Vicksburg*, 56–57.

[74] Gregory, "Vicksburg during the Siege," 117.

the loss of blood." He continued, "Flies swarm around the wounded—more numerous where the wound is severest." [75]

The hospitals themselves also could be dangerous, being sometimes located in areas of the city most exposed to shelling. Over three days, a surgeon at a hospital complex reported that his hospital buildings had been hit by shells twenty-one times and "6 wounded men re-wounded." The re-wounded men, "nerves already shattered by wounds, bear this very badly." On another occasion he reported that shells from Union mortars "penetrated my main building, and descending to the floor, blew up the surgeons' room...destroying the entire stock of drugs, except some morphine and quinine, and breaking the leg of Surgeon Bretts so badly as to require instant amputation." Shelling of hospitals, whether intentional or not, continued despite their flying a yellow flag, the equivalent of today's red cross.[76]

To deal with the overcrowding and danger, on June 5 the acting medical director of the army in Vicksburg, E. H. Bryan, sent the "slightly wounded...[back] to the field infirmaries to the care of the Asst Surgeons."[77]

Manning and the Men of the 43rd

There Manning continued to care for the sick or wounded men of the 43rd. However, he could not save all his patients. During the siege at least six of the 43rd died of unspecified causes and at least one died shortly after the siege was over from wounds received during it. In addition, Private William Peeler of Company E was badly wounded in June "while in the ditches at Vicksburg...by a piece of shell." After treating him, Manning sent him to a hospital "where he died the ninth day after being wounded." Another, Private Lewis Stovall of Company E, died in a hospital on June 20 "from relapse of Measles & Diarrhoea," and still another, Private William G. Goodno of Company A, died June 8 "from the fatigue of Siege."[78]

Confederates Seek Terms of Surrender

General Pemberton had been monitoring the deteriorating condition of his men while hoping that General Johnston, who had some thirty-thousand soldiers on the far side of the Union's lines, between the Federals and the city of Jackson, would come to his aid. On June 28 or 29, however, he received a particularly

---

[75] Alison, "Joseph Dill Alison Diary," 16 (1st quote); Hoehling, *Vicksburg*, 113–14 (2nd quote); Smith, *Siege of Vicksburg*, 302 (3rd quote); Loughborough, *My Cave Life in Vicksburg*, 77.

[76] *OR*, ser. 1, vol. 24, pt. 3, 913 (1st quote) and ser. 1, vol. 24, pt. 2, 423 (2nd quote); Hoehling, *Vicksburg*, 105; D. Miller, *Vicksburg*, 439–40.

[77] Service records of E. H. Bryan; *OR*, ser. 1, vol. 24, pt. 1, 294.

[78] William Peeler service and pension records; Lewis Stovall service and pension records; William Goodno service records; *OR*, ser. 1, vol. 24, pt. 2, 328, 424.

sobering indication of his troops' situation when a letter arrived for him from "MANY SOLDIERS." It stated that the soldiers' rations "were not enough scarcely to keep soul and body together, much less to stand the hardships we are called upon to stand." It proceeded, "If you can't feed us, you had better surrender us, horrible as the idea is.... I tell you plainly, men are not going to lie here and perish, if they do love their country dearly.... The army is now ripe for mutiny, unless it can be fed."[79]

Around this time, Pemberton had become convinced that Johnston would not come to his aid. As a result, on July 1, he asked his division commanders to inform him "as to the condition of your troops and their ability to make the marches and undergo the fatigues necessary to accomplish a successful evacuation," that is, to fight their way out.

The division commanders canvassed their brigade commanders then responded to Pemberton that a successful evacuation was impossible. Barton in particular wrote in response, "The command suffers greatly from intermittent fever, and is generally debilitated from the long exposure and inaction of the trenches. Of those now reported for duty, fully one-half are undergoing [medical] treatment. These I think are unfit for the field."

With no relief expected, little possibility his men could fight their way out, and his "defenses crumbling," Pemberton had no alternative but to seek terms of surrender from Grant. As he wrote,

> Confined to the narrow limits of a trench, with their limbs cramped and swollen, without exercise, constantly exposed to a murderous storm of shot and shell, while the enemy's unerring sharpshooters stood ready to pick off every one visible above the parapets, is it strange that the men grew weak and attenuated?.... [I]t would be an act of cruel inhumanity to subject them longer to the terrible ordeal to which for so many days and nights they had already been exposed.[80]

Major General U. S. Grant[81]

Headquarters Department of the Tennessee
Near Vicksburg, Miss., July 3, 1863
[To] Lieut. Gen. J. C. Pemberton,
Commanding Confederate Forces, Vicksburg, Miss.:

---

[79] Everhart, *Vicksburg*, 47–49; Foote, *Civil War*, 2:412–13; *OR*, ser. 1, vol. 24, pt. 3, 982–83 (quote).

[80] *OR*, ser. 1, vol. 24, pt. 1, 281–87 (Pemberton quotes), ser. 1, vol. 24, pt. 2, 347 (Barton quote); Ballard, *Vicksburg*, 396–97.

[81] *OR*, ser. 1, vol. 24, pt. 1, 60.

GENERAL: In conformity with agreement of this afternoon, I will submit the following proposition for the surrender of the city of Vicksburg, public stores, &c.:

On you accepting the terms proposed, I will march in one division as a guard, and take possession at 8 a. m. to-morrow. As soon as rolls can be made out, and paroles signed by officers and men, you will be allowed to march out of our lines, the officers taking with them their side-arms and clothing, and the field, staff, and cavalry officers one horse each. The rank and file will be allowed all their clothing, but no other property. If these conditions are accepted, any amount of rations you may deem necessary can be taken from the stores you now have, and also the necessary cooking utensils for preparing them. Thirty wagons also, counting two two-horse or mule teams as one, will be allowed to transport such articles as cannot be carried along.

The same conditions will be allowed to all sick and wounded officers and soldiers as fast as they become able to travel.

The paroles for these latter must be signed, however, while officers are present authorized to sign the roll of prisoners.

I am, generally, very respectfully, your obedient servant,
U. S. GRANT
Major-General

Notes

take possession at 8 a. m. tomorrow: Pemberton accepted Grant's terms. On the morning of July 4, the Confederate soldiers marched out of the trenches and stacked their arms in front of Union troops who were stationed opposite them. A Confederate officer observed that "the Federal troops acted splendidly." He continued, "not a jeer or taunt came from any one of the Federal soldiers."[82]

Also, after the surrender, the Federals, both individually and by Grant's order, generously provided the famished Confederates with food.[83]

paroles signed: A parole was a pledge signed by a soldier not to "take up arms again against the United States" or perform any other military useful service usually performed by officers or soldiers against the United States until officially exchanged for a Union soldier that the Confederates held prisoner.[84]

---

[82] Everhart, *Vicksburg*, 51; Loughborough, *My Cave Life in Vicksburg*, 139 (quote).

[83] *OR*, ser. 1, vol. 24, pt. 2, 201; Ballard, *Vicksburg*, 399–400; Roberts and Clark, *Atlanta's Fighting Forty-second*, 105; Walker, *Hell's Broke Loose in Georgia*, 93.

[84] The service records of Private J. R. Brock of Company D, 43rd Georgia Infantry, contain an example of a parole form signed by Vicksburg prisoners (quote); Garrison, *Encyclopedia of Civil War Usage*, 186.

A few days after the surrender, 290 men of the 43rd who were not hospitalized, and at least seventy-seven men of the 43rd who were in several Vicksburg hospitals, were paroled, each signing duplicate printed parole forms.[85]

Manning, however, was not paroled because he was not officially a prisoner. At that time, under mutual agreement between the Union and Confederate armies in 1862, captured medical officers were not considered prisoners of war and were to be released unconditionally. This agreement was reached primarily so that military doctors on both sides could continue to treat the wounded soldiers of both sides after a battle was over without the threat of being forcibly detained and transported to prison.[86]

you will be allowed to march out of our lines: After being paroled, the Vicksburg survivors were again under their Confederate officers. General Pemberton ordered those who were able to march to begin leaving Vicksburg by divisions on July 11 and to head east across Mississippi. Stevenson's division and the 43rd Georgia did not leave until July 12.[87]

Some Confederate medical officers stayed with the Confederate sick and wounded in hospital in Vicksburg. Very likely, Manning was not one of them. Those who stayed probably were officers from Mississippi and Louisiana regiments who were closer to home than officers from Tennessee and Georgia. In addition, Manning was the only medical officer for the 43rd, which had almost four times as many men marching out of Vicksburg as were staying in a Vicksburg hospital.[88]

It probably was good that Manning went with the bulk of his regiment. It now is unclear how many of the men of the 43rd were physically fit for such a long march and how many needed medical treatment along the way. Although all finally received adequate food after the surrender, some in their eagerness to head home may have persuaded themselves, and possibly Manning, that they were able to march when they were not. Also, a few had been wounded at Champion Hill, and, despite no longer being in hospital, possibly were not ready for the march either.

One who was unable was Private William H. West of Company F. He had a fever "contracted in the ditches at the siege of Vicksburg" yet marched with the able men of the 43rd toward home until reaching Smith County, Mississippi (about ninety miles east of Vicksburg), where, according to pension records, "he gave out and died." Private Jacob Bradberry of Company H did not make it that

---

[85] "List of Confederates Captured at Vicksburg, Mississippi, July 4, 1863," NARA; Gregory, "Vicksburg during the Siege," 130.

[86] H. H. Cunningham, *Doctors in Gray*, 130–33, Freemon, *Gangrene and Glory*, 82.

[87] *OR* ser. 1, vol. 24, pt. 3, 493; Connor, *Confederate Diary*, 27; Rogers, *Bible Records*, 8.

[88] "List of Confederates Captured at Vicksburg, Mississippi, July 4, 1863," NARA; *OR*, ser. 1, vol. 24, pt. 3, 494.

far. He was left behind in Simpson County, Mississippi (about seventy miles from Vicksburg), and later died of an unspecified "sickness." Somewhat luckier was Private John D. Bagwell of Company F, who shortly after leaving Vicksburg, contracted "brain fever," had to be left at a farmhouse in Smith County, and remained there "out of his senses" for some two to three weeks before he recovered. Another soldier from Stevenson's Division who "had chills" every day for several days tried to get into a hospital in Brandon, Mississippi (about fifty miles from Vicksburg), but found it crowded. "Couldn't find a surgeon or anyone who had seen one—everything topsy-turvy." He decided to go on ahead. He made it home.[89]

When the Confederates marched out of Vicksburg heading east, there was a dispute as to exactly where they were headed. Jefferson Davis intended them to march to a "parole camp" at Demopolis, Alabama, a small town about seventy miles across the Mississippi-Alabama border from Meridian, Mississippi, and a total of about 175 miles from Vicksburg. Here they were to stay together until exchanged. Then they immediately would join the fight "to serve their country in this hour of its greatest need." The men themselves, however, assumed that their paroles gave them the right simply to go home as soon as they could, and many proceeded to do exactly that.[90]

The route east paralleled the railroad from Vicksburg to Meridian, Mississippi, near the Alabama border, with train depots located every so often along the way. From Meridian, tracks led further east toward Alabama, Tennessee, and eventually Georgia. To the soldiers, boarding the train would make the trip home quicker. It was not until the men in divisions that left before Stevenson's reached the depot at Brandon, about fifty miles east of Vicksburg, that they were told that they were to go into parole camp and could not ride the railroad home. They revolted. Some of their officers had to threaten to use their side-arms in order to subdue them.[91]

General Pemberton saw that many men were stealing away from the line of march "leaving for their homes without authority." He wrote his superiors that it was impossible to keep them off the cars and otherwise making for home without an armed force. He also repeatedly recommended that the parolees be given a furlough of thirty days to go home and then be reassembled at the end of that period.[92]

---

[89] Pension records for West, Bradberry, and Bagwell; Connor, *Confederate Diary*, 28; Rand McNally, "Mississippi State Road Map."

[90] *OR*, ser. 1, vol. 24, pt. 1, 231–32; *OR*, ser. 1, vol. 24, pt. 3, 1000–1002 (quotes), 1005–1007; *Rand McNally 2019 Road Atlas*; Gregory, "Vicksburg during the Siege," 131.

[91] *OR*, ser. 1, vol. 24, pt. 1, 202; *OR*, ser. 1, vol. 24, pt. 3, 1005; Gregory, "Vicksburg during the Siege," 131; Walker, *Hell's Broke Loose in Georgia*, 94.

[92] *OR*, ser. 1, vol. 24, pt. 3, 1001 (quote), 1002, 1006–1007, 1010–1011.

In the meantime, the destination of the parolees became confused. Responding to Pemberton on July 14, General Johnston directed Pemberton to proceed to Enterprise, Mississippi, south of Meridian, rather than to Demopolis. Yet Jefferson Davis wrote Pemberton on July 16 that they still were to go to Demopolis.[93]

Finally, after an exchange of communications, it was agreed that the Vicksburg parolees would receive a thirty-day furlough. The furlough period was to commence on the day Pemberton promulgated the order granting the furlough, July 18. Although the length of the furlough later was staggered so that the soldiers furthest away would receive the longest furlough (those from Georgia receiving twenty days), it is unclear to what extent that change was enforced.[94]

The bulk of the men in Stevenson's Division, including men of Barton's Brigade and men of the 43rd, reached Enterprise, Mississippi, around July 20. As a member of the 42nd Georgia later wrote, that regiment, and probably others of Barton's Brigade, left Enterprise by train for Mobile on the July 21, or soon after. (They were retracing the route they had traveled to reach Vicksburg in December the year before.) On July 25, they arrived in Atlanta. Only then were they officially released to return to their homes.[95]

Manning very probably made it home to Lona and Nora by the same route and on the same schedule. There he stayed, for a while.

---

[93] Ibid., 1002, 1006–1007.
[94] Ibid., 1001–1007, 1010–1011, 1014–1015, 1021, 1025.
[95] *OR*, ser. 1, vol. 24, pt. 3, 1010; Goodson, *Georgia Confederate 7,000*, 2:55–56; Roberts and Clark, *Atlanta's Fighting Forty-second*, 105–106; Connor, *Confederate Diary*, 28–29; Walker, *Hell's Broke Loose in Georgia*, 94.

Chapter 21

Gettysburg: Simeon, May–July 1863

Simeon

Camp Gregg, near Guinea's Station
Va May 25, 1863
My affectionate Mother

There seems to be an impression that Gen. Lee will make a forward movement soon though we can't tell anything about it. We are in delightful camps and enjoying ourselves very much, very little to do. There is a very general revival of religion going on in our Brigade at this time, baptizing every day. There are several churches in the surrounding country that our men go to every Sabbath.... .

Your affectionate son,
S. B. David

Notes

Camp Gregg: This camp was located about eight miles below (downriver) from Fredericksburg. Simeon's regiment had returned there after fighting in the Battle of Chancellorsville as described in chapter 18. Horatio was convalescing at home in Georgia.[1]

Letter omissions: This entire letter appears in chapter 19.

impression that Gen. Lee will make a forward movement soon: Lee did. In early June, only shortly after the letter was written, he began marching his army from the Fredericksburg area toward Pennsylvania.

Lee decided on this course of action for several reasons. He wanted to go to an area that had not been ravaged by the war and where there were abundant supplies for his army. He also wanted to draw Union forces away from Virginia, particularly the Shenandoah Valley, in order to allow the area to recover, harvest crops, and be able to supply his army later.

In addition, he saw his present position at Fredericksburg as giving him only two choices, "to retire to Richmond and stand a siege, which must ultimately have ended in surrender, or to invade Pennsylvania." The latter option would give Lee more room to maneuver and might give him a victory on Union ground that

---

[1] Robertson, *General A. P. Hill*, 169; Folsom, *Heroes and Martyrs*, 118, 151; Smedlund, *Camp Fires of Georgia Troops*, 141.

would both strengthen the growing movement in the North supporting peace and encourage England to intervene on the side of the South.

Ultimately Lee and his army, including Simeon, marched toward Gettysburg.[2]

Simeon's Service Records

Medical Directors Office, Richmond, Virginia[3]
S. B. David
Capt. Co. E. 14 Regt. Ga.
Brigade: Thomas
Appears on a Register of
Medical Director's Office
Richmond, Va.,
under the head of "Furloughs and discharges."
From Genl. Hospl. No. 4
Date of injury or disease July 2, 1863
Nature of injury or disease G. S. W.
Thigh
Furloughed 40 days July 20, 1863
Discharged
Residence Cumming, Ga.

Notes

Genl Hospital No. 4: This hospital was in a building on 10th Street in Richmond that previously housed a Baptist school for girls called the Richmond Female Institute. After January 8, 1863, it treated officers only.[4]

G. S. W: These initials stand for "gunshot wound," which in Simeon's case was a wound to his thigh sustained on July 2, 1863, the second day of the Battle of Gettysburg. Simeon's pay receipt for June 30–July 31 has a handwritten notation at the bottom: "Severely wounded at Gettysburg & furloughed."

Battle of Gettysburg and Simeon—First Day

During the battle, Simeon's 14th Georgia Regiment was still one of the four regiments in General Edward Thomas's brigade. Thomas's Brigade, however, now was one of four brigades in General Dorsey Pender's division (composed of part of General A. P. Hill's former "Light Division"). Pender's Division itself was part

---

[2] Foote, *Civil War*, 2:431 (quote); Gallagher et al., *Civil War*, 169–72; Robertson, *General A. P. Hill*, 198–200; Hattaway and Jones, *How the North Won*, 397–98; *OR*, ser. 1, vol. 27, pt. 2, 305, 313.

[3] Confederate Archives, NARA, undated record copy.

[4] Waitt, *Confederate Military Hospitals in Richmond*, 11–12.

of the 3rd Corps, a new corps, consisting of three divisions, created after the death of Stonewall Jackson and commanded by a promoted A. P. Hill. All were part of General Lee's Army of Northern Virginia.[5]

The morning of July 1, Lee's army had arrived in Pennsylvania, and A. P. Hill's corps was marching at the head of the army toward Gettysburg "a farming community of about 2,400 souls," in search of a quantity of shoes that were reported to be there. Unexpectedly, it encountered a unit of Federal cavalry.

Heth's Division led the corps and was first to encounter the Union cavalry, an encounter that occurred west of the town of Gettysburg along Chambersburg Pike. (The commander of this division was the same Henry Heth who commanded the division that included Manning Alexander's 43rd Georgia when it went into and out of Kentucky in 1862; see chapter 13.) Pender's Division followed Heth's, and Thomas's Brigade marched at the rear of Pender's Division.

When other brigades of the division advanced to meet the enemy in support of Heth, Thomas's Brigade was ordered instead to take a position behind the developing front line near an artillery unit about a mile from Gettysburg. Its mission was to protect the artillery and to guard against a Union attack from the left flank.[6]

In his diary, Private Hall of the 14th Georgia reported, "soon after we cleared our camps [on July 1] we began to hear the boom of cannon ahead of us and as we advanced it became more distinct." A Confederate surgeon who also was in Pender's Division described the look on soldiers of the division when they heard the sound of the cannons: "Upon looking around I at once noticed in the contenance of all an expression of intense seriousness and solemnity, which I have always perceived in the faces of men who are about to face death and the awful shock of battle."[7]

Private Hall continued: "about 10 A. M. we formed line of Battle each side of the road and advanced through woods and fields swamps and brier thickets and presently shells began to fall and burst among us. we got orders to march by the right flank. we marched up and lay down in rear of one of our batterys that was firing at the enemy " [periods added].[8]

There the regiment remained while "bombs was falling and exploding" among them until sunset. By then the Union force had withdrawn into Gettysburg. Thomas's Brigade was ordered forward to take a position south of Gettysburg just behind Seminary Ridge and at the extreme right of the Confederate line

---

[5] Gottfried, *Brigades of Gettysburg*, 10, 639, 656; Gallagher et al., *Civil War*, 168.

[6] Gottfried, *Brigades of Gettysburg*, 639, 656; Gallagher et al., *Civil War*, 173 (quote); *OR*, ser. 1, vol. 27, pt. 2, 656; Gallagher, "Confederate Corps Leadership," 42.

[7] Hall, *Diary of George Washington Hall*, 1:43 (1st quote); Welch, *Confederate Surgeon's Letters to His Wife*, 64.

[8] Hall, *Diary of George Washington Hall*, 1:43 (quote).

that ran along the ridge a short distance south of the town of Gettysburg. The 14th Georgia was positioned within the brigade as the second regiment from the right.[9]

Battle of Gettysburg and Simeon—Second Day
The Positions and Plan

When the battle recommenced on July 2, Thomas's Brigade no longer was on the right of the Confederate line. The right of the line had moved much further south of Gettysburg as additional Confederate units gathered and were placed to the right of the brigade.[10]

That day the major Confederate action was to be an attack from this new right against the Union left. General Longstreet's Corps, on the far right of the Confederate line, was to strike the Union left wherever it was found near two hills, Big Round Top and Little Round Top, turn it, and then roll it up, sending streams of Union forces retreating toward the town of Gettysburg and toward the remainder of the Confederate army, including Simeon's 14th Georgia.[11]

A. P. Hill's 3rd Corps including Pender's Division, Thomas's Brigade, and the 14th Georgia was on Seminary Ridge now in the center of the Confederate line, north of Longstreet's Corps and a short distance southwest of the town of Gettysburg. Opposite it and about twelve hundred yards away was the Union right located around Cemetery Hill and Culp's Hill, due south of town. The Union line stretched on south from Cemetery Hill along Cemetery Ridge, a geographical feature that ran roughly parallel to Confederate-held Seminary Ridge.[12]

Between the two ridges ran the Emmitsburg Pike, a road leading north into Gettysburg. It was up this road toward Gettysburg that the Union army was supposed to flee as Longstreet attacked. The right part of Hill's Corps (Anderson's Division) was to join the attack. The primary mission of the left part, however, which included Thomas's Brigade, was to hold the Union forces in front of it in position on the opposite ridge so that they would not reinforce the Union left when Longstreet attacked. The brigade also was to protect an artillery battery that was stationed on Seminary Ridge nearby.[13]

---

[9] Ibid., 43–44 (quote); Gottfried, *Brigades of Gettysburg*, 657; J. A. Woods, *Gettysburg, July 2*, 1–2, 4n23, 13n24; Gottfried, *Maps of Gettysburg*, 143; Bachelder, "Map of the Battle Field of Gettysburg."

[10] Gottfried, *Maps of Gettysburg*, 142–43.

[11] *OR*, ser. 1, vol. 27, pt. 2, 318; Boatner, *Civil War Dictionary*, 335–36; Guelzo, *Gettysburg*, 236–37.

[12] Gottfried, *Maps of Gettysburg*, 143; Shultz and Mingus, *Second Day at Gettysburg*, 111; Bachelder, "Map of the Battle Field of Gettysburg."

[13] *OR*, ser. 1, vol. 27, pt. 2, 318; Gottfried, *Maps of Gettysburg*, 143; Boatner, *Civil War Dictionary*, 335–36; Bryan, "Letters of Two Confederate Officers," 189.

Just before dawn on July 2, most of Thomas's Brigade was positioned in an orchard on Seminary Ridge and beginning to stir from a short, fitful rest. During the night, men of the 14th had heard indications of the enemy's activities along that Union line. "Across the way came forth sure sounds of preparations by the enemy of breastworks, ditches, and the marches of multitudes gathering to do battle. Creaks of the wheels coupled with grunts of horses define without doubt the placement of cannon," a member of the 14th later wrote of that night. The 14th waited for the next day.[14]

The Battle

About two hundred yards in front of the Confederate's Seminary Ridge and running roughly parallel to it was a "sunken road," a dirt road called Long Lane that was worn down by use and bordered on each side by a bank. A post-and-rail fence ran along the top of the front bank facing the Union line.

Like a ready-made trench, this road provided some shelter for a man with a musket kneeling behind the front bank. There as the sun rose at the beginning of a hot, July day, skirmishers from the brigade, and those of another brigade to Thomas's right, were kneeling in a line, their long guns pointing out under the fence rails toward the Union line. A few yards further in front of the sunken road, other Confederate sharpshooters and skirmishers lay behind a split-rail fence in an open plain that stretched toward the Emmitsburg Pike and beyond that, Cemetery Ridge and the Union line.

Shortly after the sun had risen, Union skirmishers advanced from below Cemetery Ridge across the Emmitsburg Road toward the Confederate skirmishers. Behind "a slight rise of ground" on the Confederates' side of the road, they stopped and opened fire. For Thomas's Brigade and the 14th Georgia, the battle on the second day had begun.[15]

Fire from these skirmishers, from Union infantry on Cemetery Ridge, and cannons on Cemetery Hill soon were making things particularly hot for the men of the 14th. "[W]e lie down in line of Battle to keep the enemys Batterys from having Such affect on us," Private Hall wrote. "[C]annon balls, bombs, grape and canisters fall thick and fast around us and among us killing and wounding several of our regt." Captain Charles A. Conn of the 45th Georgia, the regiment of Thomas's Brigade next to the 14th, later wrote: "The skirmishing was the *heaviest*

---

[14] Bachelder, "Map of the Battle Field of Gettysburg"; Dewberry, *History of the 14th Georgia*, 62 (quote).

[15] Bachelder, "Map of the Battle Field of Gettysburg"; Garrison, *Encyclopedia of Civil War Usage*, 243; Shultz and Mingus, *Second Day at Gettysburg*, 80, 121–22, 145–46, 169–71; Hall, *Diary of George Washington Hall*, 1:44; L. Smith, "Recollections of Gettysburg," 300–301 (quote); Warren, "Map of the Battle-Field of Gettysburg."

I have ever heard of, being almost equal to a pitch battle all the time.... I think twas the *hottest* place I have yet been in" [emphasis original].[16]

Throughout the morning, and for most of the rest of the day, the 14th rotated men from the orchard on Seminary Ridge into and out of the sunken lane. "[E]very hour or two we relieve Skirmishers," wrote Private Hall. "[We] keep out three companies of our regiment all the time." To get safely back and forth between these positions, the men were forced to crawl or run over open ground.[17]

At one point during the day, men of the 14th in the sunken lane saw their skirmishers behind the fence to their front quickly rise and start falling back, shouting as they came that the Federals were coming across the field. Immediately came the order to prepare to advance to confront this new threat. In the lane, men formed a line of battle and waited.

Just before the Union men reached the fence to their front, the men of the 14th rose from the lane and moved forward. Their advance had the desired effect. As a Union officer later reported, "we were suddenly confronted by a regiment rising up in our front from what appeared to be an abandoned railroad cut. They advanced in line of battle and there was no alternative but retreat."[18]

After the retreat of the Union men, Confederate skirmishers and sharpshooters continued their rotation into and out of the sunken lane. Their battle with Union forces opposite persisted "well into the growing darkness" as artillery shells continued to fall around and among them, and "the pungent smell of burnt powder pervaded the evening air."[19]

General Longstreet never successfully turned the Union left, and the Union army did not come streaming north on the Emmitsburg Pike toward Gettysburg, the rest of the Confederate army, Thomas's Brigade, and the 14th Georgia. Also, the 14th did not attack further downhill toward the Emmitsburg Pike. In fact, they barely left the places on Seminary Ridge, the sunken road, and the split-rail fence where they had begun the day.[20] At some time during the day, perhaps while kneeling in the sunken road or crawling to and from the sunken road with skirmishers, Simeon was shot in the thigh.

---

[16] Shultz and Mingus, *Second Day at Gettysburg*, 396–98; Hall, *Diary of George Washington Hall*, 2:15 (1st quote); Bryan, "Letters of Two Confederate Officers," 189 (2nd quote); Bachelder, "Map of the Battle Field of Gettysburg."

[17] Hall, *Diary of George Washington Hall*, 2:15 (quote); Shultz and Mingus, *Second Day at Gettysburg*, 396–99.

[18] L. Smith, "Recollections of Gettysburg," 301 (quote); Hurst, *Journal-History of the Seventy-Third Ohio*, 70; Cline, "A Neste of Bumbelbes," 187.

[19] Shultz and Mingus, *Second Day at Gettysburg*, 396 (1st quote); M. Smith, *Smell of Battle*, 73–75 (2nd quote).

[20] Shultz and Mingus, *Second Day at Gettysburg*, 395–99; Gallagher et al., *Civil War*, 176–77; Gottfried, *Brigades of Gettysburg*, 657; Dewberry, *History of the 14th Georgia*, 62.

Simeon's Wound

After being wounded on July 2, Simeon probably was taken first to a farm building in the orchard on Seminary Ridge where an assistant surgeon was treating the regimental wounded. There the surgeon would have stopped the bleeding and bandaged his wound as best as he could, as Manning Alexander did in the Battle of Champion Hill in chapter 20.

Then Simeon would have been taken, probably by a mule or horse-drawn ambulance, to one of three or four Pender's Division hospitals located in and around a tavern and farms along the Chambersburg Pike about four miles northwest of Gettysburg. These hospitals cared for approximately thirteen hundred sick and wounded in Pender's Division. A Confederate officer recalled the scene around these hospital buildings as "a great sea of white tents, silent and still, with here and there a groan, or a surgeon passing from one tent to another relieving the pain of some poor mortal who had fallen in battle." In the tavern and in some of the farm buildings the surgeons who busily performed amputations and other surgery were, as a modern historian reported, "overwhelmed, literally struggling through the bodies and limbs, clothes smeared with the blood and guts of the dead and dying." Fortunately, Simeon's wound did not require amputation.[21]

A thigh wound may not seem serious, but sometimes it was. General Pender, the commander of Simeon's division, also was wounded in the thigh on July 2. His wound was caused by a splinter from an artillery shell. It was not thought to be serious at first, but a little over two weeks later, it caused his death.[22]

Battle of Gettysburg and Simeon—Third Day

The next day, July 3, the Confederates again attacked Cemetery Ridge in what became known as Pickett's Charge. That charge was completely repulsed with the Confederates sustaining a staggering number of casualties. That night Lee considered the numerous casualties suffered by the army in the three days of fighting and the army's shortage of food and ammunition. He decided to return to Virginia starting the following day.[23]

Battle of Gettysburg and Simeon—Fourth Day

The Confederate Retreat of the Wounded Begins

The night of July 3, Lee ordered General John D. Imboden, a cavalry officer, to take charge of evacuating the wounded. Lee told Imboden: "the care of all the wounded will be intrusted to you." He added: "The duty will be arduous,

---

[21] K. Brown, *Retreat from Gettysburg*, 56–58 (1st quote); M. Smith, *Smell of Battle*, 72–73 (2nd quote); Coco, *Vast Sea of Misery*, 152, 134–38; Gindlesperger, *Bullets and Bandages*, 98, 115–17, 121–23; *Pennsylvania Atlas & Gazetteer*, 91.

[22] Guelzo, *Gettysburg*, 377.

[23] Guelzo, *Gettysburg*, 373–78, 425–29; Foote, *Civil War*, 2:578–81.

responsible, and dangerous for I am afraid you will be harassed by the enemy's cavalry." With that in mind, Lee directed Imboden to leave early the following morning and not to stop before reaching Winchester, Virginia, on the other side of the Potomac River. The river itself was some forty miles away.[24]

The next morning, July 4, Imboden began to assemble his train of wounded. As a modern historian reported, "every able-bodied man—including band members, black servants, and drummer boys—were conscripted to gather the fallen and load them into the vehicles." By nine o'clock, however, it was evident to Imboden that "the wagons, ambulances, and wounded could not be collected and made ready to move till late in the afternoon."[25]

Making matters worse, around noon a heavy rain began falling. "The rain fell in blinding sheets," Imboden later wrote; "the very windows of heaven seemed to have opened....meadows were soon overflowed, and fences gave way before the raging streams."

"During the storm," Imboden continued, "wagons, ambulances, and artillery carriages by hundreds—nay, by thousands—were assembling in the fields along the road from Gettysburg to Cashtown [about eight miles northwest of Gettysburg], in one confused and apparently inextricable mass." The storm continued unabated throughout the afternoon as Imboden and his men struggle to bring some sort of order to the gathering. (As Imboden was assembling his train of men and vehicles, other Confederates about a thousand miles away, including Dr. Manning Alexander, were surrendering at Vicksburg.)[26]

By four in the afternoon the column of wounded finally began to move. Once it was on its way, it stretched along the road for a total of seventeen miles.[27]

Because of their location in hospitals already on the Chambersburg Pike, the wounded of Pender's Division were in the leading elements of the Confederate column of wounded. Not all of the division's wounded, however, would make the trip. Of the thirteen hundred sick and wounded in the division, seven hundred would be left behind. Simeon, however, was to go with Imboden's wagon train.[28]

On the Road with the Confederate Wounded

Most of the wagons they were riding in were Conestogas, the covered wagons that later would be depicted in western movies as typical settlers' wagons. The Conestogas were built to carry goods, not people, and particularly not

---

[24] Orrison and Welch, *Last Road North*, 134; Imboden, "Confederate Retreat from Gettysburg," 421–22 (quotes); Wittenberg, Petruzzi, and Nugent, *One Continuous Fight*, 7.

[25] Wittenberg, Petruzzi, and Nugent, *One Continuous Fight*, 5 (1st quote); Imboden, "Confederate Retreat from Gettysburg," 422 (2nd quote).

[26] Imboden, "Confederate Retreat from Gettysburg," 423; Pfanz, *Gettysburg*, 11.

[27] Imboden, "Confederate Retreat from Gettysburg," 423.

[28] K. Brown, *Retreat from Gettysburg*, 108–109.

wounded. They rolled on wooden wheels rimmed by iron and lacked springs to cushion their jolting along rough roads. In addition, very few were furnished with even a layer of straw on which the wounded could lie. The suffering men instead were forced to lie crumpled or stretched out on the wagons' bare boards. Moreover, the wagons' canvas coverings were poor protection from the rain, and frequently the men inside were drenched by the downpour.[29]

Imboden described the column of wounded he saw as he rode from near the rear of the column to its head as a "vast procession of misery":

> For four hours I hurried forward on my way to the front, and in all that time I was never out of hearing of the groans and cries of the wounded and dying. Scarcely one in a hundred had received adequate surgical aid, owing to the demands on the hard-working surgeons from still worse cases that had to be left behind. Many of the wounded in the wagons had been without food for thirty-six hours. Their torn and bloody clothing, matted and hardened, was rasping the tender, inflamed, and still oozing wounds.... The road was rough and rocky from the heavy washings of the preceding day. The jolting was enough to have killed strong men, if long exposed to it.[30]

Not all even got to ride the wagons. One Pennsylvanian standing by the road watching the column pass later wrote his brother, "all those that were just slightly wounded had to walk. I saw some walking that were shot in the arms, some shoulders, some in the face, oh! It looked awful as their wounds were not dressed yet." Moreover, not all those walking were Confederates. Union prisoners and their guards also marched along with the moving column.[31]

The rain continued all night. At daybreak on the morning of July 5, the sun broke through the clouds as the head of the column reached Greencastle, Pennsylvania, twelve or fifteen miles from the Potomac River. With the coming of day and the cessation of rain, however, the Union cavalry began "a great deal of desultory fighting and harasments along the road," Imboden reported. It was not just cavalry that began harassing the column of wounded. In the morning about thirty to forty Greencastle citizens "attacked the train with axes, cutting the spokes out of ten or a dozen wheels and dropping the wagons in the streets" until a cavalry detachment dispersed them.[32]

---

[29] Wittenberg, Petruzzi, and Nugent, *One Continuous Fight*, 7; Imboden, "Confederate Retreat from Gettysburg," 423–24; Ayers, *Thin Light of Freedom*, 73.
[30] Imboden, "Confederate Retreat from Gettysburg," 424.
[31] Wittenberg, Petruzzi, and Nugent, *One Continuous Fight*, 7, 13.
[32] Imboden, "Confederate Retreat from Gettysburg," 425.

Still, neither Union cavalry nor citizen action prevented most of the train of wounded from reaching the edge of the Potomac at Williamsport, Maryland, on the afternoon of July. 5[33]

Problems at the Potomac River

At Williamsport, Imboden discovered "the tremendous rains had raised the river more than ten feet above the fording stage of water, and we could not possibly cross then." He immediately took possession of the town and converted it into "a great hospital" for his sick and wounded. The surgeons in the wagon train "pulled off their coats and went to work, and soon a vast amount of suffering was mitigated."[34]

The next day, July 6, a large body of Union cavalry caught up with the wagon train at Williamsport. Imboden assembled a mixed command of dismounted cavalry, wounded officers, commissary and quartermaster troops, artillerymen, and teamsters (wagon drivers) and placed them artfully around the town to defend it. He managed to hold off the Union troops until Confederate cavalry from Lee's army arrived, having traveled to Williamsport from Gettysburg by a different route from the wounded. The combined force then drove the Federals from the outskirts of the town.[35]

There had been a pontoon bridge across the river at Falling Waters, a little more than four miles south of Williamsport, but it had been destroyed by Union cavalry. The only immediate way across the river was by two small, flat ferryboats. The Confederates constructed three others and kept all five busy transporting, first walking wounded and then ambulances and wagons. A Georgia private later wrote that the ferries ran along a strong wire anchored on either side of the river and stretched across it. Using that wire, the ferries were capable of "putting across one ambulance and one wagon and about seventy-five men in a trip." Most of the Confederate army, however, was not able to cross the river until July 14.[36]

Simeon Goes to Richmond

Because Simeon was in Richmond only shortly after that date, he probably crossed much earlier on one of the ferryboats. Once he crossed the Potomac, he would have been transported with other wounded by wagon or ambulance to Martinsburg, West Virginia, and from there on south to Winchester, Virginia. Then he would have traveled one hundred miles further south to the General and Receiving Hospital at Staunton. As one of the wounded wrote home from

---

[33] Ibid.; Orrison and Welch, *Last Road North*, 134, 137.
[34] Imboden, "Confederate Retreat from Gettysburg," 425.
[35] Ibid., 426–28.
[36] Wittenberg, Petruzzi, and Nugent, *One Continuous Fight*, 25, 93; Denny, *Civil War Medicine*, 214; Orrison and Welch, *Last Road North*, 138.

Winchester, "they are sending the wounded from here to Staunton as fast as they can."

Staunton was "the commercial and transportation center of the upper [southern] Shenandoah Valley." That July, the Staunton hospital, converted from the former asylum for the "deaf, dumb, and blind," treated 8,428 soldiers who had been wounded at Gettysburg. From Staunton, Simeon would have been placed on a train that could reach Richmond in ten hours.[37]

As his service records indicate, Simeon was admitted to General Hospital Number 4 in Richmond on July 15. A later service record records that Simeon was furloughed from the hospital on July 22 for forty days.

Furloughed 40 days: Almost certainly Simeon returned home during his furlough.

A forty-day furlough beginning July 22 would have expired around September 1. Again according to his service records, Simeon checked back into the hospital in Richmond on September 14, apparently for clearance to return to his regiment. On September 18 he signed a receipt indicating he received his pay for the month of August from a major in the Quartermasters Corps at Richmond.

A letter from the first lieutenant in his company, Josiah Patterson, written from camp on the Rappahannock River on October 31, records that Simeon was back with his company by at least that date and sleeping on "a nice straw bed" along with Patterson and a Sergeant McAfee using "one blanket as a sheet and cover[ing] with two blankets."[38]

Horatio's Unit at Gettysburg: Horatio's 16th Georgia Regiment was in the Gettysburg battle as part of Wofford's Brigade, McLaws's Division, Longstreet's Corps, but Horatio was not with it. He still was at home in Georgia recovering from the wound he received at Chancellorsville.

It may have been fortunate that he was not at Gettysburg. Wofford's Brigade and the 16th Georgia were part of Longstreet's right wing when it attacked the Union left on July 2. After first being held in reserve, the brigade fought in the intense actions in the Wheatfield and Stony Hill area across the Emmitsburg Road and reached the base of Little Round Top before Longstreet ordered it to go no further and to return to safety.

The brigade did not participate in the battle on July 3. Still, during the Gettysburg Battle nine men of the 16th Georgia were killed and fifty-two were wounded.[39]

---

[37] K. Brown, *Retreat from Gettysburg*, 356–83 (quote, 376); Ayers, *Thin Light of Freedom*, 83.

[38] Service records of Major John Ambler and Sergeant Joseph M. McAfee; Josiah Patterson letter of October 31, 1863.

[39] Chapter 19; Gottfried, *Brigades of Gettysburg*, 9, 24, 26, 419–22; *OR*, ser. 1, vol. 27, pt. 2, 338; Gottfried, *Maps of Gettysburg*, 176–81, 212–15; Pfanz, *Gettysburg*, 327–29, 399–400.

Chapter 22

Homefront, Late 1863–Early 1864
1863
Pillina Bell

Chulafinnee, Ala.
[October or November] 1863
Dear parents and sisters:

    I will write you a few lines this morning. We received Mother's letter of Oct. 4 some weeks ago. Were thankful to hear you were all well. We received a letter from Brother Ratio dated Oct. the 12th. He seems to be in fine spirit.

    Say to Lona [that] she has made Dr. a beautiful suit. Mother, you wished to know how my wool turned out. There was 105 lbs. when it was sent to the carder, 9 lbs. of rolls when it got home. They are very sorry rolls, badly napped.

    We are glad you have made so much nice syrup.

    Brother Beverly, our ablest Baptist preacher, died a few days ago. He was buried by the Masons. I never saw so many people at a burying as was at his. He was a very pious man. Lived three miles from us.

    Flux is raging in this county. Mr. Silas Barker, two children, and all the negro children at Papa's house had whooping-cough and the flux at the same time. Mrs. Taloe's oldest child and 3 of the little negroes have died. Mother, Dell was taken sick day before yesterday with flux. She was very sick yesterday. She thinks it will kill her. Dr. is up there now. Billy has the whooping-cough. I hope he will not take the flux. Walter and Freeman will have the cough. I do dread it. I will write again in a week or two to let you know how they are getting along.

    Corn is very high and scarce. Pork will be very scarce for so many hogs have died up. Some are dying in the pens.

    I will send you a scrap of my dress that I tried to make like Mrs. Hendricks. I made it by Lony's pattern, just like hers except the fold and buttons in front. It becomes me very much. I only got 4 yds. wove to the dollar. Provisions are so high they have to rise on the weaving.

    Dr. is not very well. I think it is caused by fatigue and exposure. Oscar's arm is well, but he can't use it much yet. We never knew that he had written to you till we received your letter. He ought to have let me corrected it for him.

    Write soon. Give us all the news. Harriet says tell Freeman that she has got the prettiest Freeman he ever saw.

                                 As ever your daughter,
                                         P. C. Bell

HOMEFRONT, LATE 1863–EARLY 1864

Notes

Date: This letter was transcribed in the 1940s, and the original is missing. There is no month or day in the transcription, but from information in the letter, it was written in late October or early November.

parents and sisters: Parents were Thirza and James, and the sisters were Annie David and Pillona David Alexander.

Dr.: He is Pillina's husband, Raymond Bell.

carder, napped: A carder is someone who vigorously combs wool, separating the fibers, removing the dirt, and arranging the fibers in an orderly way into a uniform mass of roughly even density. The process leaves a rough surface of fibers called the "nap" that then is trimmed to create an even surface. When Pillina said the rolls were "badly napped," she may have meant that the nap was poorly carded and trimmed.[1]

flux: This term refers to dysentery or severe diarrhea, an excessive discharge of fluid from the bowels. At the time Pillina was writing, it could be fatal.[2]

whooping-cough: Whooping cough is an infectious disease that is especially contracted by children and is characterized by discharge of mucous from the nose and a deep, racking cough.[3]

Papa's house: Pillina's father-in-law, William M. Bell, had moved to Alabama, probably to live near Pillina, her husband, and their children.[4]

Dell: The identity of Dell has not been clearly established. It may have been an enslaved woman belonging to the Bells. It may also have been a nickname for the Bells' daughter Ellen E. Bell, then nine years old.[5]

Billy, Walter, and Oscar: All were sons of the Bells. They were four, six, and eleven years old respectively when the letter was written.[6]

Harriet, Freeman [in Alabama], and Freeman [in Georgia]: They may have been enslaved people, the first two belonging to the Bells and the last to the Davids.

1864

Sarah Highsmith to Pillona Alexander

---

[1] Drake, *What Did They Mean by That?*, 45; Wikipedia, "Nap (fabric)," https://en.wikipedia.org/wiki/Nap_(fabric), accessed June 17, 2020.

[2] Drake, *What Did They Mean by That?*, 102; "flux," *Webster's New World College Dictionary*, 559.

[3] Drake, *What Did They Mean by That?*, 328; "whooping cough," *Webster's New World College Dictionary*, 1653.

[4] US Census, 1870, Mortality Schedules, Madison, County, Alabama.

[5] US Census, 1870, Cleburn County, Alabama.

[6] Ibid.

Polkesville
Jan 17 [1864?]
Dear friend

I seet my self to rite you A few Lines to let you no we Ar All well. hoping thes few Lines May find you And your fathers folks well.

I have got nothing new to rite More then they have ketched up the Most of the Torys And kild them. Besides times is mity hard And every thing mity high.

we hant heard from you All Sents Mr highsmith was Down At your house And we want to hear from you All mity Bad

Mr highsmith is going to Athens And I though[t] I wood rite you A few Lines. he will Bring A few of your things with him[,] your trunk And the Box of Medison. thats All he can take handily in his little wagon.

thers A good Smart of Sickness A Bout hear. Dr Rogerses wife is mity Lo And old Mr Rogers is Al most helpless. Little Nancy had Another one of them bad spells A Bout 3 weeks Ago. She ses she wants to see Norer mity Bad.

give my Best Respects to your Mother And Any And All the family. So I will close   Sarah highsmith to Mrs Perlona Alexander

[Envelope]
Mrs Perlona Davids
Alexander
Please hand this to Mr Davids

Notes

Date: The original letter contains a month and day but no year. From information in the letter, it seems to have been written in January 1864.

Sarah Highsmith: At the time the letter was written she was about thirty-nine years old and was married to John C. Highsmith, then aged about forty-eight.[7]

Polkesville: Polksville was located in the northeast corner of Hall County, probably roughly were highways 283 and 52 intersect today. This was the home of the man who provided the uniforms for Manning Alexander's short lived company, the Bell Volunteers.[8]

Dear friend: The friend was Pillona David Alexander.

Torys: This term as used in the letter refers back to the American Revolution when "Tories" were people who were part of the community but who fought and

---

[7] US Census, 1860 and 1870, Polksville, Hall County, Georgia.

[8] Dorsey, *History of Hall County*, iv; Johnson, "A. J. Johnson's Georgia and Alabama, 1863," https://archive.org/details/dr_johnsons-georgia-and-alabama-published-by-a-j-johnson-new-york-53-54-4574025, accessed March 31, 2016; *Georgia Atlas & Gazetteer*, 15.

raided for the old government of the King against the revolutionary patriots.

For Mrs. Highsmith, and others in Georgia in 1864, "Tories" meant people who raided and fought for the old government in Washington against the new Confederacy.[9]

they have ketched up the Most of the Torys And Killed them: In September 1863, there were reports in local newspapers that gangs of deserters and others were "robbing the citizens and committing other depredations," particularly in Hall County and adjoining White County. In White County in early November, a man named Lewis Pitchford, "a reliable and loyal citizen [loyal to the Confederacy]," was killed while attempting, with others, to arrest a gang of "tories and bushwhackers infesting the section."

Shortly thereafter, vengeful citizens also loyal to the Confederacy acted. In mid-November "one Jake Wofford," who was believed to have shot Pitchford, was hanged in White County:

> Circumstantial evidence against Jake being very strong, he was placed on a temporary platform, after his arrest, with a rope around his neck, and tied to a limb. Finding he was very obstinate and would not answer any questions propounded to him, some person or persons in the crowd jerked the plank from under his feet and left him suspended by his neck. In a few moments he was launched into eternity.

Not long after, it was reported that another notorious White County tory, Hamp Furgurson, was killed. The newspaper report of the killing ended, "We hope the people of that section will continue the work until they exterminate the whole gang."[10]

bring you a few of your things: Manning and Pillona may have lived in Polksville before the war, possibly in rental housing, and may have returned there while Manning was at home after Vicksburg surrendered. At least, Manning seemed to have had his medical office in Polkesville.

Little Nancy: She is Sarah's daughter Nancy O. Highsmith. At the time the letter was written, she was about eight years old.[11]

Norer: Manning and Lona's daughter Nora was five years old on the day the letter was written.

Envelope: Because the letter was to be handed to Mr. David, it seems Lona was living with her mother and father at the time it was written. She may have been living there most of the time after Manning left for the war in 1862.

---

[9] See "A Patriot's Victory" in *Southern Watchman*, January 25, 1865, 4.

[10] Dorsey, *History of Hall County*, 162–64 (1st quote); *Southern Banner*, November 11, 1863 (2nd quote); *Southern Watchman*, November 25, (3rd and 4th quotes); *Southern Banner*, December 9, 1863 (4th quote); J. D. Fowler and Parker, *Breaking the Heartland*, 36–37.

[11] US Census, 1860 and 1870, Hall County, Georgia.

Chapter 23

Manning Returns to the Army, Late 1863–Spring 1864

EXCHANGE NOTICE No. 6[1]

RICHMOND, Sept. 12, 1863

The following Confederate officers and men, captured at Vicksburg, July 4, 1863, and subsequently paroled, have been duly exchanged, and are hereby so declared: The officers and men of Gen. C. L. Stevenson's division....
R. O. Ould
Agent of Exchange

Headq'as 1st Brigade, Stevenson's Division
September 15th, 1863
General Orders No. 2.

The Brigade was duly exchanged on the 12th inst.—All officers and enlisted men will at once repair to Decatur, Ga, which is dedicated as the point of rendezvous for the Brigade. It is enjoined upon all officers to use the utmost diligence in assembling their commands.
GEN. BARTON

Notes

Exchange: The federal government later argued that this exchange concerning the Vicksburg parolees was invalid—that it was based on faulty technical grounds and that no actual exchange of men had taken place, even on paper. In effect, the Federals considered that the Confederates had arbitrarily and unjustly declared the Vicksburg men exchanged. Regardless, Manning and many of the parolees at Vicksburg returned to their units and continued to serve.[2]

General Barton transferred: September 19, four days after General Barton signed this order, the authorities in Richmond transferred him to Virginia and ordered Brigadier General W. M. Gardner to replace him as commander of what had been Barton's Brigade, which included the 43rd.

When the order was issued, Gardner was in Demopolis, Alabama, reorganizing another brigade of Stevenson's Division. He was directed to come to

---

[1] *Atlanta Daily Intelligencer*, September 24, 1863.
[2] McPherson, *Battle Cry of Freedom*, 792–93. After the war, Robert Ould, the Confederate agent of exchange, and Robert S. Northcott, a Union general, debated the legitimacy of Civil War exchanges. See McClure, ed., *Annals of the War*, 32–59, 184–90.

Georgia and assume his new command "as soon as your presence can be spared from the duties in which you are now engaged."³

1863

Manning

Adairsville Geo
Nov. 14th 1863
My Dear Lona:

Dear, you have no doubt been looking anxiously for sometime for a letter from "these head quarters" but we have been shifting about a good deal and I have been puting off writing much longer than I would have done and a great deal longer than I wished to do but I hope—I *know*—you will pardon me. And Dear you will be surprised to see my lettere headed Adairsville Geo, but let me tell you I have been troubeled [with] those pains some resently and I just came off down here [to] stay a while with Uncle John Millwee who lives in a mile of Adairsville.

Now dear don't give yourself any uneasyness about me for you know that I toled you I would write you my true condition. Well between myself and one more (you) I have been as bad off before and done duty. I have determined never to do so again. when ever I don't feel like duty I am not going to do it *any* more. So give yourself no uneasyness.

I expect to stay here two or three weeks or longer if I feel like it. I am off on permission to go to the rear to recruit my health and no limits to it. I could come home if it was not for the effect it might have having been at home so recently. but be content dear. I think I will get to see you during this winter. If you here of my being sick don't be alarmed. I will keep you posted as to my *true* condition.

Well Dear I must tell you something about our campaign in upper East Tenn. I dont know whare and how to begin. I have written you two or three short letters but had not the chance to give you anything in detail. We left Chickamauga four weeks ago to day without coocking [illegible word] tents or anything else except what we took on our backs. we went by railway to Charelston Tenn. we then took it on foot from there to Louden—38 miles—through rain and the worst mud I ever saw. It rained all most every day but we never caught the Yankees. We remaind up in that country marching from place to place till last Tuseday when we took the Cars and came *back* to Chickamauga a moove that we all regret for Upper E. Tenn. is the best country to soldier in I ever saw and Chickamauga is the poorest.

---

³ *OR*, ser. 1, vol. 30, pt. 4, 668–69.

Longstreets whole Corpse has been sent up there. They had nearly all got up there before we left. I saw a great many of my old firends. I saw some of Ratios Company. they had just heard from him and said he was not much better yet, which if true I fear it will be a long time before he gets well.

As our Command came down I got leave to go to the rear and stoped at Cleveland and had to stay over there nearly two days before I could get down to Dalton. I stayed all night in Dalton and came down here yesterday. I had a right tight squeese to get through as the officer of the guard on the train had orders not to allow any officer or soldier [to] come south of Dalton without the signature of Gen. Bragg but he agreed to let me come this far.

While at Cleveland I stayed with quite a remarkable family. there was 20 children 16 of them living 8 boys & 8 girls. the last one a girl(!) weighing 194 lbs. the largest girl weighs 286 lbs!! very good looking and well formed *so far as I could see*. just think of a woman weighing 286 lbs. why they would had to have a seperate cariage to ride in and I am not sure that, that would be the worst feture in the case. I think that they would be as much as one *bed* would hold up. Now that would be "orful" wouldn't it?

But enough about the big famely. While at Cleveland I saw Cousin Jim and Sam Lewis. They are in Jenkins brigade Longstreet Corpse. They ware boath well. I think they are as fine looking men as I have seen since I have been in service.

My opinion is that Longstreet is going [to] advance on Knoxville. They have got a pontoon bridg up there all ready to throw across the river.

I got my trunk all right. I think when I leave here I will try to get a carpet sack or vallece and only tak a part of my clothing. there is no use in having much more then we ware unless we have more transportation. I can leave my trunk here or express it home.

Jim says he don't know whether mother has any more brown wool or not. his pants ware made of some cloth she made last year. he says he think she had some at the carder but diden't know how much.

I sent him to the hospital about 12 or 15 days ago. He had "dum ague" and Diarrhoea. I learn he is at Marrietta Geo. I think he will get a detail to stay there. He said he intended to try it when he got well enough to take one. I hope he may succeed.

I think all is right now in the Regt so far [as] I am conserned. As I said in the out set I expect to stay here 3 or 4 weeks so dear you must write soon and direct as follows. M P Alexander Asst Surgeon C. S. A. Adairsville Go. If you direct as usual they may not stop here but go on to the regt. I will keep you posted as to when I leave here so direct as above till I direct otherwise.

Now my dear if you was only here we could enjoy ourselves so well. I would insist on you coming to see me but I am a witness on a case in court-marital and

I may be ordered back before I am able for duty to give in my evidence. if so I will come back again or go some place else. Give my love to all. Kiss Nora for me—
                              Yours most truly
                              M P Alexander

Notes

Adairsville, Geo: Adairsville is about halfway between Chattanooga and Atlanta. It is just off I-75 and in 1863 was a stop on the Western and Atlantic Railroad.[4]

Uncle John Millwee: According to family lore, Manning's grandmother on his mother's side was Mary Millwee. She had a brother named John who probably was this Uncle John.[5]

having been at home so recently: As indicated in chapter 20, Manning probably arrived home from Vicksburg in late July. On September 8, he purchased 114½ acres of land in Banks County. Undoubtedly this was "the little place some whare that we could do well on" that he hoped to find as mentioned in his letters from near Vicksburg. He bought the land from James L. Gillespie, who was an uncle of Mary Gillespie Alexander, Manning's brother Sam's wife.[6]

It is not clear when Manning rejoined the 43rd at Decatur, but it probably was sometime in mid-to-late September.

We left Chickamauga: The Battle of Chickamauga took its name from Chickamauga Creek in North Georgia, about five miles south of Chattanooga. The Battle of Chickamauga was fought around this creek on September 19 and 20, 1863. The 43rd missed the battle. It was still in Georgia reorganizing when it took place.[7]

On October 2, less than two weeks after the orders transferring General Barton and replacing him with General Gardner in Alabama were signed, Barton's old brigade, including the 43rd, left Decatur by train. The brigade went first to Big Shanty and then arrived in Chickamauga the next day. There they apparently were needed to replace men lost in the battle. It is unclear, however, whether

---

[4] *Georgia Atlas & Gazetteer*, 1; Wikipedia, "Western and Atlantic Railroad," https://en.wikipedia.org/wiki/Western_and_Atlantic_Railroad, accessed February 10, 2023.

[5] Draft Application for Membership in the Daughters of the American Revolution in my possession.

[6] Banks County Deed Book A, 238; Chaplin, *Riches of Bunyan* (Alexander family copy), flyleaf; certificate of death, Margarette M. Gaber, March 9, 1920, listed as daughter of Sam Alexander and Mary E. Gillespie, file no. 6848, Georgia; US Census, 1850, Franklin County, Georgia, listing for Milton W. Gillespie, father of Mary and John.

[7] Boatner, *Civil War Dictionary*, 151–53; Goodson, *Georgia Confederate 7,000*, 2:58–59; Gallagher et al., *Civil War*, 249–51.

General Gardner had arrived in Georgia from Alabama in time to go with the brigade.[8]

In the Chattanooga area in October, Barton's old brigade was again part of Stevenson's Division. The Union army had retreated into Chattanooga itself while the bulk of the Confederate army occupied Lookout Mountain and Missionary Ridge, located south and east of Chattanooga, and showed no intention of attacking the Union in Chattanooga. Instead, the Confederates had settled down to a siege.[9]

On October 17, however, General Stevenson's division and Barton's old brigade received orders to proceed northeast toward Knoxville, which was controlled by a Union force commanded by General Ambrose E. Burnside. According to reports, Burnside had sent infantry out of Knoxville south to the small town of Loudon on the way to Chattanooga and sent cavalry to another small town, Philadelphia, even closer to Chattanooga. The cavalry in particular was "laying waste" to the area around those towns. Stevenson's mission was to drive the Federal forces back toward Knoxville and gather information about the enemy's movements around Knoxville.[10]

we went by railway to Charleston, Tenn: Considering that the 43rd was unable to pack carefully, as Manning wrote, they probably left the Chattanooga area on October 17, the day Stevenson's Division received the order. When they arrived at Charleston, they were about forty-five miles northeast of Chattanooga.[11]

on foot from there [Charleston] to Louden: This is Loudon, Tennessee. It was about forty miles further toward Knoxville than Charleston, as Manning mentioned, but it still was about thirty-five miles short of Knoxville. Around Loudon was where the Federal cavalry was operating.[12]

we never caught the Yankees: Confederate cavalry brigades under Stevenson's direction did engage the Union forces around Loudon on several occasions in late October, forcing them to evacuate the town on October 27. However, the infantry in Stevenson's Division, including the 43rd, arrived at Loudon too late to be part of that action or any other action in the area.

In early November, Stevenson received orders requiring his division, including Barton's old brigade and the 43rd, to return to the Chickamauga area. Once

---

[8] Roberts and Clark, *Atlanta's Fighting Forty-Second*, 109.

[9] Boatner, *Civil War Dictionary*, 141–42.

[10] *OR*, ser. 1, vol. 30, pt. 4, 668, *OR*, ser. 1, vol. 31, pt. 1, 5, 8; *OR*, ser. 1, vol. 31, pt. 3, 581 (quote), 685; Rigdon, *Georgia 43rd Infantry Regiment*, 11; Roberts and Clark, *Atlanta's Fighting Forty-Second*, 109.

[11] Blackford to his mother, November 12, 1863; Black, *Railroads of the Confederacy*, n.p., "Numerical Key to Railroads" and following maps; Rand McNally, "Tennessee State Road Map."

[12] *OR*, ser. 1, vol. 31, pt. 3, 581; Rand McNally, "Tennessee State Road Map."

again, Manning and his regiment had done a lot of marching around, as they had done in Kentucky a year earlier, again without ever confronting the enemy.[13]

Longstreets whole Corpse: General Longstreet and his corps had left Virginia to come to the aid of General Braxton Bragg, who was in command of the Army of Tennessee in the Chattanooga area. Most of his men arrived in time to participate in the Battle of Chickamauga.[14]

After the battle, Longstreet was ordered around November 4 to take two divisions to engage Union forces at Knoxville. On November 9, he reached Sweetwater, Tennessee, about a dozen miles short (south) of Loudon, where Stevenson and his infantry were located. Here Manning saw some old friends. As Manning wrote, Ratio had not yet recovered sufficiently to come to Tennessee with his old corps.[15]

Instead of Longstreet and Stevenson and their men advancing together from Sweetwater to attack Knoxville, Stevenson had been ordered to return to the Chattanooga area while Longstreet was to stay and advance on to Knoxville alone. Shortly after Longstreet's arrival, Stevenson's Division left Sweetwater and returned to Chattanooga the way they had come.[16]

Cleveland and Dalton: On the way back to Chattanooga with Stevenson's Division, Manning, as he mentioned, felt unwell and was given leave to recuperate.

As a result, he left his regiment at Cleveland, Tennessee, located on a rail line between Charleston and Chattanooga. At Cleveland he would have changed trains to proceed almost due south, in the direction of Atlanta, to Dalton, Georgia. At Dalton, he would have changed trains yet again onto another line to travel farther south ("to the rear of the Confederate lines") to Adairsville, Georgia, where he was when he wrote this letter. [17]

Gen. Bragg: He was the commander of the Army of Tennessee of which the 43rd Georgia was a part.

Cousin Jim and Sam Lewis at Cleveland: While Longstreet himself had reached Sweetwater, which was further toward Knoxville than Cleveland, not all of his force reached there at the same time that he did, and some had gotten no farther than Cleveland. Thus, Manning was able to see cousins Jim and Sam Lewis at Cleveland. They were sons of Manning's aunt, Martha Poole Lewis. Jim

---

[13] *OR*, ser. 1, vol. 31, pt. 1, 8–10; *OR*, ser. 1, vol. 31, pt. 3, 581–82, 633.

[14] Boatner, *Civil War Dictionary*, 149–53.

[15] *OR*, ser. 1, vol. 31, pt. 1, 8–10, 455–56; Boatner, *Civil War Dictionary*, 466–68; Connelly, *Autumn of Glory*, 262–65.

[16] *OR*, ser. 1, vol. 31, pt. 1, 8–10, 455–56; Boatner, *Civil War Dictionary*, 466–68; Connelly, *Autumn of Glory*, 262–65.

[17] Black, *Railroads of the Confederacy*, n.p., "Numerical Key to Railroads" and following railroad maps.

was a private in Cobb's Legion, and Sam was a private in the Palmetto Regiment of Sharpshooters.[18]

Longstreet is going [to] advance on Knoxville: Manning was correct.[19]

my trunk: The trunk is now in my possession.

Jim: He was Manning's brother Jim, who was a private in the 43rd.

"dum ague": An abnormal fever that occurs or intensifies suddenly and irregularly.[20]

case in Court-martial: This case has not been identified.

Manning

Adairsville Geo
Nov 20th 1863
My Dear:

Although it has been but a few days since I wrote you and nothing has transpired since then in my "history" of any peticular interest, I will write again as I know it will be of interest to you.

I am yet at Uncle John Millwee's faring first rate. As to my health it is about like it was when I came here. Now I can give yourself no uneasiness about my health for as I promised I will keep you posted on that. I can injoy good enough health when protected from the wether but I dont feel disposed to expose myself and suffer from it when I can avoid it which I am going to do from this [time] out. I expect to stay here some two weeks yet. how much longer I cant tell.

I have got some money which I will send you the first oportunity. Buy a plenty of corn. let it cost what it may. get enough to do us if I should hapen to come home next year. Such a thing *might* hapen you know. the war might end. in such a contingency there would not be any chance to get anything. If we didn't need it, it would be no [drag?].

You needn't send me any more clothing till I write. I will write in time for you to send them before I need them

If you get this in time to write me in 2 weeks sent it to this office. Direct this [to]M P Alexander Asst Surg C. S. A.

If you direct as usual it will go to the regt and I won't get them soon. I left directions to have my letters remailed to this place. Dear pleas pardon this short letter

Write often and long. Give my love to all
M P Alexander

---

[18] *OR*, ser. 1, vol. 31, pt. 1, 455–56; *OR*, ser. 1, vol. 31, pt. 3, 546; Blackford letter; US Census, 1860, Anderson, South Carolina; service records.

[19] Boatner, *Civil War Dictionary*, 466–68.

[20] Dunglison, *Dictionary of Medical Science*, 418.

Manning

Adairsville Geo.
Nov 27th 1863
My Dear:

    I will drop you a line this morning in hast[e]. I know that you will have heard of the second Chicamauga battle before this reaches you and as a matter of cours be anxious to here from me. I am still at Uncle John Millwees and was not in the fight. I am improving some but not fit for the exposure of the camp. I think "the rheumattics" agree very well with me if I may be allowed to judg from my weight—I weigh 167 lbs. 13 more than I weighed when I left home. I think I just about fill your "bill" now.

    The reports from the battle are meager. no detailed account received yet, but enough has been received to decid that we have been badly whiped up to Thursday.

    The fight opened monday morning principally on our right and left. The Yankeys, I am sorry to say, stormed and took Lookout mountain Tuesday evening which surpassed anything in the annals of modern warfar. The engagement all along the line on wednesday was the most severe ever heard. at 4 oclock P. M. they succeded in taking our breastworks after one of the bloodiest struggle of the war. Our loss is refuted by passengers on the train to be from 1500 killed and from 5000 to 7000 prisoners. I fear it is much greater.

    what was done yesterday or what Bragg will do I cant say. it was thought he will fall back to Ringold. I am fearful they will cut off Longstreet. It is truly a most gloomy time, but we cant tell what a day may bring fourth.

    I will go to the Depot this morning and wait till the train comes down and send you what further news I get. Give yourself no uneasiness for me. I am doing well. I expect to stay here 10 or 12 days longer if no more. if you get this in time to write me here in that time do so. I will keep you posted as to my whereabouts.

Depot Adairsville
Nov 27 1863
Dear,

    I received yours of the 20 this morning. I was truly happy to here from you.

    No particulars from the front yet. The most of our wounded fell into the hands of the enemy. The loss in our brigade is not very heavy from what I can here. We are falling back to Tunnel hill or Dalton. I will write again in a few days.

                                              Yours Truly
                                              M. P. Alexander

Notes

second Chickamauga battle: What Manning called Second Chickamauga was the series of battles on November 23–25 that ended what now is generally known as the Chattanooga Campaign. The end was disastrous for the Confederates.

At the beginning of the series of battles, the Union army occupied Chattanooga, while the Confederates occupied Lookout Mountain, southwest of the city, and a long, steep hill or ridge called Missionary Ridge east of the city. A gap of more than two miles separated the north end of Lookout Mountain from the south end of Missionary Ridge. The ridge then extended further north about six miles.[21]

In the two months since the Battle of Chickamauga, the Union army had been reinforced by seven divisions, and it had been placed under the command of General Ulysses S. Grant. The Confederates under General Braxton Bragg also had been reinforced, by General Longstreet's two divisions, but then Bragg sent Longstreet and his divisions to Knoxville, a little over one hundred miles away, to engage the Union army there. The absence of Longstreet left the Confederates around Chattanooga with only about half the number of men available to the Federals. Observing this imbalance, Grant decided to attack.[22]

Manning's report of the battles is generally accurate. Grant's plan, as it gradually developed, was to concentrate his attack on the right wing of the Confederates at the northern end of Missionary Ridge with the objective of enveloping it. He planned to attack the Confederate left wing at Lookout Mountain earlier and take the mountain if possible but at least hold Confederate army there. In addition, he would attack the center on Missionary Ridge to hold the Confederates there in place. Once the Confederate right wing had been enveloped, the Union forces attacking the center would join with those enveloping the right and together sweep the Confederates off the ridge.[23]

His plan worked extremely well, even if not exactly as he had expected. By early morning on Wednesday, November 25, Grant's forces had occupied Lookout Mountain on the Confederate left, but the main attack on the Confederate right had stalled. Grant then ordered his men to continue to press from both ends. At the same time, he launched his attack on the Confederate center. Although the attacks against the two wings faltered, Grant's center attack was much more successful than planned. By the end of the day the Federals in the center, by themselves, had swept up and over almost the entire length of Missionary

---

[21] Lardas, *Chattanooga 1863*, 72, 76; Cozzens, *Shipwreck of Their Hopes*, 192.

[22] Cozzens, *Shipwreck of Their Hopes*, 143; McDonough, *Chattanooga*, 164.

[23] Cozzens, *Shipwreck of Their Hopes*, 112–15, 143–44; McDonough, *Chattanooga*, 108–109, 129, 161–62.

Ridge and chased Bragg and the Confederates down its far side in general disarray.[24]

"the rheumatics": Rheumatism, a general term for "any of various painful conditions of the joints and muscles, characterized by inflammation, stiffness, etc."[25]

our loss: The Confederacy's Army of Tennessee reported to Richmond 361 killed, 2,180 wounded, and 4,146 taken prisoner. Grant, however, reported that he had captured 6,143 prisoners.[26]

what Bragg will do I cant say. It was thought he will fall back to Ringold.... We are falling back to Tunnel hill or Dalton: Most of what remained of the Confederate Army of Tennessee retreated first to near Ringgold, about ten miles southeast of Chattanooga as the crow flies, and then to Dalton, another dozen miles or so southeast of Ringgold. They began to arrive at Dalton the night of November 27. On the night of November 28–29, General Bragg offered his resignation as head of that army. It was quickly accepted.[27]

The loss in our brigade is not very heavy: The report was correct. The brigade sustained only eighty-four casualties, and the 43rd Georgia lost no men killed or wounded. Only two of its men were listed as missing. The actions of the 43rd Georgia during the Battle for Missionary Ridge were as follows.[28]

On November 12, shortly after Stevenson's Division returned from the Knoxville area and shortly before the climactic battles of the Chattanooga Campaign, General Bragg began reorganizing the Army of Tennessee. He placed Barton's old brigade under the command of General Marcellus A. Stovall, from Augusta, Georgia, who during the Battle of Chickamauga had commanded a mixed Florida, Georgia, and North Carolina brigade. On November 20, he then transferred the brigade from Stevenson's Division to that of General Alexander P. Stewart in General John C. Breckinridge's corps.[29]

When the Battle for Missionary Ridge began on November 25, Breckinridge's Corps had been placed in the center of the Confederate line on the ridge, which ran generally from the north to the south and faced west toward Chattanooga and the Union army. Stewart's Division was on the Confederate left (south) and Stovall's Brigade was assigned to a position at the extreme left of the

---

[24] Cozzens, *Shipwreck of Their Hopes*, 159–346; McDonough, *Chattanooga*, 117–205; Boatner, *Civil War Dictionary*, 144–47.

[25] Dunglison, *Dictionary of Medical Science*, 901; "rheumatism," *Webster's New World College Dictionary*, 1246 (quote).

[26] Boatner, *Civil War Dictionary*, 147.

[27] Cozzens, *Shipwreck of Their Hopes*, 366, 394–97; McDonough, *Chattanooga*, 225–26; Horn, *Army of Tennessee*, 305; *Georgia Atlas & Gazetteer*, 13.

[28] *OR*, ser. 1, vol. 31, pt. 2, 745.

[29] *OR*, ser. 1, vol. 31, pt. 2, 657, 660–61; *OR*, ser. 1, vol. 31, pt. 3, 685.

division, making it the brigade farthest to the left of the Confederate line defending the ridge.[30]

Stovall, however, had been ordered to assign two of his regiments to a position even further to the left of the Confederate line and away from the rest of the division and brigade. The two regiments were to guard the Rossville Gap, which ran roughly west-east between the northern end of Lookout Mountain, then occupied by part of the Union army under General Joseph Hooker, and the southern end of Missionary Ridge. Through the Gap passed a road that offered to Hooker's force an easy route east to behind Missionary Ridge and behind the Confederate line on the Ridge. The role of the two regiments was to guard the gap and prevent Hooker's force from using it to get behind or to the flank of the Confederate army on the ridge.[31]

Stovall chose the 43rd and 42nd Georgia and a four-gun battery of artillery and placed them under the overall command of Colonel Robert J. Henderson, commander of the 42nd. Henderson arrived with his small command at its assigned location about daybreak on November 25. He placed his infantry in line of battle at a position "in the front of [the] gap, about 300 yards" with skirmishers forward another 150 yards, as he later reported. He then placed his artillery between the regiments at the crest of a small hill. His right (north) flank was anchored on Missionary Ridge, but his left (south) flank was unsupported.[32]

Around eleven o'clock, Hooker's men attacked. Heavy skirmishing between the Union and Confederates continued for about two hours. Henderson probably was not aware, but this initial attack of one Union regiment was only a holding action while more of Hooker's men rebuilt and crossed a bridge over Chattanooga Creek that Confederates had destroyed earlier and that separated Hooker on Lookout Mountain from Henderson's men. He also may not have been aware that ultimately he would be facing three Union divisions (those of Osterhaus, Cruft, and Geary) composed of over forty regiments, plus artillery. To stop their advance, Henderson had his two regiments and a battery of artillery.[33]

Soon, however, he learned he was facing this "superior force" when "long lines of infantry were discovered moving to the right and left, which I at once conceived to be a flank movement for the purpose of surrounding me," as he later

---

[30] Cozzens, *Shipwreck of Their Hopes*, 302–303.

[31] Elliot, "This Grand and Imposing Array of Brave Men," 110–14; Hewett, Trudeau, and Suderow, *OR Supplement* (*ORS*), pt. 1., vol. 6, ser. 6, 104–106; Cozzens, *Shipwreck of Their Hopes*, 313; McDonough, *Chattanooga*, 123; Powell, *All Hell Can't Stop Them*, 84–85.

[32] Elliot, "This Grand and Imposing Array of Brave Men," 110–14; *ORS*, pt. 1, vol. 6, ser. 6, 105–106, 170 (quote).

[33] Elliot, "This Grand and Imposing Array of Brave Men," 111; *ORS*, pt. 1, vol. 6, ser. 6, 170–71; 175–77; *OR*, ser. 1, vol. 31, pt. 2, 400; Powell, *All Hell Can't Stop Them*, 82; Cozzens, *Shipwreck of Their Hopes*, 399–400, 402, 406.

reported. He immediately ordered a retreat up the ridge, where his small force formed a line that held for another hour until the Federals again began to flank it, and Henderson again ordered a retreat.[34]

As he retreated, he was uncertain where to go next. He had not had contact with the rest of his brigade since he was ordered to take his position at Rossville Gap. As he later reported, "Being ignorant of where my command was, in consequence of an isolated position during the day [and] having no knowledge of the country, I was greatly confused as to the direction I should take." Moreover, scattered cavalry and civilians that he encountered gave him reports of "flying and frightened [Confederate] cavalry and infantry" that increased his confusion. In this state he came upon a road that led east down from Missionary Ridge and away from the Federals. He took that road.[35]

About five o'clock that afternoon, he and the 42nd and 43rd regiments arrived at a bridge over West Chickamauga Creek. The place was called Red House Ford, and it was roughly four miles from the crest of Missionary Ridge. There he halted and sent a courier to make contact with the rest of the Confederates. The courier finally found General Breckinridge, who told Henderson to destroy the bridge and guard the ford, which Henderson did until about nine o'clock the following morning. Then he gradually retreated to Ringgold, Georgia, about a dozen miles south of Missionary Ridge, where he was reunited with the rest of his brigade.[36]

Manning

Adairsville Geo
Nov 29th 1863
My Dear

I received yours of 25th yesterday—Saturday—I was truly glad to here from you so soon.

Dear dont give yourself so much trouble for me. I am doing well. the pain is prety much in the same place as when I was at home, but not half so bad. Now I am improving very fast. But you know I toled you I was going to take better care of myself than I have done before. there is too little hope of any thing good resulting from this thing for me to expose myself much more for it—but *best keep that to yourself.* Dont be scared about my giting lean—I am flesher than I ever was in my life. My old pants are so small I can just get in them. If I get much fatter I will have to hang them up and jump into them.

---

[34] *ORS*, pt. 1, vol. 6, ser. 6, 171–73 (quotes), 175–77; Powell, *All Hell Can't Stop Them*, 85–86.

[35] *ORS*, pt. 1, vol. 6, ser. 6, 171–73; Powell, *All Hell Can't Stop Them*, 85–86.

[36] *ORS*, pt. 1, vol. 6, ser. 6, 172–73, 175–77; Powell, *Chickamauga Campaign*, 59.

I am going to send enough money home when I go to the regt. to pay Mr. Hendrix. I am a little uneasy about that. I am going to try to come home some time this winter, but I cant tell when.

Dear, I dont need a hat now but maybe we had as well have one made when you have a good chance. I would like very well to have a vest but don't disfurnish yourself. I ware No 7¼ hat so you can have it made to fit some one who wares that number.

I got a letter yesterday from which I learned that Sam is up at Chicamauga. He was there I suppose when I was up there but I had no though[t] of his being there. he was not well. I am surprised that he stays there. Bob is at Savanna. Jim was at Mairetta when I heard from him last.

Every thing is in perfect confusion since Braggs disgrecfull defeat. The whole army is perfectly domiralized and retreating. nobody knows where. The report yesterday was that Bragg was going to make a stand at Resaca 15 miles above here and 15 this side of Dalton. We cant get any peticulars. we lost all our artilery (150 pieces) a large number of small arms and a great many wagon. our loss in killed and wounds is comparatively small. Our loss in prisoners is large. It is reported that 7000 of [o]ur me[n] threw down their arms and went over to the Yankees. How true that is I cant say but there are serious aprehentions about it. The latter statment had maybe not be circulated. The report this morning is that Braggs wagon train is in this neighborhood. I will not close till the train comes down this morning so that I can give you the latest dispatch.

Depot—Nothing more from the front. It is not true that the wagons are in the neighborhood. We will stand at Dalton. Write soon to this place.

Yours most Truly
M. P. Alexander

Notes

Sam, Bob, and Jim: All were Manning's younger brothers. Sam was serving as a private with the 29th Georgia Infantry Regiment. Jim was serving in the 43rd. As Manning mentioned in an earlier letter, Jim was sick in the hospital in Marietta. Bob may have been serving with the Confederate or Georgia state army in Savannah, but in a history of Franklin County, his home county, he is not mentioned in a list of members of various Confederate army units from that county.[37]

Bragg was going to make a stand at Resaca: Bragg had planned to retreat to Resaca and had started moving his army there. On November 29, however, the

---

[37] US Census, 1870, Franklin County, Georgia; Chaplin, *Riches of Bunyan* (Alexander family copy); service records; Tabor, *History of Franklin County, Georgia*, 754–61.

day Manning wrote this letter, Bragg learned that the Union army was not pursuing and decided to keep his men at Dalton.[38]

we lost all our artilery (150 pieces): A modern historian reports that "Forty cannon and sixty-nine limbers and caissons had been surrendered or abandoned" by the retreating Confederates.[39]

Our loss in prisoners is large. It is reported that 7000 of [o]ur me[n] threw down their arms and went over to the Yankees: The 7,000 number is closer to the number of Confederate prisoners Grant reported (6,143) than to the number reported by Bragg (4,146).[40]

Manning

Adairsville Geo.
Dec. 6th 1863
Well My Dear,

I will drop you but a line or two this time and promis to do better next time.

I am going to the command next tuseday if nothing hapens. so you need not wright any more till you here from me again. Things are so squaly up there I am going to leave my trunk here. I can borough a carpet sack and take what chothing I will need soon and leave the rest here. I should not be surprised if we ware to fall back here any day.

I will get that money and send it home as soon as I can. I am uneasy about it. May be it would be better for you to get the money from someone else and pay Mr. Hendrix.

Try to get corne enough to do next year for my opinion is that it is going to be imposable to get it next year.

There is but one way—in my opinion for this war to end (you know how that is) which will make the hardest times we ever saw.

The latest and most reliable news from Gen. Longstreet is that he is retreating from Knoxville in the direction of Abingden Va. He is intirly cut off from Hardee. Wheeler had a fight yesterday (saturday) at Cleveland Ten and was repulced. All seems to be quiet about Dalton. We cant get anything correct about our loss in the late battle. It is said now that we only lost 50 pieces of artillery and 15000 or 20,000 stand of small arms. I have heard from Sam since the fight. He was sent off withe the wagon train and was not in the fight. He was not well but on duty. I am going to see him when I go back and do something for him if I can.

---

[38] Cozzens, *Shipwreck of Their Hopes*, 395.
[39] Ibid., 389.
[40] Ibid.

Tell Ratio he can stay at home now as he can't get to his command. It was damp and cool this morning but very pleasant now. I would be glad to be at home this evening. I expect there are two of us in that fix?

I am doing very well.

Ours Most Truly
M P Alexander

Notes

squaly: Troubled or disturbed as though blown about by a wind or a squall.[41]

Gen. Longstreet: By November 18, General Longstreet had chased Union General Burnside into Knoxville. Then, on November 29 he attacked a fort protecting Knoxville, but this attack was a miserable failure. As Manning wrote, Longstreet abandoned his Knoxville campaign and began to withdraw toward Virginia the night of December 3.[42]

Hardee: He was General William Joseph Hardee. General Hardee became the temporary commander of the Army of Tennessee after Bragg resigned. General Joseph E. Johnston was appointed Bragg's permanent successor and arrived in Dalton to take command on December 27.[43]

Wheeler had a fight yesterday (saturday) at Cleveland Ten and was repulced: Wheeler was General Joseph Wheeler, commander of a Confederate cavalry corps. Manning may have been mistaken concerning this fight. There appears to be no report of such a fight in the *OR*, although Wheeler was in the Cleveland area on that Saturday (December 5) and may have encountered some Federal troops.[44]

Ratio and his command: Horatio did rejoin his command, which was part of Longstreet's army, but not until later, probably in late January 1864 (see chapter 24).

Manning

Camp 43d Geo Near Dalton Geo
Dec 11th 1863
My Dear:

I have but a few minuets to write as I have just learned that William White is going to start home this eavening. I came to camp Thirsday. I am doing tolierly

---

[41] "Squall," *Webster's New World College Dictionary*, 1408.

[42] Hallock, *Longstreet in the West*, 69–80; Boatner, *Civil War Dictionary*, 468; Cozzens, *Shipwreck of Their Hopes*, 386–88.

[43] Cozzens, *Shipwreck of Their Hopes*, 397; Horn, *Army of Tennessee*, 307–11. Connelly, *Autumn of Glory*, 281.

[44] Cozzens, *Shipwreck of Their Hopes*, 413–14; *OR*, ser. 1, vol. 31, pt. 3, 785–86.

well. I will send eight hundred dollars home, and keep two hundred with me. I have a [illegible] to sleep under. I left my trunk at uncl John Millwee's. I only brought a change of chothes with me.

I will write again soon. You need not try to send me anything this time.

Yours in Great hast[e]
M. P. Alexander

Notes

Dalton: Dalton was described by a Union soldier as "a respectable village containing at that time [1864] perhaps 1,500 inhabitants." It was located about thirty miles southeast of Chattanooga and ninety miles northwest of Atlanta. At the time the letter was written, the remains of the Army of Tennessee were encamped around the town.[45]

William White: Written on one edge of the envelope into which this letter was placed is "Politness of Segt White." He was Sergeant William J. White of Company G, 43rd Georgia, from Jackson County. He had been captured at Champion Hill in May 1863 and exchanged on July 4 of the same year.[46]

Manning

Camp 43rd Ga. Regt
Near Dalton, Geo
Dec 28th 1863
Well my Dear,

After a very heardy breakfast of sasage and sassafras tea sweetened with "gineuine" sugar, I seat myself to drop you a line or two in response to your very kind favor of 21st which was received 26th. I was truly glad to here from you as it had been some time since I had heard from my dear ones at home. The sausage, butter, potatoes and Nora apples was received and duly appreciated. Tell Nora pa eat the apples and thought of her.

My health is about as usual. I am still troubled some with pains but not enough to get home upon. But I will tell you my dear what I am going to do. If I don't get better by the last of this week I am going to the Hospital.

Now Dear don't think I am very sick, but the *secret* is it is all the way I can get to see you. So have your "tricks" all fixed up ready to come to see me and just as soon as I get to the place I expect to stay at, I will write and you can come on "immediately or sooner." Bring Nora with you. You see there are hospitals for

---

[45] *Georgia Atlas & Gazetteer*, 1; Horn, *Army of Tennessee*, 305, 311; Gould and Kennedy, *Memoirs of a Dutch Mudsill*, 237 (quote).

[46] Service records.

officers alone so I will fare well and be out of the weather and I have another object in view which I will let you know when I see you.

I am needing a pair of socks and will need a pair of pants by the last of January. I have written to father to buy Parsons land—that place near Carnesville. Mother wrote me he would wait till Christmas. he had been offered more than his price but was waiting on me. I think it the best investment we can mak so if any of them come after the money let them have as much as $500 dollars if you can spare it as that is all he wants now. I directed them to give my note for the rest payable in Confederate money.

Now dear if I write for you, you must be *sure* to come. I will make arrangements for your accomodation.

We have had a great deal of rain resently. it is very pleasint this morning.

You need not write again till you here from me.

       Yours Truly
       M P Alexander

Note

Carnesville: This is a town in Franklin County, Georgia. Manning was raised near there on the farm where his mother and father still lived when the letter was written.

1864

Manning

Atlanta Ga
Jan. 5th 1864
Dear Lona:

You will be somewhat surprised I expect to get a letter from me from Atlanta. Well I wrote you last week which I suppose you have received before this. I have come here as a hospital patient but don't be alarmed for I am by no means dangerous now this is the truth. I am going to Madison Geo. to the officer's Hospital at that place.

Now my dear I want you to come to see me without fail. You will get this friday [January 8] if nothing hapens. Madison is about 25 miles above union point on the georgia rail road. I will go there to morrow [Wednesday, January 6] . I will have every arrangement made for you. Lieut Davis of Hall Co. is with me. He is well acquainted at Madison. he says he will assist me in geting a room for you or rather for *us*.

If you get this firday I will look for you Sunday [January 10]. You can come to Athens Saturday [January 9] and by 2 oclock Sunday you can get here. You can bring Simon[,] Dyse[,] or som one with you. I will pay all expences.

Now be sure to come for it will be the only chance we will have soon to see each other. Should you not get this till monday [January 11] you cannot get here till Wednesday [January 13]. I don't know what regulation there is at the hospital at Madison but if I can get leave of absence 24 hours I will meet you in Athens Saturday night [January 9] but don't depend on that for it is altogether uncertain about geting that. It might be best to bring somthing along to eat. I think we can arrange to board urselvess but don't stand on that. Come right on. bring Nora with you.

I will meet you at the Depot. You can have your bagage checked at Athens to Madison and it will be no more trouble to you. Should any thing happen (which I have no idea [it] will) I will write a letter and direct it to Athens so you can send to the [post] office when you get there and if I am any whare else you will know it. Should Saturday be a bad day I will not much look for you till you have a good day to come to Athens in. I will be at the depot every day from sunday till you come.

Most Truly
M P Alexander

Notes

I have come here [Atlanta] as a hospital patient: The register for the Atlanta Receiving & Distribution Hospital records that Manning was admitted to that hospital on January 5, 1864, suffering from neuralgia and that the following day he was transferred to a hospital in Madison. (The register mistakenly lists Manning Poole Alexander as "Alexander, P. W.")[47]

In this first paragraph, "here" means Atlanta. In the third paragraph, however, Manning seems to be thinking ahead, and "here" means Madison.

Dictionary of Medical Science printed in 1874 defines "neuralgia" as a "generic name for a number of diseases, the chief symptom of which is a very acute pain, exacerbating or intermitting, which follows the course of a nervous branch, extends to it ramifications, and seems, therefore, to be seated in the nerve."[48]

Madison: Madison is about sixty miles east of Atlanta on the way to Augusta.[49]

You can bring Simon or Dyse: They were enslaved servants of Thirza and James David (see earlier letters).

Depot: The depot in Madison.

---

[47] B. Harris, *Confederate Hospitals of Madison, Georgia*, 351.
[48] Dunglison, *Dictionary of Medical Science*, 698.
[49] *Georgia Atlas & Gazetteer*, 1.

Manning

Madison Geo
jan 10th 1864
My Dear:

I will drop you a line this evening as I fear that you did not get my letter of the 5th inst. I was a little disappointed to day when the train came up. I looked for you. I am afraid you or dear little Nora is sick though I hope not. You could not have got my letter till friday so unless you started saturday you could not have got here today. If you did not get it I want you, my dear, to start the next morning after you get this. I never wanted to see you so badly in all my life.

I am at Madison Geo 25 miles above Union Point. I am in the Hospital but by no means dangerous. I[n] fact I am nearly well. Come sure for I dont know when there will be an oportunity for us to see each other again. I will meet you at the Depot. I will go there every day till you come or I here from you. I have made arrangements for your board so come *right straight* along. This is a tolrebly fassionable place but that makes *no* difference. I am needing some socks and pants but *dont wait one minute* for that. Bring Nora. I will look *im*pationatly for you every day. Most Truly

M P Alexander

Note

I am in the Hospital: The register of patients for Blackie Hospital in Madison indicates that Manning was admitted there on January 6, 1864. For more information about Blackie Hospital see a note in chapter 26.[50]

Manning

Madison Geo
Jan 12th 1864
My Dear

I will again drop you a line—which is the second since I have been here. I wrot you from Atlanta that I was coming to this place—Madison, Geo. as patient in the Hospital. I wrote you to come to see me while here. I have been looking for you ever since Sunday but have been so far disappointed. Oh how I long to see my dear for when I leave here I dont know when an other oportunity will offer that we can get to see you. Now my dear you must not wait one moment after you get this. I am needing some socks but dont wait one hour for that. I neve wanted to see you so badly in my life. Come to Athens and you will reach Madison by three oclock next day. I will meet you at the Depot. I will go there evey

---

[50] B. Harris, *Confederate Hospitals of Madison, Georgia*, 105.

day till you come. Dont wait an hour. bring Nora with you. I have board ingaged for you. at a very clever place. Come on come quick.

Most Truly Yours
M P Alexander

[Envelope]
Mrs M. P. Alexander
   Wall Street
      Geo

Manning

Madison Geo.
Jan 15th 1864
My Dear:

    I have just received your very kind letter of 13 inst. I am truly disappointed that you cant come any sooner. I have been looking so anxiously for you all week. Now Dear come right along don't wait for *anything*. I am *exceedingly* anxious to see you. I am so sorry to learn that dear little Nora is sick. I hope she is better before this time. I hope you will have started before this reaches you. This will reach you by Monday's mail if it goes through then. I know you will be here by Wednesday [January 20]. Come right strait along. Now *don't wait* for anything except very *bad* sickness. I don't know how long I will stay here not long I think though so come *immediately*. Bring Nora with you if she is able. I have board ready. I will go to the Depot every day till you come.

    I am at the Blackie Ho[spital]. There will be no chance for [me] to come by home.

Yours in Great Ha[ste]
M P Alexander

Manning

Madison Geo.
Feb. 3rd /64
My Dear:

    I will write a line to-day and mail it this evening so that I think you will be sure to get it firday.

    I have missed my Chill ever since you left here. I am improving very fast. I settled with Miss Hollingsworth yesterday. She charged me *six dollars* a day. I think she was quite extravagant taking every thing into consideration. Mr. Thrasher, who keeps a first rate table only charges $150.00 per month, which would have been but little more than she charged. But let it go. I have drawn two months pay, which will keep me all right.

Gen. Cobb made a very good speech full of truth but I don't think the narrow hearted people of this section will be benefited by it. They intend to hold on to every pound of meat they have got till the soldiers are compeled to leave the field for want of bread and meet.

I hope you an Nora got home safe. I will look for my papers about Saturday, though it may be a week before they come yet. If they are disapproved I will write you immediately.

Lieut Morris Quarter-master of our Regt was here yesterday on business for the Regt. He was surprised to see me looking so badly. Dr. Howard of the 52nd Geo. Regt. has been ordered on duty here. He got a transfer to Hospital duty

It is quite cold here now. The water is cold enough here now but I am not so anxious for it. I will close. I look for a letter from you Friday. Most Truly

M P Alexander

Notes

I have missed my Chill ever since you left here: Manning probably meant that he had not suffered from chills after Lona left Madison.

Gen Cobb: He was the same General Cobb who was speaker of the US House of Representatives before the Civil War and Horatio's brigade commander in 1862. At the time this letter was written, he was commander of the Georgia State Guard, a unit composed of Georgia militia and other Georgia forces. In September 1863, Governor Brown had ordered Cobb to organize the Guard into a force to be used by the Confederate army to defend Georgia. During the following eight months, Cobb also spoke at citizens' meetings, planters' gatherings, and other public assemblies pleading the Confederate cause and chastising extortionists who raised prices when there was a shortage of goods due to the needs of the army.[51]

I will look for my papers: These were papers he had requested that would grant him leave to go home before returning to his regiment, then in winter quarters near Dalton. The patient register for Blackie Hospital lists Manning as being furloughed on February 5, 1864, two days after this letter was written. The furlough was for thirty days.[52]

Dr. Howard: He was N. F. Howard former surgeon of the 52nd Georgia Regiment. At Vicksburg, the 52nd had been part of Barton's Brigade with Manning's 43rd. It also was part of Stovall's Brigade with the 43rd when the Confederate Army of Tennessee was reorganized just before the Battle of Missionary Ridge.[53]

---

[51] H. Montgomery, *Howell Cobb's Confederate Career*, 98–99, 112–13.
[52] See chapter 26; B. Harris, *Confederate Hospitals of Madison, Georgia*, 111.
[53] Service records; McDonough, *Chattanooga*, 276.

Chapter 24

Simeon and Horatio Continue the Fight, Early–Middle 1864

Horatio

Camp McTavis near Russelville,
Tennessee
February the 2nd, 1864
Dear Mother:

    I received a letter from you this morning and was very sorry to learn that Dr. Alex was so sick and glad to hear that Lon had gone to see him for I know what a good nurse can do.

    Mother, I am much stouter than I ever was. Last Thursday we left our camp and marched 30 miles in the direction of Knoxville to fight the Yanks, but they did not give us a chance for running themselves but none of us cried about it. We then came back to camp.

    Mother if you could be here and hear and listen to the boys talk you would not think of the Yanks whipping us. Capt. McRay is in command of the regt. none of the lieuts at camp and he made choice of me to command his company.

    Mother, there is some officer in our regt are entirely barefooted. Their names Capt. McRay, Capt. Moss, Lt. Cox, Lt. Stead, Lt Dyer, Capt Ross, and some others. I saved all my clothes and trunk. I spent all my money but 55 dollars but today I draw 123 dollars.

    Lt. Cox has leave of absence for 30 days. If you have time go see him. He can tell you more than he ever heard of. We had 3 men killed at Knoxville, J. M. Arthur, Matiron Waller, and Warren Chronic. John Deverel got to us yesterday. Our rations plenty, quarters good. Give my love to Father and Anna.

                                  H. J. David

Notes

    Russelville, Tennessee: After Horatio was wounded at Chancellorsville and returned home to recuperate, General Longstreet's Corps, of which Horatio's 16th Georgia was a part, fought at Gettysburg in July (see chapter 21). In September it was sent to join the western army in East Tennessee, where part of his corps (not including the 16th Georgia) arrived in time to fight at Chickamauga.[1]

    In early November, Longstreet's Corps was on the march again, this time to Knoxville. Longstreet's attack on that city was unsuccessful, and after a short

---

[1] Boatner, *Civil War Dictionary*, 490–91.

siege, Longstreet moved his men in early December some fifty or sixty miles northeast of the city to Rogersville, Tennessee, north of the Holston River. About December 17, he again moved his army, this time to the south side of the river to Russellville, about a dozen miles closer to Knoxville.[2]

February 4, 1864: It is unclear exactly when before this date Horatio rejoined Company B of the 16th Georgia. From the contents of the letter itself, it sounds as though Horatio arrived only a short time before it was written. In February 1864, the 16th Georgia was part of Wofford's Brigade of Kershaw's Division of Longstreet's Corps.[3]

Capt. McRay is in command of the regt... he made choice of me to command his company: Captain J. H. D. McRae was commander of the regiment only temporarily. Its previous commander, Colonel Henry P. Thomas, had been killed on November 29 during the assault on Knoxville. Apparently, Lieutenant Colonel B. Edward Stiles, who was promoted to be the full-time commander of the regiment, was away on leave, and McRae was appointed temporary commander. McRae had been commander of Company F, and he returned to that position after Lieutenant Colonel Stiles returned.

Horatio was a lieutenant in Company B. Apparently none of the lieutenants of Company F were in camp when McRae was the temporary regimental commander, and McRae named Horatio the temporary commander of his old company.[4]

barefoot officers: These were the new temporary regimental commander, the commanders of Companies I and G, and lieutenants in Companies B, C, and G.[5]

J. M. Arthur, Matiron Waller, and Warren Chronic: All were privates in Horatio's company, Company B, although "Matiron Waller" in this old transcription probably should have been transcribed as Madison Wallis. All were killed in Longstreet's attack on Knoxville on November 29, 1863.[6]

John Deverel: John H. Deverell was a friend of Horatio's from Jackson County. A private in Company B, he had been badly wounded and captured at Gettysburg during the battle in July 1863, exchanged in late August, and furloughed home from a Confederate hospital in early September. He had just rejoined his regiment.[7]

---

[2] Wagner, *Timeline of the Civil War*, 158; Dickert, *History of Kershaw's Brigade*, 317–10, 325; Rand McNally "Tennessee State Road Map."

[3] Service records; Byrd, *Confederate Sharpshooter*, 124–25.

[4] Rigdon, *Georgia 16th Infantry Regiment*, 71, 160; service records of McRae and Stiles; Byrd, *Confederate Sharpshooter*, 131.

[5] Rigdon, *Georgia 16th Infantry Regiment*, 96, 115, 177; Moss's service records.

[6] Rigdon, *Georgia 16th Infantry Regiment*, 97, 99, and 113.

[7] Ibid., 101; service records; see also chapters 15 and 17.

Horatio

[Febry] the 18, 1864
Camp 16th Ga. Regiment near Strawberry Plains
Dear Sister [Pillona Alexander]:

I have just finished eating a nice dinner. It was composed of bacon, bread, and gravy thickened with flour. We get ½ lb. of bacon and a pint of flour, some salt (can't estimate the quantity) per day.

Lony, my health is very good now. I am much heavier than when you saw me. My bowels were affected slightly a few days back, but I took some burnt brandy and it checked them immediately.

Sister, I have seen 2 men shot today. It was a horrid sight. It nearly makes my blood run cold to think of it, but it must be done. One of them belonged to the 24th Ga. Regt. We are compelled to witness it, and worst of all, their own company have to shoot them.

We have a nice tent with a chimney to it, which makes it nearly as comfortable as a house. I will give you the names of the men in our mess. Capt. John M. Venable, D. G. Hardigree, John H. Deverel, and H. J. David. We wallow about in each others laps as though we were [letter is torn here].

I hope Dr. is at home with you all. Tell Nora I will bring her a pretty when I come home. Give my love to all the family. Write soon. H. J. David

P. S. Lony, I want you to make me a nice pair of cotton gloves dove color so that they will do for parade gloves. Knit them close and small so that they may fit tightly. Tell Cousin Helen, Nancy, Bell and George the reason that I did not write to them is because I cannot get stamps. John Deverel is well.

Notes

Date of Letter: The original of this letter is missing, and what remains is an old transcription of the original. The month given in the old transcription, "*July 18, 1864* [my emphasis]," however, is wrong. For several reasons, the correct month is February.

Horatio's unit was close to two "Strawberry Plains" in 1864, one in Virginia and one in Tennessee. The one in Virginia was on the north side of the James River near Malvern Hill and Deep Bottom. Horatio's unit actually was at the Strawberry Plains in Virginia in late July 1864, but as will be indicated in chapter 27, on July 18, the date in the transcription, the unit still was on the south side of the James. Moreover, the letter that is the subject of this note could not have been written in July 1864. Service records clearly indicate that two of Horatio's tent mates mentioned in the letter, Captain Venable and John Deverell, were no longer with the unit in July 1864. They were, however, with the unit in February 1864. Also, it is unlikely that Horatio would have written from Virginia in July about his tent having a chimney in it that makes it comfortable. In addition, as mentioned in the following notes, other information in the letter indicates that the unit was at Strawberry Plains, Tennessee, when it was written.[8]

Strawberry Plains: Strawberry Plains, Tennessee, was the site of a strategically important trestle railway bridge over the Holston River about fifteen miles northeast of Knoxville.

In early January, Union forces occupied the area, and General Grant even had visited the site. On January 22, however, the forces there were ordered to destroy the bridge, retreat, and occupy a position much closer to Knoxville.

Around February 10, Longstreet began advancing his army to Strawberry Plains with the ultimate aim of attacking and seizing Knoxville. At Strawberry Plains, however, the army stopped while Longstreet corresponded with Richmond requesting additional troops. During several days of correspondence, he received word that they would be sent to him, but then he received an order to send his cavalry to Georgia. Compliance with that order made his assault of Knoxville impractical, and on February 22, he abandoned it. On February 25, he ordered Kershaw's division to relocate his men to Greeneville, Tennessee.[9]

I am much heavier than when you saw me: Horatio had returned only recently to his unit after being home recovering from his wound at Chancellorsville.

I have seen 2 men shot today: The man shot who belonged to the 24th Georgia probably was Private William T. Gunning or Gunion of Company F, a company that was recruited in Gwinnett County. He was sentenced to death on February 3, 1864, probably for desertion.[10]

Only about two months earlier, while the division was in Rogersville, Tennessee, another man of Horatio's division was executed for desertion. Horatio had not yet rejoined his unit, but a member of the division later described in some detail what took place then. It is likely that much the same took place at the execution Horatio witnessed.

At nine o'clock in the morning the four brigades of the division marched to the field where the execution was to take place and there formed three sides of a hollow square: one brigade on the left, another on the right, the third closing one end of the square, and of the fourth brigade, one half was aligned with the brigade on the left and the other half aligned with the brigade on the right. The fourth side of the square remained open, and there a member of the division had driven a "rude stake" into the ground.

---

[8] Service records for Venable and Deverell.

[9] Rand McNally, "Tennessee State Road Map"; Cox, *Military Reminiscences of the Civil War*, 101–10, 122–28; Longstreet, *From Manassas to Appomattox*, 538–40; *OR*, ser. 1, vol. 31, pt. 2, 389, 415, 428, 433, 728, 802.

[10] Bunch, *Roster of the Courts-Martial*, 142; Lowry and Laska, *Confederate Death Sentences*, 14; Henderson, *Roster of the Confederate Soldiers of Georgia*, 3:v.

At a signal, a platoon of guards, with their arms reversed, entered the open end of the square. Following them was a band playing the "Dead March." Then came the condemned man. A second guard platoon brought up the rear. As the cortege marched in front of each side of the lined-up troops, it kept step with the "slow and dismal sounds" of the march.

After the procession completed the circuit of the square, the condemned man was led to the stake. He was described as "an ignorant mountaineer" who "in an ill-fated moment [had] allowed his longings for home to overcome his sense of duty, and deserted his colors—fled to his mountain home and sought to shelter himself near his wife and little ones."

The man knelt in front of the stake and allowed himself to be tied to it. Facing him were thirty armed men, fifteen of whose guns had been loaded with powder and shot and fifteen with powder only.

"The officer in charge gives the command, 'ready,' thirty hammers spring back; 'aim,' the pieces rise to the shoulders; then only, the tension broke, and the unfortunate man, instead of the officer, cried out in a loud, metallic voice, 'fire.' The report of thirty rifles rang out...."[11]

mess: In the Confederate army this term generally referred to five to ten men "who ate together and took turns cooking and cleaning," shared clothing and even the same blanket at night. "Messmates formed an extended military family" that fostered close "physical and emotional relationship" that "often continued on the battlefield, where messmates were shoulder to shoulder, linked together as a band of brothers who overcame fear through their collective demonstrations of strength."[12]

I hope Dr. is at home with you all: See chapter 26.

Simeon

Camp 14th Ga Regt near
Orange C. H. March 21—1864
My dear Mother:

Your affectionate and patriotic letter of the 12th came to hand yesterday evening and found me in the enjoyment of good health. I have never had better health during the war than this winter though we have had a remarkably arduous winter campaign. We left our pleasant and delightful quarters at Harrisonburg in the valley of Virginia three weeks ago tomorrow morning and have come back to our old camp near Orange Courthouse. We left the Valley with great reluctance, as we fared most sumptuously over there. Our Brigade marched about 500 miles

---

[11] Dickert, *History of Kershaw's Brigade*, 319–21.
[12] Garrison, *Encyclopedia of Civil War Usage*, 158 (1st quote); Carmichael, *War for the Common Soldier*, 43 (2nd quote).

while we were in the valley and during the time of that dreadful cold weather but for all that, the whole of the Brigade would rather stay there than anywhere in the Confederacy.

I do not remember whether I wrote you that my company was detailed as a Provost Guard for the town of Harrisonburg in Rockingham county, Va. for the period of a month, a most delightful berth it was too. The people were just as kind to me and my company as we could have desired. As much as I have been exposed this winter I have not had a cold during the whole winter. I was sorry to hear of the affliction in your family but am glad that it was not more serious. I hope Dr. Alexander's health is restored before now.

About two weeks ago, I sent up an application for a furlough. About the time it should have been granted the roads in North Carolina were taken possession of almost exclusively for the transportation of the "Tax in Kind" from North Carolina to Richmond, and the granting of furloughs was temporarily suspended and an order from Gen Lee [was addressed] to all persons to whom furloughs had been granted to wait until further orders. The fact of its [the furlough's] being sustained by Gen Lee and not sent back disapproved is very strong that it will be approved in a few days. But for the fact that I have been expecting my furlough every day for the last ten days I would have written [earlier].

My company is in fine health except one man who is suffering from an attack of pneumonia. I have received six recruits to my company this winter and expect more. I am looking for my prisoners in a few days when my company will number some 70 men. I have enjoyed myself more this winter than I have ever done since I have been in the army. If I should get to come home, I will only get 24 days leave of absence, which will only leave me 10 or 12 days to be at home, and it being such a busy time of year I am fearful it will be out of my power to visit you. If I cannot, you must visit me. My love to Father, Sister and the negroes. Write soon.

Your affectionate son,

S. B. David

P. S. I received a letter from Ratio a few days ago. I suppose he is at home now. S. B. D

Notes

the Valley of Virginia: The Shenandoah Valley.

Our Brigade marched about 500 miles while we were in the valley: Around January 1, 1864, General Thomas's brigade, of which Simeon and the 14th Georgia were a part, was detached from Lee's Army of Northern Virginia and sent to the Shenandoah Valley to serve under General Jubal A. Early. Their mission there apparently was, in the words of a Union report, "to prevent raids and to collect men, animals, provisions, and forage from the Shenandoah and other valleys accessible to them." As Simeon wrote, however, his company spent February detached from the brigade and serving as provost guard in Harrisonburg, Virginia.[13]

Provost Guard: "A police detail usually charged with guarding prisoners or retrieving stragglers."[14]

Harrisonburg: Harrisonburg consisted of a courthouse in the center of the town square, "several stores, two or three hotels, half a dozen churches, two printing offices and many fine residences," as well as "a mammoth spring" on the square covered by a dome-shaped roof atop eight pillars with stone steps leading to a stream running from the spring to make drinking the water easier.[15]

transportation of the "Tax in Kind": On April 24, 1863, the Confederate government enacted a law requiring each farmer and planter, after deducting a certain amount for his own use, to deliver to the Confederate government by March 1 of each year one tenth of his previous year's production of certain crops, including corn, sweet potatoes, rice, hay, fodder, molasses, cotton, and tobacco.

Each farmer or planter also must provide one tenth of the weight of hogs slaughtered during the year to the Confederate government, the weight to be paid in cured bacon, at a rate of sixty pounds of bacon to one hundred pounds of pork, or the equivalent in salt pork. These products were to be provided in place of a monetary tax.[16]

Simeon's furlough: There is no indication in Simeon's service records, or apparently elsewhere, concerning when or whether Simeon got his furlough.

I am looking for my prisoners: Simeon probably is referring to men in his company who previously had been taken prisoner but now had been exchanged and could return to serve in his company.

I suppose he is at home now: As indicated in the previous letter, Horatio already had returned to his regiment.

Thirza

June 1 1864
Dear Pillina Dr and Children [Bells]

I have this evening returnd from Marys & Fannys. I had little Sally here, and I knew after her Fathers death her Poor Mother wanted to see her more than before, and I determined to carry her home. She has recd a letter from one of her cousins Mr. Mcafee Stating that our Dear Simeon was killed on the evening of the 5 May about 2 hours by sun by a Minnie ball entering below the left eye. [He] died allmost without a Struggle never Spoke a word. I am so thankfull that he did

---

[13] *OR*, ser. 1, vol. 33, 43–44, 486 (quote), 1060–1062, 1075–1076, 111, 1135, 1157, 1191.
[14] Garrison, *Encyclopedia of Civil War Usage*, 199.
[15] Boyce, "Story of the Shenandoah Valley," 199.
[16] Lester and Bromwell, *Military and Naval Laws of the Confederate States*, 177–84.

not suffer long. I have no doubt but that our and his countrys loss is his eternal Gain.

Fanny recd a letter from him dated 3 May in whitch The Dear child discribes one of the greatest revivals of Religion he ever saw that was then going on in his brigade in whitch Simeon was an active participant. So my dear Pillina he is not dead but is Gone before us to draw us from this poor world, and if all my loved ones were gone I could go with a shout. I have heard of sevral letters in Forsyth Cty in whitch his Men lament for him like he had been their Father. The Dear Child was going into Battle before his men encouraging them when no doubt a Sharp Shooter Singled him out.

Our dear little James Neal arrived at home Sunday night and rejoiced our Sad hearts. Fanny was there with us. Thank God his wound is not dangerous we hope. the ball worked out by riding home from Atlanta on Horse Back and was lodged in his drawer leg.

Dear little Ratio was unhurt the 21 may. Ratio says Mother don't grieve about Brother. he is better off than you or I. but for his poor little children I could bear it better thoug we are compelled to bow.

I went out with a two horse waggon and brought away Annolivia[,] Marys best bedding[,] and provisions. John also came with us. We could hear the cannon distinctly Sunday night. 19 miles was the nearest place of the Enemy to Mary. If they appear to be gitting nearer Mary James and Jessy will come. Dear Fanny will come too and bring her Negros and Mules and stock and all that she can.

Oh Child I wish we were all here together. I dread the thought of being divided by the Enemy. Write as Soon as you receive this and let us know how you are doing. I must close, all here Join in love to you. believe Me as ever Your afflicted but affectionate
Mother T D

This is a scrap of our drapes

Notes

Mary, Fanny, and Sally: Mary was Mary Neal, Thirza's oldest child and Simeon's oldest sister. Fanny was Simeon's wife and Sally was their third child, then age four.

one of her cousins Mr Mcafee: He was Joseph J. Miller McAfee, Fanny's first cousin once-removed, the son of the granddaughter of Fanny's uncle. He was a sergeant and later became the company commander of Simeon's company. He also was the "Sergeant McAfee" who shared a bed with Simeon and Josiah Patterson as mentioned in a letter from Patterson referred to in a note to a letter in chapter 21.

According to an interview with McAfee printed in the *North Georgia Tribune* in 1921 and reprinted in that paper on April 7, 1960, McAfee served to the end of the war participating in all the battles in which the regiment was engaged. He was one of the only two men of his, and Simeon's, company who went through the war unwounded.[17]

the 5 May: The day when Simeon was killed, May 5, 1864, was the first day of the Battle of the Wilderness, which was fought roughly ten miles west of present-day Fredericksburg, Virginia, and not far from where Simeon fought in the Battle of Chancellorsville almost exactly a year earlier. It was the beginning of a series of almost continuous battles in Virginia over forty-two days between Grant and Lee known as the Overland Campaign.[18]

Grant Crosses the Rappahannock and Rapidan Rivers and Confronts Lee

On March 10, about two months before the battle, General U. S. Grant became commander of all the Union armies. Shortly afterward, he implemented a plan for the Army of the Potomac to march south with its "first great objective" being "to get possession of Lee's army." He believed that "With the capture of his army Richmond would necessarily follow." Thus on April 9, Grant wrote to General George Meade, commander of the Army of the Potomac situated north of Virginia's Rappahannock River, "Wherever Lee goes, there you will go also."

Part of the plan was that Grant would travel with Meade and the army wherever they went. While Meade was technically in charge, Grant, as it turned out, would be the actual commander.[19]

Opposite Grant and south of the Rapidan River (a river in Virginia south of the Rappahannock), General Robert E. Lee had been following the buildup of Union forces for over a month. In response, he had begun consolidating his own Army of Northern Virginia. In mid-April, he contemplated a move against Grant's forces before Grant moved against his, but in early May, he still was gathering his army when he learned that Grant and Meade's army already had crossed the Rappahannock and was marching south toward Richmond and toward him.[20]

In the approaching confrontation, Grant had at his disposal some 120,000 infantrymen, cavalry troopers, artillerymen, and assorted others, only a little over half of them seasoned soldiers. Lee had only approximately forty-five to fifty thousand men, but most were veteran fighters. In addition, in late April Longstreet's Corps, including Horatio's regiment, had arrived in Virginia from Tennessee and again come under Lee's command. Lee could have added its fifteen thousand men immediately to his total of troops available to confront Grant south

---

[17] David Hopper (a descendent of Simeon's) email to me, July 25, 2017.

[18] Rhea, "Overland Campaign," 293, 312.

[19] Grant, *Memoirs and Selected Letters*, 481–82 footnote, 485, 1136; Rhea, *Battle of the Wilderness*, 43–46.

[20] Dowdey and Manarin, *Wartime Papers of R. E. Lee*, 684–709, 712–13; 719–20; Rhea, *Battle of the Wilderness*, 2.

of the Rapidan, but he had decided to leave them near Gordonsville, about a day's march away, to protect Richmond if needed.[21]

On May 4, most of the Army of the Potomac crossed the Rapidan and marched southeast in two columns. In addition, a third large body of Union soldiers was held in reserve and available to enforce either column as needed. At the close of day, the Federals' two columns had encountered no serious Confederate opposition. They camped for the night.[22]

Lee Responds

On May 3, the day before Grant crossed the Rapidan, General Lee began to receive reports that activity was intensifying in the Union camp. Most of Lee's army was then encamped near Orange, Virginia, about twenty-five miles west of Grant's prospective fording places on the Rapidan. As Grant advanced his men in two columns, Lee began to advance his men from the Orange area in two columns to intercept them. He hoped Grant's men would be moving slowly enough that he could reach them in time to hit them on their right flank as they headed south.

As part of his plan, he ordered Lieutenant General Richard S. Ewell, commander of the 2nd Corps, to begin marching the northern-most column east along the Orange Turnpike, roughly today's Route 20. When he learned the next day that Grant had crossed the Rapidan, he ordered General Ambrose P. Hill to take the southern-most column, two divisions of his 3rd Corps, and march them east on the Orange Plank Road. Hill's Plank Road ran roughly parallel to Ewell's Turnpike and was about two and a half miles south of it.

Both roads led east to the Germanna Plank Road, roughly today's Route 3, which ran north-south and was the route south Grant would take. Near that road was the likely place where the Confederate and Union columns would meet.[23]

On each side of the Turnpike and Plank roads lay an area known as the Wilderness. There for decades before the war "loggers had cut and recut the forests to fuel nearby iron furnaces." As a result, on the old ground flourished a dense mix of re-emerging growth, stunted pines, thick bushes, briars, and entangling vines, interrupted occasionally by swamps and boggy streams. A few small farms provided the only clearings among this encumbering plant life. One Confederate soldier wrote, "This is a dreary dismal country most fitly called the Wilderness. For many miles not a house or open field. Nothing but a wilderness of trees and

---

[21] Rhea, *Battle of the Wilderness*, 26–27, 34–35; *OR*, ser. 1, vol. 33, 1286, 1306–1307; *OR*, ser. 1, vol. 36, pt. 2, 940; Gallagher, *Fighting for the Confederacy*, 345–49; Dowdey, *Lee's Last Campaign*, 71.

[22] Rhea, *Battle of the Wilderness*, 54–57, 62–66, 74–77.

[23] Ibid., 62, 78–82; Robertson, *General A. P. Hill*, 251–52; Dowdey, *Lee's Last Campaign*, 34–35, 52–55.

underbrush and marsh." In addition, a journalist reported that what few roads there were through this wasteland "were narrow and easily choked up by troops." These characteristics of the land were to affect significantly the battle to come.[24]

For one thing, Lee understood that in this environment, Grant would find it difficult to maneuver his cavalry, artillery, and numerous infantry effectively. It was in the Wilderness, where the Union's numerical advantage would be limited, that Lee intended to fight.[25]

Simeon's Regiment Advances

As at Gettysburg, Simeon's regiment was part of General Thomas's brigade. After serving in the Shenandoah Valley as described in a previous letter in this chapter, Thomas's Brigade returned east to be one of four brigades in General Cadmus M. Wilcox's division (Wilcox had replaced Pender as division commander after Pender died from a wound received at Gettysburg). Also like Gettysburg, that division was part of Hill's 3rd Army Corps and thus would be advancing along the lower road, Orange Plank Road.[26]

About midmorning on May 4, Hill's soldiers began marching east on Plank Road toward the Union army. Major General Henry Heth's division marched in front and General Wilcox's division, including Simeon's regiment, was next in line. Traveling along with them was General Lee.

When they camped that night, they had yet to encounter the enemy. They were, however, some twelve miles closer to that confrontation.[27]

At dawn the next morning, May 5, Hill's men resumed their march east up Plank Road, Simeon leading his company. As on the day before, Heth's Division led the advance and Wilcox's Division followed. About nine o'clock, they heard the sound of muskets and artillery firing off to their left. The realized that Ewell's column marching east on the parallel Orange Turnpike had encountered Federals moving toward them, and the battle had started.[28]

About an hour later, Simeon and members of his regiment heard more sporadic rifle fire, this time from directly ahead of them where Heth's Division marched. They stopped and left their heavy backpacks in wagons nearby then

---

[24] Interpretive sign, Wilderness Battlefield, National Park Service, encountered on November 23, 2015 (1st quote); Dowdey, *Lee's Last Campaign*, 52–53; Powers, "Philip H. Powers Letters," May 5, 1864 (2nd quote); "The Campaign in Virginia," *Army and Navy Journal*, May 14, 1864 (3rd quote).

[25] Rhea, *Battle of the Wilderness*, 27–28.

[26] Ibid., 468–69; chapter 21 above; Dowdey, *Lee's Last Campaign*, 113.

[27] Rhea, *Battle of the Wilderness*, 82, 84–85; Wilcox, "Lee and Grant in the Wilderness," 488; W. K. Alexander, "Colonel Clark Moulton Avery," 59–60; Robertson, *General A. P. Hill*, 251–52.

[28] Rhea, *Battle of the Wilderness*, 123–25; Wilcox, "Lee and Grant in the Wilderness," 489–91; Champion, "Reminiscence of the Sixties," 21–22; Robertson, *General A. P. Hill*, 252–54.

resumed marching toward the firing. As they advanced, one Confederate noted, "The road was literally strewed with packs of playing cards thrown away by superstitious soldiers as they went into the fiery focus." Also as they advanced the sound of firing, the "fiery focus," advanced before them, and they passed on the side of the road a few dead Union soldiers.[29]

At that time, Heth's Division had encountered only Union pickets, who fought briefly then withdrew. Around three o'clock, however, the division confronted more Union forces, now in significant numbers. Lee then knew that both Ewell to the north and Hill's men with him to the south had encountered the enemy in some strength. Moreover, he realized his two columns were completely separate. Between them was a gap of about two to three miles that was as yet unoccupied by either Confederates or Federals. If the Confederates columns fought separate battles along their parallel roads, the Union army could rush forward to occupy the gap and then turn right or left to attack the flank of either of the Confederate columns. Lee needed to make a decision.

Based on couriers' reports, he decided Heth had sufficient men to handle the enemy there and ordered Wilcox to march his division north to close the gap between the two Confederate columns.[30]

Wilcox led his four brigades off Plank Road onto a dirt trail that led through the approximately two to three miles of wilderness north toward the right flank of Ewell's column. After marching about half a mile up the trail, Wilcox left two of his brigades at a farmhouse and its surrounding fields. Then with his two other brigades, one of which was Thomas's Brigade, including Simeon and his 14th Georgia Regiment, he continued up the trail toward Ewell.

Just as Wilcox established contact with Ewell's right flank, he was surprised to see a courier riding toward him from the direction of Plank Road. The rider brought orders from Lee: Wilcox was to return his brigades to Plank Road immediately. The Union army in front of Heth had been heavily reinforced and had attacked Heth's roughly sixty-seven hundred Confederates with some seventeen thousand Union soldiers. (Before the day was over, the Union army there would swell to around thirty-three thousand.) Only Heth's one division confronted them, and its situation was rapidly deteriorating. Already Lee had ordered the two brigades Wilcox had left at the farmhouse to Heth's aid, but they were insufficient. He needed Wilcox's other two brigades also.[31]

---

[29] Rhea, *Battle of the Wilderness*, 121–22; Wilcox, "Lee and Grant in the Wilderness," 489; Dewberry, *History of the 14th Georgia*, 76–77; W. K. Alexander, "Colonel Clark Moulton Avery," 59–60; Wheeler, *On Fields of Fury*, 109.

[30] Rhea, *Battle of the Wilderness*, 129; Wilcox, "Lee and Grant in the Wilderness," 489, 491–92; W. K. Alexander, "Colonel Clark Moulton Avery," 60; Robertson, *General A. P. Hill*, 254–55.

[31] Rhea, *Battle of the Wilderness*, 129, 193–94, 208, 222–25; Wilcox, "Lee and Grant in the Wilderness," 492; Steere, *Wilderness Campaign*, 219–20; Caldwell, "Another Struggle with Death,"

Wilcox himself rapidly made his way back to Plank Road. Thomas and the leader of Wilcox's other brigade were to follow with their men as quickly as possible.[32]

Simeon Joins the Battle

When Wilcox again reached Plank Road, his view of the fighting was hidden by smoke from Federal and Confederate guns and from the burning brush and fallen trees the guns had set on fire. Wilcox later wrote that "the rattle of musketry alone indicat[ed] where the struggle was severest, and the points to which the reinforcing brigades should be sent."[33]

Around six thirty, when Thomas's Brigade arrived at Plank Road, Wilcox ordered it to advance to replace some of Heth's exhausted fighters on the left (north) side of the road. Once in this position, the brigade would be at the extreme left of the Confederate line facing the Federals. On the brigade's own left there would be no friendly Confederate troops. Whether Union troops might be there somewhere in the thick brush was as yet unclear.[34]

As the brigade entered its new position, accounts of its movements become confused as its regiments and companies became fragmented while stumbling through the dense thickets. Its men likely shared the experience of a Union soldier: "The underbrush and briars scratched our faces, tore our clothing, and tripped our feet from under us, constantly." A Confederate officer in Wilcox's Division later wrote, "if you must relieve one line with another, [the Wilderness] is the worst place in the world. It is impossible to keep even a regiment well dressed. Then the enemy open[s] fire on you. Some men invariably return this fire. Gradually all join in it, and once the whole roar of battle opens, there is an end of unison action."[35]

It appears that as Thomas's Brigade marched forward to take up its position, its skirmishers patrolling out from its exposed left flank discovered a strong Union force there. Even before reaching Heth's men, the brigade turned to face the newly discovered enemy, leaving its back to Plank Road, and attacked. A modern historian described what happened next: "Soon Thomas's men were fighting at

---

90–91; W. K. Alexander, "Colonel Clark Moulton Avery," 60; Robertson, *General A. P. Hill*, 255–56.

[32] Wilcox, "Lee and Grant in the Wilderness," 492.

[33] Ibid., 492–93 (quote); Rhea, *Battle of the Wilderness*, 232–33.

[34] Wilcox, "Lee and Grant in the Wilderness," 492–93; Rhea, *Battle of the Wilderness*, 233; W. K. Alexander, "Colonel Clark Moulton Avery," 61; Gottfried, *Maps of the Wilderness*, 120–21.

[35] Buell, "Fighting in the Wilderness," 980 (1st quote); Caldwell, "Another Struggle with Death," 94 (2nd quote).

right angles to one another, and, in some places, back to back. Visibility [in the underbrush and smoke] was twenty yards at most."[36]

Later Wilcox reported that the firing on his position had been "of the severest kind." A member of Simeon's regiment remembered the fighting had been "fierce and deadly at close quarters." A Union private wrote, "It was a blind and bloody hunt to the death, in bewildering thickets, rather than a battle."[37]

Around this time, Union Brigadier General James S. Wadsworth's Fourth Division, accompanied by a brigade of another division, advanced to attack the area where Thomas's Brigade was fighting. Confederates detected them and informed Hill. Hill, knowing Thomas's men were fully occupied, directed a small Alabama detachment that had been guarding prisoners forward to meet Wadsworth's troops. The Alabamians charged, letting loose the Rebel yell, and the Union men, who had been stumbling through woods and wasteland much of the day while being shot at by Confederates they could not see, abruptly stopped. Before they could be motivated to march on, darkness halted the confused battle.[38]

A member of Simeon's regiment later wrote that when the fighting ceased that evening, "our brigade was somewhat in advance of the [Confederate] line in the shape of a horseshoe, lying outward toward the enemy from the Plank Road." The brigade history recorded, "Thomas' [Brigade] was left with the enemy in line in its front and rear, and on its right flank, totally unconnected with the balance of the [Wilcox] division or any other supports."[39]

In addition, individuals and small groups of the brigade's men had become separated from others in the dense thickets, and now the darkness. Another member of Simeon's regiment recalled, "So thick and heavy were the forest entanglements in this area that no one could see far in any direction and didn't dare move throughout the night for fear of stumbling into the enemy. The slightest sneeze triggered hundreds of shots from every direction."[40]

By that time, however, Simeon was dead.

Simeon was killed on the evening...about 2 hours by sun: At a time when watches were uncommon, people told time by the sun. Two hours by sun in the evening meant two hours before sunset.[41]

---

[36] Champion, "Reminiscence of the Sixties," 22; Folsom, *Heroes and Martyrs*, 121; Dewberry, *History of the 14th Georgia*, 77; Robertson, *General A. P. Hill*, 256 (quote); Caldwell, "Another Struggle with Death," 93; Wilcox, "Lee and Grant in the Wilderness," 494.

[37] Wilcox, "Lee and Grant in the Wilderness," 493 (1st quote); Champion, "Reminiscence of the Sixties," 22 (2nd quote); Buell, "Fighting in the Wilderness," 979 (3rd quote).

[38] Robertson, *General A. P. Hill*, 259; Rhea, *Battle of the Wilderness*, 231, 237–38.

[39] Champion, "Reminiscence of the Sixties," 22 (1st quote); Folsom, *Heroes and Martyrs*, 121 (2nd quote).

[40] Dewberry, *History of the 14th Georgia*, 77; Rhea, *Battle of the Wilderness*, 238–39.

[41] Hendrickson, *Dictionary of American Regionalisms*, 376; Shands, *Some Peculiarities of Speech*, 22.

In Richmond, Virginia, on May 5, 1864, the sun set at 6:51 p.m. The fighting at the Wilderness, however, did not stop until after darkness had fallen, about eight thirty or nine. As can be seen in the previous note, Simeon's regiment did not go into battle until around six thirty, closer to two hours before darkness rather than two hours before sunset. Possibly distracted by fighting, soldiers paid little attention to the position of the sun until it had been down for some time and actual darkness had settled in. Also, whether a soldier was in a thicket or a clearing made a difference. Sergeant McAfee, who reported Simeon's s death, may have incorrectly estimated the time Simeon was killed.[42]

Simeon probably was killed between six thirty and seven o'clock, just as the 14th Georgia, along with the other regiments of Thomas's Brigade, began to move into its new position and to confront the enemy. James Thomson, a corporal in Simeon's company, later told Fanny, Simeon's wife, that Simeon had "remarked before he went into the battle that he was going in and felt confident that he would be killed but rushed forward in advance of his company with his sword waving in his hand and fell with it grasped there."[43]

Wrapped in an army blanket, he was buried on the battlefield.[44]

Minnie or Minie ball: The Minie ball was not a ball but was a soft lead, cone-shaped bullet that, for its time, was unusually destructive.

> Unlike a solid ball, which could pass through the human body nearly intact, leaving an exit wound not much larger than the entrance wound, the soft, hollow-based Minie ball flattened and deformed upon impact, while creating a shock wave that emanated outward. The Minie ball didn't just break bones, it shattered them. It didn't just pierce tissue and internal organs, it shredded them. And if the ragged, tumbling bullet had enough forced to cleave completely through the body, which it often did, it tore out an exit would several times the size of the entrance wound.[45]

James Neal's wound: According to his service records, James Neal, Mary Neal's son and a member of Company B, 38th Georgia Volunteer Infantry Regiment, was admitted to General Hospital Number 9 in Richmond on May 12 with a gunshot wound to his right hip. He was given a furlough on May 26, and as the letter stated, got home on Sunday, May 29.

---

[42] R. K. Krick, *Civil War Weather in Virginia*, 129; Dowdey, *Lee's Last Campaign*, 91; Furguson, *Chancellorsville 1863*, 171, footnote.

[43] Rhea, *Battle of the Wilderness*, 237–39; letter from Fanny David, February 25, 1865, included in chapter 29.

[44] Application of Lena David Pittman, one of Simeon's daughters, to join the United Daughters of the Confederacy, May 27, 1903.

[45] Leonard, "The Bullet That Changed History," 372 (quote); Garrison, *Encyclopedia of Civil War Usage*, 159.

The 38th Georgia was part of General Ewell's 2nd Corps and participated in both the Wilderness battle and Spotsylvania battle that soon followed. The Federals attacked Ewell's Corps at the "mule shoe" at Spotsylvania at dawn on May 12, and it likely was then that James Neal was wounded.[46]

Ratio was unhurt on May 21: May 21 occurred during a series of marches and battles by Lee and Grant that took place May 13–25 between Spotsylvania and the North Anna River about twenty-five miles north of Richmond (see the immediately following letter and notes).[47]

We could hear the cannon distinctly Sunday night: Sunday night was May 29. By this time, General Sherman's Union troops had invaded Georgia and advanced deep into the northwest part of the state on their way to Atlanta. Although there were no major engagements the night of May 29, there had been extensive fighting on May 25 and 27 northwest of Atlanta along a line from Dallas to New Hope Church to Pickett's Mill, and there may have been some skirmishing and cannon fire on May 29 as the Federal troops moved their positions south-eastward toward Atlanta.[48]

The major fighting on May 25 and 27 was about thirty miles from Mary's home in Freemansville, now in Fulton County north of Alpharetta. People in Atlanta twenty-five miles from the front lines reported hearing cannon fire. Also, units of the enemy Union cavalry may have been closer.[49]

19 miles was the nearest place of the Enemy to Mary: Although the bulk of the Federal troops were some thirty miles from Mary's home, there may have been cavalry units or other soldiers closer.[50]

AnnOlivia, Mary, John, James, and Jessy: As mentioned in an earlier note, Mary Neal was Thirza's oldest child, and Ann Olivia, John, James (of the 38th Georgia), and Jessy Neal were Mary's children. At the time the letter was written, they were seventeen, nineteen, twenty, and fourteen respectively.

Horatio

May 25, 1864
Camp North Anna River
[To his mother]

...We are yet lying in fortification on the bank of the North Anna River waiting the approach of the enemy; since we left the wilderness we have not attack the enemy, we let them charge us and then O! love they taste the dirt. I know

---

[46] Nunez, *Wilderness and Spotsylvania*, 20, 75–80.
[47] Rhea, *To the North Anna River*.
[48] Hess, *Kennesaw Mountain*, 4–5; Connelly, *Autumn of Glory*, 354–57.
[49] Wortman, *Bonfire*, 231.
[50] Flinchum, *Crossroads, Creeks & Clashes*, 8.

that our loss is not more than 15000 but that is worth more than the whole yankee nation. Do not think because we left the Wilderness that we were pressed so to do for we were not, the enemy flanked our right and we came here to get between them and Richmond. Many of us has fallen and many more will fall, but you need not be uneasy for the whole north cant take Richmond if our general officers will let us fight them.

Our Brigade has been under fire at least 15 days since the fight began. I know that our Brigade has killed at least 10 to 1. some times they would charge our works and we would kill hundreds of them, when they [would] not even wound 1 of our boys.

Mother my will was always good to fight, but now it is as good again as ever since Brother Sim was killed in the fight of the Wilderness. while we was fighting the enemy and had them routed[,] there was a Brigadier Gen. Wadsworth charging down his lines trying to rally his men. at the time one of our boys shot him and hollered out; there Lt. is some blood in lieu of your brothers, and before he died they had him stripped of his clothes. he was then carried to the hospital lied all night and died in the morning.... .

I have been in command of the co since the fight began no officer to assist me but our co is no trouble. they will fight anyway. the best little co in the world...

[Horatio David]

Notes

Letter source: This partial letter is from an old catalogue of Raynor's Historical Collectible Auctions. It was found at the Fredericksburg & Spotsylvania Military Park Research Center by Donald Pfanz.

Camp North Anna River: Horatio's camp on the North Anna River was located about twenty-five miles north of Richmond. Around April 22, 1864, General Longstreet and his command, including Horatio's 16th Georgia Regiment, returned to Virginia from Tennessee and camped near Mechanicsville, about five miles southwest of Gordonsville. As 1st Corps they immediately again became part of General Lee's Army of Northern Virginia. How and why Lee's army got to the North Anna River is detailed in the immediately following notes.[51]

Horatio's "fight of the Wilderness": After returning from Tennessee to Virginia in late April, General Longstreet's 1st Corps and Horatio's 16th Georgia camped near Mechanicsville, some forty-two miles by road from the scene of the Wilderness Battle. They were not to remain there long, for they were to take part in that most important second day of the battle.

---

[51] Rhea, *To the North Anna River*, 11; Gallagher, *Fighting for the Confederacy*, 345.

About midmorning on May 4, most of Lee's 2nd and 3rd Corps began marching to meet Grant after he crossed the Rapidan River. Even though further away from Grant, Longstreet's Corps did not begin its march until four o'clock that afternoon. They did not arrive at the Wilderness until the early morning of May 6, after Simeon was killed the evening before.[52]

Longstreet Joins the Wilderness Fight

General Ewell's 2nd Corps and General Hill's 3rd Corps, including Simeon's regiment, were the first to confront Grant's Union army, and they did so on May 5th, when Simeon was killed as described in a note to the previous letter.

The confrontation took place along two roughly parallel roads running west-east in the Wilderness, several miles from Fredericksburg. General Ewell and his men were on the northernmost road, the Orange Turnpike, traveling east, and Hill on the southernmost, Orange Plank Road, also traveling east. At its eastern end, Hill and Simeon's Plank Road intersected a road running north-south called Brock Road. On May 5, General Grant's forces were traveling south on Brock Road when Hill confronted them, and the battle on that road began. It continued as described in the earlier note until it grew dark, and by then Simeon had been killed.

In the early morning of the following day, May 6, Hill's Corps on Plank Road was exhausted from the previous day's fighting and disorganized. At five o'clock, Union General Hancock's corps attacked, advancing west straight down Plank Road toward the confused and fragmented Confederate line. At the same time, Union General Wadsworth's division, attacking from the north, struck the left of the line. A modern historian later wrote, Hill's men "crumpled under the Union onslaught." As the overwhelmed Confederates streamed back down the road, Hill, and Lee who traveled with Hill, tried to restore order but with little success.[53]

About six thirty that morning, to loud Confederate cheers, much needed Confederate reinforcements began arriving on Plank Road. Longstreet's 1st Corps with its two divisions (Field's and Kershaw's) had arrived. Longstreet immediately ordered an advance toward Hancock's Federals, Field on the left (north) side of the road and Kershaw on the right (south).[54]

Field and Kershaw each had three of his four brigades with him. (Wofford's Brigade, Kershaw's 4th, including Horatio's 16th Georgia, was guarding the 1st

---

[52] Gallagher, *Fighting for the Confederacy*, 349–50; Rhea, *Battle of the Wilderness*, 82–86; *OR*, ser. 1, vol. 36, pt. 1, 1054.

[53] Rhea, *Battle of the Wilderness*, 283–93 (quote, 285), 298.

[54] Ibid., 297–99; Gallagher, *Fighting for the Confederacy*, 358; *OR*, ser. 1, vol. 36, pt. 1, 1054–55.

Corps' wagon train and still was behind the rest of the corps.) Each general sent his brigades forward one after another to confront the Federals and stop them.[55]

On the north side of the road, Field's brigades halted the Union advance. Then, however, Union General Wadsworth's full division struck Field's brigades on their left. What could have been a catastrophe was saved by an alert Alabama regiment of veterans who wheeled around to face the attackers. Even though the Alabamans were greatly outnumbered, Wadsworth's Division was filled with men straight from easy duty guarding Washington. It was outmatched. In short order the division became, at least temporarily, "no longer a functioning combat force," a modern historian wrote.[56]

On the other, south, side of the Plank Road, Kershaw's three brigades also were successful. Initially Field on the left of the road had pulled ahead of Kershaw, but by around eight o'clock that morning, Kershaw's men had pulled even with Field's so that Longstreet's Corps "ran in an unbroken line across the Plank Road into the woods on each side." But by then the Confederate counterattack was a spent force.[57]

The Union brought up reinforcements. However, the addition of units from different commands and the loss of some unit commanders created confusion, particularly concerning which general was in charge where. This confusion, plus the difficulty of the thickly entangled terrain, prevented the Federals from assembling a coordinated assault of sufficient strength to push back the reinforced Confederates. The battle was at a stalemate. "At eleven o'clock the firing died away," a Union soldier later wrote, and there was a lull in the fighting.[58]

Wofford's Men Make a Discovery

Meanwhile, Wofford's Brigade, including Horatio's 16th Georgia, finally had left the supply train and was approaching the scene of the battle. As Horatio wrote, he now commanded his company, a company composed of some forty or fifty men, mostly veterans of hard-fought battles. When back with the supply train, they had left items that might hinder them in battle—knapsacks, blanket rolls, jackets—and had kept things they would need—muskets, tin canteens, cartridge boxes, and boxes of percussion caps.[59]

By this time in the war, little was uniform about their dress. One still might wear a pair of threadbare pants from his uniform, but these pants now were matched with an old store-bought shirt and a battered hat with a broad, drooping brim. Another would wear a different combination of shirt and pants. A Union

---

[55] Rhea, *Battle of the Wilderness*, 297–312.
[56] Ibid., 291–308 (quote, 308).
[57] Ibid., 308–15 (quote, 312).
[58] Ibid., 336–43; Goss, "Private Goss Describes the Battle of the Wilderness," 981 (quote).
[59] W. C. Davis, *Rebels and Yankees*, 224–25, 230–31.

soldier described Confederate soldiers' clothing in the Wilderness as "a medley of [the contents of] all the dry goods store of the Confederacy."[60]

As Horatio and his men marched toward the sounds of battle, they met scattered members of brother Simeon's 14th Georgia retreating in disorder from the earlier morning's fight. From them Horatio and his company learned of Simeon's death the evening before. They quickened their pace.

When they caught up with the rest of the 1st Corps, Longstreet positioned them, and the rest of Wofford's Brigade, on the south side of Plank Road at the far right end of the Confederate line. When the brigade's skirmishers explored the woods further to their right, they discovered, to their surprise, an unfinished railway roadbed that led from the Confederate right eastward almost parallel to Plank Road. It even continued all the way past the left wing of the Union line. No rails or wooden crossties had been installed in the roadbed, so troops could move along it easily. More important, the roadbed was concealed from the Union army by leafy woods. Thus, a Confederate force could march up the railroad roadbed unseen and emerge on the flank of the Union army, or even behind it, and attack.

The chief engineer of Lee's army also discovered the concealed railroad bed. Both Wofford and the engineer reported these findings to Longstreet, who quickly assigned three brigades, including Wofford's, to march out the roadbed and make the flanking attack.[61]

Longstreet Attacks the Union Left Flank

Quickly the brigades filed east along the roadbed, and still unseen by the Federals, stopped and formed a line of battle facing the left end of the Union line. By now part of a fourth brigade had joined the attacking force, the brigade of Brigadier General Joseph R. Davis, commanded that day by Colonel John M. Stone. Wofford's Brigade was the center brigade with Brigadier General George T. Anderson's brigade on its right, Brigadier General William Mahone's brigade on its left, and the newly joined Davis's Brigade behind or on the left of Mahone.[62]

There is some disagreement among historians about the arrangement of the Union left wing south of Plank Road that the Confederates faced. It seems to have consisted of eight brigades (or possibly only seven) arranged in three columns parallel to the road—the nearest column to the Confederates consisted of three brigades, the next of three additional brigades, and the last of two brigades.

---

[60] Rhea, *Battle of the Wilderness*, 430–31 (quote); Glatthaar, *General Lee's Army*, 331–32.

[61] Rhea, *Battle of the Wilderness*, 351–55; "Wofford's Georgia Brigade," *Southern Confederacy*, June 15, 1864; *OR*, ser. 1, vol. 36, pt. 1, 1061–62.

[62] "Wofford's Georgia Brigade," *Southern Confederacy*, June 15, 1864; R. K. Krick, "Like a Duck on a June Bug," 241–45, 260n18; Gottfried, *Maps of the Wilderness*, 196–97.

There is agreement, however, that all faced down Plank Road (to the west) toward the Confederates aligned there. None faced left (south) toward the waiting Confederates in the unfinished railroad bed.[63]

The Confederates waited no longer. "With a step that meant to conquer," reported the commander of one of the brigades, they began striding toward the enemy's left. At roughly the same time, the Confederates on the Plank Road who faced the front of the Federal line also attacked.[64]

As Horatio and his men approached through the undergrowth, their tin canteens bumping against bushes, they saw through the trees that the Federals ahead of them were taking it easy. Some lay spread out on the ground. Others were lighting fires and brewing coffee. They were totally unprepared, "apparently bivouacking and little expecting any attack from [our] direction," a Confederate later wrote.[65]

Brigade officers gave the command to charge and "the boys raised the old rebel yell and went on them like a duck on a June bug," a private in Wofford's Brigade reported. A member of another brigade in the charge wrote that the men in line of battle moved forward rapidly "loading and firing as they moved forward, all yelling and cheering as they saw the enemy hastily retiring, the woods echoing with the rapid discharge of musketry and the 'rebel yell'" He continued, "The move through the woods in pursuit of the retreating Federals was highly exciting, the men seeming to have lost all sense of danger."[66]

The Union left was taken by surprise. To one Federal officer, the Confederates seemed "like an army of ghosts rising out of the earth." Bullets flew "from my front, on my left flank, and my rear," recalled another Union officer. "The whistling and shrieking and pinging of the balls…went on unceasingly."

Federal soldiers went "one by one, then in twos and threes, until at last [they] went in such numbers as to give the appearance of a general skedaddle." Heading away from the swarming Confederates, they ran through the briars, bushes, and brambles, some with their eyes closed "or we would have had our eyes put out." One soldier recalled, "A man would come against some elastic chinkapin tree,

---

[63] Rhea, *Battle of the Wilderness*, 352; R. K. Krick, "Like a Duck on a June Bug," 245; Gottfried, *Maps of the Wilderness*, 197.

[64] *OR*, ser. 1, vol. 36, pt. 1, 1090–91 (quote); R. K. Krick, "Like a Duck on a June Bug," 247; Rhea, *Battle of the Wilderness*, 357–60, 363.

[65] Rhea, *Battle of the Wilderness*, 357–58; Turner, "Battle of the Wilderness," 88 (quote), 99; Coffman and Graham, *To Honor These Men*, 204–205.

[66] Coffman and Graham, *To Honor These Men*, 204 (1st quote); service records for A. J. McWhirter; Byrd, *Confederate Sharpshooter*, 75–78; Turner, "Battle of the Wilderness," 91–92 (last quotes).

bending it down before him, when it would suddenly spring back with a vicious blow in the face of the man behind. Our clothes were literally torn to shreds."[67]

"Once the Confederate line struck," a modern historian wrote. "Union defenses toppled in sequence," one after the other. Soon Union resistance south of Plank road ceased to exist. General Hancock, the general in command of the Union forces there, told Longstreet after the war: "You rolled me up like a wet blanket."[68]

Wofford North of Plank Road

Continuing their charge, Wofford's Brigade, along with Longstreet's other brigades, dashed across Plank Road to its north side and into Wadsworth's troops. Wadsworth's men were caught facing west down the road toward the Confederates advancing from their front. Unfortunately for them, this positioning exposed their left flank also to the Confederates advancing across the road from the south. Finding Confederates to their front and now to their left, Wadsworth's Federals reacted as did those to the south of the road—they fled, "in utter confusion and rout" one Confederate later wrote. "The enemy continued to rush pell mell through the dense thicket of underbrush on the left [north side] of the road," a report from General Wofford's brigade appearing in an Atlanta newspaper recorded, "our men pursuing rapidly and pouring a destructive fire into their scattered ranks."[69]

As Wofford's men moved further north, they ran into a Federal force attempting to make a stand atop rising ground on the other side of a stream called Wilderness Run. Horatio's 16th Georgia was leading, and at a command, quickly formed a line of battle on the south side of the stream, and while lying down or kneeling, began firing at the Federals on the crest of the rise. The Federals promptly returned their fire.

After a while, the firing paused. To the great surprise of the Confederates, about halfway up the hill between the two battling forces, a Federal officer sat up from behind the root ball of a fallen pine tree where he had been sheltering. He energetically waved his hand and called out to the Confederates to come take him out of his exposed and unsettling position.

---

[67] Rhea, *Battle of the Wilderness*, 359–60 (1st, 4th, 6th quotes); Gottfried, *Maps of the Wilderness*, 194–99 (2nd quote); Adams, "In the Wilderness," 377 (3rd quote); R. K. Krick, "Like a Duck on a June Bug," 246 (5th quote); "Wofford's Georgia Brigade, *Southern Confederacy*, June 15, 1864; Priest, *Victory without Triumph*, 80–82, 89–94; *OR*, ser. 1, vol. 36, pt. 1, 1090–91.

[68] R. K. Krick, "Like a Duck on a June Bug," 247 (1st quote); Rhea, *Battle of the Wilderness*, 361–62 (2nd quote).

[69] Rhea, *Battle of the Wilderness*, 362–68 (1st quote); "Wofford's Georgia Brigade," *Atlanta Southern Confederacy,* June 15, 1864 (2nd quote); Priest, *Victory without Triumph*, 116–25, 132–33; R. K. Krick, "Like a Duck on a June Bug," 248; *OR*, ser. 1, vol. 36, pt. 1, 1062.

Colonel Stiles, the 16th's commanding officer, ordered a couple of men to go to his aid. When they reached him, they discovered that a Confederate bullet had broken two bones in one of his legs, and in an effort to flee, he had injured the leg further causing the sharp ends of the broken bones to cut into his flesh. He obviously was unable to walk, so the men lifted him and carried him back to their line.

The wounded officer was Captain Z. Boylston Adams, commander of Company F of the Fifty-sixth Massachusetts Infantry Regiment. He had been wounded while fighting Wofford's Brigade along the north side of Plank Road. As Captain Adams later wrote, Colonel Stiles "had me placed comfortably on the edge of the brook, gave me some corn from his haversack, and sent one of his men to find me a cap." (Adams's hat had been taken from him earlier by a passing Confederate soldier.)

Apparently, the Federals the 16th had been fighting now continued their retreat. For about fifteen minutes Adams and Styles talked about various things as some of the soldiers crowded around to listen. Adams wrote, "[S]uddenly an order was passed along the line. The colonel sprang to his feet, the men resumed their places and all was changed. 'Attention! Forward, Right Wheel,' and they were gone." As Adams watched them heading back to Plank Road, he "remarked the excellence of their discipline, their soldierly bearing and fine physical condition." Horatio and his company would have been part of this group of soldiers from the 16th Georgia.[70]

As Adams watched, the 16th and others in Wofford's Brigade headed back to Plank Road in order to take part in an attack on Union forces behind breastworks at Brock Road where Plank Road intersected it. There the Federals had fled as a presumed place of safety. Longstreet was planning to attack, hoping to strike before the Federals had time to regroup.[71]

Before the attack could begin, however, General Longstreet was wounded and taken from the field. Command of the corps devolved on General Richard

---

[70] Adams, "In the Wilderness," 380–84. Adams reported that the officer he met was "Colonel Styles, commanding the 14th Georgia of A. P. Hill's Corps." However, he was mistaken. The 14th Georgia, of course, was Simeon's regiment. As has been indicated in previous notes, it had been fighting the day before; earlier the morning of the 6th, it had been driven back down Plank Road. It had not been part of Longstreet's flank attack, and when the flank attack took place, it probably was still being reformed for future fighting. Also, during the Battle of the Wilderness, the 14th's commander on the first day was Colonel Robert W. Folsom (Folsom, *Heroes and Martyrs*, 153–54). After he was mortally wounded, he was succeeded on the second day by Lieutenant Colonel Richard Paul Lester (R. K. Krick, *Lee's Colonels*, 235). Neither was a Colonel Styles. During the Wilderness battle, Lieutenant Colonel B. Edward Stiles was in command of the 16th Georgia (Byrd, *Confederate Sharpshooter*, 131). It was he whom Captain Adams met.

[71] Rhea, *Battle of the Wilderness*, 366–68; *OR*, ser. 1, vol. 36, pt. 1, 1062.

Anderson. Anderson, however, had just arrived on the battlefield and was unaware of how the ground lay and where his subcommanders and troops were located. As a result, Lee himself took command of the proposed attack.

The troops, however, were in much confusion—units were almost hopelessly entangled with each other and were scattered around the densely wooded battlefield facing in various directions. It took some time for Lee to organize his men for the attack. When reorganization was complete, he positioned Kershaw's Division at the right of the Confederate line, its right flank at the railroad cut.

The attack finally began around four o'clock in the afternoon. After heavy fighting, the Confederates were repulsed. Kershaw's Division apparently took little or no part in the offensive.[72]

Meanwhile, before the Confederate attack commenced, Union General Burnside and his Ninth Corps, newly arrived, had attacked the left of the Confederate line forming for the attack. It was defended by two Confederate brigades. They were in the process of being overwhelmed by Burnside's superior force when one of the brigades' commanders asked Lee for reinforcements. Lee sent Wofford's Brigade.

Men from one of the Confederate brigades were in retreat when Wofford's Brigade, in the words of the retreating brigade's commander, "swooped down upon the enemy in the midst of their exultation and confusion, and swept them away like chaff." Soon other Confederate units also came to help. Not long afterward, darkness fell, and the day's fighting ended.[73]

Events then proceeded as described in a note below about additional events in the Overland Campaign.

There was a Brigadier Gen. Wadsworth charging down his lines trying to rally his men: Just before Longstreet's flank attack, General Wadsworth had been placed in charge of all of the Union forces north of Plank Road. At fifty-six, Wadsworth was one of the oldest men in the Union army. A wealthy landowner from New York, he had been an influential member of the new Republican Party, a strong Lincoln supporter, and the unsuccessful Republican candidate for the governor of New York in 1862. As detailed in a note to Thirza's letter above, he had been the commander of the Union attack on Thomas's Brigade that probably killed Simeon.[74]

Wadsworth...charging down his lines trying to rally his men at the time one of our boys shot him and hollered out; there Lt. is some blood in lieu of your brothers: As

---

[72] *OR*, ser. 1, vol. 36, pt. 1, 1062; "Wofford's Georgia Brigade," *Atlanta Southern Confederacy*, June 15, 1864; Rhea, *Battle of the Wilderness*, 367–74, 389–98.

[73] Rhea, *Battle of the Wilderness*, 380–87, 398–403; Perry, "Reminiscences of the Campaign," 59–62 (quote); *OR*, ser. 1, vol. 36, pt. 1, 1062; Gallagher, *Fighting for the Confederacy*, 363.

[74] Rhea, *Battle of the Wilderness*, 362; Mink, "Death, Retrieval, and Remembrance," 77–81, 90–91.

Longstreet's flank attack moved toward Plank Road, Wadsworth, waving his sword overhead and shouting from his horse, managed to get one of his regiments turned from the front to face the new Confederate threat. Then he personally began to lead the regiment forward in an attempt to blunt the new attack; however, he rode too far ahead.

Suddenly he realized that he and an aide were isolated in front of the oncoming Confederates. As he turned his horse around, a Confederate bullet tore through the back of his head and knocked him to the ground. At the same time his aide's horse was shot, and the aide was thrown to the ground beside him. The aide, however, was unhurt. Seeing his general lying with blood pouring from his head, the aide concluded he could do nothing to help. He quickly grabbed Wadsworth's horse, mounted it, and galloped away, leaving the general lying where he fell. It turned out, however, that Wadsworth, though seriously wounded, was not dead.

Confederates swept by the place where Wadsworth lay, and as Horatio wrote, soldiers stripped Wadsworth of his boots, silver spurs, gold watch, engraved field glasses, wallet and ninety dollars, and even the buttons off his coat. Finally, Confederate stretcher bearers came upon Wadsworth, who still breathed, and carried him to an ambulance. The ambulance transported him to a Confederate field hospital on the Pulliam farm about four miles from the battle site where he died two days later.[75]

It is unclear which unit fired the bullet that wounded and eventually killed the general. After the war, "four Confederate regiments claimed or were given credit for wounding the Union general," wrote a modern historian. To those four might be added a Virginia regiment, according to a former private in the 12th Virginia of Mahone's Brigade, a brigade that was part of the flank attack. He wrote that General Wadsworth "was found wounded (it is believed mortally) in that portion of the field over which the left of our brigade charged, and is therefore supposed to have been wounded by our brigade."[76]

In addition, it seems that, based on Horatio's letter, the 16th Georgia should be added to the list of those who claimed the mortal shot. A member of the 16th who knew Horatio, knew of the death of his brother, and was in close proximity to Horatio might have shot Wadsworth as Wadsworth was trying to rally his troops. Then that soldier, as Horatio wrote, called to Horatio to tell him of his revenge for Simeon. By that time in the day's fighting, elements of different

---

[75] Mink, "Death, Retrieval, and Remembrance," 93–100; Adams, "In the Wilderness," 389–94; "Wofford's Georgia Brigade," *Atlanta Southern Confederacy*, June 15, 1864; Rhea, *Battle of the Wilderness*, 364–68.

[76] Mink, "Death, Retrieval, and Remembrance," 94, 114n104 (1st quote); Bernard, *War Talks of Confederate Veterans*, 93 (2nd quote).

Confederate units had scattered and become mixed here and there with one another. Someone from Horatio's regiment, separated from most of the rest, may have ended up close to Wadsworth, shot him, and then called to Horatio of his revenge.[77]

Our Brigade has been under fire at least 15 days since the fight began: The fifteen days under fire Horatio referred to consisted of the first three battles of what became known as the Overland Campaign, plus other more minor actions between these battles. The three battles were the Wilderness, Spotsylvania Courthouse, and North Anna River. Although these battles and the time between them covered nineteen days, Simeon's regiment apparently was not under fire during that entire time.

The Overland Campaign

After the Battle of the Wilderness ended on May 6, the two armies remained in place until the night of May 7–8. Then began a series of movements by Grant and countermoves by Lee as the armies moved southeast toward Richmond in what, along with the Battle of the Wilderness, became known as the Overland Campaign. The Overland Campaign covered about forty-two to forty-six days of intense battles interspaced by periods of unnerving cannon fire and rapid marches—all of which Horatio and the Confederates endured.[78]

Throughout the Overland Campaign, as a modern historian summarized, "Grant tried to swing around Lee's right [east] flank, compelling the Confederate general to fight on the ground of Union choice. Each time, Lee beat the Federals to the spot, sometimes narrowly." At that spot, frequently, a battle ensued. As Horatio wrote more succinctly, "the enemy flanked our right and we came here to get between them and Richmond." The Battle of the Wilderness was followed by the Battle of Spotsylvania Courthouse.[79]

Spotsylvania Courthouse

As mentioned, the night of May 7–8, right after the Battle of the Wilderness had ended, Grant began what he hoped would be a march around Lee's right. Lee, however, moved his men faster than Grant, and beat him to the area around Spotsylvania Courthouse where Grant was headed.

Meanwhile, Horatio's corps had received a new commander. General Longstreet had been wounded during the Battle of the Wilderness, and General Richard H. Anderson was appointed to lead the 1st Corps in his place. Horatio and the 16th Georgia were part of Wofford's Brigade in Kershaw's Division in

---

[77] See "Wofford's Georgia Brigade," *Atlanta Southern Confederacy*, June 15, 1864.

[78] Rhea, *Cold Harbor*, xi; Nunez, *Wilderness and Spotsylvania*, 60–61; Rhea, "Overland Campaign," 293, 312.

[79] Glatthaar, "Union and Confederate Final Strategy," 57.

the 1st Corps. Under its new commander the 1st Corps was heavily involved in the fighting May 8–12 around Spotsylvania Courthouse.[80]

Lee ordered Anderson's 1st Corps, along with Horatio's 16th Georgia, to march from the Wilderness to the town where Spotsylvania Courthouse was located, a march they began the night of May 7–8. They reached the courthouse area early in the morning of May 8 to find a Confederate cavalry unit already engaged with a Union cavalry division and a Union infantry corps, both of whom advancing from the Wilderness. Not only was the Confederate cavalry fighting that force to its front, it also was threatened from behind by another Union cavalry division at the town where the courthouse was located.[81]

Anderson ordered two of Kershaw's four brigades to help stop the Union force coming from the Wilderness and Wofford's Brigade and Kershaw's 4th Brigade to confront the cavalry at the courthouse town. For Horatio, the Battle of Spotsylvania Courthouse began that morning when his brigade marched to the town and helped chase the Union cavalry away, firing at them as they rode out of town. That evening, Wofford's men were also part of the stronger Confederate force that repulsed a Union attack at Laurel Hill northwest of the courthouse.[82]

The Confederates, however, knew that repelling those attacks would not end the fighting. That night they "dug trenches with bayonets and tin cups, stacked timber and fence rails in front, and then tossed dirt against the face of the completed works," a modern historian reported. "They [then] laid logs on top to create loopholes for firing."

These rough fortifications formed a line running generally west-east. Not far from its eastern end there was a bulge in the overall line, a salient called the "Mule Shoe." Shaped like a mule or horseshoe, the salient jutted out about a mile from the rest of the Confederate line like a wide, upside down "U" that pointed generally north toward the Union forces. This bulge was particularly vulnerable because, unlike the remainder of the line, it could be attacked from three sides, west, north, and east, and its northern part could become a trap if Federals broke through on either its west or east side.

Wofford's Brigade was posted at the spot in the line just west, or to the left, of where it began to turn north to form the salient.[83]

---

[80] *OR*, ser. 1, vol. 36, pt. 2, 967; *OR*, ser. 1, vol. 36, pt. 1, 788–89, 1056–57; Nunez, *Wilderness and Spotsylvania*, 20.

[81] Rhea, *Spotsylvania Court House*, 40–53.

[82] *OR*, ser. 1, vol. 36, pt. 1, 788–9, 1056, 1065; Rhea, *Spotsylvania Court House*, 52, 65–67, 69. 82–85; "Woodford's Georgia Brigade," *Southern Confederacy*, June 15, 1854; Gallagher, *Fighting for the Confederacy*, 367–68.

[83] Rhea, *Spotsylvania Court House*, 89–91 (quote), 166; Gallagher, *Fighting for the Confederacy*, 367, 372; Dowdey, *Lee's Last Campaign*, 195–97; Byrd, *Confederate Sharpshooter*, 138; Wert, *Heart of Hell*, 40.

Little fighting of consequence happened on that line on May 9, but on May 10, the Federals attacked. At first light they began probing the part of the line defended by Wofford's Brigade and others seeking a weak spot. They were repulsed, however, with heavy losses, and late in the morning, they gave up, temporarily.[84]

That evening, the Federals struck again. Now reinforced, they concentrated more on the Mule Shoe salient just to the northeast of Wofford's Brigade, but they also struck the brigade itself. A reporter from the *London [England] Morning Herald* wrote that Wofford's Brigade, including Horatio, "received the shock [of the Union attack] in terrible force but could be seen...to hold its ground as steadily as if it were on a dress parade. Rapidly and regularly it threw up cloud after cloud of smoke, and the flash of its fire burst along its front every few minute." After fierce fighting, again the Union attacks were repelled.[85]

The Mule Shoe Again, in Strength, and the Bloody Angle

The following day, May 11, Grant wanted to renew his attack, but his troops were exhausted and the battlefield was deluged by a violent rainstorm accompanied by heavy wind and hail. Grant chose to wait. He used the day instead to prepare plans for a concentrated attack the following day on the Mule Shoe salient. He decided to strike all three of its sides at once.[86]

The attack began with a Union charge at 4:35 on the foggy morning of May 12. To the Confederates behind the earthworks, the Federal soldiers suddenly appeared in front of them as "indistinct, specters emerging from the early morning gloom," wrote a historian.[87]

This initial Union charge forced the Confederates back and propelled the Federals beyond the Confederate earthworks on all sides of the salient, west, north, and east, and into the salient itself and its rifle pits. A Confederate counterattack, which included James Neal's 38th Georgia, pushed them to the upper (north) part of the salient, while other Confederates frantically began building a second line of defense across the salient's southern base. Grant responded by pouring in more Union troops.

For much of the morning, the opposing sides struggled in face-to-face, hand-to-hand combat inside and outside the salient. "A dense, surging mass" of men fired pistols and muskets point blank, swung muskets like clubs or threw them, bayonets first, like harpoons. Neither side, however, dominated the other.[88]

---

[84] Rhea, *Spotsylvania Court House*, 121–30.
[85] Ibid., 161–85; "Another Interesting Letter," *Confederate Union*, June 21, 1864.
[86] Rhea, *Spotsylvania Court House*, 212–19; Byrd, *Confederate Sharpshooter*, 139–40.
[87] Wert, *Heart of Hell*, 85.
[88] Rhea, *Spotsylvania Court House*, 232–66 (quote 251); Byrd, *Sharpshooter*, 140; R. K. Krick, *Civil War Weather in Virginia*, 123–24; Gallagher et al., *Civil War*, 197.

Particularly hard hit by the Union attacks was an angle on the western side of the salient known later as the "Bloody Angle." Lee quickly realized his men there were being pushed back and sought reinforcements.

He extended the lines of Kershaw's Division, including Wofford's Brigade and Horatio's 16th Georgia regiment, toward the salient, even while the division itself was under attack. With this shift men from the division replaced two brigades of another division that were closer to the salient. Those closer brigades dashed to the aid of the defenders at the Bloody Angle.[89]

Only for a moment, however, did these reinforcements halt the advance of Grant's men. Realizing his earlier reinforcements had been inadequate, Lee ordered Wofford's Brigade to rush into the angle. Two regiments of the brigade, the 18th and 24th Georgia, led the advance, and the remainder of the brigade, including the 16th Georgia, followed. The first two regiments hit the right flank of the Union forces within the breastworks, helping drive them back from ground they had captured earlier. Then the 16th joined the fight.

By now a driving rain had begun falling. A Confederate from another brigade, rushing into the salient about the same time, later described the scene: "The trenches, dug on the inner side [of the breastworks, the Confederate side] were almost filled with water. Dead men lay on the surface of the ground and in the pools of water. The wounded bled and groaned, stretched or huddled in every attitude of pain. The water was crimsoned with blood.... The rain poured heavily, and an incessant fire was kept upon us from front and flank." He continued, "At one or two places, Confederates and Federals were only separated by the works, and the latter not a few times reached their guns over and fired right down upon the heads of the former."

However, as the Confederates reinforced their men in the angle, Grant reinforced his. Once again he thrust more troops into the salient and the angle.

In the rifle pits, at the log and dirt breastworks, and all around and among the 16th Georgia, Union and Confederate soldiers fought each other in a "seething, bubbling, roaring hell of hate and murder," one veteran remembered. Another wrote, "Nothing can describe the confusion, the savage blood-curdling yells, the murderous faces, the awful curses, and the grisly horror of the melee." A historian wrote of the fighting at the Bloody Angle, "These were the red hours of the conflict, hours no man who survived them would forget, even in his sleep, forever after. Fighting thus at arm's length across that parapet, they were caught up in a waking nightmare...." For the remainder of the day, the Confederates—

---

[89] Rhea, *Spotsylvania Court House*, 247, 255–61; Glatthaar, *General Lee's Army*, 369; *OR*, ser. 1, vol. 36, pt. 1, 1072.

Wofford's Brigade, the remains of earlier brigades, and additional reinforcements who were rushed in—held their ground.[90]

The fighting slacked off after dark but still continued until around three o'clock in the morning of the 13th. Then as officers whispered orders along the ranks, weary Confederates withdrew to the new line of entrenchments that finally had been prepared across the base of the Mule Shoe salient. Battle had been continuous for close to twenty-four hours.

"Everyone looks as if he had passed through a hard spell of sickness, black and muddy as hogs," one Confederate stated. Another from Mississippi wrote, "No Mardi Gras Carnival ever devised such a diabolical looking set of devils as we were. It was no imitation of red paint and burnt cork, but genuine himan gore and gun powder smoke."

They left behind, as one Union soldier recorded later, "Dead and dying heaped in piles." Some piles were several bodies deep with men wounded, but still living, lying beneath several layers of the dead. "Brush and logs were cut to pieces," and "[l]arge standing trees were literally cut off and brought to the ground by infantry fire alone, their great limbs whipped into basket stuff that could be woven by the hands of a girl." [91]

At night, after the battle was over, a private from Georgia later wrote that:

> [O]ne of our bands began to play "The Dead March" just in the rear of the "death angle." You could hardly ever hear a man speak, and it seemed that we all wanted to shed tears of real sorrow; some that had lost relatives or dear friends did have to wipe their eyes. When our band ceased playing, one of the Union bands played "Nearer, My God, to Thee;" then our band began to play "The Bonny Blue Flag," after which the Union band played "The Star Spangled Banner;" then our band played "Dixie Land," and the Union band finally struck up "Home, Sweet Home;" this probably brought tears rolling down many powder-blackened cheeks in both armies.[92]

Losses

In the ten days of marching and fighting since the Union army began maneuvering to cross the Rapidan River on May 3, the Federals had lost an estimated thirty-three thousand men dead, wounded, or captured, or 28 percent

---

[90] Caldwell, "Bloody Angle," 125–26 (1st and 2nd quotes); Rhea, *Spotsylvania Court House*, 266–307 (3rd and 4th quotes, 293); *OR*, ser. 1, vol. 36, pt. 1, 1057; "Wofford's Brigade," *Southern Confederacy*, June 15, 1864; Foote, *Civil War*, 3:221(5th quote), quoted in Gallagher, *Enduring Civil War*, 153.

[91] Wert, *Heart of Hell*, 176 (1st and 2nd quotes); Rhea, *Spotsylvania Court House*, 236 (3rd quote), 266–311(5th quote, 292); Gallagher, *Fighting for the Confederacy*, 378–79 (4th quote).

[92] Nichols, *Soldier's Story of His Regiment*, 159–60 (quote); Rhea, *Spotsylvania Court House*, 176–77.

of the men they started with. During the same period, the Confederates had lost about twenty-three thousand men, or a third of their force, a slightly greater percentage of men lost than Grant. At the end of the period, the Confederates only had some forty thousand men to the Union's roughly seventy-three thousand.[93]

For the period May 6–16, which included the Wilderness and Spotsylvania, the 16th Georgia lost twenty-one killed and fifty-four wounded. Of those losses, Horatio's Company was fortunate to lose only one killed and eight wounded, although of the wounded, three later died of their wounds and one had to have a foot amputated.

It is difficult to determine how many men were serving with Horatio's regiment and company then and what percentage the losses may have been of the men available. In spring 1864, another Georgia regiment listed 425 men on its rolls. A Virginia company listed eighty on its, a number that probably was high. Assuming the same number were available to serve in Horatio's regiment and company, the losses would be 18 percent of the regiment and 11 percent of the company.[94]

Grant Tries Once More

For the next several days, May 13–17, Grant shifted forces back and forth along his front near Spotsylvania seeking to attack Lee at his weakest spot. Lee shifted forces along his entrenched line to counter Grant's movements, including at one point shifting Horatio's division from the left of the Confederate line to the right. Tired Union troops moving in darkness, rain, and mud delayed Grant's movements to the extent that Lee was able to get his men in position to foil Grant's plans. During this period, as with all periods throughout the Overland Campaign, when the Union army was not attacking in force, the Federals were subjecting the Confederate lines to continual "bitter sharpshooting and angry artillery practice," a Confederate officer observed.[95]

On May 18, the rain let up, and Grant decided to attack, primarily the Confederate left wing. His assault began with artillery bombardment at four in the morning, and shortly after, the infantry moved out toward Lee's earthworks across some of the same ground they had covered on May 12. The Confederates were ready for them with cannons and muskets. Crossing a long distance in broad daylight, the Union soldiers were slaughtered, and, by nine o'clock, Grant called

---

[93] Rhea, *Spotsylvania Court House*, 319, 324; Rhea, *To the North Anna River*, 19.

[94] "Sixteenth Georgia Regiment," *Southern Watchman*, July 27, 1864; service records for G. A. Delay, Aaron Eades, D. A. Hughey, and J. J. Melton; Glatthaar, *General Lee's Army*, 401–402.

[95] Rhea, *To the North Anna River*, 65–128; Gallagher, *Fighting for the Confederacy*, 373 (quote).

off the offensive. Lee had an easy victory. Horatio's regiment at the opposite part of the Confederate line had a comparatively light day.[96]

Finally, Grant realized it was fruitless to attack the Confederates again at their current location. A *New York Times* reporter wrote, "[J]ust in proportion as we [the Union forces] stretched to the left, Lee extended his right to conform to our line, and intrenched himself, till finally he came to have a front practically impregnable." And as Horatio recorded, "we have not attack[ed] the enemy, we let them charge us and then O! love they taste the dirt."[97]

To the North Anna River

On May 19, Grant began to move his army on another march to the east and south around Lee's right wing and between Lee and Richmond. Again, as there had been a race from the Wilderness to Spotsylvania, Grant and Lee raced to another spot, the North Anna River. In particular, both recognized the importance of Hanover Junction, a railroad junction just south of the North Anna and about twenty-five miles north of Richmond. There a railroad from the Shenandoah Valley joined a rail line to Richmond. If Grant could seize this junction, he could cut off a Confederate army in the Valley from Lee's army, with serious consequences for the Confederacy. He also could prevent supplies from the Valley getting to Lee.[98]

But again, Lee deduced Grant's plans, and when Grant reached the North Anna, he found Lee already set and heavily fortified on the river's opposite (south) side. Lee had arranged his defenses in the shape of an inverted "V" with the apex of the "V" pointing toward the North Anna River and the Union Army. Anderson's Corps, including Horatio's regiment, was entrenched behind earthworks on the right (east) side of the "V," with its left wing at its apex and anchored on bluffs overlooking the river. The remainder of its line extended southeast to Telegraph Road, a major road connecting Richmond to the north, the I-95 of its day.[99]

The Confederates were learning earthwork construction by experience. Generally, they built barricades of packed dirt made higher with logs or sticks, under the highest of which narrow slits were left for the men to shoot through and remain protected. Behind these earthworks were trenches where defenders could load in relative safety. Ledges were placed along the bottom of the trenches onto which a Confederate could step, stand, aim, and shoot. Stuck into the front side of the works were rows of felled trees, one end lodged in the earthen walls and the other sharpened and pointed outwards towards an approaching Union

---

[96] Rhea, *To the North Anna River*, 127–55.
[97] Ibid., 155.
[98] Ibid., 156–260.
[99] Ibid., 258–61, 320–27.

soldier. These sharpened trees would force that Union soldier to hesitate before scaling the earthworks, making him a better target, and would hinder him if he continued forward. In addition, at strategic points along the line, artillery was placed and fortified, ready to fire.[100]

The morning of May 24, Grant attacked all along the Confederate line, including opposite Anderson's Corps and Horatio's company. Anderson's men inflicted severe losses on General Winfield S. Hancock's units that attacked their position. "Nowhere had Hancock seriously threatened their line," a modern historian summarized the effectiveness of Anderson's defense. Again, the Union was repulsed.

One Confederate officer later reported that Grant lost an estimated 570 killed and 2,100 wounded at North Anna, while the Confederate losses were estimated to be about 300 killed and 1,500 wounded. This ratio of losses was not the ten to one that Horatio wrote resulted when the Federals "charged our works," but it favored the Confederates.[101]

The next day, May 25, Grant spent probing the Confederate line. As a result, once again he determined, as he had at Spotsylvania, that Lee's position was too strong to be attacked successfully. The following day, Grant began to withdraw. Again he was moving his men east and south.[102]

May 25 was quiet enough to give Horatio an opportunity to write this letter about some of the happenings of the last fifteen days.

Horatio

near Gains farm
Camp 16th Ga Rgt
Sunday June the 5th 1864
Dear Mother I am still a live and healthy
on the 1st and 3rd we fought very hard. lost 51 men in our Rgt. the enemy acknowledge Theirs are thought to be 10,000. ours will not excede 1,000. if the yanks continue to charge our works we will kill all of them.
H. J. David
Write very often to me and send paper

---

[100] Ibid., 131–32, 337–38.

[101] Ibid., 325–53 (quote, 349); Gallagher, *Fighting for the Confederacy*, 391. Rhea reported that "Casualties reported by Confederate and Union sources varied widely" (*To the North Anna River*, 445n32).

[102] Rhea, *To the North Anna River*, 355–62, 367.

Notes

near Gains Farm: This area is better known as Gaines Mill. It was about seven or eight miles northeast of Richmond near Cold Harbor. Two years earlier, on June 27, 1862, the Battle of Gaines Mill, Lee's first great victory, had been fought at this place as part of the Seven Days Battles described in chapter 12.[103]

After the stalemate at the North Anna River as described in a note to the previous letter, Grant again attempted to get around Lee's right flank and on to Richmond. For most of the week May 26–June 1, the armies drifted slowly to the southeast toward Richmond with Lee continuing to place himself between Grant and Richmond until both armies met at Cold Harbor.[104]

on the 1st and 3rd we fought very hard: This fight was the Battle of Cold Harbor. Old Cold Harbor was described by a modern historian as the site of

> a seedy-looking tavern, squatting by a dusty crossroads 8 miles from Richmond.... There wasn't a harbor for miles and it was anything but cold. It was the only Cold Harbor in the United States, although there were many Cold Harbors on the stagecoach routes along the Thames River in England. The name indicated a place to get a bed for the night and something cold to drink, but not hot meals.

This unlikely-named place was possibly Grant's last chance to flank Lee and get between him and Richmond. If Grant were to try again and Lee were to beat him to the next spot, Lee would be in the entrenchments around Richmond with other Confederate soldiers, which Grant did not want.[105]

June 1

The morning of June 1, Horatio and the 16th Georgia were still in Wofford's Brigade in Kershaw's Divison. That morning, Kershaw's old brigade, now under General Lawrence M. Keit, led an attack against three brigades of dismounted Union cavalry near Old Cold Harbor. The attack was repulsed with only Kiet's and one other brigade of the division being engaged.

Wofford's Brigade was uninvolved in the morning fight. After this brief engagement, the whole division retreated and began to construct entrenchments on the left or northern part of a new Confederate line that ran north-south, slightly west of Old Cold Harbor. A division led by General Robert F. Hoke formed the right or southern part of the line. Richmond lay to the southwest.[106]

During that afternoon, the Union gathered its forces to attack Lee's north-south line head-on. About six o'clock, its attack commenced. Despite what

---

[103] Gallagher et al., *Civil War*, 199.
[104] Rhea, "Two Generals Who Resist Each Other," xx (map).
[105] Cullen, "Richmond National Battlefield Park," 29–30.
[106] Rhea, *Cold Harbor*, 195–203; *OR*, ser. 1, vol. 36, pt. 1, 1059.

Horatio wrote, this initial fight did not go well for Wofford's Brigade. It was positioned on the far right of Kershaw's Division, facing the enemy gathering to the east. Its own right flank was on the edge of a roughly seventy-five-yard wide ravine with a stream running through it. (The stream was called Bloody Run, named for two much earlier battles involving colonists and Indians.)

Three of General Hoke's four brigades manned the heights further to the right on the opposite side of the ravine. The ravine itself was defended initially by Hoke's 4th Brigade positioned about 150 yards to its front. Before the battle began, however, Hoke moved this brigade from the front of the ravine to the heights on the ravine's south side to strengthen his other brigades there. That move exposed Wofford's Brigade's right flank to any Federal force that thrust into the largely unprotected ravine. That is exactly what the Federals did.

Union forces in large numbers fought their way into the ravine and onto the Wofford Brigade's right flank and rear. At the same time, other Federals attacked the brigade's front. Wofford's men gave way—some surrendered, but most ran. Men from the Confederate brigade on Wofford's left also rapidly retreated, and most of Hoke's nearest brigade on the opposite side of the ravine also gave way.[107]

However, enough Confederates on both sides of the ravine held together so that when reinforcements arrived they were able to counterattack. In the counterattack, the Federals were pushed back up the ravine, and most of the ground the Southerners lost earlier was retaken.

That evening, the Confederates in this sector adjusted their line and closed gaps between brigades. Lee also strengthened his position and extended it further south of the ravine. By June 3, what had been the right of Lee's army on June 1, where Wofford's and Hoke's men were, and now remained, had become the center, and that center was well dug in. Still, Grant decided to attack simultaneously all along the now six-mile-long Confederate front.[108]

June 3

The Union attack was supposed to start at half past four in the morning. In the northern sector, however, the attack was delayed for two and a half hours. Then when it came it was unsuccessful.[109]

---

[107] Rhea, *Cold Harbor*, 202, 224–33, 239, 243–50; Bohannon, "Breastworks Are Good Things to Have on Battlefields," 118–19; Sanders, "Charles Sanders to His Sister," 297–98; *OR*, ser. 1, vol. 36, pt. 1, 1059; "Battle of Bloody Run," Wikipedia, https://en.wikipedia.org/wiki/Battle_of_Bloody_Run, accessed July 24, 2020.

[108] Rhea, *Cold Harbor*, 253–56, 264–65, 284–86, 291–95, 307–309, 312–17; Byrd, *Confederate Sharpshooter*, 145; Bohannon, "Breastworks Are Good Things to Have on Battlefields," 119–23; Rhea, "Overland Campaign," 307–309.

[109] Rhea, *Cold Harbor*, 309, 312, 318–19, 368–74, 379–82.

In the center part of the line, where Kershaw's Division and Horatio were positioned, the attack began roughly on time. Even there some of the Union units advanced tentatively and stopped well short of the Confederate line, halted by the strength of the entrenched Confederate defenses. It was in front of brigades from Kershaw's and Field's divisions, however, that the Federals advanced with the most energy and where they suffered probably the largest percentage of casualties for the number of men involved.[110]

There the Federals faced the same ravine along Bloody Run they had faced on June 1. It was shaped somewhat like a funnel, with a wide mouth that tapered to a narrower end. The wide mouth faced east toward the Federals.

On June 2 and into the night the Confederates had entrenched on both sides of the ravine. They also dug trenches across its base, the narrower end, blocking its use as an exit. They then manned their trenches heavily with infantry and with artillery double-shotted with canister—this time facing into the ravine as well as to the front. In addition, the ravine ground was swampy, slowing Union men trying to advance through it, and ravine's sides were thick with trees, making visibility to the front and sides difficult for men in the ravine.[111] Unknowingly, the Federals advanced directly into this trap. The Confederates opened fire.[112]

Wofford's Brigade was in reserve behind the front firing line, but they weren't idle. When the firing began, they passed loaded muskets to the men in the firing line, who in return passed back their empty muskets to be reloaded and then handed forward in exchange for the original guns, now empty and in need of reloading.[113]

This rapid firing overwhelmed the advancing Union men. "Men bent down as they went forward, as if trying, as they were, to breast a tempest," a Federal soldier remembered. "The files of men went down like rows of blocks or bricks pushed over by striking against each other." This onslaught came "midst deafening volleys of musketry, thundering artillery, and the wild, mad yell of battle," wrote another. The attackers' situation was desperate. "We couldn't retreat without being killed," recalled a soldier from Massachusetts, "and to stand where we were meant death."[114]

"It was deadly and bloody work," a Confederate gunner recorded. "They [the Federals] were a helpless mob now; a swarming multitude of confused men. [They] simply melted away under the fury of our fire." "I had seen the dreadful carnage in front of Marye's Hill at Fredericksburg, and on the 'old railroad cut'

---

[110] Ibid., 348–64; Byrd, *Confederate Sharpshooter*, 145.

[111] Rhea, *Cold Harbor*, 307–309, 348–51; Law, "From the Wilderness to Cold Harbor," 138–39; Gallagher, *Fighting for the Confederacy*, 405–406.

[112] Rhea, *Cold Harbor*, 351–59.

[113] Ibid., 350; G. J. Smith, *"One of the Most Daring of Men,"* 126.

[114] Rhea, *Cold Harbor*, 353 (1st and 2nd quotes), 356 (3rd and 4th quotes).

which Jackson's men held at Second Manassas," Confederate General Evander Law recollected. "[B]ut I had seen nothing to exceed this. It was not war; it was murder."[115]

Before eight o'clock that morning, the battle, in effect, was over, but only after the stubborn Union army had made fourteen assaults on the Confederate line.[116]

the enemy acknowledge Theirs [losses] are thought to be 10,000. ours will not excede 1,000: Horatio appears to refer to the losses for fighting on June 1 and June 3. A modern historian has examined the casualty figures reported by the participants and estimated that on June 1, the Union lost about twenty-two hundred and on June 3 lost about six thousand for a total for the two days of eighty-two hundred. The Confederates lost on June 1 about eighteen hundred and on June 3 between one thousand and fifteen hundred for a total for the two days of about thirty-one hundred.[117]

The Union losses were not the ten to one that Horatio reported; they were closer to two and a half to one. Horatio, however, may have been thinking only of the comparative losses on June 3. Then the losses were a little more uneven, about four and a half to one.

Pillina Bell

Chulafinnie, Ala July the 9 1864
Dear Mother

We received your kind letter of June 1st some time since but as I started you a letter the same day you wrote yours to us I thought I would wait a while.

We were are all grieved very much when we got your letter and learned Brother Simeon was killed, poor fellow. I get out of my mind. I do not expect there ever was a sister treated more kindly by a Brother [than] I was by him. I never can forget it.

We are all well. I am not stout though keep [my energy] up only when I ly down to rest.

Dr. says there is about a half a wheat crop. Our[s] is tolerable good. the prospect for corn is fine though the dry weather could ruin the corn yet. our indigo looks very well. a great many failed to dye with there mud last year. I think it was because they did not understand manuering of it.

I wish you would send me a scrap of Janes black & pale blue mixed. if Dr likes it I will make him a coat. also [send] directions.

---

[115] Ibid., 356 (1st quote); Law, "From the Wilderness to Cold Harbor," 141 (2nd quote).
[116] Law, "From the Wilderness to Cold Harbor," 142; Byrd, *Confederate Sharpshooter*, 145.
[117] Rhea, *Cold Harbor*, 266, 268, 382.

I cant write you any thing that would interest you this morning & so no more. write as soon as get this. let me hear from Sister Mary & Fannies families from Ratio & Dr. Elie.

Dr and the children join me in love to you all. as ever your devoted daughter
P C Bell

give me ratio address
let me know [where] Brother S B
was buried

Notes

Dr.: He is Pillina's husband, Dr. Raymond Bell.

A great many failed to dye with there mud last year. This sentence possibly means that many failed to make indigo dye from there mud, or paste, last year. Producing a paste from the indigo plant is a part of the process of producing indigo dye.[118]

Janes: This term refers to the cloth that was used to make the blue jeans of that period.[119]

Dr. Elie: He is Dr. Manning Alexander.

Horatio

Camp 16th Ga Regt
Petersburg Va
June the 28th 1864
Dear Mother.

As Mr. Harrison is going to start home this morning I will write a short letter and send by him to be mailed some where on the rout as one of the railroads is in critical position.

I have no news of importance to communicate to you. the enemy is lying still at present, but keep up a continual sharp shooting and cannonading but with little effect.

Mr. A [illegible] of the 24th Ga Rgt started home yesterday, and I sent by him the hat of Brother S. B. D. as there was no chance to send it to Fanny, and I sent his packet Book containing $167.50 and papers by

[A second page begins here. In a blank space at the top of that page above the ruled lines the following is written.]

167½
80

---

[118] "The Process: Indigo from Plant to Paste," Kindcraft, https://thekindcraft.com/the-process-indigo-from-plant-to-paste/, accessed July 28, 2020.

[119] Drake, *What Did They Mean by That?*, 168.

247½"
Mr. N. A. Robinson, and directed him to leave it with Mr. D. R. Lyle of our county, pleas get it and take care of it for his wife. The book when given to me, contained $247 ½ and some shin plasters that were useless. at the time my self and company were out of money, and I kept 80 dollars for our use, and put my note for 60 in the Book, and will send in this letter one for 20.

If I am able to draw all my wages at one time, I will send it immediately to her. Pleas send all the things to her as soon as possible. There was no chance for me to send it to Fanny, and it would have been in danger if I had kept it here. This leaves me in excellent health.

H. J. David

Notes

Petersburg: Petersburg was twenty-three miles south of Richmond on the Appomattox River. Vital road and railroad supply lines both for the Confederate capital and for Lee at Cold Harbor ran through the city.

After the Battle of Cold Harbor, Grant planned to continue his attempt to move around Lee's right flank. This time, however, he decided to move his army completely around Richmond all the way south to Petersburg, placing his men behind both Richmond and Lee. He then could attack and capture Petersburg, cut those supply lines, and force Lee to abandon both his strong position at Cold Harbor and Richmond itself.[120]

By June 15, Grant had moved one army corps to a position from which it could launch an attack that day on the Confederates in Petersburg under General P. G. T Beauregard. Beauregard's men were protected by trenches that completely encircled Petersburg except for a stretch that ran along the south bank of the Appomattox River. The Federal attack began shortly after seven o'clock that night, but after an initial success, the advance was ended by darkness.

During the night and the following days, Grant transferred virtually all his men from Cold Harbor to the Petersburg area. They attacked the Confederates there again on June 16 and 17 with little success. Lee, somewhat belatedly, realized Grant's intentions and on the June 18 began transferring his own troops from Cold Harbor to the defense of Petersburg.[121]

At three o'clock in the morning of June 18, Kershaw's division and Horatio's 16th Georgia left the Gaines Mill area for Petersburg. They were the first of Lee's force to be transferred there, and they arrived later in that morning, giving General Beauregard much needed reinforcements. Soon after arriving, they went into

---

[120] Lykes, *Campaign for Petersburg*, 7–9; Rhea, *On to Petersburg*, 24–27, 62–65, 310–11.
[121] Lykes, *Campaign for Petersburg*, 10–17; Rhea, *On to Petersburg*, 319–20; Beauregard, "Four Days of Battle," 540–44.

the front line trenches.[122]

That day, several Union assaults on the reinforced Confederates again were ineffectual. By the time Horatio wrote this letter on June 28, the situation at Petersburg had evolved into a Union siege of the Confederates fortified around the city plus Union cavalry thrusts against the southern railroads.[123]

the enemy is lying still at present, but keep up a continual sharp shooting and cannonading but with little effect: This is a good description of the events from the time Horatio's regiment arrived in the trench line at Petersburg and the time he wrote this letter. Wofford's Brigade, of which the 16th Georgia was a part, was in the line the whole time and not relieved until the day after Horatio wrote.[124]

D. R. Lyle: He was Dilmus Reid Lyle, a forty-eight-year-old merchant living in Jackson County. He had been one of three representatives of Jackson County at the convention to decide whether Georgia should secede. At the convention in January 1861, he voted for the Ordinance of Secession. His wife presented the flag to Horatio's company, the Centre Hill Guards, as they prepared to leave for the war. Horatio's brother, Tom, gave the response on behalf of the Guards.[125]

Mr. N. A. Robinson: He probably was related to one of the several Robinsons from Gwinnett County in Company I of the 16th Georgia. Gwinnett joins Jackson County to the south.

He may even have been the thirty-one-year-old Private A. N. Robinson of Company I who had a wife and three small children living in Gwinnett County. In the next letter, Horatio refers to Robinson as "Mr. A. N. Robinson." However, it seems unlikely that Lieutenant Horatio would have referred to a Private Robinson as "Mr."[126]

Mr. Harrison and Mr. A: They have not been identified.

shin plasters: Originally "a plaster or poultice for use on sore shins." It also came to mean paper money whose worth had diminished to less than a dollar, that is, to so little value that it could be used as shin plasters.[127]

---

[122] Beauregard, "Four Days of Battle," 540–44; *ORS*, pt. 1, vol. 7, ser. 1, 250–51.

[123] *OR*, ser. 1, vol. 40, pt. 1, 761; Beauregard, "Four Days of Battle," 540–44; Lykes, *Campaign for Petersburg*, 15–17.

[124] Dickert, *History of Kershaw's Brigade*, 386–89; *OR*, ser. 1, vol. 40, pt. 1, 761.

[125] US Census, 1850, Jackson County; *Southern Watchman*, December 25, 1860; *Southern Banner*, January 30, 1861; Gary, Adams, and *Jackson Herald* staff, *Our Time and Place*, 1–36, ch. 11.

[126] US Census, 1850, Gwinnett County; service records.

[127] "Shinplaster," *Webster's New World College Dictionary*, 1340 (quote); Drake, *What Did They Mean by That?*, 271.

Horatio

Camp 16th Ga Rgt
Petersburg Va
June the 28th 64
D. R. Lyle: Sir—

I send [by] Mr. A. N. Robinson a packet Book belonging to the Wife of Capt. S. B. David containing 167½ dollars and one half.

Return this to my father J. H. David. he will give it to his [Simeon's] wife.

pleas call on A. N. Robinson for the packet Book as soon as you get the note. by doing so you will oblige your
   Friend
   H. J. David

Chapter 25

A Wagon Journey: Thirza and Fanny, Mid-July 1864

Manning

Aug 6th/64
My Dear [Pillona Alexander],
   Your very kind letter of 1st Aug. was received on the evening of the third- that of 24th July on the morning of the 4th inst....
   I am very sorry to here of pore Fannies condition, but I hope she will recover.... .

Note

Partial letter: The remainder of this letter is in chapter 28.

Horatio

[This letter is very badly stained and faded.]
August the 15th 1864
Dear Sister [Pillona Alexander], I received a letter from you while on the [two lines illegible]
   I was pained greatly when I read that Sister Fanny was deranged, it seemes that we have more to trouble us than any one else, but we must bear it all with fortitude. I was [illegible] surprised to hear any thing of [illegible] so much that I have become so that tears are almost forgotten to me the fountain is almost dried.
   I am sorry that I ever sent Brothers hat home. it may be possible that the sight of that injured Fanny to some extent and I also blame Mr. Harris very much for not letting her go with Mother. he must be a hard harted old fellow....

Note

Partial letter: The full letter is in chapter 27.

Manning

Aug 20/64
My Dear [Pillona Alexander]:
   ...I never was more anxious to here from you. The last you wrote you toled me about your Ma going to Forsythe. I was very fearful the Yankeys would get her horse or give her some trouble some way....

Note

Partial letter: The full letter is in chapter 28.

Excerpt from a Biographical Sketch of Thirza David (c. 1910)

At the Battle of the Wilderness, Va. May 5th 1864 Capt. S. B. David was killed. He left a wife and four small children in Forsyth County. When the wife heard of the death of her husband she became temporarily insane. Mrs. David [Thirza], learning of her unfortunate condition, determined to see her as early as possible, although in order to do she must pass through the Federal lines. With a blind horse and wagon and a small negro boy who was crippled, she set out on her errand, passing the Federal lines at Browns Bridge, Hall County, going and coming with perfect safety. With her she brought back the insane daughter-in-law and four children, attracting quite a great deal of attention along the way by the singing of the insane woman.

Notes

Biographical Sketch: This is an excerpt from a biographical sketch prepared by Gussie Carr to explain to the members of the United Daughters of the Confederacy the reason for naming the Maysville chapter of that group the "Thirza David Chapter." The chapter was formed on March 7, 1910, and the sketch probably was prepared around that time. In 1910 Gussie Carr was an unmarried schoolteacher, about twenty-six years old, living in Maysville.[1]

The sketch is based, at least in part, on an undated, handwritten paper titled "Facts gathered by Mrs. G. P. Boone concerning *Mrs. Thirza David*," in the David Family Papers at the Hargrett Rare Book and Manuscript Library, University of Georgia Libraries, Athens. Mrs. Boone was Nora Alexander Boone, the daughter of Pillona David Alexander and Dr. Manning Poole Alexander. She also was Thirza David's granddaughter. As their oldest child (b. January 17, 1859), she is mentioned frequently in letters written by the Alexanders before and during the Civil War. At the time the events recorded in the sketch took place, she would have been about five and a half years old. When she recorded those events, assuming they were prepared close to the time Gussie Carr wrote her sketch, she would have been around fifty-one years old.

In a later, typewritten version of the sketch, someone, probably Lilly Alexander Edwards, another of Thirza's granddaughters, added that Thirza kept Fanny and the children "at her home until her [Fanny's] health had been restored."

---

[1] US Census, 1910, Banks County, Georgia. The original sketch, written in pencil and signed by Gussie Carr, is in my possession. The original charter of the Maysville chapter is in the possession of Susan Gaither Jones.

When the events took place, Nora was living with her mother, Pillona. Her mother clearly knew about Simeon's wife Fanny's condition as indicated in the excerpts from Manning's and Horatio's letters to her.

Also, at that time, Pillona and Nora were living with Thirza or near her, as indicated by letters in earlier chapters of this book. Young Nora probably had seen Fanny's condition for herself. Even if she had not, she would have been told the story often as she grew older. By the time Nora wrote her paper for the U. D. C. chapter, however, the story may have become somewhat embellished with the passage of time and retelling.

The Journey: Some parts of the story can be verified. The date and place of Simeon's death is accurate (see letter from Thirza dated June 1, 1864, in chapter 24). The fact of his having four children and the place where they lived also is accurate (see letters in earlier chapters). Also, the 1860 slave schedule indicated that James and Thirza David owned an enslaved male child who then was ten years old. He would have been about fourteen when the journey took place. There was no place in the schedule to indicate whether an enslaved person was crippled.

In addition, as indicated in Horatio's letter of August 15 above, Simeon's wife, Fanny, did become temporarily insane, although apparently not directly after learning of Simeon's death. Horatio also indicated in that letter that he believed his sending Simeon's hat to Fanny may have been the final act that caused her disability. In the letter of June 28 in chapter 24, Horatio mentioned that he did not send the hat until the day before, June 27, and then he apparently did not send it directly to Fanny. It is unclear when she actually would have gotten the hat, but it would likely not have been until at least early July. (Horatio also indicated in his letter of August 15 that Pillona told him that Fanny's father, Mr. Harris, would not allow Fanny to go to Thirza's home. It seems that Mr. Harris changed his mind and that the news of his change was slow to reach Horatio. Perhaps Mr. Harris thought that Thirza might be the best person to take care of Fanny and the four children, with the younger Pillona's help.)

Did Thirza's cross the Union lines at Brown's Bridge as the sketch says? As a map of the area indicates, the best way to get between Maysville and Fanny's home in the Vickery's Creek area of Forsyth County, a round-trip of more than sixty miles, would have been by way of Gainesville and Brown's Bridge over the Chattahoochee River (a bridge is still at roughly that location). Simeon mentioned taking this route in 1850 when he returned to Cherokee County, the next county west of Forsyth. (See letter from Simeon to Thirza, February 18, 1850, in chapter 1.)

Around the middle to last of July 1864, however, the Federal lines had not extended as far up the Chattahoochee River as Brown's Bridge, which was about six miles west of Gainesville. By July 9, the Union army had crossed the Chattahoochee near Roswell, about thirty miles southwest of Brown's Bridge, and established its northernmost line there. They remained there until July 17 when they moved south, closer to Atlanta, to fight the Confederate forces there.[2]

The *Southern Watchman*, however, recorded in its July 20 edition, "Among other things, it was reported that a Yankee raid was approaching by way of Brown's bridge, a point on the Chattahoochee, between Gainesville and Forsyth. Inasmuch as we have heard nothing more of this raid, we suppose it has 'fizzled out.'" Also, the *Southern Banner* in its edition of July 20 reported, "The enemy are massing in heavy force on our [illegible] near Roswell. A small party of about two or three hundred were in Forsyth County, last week, near Brown's Bridge; supposed to be a foraging party." While not denying these reports, in later editions both papers wrote that any implication from them that those Union forces were moving toward Athens turned out to be inaccurate.

Entries in the *Official Records* tend to support the newspaper reports. On July 14, a party of four or five hundred Union cavalrymen under Colonel Charles B. Seidel of the Third Ohio left Roswell headed for Cumming in Forsyth County to confront a force of some two or three hundred Confederates that Union scouts had reported to be there. The party reached Cumming about four o'clock the morning of July 15 but found no Confederates there. Instead, according to Col. Seidel's report, they "captured a large amount of tobacco and a number of horses and mules, and returned to camp [at Roswell] the same day." When gathering these items, they did not remain solely within the limits of the town of Cumming, but ranged around in various directions seeking additional useful items.[3]

Seidel's force probably is the "Yankee raid" and the "small party of two or three hundred" referred to in the Athens newspaper reports. Although Cumming is about thirteen miles southwest of Brown's Bridge, it is between Brown's Bridge and Fanny's home at Vickery's Creek, which is several more miles southwest of Cumming. Thus, although Thirza and the group in her wagon did not cross the main line of the Union army at Browns Bridge, Seidel's cavalrymen were in the area they had to cross to get to the bridge at roughly the time they were passing through it. They may have crossed paths with them at least once, either coming from or going to Forsyth County, and that confrontation was what was recorded later. (See also the portion of Manning's letter of August 20 above. In that letter, Manning mentions receiving a letter from Lona dated August 1, in which she mentions that Thirza had gone to Forsyth County.)

---

[2] *Georgia Atlas & Gazetteer*, 20–21; *OR*, ser. 1, vol. 38, pt. 1, 70–71; Sherman, *Memoirs*, 542–43.
[3] *OR*, ser. 1, vol. 38, pt. 2, 846; Evans, *Sherman's Horsemen*, 72–74; Southern Claims Barred and Disallowed, Georgia, Forsyth County, Petition of Adaline M. Hutchins, November 15, 1873, https://www.fold3.com/image/609776 (subscription only), accessed February 1, 2016.

Chapter 26

Manning Reassigned:
Manning and Pillona, Early 1864

Manning

Camp 43 Geo. Regt
Near Dalton March 7th/64
My Dear,

I have just got to arrived at camp today. I got all through safe. I was quite sick the day I left home. Next day I was better. Yesterday I was quit sick again. I, Billy White and Lieut DeLay came together. When we got to Dalton I stayed with the bagage while they went for a wagon but I took a chill before they got back and went to the Hospital and stayed till this morning. I am feeling prety well today. I hop I will improve now.

My eggs came through all whole. Dr Galloway is looking for his leave of absence. He will be gon 14 days. If the order is not countermanded by that time I will try for one.

Our camp is about 2 miles nearer Dalton than it was before but we have about as good quarters as we had before. My mess have a very comfortable cabbin.

It is raining this evening. I will not write much this time. Write as soon as you get this. excuse this short letter. Give my love to all. Keep a full supply yourself. Most Truly,

M. P. Alexander

Notes

Dalton: The Army of Tennessee still was encamped around Dalton when Manning returned.[1]

I was quite sick the day I left home: As indicated in chapter 23, after being in the hospital at Madison and before returning to his regiment, Manning received a furlough, which he spent at home.

Billy White: He was either Sergeant William J. White of Company G, 43rd Georgia, from Jackson County, who was mentioned in chapter 23, or Private William P. White of Company I, 43rd Georgia, from Forsyth County.[2]

Lieut. DeLay: He was 2nd Lieutenant Russel V. Delay of Jackson County.[3]

---

[1] Horn, *Army of Tennessee*, 311–19.
[2] Service records.
[3] Service records.

Dr. Galloway: He was Nathan L. Galloway who had been serving at the assistant surgeon of the 42nd, but in February 1864 had been promoted to surgeon and transferred to the 43rd the same month.[4]

Manning

Camp 43 Geo Regt
Near Dalton March 11th /64
My Dear:

As I feel much better this morning than I have since I left home I will write you again. I wrote you the other day but I felt very dull and badly and did not write all I should. I have not had a chill in severel days and am improving very fast. I am now on duty. Dr. Gallaway is gon on 14 days leave of absence. He will be back about 22nd but my chance will be rather bad as all the field and staff will not be present and in that case a special application has to be made out which I don't know that I can do.

I have not got any pants yet, neither do I know that I will have an oportunity to get any. The Quartermaster has none on hand. You had as well make me some and send them by the first oportunity. Ansin Culpepper is at home but that will be very unhandy for you to get them to him. Lieut Shankle started home Thursday evening but I did not know he was going. I suppose he will be at home 10 days but I don't know whether he would be trouble[d] with them or not. I can do very well a month. If I new I would get to come home about the last of this month I would not have them sent but there is but little probability of that.

I believe I wrote you about the receipt for the money that I deposited at the bank. I left it at Mr. Newton's. any time between now and 1st of June will do to call for the bond.

We are having March weather now.

Congress has passed an act allowing officers to draw rations but we are not drawing yet. Some say they will be commuted at $250 a day which will cover the account so it wont make any difference. I believe I would rathar have the $250 than the rations for I think it will not cost that much.

Well Dear I must close. Write me often and long

Give my love to all but keep a full shair for yourself and Nora.

Most affectionally
M P Alexander

---

[4] Rigdon, *Georgia 43rd Infantry Regiment*, 60.

Notes

Ansin Culpepper: He was Private Ansel M. Culpepper of Company G, 43rd Georgia and Jackson County.[5]

Lieut Shankle: He was 2nd Lieutenant Thomas S. Shankle of Company G, 43rd Georgia and Jackson County.[6]

Receipt for the money that I deposited at the bank: The receipt reads,

> Confederate States Depository, Athens, Ga., Mch. 7 1864. This will certify, that M. P. Alexander has paid in at this Office Five hundred (500) Dollars, for which amount Registered Bonds of the Confederate States of America, bearing interest from this date, at the rate of four percent per annum, will be issued to him, under the Act approved February 17th, 1864, upon the surrender of this Certificate at this Office, with his indorsement thereon.[7]

Congress has passed an act allowing officers to draw rations: Manning probably is referring to Chapter XLV of the Statutes at Large of the Confederate States of America, Fourth Session, First Congress, 1863–1864. The chapter is titled "An Act to allow commissioned officers of the army rations and the privilege of purchasing clothing from the Quartermaster's Department."[8]

The act, approved on February 17, 1864, would allow each officer while on duty in the field one ration equal to that allowed by law to privates. The act does not mention a specific dollar amount.

Commuted at $250 a day: When something is "commuted," it means that cash is given instead of certain necessities, such as rations. Rations are food the army provides to soldiers; $250 a day sounds generous. Perhaps that is why Manning would rather have the cash. In a later letter, it seems he actually got less than that.[9]

Reassignment of Manning Poole Alexander

Head-Quarters Army of Tennessee
Dalton, Georgia
March 16, 1864
Special Orders)
No. 74)

---

[5] Service records.
[6] Service records.
[7] The receipt is in my possession.
[8] *Documenting the American South*, University of North Carolina, http://docsouth.unc.edu/imls/23conf/23conf.html, accessed March 16, 2018.
[9] Garrison, *Encyclopedia of Civil War Usage*, 53, 207–208.

XII. *Asst.—Surgeon, M. P. Alexander* is relieved from duty with the 43rd Ga. Regt. and will report to *Surgeon S. H. Stout. Med*, Direct. Hosp. Atlanta, Ga.
By Command of GENERAL JOHNSTON,
Signed Kinlock Falconer A. A. G.
"Official",

G. A. Williams

Asst. Surg. M. P. Alexander

A. A. Genl.

Thro

Lieut Genl Hoode.

[Reverse side of Special Order No. 74]

Office of Med. Lee's Hospital
Atlanta Mar 19 1864

Asst. Surg M. P. Alexander will report for duty to Surg. S. Meredith the [illegible] in charge of Hospitals at Madison, Ga.

S. H. Stout
Med Direc of Hospitals

Off Surgeon in Chg of Hospls
Madison Geo. Mch 20th, 1864

Asst Surgeon M. P. Alexander will report to Surg. J. G. Boatwright in charge of Blackie Hospital for duty in that Hospital

S. Meredith
Surgeon in Chg Hospitals

Notes

Reassignments: The result of these sequential reassignments was that Manning was reassigned from the 43rd Georgia to Blackie Hospital in Madison, Georgia. His reassignment to duty in a more permanent hospital than a regimental field hospital came about because he had been ruled temporarily unfit for field duty due to "neuralgia + intermittent fever." A modern historian wrote, "Duty in this type of hospital [a more permanent hospital] was considered less arduous than that in a field hospital, so that numerous surgeons—wounded, debilitated, ill, or overworked—were transferred there from the field permanently or for a working convalescence."[10]

"Neuralgia" was defined in 1874 as "A generic name for a number of diseases, the chief symptom of which is a very acute pain, exacerbating or

---

[10] B. Harris, *Confederate Hospitals of Madison, Georgia*, 2 (2nd quote), 45, 98 (1st quote).

intermitting, which follows the course of a nervous branch, extending to its ramifications, and seems, therefore, to be seated in the nerve."[11]

The reassignments also were necessary because the Battle of Chickamauga (September 19–20, 1863) had demonstrated the total inadequacy of the Army of Tennessee's medical department to handle the carnage left in the wake of such a large-scale battle. As a modern historian reported, the battle produced "14,474 Rebel wounded (more than twice that anticipated) and 2,500 Union wounded who fell into Confederate hands." In addition, in the weeks following the battle thousands more soldiers were disabled by sickness.

Anticipating more massive battles in the spring of 1864, medical director Samuel H. Stout began to expand the department's ability to handle the numerous casualties anticipated. In September 1863, the department's hospital system had a staff of 1,543, including 53 surgeons, 43 assistant surgeons, and 34 contract doctors. In July 1864, the staff had increased to 2,533 personnel, including 73 surgeons, 66 assistant surgeons, and 36 acting assistant surgeons. Manning was one of the new assistant surgeons.[12]

Madison, Georgia: Madison was a cotton town about sixty miles east of Atlanta, a stop on the Georgia Railway on the way to Augusta. A modern historian described it as being "well supplied with fresh water from numerous streams and springs, and situated on an elevation and surrounded by low, rolling hills of fertile farm and pastureland." Before the war, the population of Morgan County, which included Madison, was 9,997, of which 70 percent were enslaved African Americans.[13]

Blackie Hospital: Blackie Hospital was the same hospital where Manning was a patient in January as described in chapter 23. It was located in the three-story building that was the former home of the Madison Female College owned and operated by the Methodist Episcopal Church. Situated at the corner of today's Academy and Kolb Streets, it was 1/3 mile from Madison's railway depot. It contained space for approximately 250 wounded soldiers, although after big battles many more were crowded in, most of whom would arrive by rail.[14]

It had begun life in Atlanta in late 1863 as Blackie and Winship Hospital. It probably was named, in part, after George S. Blackie, who provided medical supplies to Atlanta's hospitals and worked closely with the medical director of hospitals of the Army of Tennessee. In November 1863, it was moved to Dalton

---

[11] Dunglison, *Dictionary of Medical Science*, 698.

[12] Daniel, *Conquered*, 200–12.

[13] *Georgia Atlas & Gazetteer*, 28; B. Harris, *Confederate Hospitals of Madison, Georgia*, 3, 4, 7 (quote).

[14] B. Harris, *Confederate Hospitals of Madison, Georgia*, 7, 98.

where it became known simply as Blackie Hospital. It stayed in Dalton, however, only about two weeks before again moving, this time to Madison.[15]

Manning

Madison Geo
April 11th 1864
My Dear,

    I will drop you a line this evening, but I have nothing that will interest you peticularly. I got back to Madison Thursday much easier than you got home. I have moved my boarding to Mr Cary's. I give 75 dollars per month which is much better than 150. I room there also. I furnish my own bed and get a room free of charge.

    My Commutation will average $75 per month so if I can continue to get board even at that seeming high price I will be doing as well in the way of saving money as I would in the field and infinitely better every other way. The fair at Mr Cary's is not so much after the *county* style as at Mr Thrashers but it is very good. They have plenty of milk and butter and beef so you see I am very well accomodated.

    When you send my clothing send my Bible. we are going to organize a Bible class under the supervision of Rev Mr Kindrie Baptist minister latly from Charleston S. C.

    I have but five patients. My health is improving fast. (*It didn't give me chills this time*)

Write soon
        Most truly
        M. P. Alexander

Notes

Mr Cary: He probably was Isaac L. Cary, whose wife was one of several Madison wives who sold food to Madison Hospitals. He also rented a room to an officer in the engineer corps to use as an office.[16]

Commutation: This term referred to the Confederate army's paying cash to soldiers instead of supplying such necessities as housing, food, and fuel.[17]

county style: Manning probably was referring to what today would be Southern country-style food, such as pork sausage, country ham, fried chicken, corn bread, okra, butter beans, black-eyed peas, sweet potatoes, and hominy grits.[18]

Mr. Thrasher: He probably was Early W. Thrasher, a Madison farmer who hired two enslaved women, Betty and Emanda, to Blackie Hospital to work as

---

[15] Ibid., 96–98.
[16] Ibid., 26, 165, 300, 309.
[17] Garrison, *Encyclopedia of Civil War Usage*, 53; "Commutation," *Webster's New World College Dictionary*, 302.
[18] C. Wilson and Ferris, *Encyclopedia of Southern Culture*, 614–15.

laundresses, cooks, or nurses and received $20-$25 a month for their services; Mr. Thrasher sold wood and straw to the hospitals and used his wagon to haul various commodities for them.[19]

Manning

Stout Hospital
Madison Geo July 23rd /64
My Dear,

    We are in the midst of the greatest excitement I have seen since the siege of Vicksburg. The Yankies ware at Covington yesterday at 11 oclock. they burned the bridg ove Alcova river yesterday. It is reported that they are coming here but I don't think that they will come here at present. There is a general engagment going on at Atlanta. Should Atlanta fall (which I am fully convinced it will) then this whole county will be open to the enemy. In fact we are now in the rear of Shermans army. I am very fearful that Johnstons army will be anhilated.

    We are now sending off our patients to Greensboro. There is no mail from here now. I will send this letter to Greensboro by one of the sick. We have no orders yet to evacuate the place but are expecting it every day or every hour. I don't want to be captured but should I be so unfortunate give yourself—my dear—as little uneasiness as possable. I will make it go easy.

    Dear should Atlanta go up it will be very uncertain whether we will have the oportunity to here from each other oftin as this whole county will be subject to raids

    My Dear should you fall within the enemys lines try to get along as cherfull as posable. I hardly know what advice to give you in regard to the provisions. I think I would try to conceal of a portion of the meet and flour should the enemy come in the country, provided you can do it without the negros knowing it. Give yourself no uneasyness for me. I will take care of myself.

    I have got plenty of clothing to do me next winter. I got a good pair of jenes pants from the Quartermaster for 12.00 dollars and three pair of drawers—the drawers are very good—made of good drilling—they fit me very well.

    Well my Dear I will close. I will write you again in a few days *provided* I have the oportunity to do so—Mr Shearman—my Dear may order me not to do so.

    Give my love to all—and kiss Nora for me and tell her to be a good girl.

Most Truly
M P Alexander

[The remainder of the letter is written in pencil and is now very faint.]

---

[19] B. Harris, *Confederate Hospitals of Madison, Georgia*, 6, 98, 301–304, 308.

Union Point
July 24/64

My Dear, Since writing the above we have evacuated Madison and are going to Augusta. The Yankies were in eleven miles of there when we left and from reports the Yankies are in Athens by this morning.

Dear I think it very [illegible] whether this letter reaches you [illegible]. We got off most of our hospital [illegible] off. The Blackie [illegible] got but little. Sam was left in charge of the Hospital [illegible]. I am very fearful the Yankies will get him for I think they will be there before another train can go there. I advised him to take the woods if they come there. It is sespected that our army is demoralized I will mail this here or before here some place.

Most affectionately
MPA

Notes

Stout Hospital: This was another hospital in Madison. It was named after Samuel H. Stout, the medical director for hospitals for the Army of Tennessee and was located in "a defunct factory building, most recently a prison for Federal soldiers." It also was the closest of the Madison hospitals to the railroad, and Manning probably wrote at least part of this letter from this hospital as he was supervising the evacuation his patients to Greensboro by rail.[20]

The Yankies were in Covington yesterday at 11 oclock. they burned the bridg ove Alcova river: General Sherman had sent cavalry under General Kenner D. Garrard on a raid several miles east of Atlanta. Its primary purpose was to destroy railroad bridges and tracks to prevent Lee in Virginia from sending reinforcements by rail to support the Confederates in and around Atlanta.[21]

The evening of July 21, Garrard and some thirty-five hundred horsemen left Decatur, Georgia, about five miles east of Atlanta, heading for Covington and nearby railroad trestles. (Covington was another thirty miles further southeast from Decatur, and Madison was about twenty-five miles farther east from Covington.) The next morning detached troopers rode to the railway trestle over Yellow River, west of Covington, and burned it. Another group of cavalrymen destroyed two miles of track leading into the town.

Garrard's main force arrived in Covington about midmorning. Immediately the Federals went to downtown stores and began removing "boxes, barrels, and sacks of tobacco, sugar, meat, flour, coffee, salt, soda, rice, corn, syrup, soap, candles, nails, cutlery, shoes, clothing, and yard goods," loading them into large wagons, and carrying them away. Garrard's men also burned the Covington train

---

[20] Ibid., 1 (quote), 2, 7, 451.
[21] Evans, *Sherman's Horsemen*, 89–90, 175.

depot and captured several Confederate soldiers working as orderlies in one of Covington's two military hospitals and several soldiers who were convalescing there.

Meanwhile, other elements of Garrard's unit burned the covered bridge over the Alcovy River, about seven miles east of Covington, as Manning reported.[22]

I don't think they will come here at present: Manning was correct, although many others in Madison continued to believe the Federals were coming there.

Garrard and his men left Covington late in the afternoon of the 22nd, and over the following two days continued their looting and destruction as they returned to Decatur. While proceeding to and from Decatur, in addition to burning the railroad bridges and looting the Covington stores, Garrard's men burned a locomotive, several baggage cars and flatcars, two thousand bales of cotton, and a number of buildings. They also captured 151 prisoners; seized mules, horses, watches, cash, chickens, hams, an overcoat, and other personal items from homes along their way; and freed about two hundred enslaved African Americans.[23]

There is a general engagement going on at Atlanta....I am very fearful that Johnstons army will be anhilated: On July 20, three days before the first letter was written, the Confederates launched an attack on the Union army north of Atlanta. This was the Battle of Peachtree Creek. The attack, however, was a failure. The Confederates lost more than twenty-five hundred men killed or wounded while the Union lost about nineteen hundred killed, wounded, or missing. At the end of the day, the situation of the two sides was much as it was before the attack started.[24]

The Confederates tried again on July 22, the day before the first letter was written, in what has been called the Battle of Atlanta. They again failed, losing this time approximately fifty-five hundred men. The Union lost about thirty-seven hundred.[25]

The Confederates' particularly aggressive action was under a new commander. Although Manning did not know it, on July 17, almost a week before the first letter was written, General John Bell Hood replaced General Joseph E. Johnston as the commander of the Confederate forces around Atlanta. Those forces no longer were "Johnstons army," but they were closer to being annihilated.[26]

---

[22] *Georgia Atlas & Gazetteer*, 26–27; Evans, *Sherman's Horsemen*, 90, 175–94 (quote, 182); Bonds, *War Like the Thunderbolt*, 126.

[23] Evans, *Sherman's Horsemen*, 175–94.

[24] Bonds, *War Like the Thunderbolt*, 85–111; S. Davis, "Atlanta Campaign," 80.

[25] Bonds, *War Like the Thunderbolt*, 141–76, casualty figures on 172; S. Davis, "Atlanta Campaign," 80.

[26] Bonds, *War Like the Thunderbolt*, 65–68; Wortman, *Bonfire*, 259–60.

Greensboro: This town, about twenty miles east of Madison, was the next stop to the east on the Georgia Railroad.[27]

Union Point: This town was about eight miles east of Greensboro, and it was the next stop to the east after Greensboro on the Georgia Railroad. Here the Georgia Railroad intersected with a branch line leading north to Athens.[28]

from reports the Yankies are in Athens by this morning: Although there were reports that Union forces were advancing toward Athens, and Athenians were upset, the reports were false.[29]

Sam: Sam was Samuel H. Alexander, one of Manning's younger brothers. He was a private in Company B of the 29th Georgia and thirty-one years old, married with two children, when this letter was written.[30]

He had been admitted to Blackie Hospital on December 19, 1863, suffering from "catarrhal febris" or "catarrhal fever." That term referred to a group of respiratory infections, such as the common cold, influenza, and pneumonia, characterized by a watery mucous discharge from a membrane of the respiratory system accompanied by fever.[31]

He was furloughed about three weeks later, on January 9, 1864, and then readmitted still later, on March 27. At some point afterward, Manning apparently obtained a position as an orderly for his brother. According to Sam's service record, he also had been hospitalized in early 1863 in North Carolina and even been attached for duty to a hospital in Mississippi in August 1863.[32]

---

[27] *Georgia Atlas & Gazetteer*, 28; Evans, *Sherman's Horsemen*, 292; B. Harris, *Confederate Hospitals of Madison, Georgia*, 13.

[28] *Georgia Atlas & Gazetteer*, 28; Black, *Railroads of the Confederacy*, xxv.

[29] Evans, *Sherman's Horsemen*, 191–92.

[30] B. Harris, *Confederate Hospitals of Madison, Georgia*, 409; Chaplin, *Riches of Bunyan* (Alexander family copy); US Census, 1870, Franklin County, Georgia.

[31] B. Harris, *Confederate Hospitals of Madison, Georgia*, 351, 454; Dozier, *Gunner in Lee's Army*, 116n59; Dunglison, *Dictionary of Medical Science*, 182–83, 406.

[32] B. Harris, *Confederate Hospitals of Madison, Georgia*, 106, 126, 409; service records.

Chapter 27

Horatio's Last Battle, July–August 1864

Horatio

Camp 16th ga Regt
near Petersburg Va
July the 10th 64
Dear Mother,

    I will write you a short [letter] to inform you of my condition and whereabouts, we are still lying near Petersburg, but I don't think we will remain here long for the enemy is moving in some direction. we will soon follow them, it will take but little to whip them now if we strike at the proper time and in the right place.

    The health of the men is very good, my health is as good as ever it was in my life. The wound does not hurt me much. I am able to march as far and fight as much as any body.

    Cousin Highram Bowen, son of Uncle Highram come over to see me yesterday, and we had a nice dinner composed of cabbage, squashes, bean pickles, irish potatoes, bacon, beef, cornbread, biscuits etc, etc. other nice things to tedious to mention.

    The last letter I reced from you was written the 15th 1864. write oftener and tell me about Will White and the other boys in that army, send my clothes as soon as possible.

    H. J. David

    I cant write to day and am in a great hury as I have business to attend to this morning

Notes

the enemy is moving in some direction. we will soon follow them: On July 8, Grant had ordered cavalry and an infantry corps to move south from Petersburg the night of July 10 to keep the Confederates from repairing a railroad there. Horatio may have heard of that movement. More likely, he was referring to reports in the Richmond papers that Grant was withdrawing his army. Those reports were untrue.[1]

The wound: This probably refers to the wound he received at Chancellorsville.

---

[1] *OR*, ser. 1, vol. 40, pt. 1, 37.

Cousin Highram Bowen, son of Uncle Highram: It is difficult to determine who Cousin Hiram is. Uncle Hiram Bowen did not have a son named Hiram. Perry Bowen, another of Horatio's uncles, did have a son named Hiram Cox Bowen, but his service records with the 29th Georgia indicate that he was wounded in 1863 and apparently was at home in Georgia rehabilitating in July 1864. Even if he had returned to his unit, it was part of the Confederate States' Western Army and did not fight in Virginia.[2]

Horatio

Camp 16th Ga Regt Va
near Chesterfield hights
Aug the 2nd 64
Dear Mother,

James and myself sit down to write to you all again, he arrived on the 31st July. I have had so many questions to ask, and so much to talk about that I have detained him until now. he got on safely with the clothing you sent me and when I washed and put on the clothes I was compelled to feel a little proud. I almost had to speak to tell whether it was Rash or not, I look so much cleaner than any one else that it made me feel a little shamed.

also Mother I have been told that you are suffering some uneasiness concerning me and a young lady in the settlement. I had no idea that you had any scruples about it. if I had I would have made it satisfactory to you long ago. Don't unease your self about it at all, for I care nothing about her, only the respect that I ought to have to any women. I will do as you wish. I will bring our corespandence to an end as soon as I can, for it not to be noticed. some of the family use their gab to freely anyway.

I wish [I] had been at home when that negro scruful took place. I will make some of them sing low yet about that rascality. I do hope that I will be permitted to stay at home with you soon. Then rascality must cease or blood will flow. I expect to give our honerable justice a part of my sentiment soon and a part of my little strength soon or late. Since Brother Sim is gone they think that there is no one to protect you but if I get home I will show them that there is one left that will try to defend you.

You sent word to me by Jimmy that [you] wanted me to come by to see if you were alive. Why do you send me such word as that. I would suffer my head choped off, rather than leave you without defense if the war was over.

---

[2] Service records; "Bowen Bible Records," 36–37; "The Bowen Family: Biographical Sketches, Chart III," n.p.

I must stop writing. I will write you again soon. I am to mad that I can't write with any sense. I do want you to write me every thing that takes place in the country. give my love to sisters family. Rash

Notes

near Chesterfield Hights: Chesterfield Heights was located across the Appomattox River from Petersburg, about two miles northeast of the city.

During the Petersburg siege, a Confederate artillery battery was mounted on the heights opposite the right of the Union line. Horatio's unit probably was camped behind the battery somewhere near Swift Creek.

Horatio and the 16th Georgia had settled near Chesterfield Heights after returning from the north side of the James River where they had participated in what came to be called the First Battle of Deep Bottom.[3]

First Deep Bottom

On July 23, a dozen days before Horatio wrote the letter, the 16th Georgia of Wofford's Brigade and other brigades in Kershaw's Division crossed to the north side of the James River at Chaffin's Bluff, about six miles south of Richmond and several miles northwest of Deep Bottom, where they were headed. General Lee had heard that Federals were reinforcing their units on the north side of the James at Deep Bottom and had ordered Kershaw's Division to cross the river and to "reconnoiter the enemy and ascertain his position, intentions, &c."[4]

That night after crossing the James, the division marched to an outer line of earthworks defending Richmond. The earthworks were about ten miles southeast of Richmond and extended eastward from the James River at Chaffin's Bluff about five miles to New Market Heights. To their front, south of New Market Heights, was Deep Bottom, an area at the top of a long, northern loop of the James River. Kershaw confirmed to Lee that the Federals there had constructed two pontoon bridges across the James and seemed to be making arrangements for future operations in the area. In response Lee wrote he wanted Kershaw "to endeavor to dislodge the enemy, drive them across the river, and destroy the bridges" if practicable.[5]

---

[3] *OR*, ser. 1, vol. 40, pt. 1, 273–74, 665; Abbot, *Siege Artillery*, 134; Greene, *From the Crossing of the James to the Crater*, 140, 339.

[4] *OR*, ser. 1, vol. 40, pt. 1, 211, 762; *OR*, ser. 1, vol. 40, pt. 3, 795–96 (quote); Gallagher, *Fighting for the Confederacy*, 476.

[5] *OR*, ser. 1, vol. 40, pt. 1, 806; *OR*, ser. 1, vol. 40, pt. 3, 309, 796 (quote); Dickert, *History of Kershaw's Brigade*, 389; J. Salmon, *Official Virginia Civil War Battlefield Guide*, 416–18; Greene, *From the Crossing of the James to the Crater*, 222; ORS, pt. 1, vol. 7, ser. 1, 252; Trudeau, *Last Citadel*, 142–43.

On July 25, Grant, not knowing then of Kershaw's Division's movement to the north side of the James, ordered "a demonstration" to be made on that side of the river "having for its real objective the destruction of the railroad on that side [the Virginia Central Railroad linking Richmond to the Shenandoah Valley]." Grant even thought "it was barely possible" that if the Union forces were to find the Richmond defenses in the area lightly guarded and strike "boldly," they even might take Richmond itself.

Later when he learned of Kershaw's arrival on the north bank, he still determined that the "demonstration" should go ahead with faith that his forces there would break through the Confederate lines or at least force Lee to weaken his force in front of Petersburg so that a planned attack later known as the Battle of the Crater would have a better chance of succeeding.[6]

In the fighting between Federals and Confederates that ensued on the north side of the James from July 25 through July 28, Wofford's Brigade and Horatio's 16th Georgia either served in a reserve capacity or were positioned in the rear of an advance. These roles may have been selected for them because General Wofford himself was absent on leave in Georgia to be with his wife for the birth of their third child. The brigade was left under the command of a substitute, Colonel Dudley M. DuBose from Field's division, who was generally unfamiliar with the men he now led.[7]

The fighting concluded in a stalemate. By July 29, leaders, both Federal and Confederate, realized that their opponents were more powerful than they originally had expected and the aggressive actions both had planned were unrealistic.

Lee did send reinforcements for the local commander to use in his discretion either to attack the Federals or to support defenses at Deep Bottom to protect Richmond. The local commander decided to support the defenses. Thus, for a short time, Kershaw's Division and Horatio's 16th Georgia remained in position in the line around New Market Heights before returning to the Petersburg area.[8]

For his part, Grant understood that he must abandon his plan to attack the Virginia Central Railroad and to take Richmond. However, he also realized that his ancillary goal of persuading Lee to weaken his defenses fronting Petersburg had been achieved.

---

[6] *OR*, ser. 1, vol. 40, pt. 1, 309; *OR*, ser. 1, vol. 40, pt. 2, 709; *OR*, ser. 1, vol. 40, pt. 3, 437–38 (1st two quotes), 451, 458; Greene, *From the Crossing of the James to the Crater*, 393–94, 399.

[7] Greene, *From the Crossing of the James to the Crater*, 271, 393–418; G. J. Smith, *"One of the Most Daring of Men,"* 127–29; Johnson and Buel, "The Opposing Forces at Petersburg and Richmond," 4:593; J. Salmon, *Official Virginia Civil War Battlefield Guide*, 416; Price, *Battle of First Deep Bottom*, 89.

[8] *OR*, ser. 1, vol. 40, pt. 3, 562, 593, 599, 809–16; Greene, *From the Crossing of the James to the Crater*, 413–15; Byrd, *Confederate Sharpshooter*, 148.

The night of July 28–29, Grant began moving his men back across the James River and into a support position behind the Union forces before Petersburg. It now was time to explode the mine that Grant's men had dug under the Confederate defenses at Petersburg, which Grant did the next day, July 30, and the Battle of the Crater began.[9]

James, Jimmy: This was James Neal, Horatio's cousin, who was a private in the 38th Georgia. According to his service records, he was wounded in May 11 or 12 at Spotsylvania as part of Gordon's Brigade, Early's Division, Ewell's 2nd Corps. He was sent to a hospital in Richmond and on May 26 was furloughed home.[10]

when that negro scruful took place: According to modern usage, a scuffle is "a rough, confused fight; close, haphazard struggle." The scuffle Horatio referred seems to have involved the Davids' enslaved people. Whatever precisely happened may have been the result of restlessness or rebelliousness among them due to the relative proximity of Sherman's Union army and the opportunity that posed for enslaved people to escape to freedom. In particular, there were rumors in nearby Athens during the week of July 18 that a Union raiding party was headed toward the town. Raiders never came, but according to local papers, the rumors still caused "a fearful state of excitement" in the town.[11]

Horatio

August the 10th 64

All in fine health and spirits to day. we have been fishing to day and had good luck.

H. J. David

Notes

Letter: Horatio hurriedly wrote this short note on a scrap of paper torn from a bigger piece. It now is in Hargrett Library at the University of Georgia in Athens.

Addressee: Horatio probably wrote the note to his mother.

Origin: The note was written from east of the Blue Ridge Mountains near Culpepper, Virginia.

On August 6, four days after Horatio wrote the previous letter, Kershaw's Division, including the 16th Georgia, left the Petersburg area by train on its way

---

[9] *OR*, ser. 1, vol. 40, pt. 1, 311–12; *OR*, ser. 1, vol. 40, pt. 3, 596, 599–603; Greene, *From the Crossing of the James to the Crater*, 415–20, 432ff.

[10] Rhea, *Battles for Spotsylvania Court House*, 342.

[11] "Scuffle," *Webster's New World College Dictionary*, 1307–1308; Sherman, *Memoirs*, 724–25; *Southern Watchman*, July 27, 1864; *Southern Banner*, July 27, 1864.

to support General Jubal Early in the Shenandoah Valley. Accompanying Kershaw was a cavalry division and three artillery batteries. All were under the command of General Richard H. Anderson, who, at the time he was given this command, still was serving in Longstreet's place while Longstreet was recovering from his wound received at the Wilderness.[12]

Almost two months before, General Lee had ordered Early and his 2nd Corps to leave the general Richmond area for the Valley. There they were to protect Lee's rear and flank, as well as citizens in the Valley, from a Union army that had been operating savagely in the Staunton-Lexington area of the upper Valley. Since that time, Early had defended the Valley successfully and in early July had even threatened the Union capital in Washington. In addition, his men had burned a town in Pennsylvania. In early August, however, Early had moved back into Virginia. On August 12, he had fallen back to Fisher's Hill, about two miles west of Strasburg in the northern Shenandoah Valley.[13]

On August 8, the last of Kershaw's Division arrived at Mitchell's Station on the Orange & Alexandria Railroad about seven miles south of Culpepper. They stayed in the area on August 9, 10, and 11, awaiting the arrival of the artillery and cavalry. This wait gave Horatio time to fish and scrawl this scrap of a letter. They left on August 12, heading north toward Front Royal.[14]

Horatio

Front Royal Va
August the 15th 1864

Dear Sister [Pillona Alexander], I received a letter from you while on the [two lines illegible]

I was pained greatly when I read that Sister Fanny was deranged, it seemes that we have more to trouble us than any one else, but we must bear it all with fortitude. I was [illegible] surprised to hear any thing of [illegible] so much that I have become so that tears are almost forgotten to me. the fountain is almost dried.

I am sorry that I ever sent Brothers hat home. it may be possible that the sight of that injured Fanny to some extent and I also blame Mr. Harris very much for not letting her go with Mother. he must be a hard harted old fellow

Sister we have had a disagreeable time marching to this place, but we lived highly, plenty of butter and milk apples given to us. it is 130 miles to Richmond

---

[12] Patchan, *Last Battle of Winchester*, 34–35; Dickert, *History of Kershaw's Brigade*, 416–17.

[13] *OR*, ser. 1, vol. 40, pt. 1, 1018–24; McPherson, *Battle Cry of Freedom*, 737–39, 756–58; Patchan, *Last Battle of Winchester*, 12–15, 34; *Virginia Atlas & Gazetteer*, 74.

[14] *OR*, ser. 1, vol. 42, pt. 1, 873; Dickert, *History of Kershaw's Brigade*, 417; *Virginia Atlas & Gazetteer*, 68; *ORS*, pt. 1, vol. 7, ser. 1, 253–54.

and 40 miles from this place to the line of Maryland. I do not know whether we will invade that country or not. I think we have come to this part of the state more to gather the enormous wheat crop than anything else, and to repose our worn out bodies in this beautiful valley, there is [illegible] in this country but we can soon dispatch them.

Lona some times when I think of days past, it makes me fairly shudder to think howe I have escaped, so many days of hard fighting, and not even a mark marking my clothes.

I saw James Neal as we passed through Richmond. he was waiting for a company to go with him.

If there was nothing to trouble me I would enjoy my self well here, there is a large number of [illegible] ladies here. you must not expect to hear from me as often now as when we were around Richmond. Give my love to ours and Sisters familys H. J. David

Notes

Condition of this letter: The letter is very badly stained and faded and difficult to read.

Front Royal Va: The town is in Warren County on the South Fork of the Shenandoah River about forty miles north of Culpepper and twenty-five miles south of Winchester. Kershaw's Division and the 16th Georgia had reached Front Royal the afternoon of August 14.[15]

Fanny was deranged: See the note in chapter 25 following "Note from a Biographical Sketch of Thirza David."

howe I have escaped, so many days of hard fighting: On the date of the letter, Horatio still was the commander of his company, although still a lieutenant. Because of sickness, casualties, and recruitment of a new battalion of sharpshooters from the company the year before, it was a company much reduced in numbers compared with the one hundred men authorized at the beginning of the war in 1861. One report lists the number of men in the whole 16th Georgia Regiment as only 151—seventeen officers and 134 men. If these numbers are reasonably accurate, if the regiment still was divided into ten companies, and even if the number of officers did not include the regimental staff, there would have been an average of fewer than twenty soldiers per company.[16]

there is a large number of [illegible] ladies here: The family of at least one of the ladies, Miss Sue Richardson, living on North Royal Avenue in Front Royal, fed Confederate soldiers breakfast and continued feeding soldiers throughout the day

---

[15] *Virginia Atlas & Gazetteer*, 69, 74; *OR*, ser. 1, vol. 42, pt. 1, 873; Byrd, *Confederate Sharpshooter*, 76–77.

[16] Holley, *Company K, Ramsey Volunteers*, 28.

on August 14, despite it being "hard for us to get along, everything so scarce. No vegetables."[17]

H. J. David
Lt. Co. B. 15-Regt. Ga.
Appears on a
Report of the Examining Board
in General Hospital No. 4
at Richmond, Va.,
for furloughs.

Sept. 8, 1864
Brigade: Woffords
Date of injury Aug. 16, 1864
Disease or injury: V. S. Right Temple fracturing molar bone & sight right eye
Destination: Wall Street Ga.
Time 60 days

Notes

V. S.: These initials stood for *Vulnera sclopetaria*, a gunshot wound.[18]

Date of injury August 16, 1864: What is known as the Battle of Guard Hill (or Crooked Run or Cedarville) was fought on that day. In this battle, Horatio received, as indicated in this report, a gunshot wound to his right eye.[19]

Battle of Guard Hill

General Richard Anderson, in overall command of Kershaw's Division, a cavalry division, and three artillery batteries, realized that in order to advance north of Fort Royal toward Winchester and to coordinate more easily with General Early on the opposite side of Massanutten Mountain, he would have to pass over ground dominated by Guard Hill, located a little over two miles north of Front Royal on the north bank of the North Fork of the Shenandoah River. He also understood, however, that Union cavalry occupied Guard Hill.[20]

To remedy this situation, Anderson sent a cavalry brigade to attack Guard Hill directly from the south while he assigned Wofford's Brigade of Kershaw's Division, including Horatio's 16th Georgia, to swing around to the east of Guard

---

[17] S. Richardson, "Diary of Miss Sue Richardson," 2.
[18] Dunglison, *Dictionary of Medical Science*, 934, 1111.
[19] Patchan, *Last Battle of Winchester*, 90.
[20] Hotchkiss, "Sketch of Action at Guard Hill"; Patchan, *Last Battle of Winchester*, 34–35, 73, 79–80; *ORS*, pt. 1, vol. 7, ser. 1, 254.

Hill, cross the Shenandoah River and "a deep stream with steep banks" called Crooked Run, and attack the left flank of the Union position.[21]

About three in the afternoon on August 16, the Confederate cavalry riding north crossed the North Fork of the Shenandoah, charged the Union cavalry below and atop Guard Hill, quickly dislodged them, and occupied the hill, advancing artillery to its top. The Federals reacted immediately by sending in cavalry and artillery reinforcements, including a cavalry brigade headed by General George Armstrong Custer. For the rest of the afternoon, attacks and counterattacks between Confederate and Union cavalry, mounted and dismounted, and counter artillery fire continued around the hill.[22]

Meanwhile, the soldiers of Wofford's Brigade were beginning to wade across the Shenandoah River. Custer, whose men occupied some low hills to the east of Guard Hill on the extreme left of the Union line, moved part of his artillery to a ridge overlooking first Crooked Run, and then a little farther away, the river where Wofford's soldiers were crossing. His artillery opened fire.

Wofford had noticed the repositioning of the artillery and noted also that no infantry were on top of the ridge to protect the guns, making them an especially inviting target.

Once his men had crossed the river, Wofford formed two regiments, the 16th and 24th, and Cobb's Legion into a line of battle. He held the 18th Georgia in reserve. On Wofford's order they advanced to Crooked Run, still between them and the artillery, waded across to the opposite bank, and quickly reformed in the shelter of the trees and brush that lined the bank. An open field now stretched before them leading to the ridge and the Union artillery. Wofford ordered a charge. With a shrill yell "like so many demons," his men rushed out of the sheltering trees and into the open field toward the unprotected Union guns.

Those guns, while unprotected by infantry, were not defenseless, as Wofford's men soon felt. Grapeshot and canister fired from the Union artillery tore gaps in their line. The line of veterans, however, continued forward.

As these Confederates rushed forward, the unexpected occurred. Suddenly there appeared on the ridge around and among the artillery a large number of dismounted cavalry armed with seven-shot, repeating carbines aimed their way. A Union reporter watching the action recorded, "for a few minutes there was [from the Federals] one incessant roll of musketry."

Unknown to Wofford's charging Confederates, Custer had ordered part of his cavalry to dismount and hide in a ravine behind the ridge on top of which stood his artillery. Thus, to the Georgians rapidly crossing the open ground on the other side of the ridge, they were invisible. At the right moment, the Federals

---

[21] Patchan, *Last Battle of Winchester*, 80–81 (quote).
[22] Ibid., 81–85.

"rose from the grass [in the ravine] as one man," rushed "on the double-quick" to the top of the ridge and opened fire with their rapid-shooting carbines. In the open in front of them, Wofford's men faltered. Then Custer's men on the ridge charged.

The Confederates, stunned by the onslaught of men and bullets, fell back toward Crooked Run. Short of the run and still in open ground, they were reinforced by the remaining regiment of Wofford's Brigade, which had been held in reserve, and all began to make a stand. Then, however, they received an even more terrible surprise.

Custer had positioned mounted cavalry to the right of the ridge, and he now ordered them to attack. When Wofford's men saw the horsemen swinging their sabers and charging toward them from their left across the open ground, many began to flee back to Crooked Run, throwing away their muskets as they ran. Part of the Union cavalry, however, swiftly got between the fleeing Confederates and Crooked Run, cutting off their retreat.

Some Confederates still made it safely back across to the opposite bank of the stream but some did not. Roughly 150 were captured, and a few others drowned in their haste to get across the run. Those who made it across continued across the Shenandoah River and on its other side began to regroup.

By this time, it was nearly dark, and the battle was over. To the west, the Confederate cavalry and artillery still held Guard Hill, and to the east, Wofford's remaining men, reinforced by another Confederate infantry brigade, managed to hold the fords crossing the Shenandoah. The Confederates, however, had lost three hundred irreplaceable men.[23]

The 16th Georgia had been in the front of the Confederate charge. The regimental color bearer, Sergeant Wave Ballard, holding high the regimental flag on its staff, had advanced to within a few yards of the ridge when the dismounted cavalry on top of the ridge fired and charged. Sergeant Ballard looked back and saw that except for the regimental commander, Lieutenant Colonel B. E. Stiles, and himself, the rest of the Confederates were falling back. He also saw Colonel Stiles, wounded, fall to the ground.

Still holding the flag, Ballard ran to the fallen colonel. He realized immediately that the colonel was dying. Nothing could be done for him. At that moment a Union corporal who had run forward grabbed the flag staff. Ballard quickly tore the flag from its staff, leaving the startled Union corporal holding only the staff,

---

[23] Patchan, *Last Battle of Winchester*, 85–91 (1st and 3rd quotes); Byrd, *Confederate Sharpshooter*, 150–57, 154n20; *New York Times*, August 25, 1864 (2nd and 4th quotes); *OR*, ser. 1, vol. 43, pt. 1, 439.

and sprinted back to the remainder of the regiment, bullets flying around him, one slightly injuring his wrist.[24]

At some point during Wofford's Brigade's attack, Horatio was wounded in the right temple and lost the sight of his right eye

He probably got the wound when the Union dismounted cavalry first appeared on the crest of the ridge and fired on the advancing Confederates. When the Union soldiers then charged down from the ridge, he, probably with the help of one or more of his men, already had started back toward Crooked Run with others of his brigade.

When the brigade was reinforced and then made a stand, he and the men helping him would have had enough time to make it back across the run before the brigade's retreat was cut off by Custer's charging horse cavalry. They then could have retreated back across the Shenandoah.

As it turned out, eight men in his company were captured when their retreat was blocked by the mounted cavalry. Three company men were killed, Sergeant Matthew Pentecost, Private R. M. King, and Private Morgan Watts. With the addition of Horatio, his small company of about twenty men had lost twelve, 60 percent.[25]

Soon Horatio would have been taken back to Front Royal. A woman living there wrote in her diary on August 16 that "Ambulances passed [by her house in town] with wounded till 10 o'clock at night." Another Front Royal diarist wrote that "many soldiers were brought to town, and a hospital fixed there."[26]

From Front Royal an ambulance probably took Horatio to the railroad station near Culpepper where the brigade had disembarked earlier when coming from Richmond. A train took him from there to Gordonsville, where he arrived on September 6. The same day he was sent on to Richmond. He arrived in Richmond on September 7 and was assigned to Hospital Number 4, the same hospital where Simeon was taken after he was wounded at Gettysburg.[27]

As the register entry indicates, the next day he was furloughed home. Possibly he was sent home so quickly because a little over two months earlier a special

---

[24] Holley, *Company K, Ramsey Volunteers*, 27–29; service records for Wave or Wade Ballard; Patchan, *Last Battle of Winchester*, 86–87, 508. Lieutenant Colonel Stiles later died of his wounds (*Southern Watchman*, September 7, 1864). He was the leader of the 16th during the Confederate flanking movement in the Battle of the Wilderness when he saved the wounded Union officer, Captain Adams, who had become stuck between the Union and Confederate lines.

[25] *Southern Watchman*, September 7, 1864; service records for Lt. H. J. Cox; Sergeants M. J. P. Pentecost and J. J. Wallace; and Privates L. H. Adams, M. T. Adams, S. Cook, M. A. Edwards, P. J. Hall, R. M. King, J. J. Smith, and Morgan Watts.

[26] S. Richardson, "Diary of Miss Sue Richardson," 2; Eckart, "Diary of Dr. Charles Eckart, Music Teacher," 1.

[27] Horatio's service records; chapter 21.

infirmary had been opened in one of university buildings in Athens, only a few miles from his home. Its mission was specifically to treat soldiers suffering from eye wounds.[28]

Wall Street, Georgia: This was the name of the post office in Maysville during the Civil War when the federal government no longer operated the postal system. Many letters, however, still were addressed to Maysville.[29]

Walter C. Johnson to Horatio David

Nov 19th [1864]
[Richmond area]

As I did not get to mail my letter yesterday, I will add a postscript, learned yesterday from a man who had Just come from Richmond that your Division was there, and hope it is true for we are needing help on this part of the line; last night about nine (9) o clock we were roused from our peaceful Slumber by the roar of musketry and Artillery on the right of our line, the firing was near the River but I have not heard the result of it yet, I Suppose that Some of the Pickets got lonsome, and wanted company.

Is it possiable that you cannot enjoy yourself at Home; I would like to know the reason of it. Give my respects to Relations & acquiances and Recive the same, beshure and write Soon and give me all the Inst. I directed your letter to Gillsville but thought of myself, & corrected the mistake

     Write soon
         Respectfully your
         Friend

           Walter C. Johnson
           O S Co A 11th Ga Reg

Notes

Nov 19th [1864]: The letter's date lacks a year; however, the only time the 11th Georgia was in the Richmond area in November was in 1864.[30]

Postscript: This postscript is all that has survived of this letter.

Cannot enjoy yourself at home: The beginning of the letter and any indication to whom it is addressed has not survived. In 1864, the only person in the David family who had served in the war and was then at home was Horatio David. As the order immediately above indicates, he was given leave for sixty days from

---

[28] *Southern Watchman*, June 29, 1864.
[29] Old envelopes in my possession; Dorsey, "Brick Store."
[30] Austin, *Georgia Boys with Stonewall Jackson*, 59, 70–71.

September 6, 1864, to go home. Other entries in his service records indicate that he still was in Georgia in November 1864.

Walter C. Johnson: According to his service records, he was 2nd sergeant of Company A, 11th Georgia, at the time this letter was written.

Chapter 28

Manning to Augusta, July–November 1864

Manning's Reassignment

Office Senior Surgeon
Augusta Georgia
July 30th 1864,
Asst Surgeon *Manning P. Alexander*
    Will report without delay to Surgeon Boatwright in charge of Blackie Hospital Augusta Ga for duty
    J. P. Logan
                        Senior Surgeon in Chg
                        Asst Surgeon M P Alexander
                                Augusta Ga
                     [On the back of this document]
                      Office Blackie Hospital
                      Augusta Ga July 30 1864
                        Reported for Duty
                          J. G. Boatwright
                    Surgeon [illegible] in chg

Notes

Augusta: Augusta is located on the western bank of the Savannah River across from South Carolina. It is about 150 miles east of Atlanta, 90 miles southeast of Athens, and 130 miles northwest of Savanna. Augusta then was a city of thirteen thousand inhabitants, half of whom were enslaved people.[1]

Blackie Hospital, Augusta: Blackie Hospital was removed from Madison to Augusta the night of July 23 (see chapter 26). In Augusta it occupied buildings of the "recently vacated and renovated Officers Hospital," which was said in December 1864 to be located "at the corner of Washington [now Sixth Street] and Fenwick streets, and in May 1865 as Washington and 'Wadkins' [Watkins] streets." The hospital complex was described as having "seven frame wards containing about 25 beds each" located in a semicircle around the larger main building, which was over three hundred feet long and contained more than one hundred beds.[2]

---

[1] *Rand McNally 2019 Road Atlas: United States, Canada, Mexico*; Berg, *Wilson*, 30.
[2] B. Harris, *Confederate Hospitals of Madison, Georgia*, 99–100.

Surgeon J. G. Boatwright: This was John Guerrant Boatwright. He had been the surgeon in charge of Blackie Hospital in Madison and now held the same position in Augusta.

He was a Virginian who had worked for over two years in several military hospitals in Virginia before being assigned to Blackie Hospital, then in Atlanta, in October 1863. When Manning's reassignment was made, Boatwright was thirty-three years old, a few months younger than Manning.[3]

Manning

Blackie Hospital
Augusta Geo July 31st 64
My Dear

I will just drop you a few lines this morning by Mr Willis. I have just met him and he is going home as [illegible] communication is cut between this and Macon Geo. We are still here and likely to remain as communication is cut in every direction. We are opening some buildings for hospital accommodations but there is not much probability of us having many patients soon, as we are in communication with no army except the Va army and it is not probable that we will receive many patients from there. We get no direct news from Atlanta now as all the roads are cut. Our army is in a more critical position now than it ever has been. I am very fearful they will be broken up. The Confederacy is again severed. It is feared that the raiders are making their way to Andersonville to release their prisoners.

Dear, every time I write I think it is very probable it will be the last letter I will get to you. Unless things greatly change we will certainly be cut off.

It is nearly time for the train to leave so I will close. Give my love to all. Write often Dear as long as communication remain open.

                              M. P. Alexander

[The following was written in pencil.]
P. S. Have fighting at Atlanta [by] the latest account. No peticulers known. I am in good health
M P A

Notes

communication is cut in every direction: It is a little puzzling that Manning wrote that "communication is cut in every direction," yet he wrote also that Mr. Willis was able to take a letter to Lona in Jackson County by train and he asked Lona to write often "as long as communication remain open." Probably he was thinking in the first instance of communications with the Confederate army in

---

[3] Ibid., 96.

and around Atlanta. That army had been the source of hospital patients while the hospital was in Madison, but it could be a source no longer if the Union army had severed communications with it. At the same time, however, Manning believed that the railroad between Augusta and Athens was still open.

It is feared that the raiders are making their way to Andersonville to release their prisoners: Andersonville, Georgia, a little over one hundred miles southeast of Atlanta, was the location of an infamous Confederate prison for captured Union soldiers. There were approximately thirty thousand enlisted men held there.[4]

When Union raiders under General George Stoneman Jr. were in Covington, Georgia, on July 28, they boasted loudly about proceeding to Andersonville to free the prisoners. Later the same day, the raiders left Covington headed south in the direction of Andersonville. Word of this boasting and the direction the raiders were heading may have been the source of Manning's information.[5]

On their way to Andersonville, however, the raiders came to Macon, about sixty miles north of their destination. There a strong Confederate force prevented them from proceeding further south. As a result, Stoneman decided he had done all he could and began retreating to Atlanta. Some of his raiders, however, never made it and on the way back were captured and later imprisoned in Andersonville.[6]

fighting in Atlanta: On July 28, three days before the letter was written, the Battle of Ezra Church, or the Battle of the Poor House, had been fought, and the Confederates had been beaten badly. The bombardment of Atlanta itself had begun on July 20 and was continuing.[7]

Manning

Blackie Hospital
Ga
Aug 6th/64
My Dear,

Your very kind letter of 1st Aug. was received on the evening of the third—that of 24th July on the morning of the 4th inst.

Dear, you may be sure that I was highly delighted to here from you. It is always of great pleasure to here from those most dear, but in trying times like these it is almost the only solace we have. I am very sorry to here of pore Fannies condition, but I hope she will recover. I sent a letter by Mr Willis that you had not received when you wrote.

---

[4] Evans, *Sherman's Horsemen*, 205–206.
[5] Ibid., 292–93.
[6] Ibid., 311–18, 358–59.
[7] Bonds, *War Like the Thunderbolt*, 177–209, 211–13.

My Dear if you have a good oportunity I would be glad if you could send me at least one shirt. the weather is so warm that I am compeled to change twice a week and having but three shirts it is rather dificult to get them washed. I think I will get some money in a week or two. When I get it I will have the two old shirts I have fixed

Dear you n'd'nt send my overcoat till cold weather unless you have a good chance. I can take care of it here. You need not make me any more clothing. I can get it from the Quartermaster. If you will work get something for yourself. I intend the government shall keep me going from this [time] out.

If you can make any arrangement to get corn do it. I will send you some money when I get it. When the Quartermaster gets some cloth that suits me I will get a suit or at least a coat. I think of getting it cut here and sending [it] up and you can get Mrs. Willson to make it for me. If Communication should be cut off, I can get it made here by a tailor in the Hospital for thirty five dollars. I can get very good pants for 12.00 dollars by getting a soldier to draw them for me. Jacketts for 15.00 dollars. that dear is less than one yard of the cloth you made. I intent to get all I can in that way. If I get more than I need I can send them home. they will be worth more than the money. You might be able to get something for them that you need in the way of corn, meet or something for you and Nora. But say nothing about that as some might talk about it. Don't you think I had as well get all the shirts and drawers I can at 3 dollars a piece.

My Dear I see no chance that I will have to come to see you. I am making some acquaintance here and if I can make any arrangement I intend for you to come down to see me after while. Don't think because it is Augusta you can't come for you can come here nearly as soon as you could go to Madison and as for the people there is less pomp and vanity here so far as I have seen than there is in Madison

I received a letter from Ratio this morning written 21st inst. It had been sent to Madison. I am going to write to him this evening. He was not very well when he wrot.

Dear the 2d Lieut (Prater) who ran against & defeated me when Reaves Company was organized was killed on 22nd inst. How thankfull I am that I was not elected that time.

Tell Nora Pa red her letter. she must write some next time
Write often my Dear,
Yours Most Truly
M P Alexander

Direct this
    M P Alexander
        AsstSurg. P. A. C. S.
            Blackie Hospital

Augusta, Geo
PS Send me some stamps if you have them
MPA

Notes

pore Fannies condition: See chapter 25.

I can get very good pants for 12.00 dollars by getting a soldier to draw them for me: Manning probably means that he will get a soldier to get (draw) the pants from the quartermaster as part of the soldiers' clothing allotment.

I received a letter from Ratio this morning written 21st inst.... He was not very well when he wrot: Manning means July 21. Then Ratio was near Petersburg (see chapter 27).

2d Lieut (Prater) who ran against & defeated me when Reaves Company was organized: John Rives's Company was Company K of the 43rd Georgia, which had been organized in Hall County, Manning's home county. Manning had been a private in the company before becoming assistant surgeon of the regiment. At some point before he became regimental assistant surgeon, he must have run for lieutenant of the company and lost to Josiah Prater. Prater was killed in Atlanta on July 22.[8]

Asst Surg PACS: P. A. C. S. stood for the Provisional Army of the Confederate States. The provisional army was established by the Confederate government in late February 1861 when it enacted a law authorizing President Davis to take into Confederate service for at least twelve months state units that were either tendered by the state to the regular army or volunteered for the regular army and had the state's consent to join it.

A week later, the Confederate government enacted a law giving President Davis additional authority to enlist volunteers directly into the regular Confederate army to serve for twelve months, or longer if needed.

The Confederate government soon modified the provisional army statute to allow President Davis to accept, without state consent, state units who volunteered to join the provisional army. He also was authorized to treat them generally as if they were in the regular army. Most of the war was fought by the provisional army treated like the regular army.[9]

---

[8] Rigdon, *Georgia 43rd Infantry Regiment*, 208, 210; service records.
[9] Confederate Statutes, Provisional Congress, Session I, chapter XXII, February 28, 1861; chapter XXVI, March 6, 1861; Provisional Congress Session II, chapter VIII, May 11, 1861; https://docsouth.unc.edu/imls/19conf/19conf.html, accessed September 20, 2023.

Manning

Augusta Geo
Aug 20th/64
My Dear:

    I received you very kind and precious letter yesterday evening. Dear, I was very sorry to hear that you had not got my letters. I have writen two or three letters for you since I received any from you. Yesterday evening was the first time I have heard from you since the 1st of August. The letter you sent by Capt Harden I have not received yet. I never was more anxious to here from you. The last you wrote you toled me about your Ma going to Forsythe. I was very fearful the Yankeys would get her horse or give her some trouble some way. I mailed a letter to you last Monday: it should have reached you last Wednesday.

    Who is Capt Harden?

    My Dear there is but little of interest for me to write. All the Army news we have here now I suppose you will get by the time this reaches you. As is to my health dear it is as good as usual at this season. I am quite lean now. I would not "fill the bill" as well as I did last winter although I feel very well. I have a boil in my nose that is giving me some trouble just now. It seams that we are boath troubled with boils just now but not on the sam locality. My Dear I would give any thing to be at home now. I think I could injoy home now as well as I ever did in my life and then that good old fassioned eating I could do full justice to and fully appreciate.

    Dear dont trouble youself about my overcoat. if you cant dye it let it alone.

    Dear I cant give up the idea of your coming to see me some time between now an Christmas. I don't know that I can make any arrangements for you to come but if I should you must not, my dear, let work keep you from coming. If you shoud be cut off I could send you home through South Carolina.

    I will write to Nora in a day or two. I got a letter from Mother dated 1st Aug. She was improving. The weather is very warm here now. send me some fruit dear if you can by any one passing [this way].

    Writ often dear while you have an opportunity
      Yours most Truly
      M P Alexander

Note

Capt Harden: He still has not been identified.

Manning

Augusta Geo
Aug 27st /64

My Dear:

Yours of 24st was received last night. Dear what a precious privalage it is to here from those most dear. As it becomes more and more probable that we will be seperated—that *our* communication will be interrupted by raids if not permanently— the more I appreciate and value the privielage we now injoy. I have always been of the opinion—as you have oftin herd me say that I would not leave home and I yet think I would not if I had property that could be damaged, but of late, since the enemy have come as near and (in my opinion) will come nearer, I have been thinking somewhat serious about not leting you fall behind the line.

Dear it is a very hard thing for me to reconcile myself to the idea of being cut off from you and not knowing what insults and suffering you might have to endure. I would rather live on bread and water than be so situated that I would not know what you was having to suffer. I know you will be cared for as long as there is any thing in the country to be had but who knows what hour every thing may be swept away and nothing left to subsist upon and again who can protect you from the base insults and injuries the fiendish vilans may offer. But Dear, I ought not to wright this. I fear I will cause you unnecessary alarm and trouble

There is considerable excitement now about the Chicago Convention. An Armistas etc. I go but little on any thing of the kind myself, and I think those who build hopes upon any thing of the kind will see them all crumble and fall.

I am very sorry to here of your fathers' misfortune. I hope he has got the horses before now. Your ma should have called upon the Capt of the Company when she saw the horse. I am fearful they will trade them before they get to Athens.

I will be very thankful to receive the fruit, but dear don't give yourself much trouble about it.

My pay & commutation is now $203 per month now. It will be $320 in the winter months My health is very good—the wether is exceptionly warm. I have written to Nora this morning. Dear have you done anything with that Bond yet.

Write often my Dear. Most Truly
M. P. Alexander

Notes

the enemy have come as near and (in my opinion) will come nearer: When the letter was written, the Union army still was concentrated at Atlanta and had not yet captured it. Sherman had not yet started his march to the sea. On August 3, however, several of Stoneman's raiders had ridden to just south of the Mulberry River, near the current border between Barrow County to the south and Jackson County to the north in the area where present-day Highway 53 crosses the river. There Confederate cavalry attacked them. After a bloody confrontation, the raiders turned back toward Atlanta and rode away.

If they had proceeded further north and crossed the Mulberry River, they would have been about twenty-five miles south of the Davids' home where Lona was staying. If they had proceeded still further, they could have cut communications between Lona and Manning, at least for a while.[10]

Chicago Convention An Armistas etc : The Democratic Party's convention to nominate the party's candidate for president was to be held in Chicago August 29–31. There it was expected that General George B. McClellan, who opposed President Lincoln's war policies, would be the party's nominee. That is what happened.

On July 18, representatives of President Lincoln had opened peace discussions in Canada with Confederate agents. These discussions proved unproductive. At the same time, unofficial northern peace negotiators met with President Jefferson Davis in Richmond. These negotiators also failed to reach an agreement. Both efforts were widely reported and discussed in the press, but as Manning predicted, there was to be no armistice.[11]

I am very sorry to here of your fathers' misfortune: The *Southern Watchman* for August 10, 1864, contained an article complaining that Confederate authorities were retaining horses and mules the Confederate army had captured from Union army raiders. These horses and mules, however, were the same ones the Union raiders had taken only a few days earlier from the stables and pastures of Georgia farmers. Confederate authorities were keeping them rather than returning them to their rightful civilian owners. This Confederate practice may be what Manning was referring to. It also is possible that Confederate soldiers simply took some David horses without authority.

Manning

Dear

The funerel of Gen Gerardy came off to-day at the Catholic Church. It was a very imposing thing—The Priest officiated. He was buried with military honors

The Graining Mill connected with the Powder Mills at this place caught fire and was blown into attoms. There was eight men in the mill-they ware blown into fragments.

Most Affectionately
M. P. Alexander

---

[10] Evans, *Sherman's Horsemen*, 292, 349–53; *Georgia Atlas & Gazetteer*, 21–22.

[11] McPherson, *Battle Cry of Freedom*, 760–73; Wagner, *Timeline of the Civil War*, 196–97, 199, 202–203.

Notes

Date and place: There is no date or place in this short letter, which appears to have been written on a scrap of a larger piece of stationery. Because of the mention of General Girardy and the information about his funeral and the mill explosion, the letter probably was written from Augusta sometime in late August or early September.

The funerel of Gen Gerardy: According to *The Daily Richmond Examiner* of August 17, 1864, Brigadier General Victor J. B. Girardy was killed near Richmond on August 16, 1864, and his body was being transported to Augusta where his family lived.

The Graining Mill explosion: The *Southern Banner* of August 31, 1864, contained an article from an Augusta newspaper of August 28 about an explosion at the Augusta Powder Works that involved the nearby Granulating House. Eight employees were "blown into fragments" by the explosion. The cause of the disaster was unknown at the time the article was written.

Manning

Augusta Geo
Sept 15th /64
My Dear

Your precious favor was received wednesday night.

I should have answered it that night but as it seems that my letters do not go through by regular mail. I thought I would not write until to-day so that it will have two days to go to Athens. Why is it that my letters do not go through by regular mail? I always receive yours regularly.

My Dear, there is so little news going now that I cant get up a readable letter There is not much excitement in the City just now. Every thing has settled down to a deep conviction that if something is not done and that something speedily Georgia will be overrun and the Confederacy severed again.

It is rumored that Gen. Boreguard will take Command of the Army in Georgia. How much truth there is in the report I cant say, but this much I can say, it matters not who is put in command it is very evident that they will meet with the same fate that Johnston and Hood have met unless they are largly reinforced. But the question is where are reinforcements to come from?

We have but two other armies to draw from. The army of Va. and the Trans-Miss. We cannot spare them from the former for Grant is reinforcing reinforcement evey day. And I dont think the army can cross the Miss. River. The Yanks keep it too closely watched. It is greatly to be lamented that so many noble and brave men should be sacrificed without any advantage. It is confidently believed although you may not here many speek out—that as soon as Sherman gets ready he will move upon Macon with the same result [as] that of Atlanta. This may be called "Croking" by some but it seems to me that it requires but little segasity to see that it must follow as true as cause and affect. Grant has extended his lines at Petersburg to Poplar Spring Church. Ratio can tell you where the church is I suppose.

I got my overcoat but forgot to mention it in my last.

Who is Capt. Bruster? Where is he from and what is he doing. That was quite a complement I think. I don't know either whether it should be considered a complement or not. If a mear statment of facts are to be taken as complementry why it was a complement, otherwise it was not. *My opinion is that he only said what is really true.* At least I am satisfied that, if he can't prove it nearer home if he will just send down to Augusta he can get a witness. *That's so.*

My Dear I would like most exceedingly well to spend a few weeks at home but there is no probability that I will have an opportunity to do so soon. I am going to try to get to come home after while but it is quite uncertain about it and if I do it will be but 3 or 4 days

I hope dear little Nora is better by this time. I would give anything to get to see her now.

My Dear buy as much wheat as will mak a sufficiency and ingage corn if you can. I think your idea of geting some more hogs is a good one. I have not drawn any money yet—there is none in the City

Well my dear, I will close for this time. Now dear write often whether you have anything to write or not. If it is but a line it is offordes me more pleasure than any and every thing else together.

Yours Most Affectionately
M. P. Alexander

Notes

the Confederact severed again: The Confederacy was severed the first time with the Union took control of the entire length of the Mississippi River.

It is rumored that Gen. Boreguard will take Command of the Army in Georgia.... [he] will meet the same fate that Johnston and Hood have met: After General Joseph E. Johnston replaced Braxton Bragg as commander of the Army of Tennessee in December 1863, he led his army in a retreat south through northern Georgia to a position in early July 1864 only four miles from Atlanta. He was viewed by many in the South as reluctant to fight and was replaced by General John Bell Hood on July 17, 1864. Hood was more aggressive, but on September 2, 1864, Atlanta fell to General Sherman.

After Atlanta's fall, Hood took the Army of Tennessee, the army that had been defending Atlanta, away into Alabama and then Tennessee in an effort to disrupt Sherman's supply lines and take Sherman away from Georgia. Remaining in Georgia to oppose Sherman if he did not follow Hood, as he did not, were about eight thousand cavalrymen and a few units of Georgia militia.

General P. G. T. Beauregard did not become their commander. Instead, General William J. Hardee was placed in overall command of Georgia's defense. As Manning predicted, he was no more successful in stopping Sherman than Johnston and Hood had been.[12]

"Croking": Manning probably means "croaking," one meaning of which is "to talk dismally; foretell evil or misfortune; grumble," possibly referring to the somewhat mournful croaks of a frog.[13]

Poplar Spring Church: Poplar Spring Church was located about four miles southwest of Petersburg. The Union army held the ground to the east and southeast of Petersburg. The appearance of Union troops near Poplar Spring Church was part of General Grant's effort to extend his line westward in order to compel Lee also to extend his line westward, making Lee's defenses along his whole line more thinly manned than they already were.[14]

Ratio can tell you: Manning would have known that Ratio had been near Petersburg (see chapter 27) and that Ratio likely would know the church's location. Although Manning may not have known where Ratio was when he wrote this letter, he knew, or assumed, that Lona was in contact with him by mail and could ask him.

On the other hand, after Ratio was wounded at Guard Hill, he received leave to go home (previous chapter). Possibly he had gotten to Jackson County in time for Lona to let Manning know he was home, and Manning knew she could ask him personally. At any rate, as the next letter makes clear, by the following week Manning knew Ratio was home.[15]

Capt. Bruster: He has not been identified.

Manning

Augusta Geo
Sept 21st 1864
My Dear,

I have a proposition my dear to submit to you this morning. How would you like to have a position in the Hospital with me. This may surprise you my dear but I have made all the arrangements for you to come. I will tell you what your duties will be if you consent to come. You will be ward matron in my ward. Your

---

[12] Horn, *Army of Tennessee*, 308; Bonds, *War Like the Thunderbolt*, 5–15, 58–68, 364–65; Inscoe, *Civil War in Georgia*, 10, 74–82, 94; Glaze, "Georgia Campaign," 315–36.
[13] "Croak," *Webster's New World College Dictionary*, 352.
[14] McPherson, *Atlas of the Civil War*, 184–85; Gallagher et al., *Civil War*, 211–13.
[15] Horatio's service records.

duties will be to see that the ward is kept in good condition—that the beds are properly made up, that the ward is swept regularly–that the beding is clean, and that the diet is properly distributed to the patients who are not able to go to the table.

There will be eight nurses & two negros to do this work assted by the wardmaster (Sam). It will not require more than half your time, and not much [illegible] on your part further than see that is done and the wardmaster will assist in that. Your pay will be thirty (30) dollars per month & rations. Dr Boatwright will not promise to give Nora her rations but we can bring three months rations with you. By the time that is out I think there will be no doubt that I can have her rationed in the hospital. Should I fail to do it I surely can buy as much as she will eat.

We will have a good room in a building not connected with the hospital whare Mrs Nyle (the chief matron) Dr Boatwright and the linen matron stay. Mrs Nyle is a lady whos character is above suspition. You will have ample time to do all your own work. You will have no washing or any thing very fateaguing to do.

Well now my Dear what do you think of it? I have been turning this thing over in my mind ever since the fall of Atlanta and taken every thing into consideration—the possibility of my being ordered away from here, the highly probability of us being separated and every thing bearing upon the subject and have decided for you to come if you can get your own [illegible]. I am now satisfied that if Sherman will advance as soon as he gets ready and that will be before long in my opinion. He will occupy Athens in my judgment before the last of October and then we would be separated.

I know you will not feel so free and easy as when at home [but] it seems that if we don't adapt some such cours we will not have the satisfaction of each other society soon again. I have no fears but what you can give perfect satisfaction. I will be with you all the time and give you all the instruction necessary. If it should so happen that I should be ordered away at any time and you could not go me you can discontinue the business at any time you choose.

As to your dressing you need not hesitate about that for you can go into society or not here as you choose. It is not like it is in a little place like Madison where every one in the place knows you are there in less than 24 hours after geting to the place. We are in rather a retired part of the city.

When I mentioned it to Dr Boatwright and asked his advice he gave it his hearty approval and said that if his family was not so large he would have them all the time. If you conclude to come (which I hope you will do) and can have Nora a pair of shoes made it would be well. I think my dear we can live almost as [illegible] here as at home taking into consideration your rations and then we will be together.

I want you to write me dear as soon as you get this and let me know what you think of it. In the mien time I shall be making such arrangement as are necessary for you to come. If you elect to come I will try to get 6 or 8 days to come after you. Should I come I think now that I will try to come about Wednesday the 5th of Oct. Should I not have an oportunity to come or should Sherman threten our communication just lock up at any time and come on. Ratio could come with you.

It will not be necessary for you to bring but one bed and beding and not that if you can offerd to sleep on a straw matrass. I can furnish beding for Nora. I have a good cotton matrass (narrow) and two blankets and can get as many hospital comforts as I wish. fifty lbs flour & thirty lbs bacon would make Noras rations three months. You could also bring some fruit Syriup or preserves, Butter &c&c as our part of "extras" all of which you could have put In a box and marked as Hospital supplies so that you could get them th[r]ough easier.

Tell [illegible] Ratio that there is no money nor goods here yet but I think there will be some of the former in a few days. I will write him again soon and keep him posted.

I will write you again dear in a few days. Hold yourself ready to come at any time and if Sherman advances—come right along. everything is now ready.

Yours most Truly
M P Alexander

P. S. I have just drawn 400 dollars commutation. I will send soon to you the first chance if you need it. I think you will be with me in a short time.

Notes

Sam: He was Manning's younger brother who had been with him as an orderly in Blackie Hospital in Madison. He was left in charge of the hospital there when Manning and most of the patients left as the Union army advanced toward the town. He seems to have escaped capture and made his way to Augusta (see chapter 26).

the fall of Atlanta: Atlanta fell to the Union army on September 2, 1864.[16]

Manning

Augusta Ga Oct 17th/64
My Dear,

Yours of the 12th inst was received Friday evening.

I was considerably disappointed to learn that you would not be here til the 26 int. My expectations ware wrought up to the highest pitch that you would be here this week at furthest. I feel just like somthing will hapen yet that will prevent

---

[16] Boatner, *Civil War Dictionary*, 33; McPherson, *Battle Cry of Freedom*, 774.

your coming. You know I don't believe in presentiments but I cant help having some misgivings about it some way. It may be because I am so anxious to see you. I *do wish* you could have come this week. But may be it is best for you to get ready first for if I stay at this hospital it is a little uncertain when you get back home again.

There is no chance fer me to get a leave of absence for any length of time. I would be very glad to meet you in Athens but there is no chance whatever.

If you cant git that bond off bring it with you. If you can get fifty cents in the dollar for it let it go. That is the most they are brining here and I am afraid they won't be worth that long as they have a downward tendancy now. Fifty cent in a dollar is a heavy loss but it is better than nothing.

You need not bring any bedding but comforts and pillows. I can get a bed tick and sheets from the hospital. I have pillows that will do for Nora. I will not have my coat made til you come.

Now Dear *pleas don't put it off any longer.*

There are a great many rumors about what Hood is doing and whare he is going. I think his position is a very critical one. I am very fearful he will not accomplish much. He seems to be going into North Ala. He has left the State Road and gone to Blue Mountain which is in Ala. Near Jacksonville I think. Hurry my dear. The time goes slowly along.

Yours Truly
M. P. Alexander

Notes

bed tick: "[A] bag made of heavy cloth, usually canvas…filled with straw, feathers, or rags" and used as a mattress.[17]

what Hood is doing: General John Bell Hood, who was in charge of the Confederate troops in the Atlanta area, had left Atlanta with most of his troops and marched north toward Tennessee, heading back the way Johnston had retreated earlier. It is not surprising that people were uncertain where Hood was headed. On the day Manning wrote this letter, Hood, who was camped near LaFayette, Georgia, began marching his men to Gadsden, Alabama on his way into Tennessee.[18]

Manning and Pillona

Blackie Hospital
Augusta Geo Nov 26/64
Dear Fath & Mother [Thirza and James David]

---

[17] Drake, *What Did They Mean by That?*, 305.
[18] Horn, *Army of Tennessee*, 375–79; Hood, *Advance and Retreat*, 263–64, 266–68.

We received yours of 20th inst Wednesday morning—were glad to here from you.

There is not altogether as much excitment in the City as was a few days ago—but it is not certin yet whether Sherman intends coming here or not. Gen Bragg—who is here—says he will be able to decide where he is going in the next 12 hours or at least to determine whether he is coming here or not. The lates infermation is that a small cavely force are in the neighborhood of Sparta Hancock County—that the main force has crossed the Oconee river and are in the neighborhood of Sandersville, Washington Co. The Yankees are laying waist the country wherever they go burning houses, taking off provisions, taking all the stocke they want as shooting what they cant take off. Their force is variously estimated at from 20,000 to 60,000.

It is now prety well acertained that Sherman has about 25,000 men—a much larger force I fear than we are prepared to meet. Should Sherman advance on this place we will go to S. C.—to Columbia I suppose.

Tell Ratio to get another extension if he can, but if he cannot to report here and stay in hospital until he gets well.

[Tell Maison Parks that I think it very uncertain about his geting a transfer to Cavely from any of the Boards at this place as they are very ridged, but should he come I will take pleasure in rendering him any service in my power.]

I will not close this. Lona will write some.

Dear Father and Mother

I wrote you in last saturday which I suppose you recd Wednesday. I thought it probable that would be the last you would hear from us soon, but our communication is open yet and I hope will remain so. The cars did not go up to Athens sunday and monday.

The Linen and all the surplus baggage belonging to this Hospital has been packed up ever since last sunday ready to move at a few hours warning. All our sick that are able to travel will be sent over to Carolina to morrow to give place for wounded men. The convalescence will be kept here for duty. There is about 80 galvanized Yankees in this Hospital.

I saw John Lipon a day or two ago. he is well but he cant leave here till this excitement gets over. They will not let a man leave now. there is said to be between 8 and 10,000 thousand troopes here now.

Last Sunday and monday were verry wet days here. monday night it faired off verry cold and has been cold all the week. wednesday morning the ice was 2 inches thick or more. the weather has been verry warm ever since we have been here until this week.

Mother we have not sold your Janes yet. we have not been offered more than 25 dollars for it yet. but we will not take less than 28 until we hear from you. the privates want it but have not got the money and the officers are getting the confederate gray. if we were to happen to meet up with some one that wants that kind of cloth I think may be we could get 30 dollars. we will do the best we can with it. Let Deir have those pants of Drs even if some one else will give more.

from what we have heard this evening, I fear this letter will not reach you. We are all well. I have a severe cold this week. if we are cut of from you dont be uneasy about us. we will get along some way. I will not be surprised if we leave here any day. give our love to all. As ever you[r] children.

M. P. and P. W.

Nora sends howdy to all

Notes

whether Sherman intends coming here or not: Sherman's men had begun marching from Atlanta November 15–16, about ten days before Manning wrote this letter.[19]

Gen Bragg—who is here: General Bragg had arrived in Augusta two days earlier. Jefferson Davis had ordered him "to direct efforts to assemble and employ all available force against the enemy now advancing into Southeastern Georgia." The day after Manning wrote, however, Bragg wrote the Confederacy's secretary of war of his belief "that no practical combinations of my available men can avert disaster." He did little after that, and in mid-December, Davis sent him to Wilmington, North Carolina, to command all of North Carolina east of the Blue Ridge.[20]

a small cavely force are in the neighborhood of Sparta Hancock County: Sparta was about sixty miles southwest of Augusta. Manning's information about the cavalry was correct.[21]

the main force has crossed the Oconee river and are in the neighborhood of Sandersville, Washington Co: Sandersville also was about sixty miles southwest of Augusta, a little further east than Sparta. Again Manning's information was correct.[22]

Their force is variously estimated at from 20,000 to 60,000: According to Union strength reports, Sherman's force was between sixty-two thousand and sixty-six thousand men.[23]

Lona will write some: Apparently Lona had accepted the proposal in Manning's letter of September 21 to become a ward matron at his hospital. In that

---

[19] B. Davis, *Sherman's March*, 3; *OR*, ser. 1, vol. 44, 8, 788.

[20] B. Davis, *Sherman's March*, 51, 82, 84; *OR*, ser. 1, vol. 44, 881, 895; Hess, *Braxton Bragg*, 242–43.

[21] *Georgia Atlas & Gazetteer*, 1; *OR*, ser. 1, vol. 44, 376, 379–80, 589.

[22] *Georgia Atlas & Gazetteer*, 1; *OR*, ser. 1, vol. 44, 8, 789, 899.

[23] *OR*, ser. 1, vol. 44, 7, 16.

position she could have witnessed scenes such as that described by a woman visiting a friend's sons in an Augusta hospital on September 28, 1864:

> Yesterday as I went in to them in the morning I observed a poor soldier lying near them, evidently near his end. I gave him some blackberry wine, which he took from a spoon; and although he could not converse, I shall long remember the expression of his dying eyes as he would fix them intently on me. After dinner I went back. Only the narrow, naked pine bedstead remained. The poor soldier had been removed to the dead room to await interment, or perhaps to be sent home to his sorrowing friends.[24]

galvanized Yankies: A galvanized Yankee was: "A Confederate deserter or prisoner of war who took the oath of allegiance to the Union."[25]

there is said to be between 8 and 10,000 thousand troopes here now: On November 22, before General Bragg arrived, the commander of the Confederates in Augusta reported having only 4,000 men for its defense.[26]

Mason Parks, John Lipon, and "Dier": They have not been identified, although "Dier" may have been someone with the last name of Dyar, or possibly he was one of the Davids's enslaved men.

---

[24] Meyers, *Children of Pride*, 1208.
[25] Garrison, *Encyclopedia of Civil War Usage*, 90.
[26] *OR*, ser. 1, vol. 44, 883–84.

Chapter 29

Horatio and Fannie Recovering, January–March 1865

Manning

Blackie Hospital
Augusta, Geo Jan 21st/65
My dear... .
Ratio has had his suit cut. He had a jacket. He has enough left to make he and I a vest. He wants you to send his buttons off his blue jacket by the first oportunity... .
Most Truly
M. P. A.

Note

The remainder of this letter is in chapter 30. Apparently, when this letter was written in January 1865, Horatio was in Augusta. As appears from other letters in chapter 30, Manning seems to have gotten him assigned to Blackie Hospital. About this time, Horatio applied for retirement.[1]

Fanny

Feb 25th 1865
Dear Mother [Thirza]
I seat my self this morning to try to write you a few lines as it is the first opportunity I hav had of writing you a letter since John came back. he stayed here last Sunday knight and sayed you wished to hear from me as soon as possible in relation to Simeons Funeral. it will be out of my power [to] go to Jackson at the time John spoke of as it will be such a busy time but I will hav it given out to be at Bethlehem the first Sabbath in April the day you hav set apart for the occasion. it will suit me as well then as any time. I had been thinking of having it preached the first Sabbath in May and hoped some of you could come out here but as I know the relations on either side would wish to hear it I think it would suit best to have it at both places on the same day.
James Tomson who went back with Simeon to va the last time he was at home has just come in. he sayed he was standing in a few steps of him when he fell. He sayed Simeon remarked before he went into the battle that he was going

---
[1] Service records of Horatio David.

in and felt confident that he would be killed but rushed forward in advance of his company with his sword waveing in his hand and fell with it grasped there. Oh he says the comp has felt ruined ever since. The men are nearly all at home round here and say they are not going to fight any longer but they are a class that hav never hurt them selves.

John spoke of coming back here in a few days to recruit his horse a little but has not come yet.

we are having some desperate weather now. the water courses are very high and still raining.

to my dear little Elen and Lina[:] Mother was so glad to hear you were learning so fast and looking so hearty and well. Mother you dont know how glad I would be to see them. I intend if nothing hapens to go and see you all after crops are laid by if not before. I intend making the children some nice homespun dresses and sending to them if I hav an opportunity.

Cousin Gilford Harris is here uncle Ezekils Son just from home near Ringold. he says his Mother has plenty to live on and has learned to get along with the yanks finely. he says the yankys hav partys round there and plenty of Ladys go to them. he says a great many of them are marrying Georgia Ladys. Cousin Mat Harris is still here and will probably stay all the Summer,

in relation to that black muslin dress I am anxious for you to get it and if you hav not used the money Pap gave you you can appropriate what the dress calls for to your own use if you will take money. if not I will satisfy you in something else. I don't see how I will ever get the dress here.

Mary if you have any scraps of the bonnet you gave me I would be gad [if] you would send me a small slipe to pice it at. The [illegible] as it is rather short you could send it in a letter and send me a pretty stripe to make me a dress by.

I believe I have written all that would interest you. Sally says tell Elen and Lina howdy for her. She is right smartly deaf caused by the ear ache. Ginney is as fat and harty as a little Pig. as for my own health I never felt stouter in my life. I hav been thinking of going down to Marys old place after her loom as I supposed she would have no objection. my old one is so slavish to weave on. Ma and Granny sends their Love to you. write often. yours affectionately

F. E. David

Notes

John: He may have been John W. Neal, son of Thirza's oldest child, Mary Neal. When this letter was written, John Neal was twenty years old.

Simeons Funeral: As noted in chapter 24, Simeon was buried on the Wilderness battlefield. There is no indication that his body was moved for the funeral in Georgia. Instead, the funeral seemed to have been the preaching of a sermon and nothing more.

Bethlehem: Simeon had been a member of this church, Bethlehem Baptist Church, in Forsyth County.[2]

James Tomson: He was James R. Thompson, a private in Simeon's company. His service records indicate he was ill and home on furlough.

The men are nearly all at home round here and say they are not going to fight any longer: At least some of them did fight longer, and when they surrendered at Appomattox, there were only thirteen men left in the company.[3]

Elen and Lina: Elen was Mary Eleanora "Ellen" David, Simeon and Fanny's oldest daughter. When this letter was written, she was eight years old.[4]

Lina was Thirza Lena David, Simeon and Fanny's next oldest daughter. When this letter was written, she was seven years old.[5] Apparently they had been staying with Thirza for a while.

Ringold…Yankys: Ringgold was in the far northwestern corner of Georgia close to Chattanooga. It had been occupied by the Union army for over a year.[6]

Mary: She very probably was Thirza's oldest child Mary Juliette David Neal, who was thirty-six years old when this letter was written. She apparently was living with the Davids then.

Sally and Ginney: Sally was Sarah B. "Sallie" David, Simeon and Fanny's third daughter. She was five years old when this letter was written.[7] Ginney was Virginia Frances David, Simeon and Fanny's youngest daughter. She was two years old when this letter was written.[8]

Manning

Greensboro Ga
Feb 27st—65
My Dear, …

"Tell Ratio to come immediately as Boatwright might report him.… I am sorry that Rash can't get to stay at home any longer but I think he can get a recommendation and get a furlough. severel furloughs have come back approved by Gen Fry since Rash left.…

---

[2] Shadburn, ed., *Pioneer History of Forsyth County, Georgia*, 124.

[3] *North Georgia Tribune*, April 7, 1960, reprinting an article from the *Cherokee Advance* printed in the 1920s.

[4] Simeon's letter of April 29, 1856, in chapter 5; tombstone, Old Taylorsville Church Cemetery, Polk County, Georgia (Ella David Hagan Trippe).

[5] Tombstone, Lime Branch Cemetery, Polk County, Georgia (Lena David Pittman).

[6] Horn, *Army of Tennessee*, 301–303.

[7] Tombstone, Rose Hill Cemetery, Rockmart, Polk County, Georgia (Sallie B. Lowry).

[8] Simeon's letters of December 5, 1862, and January 21, 1863, in chapter 15; tombstone, Grandfield Cemetery, Tillman County, Oklahoma (Virginia Tant).

Yours most Truly
M. P. Alexander

Notes

The remainder of this letter is in chapter 30.

Greensboro Ga: The hospital had moved to Greensboro, Georgia. It is about seventy-five miles west of Augusta (back toward Atlanta) on the Georgia Railroad.[9]

Boatwright: Surg. J. G. Boatwright was in charge of Blackie Hospital.[10]

Boatwright might report him: Boatwright had left the hospital temporarily, and Manning had allowed Horatio to go home for a while. Now Manning had learned that Boatwright was coming back, and Horatio needed to come back also.

Gen. Fry: He was Brigadier General B. D. Fry, Confederate commander of the Military District of Georgia, whose headquarters was in Augusta.[11]

Horatio

H. J. David
2 Lt Co B 16 Ga Regt
Appears on a
Register
Of the Invalid Corps. P. A. C. S.
Date of retirement Mch 11, 1865
When assigned to duty S. O. 61 Mar. 15, 1865
Where assigned Supt Bu of Cons
Remarks: D 316

Notes

Invalid Corps.: In February 1864, the Confederate government established an Invalid Corps composed of men a medical examining board had certified as disabled because of wounds, other injuries, or disease received or contracted in the line of duty. Soldiers so certified were considered retired. The medical board, however, still could assign them to duty it determined they were qualified to perform.[12]

P. A. C. S.: Provisional Army of the Confederate States. The provisional army was established by the Confederate government in late February 1861 when

---

[9] *Georgia Atlas & Gazetteer*, 1; Black, *Railroads of the Confederacy*, xxiii, xxv; B. Harris, *Confederate Hospitals of Madison, Georgia*, 13.

[10] B. Harris, *Confederate Hospitals of Madison, Georgia*, 96–100.

[11] *Augusta Chronicle*, February 23, 1865.

[12] Confederate Statutes, First Congress, Session IV, chapter LVI, February 17, 1864, https://docsouth.unc.edu/imls/23conf/23conf.html, accessed September 20, 2023.

it enacted a law authorizing President Davis to take into Confederate service for twelve months state units that were either tendered by the state or volunteered and had the state's consent.

A week later, the Confederate government enacted a law authorizing President Davis to seek volunteers to form units of a regular Confederate army to serve for twelve months, or longer if needed.

The Confederate government soon modified the provisional army statute to allow President Davis to accept, without state consent, state units who volunteered to join the provisional army and to treat them generally as if they were in the regular army. Most of the war was fought by the provisional army.[13]

S. O. 61: This abbreviation probably refers to the 61st Special Order issued by a specific headquarters. Special orders generally dealt with individual soldiers, as opposed to general orders, which dealt with units.[14]

Supt Bu of Cons: This abbreviation stands for Superintendent, Bureau of Conscription. The Bureau oversaw the granting of exemptions from service in the Confederate army.[15]

---

[13] Confederate Statutes, Provisional Congress, Session I, chapter XXII, February 28, 1861; chapter XXVI, March 6, 1861; Provisional Congress Session II, chapter VIII, May 11, 1861; https://docsouth.unc.edu/imls/19conf/19conf.html, accessed September 20, 2023.

[14] Garrison, *Encyclopedia of Civil War Usage*, 92.

[15] Circular No. 8, Confederate States of America, Bureau of Conscription, *Documenting the American South*, https://docsouth.unc.edu/imls/circular8/circular.html, accessed February 16, 2023.

Chapter 30

Sherman Leaves Savannah:
Manning and Pillona, January–March 1865

Manning

Blackie Hospital
Augusta Geo. Jan 16th /65
My Dear—

    I will just drop you a few lines this eavning. I have succeeded in geting a boarding place. Also a place to lodg but at different places—boath convenient. I take my meals just below the third Geo Hospital on the same street. I lodg just back of the orphen Asylum. I like my boarding house very well. I think I will fare very well. I dont much like my lodging, but I will make out till I can do better. I get board for my rations and $75.00 per month. I get a room for thirty and furnish it myself. I moved this morning.

    Dear I have been some what uneasy about your geting home. I fear they did not get your letter in time to come after you. Peter Hawkins came down the day before you went up. He told me the Bridg at Athens was washed away. Also the Sandy Creek Bridg.

    I sent you three bunches No 12 by him. I gave $55.00 per bunch. I got No 12 as there was no difference in the price of No 12 and 10.

    Sam has not got back yet. I am somewhat uneasy but I suppose the bridges are washed away. I received a letter and a very acceptable package from your ma. the letter did not reach here till saturday night.

    I could write you a great deal if I had time I will write again in a few days

    It is rumored that Sherman is advancing upon this place with one collum and an other upon Charelston. The Yankey took Pocataligo yesterday. It is said we brot every thing off.

    I will close for the present. I am very anxious to here from you. I don't know whether you can read this. I writ with a quill pen. Most Truly
    M. P. A.

Notes

I take my meals just below the third Geo Hospital on the same street: The Third Georgia Hospital was on Telfair Street in downtown Augusta. Also, on the corner of Telfair Street and MacIntosh (now 7th) Street, was the manse of the First Presbyterian Church where eight-year-old Woodrow Wilson, future president of the United States, lived during the Civil War. His father's church also on Telfair

Street was used as an auxiliary hospital during the war, taking overflow patients from other Augusta hospitals. The future president must occasionally have ventured into the church-hospital, and possibly he and Manning crossed paths.[1]

I lodg just back of the orphen Asylum: The Augusta Orphan Asylum was located on Walker Street, the next street south of and parallel to Telfair Street.[2]

Peter Hawkins: He has not been identified.

Bridges washed away: Heavy rain had fallen in the Athens-Augusta area causing the Savannah River and other bodies of water to rise to unusual heights.[3]

bunches No. 12: Manning probably is referring to bunches of yarn, probably cotton yarn. Generally, the lower the number, the thicker or coarser the yarn; the higher the number, the finer the yarn. Very fine yarns can be recorded as high a number as No. 80. Numbers 10 and 12, thus, were both coarse yarns.[4]

Sam: He was one of Manning's younger brothers. At the time this letter was written he was thirty-two years old.[5]

The Yankey took Pocataligo yesterday: Despite what was feared earlier, on his way to Savannah from Atlanta, Sherman did not come to Augusta, or send troops there. Instead, he bypassed Augusta and went straight to Savannah, which he occupied on December 21, 1864. He then spent much of the next month consolidating his hold on the city and refitting his men for their next move.[6]

Not all of his units needed refitting. On January 3, the first of Sherman's units to advance into South Carolina embarked on boats headed for Beaufort, about forty miles northeast of Savannah. They landed there the next day without opposition. Other units followed, and on January 13, the force advanced from Beaufort toward Pocataligo on the Charleston and Savannah Railroad, some twenty-eight miles northwest of Beaufort and eighty miles southeast of Augusta. Two days later, as Manning reported, the Federals captured the town.[7]

When the letter was written, it was unclear to Confederates what Sherman would do with the remainder of his army.

---

[1] Writers' Program, *Georgia*, 194–95, 202–203; Corley, *Confederate City*, 10, 68; Berg, *Wilson*, 30–38; "History of the Manse," Boyhood Home of President Woodrow Wilson, https://www.wilsonboyhoodhome.org/learn/about-boyhood-home/history-of-the-manse/, accessed February 16, 2023.

[2] Writers' Program, *Georgia*, 194–95; Corley, *Confederate City*, 17.

[3] *Augusta Chronicle*, January 13 and 14, 1865.

[4] Marks, *Fairchild's Dictionary of Textiles*, 620; J. Montgomery, *Practical Detail of the Cotton Manufacture of the United States*, 30–31, 167.

[5] Chaplin, *Riches of Bunyan* (Alexander family copy).

[6] Wagner, *Timeline of the Civil War*, 213; B. Davis, *Sherman's March*, 113–16, 128–29, 131, 139–42; *OR*, ser. 1, vol. 47, pt. 1, 17.

[7] *OR*, ser. 1, vol. 47, pt. 1, 91, 191–92, 374–75; McPherson, *Atlas of the Civil War*, 208–209.

a quill pen: It was a pen made out of a large feather from a bird, such as a goose. The feather was cut in half, split lengthwise, and fitted with a nib.[8]

Manning

Blackie Hospital
Augusta, Geo Jan 21st/65
My Dear,

I should have written to you several days ago but have put it off till now.

I received yours of the 16 inst last Thursday. was very glad to here from you. I am glad you met with company that was agreeable on the way. You ought to have passed as a single lady. You will know how to do next tim.

Ratio has had his suit cut. He had a jacket. He has enough left to make he and I a vest. He wants you to send his buttons off his blue jacket by the first oportunity.

Sam got back last thursday night with an order from his Capt (Cap johnston) to report to him at Athens. He left here this morning for Athens. He has mad arrangements with Capt. Johnston to get an indefinit furlough to go home. I am very glad he got the order from Johnston. It will deprive Boatwright the pleasure of ordering Him to duty which he would have been sure to have done. I had mad arrangements for him to have him put on duty here in the City but as it is[,] it is better. he will now get home for a while.

I am geting on finly now. When I got back to the hospital the morning you [s]tarted home[,] Mrs. Kyle had saved me some breakfast—stake and *Busqet*. the fare was very good up to monday when I left which afforded great relief to some of them I have no doubt. Boatwright moved out the same evening to his house. Dr Phillips returned wednesdy night bring[ing] the sad (to some body) intelligence [t]hat Boatwright family was not coming. On thursday he moved (sneaked) back to the hospital and now occupies the room he moved out of; after declaring to me and Dr Howard that he was not going to take rooms in the hospital any longer no[r] permit any one else to do so. Low down unprincipold, vindictive, bigoted, selfish and *a lier*. He still takes his meals in the "Pantry." Dr Howard you know says but little—He says that Boatwright bears more personal feelings than any man he ever saw....

I have settled up all my debts except that one in Madison. have lent Ratio 60 dollars and have but 150 dollars left. I am afraid I will run out of money. if we stay here till the last of the month I will get more.

I got a letter from Wm yesterday he was well.

---

[8] Drake, *What Did They Mean by That?*, 245; "Quill," *Webster's New World College Dictionary*, 1193.

ware atmosphere still looks gloomy—Wilmington has fallen or Ft. Fisher, which is the same thing. Shermans whereabouts is not positively known. He is thought to be moving on Branchville & Charleston. Our last Port of any value is now gon. I will send you a paper if I can get one. It has been raining here all night and all day—looks like we will have another freshet.

Write me soon Dea. Give me all the news. tell Nora to be a smart girl and learn fast

Most Truly
M. P. A.

Notes

Capt Johnston: He was Captain John Johnston, company commander of Company B, 29th Georgia Infantry.[9]

Dr. Howard: He probably was Nicholas F. Howard. He had served in the Western Theater with the 52nd Georgia in the same brigade as Manning and the 43rd Georgia, and he had been assigned to Blackie Hospital in Madison in February 1864. Later he was assigned to Asylum Hospital in Augusta.[10]

Wm: He was William P. Alexander, Manning's older brother, then thirty-seven years old.[11]

Wilmington—Fort Fisher: Wilmington was a port on the coast of North Carolina, and Fort Fisher guarded the port. Fort Fisher fell to the Union on January 15. The force that captured Fort Fisher was not part of Sherman's army.[12] Wilmington was not occupied until February 22.

Branchville: Was a railroad junction where the rail line west-east from Augusta to Charleston intersected with a line going north to Columbia. It was located roughly seventy-five miles southeast of Augusta.[13]

Our last Port of any value is now gon: Manning was referring to Wilmington. It had been the only remaining port of any significance that Confederate ships running the Union blockade could have entered bringing supplies from abroad for the Confederate army.[14]

another freshet: A freshet was an "annual or regular period of high water in rivers and streams." The high water that washed away bridges that Manning mentioned in his letter of January 15 above was described in contemporary newspaper accounts as a "freshet."[15]

---

[9] Service records.
[10] Service records.
[11] Chaplin, *Riches of Bunyan* (Alexander family copy).
[12] Wagner, *Timeline of the Civil War*, 213, 214–15. Gallagher, et al, *Civil War*, 292.
[13] Rand McNally, "South Carolina State Map"; Black, *Railroads of the Confederacy*, xxix.
[14] Wagner, *Timeline of the Civil War*, 214–15.
[15] Drake, *What Did They Mean by That?*, 129.

Manning

Blackie Hospital
Augusta Geo Jan 25th 65
My Dear

    I have not heard from you but once since you left but I hope you are well and all right.

    I have but little to write this morning. there is but little news as you will see from the paper I send you. you will see one order in the paper requesting the citizensre to leave the city which has created sone excitiment but from all the news that I have I am inclined to think that Shermans movements are not yet developed.

    I saw a Lieut Col Rich a cousin of Jeny Rich of Athens yesterday morning. He toled me we ware evacuating Willmington and Charleston boath—he thought Charleston would be given up without the fire of a gun.

    All the negros are being impressed this morning to work on the entrenchments. There is considerable excitement moving coton &c this morning. As I write there is a negro running from the "Conscript" down the street and an officer after him shooting at him.

    I am assured though semi-official authority (Smith & Logan's Clerk) that in the event of Shermans coming here and any med officers leave here[,] I will be one of them.

    I am still well pleased with my boarding place. Get that butter I wrote you about last week if you can. By so doing I will be enabled to get my board on the sane term that I do now. Dr Howard sends his respects and says tell you we get *plenty* to eat now and that, that is *good*. I am very cumfortably situated.

    I will write you again in a few days—write oftener. Give my love to all—peticularly Nora.

    Most Truly
    M P A

Notes

you will see one order in the paper requesting the citizensre to leave the city: A "Special Notice" appeared on page two of the *Augusta Chronicle* of January 25, 1865, that read in part, "All non-Combatants are respectfully requested to leave the City immediately. If their removal be delayed until the emergency shall arrive, no Railroad facilities can be allowed them. In the class of non combatants, are included all young gentlemen who have no relish for the trenches. These are exhorted to leave at once under escort of the old ladies." The notice was signed by D. H. Hill, Major General Commanding.

Lieut Col Rich a cousin of Jeny Rich of Athens: He was Lieutenant Colonel William Wofford Rich, commander of Phillips Georgia Legion's cavalry battalion. The kegion had both an infantry unit and a cavalry unit. Rich's cavalry unit served under General J. E. B. Stuart in the Army of Northern Virginia. Lt. Colonel Rich resigned his commission on January 9, 1865, after the legion's surgeon diagnosed him as suffering from chronic hepatitis and apoplexy.[16]

we ware evacuating Willmington and Charleston boath—he thought Charleston would be given up without the fire of a gun: The *Augusta Chronicle* of January 25 reported "that the inhabitants, with the exception of a very few families, had left the town [Wilmington]; that the Government stores and ammunition had all been removed, and the town would fall an easy prey to the enemy...." Still, the Union army did not enter the town until February 22.[17]

Sherman's force may have seemed to some Charlestonians to pose a threat to the city when Manning wrote this letter, and probably some individuals began evacuating. Generally, however, according to the *Augusta Chronicle*, things along the Confederate lines near there were quiet.[18]

The army did not evacuate the city until the night of February 17. They did so, however, without putting up a fight of any significance. The Union army moved in unopposed the following day.[19]

There is considerable excitement moving coton &c this morning: On December 30, 1864, Confederate General Hardee wrote to Governor Brown noting that when Union forces took possession of Savannah, they seized the considerable amount of cotton stored there and converted it to the use of the federal government. In order to prevent a recurrence of these losses if the Federals took Augusta, he urged that "all Cotton in Augusta or vicinity, to be removed to a place of security." He continued that the people should be given notice that "in case Augusta should be endangered, all Cotton will be destroyed by the military authority."

On January 19, this letter was followed by an order from the commander of the Augusta district, General D. H. Hill, stating that General Hardee had ordered him "on the approach of the Yankees" to burn all cotton in Augusta, an order he was "bound to execute": "It is to be hoped that your patriotic citizens will at once remove this temptation to Yankee invasion, either to distant points or to the common, where the torch can be applied when the exigency shall occur."[20]

Smith & Logan: This entity has not been identified. The "Logan" in the name may refer to Dr. J. P. Logan, the senior surgeon in charge of the hospitals

---

[16] Coffman, *Going Back the Way They Came*, 95; Sifakis, *Compendium of the Confederate Armies*, 167–68, 284–85.

[17] *Augusta Chronicle*, January 25, 1865; Gallagher et al., *Civil War*, 291–92.

[18] *Augusta Chronicle*, January 14, 20, 24, 25, 1865.

[19] *OR*, ser. 1, vol. 47, pt. 1, 1007–1008, 1018–20, 1049.

[20] *Augusta Chronicle*, January 20, 1865.

in Augusta at the time the letter was written. A doctor named Smith, however, has not been found.[21]

Manning

Augusta Geo Feb 1st 65
My Dear,
I will only drop you a line this morning. There is still some excitement in the city in regard to Shermans operation. It is reported—as you will see from the paper—that Sherman is still advancing. I am of the opinion that the repert is true. Robertsville is about 40 miles above Savannah, whare the Federals are now.

Three brigades of the Army of Tenn. have arriveed here [and] have gon down on this side of the River—the Bridg. are very small—numbering about 500 each—Tis a sad reflection to think of a brigade that once numbered 4000 now has but 500. None of the Geo troups have arrived yet. they will probably be here to-night.

every thing is on "tip toe" about the peace commissioners. I don't think they will accomiplesh much.

Gen Lee has been made Commander in chief of the Confed-Army.

I sent you three bunches thread by Peter Faulkner. you never said whether you received it or not. I am having my new vest made. I will have a "patern" cut.

It is rumored that the Yanks have crossed over into S Ca.

I have drawn my comutation fer Jan, so I am on my feet again. It has been very cold here for a week, but now it is very pleasent.

Write me often my Dear. Give my love to Nora and all the famely—Most Truly
M P A

Notes

Sherman is still advancing.... Robertsville: Robertsville, South Carolina, is about seventy-five miles southeast of Augusta as the crow flies. As the *Augusta Chronicle* of February 1 reported, and Manning thought accurate, Union forces had occupied Robertsville. They did continue to advance.[22]

Three brigades of the Army of Tenn. have arriveed here [and] have gon down on this side of the River....None of the Geo troups have arrived yet. they will probably be here to-night: General John Bell Hood's Confederate army in Mississippi (called the Army of Tennessee) had been disbanded, and parts of it were making their way to Georgia and on to South Carolina. One of those parts going to Georgia was General Benjamin F. Cheatham's division. It was composed of four brigades,

---

[21] Corley, *Confederate City*, 70; *Augusta Chronicle*, January 25, 1865.
[22] Rand McNally, "South Carolina State Map"; *OR*, ser. 1, vol. 47, pt. 1, 17–19, 591–92.

one of which contained Georgia regiments. Possibly the three non-Georgia brigades arrived first and went on down river while the Georgia brigade arrived later.[23]

the Bridg. are very small—numbering about 500 each: Manning's source for this information is unclear. Undoubtedly, though, the brigades coming from Mississippi were much depleted.[24]

the peace commissioners: The Confederate peace commissioners arrived in Petersburg, Virginia, under a flag of truce on January 29th, and Lincoln met with them on February 3. No agreement was reached, however, as Manning predicted, and two days later, the peace commissioners returned to Richmond.[25]

Gen Lee has been made Commander in chief of the Confed-Army: President Jefferson Davis made the appointment on January 31. Previously, he had been only commander of the Army of Northern Virginia.[26]

I sent you three bunches thread by Peter Faulkner: Manning probably is referring to the bunches of yarn mentioned in his letter of January 16 above. Peter Faulkner was a fifty-eight-year-old farmer from Hall County.[27]

It is rumored that the Yanks have crossed over into S Ca: As mentioned in this and earlier letters, some Federal troops already had advanced across the Savannah River into South Carolina. What Manning probably is referring to in this letter is that the bulk of the Union forces who had occupied Savannah left it around February 1 and headed for South Carolina, leaving only a small number of men in Savannah. The *Augusta Chronicle* of February 1, 1865, reported Federal troops crossing from Georgia into South Carolina at Sister's Ferry. The ferry was about thirty-five miles upstream from Savannah, and the troops crossing there were Sherman's southern wing under General Henry Slocum.[28]

Manning

Office Blackie Hospital
Augusta Geo Feb 8th/65
My Dear,

I will just drop you a line this morning to let you know whare my whareabouts will be for the future. We are ordered to Greensboro. Our Hospt. will leave to-night and to-morrow. I will go up with the train to-night.

---

[23] Horn, *Army of Tennessee*, 422–23; *OR*, ser. 1, vol. 45, pt. 1, 664–67; *OR*, ser. 1, vol. 47, pt. 2, 800–802.

[24] Horn, *Army of Tennessee*, 422–23.

[25] Wagner, *Timeline of the Civil War*, 217, 218; McPherson, *Battle Cry of Freedom*, 822–24.

[26] Wagner, *Timeline of the Civil War*, 217.

[27] US Census, 1850, Hall County, Georgia.

[28] McPherson, *Battle Cry of Freedom*, 825–26; B. Davis, *Sherman's March*, 142; *OR*, ser. 1, vol. 47, pt. 1, 17–19.

I have not had a letter from you in severel days. I think I would get one tonight if I was not going off, but if any letter comes it will be sent to me to-morrow.

It is thought that we will not stay at Greensboro long—that we will come back. I cant tell how that will be. I am of the opinon that we will stay. Sherman struck the S. C. Rail Road about 50 miles below here yesterday. It is not known which way he will go. Whether here to Charleston or Columbia. All the cotton and tobaco is being moved out—the cotten will be burned should the enemy threaten the City. There is the greatest excitment here and has been for two weeks. I would make some effort to get a transfer but I am fearful I would be left here. when evey thing gets quiet I will try my hand. I was in hope that we would go to Athens, but Boatwright was not pleased with the place.

I will close for the present as I am in a great hury

Address me at
Greensboro
Yours Truly
M. P. A.

Notes

Greensboro: Greensboro, Georgia, is about seventy-five miles west of Augusta (toward Atlanta) on the Georgia Railroad.[29]

Sherman struck the S. C. Rail Road about 50 miles below here yesterday: The Union army struck the Blackville-Barnwell, South Carolina area, about forty-seven miles southeast of Augusta, on February 7.[30]

All the cotton and tobaco is being moved out—the cotten will be burned should the enemy threaten the City: See the note to Manning's letter of January 25 above on excitement about cotton.

Manning

Greensboro Geo
Feb 22d . 65
My Dear,

Yes, you may call me that too. I have just received three letters from you this evening. One written 10th inst—the one you wrot befor you left home and yesterday in "Athens."

"Dear" I regret so much that I did not know that you was coming to Athens. Boatwright was at Augusta so I could have come over easily. But never mind. may be it will all come out right yet.

---

[29] *Georgia Atlas & Gazetteer*, 1; Black, *Railroads of the Confederacy*, xxix; B. Harris, *Confederate Hospitals of Madison, Georgia*, 13.

[30] *Augusta Chronicle*, February 8, 1865; *OR*, ser. 1, vol. 47, pt. 1, 19–20.

Boatwright got back from Augusta to day—He is going back to Augusta with the Hospt. but Dr Logan is going to establish a small hospital here and put Dr Greene in charge. I have written to Dr Logan to night to let me remain here. I think he will comply with my request. He was here last week. I toled him I wanted a transfer. He asked me whare I wanted to go. I toled I did not care so that I got away from Boatwright.

I suppose it will be some week or 10 days before the hosp. goes back. The patients will remain here. I will keep you posted. Should I be so fortunate as to get to stay here you have got to come and stay with me a while or longer if I can make the arrangements. You need not go to making any excuse. you must come.

Make your figurs to come in about 3 or 4 weeks. The hospital may not remain here long. That is my impression from the "tone" of Dr Logan's letter to Dr Greene. I think I can make living arrangements by you bringing your provisions with you. Come and stay with me while you can—there is going to be some mighty changes take place in the Confederacy soon. A mighty storm is threatening us. My opinion the great battle that will decide our national fate will be fought soon. Upon its result hangs the destiny of the Southern people. Write me soon when you can come so that I may be making my arrangements accordingly.

Dr Howard got back yesterday. I was glad to see the old fellow. He stayed at Capt Deadington as he came down.

Most Affectionately
M. P. Alexande

Notes

Dr. Logan: He was Dr. J. P. Logan, the senior surgeon in charge of the hospitals in Augusta.[31]

Dr. Greene: He has not been identified.

Dr. Howard: He probably was Nicholas F. Howard, who had served in the Western Theater with the 52nd Georgia in the same brigade as Manning and the 43rd Georgia. He had been assigned to Blackie Hospital in Madison in February 1864. He later was assigned to Asylum Hospital in Augusta.[32]

Capt. Deadington: He has not been identified.

Manning

Greensboro Ga
Feb 27st—65

---

[31] Corley, *Confederate City*, 70; *Augusta Chronicle*, January 25, 1865.
[32] Goodson, *Georgia Confederate 7,000*, 1:85, 139; service records, N. F. Howard; B. Harris, *Confederate Hospitals of Madison, Georgia*, 59.

My Dear,

Boatwright got back from Augusta this evening and every thing has changed. The whole hospital is going back to Augusta.

I am now convinced that he went to Augusta to prevent a hospital from being established here. So my dear I will have to go back to Augusta, but worst of all is that I will still be with him. But I am going to make application for a transfer just as soon as we get back. I will ask to go to Madison if there is any medical officer wanting there. I am going to leave the bigoted selfish upstart. I don't care whare I go to. I will keep you posted as to my movements.

Tell Ratio to come immediately as Boatwright might report him. I don't *know* that he would, but Dr Greene toled me to write to him to come right along. Dr Greene will not go down till friday—so if Rash can get off thursday he will meet him at Union Point friday and come down with him. I am sorry that Rash can't get to stay at home any longer but I think he can get a recommendation and get a furlough. severel furloughs have come back approved by Gen Fry since Rash left

Write me how you are getting along with my suit.

Make your preparations to visit me this spring. I will make some arrangements for you to stay with me a while. any how I doubt whether we stay long in Augusta. The place is too much exposed. It is now prety well confirmed that Sherman has burned three thousand cars & engines near Charlotte N. C. I will go down about Wednesday.

Kiss Nora for me.
Yours most Truly
M. P. Alexander

Notes

Union Point: Union Point is where the branch line of the Georgia Railroad from Athens meets the main line from Atlanta to Augusta.[33]

Gen. Fry: General B. D. Fry was the Confederate commanding officer at Augusta when the letter was written.[34]

Sherman burned cars and engines near Charlotte: The Union army destroyed about forty-four miles of the railroad from Columbia north toward Charlotte, North Carolina, a distance that stretched from Columbia to a little north of Winnsboro, South Carolina. That still, however, was well short of Charlotte. Sherman intended to feint toward Charlotte in order to hold Confederate troops

---

[33] Black, *Railroads of the Confederacy*, xxv.
[34] *OR*, ser. 1, vol. 47, pt. 1, sec. 2, 1063, 1109, 1184; *Augusta Chronicle*, January 21, 1865.

there while his true intention was to go to the northeast and the state capital of Raleigh.[35]

Manning

Blackie Hospital
Augusta Geo
March 11st 1865
My Dear

As Ratio is going to start home in the morning I will write you a few lines.

I thought this morning that I would make an application for a few days leave and accordingly sent up an application. After doing so I learned that all application for leave had to have the Approval of the Surgeon Gen, so that puts at rest any probability of my geting to come home.

So you see my dear there is no other chance for us but for you to come to see me. And that I want you to do if I can get my wages. So I want you to be ready to come when I write for you. let that be when it may. I can get avey good room for fifty dollars per month so you can bring you provisions with you and be at no extra expenses. I am still determined to leave here if I can but it seems that I am not succeeding very well yet but I am going to keep trying.

You need not trouble yourself about sending those pants. I can do very well without them till I get my new ones if it is till June.

Jimi stayed with me last night and part of to-day—his command has come back from S. C. They are going to Waynesboro. Robert is gon on a scout to Columbia or beyond there. There is no war news. Sherman was still going on when last heard from—I think the evacuation of Va is inevible. The R. R. can't be repaired in 12 months and it is certain that the Army cant be fed that long there—My fears are that they will come out throug our country and sweep every thing before them. Kiss Nora for me give my love to all the family
Most Truly
M. P. Alexander

Notes

Surgeon. Gen.: The Confederate surgeon general, Samuel Preston Moore, was the head of the entire Confederate medical department and was located in Richmond. Manning had reason to think his chances of leave were remote.[36]

---

[35] *OR*, ser. 1, vol. 47, pt. 1, 22, 171; B. Davis, *Sherman's March*, 185.
[36] Schroeder-Lein, *Encyclopedia of Civil War Medicine*, 216–18.

Jimi: He was James D. Alexander, one of Manning's younger brothers. He was then twenty-five years old and a lieutenant in Company D of the 11th Georgia Cavalry.[37]

Waynesboro: Waynesboro, Georgia is about twenty-five miles south of Augusta.[38]

Robert: He was Robert C. Alexander, another of Manning's younger brothers. He was then nineteen years old and a corporal also in Company D of the 11th Georgia Cavalry.[39]

Sherman was still going on when last heard from: "Sherman still going on" refers to Sherman's going on from Augusta and Georgia generally, which he continued to do. Despite the concerns of Manning, Lona, and the citizens of Augusta, Sherman never intended to attack Augusta. However, he wanted to give the impression of being about to attack both Augusta and Charleston, South Carolina, in order to hold Confederate forces there while he moved on to Columbia and further north.[40]

The evacuation of Virginia and the inability to repair the railroad: Most of the supplies for Lee's army around Richmond came from the south. Grant's actions on the railroads south of Petersburg in December 1864 and February 1865 had severely affected Lee's supply chain. In addition, as Sherman had done between Columbia and Charlotte, he was continuing to destroy important railroads south of Virginia. These actions were making it more and more difficult for Lee to remain in static defense around Richmond. In less than a month, Lee would abandon Richmond in what would be a futile attempt to leave Virginia, find supplies, and join Confederates in North Carolina.[41]

Manning

Blackie Hospital
Augusta Geo
March 12st '65
My Dear—

To my great surprise and delight my application of leave came back yesterday "Respectfully returned approved."

I will leave here next friday morning. I will get to Athens friday night if I have no bad luck. I will get home Saturday night I would like for you to make

---

[37] Chaplin, *Riches of Bunyan* (Alexander family copy); service records.
[38] *Georgia Atlas & Gazetteer*, 1.
[39] Chaplin, *Riches of Bunyan* (Alexander family copy); service records.
[40] B. Davis, *Sherman's March*, 139; Sherman, *Memoirs*, 702.
[41] Gallagher et al., *Civil War*, 210–13, 222–25; Trudeau, *Last Citadel*, 284–85, 315–27, 403; Lykes, *Campaign for Petersburg*, 44, 46–48, 70.

some arrangements to meet me on the way Saturday. I will either come out a part of the way friday night or start very early Saturday morning. I know you[r] pa will be so busy that I cant ask him to send to meet me. I will walk half way if you can get some one to meet me Saturday. It will help me along very much. I don't think I can walk all the way in one day

Tell Rash to look about for us some conveyance to go down to fathers in. I will come the direct road—by Moons, Nashez tc

Tell Rash to write me whether there is any foot way across Sandy Creek about the Bridg or not.

There is no news from Sherman further than he is going toward Wilmington. It is reported that his left wing has been defeated. It is thought that Mobial [Mobile] will be attacted soon.

Hoping soon to See you
I remain Yours Most Truly
M. P. Alexander

Notes

I know you[r] pa will be so busy that I cant ask him to send to meet me: It is interesting that Manning did not ask to be met by one of the Davids' enslaved people as he and other family members had done previously.

fathers: This was Lona's father, James Horatio David.

I will come the direct road—by Moons, Nashes &c; across Sandy Creek: Manning appears to be planning to travel from Athens to the David family farm northwest of Maysville (a trip of around twenty-five miles) roughly along present-day Federal Highway 441 and State Road 98.

He would pass over Sandy Creek, a tributary of the North Oconee River, shortly after leaving Athens. He then would proceed toward what today is the town of Commerce, but then would have been the community of Harmony Grove. About four miles south of Harmony Grove, the Nash family had a big house, which later became an inn, on the "Clarksville Road" (today's Highway 441). This house may have been what Manning was referring to as "Nashes."

From Harmony Grove, he would have proceeded northwest to Maysville along what is today State Road 98. ("Moons" has not been identified.)[42]

Sherman going toward Wilmington: Sherman's forces already had taken Wilmington, North Carolina. They had entered it on February 22.[43]

---

[42] Rand McNally, "Map of Athens"; G. Wilson and White, *Early History of Jackson County, Georgia*, 228; *Georgia Atlas & Gazetteer*, 22.

[43] *OR*, ser. 1, vol. 47, pt. 1, 930.

his left wing defeated: When Sherman's forces left Savannah and moved into South Carolina, they had been divided into a right and a left wing. The right wing moved generally closer to the coast, and the left wing moved more inland.[44]

Manning may have been referring to the temporary success of Confederate cavalry General Wade Hampton over Union cavalry General Judson Kilpatrick of the left wing on the morning of March 10 near the South Carolina–North Carolina border. Sherman in his general report recorded the action:

> During the night of the 9th of March his [Kilpatrick's] three brigades were divided to picket the roads. General Hampton detecting this dashed in at daylight and gained possession of the camp of Colonel Spencer's brigade, and the house in which General Kilpatrick and Colonel Spencer had their quarters. The surprise was complete, but General Kilpatrick quickly succeeded in rallying his men, on foot, in a swamp near by, and by a prompt attack, well followed up, regained his artillery, horses, camp, and everything save some prisoners whom the enemy carried off, leaving their dead on the ground.[45]

Mobial [Mobile] will be attacted soon: Union forces began to mobilize in the area of Mobile Bay in mid-February, but it was not until mid-March that the entire Union force that was intending to attack Mobile was gathered at, or was on its way to, its various rendezvous points. General movement of the force for the attack began on March 17. The Union forces finally occupied Mobile on April 12, after Lee had surrendered in Virginia.[46]

---

[44] Ibid., 17–18.
[45] Ibid., 23.
[46] *Augusta Chronicle*, March 12, 1865; *OR*, ser. 1, vol. 49, pt. 1, 87, 91–93; Gallagher et al., *Civil War*, 241, 312.

Chapter 31

The War Ends: Manning, Pillona, and Horatio, April–May 1865

Pillona

At home April 24th 1865
My Dearest *precious one*,

    I have written you a great many letters but but never with such feelings before as I am writing to night. I feel that it is almost impossible to compose my mind enough to write any kind of a letter, but we are compelled to bear it, and every thing that is put upon us. Oh! My Dear how hard it is that the *blood* of our precious brothers should all be spilt in vain. I feel like if we only had them back I could reconcile it to my feelings a great deal better. I am so very anxious to see result of this armistice. My Dear your precious letter of 22 inst. came to hand this evening and also the papers. although its contents were sad it was received with a great deal of pleasure. My Dear I have expected for some time it would come before a great while but it came sooner than I expected.

    My Dear I am afraid to help myself up with the idea of your coming home to stay soon. if we only could have our liberties and you at home my joy would be inexpressible. We heard saturday evening that Lincon was killed and Seward stabbed but did not believe it although Ratio saw a man that saw it in the Yankee papers in the vicinity of Atlanta. We heard yesterday of the capture of Gen. Lees army. it seemed to be authentic information but yet we hoped it was untrue.

    There was 4 men went up in the hack this evening that belonged to Phips Legion that were captured and paroled. they said there was only 8 thousand 8000 men lives [alive?] when they were paroled. the remainder were stragling over Va. We have not heard one word from poor little Jimie Neal. if we could but know his fate. We hardly have any grounds to hope that he was alive.

    Ratio wants to go to Athens this week to see if he can draw his rations. he will bring the box if he does. if [he does] not go I will send for it the first good opportunity. Hogs are very scarce in this country. I went to see Mr. Savale this morning. he told me to look around in the country and if I couldnt git any he would try to let me have one.

    [he never said what it was worth but I don't know whether he will let me have it now or not. I would have written you a long letter to day but I heard this morning that the roads was cut between Athens and Augusta and did not know whether to write till I heard from you]

Notes

This letter: Lona wrote this letter on the front and back of a single sheet of poor-quality paper. She ran out of room at the bottom of the back side of the paper, so she turned the paper upside down and wrote the bracketed words in the top margin of the back of the paper that she originally had left blank. She had no room left for her signature.

this armistice: On April 18, General Sherman for the Union and General Joseph E. Johnston for the Confederates signed an armistice agreement near Durham Station, North Carolina. The terms Sherman agreed upon, however, were found by President Andrew Johnson, now president after Lincoln's assassination on April 14, and the cabinet to be too generous, and they rejected them. With the aid of General Grant, new terms for surrender of Johnston's Army of Tennessee were presented, and the surrender was signed on April 26. The document signed was not an armistice (that is, a cease fire with peace terms to be negotiated later) but was surrender by the Confederates under terms dictated by the Union.[1]

Lincon was killed and Seward stabbed: President Lincoln was shot by John Wilkes Booth on April 14 and died the next day. Also on April 14, William Henry Seward, secretary of state, was stabbed by one of Booth's co-conspirators, but Seward survived.[2]

capture of Gen Lees army: General Lee surrendered the Army of Northern Virginia at Appomattox, Virginia, on April 9.[3]

hack: A "hack" was horse-drawn vehicle, such as a carriage, coach, or wagon, that was for hire.[4]

Phips Legion that were captured and paroled: Lona is referring to Phillips Georgia Legion, which had been divided into an infantry unit and a cavalry unit. Phillips Legion infantry surrendered with Lee at Appomattox while Phillips Legion cavalry surrendered with Johnston in North Carolina. Because the men Lona had talked with mentioned stragglers in Virginia and because Lee surrendered before Johnston, they probably were with the infantry unit.[5]

Jimie Neal: James R. Neal, son of Mary Juliette David Neal, surrendered with Lee at Appomattox on April 9. He had survived the war and later returned home to Georgia.[6]

---

[1] Gallagher et al., *Civil War*, 312; Wagner, *Timeline of the Civil War*, 227–28.
[2] Wagner, *Timeline of the Civil War*, 227.
[3] Ibid., 226.
[4] "Hack," *Webster's New World College Dictionary*, 651.
[5] Coffman, *Going Back the Way They Came*, 95; Sifakis, *Compendium of the Confederate Armies*, 167–68, 284–85.
[6] Service records.

Mr. Savale: There were at least two older male Savalls in Jackson County then, Isaiah and William. Both were farmers and both about sixty-four years old. Possibly the one Lona wrote about was William. He and Manning had a later connection when in 1875 Manning apprenticed the orphan daughter of woman who had once been enslaved by William (see chapter 32).[7]

Manning

Blackie Hospital
Augusta Geo
April 29th/65
My Dear

I will write you a few lines to day although I am so low spirited that I cannot write anything interesting

I will send you a paper which contains all the news and rumors that are in circulation.

Dear—I have been fully confident for a long time—as you know—that we would finally come to our present condition. I thought I was fully prepared for the emergency but in spite of all my efforts to bear the misfortune calmly I find it very difficult to bear up under it. I feel and look five years older than I did when I was at home. And then the suspence is hardly bearable.

I am now fully satisfied that the fighting is over but how long we will have to remain here I cant tell. My opinion is that this will be the last place to wind up

I succeeded in geting two more yards of blue cloth today. I will try to buy some salt with the money I have—I cant buy anything here—Confederate money [here] is only worth $00 for one is specia to-day. Dr Howard has tendered his [torn line] days leave. He will start home tomorrow. I think I will send 200 dollars to Athens by him to buy salt.

Lieut Gramlin got here last night. he saw Ratio at the office as he came along. I received yours of 26 wednesday night.

Dear I will close. I will write soon and try to interest you more next time

Yours most Truly
M P Alexander

Notes

This letter: The letter was written on paper that was longer than usual and was folded to form an envelope addressed:
"Mrs. M P Alexander
   Wall Street

---

[7] US Census, 1850, Jackson County, for William and Isaiah Savall.

Georgia"

specia: Specie: "coin of precious metal."[8]

Dr. Howard: He was N. F. Howard former surgeon of the 52nd Georgia Regiment. At Vicksburg, the 52nd had been part of Barton's Brigade with the 43rd when Manning was with the 43rd.[9]

Lieut. Gramlin: He has not been identified.

Manning Poole Alexander to E. J. Roach, Surgeon in Charge

Office Blackie Hospital
Augusta Geo May 1st 1865

Sir:
Having been paroled, I have the honor to ask you to be relieved from duty.
Very Respectfully
M. P. Alexander
Asst Surg P. A. C. S.

[To] E J Roach
Surg in Charge
Gen. Hospitals
[Written on the back of M. P. Alexander's application]
Blackie Hospital
Augusta Ga
May 1st 1865
M P Alexander
Asst Surg PACS
Application to
be relieved
from duty
Office Blackie Hos
Augusta Ga May 1, 1865

Approved & Respectfully
Forwarded

J. G. Boatwright
Surg in ch

Office Post Surg
Augusta Ga

---

[8] Drake, *What Did They Mean by That?*, 285.
[9] Service records.

May 1st/65

Approved
E. J. Roach
Senr Surg in charge

Notes

Having been paroled: Manning would have been paroled a day or so earlier by Confederate General Birkett D. Fry, commander of the Confederate troops in Augusta. General Fry was acting under the military convention agreed to by Generals Sherman and Johnston and under specific instructions from General Johnston. In his parole, Manning agreed not to take up arms against the United States of America or provide any information or do any military duty whatever.[10]

Paroles given by General Fry, however, were questioned by a Union officer, General Emory Upton, when he arrived in Augusta on May 3 to take command of the city. Upton was concerned that the paroles had been given by a Confederate rather than a Union officer. Fortunately, when he checked with his commanding officer, that officer approved Fry's paroles.[11]

Asst Surg PACS: P. A. C. S. stood for the Provisional Army of the Confederate States. The Provisional Army was established by the Confederate government in late February 1861 when it enacted a law authorizing President Davis to take into Confederate service for twelve months, state units that either were tendered by the state to the regular army or that volunteered for the regular army and had the state's consent to join it.

A week later, the Confederate government enacted a law giving President Davis additional authority, authority to enlist volunteers directly into the regular Confederate army to serve for twelve months, or longer if needed.

The Confederate government soon modified the provisional army statute to allow President Davis to accept, without state consent, state units who volunteered to join the provisional army. He also was authorized to treat them generally as if they were in the regular army. Most of the war was fought by the provisional army treated like the regular army.[12]

---

[10] *Augusta Chronicle*, April 21 and April 28, 1865; *OR*, ser. 1, vol. 49, pt. 2, 462, 588, 650; *OR*, ser. 1, vol. 49, pt. 1, 347, 415.

[11] *OR*, ser. 1, vol. 49, pt. 2, 588; *OR*, ser. 1, vol. 49, pt. 1, 415.

[12] Confederate Statutes, Provisional Congress, Session I, chapter XXII, February 28, 1861; chapter XXVI, March 6, 1861; Provisional Congress Session II, chapter VIII, May 11, 1861; https://docsouth.unc.edu/imls/19conf/19conf.html, accessed September 20, 2023.

Excerpt from "A Reminiscence of an Afternoon Spent with a Real Daughter of the Confederacy"[13]

Mrs. Jackson recalls that he [Manning Poole Alexander, her father] said he was paroled by the Union and allowed to return to his home, but his medical instruments, except for his amputation saw, were confiscated. The old saw had seen plenty of service, he told his young daughter, but he never elaborated on this gory subject.

Notes

Undated: The author of this document records that he interviewed Lily Alexander Jackson when she was eighty-four years old. This would have meant the date of the interview was 1960 or 1961.

amputation saw: For many years this saw, framed, hung on the office wall of Dr. Alexander's great-grandson, Dr. James C. Gaither.

Capture and Parole—Horatio David[14]

H. J. David
2 Lt, Co. ____, 16 Reg't Georgia Infantry
Appears on a
Roll of Prisoners of War
captured by U. S. Forces under Brvt. Brig. Gen'l
W. J. Palmer and paroled
Roll dated—Not dated
Where captured Athens Ga
When captured May 8, 1865
Remarks:..... . [None]................
Paroled by command of Bvt. Brig Genl. W. J. Palmer at Athens, Ga., on or about May 8, 1865.
G. C. West

Note

Brvt. Brig Genl. W. J. Palmer: General Palmer of the Fifteenth Pennsylvania Cavalry was originally in Athens in pursuit of the fleeing Confederate president Jefferson Davis.

General Palmer, who in early May was in command of Cavalry Division, District of East Tennessee, was near Cowpens, South Carolina, when he received

---

[13] Colquitt Brackett, Ellen A. Crawford Chapter, Children of the Confederacy, n.d., in my possession.
[14] Service records, NARA.

orders to attempt to capture President Davis. Davis was fleeing with members of his cabinet and a cache of Confederate gold, silver, and other valuables thought to be worth several million dollars (actually valued closer to $800,000) that had been stored in Richmond and at the mint in Dahlonega, Georgia. Protected by several brigades of cavalry, he was heading south from Charlotte, North Carolina, with the ultimate goal of making it across the Mississippi River to safety. Palmer hoped to get ahead of Davis and his party and intercept them at Athens.

Palmer and his cavalry division reached Athens on May 4 ahead of Davis and his group. He ordered parts of his command to various places in Georgia to guard fords, ferries, bridges, and roads that Davis might use and to destroy rail lines to prevent him from traveling by rail.

In the end, however, Palmer did not capture Davis, but elements of his command did capture General Braxton Bragg and Major General Joseph Wheeler. By his quick movements, however, Palmer had cut Davis off from going toward the Mississippi River. Davis finally was captured in the early morning of May 10 near Irwinville, in south central Georgia, about forty-five miles east of Albany.

Palmer himself left Athens sometime before May 12. Before he left, he ordered Horatio and other Confederate soldiers found in Athens paroled. He also left Howell Cobb, former speaker of the US House of Representatives and now former Confederate general, at Cobb's home in Athens awaiting arrest for his part in the secession and the war. Howell Cobb had been the first commander of Horatio's regiment.[15]

For Horatio and Manning the war now was over.

---

[15] *OR*, ser. 1, vol. 49, pt. 1, 534–56; Inscoe, *Civil War in Georgia*, xiii, 101–104; H. Montgomery, *Howell Cobb's Confederate Career*, 14, 33–35, 132.

PART 3

AFTER THE WAR

1865–1923

Chapter 32

Manning and Pelona, 1865–1880

1865

Reminiscences of Lily Alexander Jackson[1]

When the war ended my parents were so poor they had to live in one of Grandpa David's *vacated* [emphasis original] slave houses. However, before Margie was born in December 1867 they had bought a farm home called the Brown place where Mamie was also born. Before I came, they had moved to another place, the farm you children [Margie's children] own.

Notes

Lily Alexander Jackson: She was Manning Poole and Pelona David Alexander's youngest child, born December 6, 1877. The reminiscences are undated but probably were written in 1946 when she was sixty-nine years old, or around that time.[2]

my parents: Manning and Lona Alexander.

Slave houses: The 1860 slave schedule listed James H. David as having two slave houses.

Margie: She was the Alexanders' second child, Margaret Bowen Alexander, born December 16, 1867. She married James T. Comer on July 5, 1886.[3]

Mamie: Mamie was the Alexander's third child, Mary Lee Alexander, born November 16, 1871.[4]

vacated slave houses: In an attempt to find what happened to the Davids' enslaved people after the Civil War, I worked with Elizabeth Olson, a professional genealogist with specialties in Georgia and African American research. Unfortunately, we were unable to find any definite information about where they went or what they did once they became free. The lack of records during slavery that named them, the fact that not all enslaved people took their owners' last names, the frequent movement of formerly enslaved people away from their former

---

[1] The handwritten reminiscences are in my possession.
[2] Lily Alexander Jackson to Olivia Comer Brockmann, August 8, 1946; tombstone of "Lillie Alexander Jackson," Oconee Hill Cemetery, Athens, Georgia.
[3] Tombstone of Margie A. Comer, Oconee Hill Cemetery, Athens, Georgia; Lily Alexander Jackson, genealogical notes; marriage certificate, State of Georgia, Jackson County.
[4] Tombstone of Mamie Alexander O'Kelley, Sunrise Cemetery, Maysville, Georgia; Lily Alexander Jackson, genealogical notes.

homes seeking opportunities elsewhere, the frequent uncertainty of their dates of birth, and the general lack of information about them made the task difficult, and ultimately, not possible.

1867

Reconstruction Oath

No. 80

STATE OF GEORGIA
COUNTY OF Jackson Personally appeared before me this *29th* day of *July*, 1867, *Manning P. Alexander*
who states he resides in the *465* Election Precinct of *Jackson* County Georgia, and who makes oath as follows:

"I *Manning P. Alexander* do solemnly swear...in the presence of Almighty God, that I am a citizen of the State of Georgia; that I have resided in said State for *twelve* months next preceding this day, and now reside in the County of *Jackson* in said State; that I am 21 years old; that I have not been disfranchised for participation in any rebellion or civil war against the United States, nor for felony committed against the laws of any State or the United States; that I have never been a member of any State Legislature, nor held any executive or judicial office in any State, and afterwards engaged in insurrection or rebellion against the United States, or given aid or comfort to the enemies thereof; that I have never taken an oath as a member of Congress of the United States, or as an officer of the United States, or as a member of any State Legislature, or as an executive or judicial officer of any State, to support the Constitution of the United States, and afterwards engaged in insurrection or rebellion against the United States, or given aid and comfort to the enemies thereof; that I will faithfully support the Constitution and obey the laws of the United States, and will to the best of my ability, encourage others so to do. So help me, God."

The said *Manning P. Alexander* further swears....that he has not been previously registered under the provisions of "An act supplemental to 'an act to provide for the more efficient government of the rebel States'—passed March 2, 1867 and to facilitate restoration," under this or any other name, in this or any other Election District; and further, that he was born in[left blank]and naturalized by [left blank] on the [left blank] day of [left blank], 18 [left blank] in the [left blank].

Manning P. Alexander
SWORN AND SUBSCIRBED before me
J. B. S. Davis
Register of the *33d* Registration District

Notes

Oath: The oath was required by the federal act cited in the oath, otherwise known as the Second Reconstruction Act. Enacted on March 23, 1867, the act required each male citizen of the United States (Black and White) who was twenty-one years of age and older and a resident of a state that the First Reconciliation Act had included in a military-controlled district to take the oath before being registered to vote. Ten southern states were in such districts, and Georgia was in the Third Military District.[5]

All otherwise eligible males in Georgia were required to take the oath and register before being able to vote in an election held in late 1867 for delegates to a convention to write a new state constitution. The Second Reconstruction Act prescribed the exact wording of the oath. As indicated above, Manning took the oath.[6]

1869

Manning Alexander

Richmond Daily Dispatch
July 10, 1869
A Soldier's Grave to be Identified
MAYSVILLE, Ga., July 4, 1869
Editors Dispatch:

My brother, A. O. Alexander, was killed near Gaines's mill during the seven days' fight around Richmond, June, 1862. He was buried with two other soldiers in the same grave. I have learned that the grave was marked. If that be true, perhaps the grave may be identified yet. Now, it is the earnest request of an affectionate wife, an aged father and mother, and his surviving brothers, that the papers of Richmond give this a place in their columns, so that should it fall under the notice of any one in the vicinity of Gaines's mill who is willing to trouble themselves to examine the *Confederate* [emphasis original] graves and write to the subscriber, they will at least very much oblige the bereaved family and friends of the deceased. I think the Twenty-second Georgia was the regiment that he belonged to.

---

[5] Manning's oath was found in Georgia, Returns of Qualified Voters and Reconstruction Oath Books, 1867–1869, Jackson County, 33.

[6] Encyclopaedia Britannica, *Annals of America*, 10:93–95; Coleman, *History of Georgia*, 211–12; "America's Reconstruction: People and Politics After the Civil War," Supplementary Reconstruction Act of Fortieth Congress, https://www.digitalhistory.uh.edu/exhibits/reconstruction/section4/section4_reconact1867_2.html, accessed February 16, 2023.

My post-office address is Maysville, Jackson county, Ga.

M. P. Alexander, M.D.

Notes

write to the subscriber: No response to this letter has been found.

the Twenty-second Georgia: According to his service records, Adam O. Alexander was in the 21st Georgia.

1870

Margaret and James D. Alexander

September, 1870
Dear Son

I seat myself to Drop you a few lines to let you [know] we got home safe and found all well. J D will start Friday weak and will come by youre house and stay until thee rest comes on. your father has sold his land for 12 hundred dollars to a man from south carlina. he was thar when we got home. we all exspect [to] start the last of November. J D will [tell you] all about it. it is a hard trial for me to part from any of you but I have studied it over And it may be for the best for us to go as it may be of advantage to the rest if ever you move. I hope you will come to us. you mus all come down before we move. ther is severl as old as we are a going. no more at present
your mother
Dear Brother M P

I will first say to you that I will be at your house on Saturday after the fourth Sunday on my way to Texas if nothings happens. can you not come over to Homer on that day & meet us there
Yours as ever

J. D. A.

Notes

it is a hard trial for me to part from any of you: Most of Manning's family decided to move to Texas, but Manning and his older brother William stayed in Georgia. (A younger brother, John N. Alexander, who was mentioned in Margaret Alexander's letter of 1862 in chapter 14, had died on August 28, 1863, at the age of fifteen.)[7]

Homer: Homer, Georgia, was in Banks County about ten miles from the farm outside the small town of Harmony Grove where Manning and his family had moved by 1870. (In 1903 Harmony Grove was renamed "Commerce.")

---

[7] Chaplin, *Riches of Bunyan* (Alexander family copy).

By then Manning's family had grown by the birth of a daughter, Margaret Bowen Alexander, on December 16, 1867. Manning was practicing medicine, and at least some dentistry according to a bill to him from "Samuel S. White, Manufacturer of and Wholesale Dealer in Artificial Teeth and Dentist's Materials." Also, on his farm he was growing such crops as potatoes, beans, and wheat.[8]

Democratic Meeting in Jackson[9]

JEFFERSON, GA., OCT. 10TH, 1870

According to a previous notice, the delegates from the various Districts of Jackson County, assembled in the Court House to-day, for the purpose of nominating a Democratic candidate to represent the party in the next Legislature... .

The roll of Districts was called:....

Cut Off.—T. V. Brazzleton, H. J. David, M. P. Alexander.....

Notes

Democratic candidate to represent the party in the next Legislature: In July 1870, Congress restored Georgia to the Union. In December of the same year, a sufficient number of Democrats were elected to take control of both houses of the Georgia legislature. What is sometimes called "Radical Reconstruction" had come to an end in Georgia.[10]

H. J. David: He was Manning's brother-in-law, Horatio James David (Ratio).

1871

Margaret Alexander

Wood Co Tex Jan 22d 1871
Dear Son

I with plesure tak my [pen] this butifull sabath morning for the first tim to inform you how we have got along since we left you. we have saw many strang things since we left you[,] more than I can tell you of now but we hav hadno bad luck yet. we got a long without ever being pesterd.

we went from atlata to west point & then to mongumery & the[n] to mobelive [Mobile] crost the bay and toock the cars to new orleens. in all th places we saw many strange things & all sorts of peope. we got hear on sund day evening &

---

[8] *Atlanta Constitution*, August 21, 1903; envelope from Sam to Manning sent from Jefferson, Texas, December 11, 1870; US Census, 1870, Jackson County; bill of sales for goods in 1871 in my possession.

[9] *Southern Watchman*, October 19, 1870, 3.

[10] Coleman, *History of Georgia*, 214–17.

went abord of red river bote & left monday eve[,] monday at five oclock [,] & got to jefferson sonday morning.

we stay ther two days. we got a room & fire wood for seventy five sents a day. then we went to coffyvill. we got a room for nothing and hear bob left us and went to hopkins county as we thaugt we wold go ther two but your father & sam was taken sick with dire [diarrhea] and was verry bad of[f].

your father got better & him [and] James started with a lode & your father got worse againe & thy cum on this chane which was very good & good houses & they thought had better stop as th wether was very cold & rodes bad & they though[t] they had beter stop and make a crop and lok for a place to go to. the cntry is good hear and plenty of the best of land for sail but they think ther is places that wil soote them better & so they loock before they will settle.

I can see nothing to hinde[r] peope to do well hear if they have ther health. we are all well satisfied so far but we have had no chance to [k]no[w] much yet as the wether has bin very cold.

bob is hear now. he has got a good [s]chool at ryleyes springs in Hopkins county 24 miles from hear.

I have stood the trip well so fare. have had my health well. the rest is all well. sam thinks his lungs improveing.

I will come to a close for the presant but will wright more soon. Wright as soon as you get this & let us know how you all geting a long. tell lona and the children that I think of them every day of my life. tell marga [Margie] grnma will [not?] forget her. so I remain your mother till death

Notes

Letter: Margaret Alexander wrote all of this letter as one paragraph and inserted no periods at the ends of sentences. She frequently wrote parts of words and then crossed them out and left letters out of a word or left a word out altogether. More than once, she wrote the identical words right after the other. The paragraphs and periods have been added, the crossed out parts of words and the double wordings have been eliminated, and some letters and words (in brackets) have been inserted to make the letter easier to read.

Wood Co Tex: Wood County is about eighty-five miles east of Dallas as the crow flies. Most of the family had stopped to spend winter at the very northeast part of the county near Winnsboro.[11]

Trip to Texas: Some details of the journey included in this note and notes for subsequent letters are taken from letters not included in this book but in my possession.

---

[11] *Rand–McNally 2019 Road Atlas*, 100.

Margaret and Robert Alexander, the senior Alexanders, left home in Franklin County, probably with the rest of the traveling family, in late November 1870. The group probably traveled by horse or mule-drawn wagons and arrived in Atlanta on November 30.[12]

On December 2, they left Atlanta by rail, probably after selling the wagons and animals. Their rail trip took them by West Point, Georgia to Montgomery, Alabama. There they changed trains to go to Mobile on a newly constructed line from Montgomery to New Orleans that had been in operation for only two weeks. In fact, they thought they were the first emigrants to travel on that line. Their arrival in Mobile was delayed, however, by a collision on the line, which did not hurt anyone in their party but was described as "a frightful Scene." They proceeded on to New Orleans, arriving on December 4.[13]

The next day they left New Orleans aboard the steamer *Gladiola* for a trip up the Red River. Manning's brother Sam described the Red River as "a vary ugly Stream" and the trip itself as "vary tedious." The river was low, and for much of the way upriver the boat had to be pulled by setting the anchor ahead and gradually winding the anchor chain around the capstan to pull the boat forward.[14]

The family and their baggage traveled on deck taking advantage of a cheaper rate. (A deck pass was eight dollars per person while cabin was twenty dollars per person.) They were crowded, but being in the open air, they did have a stove to cook on. At least one member of the traveling family, however, regretted the economy. Brother Bob wrote Manning that "if there is hell on earth Deck pass on Red river has its full portion."[15]

Their deck travel ended at Jefferson, Texas, where they arrived on December 11, a trip of six days. At that time a huge, hundred-mile-long logjam blocked boats from going very far north on the Red River. Instead, boats carrying people into Texas left the Red a few miles north of Shreveport, Louisiana, and traveled into Texas across Caddo Lake and Big Cypress Bayou to Jefferson.[16]

As Manning's mother indicated, they stayed in Jefferson two days and left December 13, heading west. They reached Coffeeville in Upshur County about twenty-eight miles west of Jefferson on December 14 or 15. (In 2016 Coffeeville was reported to be something of a ghost town, with only a small church building

---

[12] Sam Alexander to Manning, November 30, 1870.

[13] Sam Alexander to Manning, December 11, 1870; Bob Alexander to Manning, December 25, 1870.

[14] Sam Alexander to Manning, December 11, 1870; Bob Alexander to Manning, December 25, 1870.

[15] Bob Alexander to Manning, December 25, 1870, February 19, 1871; Margaret Alexander to Manning, May 26, 1871.

[16] Bob Alexander to Manning, December 25, 1870; Wikipedia, "Jefferson, Texas," https://en.wikipedia.org/wiki/Jefferson,_Texas, accessed January 4, 2019.

remaining). Bob already had arranged to be taken further west, and he and his wife left shortly for Sulphur Springs, about fifty miles away in Hopkins County. They had arrived by Christmas Day.

As Manning's mother indicated, the remainder of the family was to follow, but illness prevented their going very far. They decided to stay instead in nearby Wood County for at least the winter. Meanwhile, Bob and wife had moved to Reilly Springs, about twelve miles south from Sulphur Springs, for the winter.[17]

chane: The meaning of this word has not been found. Possibly "chance" was what was meant and the second "c" was left out accidentally.

William P. Alexander

Feb 16th 1871

Dear brother [Manning] I received a few lines from you Enquireing of fathr & mother. I received a letter from jim the Same male. he dident write much. Said that he had writin to me and had not received any answer. I havent received anything but this one letter since I saw you. Could not write to them unless I knew where to write. he said that father had had a verry bad spell of Dysentery but was better[,] that he Suffered a good deal in making water[,] that they wer all living on the same farm togeather [and]that he[,] that is jim[,] was well satisfied.[This] was a bout all of his letter. their post office is Winnsborough Wood County Texas. this leaves us all well. come down and see us. I am verry busy now trying to fix for a crop

       Yours etc Wm. P Alexander

Note

William P. Alexander: He was Manning's older brother, then forty-three years old with a wife and four children. Manning was then forty.[18]

Margaret and Robert W. Alexander

Wood Co Tex Feb 19th, 1871

Dear Son

After so long we have met with another favorable opportunity of dropping you a few more lines, that you may learn that we are all in very good health. And fondly hope that we will hear from you bfore long with the gladsome news that you are all well. For while we are very, yes very! far from you & many vast rivers

---

[17] Wikipedia, "Coffeeville, Texas" https://en.wikipedia.org/wiki/Coffeeville,_Texas, accessed January 4, 2019; Sam Alexander to Manning, December 11, 1870; Bob Alexander to Manning, December 25, 1870, and January 8, 1871; *Rand McNally 2019 Road Atlas*, 100.

[18] Chaplin, *Riches of Bunyan* (Alexander family copy); US Census, 1870, Madison County, Georgia.

exist betwen us yet that same strong & sacred ty that binds the parent & child together remains unbroken & the heart fills to overflow & break out in a sob of inexpressible love as the mind runs back to the old homested and sees by imagination those two dear boys with their loveing little famlys as they gase toward that sacred spot talking a bout going to fathers to bask a while in the sunshine of pleasure & add a word of comfort to the aged parents. But alas cannot;

But while these feelings linger around our hearts, we are not despondent for this is a vast country with the richest soil we ever saw & with e[c]onomy (a term almost unknown here) an[d] intdstry we see nothing to hinder us from liveing well & have all the comeforts that one could desire if the health of the country will admit of it & there is as little fatal sickness here as there is anywere but there are a greate many that have chills. But [they] are of lighter form than those in the old states.

But to sum it all in a few words I would say that the fever & ague is all the drawback there is a bout this country. For the improvement & intelligence of this country is as good as can be found anywere. The state of society will equal if not surpass that of old Jackson & Banks counties. Schools. we know of no country that excels this for schools. for instant the renowned M. H. & George Loonys are in this county teaching. And there are many schools that will tally with theirs so you see that this is not a backs-woods country. And churches of various denominations are flourishing at different in this & adjoining counties. And judgeing from the most reliable information that we can git it is the same in various other counties over the state.

Land varies considerable here in price, owing to locality improvement & quality, but the locality governes more than any thing elce. It is selling from two to ten dollars per A, the vary best of improved land & in the vary best of society is worth ten. This is the highest price with improvement & society as good as heart could desire & the man that would want a better soil ought to be hung. As you git further from these desireable neighborhoods the price of land decreases. You can git just as good land as you want unimproved in vary good settlements for three dollars for A. And it is much easier to improve land here than there. & the first crop is as good as the low ground in Ga. Cotton on new ground will do finely. it will grow & mature fore & five feet high.

We have not fully determined yet whether we will stop in this country or go further west. we would like to hear from you on that point. there is no question but wat the land is much better west than here, but it is vary scearce of timber & here we have the best of timber. J. D. has been up as far west as Grason Co. he says the land is as good as he ever saw in the old KY but the timber is retchedly scearce. we hear vary favorable reports from Bell, Hill & Johnson Countys & think perhaps will go to Johnson. It is said to be qute healty & no chills there.

We donot wish you to think that we over rate this country, for in our Judegement we dont. Neither would we have you think we are trying to induce [you]to come here for their are many sacred ties to be cut loose before one can leave their native land & bid farewell to sod that gave them birth.[It] is one of the hardest tryals of a persons life & none know the feeling but those who have undergone the tryal. But not withstanding this when we look-out on this vast country which is destined one day to be the Edon of this continent we cannot refrain from wishing all our friends were here to shear some of the good things of this country [even] if it is adulterated with some bad.

But we will drop this subject short off. We rote you before that your father had been vary sick, and is now well as ever with the exception of feet & legs. they got frostbitten in that cold weather while moveing. They have been so badly swollen & painful that we was fearful that it might terminate vary srously. You can scearcely conceive how bad they was & are still vary bad but some better.

Perhaps you think it has been a long time since we wrote so it has been. But the reason why we have not written sooner is becaus we could not procure stamps. We will write oftener. Hope we will soon hear from you—have not heard a word from you since we left you.

Direct your letters as before.
    Leesburg Upshare Co.
        Tex
Care of Wm Frederick
R. W. & M. C. Alexander

Notes

chills: A modern book defines the term: "[A] common expression meaning any chilling and feverish condition early thought to be diseases rather than symptoms."

In an earlier letter from Texas, Manning's brother Bob explained that the chills "are not bad, people do not stop work for them, only while the chill is on." He said that when the man who drove him from Jefferson had the chills, "he would lie down on the road side and wait till it was off, get up and drive on, talk and laugh like nothing had happened." (Possibly "chills" was another term for malaria?) Bob added "but I don't care to have them."

Bob also mentioned that the remedy was "a preparation containing arsenic" and asked Manning for his advice about chills and the remedy. "Chills" later would be a problem for the whole family.[19]

---

[19] Drake, *What Did They Mean by That?*, 54; Robert Alexander to Manning, January 8, 1871.

ague: "An intermittent fever and chills."[20]

M. H. and George Loonys: They were the brothers Morgan H. Looney and George C. Looney, friends of Manning from Franklin County (see chapter 2). In 1854, Alexander H. Stephens, later vice president of the Confederacy, said of Looney, "As an educator [he] has no equal in the South."[21]

Grason County: Grayson County is in North Texas about sixty miles north of Dallas.[22]

Bell, Hill & Johnson Countys: Bell County is in Central Texas about thirty-five miles south of Waco. Hill and Johnson Counties are between Dallas and Waco.[23]

we cannot refrain from wishing all our friends were here to shear some of the good things of this country [even] if it is adulterated with some bad: In her letter, Margaret mentioned some factors the family was considering as they evaluated potential home sites. She mentioned the healthiness of an area, the quality of its soil, the schools and churches it contained, the state of its society in general, the price of land, and the availability of timber to build houses, fences, and outbuildings. Other factors mentioned later in other letters were whether the weather was good; the land was good for farming or for grazing hogs, cattle, or cows; good water was available; and dangerous Indians were nearby.

Although Margaret also wrote that she would not have Manning think they were trying to induce Manning to come there, she clearly was giving him information about the place with that possibility in mind. Manning's brothers in subsequent letters also provided such information with the same thought. One letter included information on the number and quality of the doctors in the area. Manning also began asking questions on his own with the thought of coming to Texas, at least to evaluate it for himself.[24]

Leesburg Upshare Co.: Where the Alexanders stopped in Wood County was very close to the Upshur County border. Leesburg probably was the closest post office.[25]

Bob Alexander

Riley Springs
[not dated but probably May 1871]

---

[20] Drake, *What Did They Mean by That?*, 5.

[21] See chapter 2.

[22] *Rand McNally 2019 Road Atlas*, 100.

[23] Ibid.

[24] For example, see the following letters, all addressed to Manning: letters from Robert dated February 19, 1871, and May 29, 1871, and letter from James dated March 6, 1871.

[25] *Rand McNally 2019 Road Atlas*, 100.

[The letter has no a salutation, but it was written to Bob's brother Manning.]

I recieved a copy of the Athens Watchman last week which I supose you sent. I saw in it that you had left Irish potaors at the office as a sample. we had a mess the 1st Sunday in Ap[ril] large as hen eggs & that of the late pink eye variety. if we had had your kind we would have had them earlier— we had a mess of beans the first of May of the variety of which you gave mother the seed—white bean that mess. I have some of the vines 15 feet high. I think if I had a pole they would run 40 feet high. I have 3 acres of corn waist & shoulder high. will lay it by next saturday—have ½ acre in yam potatoes. we have Irish potatoes by the bushels. Texas is the greatest place for a farmer to be rewarded for his labor I ever saw. corn & cotton grows right up. my corn has had but one plowing. all it need is to keep it above the weed.

… I dont think I will settle in this part of Texas. I am certain I will not till I see more of the west. I would be satisfied here if it was not for the single word *chills*. we have enjoyed perfect health yet but I fear we will not this fall. but emegrants are scarcely ever sick the first year. they generally take the chills the 2d or 3d year.

Good thimble skein wagons are worth $100.00 & $120.00. good mules $175.00 $200 & $250.00. Such mules [as] your gray mule $150.00.

land is on a stand neither rising nor falling. some think it is as high as it will get. land in the woods $2.50 to $5.00 [per acre]. improved $10.00 to $15.00. the $2.50 land is generally in some sickly locality.

I am going to fathers next Friday. I think we will come to some conclusion as to whether father will settle in this part or go west. I know I can do better west. all a man has to do west is to buy himself a few cows and the increase soon makes him rich. I want to find a country that abounds in plenty of good water, hills & valleys etc. write soon. Your brother Bob

Note

thimble skein wagons: A thimble skein was a device used to attach a wooden axle to a wagon wheel. It was a hollow metal casing that fitted tightly over the axle end and held the wheel by a threaded nut.[26]

Sam Alexander

Leesburg Texas July 24th71
Dear brother [Manning]

---

[26] National Historic Oregon Trail Interpretive Center, https://www.blm.gov/learn/interpretive-centers/national-historic-oregon-trail-interpretive-center, accessed January 1, 2019; Sneed, "Wheels That Won the West," http://wheelsthatwonthewest.blogspot.com, accessed January 1, 2019.

According to promic I again take-up my old steel pen to let you know how we are all giting a long.

When I wrote you last some of us was not well & especialy mother and some are not in vary good health yet but all improving. mother has had a very bad spell with her bowels but is now improving vary fast & might say has got a bout well but is feeble & week. she can now sit up most all day. her bowels do not trouble her any. we hav one of the best doctors (said to be in the state) to see her. his first prescription was kino, quinine, wine & a small qunity of opium. I do not know what his last pre was as I did not see him myself but she has now quit takeing anything.

Fathers health has been quite good all summer, but is somewhat poorly at this time. He is suffering with his bladder complaint more than he has don since he has been here & I think has some symtoms of chills but if he has we will stop them immediately. It is vary seldom that old persons are troubbled with chills.

J. D. family hav all been chilling except Jim. Lily has had a very bad spell of bilious fevor but is giting better. Some of my chaps hav had symtoms of chills but I broke them up before they chilled much if any. I think Lizzie had a slight chill yesterday so I am doctor again to day. My prescription Jayne's pills, quinine & plenty of chicken & soop.

We hav had a severe drouth here which has injured some corn considerable but some is just good enough. Ours being two thick is badly injured, but we will make agood deal of corn. hav some rain to day & prospect for more.

I am teaching. hav a good school worth some fifty or sixty dollars per month. J D has a school some four miles from here. he thinks it will pay vary well.

Father has bought land in this settlement. I think I told you a bout the place in my last. So I will not say any thing this time more than father is well pleased with the place & it is one of the healthyest places in this country. Has excellent water & is well improved. The corn on the place is as good as any bottom land in that country.

we heard from bob to day. he & fany hav the chills. Bob says he cant stay where he will hav chills. Fany says she dont mind it much. Jim says he dont think he will stay in Texas any longer than [when] he gits able to git a way. I will hav to see something worce than I hav seen before I git so bad out of heart.

Samson Westbrook & John Bellamy was here last week. They liv a bout seventy miles west of this in Hunt Co. they are going to move down here. they want to git to better water & where it is not so subject to drouth.

I will close for this time as I must write to W. P. Benot [illegible word]. I will keep you posted in regard to our health. write us soon. You can chainge the direction of our letters a little as we hav become acquainted with the P M. Just say forward to Leesbrg in place of in care of Fredrick. I remain your Brother

Sam

Notes

kino: A gum obtained from certain tropical plants used in medicine as an astringent to "contract bodily tissue and check secretions."[27]

J. D.: James David "Jim" Alexander.

Lily: She is Jim's wife, Eliza. She also is called Lila.[28]

bilious fever: Bilious fever is "an inexact early description of any fever attended by yellow discoloration of the skin, usually thought to have been caused by an excess of bile and/or a liver dysfunction." General symptoms are nausea and vomiting.[29]

Lizzie: She is Sam's wife, Mary Elizabeth.[30]

Jayne's pills: Dr. Jaynes produced a wide selection of patent medicines that were said to cure almost any disease imaginable. An advertisement read, "In settlements and localities where the attendance of physician cannot be readily obtained, families will find these remedies of great service."[31]

so I am doctor again today: Sam had been an orderly working with Manning at both the hospital in Madison and Augusta, Georgia, during the war. He must have acquired some knowledge of medical care during that time.[32]

good school worth some fifty or sixty dollars per monthe: It appears that Texas had "field schools" similar to those in Georgia in which Simeon taught before the Civil War. They were not funded by a state, city, or county but instead the teacher received from a student's parents so much per student for each day the student attended.[33]

Samson Westbrook & John Bellamy: The Westbrooks were early settlers in Franklin County, the Alexanders' home county in Georgia, and a Sampson Westbrook was born there in 1816. Bellamy also was a Franklin County name. A John Bellamy Jr. was married in 1829, and a woman named Bellamy married a Westbrook, her neighbor, about the same time.[34]

W. P. Benot: He has not been identified.

---

[27] "Astringent," "Kino," *Webster's New World College Dictionary*, 88, 802.

[28] US Census, 1870, Franklin County, Georgia; James and Lila Alexander to Manning, August 4, 1871, below in this chapter.

[29] Drake, *What Did They Mean by That?*, 22; "Bilious," *Webster's New World College Dictionary*, 145.

[30] US Census, 1870, Franklin County, Georgia.

[31] *Alexandria Gazette*, November 21, 1849, April 14, 1868 (quote).

[32] See chapters 26 and 28.

[33] See chapter 1.

[34] Tabor, *History of Franklin County, Georgia*, 166, 395–96, 540.

Sam Alexander

Leesburg Tex Aug 3rd 1871
Dear Brother [Manning],

It is under different felings & sadder circumstances that I write to you this time than ever before. And O! God how can I write the sad word that tells you that our dear father is dead. None but they that hav to perform the task can tell the feelings.

But it is unnecessary for me to try to tell your feelings for it is more than I can do. But I will try to tell you something a bout fathers sickness & death. And to do so I must go back to the early part of the spring that you may understand the nature of his case the better.

From that time up till within a few weeks before his death he was in better health than he had been in for the last ten years. And we had begun to hope that his bladder complaint would never be so painful as it had been. but we were disapointed in our hopes. some four or five weeks before his death, his urinating became painful & got worce untill it was vary severe at times. A few days before he was taken so bad he complained of feeling week & bad. I thought that perhaps he was going to hav chills, but I was mistaken

last tuesday when evening when I came from school, he was walking a bout the house & yard & seemed to be improving. He made inquiry a bout my school & when I told him a bout it, he expressed himself highly delighted with the prospect of my makeing something

He then went into the house & began to talk with mother & said to her that he believed he was loosing his mind & that he was not going to live long. She said to him that we none new when we was going to die, but that he looked more like living than she did. he looked vary strait at her & said you need not be surprised if I am a corps before tomorrow morning

he went to bed & appeared to rest easy. About two or three oclock that night they called me to come in their house & do something with father I went & found him siting on the hearth I spoke to him & said father git up & go to bed, but he paid no attention whatever to what I said. He had sunk into a state of paroxysm & was unconscious of every thing. He had passed his water on the hearth & I think the severe pain had thrown him into paroxysms I put him on the bed & he soon went to sleep & rested tolerable well & did not complain of much pain.

in the morning we tryed to rouse him but he seemed to be in a deep stupor. we sent immediately for the doctor, but could not git him till eight oclock at night & at that time the second paroxysm had commenced but the doctor went to work, we all worked & arrested the paroxysm & he revived a little & rationality returned but seemed to be momentary. the doctor said that the first paroxysm had done the work. that his whole nervous cystem was parellised so there was but little or no chanch fror him. but he stood by him as long as it was necessary

The neighbors come fare & near to wait on him. men that never saw his face before came. All was don that was win the power of man to do, but alas, in vain. The Great & Good One saw fit to take him out of his sufferings & he had to go. And I beleive (from what he said & his manner of living before he was taken so bad) that while we are mourning his loss that he is in Heaven singing praise to the Lamb with part of his family.

He lived seven days after he was taten bad but was unconscious all the time. He died a bout 9 oclock July 31st & was buried Augist 1st He was buried at a church & was put away as nice as I ever saw anyone. his coat pants & vest cost twenty five dollars. Johnson Weemes made his coffin. One Mr Acker[,] a second cousin of fathers[,] Mr McCartha & Mr. Weemes dressed him. Every[thing] upon which he urinated was dyed a bout a deep red copper as culor, his urin a bout the color of strong lye.

Father had bargained for a place but had not drawn writes so the trade was not completed, but the man says mother can have the place if she wants it. But mother is at a loss to know what to do a bout it, and she wants your advice a bout what to do. Mother myself James & Bobb hav concluded to leave it with you & Willian to say what will be best for mother to do in future & whatever you say will be don. so see Willian immediately & consult with him & let us hear from you soon so that she may know what you want her to do whether to buy land here or go further west, or go back. be sure to let her know just what you think best. Uncle Wm O. A. has bought land in Johnson Co & writes for us to go there. Mother says she thinks if she had a farm in this country that she could make a good living if she could have her health.

We want mother to keep all that father left as long as she lives. I thint it best to let her have full controle of all & have no administration if it can be a voided I dont know what the laws of this state are in regard to such matters but will find out before long & if she cant do as she pleases with what she has got I thank she had best retreat. but if she can do as she pleases I think she can do well in this country. but we will wait to hear from you & just what you say for her to do will be don so say just what you think best. I assure you that all that are here will be satisfied with what you & Wm P says for that is what mother wants to do & the rest of us think it best.

I will write more soon. this leaves us all in tolerable good health. Mother has got well.

I remain as ever your brother

Sam

Notes

I will try to tell you something a bout fathers sickness & death: From the symptoms that were described in the letter, it appears as though Robert Alexander, the brothers' father, age seventy-one, had an enlarged prostate that prevented him from completely emptying his bladder. The trapped urine then remained in the bladder for a sufficient time for bacteria to get into both the bladder and the urine. Infection and pain in urination resulted.

Eventually, the bacteria in the urine infected the blood. The paroxysms mentioned in the letter were probably the resulting bouts of high fevers, chills, and delirium. Apparently, the condition was treated inadequately or too late, and low blood pressure, multiorgan failure, and death resulted, which can happen over a period of days to weeks.[35]

paroxysm: "A periodic exacerbation or fit of a disease."[36] "A sudden attack, or intensification of the symptoms, of a disease, usually recurring periodically."[37]

Weemes, Acker, McCartha: Members of the Weems family lived in Franklin County, but they may not be connected to the Weemes in Texas. Acker and McCartha have not been identified other than the connection that appears in the letter.[38]

Uncle Wm O. A.: He was Robert Alexander's brother. He had traveled with Manning's family from Atlanta to Montgomery, Alabama. There he left them to go to Galveston, Texas, by way of the Gulf of Mexico.[39]

Johnson County: Johnson County, to the south of Fort Worth, now is considered part of the Dallas-Fort Worth-Arlington Metropolitan Statistical Area.[40]

James and Lila Alexander

Leesburg Texas
August 4th [1871]
Dear Brother & family [Manning and family]
I will just drop you a feew lines to informe you of our health &c. we air not vry well but all up—as Sam has just rote you a bout fathers death Sickness &c I will not Say any thing a bout it—but will let you no more a bout what Mother wants to do.

---

[35] Email from Stephen M. Minton, MD, Alexandria, Virginia, January 18, 2019.
[36] Dunglison, *Dictionary of Medical Science*, 760.
[37] "Paroxysm," *Webster's New World College Dictionary*, 1063.
[38] Tabor, *History of Franklin County, Georgia*, 286, 306, 350.
[39] Robert Alexander to Manning, February 19, 1871.
[40] Wikipedia, "Johnson County, Texas," https://en.wikipedia.org/wiki/Johnson_County,_Texas, accessed February 16, 2023.

Sam did not write just as She wanted him to do. puting it in few words She wants to go back the worst of any thing elce if She cold See any way to get Back and then live after She gets Back. She Ses if She was back there & you had her money that you cold make it suport her better than for her to be vext [vexed] with a farm. So I think if Shee lives She had best go back as She will never be Satisfied here any more. if you think it best for her to go back the Sooner the better.

Just here let me Say to you that if She Stays here Sams familey will Soon run threw with what She has got. no mistake a bout that. I See how it will go.

I cant write mutch as I have a light Billious attact. I am teaching School a bout 4 miles from Mothers. I am living a bout 3 Miles from her. I have a vry good School.

I will close by Saying I do not exspect to make Texas my home many years.

[This following note from Lila, James's wife, is continued on the same page.]

Sister Lona after along time I will try to write you a little tho I am So neurvis. I make [illegible word] owt. I have bin Sick for the laste 6 weeks and am juste able to do my little Hause worke now. Ive had the fevar, becides other aflictions Im laberin under. Iv [illegible word] disead that I've Sufferd a grate deal with this year. I think it is a grate deal worse than your Sick Stomache. I had rather have the Sick Stomache any way.

the children have bin chilling & loock very bad. this cowntry don't sute N. E. Ga. thr is no plasure in all waise having to take strong medisan.

we nead not regret that Father came to Texas. I havante a doute but if He had remaind in Franklin He wold have bin taken from us. He dide with His olde diseas that He Sufferd So longe with & He was so well Satisfide hear. I have herde Him Say often he never wanted to be berrid in Franklin Co. Mother had Him put away juste write. Bough[t] a redy made sute of close, (black [illegible word]) coate pantes & veste. He had never wore His shoose. He had [them] made before He cam to Texas. we put them on Him. they wer nice as any we cold have got.

Mother toock it very harde. Mother Sed Father had been better of this olde diseas this year than He had bin in several years, until about a month ago. He began to get worse, & He has bin going down hill ever Since. He was able to go about untill wednsday before He dide on Monday. He never new any thing after Thursday. Bobb cam Thursday. Father never new after He got thar.

I think if Mother was backe thar with Brother Maning, wher She cold get medisan from Him She wold be mutch better Satisfide. She tells us when we air wating on her if Maning was thar He cold fix it but we did not know how.

I must close as I want to write to Ma to day
    as ever your Sister Lila

Sam Alexander

Leesburg Tex
[circa October 1, 1871]
Dear Brother & sister [Manning and Lona].

Again we have taken up the old pen to try to tell you how we are giting a long. in so doing we have to record the sad news that our dear little daughter Mattie is dead. None but those that have lost a darling child can immagin how hard it is to give them up. She died of wormes. she was taken vary suddenly with a spasom. the doctor was here in a few minutes after she was taken [illegible word] could do no good. she only lived four days after she was taken & died sept 4th.

our health is now improving some I think except myself, my cough is vary bad & has been for sometime. little magga looks vary badly, she got a fall from the table & bruised her liver some six or eight weeks a go & has looke vary bad ever since. but I hope she may soon git better.

J. D. is chilling some. the rest of his family is well. Susan children are chilling some but I think have got them broken up. Mothers health is tolerable good. she went up to Bobbs & stayed two weeks & had some chills while there. so you can now see why we have delayed writing so long waiting for her to come home.

We have received three letters from you since we wrote you a bout fathers death. And have duly considered them & mother has a bout come to the conclusion to go back to Georgia. she thinks it will be the best for severile reasons. J. D. has determined long since to go back & Bobb will go [move] to the southwest which is some three or four hundred miles & mother does not feel able to undergo the fatigue of so long a move. And as James is determined to go back there would be none but myself to stay with her & look after her & Susans affairs. And she thinks if my health does not get better that I could support susan if she should not live.

Mother I think would be wiling to go as far west as the Brazos River. But that does not seem to satisfy Bobb. She says to tell you that she thinks that she could live easier in this country than a most any where elce if we would all stay together. she says tell you that she is not out of heart a bout the country yet. She says tell you that she thinks that James had better stayed another year any how.

Mother has not decided yet how she will live if she goes back, but thinks she will buy a small farm if she can git it & get a boy to do the plowing & let susan & the children do the hoeing & make their support & she could stay with you the most of her time. but when she gits back you can consult & see what will be best to do.

She will come back with James when he go. I cant say yet when she can git off as the mules & wagon will have to be disposed of & the crop. I dont know how much corn we will make but I suppose a bout a half crop. it has been vary dry this year. has been no rain since the last of May. Still the average crop is a bout as good as bottom land in that country. But ours is not that good. we had two much planted & could not cultivate it as it should hav been.

We would be glad if you would have fathers obituary published. He Joined the Pesbyterian Church at Brandaway S. C. Sept 1828. And was soon after chosen ruling elder of that church which office he filled till the day of his death. He had not put his letter in any church here.

Confidential

Brother M. P. you know that I am no hand to complain at the doings of others. But I think that James & Boobb have been two hasty in their decisions as to what they are going to do. James affirmed that he was going back long before we heard from you, & even before Mother had time to consuld her own mind. And I believe she would hav stayed if they would. And as she came with them here I think it should have been the last thing to leave her. I could not I would not have made no such decision untill I new what she was going to do. Had she staid here or dos stay I feel bound to stay with her. So long as she lives

As ever your Brother Sam

Notes

our dear little daughter Mattie: She was Martha Alexander, aged two or three.[41]

wormes: A disease, usually of the intestines, caused by the presence of parasitic worms.[42]

little magga: She was Margaret Alexander, aged four or five.[43]

Susan: She was the widow of Manning's brother Adam. She had three children, aged nine to fourteen.

He had not put his letter in any church here: This is a type of letter that verifies a person is a member of a particular Presbyterian church. When the person hands this letter to another church, it is at least the first step in becoming a member of the other church.[44]

Manning Alexander

Harmony Grove Geo
Oct 19th 1871

---

[41] US Census, 1870, Franklin County, Georgia.

[42] Dunglison, *Dictionary of Medical Science*, 1124; "Worms," *Webster's New World College Dictionary*, 1668.

[43] US Census, 1870, Franklin County, Georgia.

[44] Walmsley, *Handbook for Clerks of Session in the Presbyterian Church (U.S.A.)*, 3.

Dear Brother—[William]

I received a letter from Sam wednesday which I send you. The letter is not dated but from the post mark I suppose it was written about 1st of Oct. It was mailed 2nd oct. I dont think it necessary for us to meet next Sunday. Should you here any thing that you want to see me about come up any time. I suppose you will get a letter too this week. I think Sam is just right about Jim and Bobb. course I have written to them by todays mail.

Yours Truly
M P Alexander

James Alexander and Margaret Alexander

Texas
Daingerfield
Oct 31, 1871
Dear Brother [Manning]

This is to let you no that me & Mother air onn our way back to Geo. we air now att Thomas Pulliams. will leave here on to morrow morning.

we air coming in wagons. Mother is going to Stay with the wagons as long as She Stayes well or the weather gets bad, in eather case she is going to take the RR. One Mr Davis is driving her wagon. one of Jim Burrouhs Boyes is with us. if Mother takes the cars one [of them] will See her threw.

Mr Burroughs own reasons for coming with wagons air this[:] the Scarsity of money high Tax &c is pressing the people So tight that is hard to Sell Stock for there worth. Mother Sez tel you She wants you to look her out Some Corne. We air all well except Lula & Baby. they air chilling and look badley. I exspect to Stop in Cherokee Georgia

I will rite more next Sunday
Your brother

Notes

Daingerfield, Texas: Daingerfield is about twenty miles northeast of Leesburg.[45]

Thomas Pulliams: William and Joseph Pulliam fought in the Revolutionary War, received land bounties in Franklin County, Georgia, and apparently were the first of that name to live in Franklin County, the Alexanders' home county. In 1853, the Board of Commissioners of the Poor School Fund of Franklin County examined a Thomas Pulliam for fitness as a teacher in a school in the

---

[45] *Rand McNally 2019 Road Atlas*, 100.

County. There is no known relationship between this branch of the Pulliam family and me.[46]

One of Jim Burroughs Boyes: Jim Burroughs may be the James Burroughs who lived and died in Franklin County. He came to Franklin County from Anderson County, South Carolina, the same place that Manning and his family had come from. He also had two sons who died in Texas.[47]

Lula and Baby: Lula is James's wife, and Baby was Robert W. Alexander, about eighteen months old.[48]

James Alexander and Margaret Alexander

Camden Ark
Nov 10 1871
Dear Brother [Manning]

I rote you at Daingeald Texas. this is the next opportinuty and now the chance [is] bad around a camp but I no the thing you most want to no is how Mother is geting a long. She is doing as well as She did at Home before we Started. Mothers mules have improved evry day. I am driving large yoke of oxes a bout as fast as I can. [...] they improve boath in flesh & [in] [illegible] they keep up with the mules. I have allso a vry good [illegible] Wagon!

we have travild a bout 200 Miles. Mother has not decided yet whether She take publick coneveyance or not. if She Shold I will let you no. Mother aimes to leeve Susan at her Brothers & Sisters this year. I will rite more Some Sunday when we air resting. wee have a killing frost this morning. the first.

Your Mother & J D A
I will tell you in my next what I think of Ark.

Notes

Camden Ark: By direct lines, Camden is about seventy miles east of Texas-Arkansas border and fifty-five miles north of the Arkansas-Louisiana border. Jim and his mother returned to Georgia by a different route from the way they had come. They apparently wanted to avoid traveling on the Red River and instead went overland through Arkansas, Mississippi, and Alabama, and then into Georgia.

This is the last letter from Jim and his mother written on their trip back to Georgia. It is not clear where they stayed when they got to Georgia. Possibly they

---

[46] Tabor, *History of Franklin County, Georgia*, 63, 68, 69, 171–76.
[47] Tabor, *History of Franklin County, Georgia*, 414–15; Ancestry.com, Burris/Buress, Burroughs Family Tree, accessed January 29, 2019.
[48] US Census, 1870, Franklin County, Georgia.

stayed at William's or Manning's house for a while until they got settled in their own places. It also is unclear whether Manning's mother ever boarded a train.[49]

Susan: Susan Alexander was the widow of Manning's brother Adam Alexander, who was killed on June 27, 1862, during the Civil War. She and her children returned to Georgia with Margaret.

Henry Hunter

November 15th—1871
Cherokee Mills
Ga

Dear Cousin [Manning]it is withe great pleasure that I have the oppertunity of takeing my pen in hand to write you a short letter. this leaves us all well. hopeing that those few lines will find you all enjoying the same.

I have not any thing to write that would interest you. my object of writeing to you is Pa wants me to read medicine; and as I had rather read under you as any other phisician that I kow of any where and if you will take me under your care to read medicine and practice writhe you until I pay you I will com out thire soon after chrismass. for I expect to read medicine some where. write soon and let me know what you do[,] so I will know how arrang my beuisiness....

Ma and all the rest send houdy to you all
Direct your letters to
    Cherokee mills Ga
To Mr M. P. Elesandra
    Henry Hunter
I will practice with you till I pay you or longer if you want me to
    write soon and let me know
        Henry Hunter

Notes

Cherokee Mills: It was in Cherokee County about eight miles southwest of Canton on Lake Altoona.[50]

Henry Hunter: He was a distant cousin of Pillona Alexander's. Pillona's great-grandmother on her father's side was a Hunter.

1875

---

[49] *Rand McNally 2019 Road Atlas*, 10.
[50] *Georgia Atlas & Gazetteer*, 20; Marlin, *History of Cherokee County*, 30, 134.

Indenture of Apprenticeship

Jackson County, Georgia
State of Georgia
Jackson County

This indenture made & entered into this 27 day of May 1875 between Wiley C. Howard, Ordinary in & for said County of the one part & Dr. M. P. Alexander of said County of the other part, witnesseth that Wiley C. Howard, Ordinary as aforesaid, does hereby bind to the said M. P. Alexander the following named child, to wit Emma Saveall (Col.), an illegitimate orphan girl about Nine years old, the minor orphan of Rhoda Savall, dec'd, as apprentice to the said Alexander until the said Minor shall attain the age of twenty one years (1) it having been made satisfactorily known to the said Ordinary that said child is an illegitimate child whose mother is dead & who has no Estate of any kind to support & maintain her (2) it is agreed on the part of the said M. P. Alexander in consideration of the above stipulation that he will furnish said Minor orphan with suitable provision, clothing, & medical attendance during her minority, or term as apprentice, and will teach her the occupation or business of home service, cooking, washing, ironing, etc & to govern her with Humanity & kindness using only the same degree of force to compel her obedience as a parent may use with a minor child, And he further agrees to teach her habits of morality & industry.

Witness our hands and Seals in Duplicate—day & date above written
Wiley C. Howard, Ordinary [Seal]
M. P. alexander [Seal]
Recorded May 27, 1875

Note

Indenture of Apprenticeship: Manning had applied for the apprenticeship of Emma on April 15, 1875.[51]

The application was made under a law passed by the Georgia General Assembly two years earlier, on February 20, 1873. That law provided that the trustee of the Orphans' Home of the North Georgia Conference of the Methodist Episcopal Church, South, could apprentice orphans in their charge for "some useful trade or calling or occupation" if the apprenticeship was approved by the Ordinary [Judge of the Probate Court] of the county where the orphan resided.[52]

---

[51] *Jackson County Ordinary Minutes, 1873–1878*, 241–42; *Jackson County Ordinary Apprenticeship, Indentures, 1872–1906*, 29.

[52] *Acts and Resolutions of the General Assembly of the State of Georgia, Passed at the Regular January Session 1873*, vol. 1, 184; Amendment 4, "Georgia Office and Court of Ordinary Amendment," Amendment 4 to the Constitution of the State of Georgia (1974), "Georgia's Official Register 1973–1974," https://ballotpedia.org/Georgia_Office_and_Court_of_Ordinary,_Amendment_4_(1974), accessed September 20, 2023.

Savaell, Savall: These are the spellings of Emma and Rhoda's last name as they appear in the indenture recorded in Jackson County.

In the 1870 federal census for Jackson County, however, five years before the apprenticeship agreement, "Roda" and Emma Savell are listed as living in the home of William and Mary A. Savell. Roda is listed as being twenty-five years old, and Emma as four They are almost certainly the Emma who was apprenticed to Manning and her mother, Rhoda, and the Savells likely earlier were the owners of Rhoda, who was born in slavery.

In the 1880 census for Jackson County, five years after the apprenticeship agreement, Emma is listed as living in Manning's home, except she is listed there as "Emma Henderson, B [Black], 13, Bound." It is unclear why her last name was changed.

The 1890 census for Jackson County, Georgia, was lost in a fire at the US Commerce Department in 1921, along with most of the other census records for that year.

On July 8, 1886, a Black child named Emma was born in an unknown place in Georgia. She died as Emma Blount or Blunt in Athens, Georgia, in January 1980 at the age of ninety-three. For a number of years, she had been the cook and companion of Lily Alexander Jackson, Manning's youngest daughter, who was born December 6, 1877, and died June 2, 1970.[53]

This Emma Blount possibly was the daughter of the apprenticed Emma Savell/Henderson. When Emma Blount was born in 1886, Emma Savell/Henderson would have been about twenty years old and likely living with Manning because her apprenticeship had not yet expired. Lily Alexander would have been nine years old and living also with Manning. If Emma Blount was the daughter of Emma Savell/Henderson, Lily would have gotten to know her and perhaps even helped to take care of her. A relationship likely would have developed that led to Emma Blount's being Lily's long-term cook and companion.

1876

Mary Juliette David Neal Epperson
Staffords pond Fla Aug. 27, 1876
Nora Dear Niece [Nora Alexander]

I was thankful to hear through your Ma's letter that you hade made a public profession of your faith in Christ by joining the church. My precious Nora how

---

[53] The dates for Emma Blount's birth and death are in the entry for Emma Blount in the *U. S. Social Security Death Index, 1935–2014*, master file, Social Security Administration; tombstone, "Lillie Alexander Jackson," Oconee Hill Cemetery, Athens, Georgia; Emma Blunt to Allie Comer Gaither (Manning's granddaughter), January 11, 1974; and Comer family tradition.

much I wish you to be a humble useful working Christian having *God* in view and the good of Souls.

I think you would enjoy our Bible lessons. The subject for the first L[esson] in this month was Intemperance, the 2 Sabbath[,] the Excellent Woman, Proverbs 31 chap. 10–31. The 3 Sab[,] A Godly Life or the Wisdom of early Piety. Eccelsiastis 12 chap 1–14

Dear Nora I would very [much like] to have a letter from you. visit Livia please. I will try to wite to her soon also to Father and Annie. Mr. E joins in much love to all yours. Ant Mary

Notes

Mary Juliette David Neal Epperson: She was Lona's sister, and Nora's aunt. She had married John Ira Epperson on October 16, 1870. When she wrote this letter, she was forty-nine years old.[54]

Nora: She was Manning and Lona's oldest daughter. She was seventeen when this letter was written.[55]

Proverbs 31 chap, verses 10–31: This biblical selection begins, "Who can find a virtuous woman? for her price is far above rubies" (KJV).

Ecclesiastes 12 chap, verses 1–14: This selection begins, "Remember now thy Creator in the days of thy youth, while the evil days come not, nor the years draw nigh, when thou shalt say, I have no pleasure in them...." (KJV).

Livia: She was Ann Olivia Neal, Mary's daughter. She would have been twenty-nine years old when this letter was written, and she had married James M. Lyle on August 4, 1870.[56]

1879

Susan Alexander and Margaret Edwards

[1879]
Dear Brother [Manning]

I will rite you a few lines to let you no that I am Well at [this] time and I hope it may find you the same. I Want you to come to see me. Tel loney howdy for me. I Would be glad to see all of you and Would have bin glad to see mother before she died and Sam to. I hope they air goan to rest. our Small loss Will be their great gain.

---

[54] *Banks County Marriage Licenses, Book A, 1859–1873*, 142; David Family Bible.
[55] Tombstone of Nora Alexander Boone, Sunrise Cemetery, Maysville, Georgia.
[56] *Jackson County Marriages Book E, 1869–1873*, 13; tombstone of A. Olivia Lyle, Sunrise Cemetery, Maysville, Georgia.

So I must come to a close by asking you to rite.
Susan Alexander
To Dr. mp Alexander
don't forget to rite to us
Rome Floyd Co. Ga
[new page]
Rome Floyd Co
Georgia

Dear uncle it is with the greatest of pleasure that I seat myself to answer your kind letter. you rote me sad news that grandmother Was dead. I [am] very [sorry] to hear it. it geaves me very much and so uncle Sam Was dead and uncle Jim near bout blind. it is sad to me to hear of so much bad luck.

Mr. Dempsey told me that he had gotten a letter from you and presented it to me. What had become of me and mother[?]I am married and mother is living With me. I Want you to rite to me what has become of uncle Sam's children and Where uncle Jim is. I Would like to have seen grandmother before she died and Uncle Sam to[o,] uncle mannan [Manning].

You rite to me that I had hurt grandmothers feelings. I am sorry of it but my uncle done the riting [,] my uncle William Burkhalter[,] and I could not read it and he rote as he pleased. dont think heard of me for it. I did not do it.

you rote to me that you had grandmother bed for me. I Would like to have it to remember her and Would like to have a little of the estate. I think something is duiu me for my father Was one of her own children.

uncle mannan I don't want you to think hard of me for I did not do it. beged him to not do it but he Would do it eny how. don't think heard of me for it. I beg all pardin in the World for forgeaning [forgiving me] and I hope [word illegible] you told me to come to see you but I have got no chance to come to see you so I must close for this time and I Want you to rite soon to me and direct your letter to
William Edwards
Rome Floyd County
Georgi
  Margaret Edwards
  To mp Alexander

Notes

Susan Alexander and Margaret Edwards: Susan Alexander was the widow of Manning's brother Adam Alexander who was killed on June 27, 1862, during the

Civil War. Margaret Edwards was her daughter and the wife of William Edwards.[57]

Date: The letter was undated, but the information it contains indicates it was written in 1879.

mother: She was Margaret Alexander, who died January 22, 1879, age seventy-two.[58]

Sam: He was Sam Alexander, who died February 23, 1879, age forty-six. He was buried in Georgia, but it is unclear whether he had returned to Georgia from Texas or his family had taken his body to Georgia for burial.[59]

uncle William Burkhalter: He was Susan Alexander's brother.[60]

Forest News, June 11, 1880

Dr. Alexander will soon bring his residence to completion, then he will move over from his plantation, and become one of our permanent citizens; after strong solicitation he commenced practicing again, he will soon erect an office near his residence.

Note

his residence: This would have been his house. It still stands on Bacon Street in Maysville, Georgia.

Forest News, November 5, 1880

Dr. M. P. Alexander and Mr. Jas. Ellison, Jr., have moved into their new dwellings.

---

[57] Chaplin, *Riches of Bunyan* (Alexander family copy); US Census, 1880, Floyd County, Georgia.

[58] Chaplin, *Riches of Bunyan* (Alexander family copy); Lily Alexander Jackson, genealogical notes.

[59] Chaplin, *Riches of Bunyan* (Alexander family copy); Lily Alexander Jackson, genealogical notes; tombstone of Samuel H. Alexander, Hebron Presbyterian Cemetery, Banks County, Georgia.

[60] US Census, 1850, Cass County, Georgia.

Chapter 33

Horatio, 1867–1883

1867

July 29
On this day, Horatio took the same Reconstruction Oath that Manning Alexander took.[1]

1868

July 14
Horatio married Teressa Ann Amanda Ellison in Jackson County on this date. Horatio was twenty-five years old; Teressa was three weeks short of her eighteenth birthday. Teressa was the daughter of James Ellison, a farmer in Jackson County.[2]

1869

April 18
A daughter, Daisy Lee David, was born to Horatio and Teressa on this date. Four other children were born to them from 1873 to 1885, three boys and one girl.[3]

1870

The 1870 federal census for Jackson County listed Horatio as a farmer.

---

[1] See chapter 32 for the oath's wording; *Georgia, Returns of Qualified Voters and Reconstruction Oath Books, 1867–1869*, Jackson County, Election District 33.

[2] Teressa's tombstone, Sunrise Cemetery, Maysville, Banks County, Georgia; David Family Bible, Marriages page in Family Records section; US Census, 1860, Banks County, Georgia.

[3] Daisy Lee David's grave marker, David Family Cemetery, Mitchell Road, Banks County, Georgia; grave markers of James Simeon David and George Thomas David, Sunrise Cemetery, Maysville, Banks County, Georgia; Horatio Bowen David's grave marker, Crest Lawn Cemetery, Atlanta; Mary Lee David McDonald's grave marker, Rose Hill Cemetery, Winder, Barrow County, Georgia.

1874

Meeting in Banks County

Previous notice being given, a large number of people of Banks county convened at the Court House in Homer, on the 4th Inst, for the purpose of selecting delegates to meet the Convention, to be held at Cleveland, White county, to select a candidate for the 9th Congressional District...[and] to select delegates for the Gillsville Convention, to nominate a Senator for the 33d Senatorial District.....

The Committee reported, through their Chairman, the following names of delegates to attend ...the Gillsville Convention: H. J. David.[4]

Notes

H. J. David: He was Horatio, Horatio James David.

delegates: Although the article does not mention it, the delegates undoubtedly were to attend a Democratic Party convention. As noted in chapter 32, in 1870, Horatio, along with Manning Alexander, was elected to an assembly to nominate a Democratic Party candidate for the Georgia legislature.

The earlier assembly was held in Jackson County, while this later convention was held in Banks County. Strangely, Horatio may have been eligible to attend both meetings in the two different counties at the two different times without moving. In 1870, the part of Jackson County where Horatio's father's farm was located and the part of Maysville north of the railroad tracks became part of Banks County. Horatio may have been living in the Jackson County area that later became part of Banks.[5]

1875

*Premiums Awarded
At the Oconee County Fair....*

Best colt between two and three years old, $5—H. J. David[6]

Note

Oconee County: Athens is the county seat of Oconee County.

---

[4] *Southern Watchman*, August 12, 1874.
[5] Elrod, *Historical Notes*, 37.
[6] *Athens Weekly Georgian*, October 20, 1875.

1882

Maysville Items

Mr. H. J. David will have his eye extracted on tomorrow by Dr. L. G. Hardman and Alexander [Dr. M. P. Alexander]. Damage was caused by a wound received in the face at Front Royal, in August 1864. Mr. David has been a continued sufferer, more or less, since that time.[7]

Maysville Items

Mr. H. J. David fills the vacancy in the Grange Store caused by Mr. Webb's departure. Mr. David is a good business man.[8]

Note

Grange Store: In 1866 an employee of the Department of Agriculture in Washington toured the Southern states, talking with farmers and planters. He discovered that they were facing great difficulties and were helpless to overcome them, primarily because they lacked "any means of expressing or enforcing their views as a body."

What was true of farmers in the South also proved true for farmers throughout the country. The following year, representatives from several federal government agencies met and formed the Order of Patrons of Husbandry, more informally known as the National Grange, and began organizing subordinate Granges throughout the country.

The overall purpose of the Granges was to help farmers, not only in business but in their social life. Women were welcome as members. An early history of the Grange expressed this two-fold purpose:

> The women and the young people, who met at evening to go through the little ceremonies of the Grangers' ritual, and pass an hour or so in decorous amusements and conversation, and song, and reading, may have fancied that they were only breaking the monotony of toil by a bit of harmless entertainment; but the Grange knew better. They were learning, and teaching others, to be better farmers, to be thrifty, to buy cheaper, to sell better, to rid themselves of creditors, to keep out of debt, and finally to check the enormous power of the railroads which have so long been driving farmers to the wall.

In particular the Grange "encouraged its members to organize local farmer-owned businesses to cooperatively purchase inputs and market commodities." The Grange store grew out of this encouragement. A store was owned and

---

[7] *Jackson Herald*, September 29, 1882.
[8] *Jackson Herald*, November 3, 1882.

controlled by community farmers who were members of the Grange and who purchased shares in the store. The store ordered its goods directly from the manufacturer, cutting out the middleman and paying less for the goods. The goods then were sold with a slight markup that produced a profit that in turn was split among the store's shareholders.

Someone who participated in the day-to-day operation of a Grange store was a popular member of a farming community like Maysville.[9]

Maysville Items

Mr. H. J. David had his eye extracted on last week in Atlanta. The operation was a painful one. He is at home and attending to his business.[10]

1883

Maysville Items

Go to the Grange Store and Mr. H. J. David will show you all that is necessary to be done with a spring mattress.[11]

Note

spring mattress: Spring mattresses in the 1880s were a new advancement in mattress construction. They were made by arranging coiled springs within a casing of strong fabric so that one's whole body was supported without sags or lumps. In the early days, makers of spring mattresses still were experimenting with their design and production. Consumers were not always familiar with the resulting products and needed help learning how they should be used.[12]

Maysville Items

Mr. H. J. David was elected General Manager of the Banks County [Grange] Cooperative Association, with Mr. Joe Sims to assist him. The duties were too much for Mr. Wills, in his declining years.[13]

Maysville Items

---

[9] E. Martin, *History of the Grange Movement*, 407–10, 416–17, 419–21, 479–80 (1st and 2nd quotes); Blackmar, *Economics*, 202–204; Brower, "Farm Cooperatives" (3rd quote).

[10] *Jackson Herald*, November 17, 1882.

[11] *Jackson Herald*, January 5, 1883.

[12] "Mattress," *Webster's New World College Dictionary*, 902; "Mattress coil," Wikipedia, https://en.wikipedia.org/wiki/Mattress_coil, accessed September 1, 2020.

[13] *Jackson Herald*, January 19, 1883.

Mr. C. T. Bacon, Rev. Mr. Hoyt and Mr. H. David are preparing to build some nice dwellings soon. The ville is on a boom, and these are enterprising gentlemen.[14]

Maysville Items

Mr. H. J. David, who has had charge of the Grange Store for some time, and shown so much interest in its management, will turn his attention to farming after this year. He says there is more pleasure in this than any thing he ever followed.[15]

Maysville Items

On Tuesday morning we buried the oldest child and only daughter of Mr. H. J. David, Miss Dasy [Daisy] David, with temperance honors, at the family burying ground near his home. Her funeral was preached by Rev. Mr. H. F. Hoyt.[16]

Notes

Daisy David: She was fourteen years old when she died.

temperance honors: The temperance movement regarded alcoholic beverages as harmful to the individual and to society. "Supposedly, drink destroyed families and reputations and brought about poverty, disorder, and crime," writes Fahey. Temperance followers urged people to sign pledges not to drink. Apparently, Daisy had signed such a pledge and was eligible to be buried with temperance honors.[17]

Rev. H. F. Hoyt: He was minister of various Presbyterian churches in Jackson County and neighboring counties, and for a time was minister of the Presbyterian church in Maysville. He also served as a chaplain in the Confederate army throughout the Civil War.[18]

In Memoriam

Daisy David died, in Maysville, July 24, 1883. Bright and lovely in her girlhood lies Daisy in her grave. Tears and anguish, bitterness of pain, our pleading prayers availed not to keep her young spirit with us, although around her clung so many loving hearts. Parents, relatives, school mates, friends—all pleading in vain for her to be spared to gladden her home. From those loving hearts and tender loving arms God has taken her unto Himself, where, basking in the bright

---

[14] *Jackson Herald*, May 18, 1883.
[15] *Jackson Herald*, June 13, 1883.
[16] *Jackson Herald*, August 3, 1883.
[17] Fahey, "Temperance Movement."
[18] *Presbyterian of the South*, July 10, 1912 (obituary).

sunshine of His love, living forever in His presence, she will ne'er more know pain nor suffering, but in joy and gladness will be another link in God's chain of love to draw the hearts of those fond parents and loving friends unto Himself. May her loving Heavenly Father send to these suffering hearts the sweetest comfort of His love and mercy....[19]

Mary Juliette David Neal Epperson

August [1883]
My Dear bereaved Brother and Sister [Horatio and Teressa]

Through Livias letter last night I heard the sad news of your only daughters death. How gladly I would write a letter of condolence but to hearts so sadly bereaved, how delicate the subject. God has not required you, as he did Abraham of old to take the life of your loved Daisie but he has made it your privilege, as well as duty, as Christians, to say Amen to the will of *Him* who is too wise to err and too good to do wrong. We are so shortsighted, here we only see for the present. Faith in God, in the promises of His holy Word, resignation to His will, will enable us to exclaim in Christian triumph, though He *slay me*, yet will I trust in Him.

My dear Tressie and Ratio, I hope you do not feel a rebellious spirit. When we are so impressed with our incapability of doing anything to comfort in such bereavement, how consoling to know that Jesus is all love all sympathy. What little we feel in comparison is only a spark derived from him. This thought consoled me after the death of our precious Mother, when reflecting that her simpathy and her prayers had ended for us, so far as we could hear. But Jesus ever lives to intercede for us.

After the death of our precious Rienza I yielded to the suggestion that it was wrong to try to be submissive to the death of so promising a child. Strange I did not know it was a temptation from the great enemy of souls. He was the *Lords*. He was only lent to us. Months afterward in conversing with Mother on the subject, she seemed surprised, urged me to try to be entirely resigned, or a heavier trial would befall me. In July1852 when I was assisted by grace to say Amen to the Devine will in the death of my dearest earthly friend, time seemed but a day compared to eternity. There was a humble [illegible word] trust in God. When temperal things seemed dark, I could feel the Lord will provide. Twice since then it has required a great effort to be entirely resigned under bereavement.

My Husband requested me to say [to] you that you have his deepest simpathy and kind regards. His oldest daughter died at 17 of Tipoid fever....

---

[19] *Jackson Herald,* August 10, 1883.

All well. Write soon to your devoted sister, MJE.
[Written upside down in a different handwriting]
Dear Brother. Come down and See us & bring Sister Annie this Fall. J. I. Epperson

Notes

Mary Juliette David Neal Epperson: Mary Juliette David Neal married John Ira Epperson on October 16, 1870.[20]

Livia: She is probably Mary's daughter Olivia Neal.

Abraham of old: He is Abraham of the Bible. He was tested by God as to his faith and his obedience to God's will when God told him to sacrifice his only son Isaac. Abraham agreed to make the sacrifice, but at the last moment, God allowed him to substitute a ram in Isaac's place (Gen 22:1-19).

the death of our precious mother: Thirza David died on May 30, 1876 (see next chapter).

our precious Rienza: He was Hiram Rienza Neal who died in June 1850 when only nineteen months old.[21]

July 1852: This was the time of the death of her first husband, Richard Neal (see chapter 1).

---

[20] *Banks County Marriage Licenses, Book A, 1859–1873*, 142.
[21] David Family Bible, first Deaths page in Family Records section.

Chapter 34

Thirza, James, and Annie David, 1876–1884

1876

Thirza David Obituary

Departed this life June 1st, 1876, at her home in Banks County, Mrs. Thirza David, wife of Deacon James David. She was the only daughter and last remaining child of Captain Owen J. Bowen. Mrs. David was born in Jackson county, Georgia, on June 20th, 1803, joining the Baptist church, at Kandler's Creek, December 1820; was married to Jas. David July 31st, 1823. She raised seven children, all of whom she lived to see profess Christ and join the church; five of these, with her aged husband, are left to mourn their loss. She resided during her life in three miles of her birth-place and the church to which she belonged. Mrs. David was truly a good wife, a faithful and affectionate mother, and devoted Christian. For many years she was the warm friend of the temperance cause, and was a Knight Templar at her death. W. F. S.[1]

Note

Knight Templar: The Knights Templar was a monastic order organized in 1120 to protect pilgrims traveling to the Holy Land. The Catholic Church formally recognized the order in 1129, and the Templars rapidly became a wealthy charity. Believers made substantial donations of money, land, and other valuable property to aid their efforts to help pilgrims and to fight in the Crusades.[2]

In the United States, beginning in the 1850s, temperance organizations named themselves "Good Templars" after the Knights Templar, partly because of the similarity of "temperance" and "Templar" and partly because they were fighting a "great crusade" against the destructive vice of alcohol. In the United States, unlike the original Templars, the Good Templars allowed women to join, and they became valuable members of the organization.[3]

W. F. S.: He was Washington Franklin Stark, a Baptist minister in Jackson County.[4]

---

[1] *Forest News*, June 10, 1876.
[2] "Knights Templar," Wikipedia, https://en.wikipedia.org/wiki/Knights_Templar, accessed February 21, 2019.
[3] Nicholson, *Brief History of the Knights Templar*, chapter 9.
[4] *Atlanta Constitution*, October 26, 1884.

Pillina C. Bell

Bells Mills Cleburnecty Ala Nov 9 1876
Dear Father and Sister [James and Annie David]

    I will write you a few lines this morning before the mails comes. We received a letter from Sister Lona some two weeks since dated oct 13. we were very glad to hear from you all and thankful that Papa was able to walk even to the lot. hope he is still improving.

    Lona wrote me that Annie health was much better than it was in the summer. Sister I am thankful. hope your health will continue good. Sister you are there with Papa. I am sure you will take care of him the best you can and be sure and hire what assistance you kneed to wait on him and then Dear Sister you can have a home under our Roof as long as we have any if you wish it.

    Dear Father I hope your health will improve so that you can enjoy life yet. my intention is to see you again.

    I will not write to Lona this time. Billy says tell Nora she can [can't?] beat him picking cotton. Margie and Mamie picked finely. Leola says tell her cousins her School was out yesterday. Sister Lona said Something to me about Dear Mother clothes. all of you do what you wish to with them. I only want some little thing to keep in rememberance of her.

    Please write soon as I am anxious to hear from you. we are all enjoying common health. as ever your devoted daughter and Sister

P C Bell

My love and best wishes to Sister Lona and family, Brother Horatio and family and also Olivia and family

P C Bell

Notes

Billy and Nora: Billy was Pillina Bell's son, then about seventeen years old. Nora was Lona and Manning's oldest daughter, then about the same age, 17.[5]

Margie and Mamie: Margie and Mamie were both daughters of Lona and Manning. Margie's age then was almost nine, and Mamie was only about a week short of turning five.[6]

Leola: She was Pillina's daughter, then about six years old.[7]

---

[5] Nora's grave marker, Sunrise Cemetery, Maysville, Banks County, Georgia; US Census, 1870, Cleburne County, Alabama.

[6] Margie Alexander Comer's grave marker, Oconee Hills Cemetery, Athens, Georgia; Mamie O'Kelley's grave marker, Sunrise Cemetery, Maysville, Banks County, Georgia.

[7] US Census, 1870, Cleburne County, Alabama.

Olivia and family: Olivia married James M. Lyle on August 4, 1870. In 1876 they lived in Jackson County and had two children.[8]

1878

Obituary

Departed this life, January 21st, 1878, at his residence, in Banks county, Ga., Deacon James David, aged 78 years and 4 months, fifty years of which he had been a member and officer of Kandler's creek Baptist church. For near two years before his death, owing to severe affliction, he was unable to attend his church meetings, in which he had been a faithful worker for Christ so long.

Bro. David was truly one of the best men I ever knew; he was faithful, honest, pious, and modest; manifesting a zeal for Christ and the salvation [of] sinners worthy of imitation, and possessing that charity which "never faileth."

In his death, his children and grandchildren have lost a faithful and affectionate officer; his neighbors a friend tried and true; his country one of her best citizens. But their loss is eternal gain. As a shock of corn, fully ripe, he has been gathered by his Savior, in the garner on high. W. F. Stark[9]

Note

Will of James H. David: In the will he notes that he already had given money to all his children. The will also directs that all his property be sold and divided equally among his children and a share to Simeon's children.[10]

1882

Mary Juliette David Neal Epperson

Oct 31st 1882
Dear Sister Annie

My Husband joins me in sending an earnest solicitation for you to spend the winter with us. hope you will be sure to come unless Dear Ratio's eye or some other affliction prevents. I do think you will enjoy the stay and I cannot express my anxiety to have you spend all the winter. don't apprehend any danger of sickness. now come while the oranges are on the trees. Some of the neighbors have began to make sugar. A very few of the ripest oranges are being shipped.

---

[8] *Jackson County Marriages, Book E, 1869–1873*, 13; US Census, 1870 and 1880, Jackson County, Georgia.
[9] Forest News, March 16, 1878.
[10] Banks County Will Book A, 515.

John Neal spoke last fall of coming next January. Please don't wait until then. the stay would be so very short. I know you will dread to come alone, but starting is the worst. you will come through so soon. come to Bronson. the train arrives at 4 PM. let us know when to meet you, and we will spend the night with Willie or Ella and come home next morning. I have intended to write for weeks but was very much hurried with my work before quarterly meeting. was sick with [illegible]

Please write immediately and let us know whether you will come Nov 2. all well. love to dear Lona and family. would be delighted to have letters from any and all of you. Your devoted Sister MJE

Notes

Letter: This letter was found placed into the David Family Bible.
John Neal: He is Mary Epperson's son.
Bronson: Bronson is the capital of Levy County, Florida. The Eppersons live in the county outside Bronson.[11]
Willie or Ella: Willie was William J. Epperson, son of Mary's husband, who then was married and living in Bronson. Ella was Lydia Ella Epperson Gronto, daughter of Mary's husband.[12]

1884

Mary Juliette David Neal Epperson
Dec 10th 1884
Dear Sister Annie

Received a letter from Olivia Saturday. So rejoiced to here you was thinking of coming to visit us. I will write giving you directions. Miss Bachman who is boarding with us come the old road from Atlanta to Macon. had to change cars at Macon then at Calahan. cost $15.15cts from Atlanta to Branson. could have come cheaper by taking a round ticket that will hold good three months but you have to go back the same route.

When we got to Atlanta 11 A M we called for the ticket office for the new R Road which is just across the street from the car Shed. there you get free transportation for yourself trunk and hand baggage to the new Depot over one mile.

at three P M you take the through train to Callahan. have no more trouble until 9 or 10 oclock next morning. there you wait until [word illegible] one hour and run down to Branson that afternoon.

---

[11] "Bronson, Florida," Wikipedia, https://en.wikipedia.org/wiki/Bronson,_Florida, accessed February 22, 2019.
[12] US Census, 1880, Levy County, Florida; *Florida, County Marriage Records, 1823–1982*.

call for directions to W. J. Epperson at Mr. Grant's store in all very near the Depot. please do not fail to come and let us know when to meet you. Love to evy one Dear loved ones in Ratio's.

Your Sister M J E

Mr E says come without fail. there will be no diffulty in coming alone.

Note

Annie's death: Annie lived until October 18, 1911, almost twenty-seven years after this letter was written. It is not known whether she ever made a trip to visit her sister, Mary. When she died, she was seventy-eight years old and unmarried.[13]

Biographical Sketch of Thirza David

Mrs. Thirza David

For whom the U. D. C. chapter organized in Maysville, Ga. On Mar. 7th, 1910 was named, was a woman of rare intelligence, and no section of our sunny south-land can boast of a woman whose more heroic deeds should be imprinted in the minds of the present generation, and shine among brighter pages of our history;

Thirza Bowen was born in Jackson County, Ga, June 29th 1803, and was the daughter of Capt. Owen J. Bowen, who commanded a section of block houses between the South Carolina and the Chattahoochee river at the time of the removal of the Indians from Ga., and who was one of the pioneer settlers of this county.

Thirza Bowen attended school at Eatonton, Ga. And later at Clinton, Ga. On July 21st 1823 she was married to James David.

For several years after her marriage she taught school, being the only woman in that section who was capable. Mrs. David was the mother of nine children, seven of whom she reared to manhood and woman hood, taking special interest in their education and moral training.

When the war between the states was declared she cheerfully sent three sons to the front, viz. Capt. S. B. David, 14th Ga. Regt. from Forsyth County; Lieutenant O. T. David and Lieutenant H. J. David 16th Ga. Regt. from Jackson County, one son-in-law, Dr. M. P. Alexander, assistant surgeon 43rd Ga. Regt., and two grand-sons, James P. and John W. Neal from Forsyth County.

All the force of her strong physical and intellectual powers were now given to the cause she so loyally espoused.

Seeing the necessity of medical aid for the wives and children of Confederate soldiers while they were at the front, she thoroughly equipped herself for this charitable work by reading a course in medicine at home, obtaining books from

---

[13] Grave marker, Thirza Ann David, Sunrise Cemetery, Maysville, Banks County, Georgia.

physicians in Athens. All physicians having gone to the war she did a successful work for many miles around her home—often riding horseback through rain or snow during the lonely hours of the night and through sparsely settled sections with a pine-knot torch as her only light.

To see the suffering of her patients allayed was the only compensation she expected; through frequently she was given a homespun dress, or coverlet, a supply of tallow candles or provisions from the pantry.

In September, 1861 she visited two of her sons at Richmond, Va., making the trip alone. One of these sons, O. T. David, being sick of measles at the time, from effects of which he afterward died.

At the Battle of Chancellorsville, Va. In May 1863, her youngest son, H. J. David, received a very severe wound; and the anxious mother made another trip to Richmond and nursed him until he was able to be brought home. Later in the Battle of Bull Run [this is the wrong battle, see chapter 27] he lost his right eye by gunshot wound, which fact he kept from his mother, knowing she would make another trip if she knew of his misfortune.

At the Battle of the Wilderness, Va. May 5th 1864 Capt. S. B. David was killed. He left a wife and four small children in Forsyth County. When the wife heard of the death of her husband she became temporarily insane. Mrs. David, learning of her unfortunate condition, determined to see her as early as possible, although in order to do so she must pass through the Federal lines. With a blind horse and wagon and a small Negro boy who was crippled, she set out on her errand, passing the Federal lines at Browns Bridge, Hall County, going and coming with perfect safety. With her she brought back the insane daughter-in-law and four children, attracting quite a great deal of attention along the way by the singing of the insane woman.

After the war ended twelve years were added to the life of this noble woman, each of them being brighter than the last by reason of the service she had rendered to her country and her Creator.

On the first day of June 1876, her earthly cares were ended and she was lain to rest near her home in Banks county, near Maysville where the memory of one who befriended so many helpless people during the four years of the cruel war will be handed down from generation to generation until time is no more.[14]

Notes

Thirza David Chapter of the United Daughters of the Confederacy: The Thirza David Chapter was chartered as chapter number 1254 March 7, 1910.[15]

---

[14] Prepared for the United Daughters of the Confederacy, Thirza David Chapter, c. 1910.

[15] Charter in possession of Thirza's great-great-great-granddaughter Susan Gaither Jones.

Biographical Sketch: This document was prepared by Gussie Carr, a young schoolteacher living in Maysville. It was based on an undated, handwritten paper titled "Facts gathered by Mrs. G. P. Boone concerning *Mrs. Thirza David*," in the David Family Papers at the Hargrett Rare Book and Manuscript Library, University of Georgia Libraries, Athens.

Mrs. Boone was Nora Alexander Boone, the oldest daughter of Pillona David Alexander and Dr. Manning Poole Alexander. She also was Thirza David's granddaughter. She was mentioned frequently in letters written by the Alexanders before and during the Civil War.

For more information about the sketch, particularly the part concerning Thirza's trip with Fanny David and children, see chapter 25. Most of the other information contained in the sketch can be found and described more fully in earlier chapters of this book.

Chapter 35

Horatio's Last Years, 1885–1923

1885

Pillina David Bell

Bells Mills Ala Oct. 5th 1885
Dear Brother [Horatio] and family
 I have been intending to write to you several weeks so I will not put it off any longer.
 I must say to you that I never expect to regret going to Ga. I am feeling so much better now than I did in May June and July. I was very unwell with a cold when we reached home and several days after. I have not been sick at my stomach any since I came home. I feel able to cook now but having Leola here to help me and her company has been a great advantage to me. I think we will send her to Oxford to School next cession.
 This morning is quite cool. I did not see any frost though some people say they did. Our crops were good though are badly injured on all low lands by wet weather. it rained here the most of the time for eight days, some times tolerable hard though most of the time a slow rain. a great deal of corn has blown down in the water and is sprouted. Cotten is also badly injured
 Dr Walter Leola and I went to Campmeeting yesterday. heard a Good Sermen preached at eleven oclock and met many of our friends and acquaintances there. had quite a nice time.
 Leola read the book that you gave her through in two weeks. She likes it very much
 Write to us and tell us about your fish pond and how you are all getting on. Billies Wife and children reached here on the 17 of Sept. Billie got here on the morning of 26 and he and his family left here on the 28 for Gadsden Ala where he moved to. he and his wifes brother Mr. Gurly that lived with Billie when he was in Arkansas have gone into business in Gadsden. Billie looks very badly. he is very lean. he says he is not able to labor on a farm. We were expecting him every day but his Pa and Walter did not know him when he called at the Mill but they came with him to the house and of course we new him. it was five years last March since we Saw him.
 Tell Simie and Tommie we have not forgotten what smart boys they were. Tell Bowen I wish I could hear him talk and see him eat drum sticks. Sister Anie do you still think you will go to Fla this winter[?]I have not written to Sister Mary

since I came home but think I will soon. You must not forget to visit us. We will be disappointed if our relations fail to visit us next year I think Margie will come to see us this winter Sister Anna if you fail to go to Fla you come with Margie to us.

We had a letter from Sister Lona a few days ago. She was not very well but I think she will get well now as she has no boarders and not so many visitors. The family joins me in love to your family and all our relations and friends back there. Write soon to your Sister

P. C. Bell

Notes

Brother: Horatio David was then age forty-two.
Leola: She was Pillina's daughter, then about fifteen years old.[1]
Oxford to School: Oxford, Alabama, is a small town that, when the letter was written, was in Calhoun County but now is partly in Calhoun and partly in Talladega County. It is about fifty miles east of Birmingham and one hundred miles west of Atlanta.[2]
Dr.: He was Pillina's husband, Middleton Raymond Bell.[3]
Walter: He was Pillina's son, Walter J. Bell, then about twenty-eight years old.[4]
Billie: He was Pillina's son, William B. Bell, then about twenty-six years old and married to the former Nannie Gurly.[5]
Simmie and Tommie: Simmie and Tommie were Horatio's sons. Simmie was James Simeon David, then about twelve years old, and Tommie was George Thomas David, then about ten years old.[6]
Bowen: He was another of Horatio's sons, Horatio Bowen David, then about three years old.[7]
Margie: She was Margie Alexander, daughter of Manning and Lona Alexander. When this letter was written, she was seventeen years old.[8]

---

[1] US Census, 1880, Cleburne County, Alabama.
[2] Wikipedia, "Oxford, Alabama," Wikipedia, https://en.wikipedia.org/wiki/Oxford,_Alabama, accessed February 26, 2019; *Rand McNally 2019 Road Atlas*, 4.
[3] US Census, 1870, Cleburne County, Alabama.
[4] Ibid.
[5] Ibid.
[6] US Census, 1880, Jackson County, Georgia.
[7] US Census, 1900 and 1910, Jackson County, Georgia.
[8] Grave marker, Oconee Hills Cemetery, Athens, Georgia.

1889

Award of Pension
No. 460
State of Georgia
Executive Department   Atlanta, Feby 13, 1889

Mr. H. J. David of the County of Banks, having filed his application in the Executive Department of an allowance under the Act approved October 24, 1887, as amended by Act, Dec. 24, 1888, and the same having been allowed for Loss of Right Eye, He is entitled to receive the sum of Thirty & 00 Dollars for such disability, the same being allowance due for year ending October 24, 1889.

The Treasurer will pay the same and hold his receipt for this voucher, and return same to Executive Department for warrant. J. B. Gordon, Governor

Note

Loss of Right Eye: Another document filed later in Horatio's pension file described the loss of eye in more detail: "he was wounded as follows: Gun shot wound in right eye ball passed out near the ear which resulted in total loss of sight of the right eye." The thirty dollars was a payment per year.[9]

Horatio was the tax collector for Banks County. The county tax collector was an elected position.[10]

1895

Affidavit for Witnesses
Horatio's Pension Application
August 1, 1895
State of Georgia
Banks County

Personally appears before me the undersigned ordinary in and for said County. G. W Brown, A. M. Chandler and W. N. Bates each of whom, being duly sworn according to law, severally say, under oath, that they are personally well acquainted with H. J. David whose application is herewith presented for a pension, that he served in Company B of the 16th Regiment of Wofford's Brigade, and from our personal knowledge he was injured by the service as follows: Gun shot wound entering the back part of right hip, passing to the back bone,

---

[9] "For Applicants Heretofore Allowed Pensions," filed February 17, 1891, in pension file for David, H. J., file no. 460, Confederate Pension Applications, Georgia Confederate Pension Office, RG58-1-1, Georgia Archives.

[10] Mize, *History of Banks County*, 256; *Banks County Observer*, January 9, 1889.

ranging upward three or four inches [and] lodging at said point greatly lacerating the muscles and tissues and fracturing the bones in the track of said ball. Said ball lodged at said point and remained there until it was located by copious and excessive wasting from that locality. Said wound greatly affects right leg in walking and also effects and renders it quite painful in bending forward and laterally. Witnesses say further that, applicant from the effect originating directly from said wound, is rendered practically incompetent to perform the ordinary manual vocations of life in making a support.

We personally know above stated facts. We were with him in the army and have known him ever since. He was honorably retired from the service before the war closed, his pay and emoluments continuing. Applicant is permanently disabled as stated and has been so to our knowledge ever since 18__ [blank in original]. We have no interest in the recovery of a pension by him.

Sworn and subscribed before me this
1st day of Aug. 1895   Signed: G. W. Brown
T. F. Hill   A. M. Chandler
Ordinary   W. N. Bates

Notes

Pension: On August 16, 1895, Horatio received a pension of fifty dollars a year for damage to hip and back. This amount was in addition to the thirty dollars awarded earlier for loss of his eye.[11]

An additional supporting document had been filed by two doctors on April 2, 1893. It describes the wound:

> There is gunshot wound of right Hip. Ball entered 1 ½ inches to right of spine—ranged upward injuring the spine. There is roughening and other visible evidence of injury to the lower lumbar vertebrae. Just at the edge of Hip bone and near spine there has been deep abscess, resulting several old scars with adhesion to the bones and injury to the nerves, especially the Sciatic, also some wasting of the limb. There are sharp pains or soreness and limping on walking or attempting other exercise or movements of the body. The limb is not entirely useless but the injury resulting from this wound is such as to disqualify him for active labor on the farm.[12]

G. W. Brown, A. M. Chandler, W. N. Bates: All had been members of the 16th Georgia Regiment. G. W. Brown was George W. Brown, a private in

---

[11] Pension file for David, H. J., file no. 460, Confederate Pension Applications, Georgia Confederate Pension Office, RG58–1-1, Georgia Archives.

[12] Affidavit of doctors V. D. Lockhart and Thomas Hayden, April 2, 1893.

Company D; A. M. Chandler was Allen M. Chandler, a private in Company A; and W. N. Bates was William N. Bates, a private in Company B.[13]

1900

Horatio

Maysville Aug 27 1900
Mr John H Bowen
Dear Cousin

No doubt you will think strange of me writing to you as we have never seen each other but I have a request to make of you and hope that you can comply with it.

I have heard that you or your son John Hunter have a letter or letters in your possession that once belonged to cousin John Jones giving a history of the Bowen family for several generatons back. I am verry anxious to get it and will be verry thankful if you will copy it or have it typewriten and send it to me.

Sister Anna David has a photograph of yourself and one of your father and mother taken a long time ago and she thinks that some of the relatives have requested it at some time but it was not sent as she did not know the address but if you would like to have them we will send them at once.

Some two weeks ago I visited my sister Pelina Bell in Ala and on my return I spent a day and night with cousin C P Bowen and he told me where you lived and gave me your address.

I hope you will write at once and please tell who of your brothers and sisters are living and if cousin Amanda Jones has some children living.[The very bottom of the last page is torn and faded.]

Notes

John H. Bowen: Horatio has two cousins named John H. Bowen. One is the son of Horatio's uncle Horatio Owen Bowen and the other is the son of his uncle Hiram Bowen. It is unclear which one is the addressee of this letter.[14]

C. P. Bowen: He probably was Caleb Perry Bowen, a son of Horatio's uncle, Thomas Jones Bowen.[15]

John Jones and Amanda Jones: John H. Jones was married to his cousin Amanda Bowen. Amanda was the daughter of Thirza's youngest brother, Hiram. John H. Jones was the son of one of Hiram's and Thirza's uncles on their mother's

---

[13] Service records.
[14] US Census, 1850, Horatio Bowen, Jones County, Georgia; US Census, 1850, Hiram Bowen, Carroll County, Georgia.
[15] Southern Historical Association, *Memoirs of Georgia*, 614.

side. Thus, Amanda Bowen Jones and John H. Jones were first cousins once removed. Letters from them are in chapters 3, 6, and 19.

letters and photographs: The letters and photographs mentioned in the letters are not known to have survived.

1906–1910

Horatio was tax receiver for Banks County.

Note

tax receiver: In Georgia, each county was required to have a tax receiver with whom most tax payers were required to file information concerning their property, such as its ownership and valuation. The tax receiver could raise the tax valuation if he or she determined it was below market value. The tax receiver was elected by the voters of the county.[16]

1920

Thirza McDonald Brooks

Description of Horatio as he looked circa 1920

"Horatio James David, a farmer-tax collector was a commanding figure and a person with which to be reckoned. He stood tall and handsome, complete with goatee, and his granddaughter loved him to pieces! He wore a patch over one eye to cover the mangled place that the Yankee bullet had left during the War Between the States, sometimes referred to 'as the late unpleasantness.'"[17]

Note

Thirza McDonald Brooks was Horatio's granddaughter, the daughter of Horatio's daughter Mary and her husband, the Reverend William Benjamin McDonald.[18]

1923

Horatio David Obituary

Mr. H. J. David, one of Maysville's muchly beloved and prominent citizens, and a noble Confederate veteran, died Tuesday night at 7:30 p. m. after an illness

---

[16] Mize, *History of Banks County*, 258; Sjoquist, "Brief History of the Property Tax in Georgia," 7; Section 48-5-210 of the Georgia Code.

[17] Brooks, "All-Day-Dinner-and-Meeting-on-the-Ground," 18.

[18] Ibid.

of several days, from leakage of the heart. The funeral services were held Wednesday afternoon at two o'clock from the Christian Church, of which he had been a member for 20 years, services being conducted by Rev. R. L. Porter, pastor of the Christian Church at Athens and interment made in the Maysville cemetery.[19]

Note

Age and survivors: When Horatio died, on February 6, 1923, he was eighty years old. He was survived by his wife, Teressa Ellison David; three sons, James Simeon David, George Thomas David, and Horatio Bowen David; one daughter, Mary David McDonald (of whom Horatio once said "I wish I had twelve daughters and that they would be all exactly like Mary"); and four grandchildren.[20]

One of Horatio's grandchildren was Admiral David L. McDonald. A graduate of the Naval Academy and a navy pilot, he served aboard aircraft carriers during World War II and from August 1, 1963, to August 1, 1967, was Chief of Naval Operations.[21]

---

[19] *Jackson Herald*, February 15, 1923.

[20] Brooks, "All-Day-Dinner-and Meeting-on-the-Ground," 18 (quote); Application for Pension Due Deceased Soldier (Widow's Pension Application), Confederate Pension Application Supplements, Georgia Confederate Pension Office, RG 58–1-1, Georgia Archives; grave markers of James Simeon David and George Thomas David, Sunrise Cemetery, Maysville, Banks County, Georgia; Horatio Bowen David's grave marker, Crest Lawn Cemetery, Atlanta; Mary Lee David McDonald's grave marker, Rose Hill Cemetery, Winder, Barrow County, Georgia;

[21] *Washington Post*, December 20, 1997; "Admiral David L. McDonald, Seventeenth Chief of Naval Operations," Naval History and Heritage Command, https://www.history.navy.mil/browse-by-topic/people/chiefs-of-naval-operations/admiral-david-l--mcdonald.html, accessed February 16, 2023.

Chapter 36

Manning and Pillona, 1881–1915

1881

There is Alexander, but not the Great,
As good a doctor as in the State,
If you send for him he will always tell
Whether he thinks you'll die or get well.[1]

1882

Maysville Items

Dr. M. P. Alexander is doing a considerable practice, judging from his traveling. He is a good physician, a high-toned gentleman, and worthy of public patronage.[2]

Maysville Items

Dr. Alexander rode 35 miles on the 13th and visited several critical cases. How is that for business?[3]

1883

Maysville Items

Ku-Klux Arrests
This morning some United States officers from Gainesville came down to the neighborhood of Maysville and arrested J. M. Neal, James and Caleb Yarborough and Stacy Linderman on United States warrants for complicity in the ku-klux outrages that have occurred over in that neighborhood.

They passed through Maysville on their way back to Gainesville, where, we presume they will have a preliminary trial before United States Commissioner

---

[1] *Jackson Herald*, October 14, 1881. This was one of twelve verses of a poem by "Nemo," the paper's Maysville reporter, describing some of the business and professional men of Maysville.

[2] *Jackson Herald*, February 17, 1882.

[3] *Jackson Herald*, March 17, 1882.

Dunlap. We hope that they will be able to prove their innocence from such serious charges. At best, it will cost them a good round sum.[4]

1883

Maysville Items

Dr. M. P. Alexander is summoned to the U. S. court in the Ku Klux shooting scrape.[5]

Note

Ku Klux shooting scrape: The Ku Klux shooting scrape mentioned in the newspaper excerpt began the night of July 13, 1883, in Banks County, a very rural county about sixty miles northeast of Atlanta. At the time, Dr. Alexander was living in Maysville, a small town of fewer than five hundred people on the Jackson County-Banks County border. Although he did not have a large part to play in the case, he very likely would have remembered the case for a long time afterwards.

The Nightriders Strike

After a day of jury selection, the trial in a US district court in Atlanta began. According to testimony given from Tuesday, October 23, through Thursday, October 25, and reported in the *Atlanta Constitution* or summarized by a court reporter, on the night of July 13, 1883, a "shrieking mob" of masked men came running into the house of an African American man named Calvin Bush. As some pointed pistols at him while he lay in bed, one of them cried out "Raise your hands, G—d d—n you."

They then hauled Bush outside into his yard where a large number of mounted and masked men waited. One ordered him "to pull off his shirt and drop down his breeches." When he hesitated, several men forced him to do so. They then proceeded to give him 175 lashes with a whip. He knew the number because, as he testified, "one of the mob counted them out aloud as they were hit." At the trial when requested by the district attorney, Bush took off his shirt and showed the courtroom his scars.

On cross examination, the defense contradicted none of this evidence. It did present testimony that Bush had been brought into court that day directly from jail, where he was being held for "cutting a negro Saturday night." Bush testified,

---

[4] *Jackson Herald*, August 10, 1883.
[5] *Jackson Herald*, October 12, 1883.

however, as the newspaper reported, that he "really didn't mean any harm to the man he cut as they were only playing."

Then the night of July 25, the mob struck again. There were about fifteen of them, all masked, and they first rode to the house of Warren Brison, a twenty-five-year-old black man. He testified that they took him out of his house and that "some fellow with long, black whiskers [apparently visible under his mask] had hit him over the head with a pistol a time or two." When he was asked whether he would raise his hat to a White man, there was some misunderstanding as to his answer, so "he was pummeled again."

They then rode to a house close by, that of Elisha Brooks, a fifty-two-year-old African American with a wife and nine children, aged from one to twenty years old. They broke into the house and grabbed Brooks. He testified that he "scuffled with them as best he could." He managed to get one of them by the legs as they tried to drag him out the door, but two of them "caught him by each big toe. Then he found resistance useless and was dragged out into the yard and whipped." He continued testifying that "someone also hit him with steel knuckles and kicked him badly." He knew one of the men, who told him, "If you know anybody in this crowd and tell on him I'll put you in your grave and put salt in your coffin and come to see you."

Later that same night, around midnight, the mob came to the house of their final victim, Berry Sanders, a forty-two-year-old black farm hand, married with seven children. Sanders testified that the mob had "roused him out [of his house]" and that he had "been shot three times, once in back, once in the hip and once in the heel." His wife said that the men "threatened to fire the house and then broke the door down, and Berry broke and jumped out and ran off. They fired at him several times." She found him the next morning bleeding, "blood was running down his pants." She said she "had to lift him like a baby" and carry him to the house.

The son of Sanders's former White owner testified that he knew Sanders to be a good man "who had belonged to his father and worked for him for years." He also testified that he had heard the mob that night and afterward saw Sanders "lying prostrate from his wounds."

Dr. Alexander Testifies

At this point in the trial, Dr. Alexander took the stand for the prosecution. He testified that he was a practicing physician in Maysville, Jackson County. "On the morning of the 26th July last [the morning after the shooting] at Berry Sanders' house, [I] found Berry Sanders suffering from gunshot wound[s] on the back and in the hip." He continued to confirm Sanders's testimony, saying that one ball (bullet) entered Sanders's body and one grazed him. He was not cross examined, and he stepped down from the witness stand.

The Riders Identified

Several of the persons injured testified that they recognized some of the men in the crowd, even though they were masked or disguised. Particularly they recognized one Jasper Yarbrough. Bush said he knew him by his voice and "his make," meaning probably his manner or his bodily appearance. Two witnesses testified that the night of July 25, one of the men wore a singular baseball cap. A deputy marshal went to Yarbrough's house, which was not far from the houses of the victims, and found such a cap, "a calico cap with a black brim and red tassels" and the name of the baseball club "Pop and Go" written on a piece of paper above the visor. The witnesses identified that as the cap worn the second night of the beatings. Yarbrough's wife later testified that "she had made the cap of pieces of one of her dresses," and Yarbrough himself testified that he often wore it "as pitcher for a baseball club well known in north Georgia."

William Anderson, testified that he lived near the houses of the victims, and that one of the victims, Warren Brison, had come to his house the night of July 25 and told him what was happening. The next day Anderson went to the houses of the first two of that night's victims and saw in some bushes the place where the nightriders had tied their horses. He testified that it had rained two days earlier and the horses' tracks were "plainly discernible in the soft earth."

Anderson tracked the party as they took a road away from the houses until they turned off that road and into the place where the victim Berry Sanders lived. He then testified that the same tracks came back out from Sanders's place and proceeded further down the road toward Jasper Yarbrough's home and separated at a fork in the road, one fork leading to the Yarbrough house.

Besides Jasper Yarbrough, other men in the mob who were identified and charged were James Yarbrough, Dilmus Yarbrough, Neal Yarbrough, Lovel Streetman, Bold Emory (described by the *Atlanta Constitution* reporter "as anything but a bold looking individual"), Stacy Landerman, and E. H. Green—all from Jackson County.

Charged Under Federal Law

Prosecutors charged these men for violating the Enforcement Act of 1870, a federal statute that prohibited the use of violence or intimidation to prevent African Americans from voting. During the presentation of the prosecution's case, one of the victims testified he heard several of the masked men swear that "they were going to make it cheerful for all the negroes that had voted for Emory Speer in the last congressional contest in the ninth district." Another victim testified that, as he was being whipped, one of the mob had said, "you see what your d-d Speer has done for you." This charge under a federal statute meant that the case could be heard, and was heard, in the US Circuit Court for the Northern District of Georgia sitting in Atlanta, rather than in what was thought to be a less friendly court in Banks County. (A court in Banks County, however, might not have been all that unfriendly. After the attacks in Banks County "a large and enthusiastic meeting of the best citizens of Banks and Jackson Counties" was held in Maysville to protest against the "lawless persons who have been going to negro houses and whipping and shooting the negroes for no cause whatever," a local paper reported.)

(In an odd series of events, Emory Speer, the man the victims had supported in the recent congressional election, was the lead attorney prosecuting their attackers in the Ku Klux Klan case. He had been elected to Congress in 1878 and 1880 as an Independent. In the 1880 election he had received the support of the Georgia Republican Party, which infuriated Georgia Democrats. The Democrats then resorted to election fraud and violence to prevent him from being reelected in 1882. Shortly after Speer lost his reelection bid, Republican president Chester A. Arthur appointed him US Attorney for the Northern District of Georgia, which meant that he was the lead prosecutor in this Ku Klux Klan case.)

The Case for the Defense

After the prosecution rested, the defense presented its case. The defense left uncontested the evidence that the African American men had been injured in the way they described in their testimony. It contended instead that the defendants had not been part of the mob that inflicted those injuries.

The defense evidence consisted entirely of alibis for the men charged. Many of the alibis were given by a cousin, niece, brother, or wife of a defendant. One of the defendants was home with a sick child, another with a sick wife, another with a sick cousin, and another with a sick mother. One non-relative testified that he was at a defendant's home where they "sat around the fire and talked" for most of the night. When on cross examination it was pointed out that the defendant was unlikely to have lit a fire in July in Georgia, the witness, according to the *Constitution*'s reporter, "quickly corrected himself."

After this testimony, the defense rested.

The Jury Decides

On Friday, the fifth day of the trial, counsel for the prosecution and counsel for the defense presented their closing arguments. The *Atlanta Constitution* reported that the courtroom "was filled to its utmost capacity, barely a foot of space being unoccupied." The lead defense counsel talked for five hours and fifteen minutes. The *Constitution*'s reporter did not record the length of the prosecution's statement, given by former congressman Speer, but he did write that it was "adroit," "sparkling," "brilliant," and "one of the most remarkable ever delivered in an Atlanta courtroom." The judge then charged the jury, and the case went to the jury that evening.

By nine thirty the following morning, the jury, composed of seven White men and five Black men, had reached its verdict. The jurors filed into the courtroom led by the foreman, a Confederate army veteran crippled by wounds. When all were seated in their places, the foreman handed a yellowish piece of paper containing the verdicts to the deputy clerk who read from it aloud. All eight of the accused were found guilty.

As District Attorney Speer said after the verdicts were announced, "the jury could do one or two things—believe the witnesses for the government or believe the witnesses for the defense. They preferred to believe the government's witnesses and that was the end of it."

The verdict may seem somewhat surprising now, but the Ku Klux Klan was not as powerful in Georgia in 1883 as it had been right after the Civil War. In the late 1860s and early 1870s, the pre-war conservative leaders in Georgia and other Southern states were members of, or at least sympathetic to, the Klan and its violent intimidation of Black citizens. Their primary reason was that they wanted to lead again, and the Klan helped them by preventing newly enfranchised Black men from voting. That tactic, along with other less violent and quieter methods, such as requiring Black men to pay a poll tax before being allowed to vote, were successful in returning state and many local governments to the control of conservative Democrats in the 1870s. Then Klan support by leaders in the community fell away, and membership in the Klan declined.

Moreover, Georgians, particularly businessmen in Atlanta, realized they needed Northern capital in order to rebuild their businesses, their state, and their towns after the Civil War. Only two years before the trial, in 1881, Atlanta held the "World's Fair and Great International Cotton Exposition" in order to "bring people to Georgia and show them why they should invest in industry in the state," as a modern Georgia historian recorded. Yet Klan violence produced instability, scared away the needed Northern capital, and invited greater federal intervention. This type of thinking was on the judge's mind when he gave his charge to the jury in the Banks County case. After describing the "hellish things" done to the victims, the judge told the jury "nothing has tended so much to bring this southern country into disgrace—nothing has tended so much to put the balance of the United States against us, as this kind of outrages." These factors seemed to have had their effect.

Aftermath

Although District Attorney Speer said the verdict was the end of the case, that was not quite so. The case still had its surprises. At a hearing on the defense motion for a new trial, five of the defendants admitted their guilt. They said also that two of the defendants, Dilmus Yarbrough and E. H. Green, had not been with them on either of the nights in question. The judge granted new trials to the latter two but sentenced the other five, plus one other defendant who was sick in jail and unable to appear at the hearing, to two years in the federal prison in Albany, New York.

The defendants appealed to the Supreme Court, but that court ruled against them in March 1884. The case finally was over. By then Dr. Alexander had long ago returned home to Maysville.[6]

1885

Pillina David Bell

Bells Mills Ala Oct. 5th 1885
Dear Brother (Horatio) and family
...We had a letter from Sister Lona a few days ago She was not very well but I think she will get well now as she has no boarders and not so many visitors. the family joins me in love to your family and all our relations and friends back there. Write soon to your Sister
P. C. Bell

Note

Letter: For the complete letter, see chapter 35.

she has no boarders and not so many visitors: According to an article in the *Jackson Herald*, December 14, 1905, titled "The Medical Fraternity of Jackson County," Manning had retired from "active practice" of medicine about fifteen years earlier after enjoying "a large practice in Jackson and Banks counties." The

---

[6] *Banner-Watchman*, August 7, November 6, 1883; *Atlanta Constitution*, October 22–28, December 22, 1863; *Columbus Daily Enquirer-Sun*, October 26, 1883; *Ex Parte Yarbrough*, 110 US 651 (1884); Aucoin, *Rift in the Clouds*, 38–40; Trelease, *White Terror*, xliv–xlviii, 226–29, 235–42, 318–35, 419; Bryant, "Ku Klux Klan in the Reconstruction Era," *New Georgia Encyclopedia*, https://www.georgiaencyclopedia.org/articles/history-archaeology/ku-klux-klan-in-the-reconstruction-era/, accessed February 16, 2023; Coleman, *History of Georgia*, 233–37; Hepburn, *Georgia History Book*, 130; Brief of Evidence, Dr. Alexander Sworn for Gov., *U.S. vs Jasper Yarbrough et al.*, Case No. 3093, 2 of 2, US Circuit Court, Northern District of Georgia, Atlanta, Civil, Criminal, Equity, & Others, 1872–1911, Acc 52A177, RG 21, box 120, NARA, Southeast Region, Morrow, Georgia.

article continues, "He and his estimable family operate the 'Alexander House.'" The author of the article further urges "when in Maysville be sure to stop there."

A register for the Alexander House has survived and is in the possession of Manning and Pillona's great-great granddaughter, Shirley Cavin Chucci. It covers the period January 2, 1897, to January 1, 1906, when the Alexander House closed.

In 1900, Maysville had a population of only 453. It also was a stop on a branch of the Southern Railway. Despite its small size, but probably because of its location on the railroad, the Alexander House register indicates it had visitors from a variety of places in the United States. As well as visitors from Atlanta and other towns and cities in Georgia, people stayed there who were from, for example, Louisville, Knoxville, Detroit, Baltimore, Chicago, and New York. A history of Jackson County reported, "The train brought numerous traveling salesmen or 'drummers,' who, after they had covered Maysville, would hire a hack or buggy and driver to carry them to surrounding communities."[7]

Jackson Herald

The town pursuant to the amended act of October 13th, 1885, organized as the town of Maysville, Ga., in the counties of Jackson and Banks on the 5th day of November, 1885. The first councilors of the town of Maysville who were qualified and inducted into office under the act were Dr. Manning P. Alexander, Hugh Atkins, George Washington Brown, Wm. Jinkins Comer, and Hope Hull Hale.[8]

1886

Margie Alexander

Gainesville, Ga.
Feb. 4, 1886
Mr. Comer

Please accept my sincere thanks for the nice basket. I assure you I enjoyed it immensely. The pictures came all O. K. and I think they are just splendid. I am going to be selfish enough to take the best one. I showed them to Birdie D. and she thinks they are very handsome.

As it has been raining ever since I came we have not been up town for a wonder but am going this morning. I had something else to tell you but I have

---

[7] Candler and Evans, eds., *Georgia*, 551–52; Alexander House register; Gary, Adams, and *Jackson Herald* staff, *Our Time and Place*, 2–15.

[8] *Jackson Herald*, June 15, 1888.

forgotten what it was so I guess I will stop. When you write to me be sure to *seal the letter*.

Truly your friend
Margie A.

I think Pa [Manning] is going to Athens some time this week or next—so please do not say anything to him unless he does [speak first]. Do you *hear*?

Notes

Margie Alexander: She was Manning's second daughter. When this letter was written, she was eighteen years old.

Mr. Comer: He was James T. (Jim) Comer, a widower with one child, a boy named Ralph, eight years old when the letter was written. Jim's wife, Alice (Allie) Thurmond Comer, had died in childbirth in September 1879. Also, when the letter was written, Jim was thirty-six years old, double Margie's age.[9]

seal the letter.... please do not say anything to Pa: According to family lore, Manning was very much against the budding relationship between Margie and Jim, probably because of the difference in their ages and the fact that Jim was a widower with a young son. Margie and Jim had to be secretive about meeting and communicated only through letters delivered by friends. This letter is one of several between the two that have survived. The first had been sent from Jim to Margie on November 16, 1885.

Eventually, Manning relented, and Margie and Jim were married on July 5, 1886, five months after this letter was written. They remained married for twenty-five years until Jim died on July 25, 1911. Six of their children lived beyond infancy.[10]

1889

Pillona

Maysville Oct 22nd /89
My darling Lillie

We rece'd yours and sister's letter today. I am so glad to hear you are so well satisfied. I hope you will be well pleased with the school and Mama is so glad to know that you are a good girl too. Your sister writes me that Perino says you are a quiet nice behaved child. Now Mama is so glad to hear that; you don't know how proud it makes me. I know you will not act wrong on purpose. You may be

---

[9] Grave markers for James T. Comer and Alice Comer, Oconee Hill Cemetery, Athens, Georgia; US Census, 1880, Ralph Comer, Clarke County, Georgia.

[10] *Weekly Banner-Watchman*, July 13, 1886; *Weekly Banner*, July 28, 1911.

a little unthoughtful sometimes. You must ask sister's and Perino's advice like you would mama and papa. They will tell you and Annie how to act. We are glad you enjoyed your trip to the exposition so much. I know you saw a great many nice things that was new and interesting to you and I think you must have enjoyed your visit to the capitol as much as anything else. A good many people went from here and this neighborhood today. The trains were crowded.

Mama must tell you about her birthday presents. Mr. Comer gave me a reference bible and papa and the children gave me a carving set. We needed that very much. Henry Comer and Mr. Boone took dinner here sunday. Had preaching at both the churches. Your little *friends* seem to miss you very much and are always enquiring about you.

Tell Nora to write me whether she can get the undervests for you or not. We have not made your flannel skirts yet. I would like to know how she is going to make Annie's winter dress before we make you one.[unintelligible word] little Lucy was rite sick today derangement of the stomach and bowels. I hope nothing serious. Margie is going to Mr Deadwilers to spend the day today Wednesday. All are quite well.

Be sure to brush your teeth and keep your nails clean and wash your neck every day. I hope you and Annie will be good children and not dispute or fall out with each other. Papa and the children send love to you all. Write often to

Mama

Notes

My darling Lillie: She was Manning and Pillona's fourth and last child. At the time this letter was written, she was eleven years old.

Years later she wrote a note on the back of the envelope in which this letter was sent: "Will some one in the family please keep this letter. Its so typical of my dear mother—was written to me when I went to Gville [Gainesville, Georgia] to school one Fall term when we did not have any school at home."

Lillie, who married but had no children, gradually became the unofficial family historian. In that role, she preserved most of the letters printed in this book.

sister and Perino: Sister was Manning and Pillona's oldest child, Nora Alexander Boone. When this letter was written, she was thirty years old. Perino Boone was her husband.[11]

---

[11] US Census, 1910, Jackson County, Georgia; grave marker for Nora A. Boone, Sunrise Cemetery, Maysville, Banks County, Georgia.

Annie: She was Nora Boone's daughter, age twelve when this letter was written.[12]

exposition: In 1881 Atlanta organized its first exposition, called the International Cotton Exposition. Its purpose was to promote investment in Atlanta businesses and help the city recover from the Civil War. Atlanta held a more regional exposition in 1887, the first held in Piedmont Park, a 189-acre former forest that had recently been cleared and on which a main building 570 feet long and 126 feet wide, as well as a racetrack, had been constructed. With much the same goal as the earlier exposition, civic leaders wanted to expand Atlanta's reputation as a place to visit and conduct business.[13]

Two years later, another exposition was held at Piedmont Park, the exposition referred to in the letter. Besides industrial and agricultural displays, it featured parades, speeches, horse races, a "balloon ascension and parachute leap," and a Wild West Show with Indians and cowboys.[14]

Mr. Comer and Henry Comer: Mr. Comer was Pillona's son-in-law James T. Comer, Margie's husband. Henry Comer was his brother.[15]

papa and the children: Papa was Manning, but it is unclear who "the children" were.

Mr. Deadwilers: This may be a reference to George E. Deadwyler who lived in Maysville and had a large family.[16]

1893

Maysville

The whole town and community was quite sad last Monday morning on hearing of the death of Mrs. Mamie O'Kelly, wife of Rev. T. W. O'Kelly. Miss Mamie passed away last Sunday night [April 23], at the residence of her father, Dr. M. P. Alexander of this place. This sad event was not unexpected, as she has been quite ill for some time. She was a good wife, a devoted Christian, and loved by every one who knew her. Her kind deeds and gentle words will make her

---

[12] Grave marker for Annie B. [Boone] Wingfield, Sunrise Cemetery, Maysville, Banks County, Georgia.

[13] "Piedmont Exposition," Wikipedia, https://en.wikipedia.org/wiki/Piedmont_Exposition, accessed May 6, 2019; Newman, "Cotton Expositions in Atlanta," *New Georgia Encyclopedia*, https://www.georgiaencyclopedia.org/articles/history-archaeology/cotton-expositions-in-atlanta/, accessed May 7, 2019.

[14] *Atlanta Constitution*, October 6 and 10, 1889.

[15] US Census, 1850, Reuben T. Comer, Athens, Georgia; US Census, 1870, Joseph Fletcher Comer, Oglethorpe County, Georgia.

[16] US Census, 1880, Banks County, Georgia.

memory a blessing to the neighborhood, the church and her sorrowing family. While we sympathize with the family in their loss, we rejoice to know that she has entered into the joy eternal in the heavens which the Lord has prepared for those who love him.[17]

Notes

Mrs. Mamie O'Kelly: She was the third daughter of Dr. Alexander. She was twenty-one years old and had been married for less than a year and a half when she died.[18]

Rev. T. W. O'Kelly: Reverend Thomas Washington O'Kelly was thirty-two years old when his wife died. He was pastor of the Hawkinsville Baptist Church in Pulaski County, and for at least part of the short time that they were married, he taught Latin at Mercer University. In 1913, he was offered the presidency of Mercer but turned it down because he loved to preach and believed that was what God had called him to do.[19]

c. 1900

Manning
[Letterhead on notepaper]
Office of

Alexander House

DR. M. P. ALEXANDER, Proprietor
HEADQUARTERS
COMMERCIAL SALESMEN.
Maysville, Ga.   190.....
This is the receipt [recipe] for Small pox
Sulphate Zinc one grain
Digitalis one grain
Sugar one half tea spoonfull

---

[17] Jackson Herald, April 28, 1893.
[18] Grave marker, Mamie O'Kelley, Sunrise Cemetery, Maysville, Banks County, Georgia; *Jackson County Marriages, Book G, 1884–1895*, 379.
[19] Mercer University, *Triennial Register and Annual Catalogue*, 39; *Atlanta Constitution*, August 1 and August 8, 1913; grave marker, Thomas W. O'Kelley, Oakwood Cemetery, Raleigh, North Carolina; "Thomas W. O'Kelley," *Biblical Recorder*, Baptist State Convention of North Carolina, Raleigh, July 20, 1927, 6:1–3.

Disolve in a wine glass of water or water that has been boiled and cooled. Take a teaspoonfull every hour. Either Small pox or Scarlet fever will disappear in twelve hours

Notes

Alexander House: See the note concerning the Alexander House related to the partial letter from Pillina Bell to Horatio above in this chapter.

the receipt: Manning wrote this "receipt," recipe, or prescription on lined paper with the Alexander House letterhead at the top. When Manning wrote it, however, he turned the paper upside down and began his writing at the bottom of the page. His recording of the recipe and keeping it suggests that from time to time he was consulted as a doctor, or at least wanted to continue being informed about medical practices, even after formally retiring from his practice.

At the time Manning wrote the recipe for curing smallpox and scarlet fever, vaccination had been recognized as effective to prevent smallpox. It was so recognized soon after vaccination was tried in 1796, yet its use still was not sufficiently widespread to prevent people from developing the disease, and a cure continued to be needed. Even now an effective cure has yet to be developed.[20]

The purported cure that Manning recorded had appeared in journals and newspapers in the United States as early as 1860, and it continued to appear in later newspapers. The *Daily Republican* of Monongahela, Pennsylvania, reported it in its November 15, 1881, edition, saying that the prescription is "as unfailing as fate, and conquers in every instance." The same article as in the *Daily Republican* appeared in the *Banner-Watchman* of Athens on May 4, 1882. The "cure" described also appeared in local newspapers in Muncie, Indiana, during an epidemic there in 1893. The Muncie papers referred to it as an "infallible" cure.[21]

1907

Manning and Pillona

Maysville Ga
April 27—1907
Dear Margie:

Well I have passed my 77th birthday and am thankful to be able to say I am almost in perfect health. I think I am feeling better than I have been in fifteen years.

---

[20] "Jenner, Edward," *Encyclopedia Britannica*, 10:133–34, "Small pox," IX:280; "Smallpox," Mayo Clinic, https://www.mayoclinic.org/diseases-conditions/smallpox/symptoms-causes/syc-20353027, accessed September 8, 2020.

[21] Tucker, *Scourge*, 35, in addition to the newspapers cited in the note.

We ware disappointed that you did not come, but since we learned how it was, we know you could not leave well. We hope to see you next week. Lily says tell you, you "sholly" missed a mighty dood dinner by not being here. Tell George I hardly think I will get off to the Reunion. May be someone from about Comer may go that he can go with.

I have sold Brownie so I have not a single living thing to look after but your Mama, and she thinks she is looking after me.

Hope to see you soon.

           Affect'
           Papa

PS. So that you may better understand my present state of halth Lily suggest that I state that I am much stronger and know a whole lot more than I did 77 years ago.

           Afft
           Papa

[In the same envelope]
Maysville Apr 27 1907
Dear Margie

As your Papa is writing to you I will write some too. We were glad to get your letter and learn that you all are well. I am sorry George has a rising. Hope it is not a carbuncle

We will be so glad for you and the children to come any time you can but I know you could not have come yesterday as the young lady was coming. Nora come and took dinner with us. Perino went to Ganesville the day before and Harry went to the picnic at Gravelly Church. The school the little set had a picnic there. They had a good time.

Well Margie I am glad to tell you that I am much better than when Mr. Comer was here. I am gaining strength but am so very thin. I am living on chicken most of the time, only eat a little light bread for supper. I am taking medicine now from Dr. Carlton. Nora saw him and got the medicine for me. I hope I will get well after a while. I have not had a [illegible word] spell in over a week. I think they are caused from indigestion but they make me so weak. I walked over to Noras this morning. She did not take Harry to Athens with her. She will write you soon.

Affect Mamma

Notes

George: He was Margie's son, then about fifteen years old.[22]

---

[22] US Census, 1900, Madison County, Georgia.

Reunion: Probably a Confederate reunion.
Comer: Margie was living in Comer, Georgia, in Madison County at that time.
a rising: In this case, something that rises under the skin, such as a boil or abscess.[23]
Harry: He was Nora's son, then nine years old.[24]
Mr. Comer: He was Margie's husband, James T. Comer.[25]

Pillona's Obituary

Mrs. M. P. Alexander

It is always pleasant to say nice things about anyone, especially so, when we feel that all we can say is less than is deserved by the one spoken of. Too much cannot be said of Mrs. M. P. Alexander who died at her home in Maysville on August 23rd, within two months of her 68th birthday. She was married to Dr. M. P. Alexander Oct. 20, 1857, and for fifty years this union was blessed of God, for no happier one could have been, and it was a continual honeymoon. Four daughters, of whom they were justly proud, were the fruit of this union. Three of whom, Mrs. J. T. Comer, of Comer, Mrs. G. P. Boone and Mrs. E. C. Jackson, of Maysville, survive her and Mrs. Thos. W. O'Kelley who died several years ago. The venerable husband in the midst of his great grief finds sweet consolation in the love of his three noble daughters whose devotion to him cannot be excelled.

For fifty-five years Mrs. Alexander was a faithful member of the Baptist Church and being profoundly in love with all good word and works she took a prominent and active part in all the institutions of her Church. A charter member of the Woman's Missionary Society, she did all that a thoroughly consecrated Christian could do to make the society a blessing to the world, and her enthusiastic zeal inspired others to take hold of the work in such a way that it is now one of the best organizations of its kind in the state, blessing thousands with its works of love.

As a Sunday School teacher she showed the depth and purity of her trust in her Savior, and her Christian love so impressed itself on those who were so fortunate as to be in her class, that today many them rise up to call her blessed. It was but fitting that her funeral services should be held at the Church she loved so well, and the tributes to her noble character by her pastor, the Rev. J. J. Kimsey and the venerable Dr. H. F. Hoyt, of the Presbyterian Church, were appropriate

---

[23] "Rising," *Webster's New World College Dictionary*, 1255.
[24] US Census, 1900, Gainesville, Hall County, Georgia.
[25] *Jackson County Marriages, Book G, 1884–1895*, 75.

indeed touching a tender chord in each heart in that vast audience, for each one there felt a distinct personal loss.

In the cemetery on the hill, beside the grave of her beloved Mamie, the remains of the dear departed will rest until the earth gives up its dead.

As a friend, we loved her dearly, and our hearts go out in loving sympathy to the sad hearted husband and daughters, and our prayer is that He who tempers the wind to the shorn lamb may send to them the consolation the world cannot give, and at last when God has called them home they will find her at the pearly gates to welcome them to the eternal home, then –

"How sweet it will be in that beautiful land
So free from all sorrow and pain,
With songs on our lips and harps in our hand
To greet one another again."

"Friends"[26]

Notes

Dr. H. F. Hoyt: He was the same minister who preached at Horatio's daughter Daisy's funeral fourteen years earlier in 1883 (see chapter 33).

"How sweet it will be....": This is a stanza from an old hymn.[27]

1912 [undated]

A Reminiscence of an Afternoon Spent with a Real Daughter of the Confederacy

Mrs. Jackson recalled how her father [Manning Poole Alexander] had enjoyed attending the old Confederate Veteran reunion, and she remembered how delighted she had been when her father allowed her to go with him to the 1912 reunion at Macon. She said that the thrill of seeing her eighty-two year old father dressed in full uniform, with his snow white beard blowing in the wind, parading down the street astride a huge horse that reared at his command, was one she can never forget. She said the coat he wore in the parade was the same one he had used all during the war.[28]

Note

undated: The document, in possession of the editor, records that the author interviewed Lily Alexander Jackson when she was eighty-four years old. This would have meant the date of the interview was 1960 or 1961.

---

[26] *Maysville News*, September 5, 1907.
[27] Hazard, *National Sunday School Teacher*, 539.
[28] Colquitt Brackett, Ellen A. Crawford Chapter, Children of the Confederacy, n.d.

1915

Manning Alexander

HEAD QUARTERS JOHN H. MORGAN CAMP U. C. V. 1330

A tribute to the memory of our deceased friend and Comrade, Dr. M. P. Alexander, who departed this life March 17th 1915 at his home in Maysville, Ga., where he had resided for many years.

Dr. Alexander was born near Anderson, S. C. April 26th, 1830. In the year 1839 he, with his parents, moved to Franklin County, Ga., where his early life was spent.

In the year 1858 [sic], Dr. Alexander was united in marriage to Miss Pelona David of Jackson County, Ga. He chose medicine as his profession and after graduating at the famous medical college in Cincinnati, Ohio, he located and practiced medicine at Homer, Ga., and afterwards moved to Hall County, Ga.

In the year 1861, when the war between the states was declared, he organized a Company of volunteers, and carried it to Savannah, Ga., but on account of a misunderstanding with the War Department, the company was not mustered into service, but disbanded, and returned to their homes.

In March, 1862, he enlisted as a member in Company K, 43d Regiment Georgia Volunteers and was mustered into the Confederate service at Big Shanty, Ga.

On July 12th, 1862, he was commissioned Assistant Surgeon, C. S. A. and served in that capacity through all of the subsequent campaigns of the Western Army until he was assigned to hospital duty at Blacky Hospital at Augusta, Ga., where he served until the surrender in 1865 when he was paroled by order of Gen. Sherman of the U. S. A.

At the close of the war, Dr. Alexander located at Maysville, Ga. where he practiced medicine for a period of thirty-five (35) years.

For a number of years, he had been an honored member and surgeon of J. H. Morgan Camp U. C. V. #1330, located at Commerce, Ga., and was universally loved and honored by each member of the camp.

Gen. Bennett H. Young, Commander in Chief of the U. C. V. had conferred a signal honor on Dr. Alexander by assigning him to a place on his staff and commissioning his Assistant Surgeon with rank of Lieutenant Colonel, an honor that anyone might covet.

During Dr. Alexander's long and exemplary life, he was honored and loved by all classes for his many virtues and his kind and genial disposition towards all he came in contact. On the 17th day of March, 1915, after a severe attack of pneumonia, Dr. Alexander after serving his day and generation well, yielded up this long and useful life to his Creator and on the following day (March 18th) he was laid peacefully to rest in the beautiful Cemetery at Maysville by his comrades, members of his camp, using their beautiful and impressive Ritual of their camp.

Therefore: Be it resolved, that in the death of Dr. Alexander that our Camp has lost an honored member and an officer, but when the Final Roll is called, we confidently hope and believe that we will meet our friend and Comrade in that final Bivouack [sic] of the faithful, true and brave, where parting will be no more.

Resolved second, that this resolution be spread upon our minutes, and a copy be sent to the *Confederate Veteran* with request to publish. Also that a copy be furnished to the family of the deceased.

G. L. Carson
H. I. [sic] David
D. D. Holland
Committee

Notes

deceased friend: Manning had been ill for two weeks with pneumonia and died from that illness while in the home of his oldest daughter, Nora Alexander Boone. Another obituary printed in the *Athens Daily Herald* read in part: "The closing scenes of a well spent life found him among those he loved, successful in life and victorious in death."[29]

This tribute is transcribed from a typewritten copy of the original found in the Alexander-Bowen-David Papers in my possession.

---

[29] *Weekly Banner*, March 19, 1915; *Athens Daily Herald*, April 12, 1915 (quote). A modified version of the tribute appeared in *Confederate Veteran* (June 1915): 271.

Chapter 37

Fanny Harris David, 1873

Fanny Harris David Davis and Van W. Davis to Thirza David

Introduction

This letter was written much earlier than the letters and other documents in the immediately preceding chapters. It is the last known surviving letter from Simeon's widow, Fanny David. This book started with a letter from Simeon, and it seems appropriate to end with a letter like one he might have written later had he lived, one Fanny wrote to tell Simeon's mother what is happening with her and Simeon's children.

Rockmart May 8th 1873
    Dear Mother I seat my self once more to try to write. your welcom letter came to hand last week. I was so glad to hear your health was improved and you had an Idia of coming to See us once more. I dont know of any thing on earth would afford me any more pleasure than to See you coming.
    Mother if I could find it in my heart to deny receving your letter away back in Nov or Dec I would do it. I hunted up Some paper the next day after I got it and had no ink and my health was awful bad along then and I kept putting it off until I got to feeling ashamed to write. I know I never was glader to recive a letter from you nor more interested in one So I hav tried to make my poor apoligy and I hope you will Sorter forgive me.
    Elen was married 19 Dec to Billy Hagen Mr Newton Hagens Son. they live in Pauldin[g] [County] on Raccoon [Creek]. Ann might have Seen Some of them when She was here. he is a mighty nice good looking young man. Weighs Hundred and 75. lacked a few days being 21. he is very Study and of a Splendid family. I was very much pleased with her Selection
    Elen weighs over a Hundred and 30. Billy is making a crop with his Father this year. Lina an Sally are boarding with them and going to School to Mr Helms at High Shoals half a mile [away]. he is called a very good teacher.
    it is 6 miles to where they live and it is very seldom I get to see any of them. I hav never been to see Elen but once since she was married. they live in a very neat little house and we fixed them up with evry thing necessary for housekeeping and a good cow and calf[,] sow and pigs. Van went to Rome and bought her a nice Bureau 15 Dollars, 2 Bedsteads 11, Safe 7, cooking Stove 20, Saddle 15, 45 pounds Feathers 33 Dollars, and 50 cts freight from Atlanta to Rockmart. we got her a nice chance of crockery, tin water Buckets, washing tub, evry thing they

neded. I will tell you what Van had desided to give them all Cow and Calf, Sow and pigs, Bed and bed clothes, Trunk, Saddle, and 2 Hundred Dollars besides or its equivolent and I divided Some of nearly evry thing I had with Elen. I think she is the nicest house Keeper I nearly ever Saw and the best cook of her age. She had peaced up and quilted Several very nice Bed quilts. She is Just as industrious as a bee.

I am afraid I wont get to keep Lina long. She is called a perfect Beauty. I dont think She will be much larger than her Aunt Any if any. Sally is the tallest and I think looks as well as Lina and poor little Giny She is at home helping me. She has grown you hav no idia and I know the best and the Smartest Childe I ever saw. I think She is very much like her Pappy. She ought to go to School this year but I cant posably spare them all.

we hav a young man hired living in the house with us. we milk 3 Cows and get the most milk and Butter from that number I ever Saw. Giny does all the Hen Setting. She has taken off over a Hundred and 60 young Chickens and lots Setting. we hav over 40 nearly large enough to Kill. I tell you Since Lina and Sally left we hav our hands full.

I will be confined Some time in July. I am poolier this time than I ever was but Van tries to fix evry thing for me convenient as he is able. he has bought me a new Sewing Mashine cost 90 Dollars the improved Wheeler and Wilson. I can use it splendidly. I reckon we are getting on as well as a Single handed man could be expected.

John Hilburn is still living with us. he is a Splendid little boy to work our Wheat. looks like makeing a very fair crop but the winter freshets injured it very much. we hav a large crop sown. we only hav in 8 Achors Cotton this year. last year we made 6 or 7 heavy Bales. we hav in a heavy corn crop for our force.

vans health has not been very good for some time but he is improveing. now he has had two attacts lately of Something like Diabetus but I think if he will take care of himself it will not return. he become very much alarmed. he works very hard more than he is able and he is just as good to Buy for the children and takes as much delight in Seeing them dressed and Sending them out as I do.

I hav forgotten to Say any thing about my little Boys. Billy is a right Smart Size little chap and Bob my Baby is the largest child I know of to his age. he was 2 years old in March. he is just like my folks black eyed. I think they are both powerful pretty and Smart and van thinks no body has got Boys but him.

Billy Hagen Elen Lina and Sally are going to hav their pictures taken this week and Send to you and the first time there is an artist handy I will get Ginnys. Mother it was as kinder offer as you could hav made to take one of the children and Send to School as you could hav made but I was not well and could not bear the idia of Seeing one Start So far but if we all live and you Still want one of them I may let Ginny go next year but I expect it would be harder for me to see her go than any of them. She is the most pleasant disposed childe I ever Saw and can do almost any thing like a Woman. not Boasting but it is generally Said I hav the Smartest Set of girls in Polk [County].

van is prepareing to put us up a good house after crops are laid by. he has 15 thousand Shingels all ready. he aims to build about half mile from where we now live if we can get good water.

the late frost killed I might Say all the fruit Irish Potatoes Bunch Beans and etc but I hav a beautiful garden considering.

I reckon you herd what Simeons land brought. three Hundred and 90 odd Dollars almost for nothing.

Our address is Rockmart. van will give you the Railroad Schedule.

If there is any thing I hav left out I will write next time. the cildren carried your letter [to me] to Pauldin and I may hav forgotten Something you wished to know. Mother I want you to Just keep it in your head to come to See us or I am afraid I will never get to go to See you all.

I dont think Billy Hagen knows what the chance will be for him to go but I hav very little Idia he will think he can spare the time. his Father has a good Plantation and a tan yard. livs in a nice white house but they are very plain common people in their ways. he speaks of fixing Billy and Elen off with a home of their own next Fall.

it is getting late. I will close for this time. dont think hard of me. I hav never written Sister Mary but 2 letters Since I was married. I will Send you a pice of Elens fare dress. my warmest love to you all. good by
             FED
Mrs David your note to me to know the fare from atlanta to Rockmart which is three dollars and fifty cents. the post office is moved to Rockmart. fanie has wrote all the nuse. I close for the present. yours as ever
             V W Davis
Ps tell Ann Dr. Allen, Mrs Jo Hichcock, Cornelia Simpson hav all Died lately. the Train leavs Rockmart at 7 in the morning and returns Sat at 5 or 6 in the afternoon.

Notes

Van W. Davis: Fannie married Van William Davis in 1866 in Taylorsville, Georgia, according to an obituary from a newspaper in Bartow County, Georgia. She was then about thirty years old, and he was about thirty-eight.

He was a widower with two young children. Fannie had the four girls from her marriage with Simeon, and she and Van together had four children. Van was a Confederate veteran having served as a private in Company C, Montgomery Artillery.[1]

Date: This letter was written almost exactly nine years after Simeon was killed.

Punctuation: Commas have been inserted in the several lists in the letter for ease of reading.

Rockmart: Rockmart is in Polk County about forty-five miles northwest of Atlanta.[2]

Fannie's children by Simeon: According to their grave markers in various cemeteries

Ellen: At the time the letter was written, she was seventeen years old. She died at Taylorsville, Georgia, in 1929, at the age of seventy-three.[3]

Lena: She was sixteen when the letter was written. She died in Bibb County in 1934 at the age of seventy-seven and was buried in Polk County.[4]

Sally: She was thirteen. She died in Polk County in 1934 at the age of seventy-four.[5]

Ginny: She was eleven. She died in 1959 at the age of ninety-seven and was buried in Tillman County, Oklahoma.[6]

Aunt Any: She was Simeon's sister Annie.

I will be confined Some time in July: Fannie was pregnant with her and Van's first daughter, Alice Doris Davis, born in August 1873.[7]

Single handed man: This phrase seems to imply that Van had lost a hand at some time. However, his pension file, which contains a doctor's evaluation of his ability to work, does not mention that he had only one hand. Perhaps it means he only had one helper (as a "farm hand").

He had filed for a pension in 1907 on the basis of age, poverty, and "feeble health." The doctor found that "besides his old age [he is] suffering from Severe Bronchitis and wholy unable to earn any part of [his] support by manual labor."

it is getting late. I will close for this time: Fannie died twenty-six years later, on April 10, 1899, at the age of sixty-two. She lived thirty-five years after Simeon's

---

[1] Hopper-Tinsley family tree in Ancestry.com; Indigent Pension Application No. 1908, Van W. Davis, signed May 28, 1907, received June 12, 1907, Georgia Archives, http://cdm.georgiaarchives.org.

[2] *Georgia Atlas & Gazetteer*, 1.

[3] Grave marker of Ella David Hagan Trippe, Old Taylorsville Church Cemetery, Polk County, Georgia.

[4] Grave marker of Lena David Pittman, Lime Branch Cemetery, Polk County, Georgia.

[5] Grave marker of Sallie B. Lowry, Rose Hill Cemetery, Rockmart, Polk County, Georgia.

[6] Grave marker of Virginia David Tant, Grandfield, Tillman County, Oklahoma.

[7] US Census, 1880, Stilsboro, Bartow County, Georgia; Hopper-Tinsley family tree, Ancestry.com.

death.[8] Van lived another seventeen years after her, dying on December 15, 1916, at the age of eighty-eight.[9]

---

[8] Grave marker, Old Taylorsville Church Cemetery, Polk County, Georgia.
[9] Ibid.

Acknowledgments

I have been fortunate while working on the book off and on for several years to have the help and encouragement of many capable and supportive people for which I am truly grateful.

In particular, my sincere thanks for their friendly efficiency and cooperation to the staffs of the institutions where I researched various aspects of the book:

In Georgia, the Jackson County Library, Courthouse, and Historical Society; Forsyth County Library; Hall County Courthouse; Banks County Courthouse and Library; Franklin County Courthouse; Elberton County Library; Georgia Department of Archives and History; Manuscript, Archives, and Rare Book Library, Emory University, especially Kathy Shoemaker; and the Hargrett Rare Books & Manuscripts Library, University of Georgia, especially Mary Linneman.

In Virginia, the Madison County Library and the Alexandria Library, Special Collections Branch, particularly Leslie Anderson.

The US Army Heritage and Education Center in Carlisle, Pennsylvania, and the Daughters of the American Revolution Library and the Library of Congress in Washington, D.C.

For their thorough research on my behalf, I am indebted to Elizabeth Olsson and Don Evans. For their thoughtful comments and suggestions after reading portions of my manuscript, warm thanks to Marya Fitzgerald, Paul Sherry, and Andrew McElwain. My thanks to Jennifer Baker, who taught a writing course in my hometown of Alexandria, Virginia, and gave a very helpful critique of my book proposal. To Bruce Swain, longtime friend, my special thanks for his suggestions on my proposal and for his continued encouragement.

Several people provided or referred me to key documents during the course of my writing, for which I am deeply grateful. Todd Dorsey, a Maysville, Georgia, historian, provided me genealogical pages from the David Family Bible and a family letter he found among the pages of that volume. Donald Pfanz, National Park Service historian, found and passed on to me an excerpt of a letter from Horatio that was vital to the story of Horatio and Simeon at the Battle of the Wilderness. My cousin, Shirley Cucci, gave me copies of pages from the old register of the Alexander family hotel in Maysville. Many thanks also to Keith Bohannon, professor of history at the University of West Georgia and excellent writer on the Civil War, for his valuable correspondence about David family letters he had found, for pointing me toward such useful sources as the letters of Simeon's tent-mate Josiah B. Patterson, Folsom's *Heroes and Martyrs of Georgia*, and Krick's *Stonewall at Cedar Mountain*, and for his insight into the uniform worn by Simeon in his 1855 photo.

I am indebted also to many others who helped in various ways, including Bowen descendants Helen Carey and Kay Gibbs for their extensive genealogical information and consultation; friend Elaine Hawes, for pointing out to me that these letters might make a good book; my able and personable internal medicine practitioner, Dr. Stephen Minton, for his precise diagnosis of Robert Alexander's terminal illness; and Marjan Khanjani of Old Town Photo Restoration Studio for excellent restoration work on the old family ambrotypes. In addition, my most grateful thanks to Tammy Wilson and Texie Doolittle, whose able and accurate transcriptions of the surviving original letters saved me countless hours, and to the late Livy and Charles Brockmann, who in the 1940s transcribed a number of key letters that later were lost.

Many people have offered continued encouragement during this long process that I greatly appreciate: my cousins, the Gaither family (especially Albert Gaither and Susan Gaither Jones), Elizabeth Chew, Sam Clark, Nancy Comer Shuford, Jim Comer, and Bill Brockmann; my morning coffee friends Jay Roberts and Dave Cavanaugh; my fellow book club members Paul Sherry, Jim Silverwood, Tom Long, and Bob Lavine; Mark Pentecost, admirable 16th Georgia Volunteer Infantry Regiment re-enactor and friend; Elaine Fowler Palencia, Michael Palencia-Roth, and Cliff Roberts of the General Barton and Stovall History/Heritage Association; Dave Phlegar, college classmate, correspondent, and guide to Athens and the University of Georgia campus; and finally to my sister, Margie Pulliam.

And my particular thanks to my distant cousin and Simeon descendant, David Hopper, for being my wise reviewer, sounding board, researcher, and adviser throughout this project.

I also am most grateful to the staff at Mercer University Press—particularly Marc Jolley, Marsha Luttrell, and Mary Beth Kosowski—for their attention to detail while guiding this volume into print.

Finally, I cannot say enough for all the love, understanding, and patience of my wife, Molly.

Bibliography

LETTERS, DIARIES, AND MEMOIRS

Alison, Joseph Dill. "Joseph Dill Alison Diary, 1861–1863." Collection Number 03267-z, Manuscript Collection, Southern Historical Collection, Louis Round Wilson Special Collections Library, University of North Carolina, Chapel Hill.

Blackford, Launcelot Minor. Letter to his mother. November 12, 1863, Louis Round Wilson Special Collections Library, University of North Carolina, Chapel Hill.

Bowen, Owen. Deposition. December 3, 1792, sent by General Elijah Clarke to Governor Edward Telfair, Hargrett Library manuscripts, University of Georgia Libraries, Athens, Georgia.

Brown, Theo V. "Gaines's Mill, June 27, 1862." In *Remembering the Civil War: The Conflict as Told by Those Who Lived It*. Edited by Michael Barton and Charles Kupfer, 142–48. Guilford, CT: Lyons Press, an imprint of The Rowan & Littlefield Publishing Group. Inc., 2020.

Bryan, T. Conn. "Letters of Two Confederate Officers: William Thomas Conn and Charles Augustus Conn." *Georgia Historical Quarterly* 46 (June 1962): 169–95.

Champion, David. "A Reminiscence of the Sixties, 1861–1865, As Told by David Champion, Lieutenant in Company 'C' 14th Georgia Regiment to his Son Randolph E. Champion of Albany Who Wrote Down His Father's Experiences as Told to Him." Drawer 283, box 21, Microfilm Collection. Georgia Department of Archives and History, Morrow, Georgia.

Cline, William. "A Neste of Bumbelbes." In *Gettysburg 1863, Seething Hell: The Epic Battle of the Civil War in the Soldiers' Own Words*. Edited by Thomas R. Pero, 187. Mill Creek, WA: Wild River Press, 2016.

Connor, Wesley Olin. *The Confederate Diary of Wesley Olin Connor of Cave Spring, Georgia*. In the Wesley O. Connor Family Papers, MS 3102. Hargrett Rare Book and Manuscript Library, University of Georgia Libraries, Athens.

David, Horatio J. Family Papers, MS 3127. Hargrett Rare Book and Manuscript Library, University of Georgia Libraries, Athens.

Eckardt, Charles. "Diary of Dr. Charles Eckardt, Music Teacher." In "Diary Accounts of Guard Hill Battle," file 175-2b-2c. Warren Heritage Society, Front Royal, Virginia.

Fowler, Washington A, Company B, 43rd Georgia. "Letters." Drawer 10, box 82. Georgia Department of Archives and History, Morrow, Georgia.

Hall, George Washington. *Diary of George Washington Hall, 1861–1865*. 2 vols. Manuscript Reading Room (Madison, LM101), shelving no. mm73040691. Library of Congress, Washington, D.C.

Hitt, David M. "David M. Hitt Letters." Confederate Miscellany, 1b: MSS 20. Manuscript, Archives, and Rare Book Library, Emory University, Atlanta.

Owen, William. "The Yankees Attack Marye's Heights." In *The Blue and the Gray: The Story of the Civil War as Told by Participants*. Edited by Henry Steele Commager, 235–39. Avenel, NJ: Crescent Books, 1995.

Patterson, Josiah Blair. Josiah Blair Patterson letters, Manuscript Collection, Civil War Miscellany, ac 61-210, mf 147, Georgia Archives, Morrow, Georgia.

Powers, Philip H. "Philip H. Powers Letters." Lewis Leigh Collection, book 19, item 103. Army Heritage and Education Center, Carlisle, Pennsylvania.

Richardson, Sue. "Diary of Miss Sue Richardson." In "Diary Accounts of Guard Hill Battle," file 175-2b-2c. Warren Heritage Society, Front Royal, Virginia.

Rogers, W. H. H. *Bible Records, Military Rosters and Reminiscences of Confederate Soldiers Copied and Compiled from the files of the Georgia Division, United Daughters of the Confederacy.* Vol. 9, 105–107. Atlanta: Georgia Division, United Daughters of the Confederacy, 1942.

Sanders, Charles. "Charles Sanders to His Sister." In *"Dear Mother: Don't grieve about me. If I get killed, I'll only be dead": Letters from Georgia Soldiers in the Civil War.* Edited by Mills Lane, 296–98. Savannah: Beehive Press, 1977.

Shankle, Thomas S. Letter to Mollie Hawes. 13 February 1863. Microfilm Collections, Georgia Department of Archives and History, Morrow, Georgia.

Storey, Joseph M. "Joseph M. Storey Collection." Eleanor S. Brokenborough Library, Confederate White House, Museum of the American Civil War, Richmond, Virginia.

Walkup, Samuel. *Writings of a Rebel Colonel: The Civil War Diary and Letters of Samuel Walkup, 48th North Carolina Infantry.* Edited by Kemp Burpeau. Jefferson, NC: McFarland & Company, Publishers, 2021.

Woods, Joseph White. "History of Service of Joseph White Woods, Soldier in the War Between the States." Vol. 21 of *Confederate Reminisces and Letters 1861–1865*, 106–12. Atlanta: Georgia Division, United Daughters of the Confederacy, 2004.

BOOKS AND ARTICLES

Abbot, Henry L. *Siege Artillery in the Campaigns Against Richmond with Notes on the 15-Inch Gun: Professional Papers, Corps of Engineers, Number 14.* Washington: Government Printing Office, 1867.

Acker, Martha Walters, ed. *Deeds of Franklin County, Georgia, 1784–1826.* Easley, SC: Southern Historical Press, 1976.

Adams, Z. Boylston. "In the Wilderness." In *Civil War Papers Read before the Commandery of the State of Massachusetts, Military Order of the Loyal Legion of the United States*, vol. 2, 373–99. Boston: F. H. Gilson Company, 1900.

Alexander, Edward Porter. "The Seven Days Begin: Virginia, June 1862 from *Fighting for the Confederacy.*" In *The Civil War: The Second Year Told by Those Who Lived It.* Edited by Stephen W. Sears, 246–57. New York: Library of America, 2012.

Alexander, Virginia, Colleen Morse Elliott, and Betty White, eds. *Pendleton District and Anderson County, S.C. Wills, Estates, Inventories, Tax Returns and Census Records.* Easley, SC: Southern Historical Press, 1980.

Alexander, W. Keith. "Colonel Clark Moulton Avery and the 33rd North Carolina Infantry, May 5–6, 1864." *Civil War Regiments: A Journal of the American Civil War* 6/4 (1999): 46–76.

Allan, William. *Stonewall Jackson, Robert E. Lee, and the Army of Northern Virginia, 1862.* Two volumes in one: *History of the Campaign of Gen. T. J. (Stonewall) Jackson in the Shenandoah Valley of Virginia from November 4, 1861 to June 17, 1862*, 1880, 1:1–172; *The Army of Northern Virginia in 1862*, 1892, 2:1–537, with a new introduction by Robert K. Krick. New York: Da Capo Press, 1995.

Ammen, Daniel. "Du Pont and the Port Royal Expedition." In *Battles and Leaders of the Civil War*, vol. 1. Edited by Robert Underwood Johnson and C. C. Buel, 671–91. New York: Castle Books, 1956.

Ancestry.com. *Alabama, Compiled Marriages from Selected Counties, 1809–1920*. Provo, UT: Ancestry.com Operations Inc., 1999.

———. *Florida, County Marriage Records, 1823–1982*. Lehi, UT: Ancestry.com. Operations Inc., 2016.

———. *Georgia Marriages, 1699–1944*. Provo, UT: Ancestry.com Operations Inc., 2004.

———. *Georgia Marriage Records from Select Counties, 1828–1978*. Provo, UT: Ancestry.com Operations Inc., 2013.

Archer, John M. *Fury on the Bliss Farm at Gettysburg*. Middletown, DE: Maury Books, 2015.

Aucoin, Brent J. *A Rift in the Clouds: Race and the Southern Federal Judiciary, 1900–1910*. Fayetteville: University of Arkansas Press, 2007.

Austin, Aurelia. *Georgia Boys with Stonewall Jackson: James Thomas Thompson and the Walton Infantry*. Athens: University of Georgia Press, 1967.

Ayers, Edward L. *The Thin Light of Freedom: The Civil War and Emancipation in the Heart of America*. New York: W. W. Norton & Company, 2017.

Baggs, Nicholas, ed. *History of Abington Presbyterian Church, Abington, Pa*. Hatboro, PA: Robinson Pub. Co., 1914.

Bagley, Garland C. *History of Forsyth County, Georgia, 1832–1932*. Vol. 1. Milledgeville, GA: Boyd Publishing Company, 1996.

Baldwin, Thomas and J. Thomas. *A New and Complete Gazetteer of the United States; Giving a Full and Comprehensive Review of the Present Condition, Industry, and Resources of the American Confederacy*. Philadelphia: Lippincott, Grambo & Co., 1854.

Ballard, Michael B. *Vicksburg: The Campaign That Opened the Mississippi*. Chapel Hill: University of North Carolina Press, 2004.

Baptist Trustees, eds. *Psalms and Hymns for Public, Social, and Private Worship; Prepared for the Use of the Baptist Denomination*. London: J. Haddon, 1862.

Barnhart, Terry A. "Apostles of the Lost Cause: The Albert Taylor Bledsoe–Alexander Hamilton Stephens Controversy." *Georgia Historical Quarterly* 96 (Winter 2012): 371–424.

Barr, Gene. *A Civil War Captain and His Lady: Love, Courtship, and Combat from Fort Donelson through the Vicksburg Campaign*. El Dorado Hills, CA: Savas Beatie LLC, 2019.

Barton, William E. *Old Plantation Hymns: A collection of hitherto unpublished melodies of the slave and freedman, with historical and descriptive notes*. Boston: Lamson, Wolffe and Company, 1899.

Bathurst, Bella. *The Lighthouse Stevensons*. New York: HarperCollins Publishers, 1999.

Beard, Dan. "How to Play Corner Ball." http://www.inquiry.net/outdoor/summer/ball/cornerball.htm. Accessed May 8, 2020.

Bearss, Edwin Cole. *The Campaign for Vicksburg: Grant Strikes a Fatal Blow*. Dayton, OH: Morningside House, Inc., 1991.

Beauregard, G. T. "Four Days of Battle at Petersburg." In *Battles and Leaders of the Civil War*, vol. 4. Edited by Robert Underwood Johnson and C. C. Buel, 540–44. New York: Castle Books, 1956.

Bell, Hiram Parks. *Men and Things: Being Reminiscent, Biographical and Historical*. Atlanta: Press of the Foote & Davies Company, 1907.

Bell, James W. *The 43rd Georgia Infantry Regiment, Army of Tennessee, C.S.A.* Hodges, SC: Lindy Publications, 1990.

Benjamin, J. P., Secretary of War. *Regulations for the Army of the Confederate States, 1862*. Richmond: J. W. Randollph, 1863.

Bennett, John C. *The Poultry Book: A Treatise on Breeding and General Management of Domestic Fowls*. Boston: Phillips, Sampson & Company, 1850.

Berg, A. Scott. *Wilson*. New York: G. P. Putnam & Sons, 2014.

Bernard, George S., comp. and ed. *War Talks of Confederate Veterans*. Petersburg, VA: Fenn and Owen, 1892.

Berkow, Robert, Mark H. Beers, Andrew J. Fletcher, eds. *The Merck Manual of Medical Information, Home Edition*. Whitehouse Station, NJ: Merck Research Laboratories, 1997.

Bigelow, John Jr. *The Campaign of Chancellorsville: A Strategic and Tactical Study*. New Haven: Yale University Press, 1910.

Black, Robert C., III. *The Railroads of the Confederacy*. Chapel Hill: University of North Carolina Press, 1998.

Blackmar, Frank W. *Economics*. New York: Macmillan Company, 1912.

Bledsoe, Andrew S. *Citizen-Officers: The Union and Confederate Volunteer Junior Officer Corps in the American Civil War*. Baton Rouge: Louisiana State University Press, 2015.

Blythe, LeGette, and Charles Raven Brockmann. *Hornets' Nest: The History of Charlotte and Mecklenburg County*. Charlotte: McNally of Charlotte, 1961.

Boatner, Mark M. *The Civil War Dictionary*. New York: Random House, Inc., 1991.

Bohannon, Keith S. "Breastworks Are Good Things to Have on Battlefields: Confederate Engineering Operations and Field Fortifications in the Overland Campaign." In *Cold Harbor to the Crater: The End of the Overland Campaign*. Edited by Gary W. Gallagher and Caroline E. Janney, 109–37. Chapel Hill: University of North Carolina Press, 2015.

———. "Dirty, Ragged, and Ill-Provided For: Confederate Logistical Problems in the 1862 Maryland Campaign and Their Solutions." In *The Antietam Campaign*. Edited by Gary W. Gallagher, 101–42. Chapel Hill: University of North Carolina Press, 1999.

Bollet, Alfred Jay. *Civil War Medicine: Challenges and Triumphs*. Tucson: Glen Press, Ltd., 2002.

Bonds, Russell S. *War Like the Thunderbolt: The Battle and Burning of Atlanta*. Yardley, PA: Westholme Publishing, LLC, 2009.

Boston City Council. *A Memorial of the American Patriots Who Fell at the Battle of Bunker Hill, June 17, 1775 with an Account of the Dedication of the Memorial Tablets*. Boston: Boston City Council, 1889.

Boyce, C. W. "A Story of the Shenandoah Valley in 1862: The First Provost-Marshall of Harrisonburg, VA." In *Under Both Flags: A Panorama of the Great Civil War as*

Represented in Story, Anecdote, Adventure, and the Romance of Reality. Edited by C. R. Graham, 198–203. San Francisco: J. Dewing Co., Publishers, 1896.

Boykin, Samuel. *History of the Baptist Denomination of Georgia with Biographical Compendium, etc.* Atlanta: Jas. P. Harrison, 1881.

Boykin, Samuel, ed. *Memorial Volume of the Hon. Howell Cobb of Georgia.* Philadelphia: J. B. Lippincott, 1870.

Bradley, Sculley, Richmond Croom Beatty, and E. Hudson Long, eds. *The American Tradition in Literature.* Vol. 1. Revised. New York: W. W. Norton & Company, 1962.

Bramblett, Annette. *Forsyth County History Stories.* Charleston, SC: Arcadia Publishing, 2002.

Brands, H. W. *The Age of Gold: The California Gold Rush and the New American Dream.* New York: Doubleday, 2002.

Brontë, Charlotte. *Jane Eyre.* New York: Penguin Classics, 2013.

Brower, Paul G. "Farm Cooperatives." *New Georgia Encyclopedia.* https://www.georgiaencyclopedia.org. Accessed January 31, 2019.

Brown, Kent Masterson. *Retreat from Gettysburg: Lee, Logistics and the Pennsylvania Campaign.* Chapel Hill: University of North Carolina Press, 2005.

Buell, Augustus. "Fighting in the Wilderness." In *The Blue and the Gray: The Story of the Civil War as Told by Participants.* Edited by Henry Steele Commager, 976–78. Avenel, NJ: Crescent Books, 1995.

Brock, R. A. *Documents Chiefly Unpublished Relating to the Huguenot Emigration to Virginia and to the Settlement at Manakin Town.* Baltimore: Genealogical Publishing Co., Inc, 1979.

Bunch, Jack A. *Military Justice in the Confederate States Armies.* Shippensburg, PA: White Mane Books, 2000.

———. *Roster of the Courts-Martial in the Confederate States Armies.* Shippensburg, PA: White Mane Books, 2001.

Burrows, J. Lansing, ed. *American Baptist Register for 1852.* Philadelphia: American Baptist Publication Society, 1853.

Burton, Brian K. *Extraordinary Circumstances: The Seven Days Battles.* Bloomingdale: Indiana University Press, 2001.

———. *The Peninsula & Seven Days: A Battlefield Guide.* This Hallowed Ground: Guides to Civil War Battlefields Series. Lincoln: University of Nebraska Press, 2007.

Byrd, Joseph P., IV. *Confederate Sharpshooter Major William E. Simmons: Through the War with the 16th Georgia Infantry and the 3rd Battalion Georgia Sharpshooters.* Macon: Mercer University Press, 2016.

Calcutt, Rebecca Barbour. *Richmond's Wartime Hospitals.* Gretna, LA: Pelican Publishing Company, Inc., 2005.

Caldwell, J. F. J. "Another Struggle with Death, Virginia, May 1864." In *The History of a Brigade of South Carolinians.* In *The Civil War: The Final Year Told by Those Who Lived It.* Edited by Aaron Sheehan-Dean, 90–99. New York: Library of America, 2014.

———. "The Bloody Angle: Virginia, May 1864." In *The History of a Brigade of South Carolinians.* In *The Civil War: The Final Year Told by Those Who Lived It.* Edited by Aaron Sheehan-Dean, 122–29. New York: Library of America, 2014.

Campbell, Thomas. *The Complete Poetical Works of Thomas Campbell, with a Memoir of His Life*. New York: J. C. Derby, 1855.

Candler, Allen D., and Clement A. Evans, eds. *Georgia: Comprising Sketches of Counties, Towns, Events, Institutions, and Persons, Arranged in Cyclopedic Form*. Vol. 2. Atlanta: State Historical Association, 1906.

Carey, Anthony Gene, and George W. Justice. "Secession." In *The Civil War in Georgia: A New Georgia Encyclopedia Companion*. Edited by John C. Inscoe, 35–38. Athens: University of Georgia Press, 2011.

Carter, Samuel Carter III. *The Final Fortress: The Campaign for Vicksburg 1862–1863*. New York: St. Martin's Press, 1980.

Casler, John O. *Four Years in the Stonewall Brigade*. 2nd ed. Columbia: University of South Carolina Press, 1995.

Chambers, Richard J. *Cemeteries and Deaths in Banks County, Georgia*. Toccoa, GA: Commercial Printing Co., Inc., 2000.

Cherokee County Historical Society. *Glimpses of Cherokee County: Celebrating Sesquicentennial, 1831–1981*. Canton, GA: Industrial Printing Service, Inc., 1981.

Chisolm, J. Julian. *A Manual of Military Surgery for the Use of Surgeons in the Confederate States Army; with Explanatory Plates of all Useful Operations*. Columbia, SC: Evans and Cogswell, 1864.

Clark, T. D. "The Montgomery and West Point Railroad Company." *Georgia Historical Quarterly* 17 (December 1933): 293–98.

Clemmer, G.W. "Some Reminiscences of the Firing Line: A War-Time Diary." *Watson's Magazine* (May 1912): 52–61.

Coco, Gregory A. *A Vast Sea of Misery: A History and Guide to the Union and Confederate Field Hospitals at Gettysburg July 1-November 20, 1863*. El Dorado Hills, CA: Savas Beatie LLC, 2017.

Coffman, Richard M., and Kurt D. Graham. *To Honor These Men: A History of the Phillips Georgia Legion Infantry Battalion*. Macon: Mercer University Press, 2007.

Coffman, Richard M. *Going Back the Way They Came: A History of the Phillips Legion Cavalry Battalion*. Macon: Mercer University Press, 2011.

Coleman, Kenneth, ed. *A History of Georgia*. 2nd ed. Athens: University of Georgia Press, 1991.

Coleman, Kenneth. *The American Revolution in Georgia, 1763–1789*. Athens: University of Georgia Press, 1958.

Coles, David J. "Richmond, the Confederate Hospital City," In *Virginia at War, 1862*. Edited by William C. Davis and James I Robertson, Jr., 71–91. Lexington: University Press of Kentucky, 2007.

Collins, Lewis. *History of Kentucky*. Vol. 1. Covington, KY: Collins & Company, 1882.

Comfort, J. W. *The Practice of Medicine on Thomsonian Principles Adapted as Well to the Use of Families as to that of a Practitioner*. 7th ed. Philadelphia: Lindsay & Blankiston, 1867.

Connelly, Thomas Lawrence. *Autumn of Glory: The Army of Tennessee, 1862–1865*. Baton Rouge: Louisiana State University Press, 1971.

Copsey, Jonathan. "Providence Baptist Turns 180 Years Old." *Alpharetta-Roswell Herald*. November 24, 2014. https://www.appenmedia.com/news/providence-baptist-turns-

180-years-old/article_07ce0132-d23c-544e-bf8e-21cee737c888.html. Accessed January 31, 2023.

Corley, Florence Fleming. *Confederate City: Augusta, Georgia 1860–1865*. Columbia: University of South Carolina Press, 1960.

Cotton, Gordon. *Vicksburg: Southern Stories of the Seige*. Vicksburg: Gordon A. Cotton, 1988.

Cox, Jacob D. "McClellan in West Virginia." In *Battles and Leaders of the Civil War*, vol. 1. Edited by Robert Underwood Johnson and C. C. Buel, 126–48. New York: Castle Books, 1956.

———. *Military Reminiscences of the Civil War*. Vol. 2. New York: Charles Scribner's Sons, 1900.

Cozzens, Peter. *The Shipwreck of Their Hopes: The Battles for Chattanooga*. Urbana: University of Illinois Press, 1996.

Crenshaw, Douglas. *Richmond Shall Not Be Given Up: The Seven Days' Battles, June 25–July 1, 1862*. El Dorado Hills, CA: Savas Beatie LLC, 2017.

———. *The Battle of Glendale: Robert E. Lee's Lost Opportunity*. Charleston, SC: History Press, 2017.

Confederate States of America. War Department. *Regulations for the Army of the Confederate States, 1863*. Richmond: J. W. Randolph, 1863.

Cullen, Joseph P. "Richmond National Battlefield Park Virginia: National Park Service Historical Handbook Series No. 33." Washington: National Park Service, 1961.

Cunningham, H. H. *Doctors in Gray: The Confederate Medical Service*. Baton Rouge: Louisiana State University Press, 1993.

Cunningham, S. A., ed. *Confederate Veteran*. 40 vols. Nashville: S. A. Cunningham, 1893–1932.

Daniel, Larry J. *Conquered: Why the Army of Tennessee Failed*. Chapel Hill: University of North Carolina Press, 2019.

Davidson, Grace Gillam, ed. *Records of Elbert County, Georgia*. Historical Collections of the Georgia Chapters, Daughters of the American Revolution, vol. 2. Baltimore: Clearfield Company, 1998.

Davis, Burke. *Sherman's March: The First Full-Length Narrative of General William T. Sherman's Devastating March through Georgia and the Carolinas*. New York: Vintage Books, 1988.

Davis, Stephen. "Atlanta Campaign." In *The Civil War in Georgia: A New Georgia Encyclopedia Companion*. Edited by John C. Inscoe, 73–83. Athens: University of Georgia Press, 2011.

Davis, William C. *Rebels and Yankees: The Fighting Men of the Civil War*. New York: Smithmark Publishers, 1991.

———. "Military Affairs in the West, 1861–1862." In *Military Strategy in the American Civil War*. Edited by James I Robertson Jr., 63–77. Richmond: Virginia Sesquicentennial of the American Civil War Commission, 2012.

———. *Look Away!: A History of the Confederate States of America*. New York: Free Press, 2002.

De Vere, M. Schele. *Americanisms: The English of the New World*. New York: Charles Scribner & Company, 1872.

Denny, Robert E. *Civil War Medicine: Care & Comfort of the Wounded*. New York: Sterling Publishing Co., Inc., 1994.
Derry, Joseph T. *Confederate Military History: Georgia. A Library of Confederate States History*, vol. 6. 1899. Reprint, Secaucus: Blue and Gray Press, 1970.
Detzer, David. *Donnybrook: The Battle of Bull Run, 1861*. Orlando, FL: Harcourt, Inc., 2004.
Dewberry, Ray. *History of the 14th Georgia Infantry Regiment*. Westminster, MD: Heritage Books, 2008.
Dickert, D. Augustus. *History of Kershaw's Brigade with Complete Roll of Companies, Biographical Sketches, Incidents, Anecdotes, Etc.* 1899. Dayton, OH: Press of Morningside Bookshop, 1973.
Dickson, Paul. *The Dickson Baseball Dictionary*. 3rd ed. New York: W. W. Norton & Company, 2009.
Dilman, Caroline Matheny. "Milton County." *New Georgia Encyclopedia*, 15 December 2003. Accessed October 23, 2020.
Dorman, John Frederick. "Henry County, Virginia, Will Book I, 1779–1799." *Virginia Genealogist* 1 (January–March 1957): 29–38.
Dorsey, James E. *The History of Hall County, Georgia*. Vol. 1, 1818–1900. Gainesville, GA: Magnolia Press, 1991.
Dowdey, Clifford. *The Seven Days: The Emergence of Robert E. Lee and the Dawn of a Legend*. New York: Skyhorse Publishing, 1992.
———. *Lee's Last Campaign: The Story of Lee and His Men against Grant—1864*. New York: Barnes & Noble Books, 1994.
Dowdey, Clifford, and Manarin, Louis H., eds. *The Wartime Papers of R. E. Lee*. New York: Bramhall House, 1961.
Dozier, Graham T., ed. *A Gunner in Lee's Army: The Civil War Letters of Thomas Henry Carter*. Chapel Hill: University of North Carolina Press, 2014.
Drake, Paul. *What Did They Mean by That?: A Dictionary of Historical and Genealogical Terms Old and New*. Westminster, MD: Heritage Books, 2008.
Dunglison, Richard J. *A Dictionary of Medical Science; Containing a Concise Explanation of the Various Subjects and Terms of Anatomy, Physiology, Pathology, Hygiene, Therapeutics, Medical Chemistry, Pharmacology, Pharmacy, Surgery, Obstetrics, Medical Jurisprudence, and Dentistry; Notices of Climate, and of Mineral Waters; Formulae for Officinal, Empirical, and Dietetic Preparations; with The Accentuation and Etymology of the Terms and The French and Other Synonyms, a new edition*. Philadelphia: Henry C. Lea, 1874.
Egle, William Henry. *Proprietary Tax Lists of the County of Chester for the Years 1765, 1766, 1767, 1768, 1769, 1771*. Harrisburg: Wm. Stanley Ray, State Printer of Pennsylvania, 1897.
Elliot, Sam Davis. "This Grand and Imposing Array of Brave Men: The Capture of Rossville Gap and the Defeat of the Confederate Army." In *The Chattanooga Campaign*. Edited by Steven E. Woodworth and Charles D. Grear, 6–131. Carbondale: Southern Illinois University Press, 2012.
Ellis, Samuel. *The History of the Order of the Sons of Temperance, from Its Organization on the 20th September, 1842, to the Commencement of the Year 1848*. Boston: Stacy, Richardson & Co, 1848.

Elrod, Frary. *Historical Notes on Jackson County, Georgia.* Privately printed, 1967.
Encyclopaedia Britannica. *The Annals of America.* 19 vols. London: Encyclopaedia Britannica, Inc., 1968.
Encyclopedia Britannica. 30 vols. Chicago and London: Encyclopedia Britannica, Inc., 1977. This edition has two sets; volumes in one set are numbered with Roman numerals.
Esposito, Vincent J. *The West Point Atlas of American Wars, Volume 1, 1689–1900.* New York: Frederick A. Praeger, Publishers, 1959.
Evans, David. *Sherman's Horsemen: Union Cavalry Operations in the Atlanta Campaign.* Bloomington: Indiana University Press, 1999.
Everhart, William C. *Vicksburg National Military Park, Mississippi.* Washington, D.C.: National Park Service, 1954.
F. A. Battey & Company. *Biographical Souvenir of the States of Georgia and Florida, Containing Biographical Sketches of the Representative Public, and many Early Settled Families in These States.* Chicago: F. A. Battey & Company, 1889.
Fahey, David M. "Temperance Movement." *New Georgia Encyclopedia.* March 10, 2003. http://www.georgiaencyclopedia.org/articles/history-archaeology/temperance-movement. Accessed October 2, 2020.
Farwell, Byron. *Stonewall: A Biography of General Thomas J. Jackson.* New York: W. W. Norton & Company, 1992.
Fehrenbacher, Don E. ed. *Abraham Lincoln: Speeches and Writings, 1859–1865.* New York: Library of America, 1989.
Felter, Harvey Wickes. *History of the Eclectic Medical Institute, Cincinnati, Ohio, 1845–1902, Including the Worthington Medical College (1830–1842), the Reformed Medical School of Cincinnati (1842–1845), and the Eclectic College of Medicine (1856–1859), with Biographical Sketches of Members of the Various Faculties and Lists of Graduates Arranged in Alphabetically and by Classes.* Cincinnati: Felter, Scudder, and Lloyd, Committee of the Alumnal Association of the Eclectic Medical Institute, 1902.
Fischer, David Hackett, and James C. Kelly. *Away, I'm Bound Away: Virginia and the Western Movement.* Richmond: Virginia Historical Society, 1993.
Fletcher, Jacqui. "Managing Wound Exudate." *Nursing Times* 5 (February 4, 2003): 51–55.
Flinchum, Gerald W. *Crossroads, Creeks & Clashes: Civil War Skirmishes in Cherokee and North Cobb Counties: 1864.* Woodstock, GA: self-published, 2014.
Flippin, Percy Scott. *Herschel V. Johnson of Georgia, State Rights Unionist.* Richmond: Press of Deitz Printing Co., 1931.
Folsom, James M. *Heroes and Martyrs of Georgia: Georgia's Record in the Revolution of 1861.* Vol. 1. Macon, GA: Burke, Boykin & Company, 1864.
Foote, Shelby. *The Civil War: A Narrative.* 4 vols. New York: Random House, 1958–1974.
Fortson, Ben W. Jr. *State of Georgia Official and Statistical Register: 1977–1978.* Atlanta: Department of Archives and History, 1978.
Fowler, H. W., and F. G. Fowler. *The Concise Oxford Dictionary of Current English.* 4th ed., revised. Oxford: Clarendon Press, 1959.

Fowler, John D., and David B. Parker. *Breaking the Heartland: The Civil War in Georgia.* Macon: Mercer University Press, 2011.

Fowler, Nolan. "Johnny Reb's Impressions of Kentucky in the Fall of 1862." *Register of the Kentucky Historical Society* 48/164 (July 1950): 205–16.

Franklin County Historical Society. *History of Franklin County, Georgia.* Roswell, GA: WH Wolfe Associates, 1986.

Freehling, William W., and Craig M. Simpson, eds. *Secession Debated: Georgia's Showdown in 1860.* New York: Oxford University Press, 1992.

Freeman, Douglas Southall. *Lee's Lieutenants: A Study in Command.* 3 vols. New York: Charles Scribner's Sons, 1942–1944.

Freemon, Frank R. *Gangrene and Glory: Medical Care during the American Civil War.* Urbana: University of Illinois Press, 2001.

Furguson, Ernest B. *Chancellorsville 1863: The Souls of the Brave.* New York: Alfred A. Knopf, 1882.

Galehouse, Maggie. "Texas Fighting for Santa Anna's Leg," *Houston Chronicle*, May 16, 2014. https://www.houstonchronicle.com/culture/main/article/Texas-fighting-for-Santa-Anna-s-leg-5483826.php. Accessed February 4, 2023.

Gallagher, Gary, Stephen Engle, Robert Krick, and Joseph Glatthaar. *Civil War: From Sumter to Appomattox.* Oxford: Osprey Publishing, 2003.

Gallagher, Gary W. "Confederate Corps Leadership on the First Day at Gettysburg: A. P. Hill and Richard S. Ewell in a Difficult Debut." In *The First Day of Gettysburg: Essays on Confederate and Union Leadership.* Edited by Gary W. Gallagher, 30–56. Kent: Kent State University Press, 1992.

———. *Enduring Civil War: Reflections on the Great American Crisis.* Baton Rouge: Louisiana State University Press, 2020.

———, ed. *Fighting for the Confederacy: The Personal Recollections of General Edward Porter Alexander.* Chapel Hill: University of North Carolina Press, 1989.

Garrison, Webb. *The Encyclopedia of Civil War Usage: An Illustrated Compendium of the Everyday Language of Soldiers and Civilians.* Nashville: Cumberland House Publishing, Inc., 2001.

Gary, Angela, Jana Adams, and staff of *Jackson Herald*. *Our Time and Place: A History of Jackson County Georgia.* Jefferson, GA: MainStreet Newspapers, Inc., 2000.

Georgia House of Representatives. *Journal of the House of Representatives of the State of Georgia at the Annual Session of the General Assembly, Commenced at Milledgeville, November 2d, 1859.* Milledgeville: Boughton, Nisbet & Barnes, State Printers, 1859.

———. *Journal of the House of Representatives of the State of Georgia at the Annual Session of the General Assembly, Commenced at Milledgeville, November 7th, 1860.* Milledgeville: Boughton, Nisbet & Barnes, State Printers, 1860.

Gilchrist, Captain R. C. *The Duties of a Judge Advocate in a Trial before a General Court Martial Compiled from Various Works on Military Law.* Columbia, SC: Evans and Cogswell, 1864.

Gindlesperger, James. *Bullets & Bandages: The Aid Stations and Field Hospitals at Gettysburg.* Durham, NC: Blair, an imprint of Carolina Wren Press, 2021.

Glatthaar, Joseph T. "Union and Confederate Final Strategy, 1864–1865." In *Military Strategy in the American Civil War*. Edited by James I. Robertson, Jr., 48–61, Richmond: Virginia Sesquicentennial of the American Civil War Commission, 2012.

———. *General Lee's Army: From Victory to Collapse*. New York: Simon & Shuster, 2008.

Glaze, Robert L. "The Georgia Campaign." In *The Cambridge History of the American Civil War*, vol. 1. Edited by Aaron Sheehan-Dean, 315–36. Cambridge: Cambridge University Press, 2019.

Goldsmith, W. L. "Cavalry versus Infantry." In *Under Both Flags: A Panorama of the Great Civil War As represented in Story, Anecdote, Adventure, and the Romance of Reality*. Edited by C. R. Graham, 219. San Francisco: J. Dewing Co., Publishers, 1896.

———. "'Stonewall' Jackson's Last Grand Blow." In *Under Both Flags: A Panorama of the Great Civil War as Represented in Story, Anecdote, Adventure, and the Romance of Reality*. Edited by C. R. Graham, 519–20. San Francisco: J. Dewing Co., Publishers, 1896.

Goodson, Gary Ray Sr. *The Georgia Confederate 7,000 Army of Tennessee*. 3 vols. Shawnee, CO: Goodson Enterprises, Inc., 1995–2000.

Goss, Warren. "Private Goss Describes the Battle of the Wilderness." In *The Blue and The Gray: The Story of the Civil War as Told by Its Participants*. Edited by Henry Steele Commager, 978–82. Avenel, NJ: Crescent Books, 1995.

Gottfried, Bradley M. *Brigades of Gettysburg: The Union and Confederate Brigades at the Battle of Gettysburg*. New York: Skyhorse Publishing, 2012.

———. *The Maps of Fredericksburg: An Atlas of the Fredericksburg Campaign, Including All Cavalry Operations, September 18, 1862–January 22, 1863*. El Dorado Hills, CA: Savas Beatie LLC, 2018.

———. *The Maps of Gettysburg: An Atlas of the Gettysburg Campaign, June 3–July 13, 1863*. New York: Savas Beatie, 2007.

———. *The Maps of the Wilderness: An Atlas of the Wilderness Campaign, Including all Cavalry Operations, May 2–6, 1864*. El Dorado Hills, CA: Savas Beatie LLC, 2016.

Gould, David, and James B. Kennedy, eds. *Memoirs of a Dutch Mudsill: The "War Memories" of John Henry Otto, Captain, Company D, 21st Regiment, Wisconsin Volunteer Infantry*. Kent: Kent State University Press, 2004.

Grant, U. S. *Ulysses S. Grant: Memoirs and Selected Letters*. New York: Library of America, 1990.

Greeman, Betty Dix. "The Democratic Convention of 1860: Prelude to Secession." *Maryland Historical Magazine* 67 (Fall 1972): 225–53.

Greene, A. Wilson. *From the Crossing of the James to the Crater*. Vol. 1 of *A Campaign of Giants: The Battle for Petersburg*. Chapel Hill: University of North Carolina Press, 2018.

Gregory, Edward S. "Vicksburg during the Siege." In *Annals of the War Written by Leading Participants North and South*. Edited by Alexander K. McClure, 111–33. 1879. Reprint, Edison, NJ: Blue and Gray Press, 1996.

Greve, Charles Theodore. *Centennial History of Cincinnati and Representative Citizens*. Vol. 1. Chicago: Biographical Publishing Company, 1904.

Griffith, Paddy. *Battle Tactics of the Civil War*. New Haven: Yale University Press, 2001.

Grimsley, Major Daniel A. *Battles in Culpeper County, Virginia, 1861–1865, and Other Articles*. Culpeper, VA: Raleigh Travers Green, 1900.

Guelzo, Allen C. *Gettysburg: The Last Invasion.* New York: Alfred A. Knopf, 2013.
Guernsey, Alfred H., and Henry M. Alden. *Harper's Pictorial History of the Civil War.* New York: Fairfax Press, 1866.
Haller, John S., Jr. *Alternative Medicine: The Eclectic Medical College of Cincinnati, 1845–1942.* Kent: Kent State University Press, 1999.
Hallock, Judith Lee. *General James Longstreet in the West: A Monumental Failure.* Abilene, TX: McWhiney Foundation Press, 1998.
Hammond, Paul F. "Campaign of General E. Kirby Smith in Kentucky, in 1862." *Southern Historical Society Papers* 9 (January–December 1881): 224–33, 246–54, 289–97; 10 (January–December 1882): 70–76.
Harding, Jeffrey J. "Death by Dew Point: Extreme Heat Conditions Affected Battle Strategy and Killed Soldiers." *Civil War Times* 61/4 (Autumn 2022): 52–59.
Harris, Bonnie P. (Patsy). *The Confederate Hospitals of Madison, Georgia: Their Records and Histories, 1861–1865.* Buckhead, GA: Bonnie P. (Patsy) Harris, 2014.
Harris, Tina, ed. *Portraits of a Southern Place: A Pictorial History of Early Jackson County, Georgia.* Commerce: Jackson County Historical Society, 2006.
Hattaway, Herman, and Archer Jones. *How the North Won: A Military History of the Civil War.* Urbana: University of Illinois Press, 1991.
Hays, Mrs. J. E., ed. *Georgia Military Record Book, 1779–1839.* Atlanta: General John Floyd Chapter United States Daughters of 1812, 1941.
———. *Georgia Military Affairs, 1793–1800.* Vol. 2, part 1. Atlanta: General John Floyd Chapter United States Daughters of 1812, 1940.
———. *Georgia Military Affairs, 1793–1800.* Vol. 2, part 2. Atlanta: General John Floyd Chapter United Daughters of 1812, 1940.
Hazard, M. C., ed. *The National Sunday School Teacher.* Chicago: Adams, Blackmer, & Lyon Publishing Co., 1879.
Hebert, Keith S. *Cornerstone of the Confederacy: Alexander Stephens and the Speech that Defined the Lost Cause.* Knoxville: University of Tennessee Press, 2021.
Hebron Historical Society. *Hebron Presbyterian Church: God's Pilgrim People, 1796–1996.* Atlanta: Darby Printing Company, 1995.
Heineman, Ronald L., John G. Kolp, Anthony S. Parent, Jr., and William G. Shade. *Old Dominion, New Commonwealth: A History of Virginia, 1607–2007.* Charlottesville: University of Virginia Press, 2007.
Henderson, Lillian. *Roster of the Confederate Soldiers of Georgia, 1861–1865.* 6 vols. Hapeville, GA: Longina & Porter, 1959.
Hendrickson, Robert. *The Facts on File Dictionary of American Regionalisms: Local Expressions from Coast to Coast.* New York: Facts on File, Inc., 2000.
Hennessy, John. "The Second Bull Run Campaign." In *The Cambridge History of the American Civil War*, vol. 1. Edited by Aaron Sheehan-Dean, 120–40. Cambridge: Cambridge University Press, 2019.
Hepburn, Lawrence R. *The Georgia History Book.* Athens: Institute of Government, University of Georgia, 1982.
Hess, Earl J. *The Union Soldier in Battle: Enduring the Ordeal of Combat.* Lawrence: University of Kansas Press, 1997.

———. *Kennesaw Mountain: Sherman, Johnston, and the Atlanta Campaign.* Chapel Hill: University of North Carolina Press, 2013.

———. *Braxton Bragg: The Most Hated Man in the Confederacy.* Chapel Hill: University of North Carolina Press, 2016.

Hessler, Iola Osmond. *Cincinnati, Then and Now.* Cincinnati: League of Women Voters, 1949.

Heth, Henry. *The Memoirs of Henry Heth.* Edited by James L. Morrison Jr. Westport, CT: Greenwood Press, 1974.

Hewett, Janet B. *Supplement to the Official Records of the Union and Confederate Armies.* 100 vols. Wilmington, NC: Broadfoot Publishing Company, 1996.

Hoehling, A. A. *Vicksburg: 47 Days of Siege.* Mechanicsville, PA: Stackpole Books, 1996.

Hollander, John, ed. *American Poetry: The Nineteenth Century.* Vol. 1, *Philip Freneau to Walt Whitman.* New York: Viking Press, 1993.

Holley, Thomas Earl. *Company K, Ramsey Volunteers, The Sixteenth Georgia Infantry Regiment, Army of Northern Virginia, Confederate States of America: The Officers, The Battles and a Genealogy of its Soldiers.* Fernandina Beach, FL: Wolfe Publishing, 1995.

Hood, John Bell. *Advance and Retreat: Personal Experiences in the United States and Confederate States Armies.* New Orleans: Hood Orphan Memorial Publication Fund, 1880.

Horn, Stanley F. *The Army of Tennessee.* 1941. Reprint, Wilmington, NC: Broadfoot Publishing Company, 1987.

Howe, Daniel Walker. *What Hath God Wrought: The Transformation of America, 1815–1848.* Oxford: Oxford University Press, Inc., 2007.

Howell, H. Grady, Jr. *Hill of Death: The Battle of Champion Hill.* Madison, MS: Chickasaw Bayou Press, 1993.

Humphrey, John T. *Pennsylvania Births: Montgomery County, 1682–1800.* Washington: Humphrey Publications, 1993.

Hurst, Samuel H. *Journal-History of the Seventy-Third Ohio Volunteer Infantry.* Chillicothe, OH: S. H. Hurst, 1866.

Imboden, John D. "The Confederate Retreat from Gettysburg." In *Battles and Leaders of the Civil War*, vol. 3. Edited by Robert Underwood Johnson and C. C. Buel, 420–33. New York: Castle Books, 1956.

Inscoe, John C. *The Civil War in Georgia.* Athens: University of Georgia Press, 2011.

Jackson, Ronald Vern, and Gary Ronald Teeples, eds. *South Carolina 1830 Census Index.* Bountiful, UT: Accelerated Indexing Systems, Inc., 1976.

———. *South Carolina 1840 Census Index.* Bountiful, UT: Accelerated Indexing Systems, Inc., 1977.

Jennings, Samuel H. "A plain elementary Explanation of the Nature and Cure of Diseases, predicated upon Facts and Experience; presenting View of that train of thinking which led to the Invention of the Patent Portable Warm and Hot Bath." In *The Medical Repository of Original Essays and Intelligence Relative to Physic, Surgery, Chemistry, and Natural History.* Edited by Samuel L. Mitchill, Felix Pascalis, and Samuel Akerly, 368–74. New York: T. and J. Swords, 1815.

Johnson, Robert Underwood, and C. C. Buel, eds. *Battles and Leaders of the Civil War.* 4 vols. New York: Castle Books, 1956.

Johnston, John Warfield. "Joseph W. Anderson, B. L." In *The University Memorial Biographical Sketches: Alumni of the University of Virginia Who Fell in the Confederate War*, 383–99. Baltimore: Turnbull Brothers, 1871.

Johnston, Rebecca. *Cherokee County, Georgia: A History*. Canton, GA: Yawn's Publishing, 2011.

Johnston, Richard Malcolm, and William Hand Browne. *Life of Alexander H. Stephens*. Philadelphia: J. B. Lippincott & Co., 1878.

Jones, Patricia K. *Annotated Abstracts of Extant Gainesville, Georgia Newspapers 1861–1910: Unfortunate Events and Items of Genealogical Interest*. Evansville, IN: Evansville Bindery, Inc., 2012.

Jones, Ron. *War Comes to Broad River: A Novel of the Civil War Based on the Diary of Isaac V. Moore*. Mustang, OK: Tate Publishing Co., 2005.

Keyes, Ralph. *Euphemania: Our Love Affair with Euphemisms*. New York: Little, Brown & Company, 2020.

Kelly, James M. *Reports of Cases in Law and Equity Argued and Determined in the Supreme Court of the State of Georgia in the year 1846*, vol. 1. New York: Edward O. Jenkins, 1847.

Kilpatrick, William H. "The Beginnings of the Public School System in Georgia." *The Georgia Historical Quarterly* 5 (September 1921): 3–19.

Kirkland, Thomas J. and Robert M. Kennedy. *Historic Camden: Part One, Colonial and Revolutionary*. 1905. Reprint, Camden, SC: Kershaw County Historical Society, 1963.

Kolakowski, Christopher L. *The Civil War at Perryville: Battling for the Bluegrass*. Charleston, SC: History Press, 2009.

Korn, Jerry. *War on the Mississippi: Grant's Vicksburg Campaign*. Alexandria, VA: Time-Life Books, Inc., 1985.

Krakow, Kenneth K. *Georgia Place Names*. 3rd ed. Macon: Winship Press, 1999.

Kratovil, Judy Swaim, ed. *Georgia Governors' Journals, 1789–1798, County, State and Militia Officers*. Fernandina Beach, FL: Wolfe Publishing, 2000.

Krick, Robert E. L. *Staff Officers in Gray: A Biographical Register of the Staff Officers in the Army of Northern Virginia*. Chapel Hill: University of North Carolina Press, 2003.

Krick, Robert K. *Lee's Colonels: A Biographical Register of the Field Officers of the Army of Northern Virginia*. 4th ed. Dayton, OH: Morningside House, Inc., 1992.

———. *Stonewall Jackson at Cedar Mountain*. Chapel Hill: University of North Carolina Press, 1990.

———. "The Smoothbore Volley that Doomed the Confederacy." In *Chancellorsville: The Battle and Its Aftermath*. Edited by Gary W. Gallagher, 107–42. Chapel Hill: University of North Carolina Press, 1996.

———. *Civil War Weather in Virginia*. Tuscaloosa: University of Alabama Press, 2007.

———. "Like a Duck on a June Bug: James Longstreet's Flank Attack, May 6, 1864." In *The Wilderness Campaign*. Edited by Gary W. Gallagher, 236–64. Chapel Hill: University of North Carolina Press, 1997.

———. "The Men Who Carried This Position Were Soldiers Indeed: The Decisive Charge of Whiting's Division at Gaines Mill." In *The Richmond Campaign of 1862:*

The Peninsula & the Seven Days. Edited by Gary W. Gallagher, 181–216. Chapel Hill: University of North Carolina Press, 2000.

Lambert, D. Warren. *When the Ripe Pears Fell: The Battle of Richmond, Kentucky.* Richmond, KY: Madison County Historical Society, Inc., 1996.

Lane, Mills, ed. *"Dear Mother: Don't Grieve about me. If I get killed, I'll only be dead.": Letters from Georgia Soldiers in the Civil War.* Savannah: A Beehive Press, 1990.

———. *Georgia: History Written by Those Who Lived It.* Savannah: Beehive Press, 1995.

Lardas, Mark. *Chattanooga 1863: Grant and Bragg in Central Tennessee.* New York: Osprey Publishing Ltd, 2016.

Lattner, W. Travis, Jr. *The Lattner Story: Farmers, Doctors, Soldiers: A Family Story.* Self-published, 2002.

Law, Evander M. "From the Wilderness to Cold Harbor." In *Battles and Leaders of the Civil War*, vol. 4. Edited by Robert Underwood Johnson and C. C. Buel, 118–44. New York: Castle Books, 1956.

LeVan, Russell G. *The Great War of Destruction.* Raleigh, NC: Pentland Press, Inc., 1999.

Leonard, Pat. "The Bullet That Changed History." In *The New York Times Disunion: 106 Articles from the New York Times Opinionator.* Edited by Ted Widmer, 369–73. New York: Black Dog and Leventhal, Publishers, Inc., 2013.

Lepore, Jill. *Book of Ages: The Life and Opinions of Jane Franklin.* New York: Vintage Books, 2014.

Lester, W. W., and William J. Bromwell, eds. *A Digest of the Military and Naval Laws of the Confederate States, from the Commencement of the Provisional Congress to the End of the First Congress under the Permanent Constitution.* Columbia, SC: Evans and Cogswell, 1864.

Linn, John Blair, and William Henry Egle, eds. *Pennsylvania Marriages Prior to 1790.* 1890. Reprint with supplemental material, Baltimore: Genealogical Publishing Company, 1994, 2001.

Longstreet, James. "The Battle of Fredericksburg." In *Battles and Leaders of the Civil War*, vol. 3. Edited by Robert Underwood Johnson and C. C. Buel, 70–94. New York: Castle Books, 1956.

———. *From Manassas to Appomattox: Memoirs of the Civil War in America.* 1896. Reprint, Secaucus, NJ: Blue and Gray Press, n.d.

Loughborough, Mary Ann Webster. *My Cave Life in Vicksburg.* Bedford, MA: Applewood Books. Facsimile of the original book published in New York by D. Appleton & Co., 1864.

Loyd, Doyal T. "Morgan H. Looney and his Gilmer School 1861–1871." *East Texas Historical Journal* 15 (March 1977): 20–23.

Lowry, Thomas P., and Lewis Laska. *Confederate Death Sentences: A Reference Guide.* Charleston, SC: Booksurge, 2008.

Lykes, Richard Wayne. *Campaign for Petersburg.* Washington: National Park Service, 1970.

MacIntyre, W. Irwin. *History of Thomas County, Georgia from the Time of Desoto to the Civil War.* Thomasville, GA: W. Irwin MacIntyre, 1923.

McDonough, James Lee. *Chattanooga: A Death Grip on the Confederacy.* Knoxville: University of Tennessee Press, 1984.

McElreath, Walter. *A Treatise on the Constitution of Georgia*. Atlanta: Harrison Company, 1912.

McLaws, Lafayette. "The Confederate Left at Fredericksburg." In *Battles and Leaders of the Civil War*, vol. 3. Edited by Robert Underwood Johnson and C. C. Buel, 86–94. New York: Castle Books, 1956.

McPherson, James M. *Battle Cry of Freedom: The Civil War Era*. New York: Oxford University Press, 1988.

———. *Embattled Rebel: Jefferson Davis and the Confederate Civil War*. New York: Penguin Books, 2015.

———, ed. *The Atlas of the Civil War*. New York: Macmillan, 1994.

Marks, Stephen S. *Fairchild's Dictionary of Textiles*. New York: Fairchild Publications, Inc., 1959.

Marlin, Lloyd G. *The History of Cherokee County*, 2nd printing. Fernandina Beach, FL: Wolfe Publishing, 2000.

Martin, Edward Winslow. *History of the Grange Movement*. Philadelphia: National Publishing Company, 1874.

Martin, Jacob. *Wills of Chester County, Pennsylvania, 1766–1778*. Westminster, MD: Family Line Publications, 1993.

Matter, William D. *If It Takes All Summer: The Battle of Spotsylvania*. Chapel Hill: University of North Carolina Press, 1988.

Matteson, John. *A Worse Place than Hell: How the Civil War Battle of Fredericksburg Changed a Nation*. New York: W. W. Norton & Company, 2021.

Matthews, James M. *Public Laws of the Confederate States of America, Passed at the Second Session of the First Congress; 1862*. Richmond: R. M. Smith, Printer to Congress, 1862.

McClure, Alexander, ed. *Annals of the War Written by Leading Participants North and South*. 1879. Reprint, Edison, NJ: Blue and Gray Press, 1996.

Meier, Kathryn Shively. *Nature's Civil War: Common Soldiers and the Environment in 1862 Virginia*. Chapel Hill: University of North Carolina Press, 2013.

Mercer University. *Triennial Register and Annual Catalogue of Mercer University, Macon, Georgia, 1891–1892*. Macon: J. W. Burke & Co., Printers, 1892.

Meyers, Robert Manson, ed. *The Children of Pride: A True Story of Georgia and the Civil War*. New Haven: Yale University Press, 1972.

Mieder, Wolfgang, Stewart A. Kingsbury, Kelsie B. Harder. *A Dictionary of American Proverbs*. New York: Oxford University Press, 1992.

Miller, Donald L. *Vicksburg: Grant's Campaign That Broke the Confederacy*. New York: Simon & Schuster, 2019.

Miller, William J., and Brian C. Pohanka. *An Illustrated History of the Civil War: Images of an American Tragedy*. Alexandria, VA: Time-Life Books, 2000.

Mink, Eric. J. "The Death, Retrieval, and Remembrance of Brigadier General James S. Wadsworth in the Battle of the Wilderness." *Civil War Regiments: A Journal of the American Civil War* 6/4 (1999): 77–119.

Mish, Frederick C., ed. *Merriam-Webster's Collegiate Dictionary*. 11th ed. Springfield, MA: Merriam-Webster, Inc., 2009.

Mitchell, Ralph Molyneux, II. "Improvisation, Adaptation and Innovation: The Handling of Wounded in the Civil War." Master's thesis. Rice University, Houston, TX, 1975.
Mize, Jessie Julia. *The History of Banks County, Georgia, 1858–1976.* Homer, GA: Banks County Chamber of Commerce, 1977.
Montgomery, Horace. *Howell Cobb's Confederate Career.* Tuscaloosa: Confederate Publishing Company, Inc., 1959. Reprint, Wilmington, NC: Broadfoot Publishing Company, 2000.
Montgomery, James. *A Practical Detail of the Cotton Manufacture of the United States of America; and the State of the Cotton Manufacture of That Country Contrasted and Compared with That of Great Britain.* Glasgow: John Niven, 1840.
Morgan, George W. "The Assault on Chickasaw Bluffs." In *Battles and Leaders of the Civil War*, vol. 2. Edited by Robert Underwood Johnson and C. C. Buel, 462–70. New York: Castle Books, 1956.
Morgan, Linda. "Fort Gaines." *New Georgia Encyclopedia.* 15 August 2013. Accessed 15 October 2015.
Morgan, Robert, *Boone: A Biography.* Chapel Hill: Algonquin Books, 2008.
Nevins, Allan. *Ordeal of the Union.* 8 vols. New York: Charles Scribner's Sons, 1947–1971.
Nichols, G. W. *A Soldier's Story of His Regiment (61st Georgia) and Incidentally of the Lawton-Gordon-Evans Brigade of the Army Northern Virginia.* Jessup, GA: privately printed, 1898. Reprint, Kennesaw, GA: Continental Book Company, 1961.
Nicholson, Helen. *A Brief History of the Knights Templar.* Philadelphia: Running Press Book Publishers, 2010.
Nicolay, John G., and John Hay. *Abraham Lincoln: A History.* Vol. 2. New York: The Century Company, 1914.
Nunez, Andy. *Wilderness and Spotsylvania 1864: Grant versus Lee in the East.* New York: Osprey Publishing Ltd., 2014.
O'Reilly, Francis Augustin. *The Fredericksburg Campaign: Winter War on the Rappahannock.* Baton Rouge: Louisiana State University Press, 2006.
———. "Chancellorsville: The Soldiers' Battle, Victory amid the Flames." *Blue & Gray* 29/5 (2013): 6–27.
Oeffinger, John C., ed. *A Soldier's General: The Civil War Letters of Major General Lafayette McLaws.* Chapel Hill: University of North Carolina Press, 2002.
Orrison, Robert, and Dan Welch. *The Last Road North: A Guide to the Gettysburg Campaign, 1863.* El Dorado Hills, CA: Savas Beatie LLC, 2016.
Osborn, Kyle. "Sectional Crisis." In *The Civil War in Georgia: A New Georgia Encyclopedia Companion.* Edited by John C. Inscoe, 29–34. Athens: University of Georgia Press, 2011.
"Our Book Table." *The Southern Cultivator: A Monthly Journal Dedicated to the Interests of Southern Agriculture* 15 (January 1857): 25.
Paine, William. *An Epitome of the American Eclectic Practice of Medicine, Surgery, Obstetrics, Diseases of Women and Children, Materia Medica and Pharmacy, with Glossary, Designed for Physicians, the Student of Medicine, and as a Domestic Practice for Families.* Philadelphia: John Gladding, 1859.

Palencia, Elaine Fowler. *On Rising Ground: The Life and Civil War Letters of Joyn M. Douthit, 52nd Georgia Volunteer Infantry Regiment*. Macon: Mercer University Press, 2021.

Parks, Joseph Howard. *General Edmund Kirby Smith, C.S.A*. Baton Rouge: Louisiana State University Press, 1992.

Patchan, Scott C. *The Last Battle of Winchester: Phil Sheridan, Jubal Early, and the Shenandoah Valley Campaign, August 7–September 19, 1864*. El Dorado Hills, CA: Savas Beatie LLC, 2013.

Perry, William F. "Reminiscences of the Campaign of 1864 Virginia." *Southern Historical Society Papers* 7/2 (January–December 1879): 49–63.

Pfanz, Harry W. *Gettysburg: The Second Day*. Chapel Hill: University of North Carolina Press, 1987.

———. *Gettysburg—Culp's Hill & Cemetery Hill*. Chapel Hill: University of North Carolina Press, 1993.

Piston, William Garrett. *Carter's Raid: An Episode of the Civil War in Tennessee*. Johnson City, TN: Overmountain Press, 1989.

Pope, Alexander. *The Temple of Fame: A Vision*. London, Bernard Lintott, 1715. Early English Books Online Text Creation Partnership. http://name.umdl.umich.edu/004809333.0001.000. Accessed September 14, 2021.

Porter, Fitz John. "The Battle of Malvern Hill." In *Battles and Leaders of the Civil War*, vol. 2. Edited by Robert Underwood Johnson and C. C. Buel, 671–91. New York: Castle Books, 1956.

Porter, Phyllis. *The Heritage of Cherokee County, Georgia—1831–1998*. Waynesville, NC: Walsworth Publishing Co., 1998.

Portraits and Sketches of the Lives of All the Candidates for the Presidency and Vice-Presidency, for 1860. Compromising Eight Portraits Engraved on Steel, Facts in the Life of Each, the Four Platforms, the Cincinnati Platform. J. C. Buttre, engraver. New York: J. C. Buttre, 1860.

Poss, Faye Stone. *Jackson County, Georgia: Deed Abstracts, Books A-D, 1796–1808*. Fernandina Beach, FL: Wolfe Publishing, 1998.

Potter, David M., and Don E. Fehrenbacher. *The Impending Crisis: America before the Civil War, 1848–1861*. New York: Harper Perennial, 2011.

Powell, David A. *All Hell Can't Stop Them: The Battles for Chattanooga—Missionary Ridge and Ringgold, November 24–27, 1863*. El Dorado Hills, CA: Savas Beatie, 2018.

———. *The Chickamauga Campaign: Barren Victory: The Retreat into Chattanooga, the Confederate Pursuit, and the Aftermath of the Battle, September 21 to October 20, 1863*. El Dorado Hills, CA: Savas Beatie, 2016.

"Prevent Painful Horse Hoof Abscesses with Proper Equine Treatments & Care." *American Horse Rider* and Horses & Horse Information. Summer 1998. http://www.horses-and-horse-information.com/articles/0398abcess.shtml. Accessed February 7, 2023.

Price, James S. *The Battle of First Deep Bottom*. Charleston, SC: History Press, 2014.

Priest, John Michael. *Victory without Triumph: The Wilderness, May 6th & 7th, 1864*. Vol. 2. Shippensburg, PA: White Mane Publishing Company, Inc., 1996.

Pruitt, Albert Bruce. *Abstracts of South Carolina Plat Books 9 and 10 (1784–1786)*. Whitakers, NC: self-published, 2003.

———. *Spartanburg County/District South Carolina Deed Abstracts, Books A–T, 1785–1827 (1752–1827)*. Greenville, SC: Southern Historical Press, 1988.
Quarstein, John V., and J. Michael Moore. *Yorktown's Civil War Siege: Drums along the Warwick*. Charleston, SC: The History Press, 2012.
Rable, George C. *Fredericksburg! Fredericksburg!* Chapel Hill: University of North Carolina Press, 2002.
Read, William A. *Indian Place Names in Alabama*. Rev. ed. Tuscaloosa: University of Alabama Press, 1984.
Reardon, Carol. "The Forlorn Hope: Brig. Gen. Andrew A. Humphreys's Pennsylvania Division at Fredericksburg." In *The Fredericksburg Campaign: Decision on the Rappahannock*. Edited by Gary W. Gallagher, 80–112. Chapel Hill: University of North Carolina Press, 1995.
Rhea, Gordon C. *The Battle of the Wilderness: May 5–6, 1864*. Baton Rouge: Louisiana State University Press, 1994.
———. *The Battles for Spotsylvania Court House and the Road to Yellow Tavern: May 7–12, 1864*. Baton Rouge: Louisiana State University Press, 1997.
———. *Cold Harbor: Grant and Lee, May 26–June 3, 1864*. Baton Rouge: Louisiana State University Press, 2002.
———. *On to Petersburg: Grant and Lee, June 4–15, 1864*. Baton Rouge: Louisiana State University Press, 2017.
———. "The Overland Campaign." In *The Cambridge History of the American Civil War*, vol. 1. Edited by Aaron Sheehan-Dean, 292–314. Cambridge: Cambridge University Press, 2019.
———. *To the North Anna River: Grant and Lee, May 13–25, 1864*. Baton Rouge: Louisiana State University Press, 2000.
———. "The Two Generals Who Resist Each Other: Perceptions of Grant and Lee in the Summer of 1864." In *Cold Harbor to the Crater: The End of the Overland Campaign*. Edited by Gary W. Gallagher & Caroline E. Janney, 1–32. Chapel Hill: University of North Carolina Press, 2015.
Richardson, Darcy G. *Others: Third Party Politics from the Nation's Founding to the Rise and Fall of the Greenback-Labor Party*. Vol. 1. Lincoln, NE: Universe, Inc. 2004
Rigdon, John C. *Historical Sketch & Roster: The Georgia 16th Infantry Regiment*. Powder Springs, GA: Eastern Digital Resources, 2004.
———. *Historical Sketch & Roster: The Georgia 43rd Infantry Regiment*. Powder Springs, GA: Eastern Digital Resources, 2004.
Ritter, W. L. "Sketch of the Third Battery of Maryland Artillery." *Southern Historical Society Papers* 10 (January–December 1882): 328–32, 392–401, 464–71.
Roberson, Elizabeth Whitley. *In Care of Yellow River: The Complete Civil War Letters of Pvt. Eli Pinson Landers to His Mother*. Gretna, LA: Pelican Publishing Company, 1997.
Roberts, W. Clifford, Jr., and Frank E. Clark. *Atlanta's Fighting Forty-Second: Joseph Johnston's "Old Guard."* Macon: Mercer University Press, 2020.
Robertson, James I., Jr. *General A. P. Hill: The Story of a Confederate Warrior*. New York: Random House, 1992.
———. *Stonewall Jackson: The Man, the Soldier, the Legend*. New York: Macmillan, 1997.

Roland, Charles P. *An American Iliad: The Story of the Civil War*. New York: McGraw-Hill Higher Education, 2002.

Salmon, Lee, and Dennis Hawkins. "Cochins." Alachua Freenet. http://www.afn.org/~poultry/breeds/cochin.htm. Accessed February 1, 2023.

Salmon, John S. *The Official Virginia Civil War Battlefield Guide*. Mechanicsville, PA: Stackpole Books, 2001

Schroeder-Lein, Glenna R. *The Encyclopedia of Civil War Medicine*. Armonk, NY: M.E. Sharpe, 2008

Scott, Hervey. *A Complete History of Fairfield County, Ohio, 1795–1876*. Columbus: Siebert & Lilley, Printers and Binders, 1877.

Sears, Stephen W. *To the Gates of Richmond: The Peninsula Campaign*. New York: Ticknor & Fields, 1992.

———. *Landscape Turned Red: The Battle of Antietam*. New York: Warner Books, Inc., 1983.

———. *Chancellorsville*. Boston: Houghton Mifflin Company, 1996.

Severance, Frank H. "Notes on the Ancestry and Descendants of Horatio Jones." *Publications of the Buffalo Historical Society* 6 (1906): 521–26.

Shadburn, Don L., ed. *Pioneer History of Forsyth County, Georgia*. Vol. 1. Roswell, GA: W. H. Wolfe Associates, 1981. Reprint, Cumming, GA: privately printed, 1996.

Shadburn, Don L., and Ted O. Brooke. *Crimson and Sabres: A Confederate Record of Forsyth County, Georgia*. Cumming, GA: Pioneer-Cherokee Heritage Series, 1997.

Shands, H. A. *Some Peculiarities of Speech in Mississippi*. Boston: Norwood Press, J. S. Cushing & Company, 1893.

Sherman, William Tecumseh. *Memoirs of General W. T. Sherman*. New York: Library of America, 1990.

Shultz, David L., and Scott L. Mingus Sr. *The Second Day at Gettysburg: The Attack and Defense of Cemetery Ridge, July 2, 1863*. El Dorado Hills, CA: Savas Beatie LLC, 2015.

Sifakis, Stewart. *Compendium of the Confederate Armies: South Carolina and Georgia*. Westminster, MD: Heritage Books, Inc., 2007.

Simmons, Henry E. *A Concise Encyclopedia of the Civil War*. New York: Bonanza Books, 1965.

Simpson, Brooks B., Stephen W. Sears, and Aaron Sheehan-Dean, eds. *The Civil War: The First Year Told by Those Who Lived It*. New York: Library of America, 2011.

Simpson, D. P., comp. *Cassell's Compact Latin-English, English-Latin Dictionary*. New York: Dell Publishing Co., Inc., 1963.

Smedlund, William S. *Camp Fires of Georgia Troops, 1861–1865*. Sharpsburg, GA: Author, 1995.

Smith, George Gilman. *The Story of Georgia and the Georgia People, 1732–1860*. Macon: G.G. Smith, 1900.

Smith, Gerald J. *"One of the Most Daring of Men": The Life of Confederate General William Tatum Wofford*. Murfreesboro, TN: Southern Heritage Press, 1997.

Smith, Gordon Burns. *History of the Georgia Militia, 1783–1860*. Vol. 1. Milledgeville: Boyd Publishing, 2000.

Smith, Joseph, Jr., Oliver Cowdery, Sidney Rigdon, and Frederick G. Williams, comps. *Doctrine and Covenants of the Church of the Latter Day Saints: Carefully Selected from the Revelations of God*. Kirkland, OH: F. G. Williams & Co., 1835.

Smith, L. A. "Recollections of Gettysburg." In *War Papers Read before the Michigan Commandery of the Military Order of the Loyal Legion of the United States*, vol. 2. Edited by Charles G. Hampton, 297–308. Detroit: James H. Stone & Co., Printers, 1898.

Smith, Mark M. *The Smell of Battle, The Taste of Siege: A Sensory History of the Civil War*. Oxford: Oxford University Press, 2015.

Smith, Timothy B. *Champion Hill: Decisive Battle for Vicksburg*. New York: Savas Beatie LLC, 2007.

———. *The Siege of Vicksburg: Climax of the Campaign to Open the Mississippi River, May 23–July 4, 1863*. Lawrence: University of Kansas Press, 2021.

Snell, Mark A. *West Virginia and the Civil War*. Charleston, SC: History Press, 2011.

Sjoquist, David L. "A Brief History of the Property Tax in Georgia." Atlanta: Fiscal Research Center, Andrew Young School of Policy Studies, Georgia State University, 2008.

Sons of Temperance of North America. *Constitutions of the Order of the Sons of Temperance of North America*. Philadelphia: Craig and Young, 1849.

Southern Historical Association. *Memoirs of Georgia Containing Historical Accounts of Civil, Military, Industrial and Professional Interests, and Personal Sketches of Many of the People*. Vol. 1. Atlanta: Southern Historical Association, 1895.

Stackpole, Edward J. *From Second Bull Run to Gettysburg: The Civil War in the East, 1862–1863*. Guilford, CT: Stackpole Books, 2018.

———. *The Battle of Fredericksburg*. Conshohocken, PA: Eastern Acorn Press, 1981.

State of Georgia. *Acts of the General Assembly of the State of Georgia Passed in Milledgeville at an Annual Session in November and December 1842*. Milledgeville: William S. Rogers, 1842.

Steere, Edward. *The Wilderness Campaign*. Harrisburg, PA: Stackpole Company, 1960.

Stoker, Donald, and Mark Elam. "Strategy, Operations, and Tactics." In *The Cambridge History of the American Civil War*, vol. 2. Edited by Aaron Sheehan-Dean, 65–89. Cambridge: Cambridge University Press, 2019.

Stovall, Pleasant A. *Robert Toombs: Statesman, Speaker, Soldier, Sage*. New York: Cassell Publishing Company, 1892.

Tabor, Anna Belle Little. *History of Franklin County, Georgia*. Roswell, GA: W. H. Wolfe Associates, 1986.

Tinling, Marion, ed. *The Correspondence of the Three William Byrds of Westover, Virginia, 1684–1776*. Vol. 1. Charlottesville: University Press of Virginia, 1977.

Trelease, Allen W. *White Terror: The Ku Klux Klan Conspiracy and Southern Reconstruction*. Westport, CT: Greenwood Press, 1979.

Trudeau, Noah Andre. *The Last Citadel: Petersburg June 1864–April 1865*. El Dorado Hills, CA: Savas Beatie LLC, 1991.

Tucker, Jonathan B. *Scourge: The Once and Future Threat of Smallpox*. New York: Grove Press, 2002.

Turner, John R. "The Battle of the Wilderness: The Part Taken by Mahone's Brigade." In *War Talks of Confederate Veterans*. Edited by George S. Bernard, 87–106. Petersburg, VA: Fenn & Owen Publishers, 1892.

"A Union Woman Suffers through the Siege." In *The Blue and the Gray: The Story of the Civil War as Told by Participants*. Edited by Henry Steele Commager, 662–68. Avenel, NJ: Crescent Books, 1995.

US Bureau of Engraving and Printing. "Redeemed Mutilated Currency." https://www.bep.gov/services/mutilated-currency-redemption. Accessed January 14, 2020.

US Department of Defense. Adjutant General. *Georgia Military Record Book*. Vol. 4, 1841–1862. Military Records RG 22, 01.004. Georgia Archives, Morrow, Georgia.

US War Department. *War of the Rebellion: A Compilation of the Official Records of the Union and Confederate Armies in the War of the Rebellion*. 128 vols. Washington, D.C.: US Government Printing Office, 1880–1901.

Vandiver, Louise Ayer. *Traditions and History of Anderson County*. Atlanta: Ruralist Press, 1928.

Vieux Seconde. "Notes on General E. Kirby Smith's Kentucky Campaign." *The Annals of the Army of Tennessee and Early Western History* 1 (April–December 1878): 193–211.

Wagner, Margaret E. *The Library of Congress Illustrated Timeline of the Civil War*. New York: Little, Brown and Company, 2011.

Waitt, Robert W., Jr. *Confederate Military Hospitals in Richmond*. 1964. Reprint, Richmond: Richmond Independence Bicentennial Commission, 1979.

Walker, Scott. *Hell's Broke Loose in Georgia: Survival in a Civil War Regiment*. Athens: University of Georgia Press, 2007.

Walmsley, Frank. *Handbook for Clerks of Session in the Presbyterian Church (U.S.A.)*. San Antonio: self-published, 1998, 2002.

Waltz, Robert B., ed. *The Minnesota Heritage Songbook*. Fort Snelling, MN: Friends of Fort Snelling, 2008. Available at www.MNHeritageSongbook.net.

Ward, Geoffrey C., Ric Burns, and Ken Burns. *The Civil War: An Illustrated History*. New York: Alfred A. Knopf, Inc., 1990.

Ward, Patricia Spain. *Simon Baruch: Rebel in the Ranks of Medicine 1840–1921*. Tuscaloosa: University of Alabama Press, 1994. (Bernard M. Baruch, adviser to presidents Woodrow Wilson and Franklin D. Roosevelt, was Simon Baruch's son.)

Warner, Ezra J. *Generals in Gray: Lives of the Confederate Commanders*. Baton Rouge: Louisiana University Press, 1995.

Webster's New World College Dictionary. 5th ed. New York: Houghton Mifflin Harcourt, 2014.

Welborn, James H., III, and Richard Houston. "Union Blockade and Coastal Occupation." In *The Civil War in Georgia: A New Georgia Encyclopedia Companion*. Edited by John C. Inscoe, 51–55. Athens: University of Georgia Press, 2011.

Welch, Spencer Glasgow. *A Confederate Surgeon's Letters to His Wife*. New York: Neale Publishing Company, 1911.

Wert, Jeffrey D. *The Heart of Hell: The Soldiers' Struggle for Spotsylvania's Bloody Angle*. Chapel Hill: University of North Carolina Press, 2022.

Wheeler, Richard. *On Fields of Fury: From the Wilderness to the Crater: An Eyewitness History*. New York: HarperCollins, 1991.

White, B. F., and King, E. J. *The Sacred Harp*. Carrolton, GA: Sacred Harp Publishing Company, 1991.

White, Ronald C. *American Ulysses: A Life of Ulysses S. Grant*. New York: Random House, 2016.

Wilcox, C. M. "Lee and Grant in the Wilderness." In *Annals of the War Written by Leading Participants North and South*. Edited by Alexander K. McClure. 1879. Reprint, Edison, NJ: Blue and Gray Press, 1996.

Wilson, Charles Reagan, and William Ferris, eds. *Encyclopedia of Southern Culture*. Chapel Hill: University of North Carolina Press, 1989.

Wilson, Gustavus James Nash, and William Ellis White. *The Early History of Jackson County, Georgia*. Atlanta: Foote & Davis Co., 1914.

Wittenberg, Eric J., J. David Petruzzi, and Michael F. Nugent. *One Continuous Fight: The Retreat from Gettysburg and the Pursuit of Lee's Army of Northern Virginia, July 4–14, 1863*. New York: Savas Beatie, 2011.

"Wofford's Georgia Brigade." *Southern Confederacy* (Atlanta), June 15, 1864.

Woods, James A. *Gettysburg, July 2: The Ebb and Flow of Battle*. Gillette, NJ: Canister Publishing LLC, 2012.

Woodward, Harold R., Jr. *For Home and Honor: The Story of Madison County, Virginia during the War Between the States 1861–1865*. Berryville, VA: H. R. Woodward Publishing, 1990.

Woodworth, Steven. "Confederate Military Leadership." In *The Cambridge History of the American Civil War*, vol. 2. Edited by Aaron Sheehan-Dean, 118–140. Cambridge: Cambridge University Press, 2019.

Writers' Program (US). Georgia. *Georgia, A Guide to Its Towns and Countryside, Compiled and Written by Workers of the Writers' Program of the Work Projects Administration in the State of Georgia*. Sponsored by the Georgia Board of Education. Athens: University of Georgia Press, 1946.

Wortman, Marc. *The Bonfire: The Siege and Burning of Atlanta*. New York: PublicAffairs, 2009.

Young, H. E. "Instructions for the Guidance of Courts Martial and Judges Advocate in this Army." Headquarters, Army of Northern Virginia, August 14, 1863.

FAMILY RECORDS

Alexander, Manning and Pillona. Alexander House Register, January 2, 1897–January 1, 1906. In the possession of Shirley Cavin Cucci, Stanley, North Carolina.

Brockman, Charles Raven, and Olivia Comer. "The Bowen Family: Biographical Sketches, Chart III." Typewritten and unpaginated. In possession of the editor.

Chaplin, Rev. Jeremiah, ed. *The Riches of Bunyan: Selected from His Works for the American Tract Society*. New York: The American Tract Society, 1850. (The Robert Alexander family, Manning's father's family, entered records of family births, deaths, and marriages in the front of this book. The book is in the editor's possession.)

Boatman, Dave, ed. "Henry White of Buckingham County, Virginia: Descendants of Henry White & Celia Page." March 1997. In the possession of Dave Boatman, Fort Worth, TX.

Boone, Nora Alexander. "Facts gathered by Mrs. G. P. Boone concerning *Mrs. Thirza David*." An undated, handwritten paper in the David Family Papers at the Hargrett Rare Book and Manuscript Library, University of Georgia Libraries, Athens.

"Bowen Bible Records." In Lockett, Mrs. P. C. and Mrs. Fred W. Thompson, eds. *Family Records, James Campbell Chapter, D. A. R., Dallas Texas (1706–1954)*. Dallas: Texas Daughters of the American Revolution, 1958.

Brooks, Thirza McDonald. "All-Day-Dinner-and Meeting-on-the-Ground: A Loving Retrospective." 1997. MS3198, Thirza McDonald Brooks papers, Hargrett Rare Book and Manuscript Library, University of Georgia Libraries, Athens, Georgia.

David Family Bible. *The Holy Bible Containing the Old and New Testaments, Translated from the Original Tongues and with the Former translations Diligently Compared and Revised*, etc., Philadelphia: C. Alexander & Co., 1834, in the possession of David Hopper of Hamilton, New York.

David, Horatio J. Family Papers. MS 3127. Hargrett Rare Book and Manuscript Library, University of Georgia Libraries, Athens, Georgia.

"The David Journal: The Official Newsletter of the Pierre David Family Association." Vol. 1, nos. 1, 2, and 3. Atlanta: David Family Association, 1983.

David, Pillina. Handwritten genealogical notes on sheets of paper stitched together with string to form a notebook, in the possession of the editor. Pillina David David was James H. David's mother. Cited as P. David, genealogical notes.

Jackson, Lily Alexander. Undated, handwritten genealogical notes in the possession of the editor. Cited as Lily Alexander Jackson, genealogical notes.

MAPS

Bachelder, John B. "Map of the Battle Field of Gettysburg: Second Day's Battle." New York: Endicott & Co., 1876.

Eastern National. "The Battle of Fredericksburg: A Self-Guided Driving Tour." Fort Washington, PA: Eastern National, 2007.

Georgia Atlas & Gazetteer. 4th ed. Yarmouth, Maine: DeLorme, 2010.

Hotchkiss, Jedediah. "Railroad Map of South Carolina, 1880." Library of Congress. https://www.loc.gov/resource/g3911p.rr003000/. Accessed September 20, 2023.

———. "No. 19. Sketch of Action at Guard Hill, Aug. 16th, 1864 to accompany report of Jed. Hotchkiss, Top. Eng. V.D." Library of Congress. https://www.loc.gov/resource/g3881sm.gcwh0008. Accessed September 20, 2023.

Johnson, A. J. "Johnson's Georgia and Alabama." New York: Johnson and Ward, 1863. hmf0079. Virtual Vault, Georgia Archives, University System of Georgia, Morrow, Georgia. https://vault.georgiaarchives.org/digital/collection/hmf/id/29. Accessed February 6, 2023.

Johnson and Ward. *Johnson's Map of the Vicinity of Richmond and Peninsular Campaign in Virginia. Showing also the interesting localities along the James, Chickahominy and York Rivers. Compiled from the Official Maps of the War Department*. "Entered according to

Act of Congress in the year 1862 by J. Knowles Hare in the Clerks office in the District Court of the United States for the Northern District of New York."

Kentucky Atlas & Gazetteer. 4th ed. Yarmouth, ME: DeLorme, 2010.

Lloyd, James T. "Lloyd's map of the southern states showing all the railroads, their stations & distances, also the counties, towns, villages, harbors, rivers, and forts." G3860 1862.L5. https://lccn.loc.gov/98688408. Library of Congress Geography and Map Division, Washington, D.C. Accessed October 13, 2020.

McElfresh, Earl B. "The Battlefield of Cold Harbor, Hanover County, Virginia 1864." Olean, NY: McElfresh Map Co., LLC, 2000.

———. "Cedar Mountain Battlefield, Culpeper County, Virginia, 1862." Olean, NY: McElfresh Map Co., LLC, 1997.

Pennsylvania Atlas & Gazetteer. 8th ed. Yarmouth, ME: DeLorme, 2003.

Potomac Appalachian Trail Club, Inc. "Map 10, Appalachian Trail and Other Trails in Shenandoah National Park Central District." Vienna, VA: Potomac Appalachian Trail Club, Inc, 2013.

Rand McNally 2019 Road Atlas: United States, Canada, Mexico. Chicago: RM Acquisition LLC, 2018.

Rand McNally. "Map of Athens," 2001.

Rand McNally. "Mississippi State Road Map," 2009.

Rand McNally. "Tennessee State Road Map," 2009.

Rand McNally. "South Carolina State Map," 2008.

Virginia Atlas & Gazetteer. 4th ed. Yarmouth, ME: DeLorme, 2000.

Warren, G. K. "Map of the Battle-Field of Gettysburg." 1868–1869, partially revised in 1873. http://www.codex99.com/cartography/125.html, accessed 7 November 2020.

PENSION RECORDS

Bowen, Thomas. "War of 1812 Pension and Bounty Land Warrant Application Files." Widow's Pension file 18,280, catalog 564415, RG 15. National Archives and Records Administration, Washington, D.C.

OTHER

Acts of the General Assembly of the State of Georgia. Volumes for 1837 and 1842.

"Compiled Service Records of Confederate Soldiers Who Served in Organizations from the State of Georgia." M266, RG 109. National Archives and Records Administration, Washington, D.C. https://www.fold3.com. Cited as "service records."

"Compiled Service Records of Soldiers Who Served in the American Army during the Revolutionary War, 1775–1783," RG 93, roll 0886, vol. 9, pg. 170, National Archives and Records Administration, Washington, D.C.

Constitution of the Order of the Sons of Temperance of North America. Philadelphia: Craig & Young, 1849.

"Eclectic Medical Institute of Cincinnati Matriculation Records." Eclectic Medical College Records, 1845–1942. Collection no. 3, series 3, box 5, vol. 6. Lloyd Library and Museum, Cincinnati, OH.

Editor conversation with Danny Elrod and other members of Unity Christian Church. July 29, 2012.

Federal Agricultural Census, Jackson County, Subdivision No. 45, 1850. https://www.ancestry.com/search/collections/1276/?name=James_David&f-F0006442=Agriculture& residence=1850_jackson-georgia-usa_1466. Accessed September 20, 2023.

General Order No. 34, paragraph II, Headquarters of the Army of Northern Virginia, 7 March 1863, and General Order No. 66, paragraph XV, Headquarters of the Army of Northern Virginia, May 25, 1853, M921, roll 1. "Orders and Circulars Issued by the Army of the Potomac and the Army and Department of the Army of Northern Virginia C. S. A. 1861–1866." Library of Congress, Washington, D.C.

Georgia Marriage Records, 1699–1944. Available through Ancestry.com.

Georgia Marriage Records from Select Counties, 1828–1978. Available through Ancestry.com.

Jackson County Deed Books, Court House of Jackson County, Jefferson, GA.

Jackson County Ordinary Apprenticeship, Indentures, 1872–1906. SLC RHS 3405, microfilm drawer 168, box 49. Georgia State Archives.

"List of Confederates Captured at Vicksburg, Mississippi, July 4, 1863." M2072, roll 1, National Archives and Records Administration, Washington, D.C.

United States Census, 1850. Database with images. *FamilySearch.* https://www.familysearch.org/search/collection/1401638. 28 December 2022. Citing NARA microfilm publication M432. Washington, D.C.: National Archives and Records Administration, n.d. Cited as US Census, 1850.

United States Census, 1860. Database with images. *FamilySearch.* https://www.familysearch.org/search/collection/1473181. 23 January 2023. From "1860 US Federal Census —Population." Database. n.d. Citing NARA microfilm publication M653. Washington, D.C.: National Archives and Records Administration, n.d. Cited as US Census, 1860.

United States Census, 1870. Database with images. *FamilySearch.* https://www.familysearch.org/search/collection/1438024. 25 October 2022. Citing NARA microfilm publication M593. Washington, D.C.: National Archives and Records Administration, n.d. Cited as US Census, 1870.

United States Census, 1880. Database with images. *FamilySearch.* https://www.familysearch.org/search/collection/1417683. 28 November 2022. Citing NARA microfilm publication T9. Washington, D.C.: National Archives and Records Administration, n.d. Cited as US Census, 1880.

United States Census, 1900. Database with images. *FamilySearch.* https://www.familysearch.org/search/collection/1325221. 28 January 2023. Citing NARA microfilm publication T623. Washington, D.C.: National Archives and Records Administration, n.d. Cited as US Census, 1900.

United States Census, 1910. Database with images. *FamilySearch.* https://www.familysearch.org/search/collection/1727033. 24 October 2022. Citing NARA microfilm publication T624. Washington, D.C.: National Archives and Records Administration, n.d. Cited as US Census, 1910.

Virginia State Highway Marker JE7. "Blue Ridge Turnpike." Near Criglersville Elementary School, Criglersville, VA.

WEBSITES

Stover, Ken. "Civil War Tents." Civil War Academy. https://www.civilwaracademy.com/civil-war-tents. Accessed February 9, 2023.

Dalton, Kyle. "'They Did Not Seem to Respect It Much': Insignia and Medical Evacuation." National Museum of Civil War Medicine. https://www.civilwarmed.org/surgeons-call/medical-evacuation-insignia. Accessed June 14, 2021.

Documenting the American South. University Library at the University of North Carolina at Chapel Hill. https://docsouth.unc.edu.

Dorsey, Todd. "'Brick Store'—Maysville's Earlier Name." January 2011. From "Victorian Maysville" blog. http://victorianmaysville.blogspot.com/2011/01/. Accessed January 31, 2023.

"Find a Grave" for photographs of grave markers

New Georgia Encyclopedia, http://www.georgiaencyclopedia.org.

NEWSPAPERS

Abbeville Banner (Abbeville, SC)
Atlanta Constitution
Atlanta Weekly Intelligencer
Atlanta Daily Intelligencer and Examiner
Atlanta Southern Confederacy
Army and Navy Journal (New York)
Augusta Chronicle
Banks County Observer (Homer, GA)
Banner Watchman (Athens, GA)
Biblical Recorder (Raleigh, NC)
Confederate Union (Milledgeville, GA)
Federal Union and *Daily Federal Union* (Milledgeville, GA)
Forest News (Jefferson, GA)
Gainesville Eagle (Gainesville, GA)
Georgia Weekly Telegraph (Macon, GA)
Jackson Herald (Jefferson, GA)
North Georgia Tribune (Canton, GA)
Presbyterian of the South (Atlanta)
Southern Banner (Athens, GA)
Southern Recorder (Milledgeville, GA)
Southern Star (Ozark, AL)
Southern Watchman (Athens, GA)
Thomasville Times (Thomasville, GA)
Thomasville Weekly (Thomasville, GA)
Weekly Banner (Athens, GA)
Weekly Georgia Telegraph (Macon, GA)

Index

Abbeville (AL) Greys, 127
Abington, PA, xv
Abolitionists, 105–109, 136
Acker, Mr. (second cousin of JHD), 492–493
Adairsvillle, GA, 73, 343–345, 347–349, 353, 355
Adalaide (horse), 16
Adams, A., *Letter*: March 19, 1863, 248
Adams, Z. Boylston, Capt. (Union), 384–385
African Americans, enslaved: *General*, 34, 67, 101, 109, 111, 142, 338, 412, 416, 431, 442, 457; *David Family's As a Group*, xxi, 3, 7, 10, 17, 23, 25, 121, 140–141, 148, 153, 156, 225, 246, 251, 256–257, 287–288, 368, 370, 406, 414, 416, 419, 422, 431, 466, 477–478; *David Family's Individuals*: A, 290–291; Ben, xxi, 10, 12, 140–141; Cinda, xxi, 29–30; Dyse (Dyer, Dise, Dire Dier), xxi, 46, 125–126, 290–291, 359, 446–447; Freeman, 28, 338–339; Harriet, 19–20, 29–30, 222–223, 338–339; Henry, xxi, 126–127; Janis, 262, 268; John, 288; Joshua, 25–26; Juddy, 288, Simon, xxi, 121, 123, 126–127, 153, 156, 257, 359; unknown, 405–406, 517; *Others' Individuals*: Betty, 413; Bill, 56–57; Dave, 44; Dell, 338–339; Emanda, 413; John, 67; *David Family's freed*, 477
African Americans, free: *General*, 101, 106–107, 109, 111, 416, 477–478, 528–530; *Individuals*: Blount (Blunt), Emma, 501; Brisson, Warren, 528–529; Brooks, Elisha, 528; Bush, Calvin, 527–529; Sanders, Berry, 528–529; Savall (Henderson), Emma, 470, 500–501; Savall, Rhoda, 470, 500–501
Alabama Infantry Regiments: 6th, 127–128, 262; 22nd, 222; 47th, 171, 175–176; 48th, 171, 175–176

Alabama, state of, and secession, 106
Albany, GA, 104, 474
Albany, NY, 532
Alexander, Adam O. (AOA) (brother of MPA), xii, 72–73, 86–87, 193–194, 196, 199, 219–221, 479–480, 496, 499, 503; *Letter*: October 11, 1858, 72–73
Alexander, Buena E. (daughter of SHA), 193–194, 219–220
Alexander family, genealogical chart, xii goes to Texas, 480–499
Alexander, Fanny (wife of RCA), 484, 488–489
Alexander, Henry C. (brother of MPA), xii
Alexander, Henry C. (son of WPA), 87
Alexander House (boarding house), 532–533, 537–538
Alexander, James D. (JDA) (brother of MPA), xii, 132, 193–194, 196–197, 199, 203, 210–211, 214, 219–221, 302, 344, 348, 354, 464–465, 482, 484–485, 489–490, 492, 495–498, 503; *Letters*: September 1870,, 480–481; August 4, 1871, 493–494; October 31, 1871, 497–498; November 10, 1871, 498–499
Alexander, James P. (son of WPA), 220–221
Alexander, John N. (brother of MPA), xii, 219, 221, 480
Alexander, Lilly (Eliza, Lila) (wife of JDA), 489–490, 493–494; *Letter*: August 4, 1871, 494
Alexander, Lily (Mrs. Jackson) (daughter of MPA), xxii, 314–315, 405, 473, 477, 501, 540, 541
Alexander, Lou Sewell (wife of WPA), xii, 43, 86
Alexander, Magga (Margaret) (daughter of SHA), 495–496
Alexander, Mamie (Mrs. O'Kelly) (daughter of MPA), 477, 513, 536–537, 541

Alexander, Manning Poole (M.P., Elie) (MPA), xi–xii, xxi–xxii, 39–41, 50–52, 55, 71–73, 146, 213–214, 218, 220–221, 255–256, 264, 278, 314-315; early education, 42–43; courting, 37–39, 43–48; marriage, 48; medical school, 73–91; reports pyromaniac, 91; leads Bell Volunteers, 131–135; enlists in Georgia 43rd, 180–193; appointed assistant surgeon, 195–198; Kentucky, 195–213; early time in Vicksburg, 296–307; Champion Hill Battle, 306–314; Vicksburg siege, 314–322; surrender, 322-324, 334; march from Vicksburg, 324–326; reports back to 43rd, 342–362, 407–410; assigned to Madison hospital, 410–417; assigned to Augusta hospital, 431–447, 453–461, 464–467, 470–473; assigned to Greensboro, Georga, 461–464; reaction war's end, 470–473; early post-war peacetime, 477–504; apprenticeship agreement, 499–501; late peacetime, 524–543; Klu Klux Klan, 526–532; obituary, 541–543; *Letters*: March 19, 1859, 74–75; March 27, 1859, 77–82; April 3, 1859, 83–85; April 18, 1859, 87–89; July 26, 1862, 195–199; August 27, 1862, 199–203; April 24, 1863, 301–305; December 6, 1863, 355–356; December 11, 1863, 356–357; December 28, 1863, 357–358; January 5, 1864, 358–359; January 10, 1864, 360; January 12, 1864, 360–361; January 15, 1864, 361; February 3, 1864, 361–362; March 7, 1864, 408–409; March 11, 1864, 409–410; April 11, 1864, 413–414; July 23, 1864, 414–417; July 31, 1864, 432–433; August 6, 1864, 404, 433–435; August 20, 1864, 404–405, 436; August 27, 1864, 436–438; late August or early September, 1864, 438–439; January 16, 1865, 449, 453–454; January 21, 1865, 448, 455–456; January 25, 1865, 457–459; February 1, 1865, 459–460; February 8, 1865, 460–461; February 22, 1865, 461–462; February 27, 1865, 450–451, 463–464; March 11, 1865, 464–465; March 12, 1865, 465–466; April 19, 1865, 470–471; April 27, 1907, 538–539

Alexander, Margaret (Mrs. Edwards) (daughter of AOA), xii, 219-220; *Letter*: 1879, 503–504

Alexander, Margaret Poole (mother of MPA), xii, 40–41, 358, 502-504; death, 504; goes to Texas, 481–496; returns from Texas, 497–499; *Letters*: May 18, 1862, 193–194; September 25, 1862, 219–221; September 1870, 480–481; January 22, 1871, 481-484; February 19, 1871, 484-487; October 31, 1871, 497-498; November 10, 1871, 498-499

Alexander, Margaret (daughter of AOA), xii, 194, 219, 221, 480-483, 496-498, 504

Alexander, Margie (Mrs. Comer) (daughter of MPA), xxii, 40–41, 315, 477, 482, 513, 520, 535-536, 538-540; *Letter*, February 4, 1886, 533-534

Alexander, Mary Elizabeth Gillespie (Lizzie, EY) (wife of SHA), xii, 193-194, 345, 489–490

Alexander, Mattie (Martha) (daughter of SHA), 495, 496

Alexander, Nancy (daughter of AOA), 220

Alexander, Nora (Mrs. Boone) (daughter of MPA), xii, 55, 75–77, 80, 82–83, 181-187, 190, 199–200, 204, 214, 219, 240, 244, 251–252, 281, 287-289, 306, 326, 341, 345, 357-362, 365, 405-406, 409, 414, 434, 436-437, 440-446, 456-459, 464, 501, 502, 513, 518, 534-536, 539, 540, 543

Alexander, Pillona David (Lona), (wife of MPA), xi, xii, xxii, xxii, 7, 21, 31-32, 37, 38, 49, 54, 55, 64, 65, 74, 89, 125, 149, 158, 185, 193, 203, 213,

INDEX

217, 219, 221, 225, 240, 242-244, 246, 251, 254, 255, 296-297, 305, 314-315, 326, 338-341, 343, 358, 362, 365, 404, 406, 407, 423, 432, 438, 441, 465, 466, 477, 482, 494, 495, 499, 502, 513, 515, 518, 520, 532, 533; student of Manning's, 37; married, 48; ward nurse on Manning's ward, 441-442, 446-44; war's end letter, 468-470; obituary, 540-541; *Letters*: July 5, 1855, 37-39; July 15, 1856 45-47; June 8, 1857, 47-48; April 3, 1859 82-83; April 18, 1859 85-87; April 1, 1862, 180-183; April 10, 1862, 183-186; April 14, 1862, 186-188; April 26, 1862, 188-189; May 4, 1862, 146-147, 189-193; November 26, 1864, 444-447; April 24, 1865, 468-470; October 22, 1889, 534-536

Alexander, Robert (father of MPA), xii, xxi, 87, 219, 221, 483, 486, 493, death, 491-493; *Letter*, February 19, 1871, 487-488

Alexander, Robert C. (RCA) (brother of MPA), xii, 219, 221, 464-465, 482-484, 486, 489; *Letter*, May 1871, 487-488

Alexander, Robert W. (son of SHA), 498

Alexander, Samuel H. (SHA) (brother of MPA), xii, 86-87, 193-194, 219-220, 345, 354, 355, 415-417, 442-443, 453-455, 482-483, 494, 497, 502, 503-504; *Letters*, July 24, 1871, 488-490; August 3, 1871, 491-493; October 1, 1871, 495-496

Alexander, Susanna Burkhalter (Susan) (wife of AOA), xii, 193-194, 219-220, 495-496, 498-499; *Letter*: 1879, 502-504

Alexander, William O. (WOA) (uncle of MPA), 219-220

Alexander, William P. (WPA) (brother of MPA), xii, 42-42, 86-87, 455-456; *Letter*, February 16, 1871, 484

Alpharetta, GA, 21, 23, 242-243, 254

Anderson County, SC, 194, 498

Anderson, Deral, 44
Anderson, George T., Gen., 382, 385-386
Anderson, Joseph R., Gen., 163-172
Anderson, Richard H., Gen. 388-389, 394-395, 422-423, 425-229
Anderson, SC, 40-41, 223, 542
Anderson, William, 529
Andersonville, GA, 432-433
Anglin, Miss, 27
Antietam, Battle of, 154-156, 179, 210
Appomattox, VA, 450, 469
Arbachoocha, AL, 124
Arkansas, state of, 32, 98, 128-129, 498, 519
Armer, Taylor, 132
Armor, James F., 307, 314
Arthur, J. M., 363-364
Athens, GA, newspapers during the war, 80; railroad route, 90-91
Atkins, Abram, 45, 46, 213
Atkins, Hugh, 35, 44, 45, 46, 533
Atlanta, (Marthasville) GA: 13, 54-55, 58, 79, 106, 199, 245, 300, 347, 370, 411, 454, 468, 493, 531, 533; Democratic Party meeting at, 62; distance from, xi, 345, 357, 359, 431, 440, 520, 521, 547; exposition in, 536; Horatio has eye extracted there, 508; KKK trial held there, 527, 530; name changed from Marthasville, 4; railroad stop, 89, 90-91, 290, 451, 464, 463, 483, 515, 544-545; Simeon in, 117, 118, *See also*, Atlanta, Battle of
Atlanta, Battle of, 378, 407, 414-416, 432-433, 437; Atlanta falls to Sherman, 440, 443; Hood leaves Atlanta, 440-441, 444; Sherman leaves Atlanta, 446
Augusta, GA, location, 431, Manning in, 431-448, 453-460, 464- 467, 470-472; Thirza and Horatio in, 288-292
Augusta Orphan Asylum, 454
Austin, Capt., 22
Austin, Jacob Newton, 183
Bacon, Mr. (our venerabe old County man), 13

581

Bacon, C.T., 508
Bagwell, 213
Bagwell, John D., Pvt., 325
Baker's Creek, Battle of. *See* Champion Hill, Battle of
Ball (horse), 16
Ballard, Wave, Sgt., 427-428
Baltimore, MD, 154, 533
Baltimore Convention, 94-101, 106
Banks, Nathaniel P., Gen. (Union), 172-173
Baptist Associations, 22-23, 31, 46, 105, 113
Baptist Union Meeting, 22-23, 25
Baptist Women's Missionary Society, 540
Barber, John P, 218
Barber, Mrs. Susan N., 277-278
Barbourville (Barbersville), KY, 199-204, 208-209
Bardstown, KY, 206-207
Barker, Silas, 338
Barton, Seth Maxwell, Gen., 296-297, 299-300, 307-314, 316, 322, 326, 342
Bates, Russell (Bassell), 35-36
Bates, William N., 521-523
Beaufort, SC, 129-454
Beauregard, Pierre Gustave Toutant, Gen., 158-159, 401-402, 441
Beaver Dam Creek, Battle of. *See* Mechanicsville, Battle of,
Beechum, Dr., 78-79
Bell, Aaron (provider of uniforms for Bell Volunteers), 131
Bell, Allen, 184
Bell County, TX, 487
Bell, Ellen E. (daughter of PDB and MJRB), xi, 33, 359
Bell, George (father of runaway wife, cousin of Hiram Parks Bell), 59
Bell, Hiram Parks, Col., 59, 112-113, 300
Bell, Jack, 59
Bell, James, (brother of MRB), 62

Bell, John C. (Nominee of Constitutional Union Party in 1860 presidential election), 106, 109, 112
Bell, John Howard (brother of MRB), 32, 34, 218
Bell, Largus R. (brother of MRB), 217-218
Bell, Leola (daughter of PDB and MRB), 513, 519-520,
Bell, Middleton Raymond, Dr. (MRB) (husband of PDB), 13, 16, 20, 25, 30, 32-34, 51, 62, 63, 86-87, 88, 122, 123, 153, 217, 218, 222, 225, 241, 281, 301, 338, 369, 395, 400, 520; married, 10-11; left for Alabama, 47; *Letter*: November 11, 1850, 18-20, August 15, 1862, 217-219, March 21, 1863, 240-242
Bell, Myrtalas X. (Mrs. Barber) (sister of MRB), 217-218
Bell, Nannie Gurly (wife of WBB), 520
Bell, Oscar (son of PDB and MRB), xi, 33, 338-339
Bell, Pillina Charity David (PDB) (daughter of JHD and TBD), xi, 3-5, 7, 11, 13, 14, 23, 25, 30, 37, 187, 123, 125-126, 153, 159, 225, 281, 285, 369- 370, 380, 538; marriage, 11; move to Alabama, 32-34, 47, 63; *Letters*: November 11, 1850, 18-20; September 11, 1854, 32-34; July 16, 1861, 124-125; August 15, 1862, 217-219; January 16, 1863, 221-223, 296; March 21, 1863, 240-242; October or November, 1863, 338-339; July 9, 1864, 399-400; November 9, 1876, 513-514; October 5, 1885, 519-520
Bell, Rayson Perry (Rasin) (brother of MRB), 2, 6, 16, 18, 19, 34
Bell Volunteers, 126, 131-135, 210, 340
Bell, Walter J. (son of PDB and MRB), xi, 338-339, 520
Bell, William B. (Billy or Billie) (son of PDB and MRB), xi, 338-339, 520
Bell, William Milton (father of MRB), 20, 33, 339

582

INDEX

Bellamy, John, 489-490
Bells Mills, AL, 513, 519, 532
Belton, SC, 41
Ben. *See* African Americans, enslaved
Bennett, Rev. Mr., 253
Berea, KY, 208
Betty. *See* African Americans, enslaved
Beverly, Brother, 338
Big Black River Bridge, Battle of, 314
Big Cypress Bayou, TX, 483
Big Hill, KY, 208
Big Shanty (Kennesaw), GA, 180,182, 184, 186, 189, 345, 542
Big Springs, VA (now WV), 121
Bill, Mrs. Gober's. *See* African Americans, enslaved
Billups, John, Gen., 134
Birmingham, AL, 245, 520
Black Republicans, 106, 336
Blackie, George S., 412
Blacks. *See* African Americans, enslaved; African Americans, free
Blackwell, Jesse, 295
Blackwell, Mary, 295
Blaine's Crossroad, TN, 204, 209
Blalock, Miss, 125
Blalock, George, 125
Block & Co., publishers, 83
Bloody Run, 397-398
Blount, Emma. *See* African Americans, free
Blue Ridge Mountains, 224, 226, 422, 446
Blue Ridge Turnpike, 226
Boatwright, John Guerrant, Surg., 411, 431-432, 442, 450-451, 455, 461-463, 471
Boatswain's Creek or Boatswain's Swamp, 164-165
Boger, Franklin, 16, 18, 19
Boger, Mrs., 17
Boger, Peter C., 17, 18
Bogle, Dr. and wife, 68
Bond's Ferry, 11
Books: *Gleanings from Memory: Stories of My Childhood*, 48; *Jane Eyre* 96, *The Scarlet Letter*, 26, *The Upper Ten Thousand: Sketches of American Society*, 85
Boone, Annie (daughter of Nora Alexander Boone), 535-536
Boone, Harry (possibly Nora Alexander Boone's son), 539-540
Boone, Mrs. G. P. *See* Nora Alexander
Boone, Perino (husband of Nora Alexander Boone), 534-535, 539
Boring, Alex, 34
Boring, Elizabeth, 3, 7, 18
Boring, Francis, 34
Boring, Isaac, 34
Boring, John P., Dr., 16, 18, 20, 34
Boring, Julian, 34
Bowen family genealogical chart, x
Bowen, Abner H. (son of HoB), x, 262, 268
Bowen, Amanda (Mrs. Jones), *See* Amanda Bowen Jones
Bowen, Amanda Helena (daughter of Caleb Perry Bowen), 295, 523
Bowen, Caleb Perry (son of TJB), x, 293-295, 523
Bowen, Charity Blackwell (wife of HiB), x, 15, 34, 295
Bowen, Hiram (HiB) (brother of TBD), x, 13, 15, 34, 103, 127-129, 142-143, 268, 293-295, 419, 523; *Letter*: November 18, 1861, 127-130, 142-143
Bowen, Hiram Cox (son of PB), x, 128, 419
Bowen, Horatio Owen (HoB), (brother of TBD), x, 130, 523
Bowen, Jesse James (Jesse) (son of HiB), x, 127-129, 191, 244, 245, 262, 268, 293, 295, 370, 378
Bowen, John (son of HiB), x, 293, 295, 523
Bowen, John Hunter (son of HoB), x, 262, 268, 523
Bowen, John S., Gen., 307, 312
Bowen, Malachi (Mac) (son of PB), x, 246
Bowen, Mary Amanda Hill (wife of HoB), x,

Bowen, Mary Ann Palina (Milly?) (daughter of HiB), x, 295
Bowen, Mary Cox (wife of PB), x, 52, 216
Bowen, Nancy Ann Jones (mother of TJB, HoB, PB, HiB, and TBD), x, xvi, xvii
Bowen, Nancy Calfenny (Cally) (daughter of (HiB), x, 128-129
Bowen, Nancy Yarbrough (wife of TJB), x, 141, 183
Bowen, Owen (son of PB), x, 128, 216
Bowen, Owen Bulow (Dock) (son of HiB), x, 49-50, 127-130, 293
Bowen, Owen Jones (father of TJB, HoB, PB, HiB, and TBD), x, xvi-xvii, xviii, xix, 39, 512, 513
Bowen, Perry (PB) (brother of TBD), x, 52, 128-130, 168, 216, 293, 419
Bowen, Perry (son of HiB), x
Bowen, Polly, *See* Mary Cox Bowen
Bowen, Reuben Hunter (son of PB), x, *Letter*, April 27, 1862, 216-217
Bowen, Roady Ann (daughter of PB), x, 128-129
Bowen, Sallie (daughter of HoB), x
Bowen, Teresa Ann (Mrs. Lindsey) (daughter of PB), x, 7, 216
Bowen, Thirza, *See* Thirza Bowen David (TBD)
Bowen, Thirza Ann (daughter of HiB), x,
Bowen, Thomas Lindsay (son of HiB), x
Bowen, Thomas Owen (son of HoB), x
Bowen, Thomas Jones (TJB) (brother of TBD), x, xvi, 141, 183, 523
Bowen, William (Willie) (son of HiB), x, 293, 295
Boyd, C. Hopson (Major?), 198
Brackett, Colquitt, 473, 541
Bradberry, Jacob, Pvt, 324-325
Bradley, Lucius C., Pvt., 313
Brady, Dr., 78
Bragg, Braxton, Gen., 201-203, 205-210, 296, 344, 347, 349-351, 354-355, 356, 440, 446-447, 474
Branchville, SC, 278-280, 456

Brandaway, SC, 496
Brandon, MS, 325
Brazzleton, T. V., 481
Breckinridge, John C., Gen., Vice Pres., 62, 106, 112, 293, 351-353
Bridgeport, AL, Battle of, 192
Brison, Warren. *See* African Americans, free
Brockmann, Olivia Comer, xxii
Brockmann, Charles, xxii
Bronson, FL, 515
Brooks, Elisha. *See* African Americans, free
Brooks, Thirza McDonald, xxii, 524
Bronston, Uncle, 203, 210
Brown, George Washington, 521-523, 533
Brown, John, 70-71
Brown, Joseph E., Gov., 131-133, 134, 182, 236, 290, 362, 458
Brown place, 477
Brown's Boys, 182
Brown's Bridge Road, GA, 11, 405-407
Brown's Ferry, GA, 10-11
Brownie (horse), 539
Bruinsburg, MS, 307
Brumley, Col., 126
Bruton, A., 69-70
Bryan, E.H., Dr., 321
Buchanan, James, Pres., 62, 71, 95
Buck (horse), 181, 183, 197, 200, 306
Buckingham County, VA, xvii-xv
Buell, Don Carlos, Gen. (Union), 206-208
Bull Run Battles, *See* Manassas, Battles of
Burgess, Lewis, 67
Burkhalter, William, 503-504
Burriss, Joseph, *See* Sylvanus Stokes
Burnside, Ambrose E., Gen. (Union), 227-232, 263, 346, 356, 386
Burroughs, Jim, 497, 498
Bush, Calvin. *See* African Americans, free
Caddo Lake, LA, TX, 483
Cain, Mrs., *See* Francis Kane
Calhoun County, AL, 218, 520

INDEX

California, state of, 16-20, 32-34, 59-60, 67-68, 97, 297
Callahan, Lt., 168-169
Camden, AR, 498
Camden, SC, xxi
Camp meetings and campgrounds: general and unspecified, 14, 33, 62; Baptist, 27, 46, 64; Bethlehem, 93; Hickory Flat, 12, 14; Holbrook, 12-13, 14, 25-27; Mossy Creek, 92
Campbell, Dr., 22
Campbell, Thomas, poet, 169
Candler, Sallie, 45
Canton (Etowa), GA, 3, 5, 35, 63, 490
Cantrell, Dr., 34
Carlisle Barracks, xxiii
Carnesville, GA, xxi, 38, 40, 42, 194, 213-214, 358
Carnifex Ferry, Battle of, 123
Carr, Gussie, 405, 518
Carrollton, GA, 221
Carson, G. L., 543
Carson, Henry D., *Letter:* April 25, 1863, 247-248
Carter, Jesse, 213-214
Carter's Depot, TN, 248
Cary, Isaac L., 413
Cashtown, PA, 334
Cedar Ford (Luttrell), TN, 196, 198
Cedar Mountain, Battle of, 172-178, 179, 225, 229
Cedar Run, Battle of. *See* Cedar Mountain, Battle of
Cedarville, Battle of. *See* Guard Hill, Battle of
Cemetery Ridge, 330-331, 333
Centre Hill Guards, 136-138, 140, 402; *See also* 16th Georgia Infantry Regiment
Champion Hill (Baker's Creek), Battle of, 306-314
Chancellorsville, Battle of, 261-273
Chaffin's Bluff, VA, 420
Chandler, Allen M., 523
Chantilly (Shantello), Battle of, 225, 238
Charleston, SC, 119, 236, 239, 413, 456, 457, 458, 461, 465

Charleston Convention, 93-96, 97, 99, 100, 101, 102
Charleston, TN, 346-347
Charleston, WV, 123
Charlotte, NC, xxii, 463, 465, 474
Chattanooga, TN, 73, 182, 186, 192-193, 197, 201, 278
Chattanooga, Campaign of, 346-356, 365
Cheatham, Benjamin F., Gen., 459-460
Chester County, PA, xvi
Chesterfield Heights, VA, 420
Chicago Convention, 437-438
Chickahominy River, 162-164, 167
Chicago, IL, 533
Chickamauga, Battle of, 343, 345, 347, 363
Chickasaw Bayou, Battle of, 297-300, 303
Christian Soldiers Association, 258
Chronic, Warren, 363-364
Chucci, Shirley, Cavin, 535
Chulafinnee, AL, 124, 217-218, 221, 296, 338
Churches, Georgia: Athens Christian, 525; Bethabra Baptist, 143; Bethlehem Baptist, 450; Candler's Creek Baptist, xix-xx, 38-39, 48, 183, 190, 512, 514; First Presbyterian, Augusta, 453-454; Friendship Baptist, 36; Gravelly, 539; Hawkinsville Baptist, 537; Maysville Presbyterian, 509; Methodist Episcopal Church, South, 500; Noonday Baptist, 10-11, 17; Oconee, 35; Providence Baptist, 23; unnamed Baptist Church, 25, 92, 141, 540
Cincinnati, OH, 55, 72-82, 83-85, 87-91, 205, 542
Cincinnati Platform, 94-96, 97, 101, 102
Cinda. *See* African Americans, enslaved
Clarksville, GA, 72, 466
Cleburne County, AL, 124, 218-219
Cleburne, Patrick, Gen., 201-202
Cleveland, TN, 344, 347, 355-356, 506
Clinch Mountain, TN, 198
Clinton, GA, xx, 6, 516

Clothing, making: boots 140, 180, 200, 211, 214; coat, 125, 148, 151, 184, 211, 257, 258, 285-286, 257, 399, 434, 444; drawers, 125, 148, 180, 200, 203, 211, 214, 260, 307, 414; dress 19, 82, 241, 243, 338, 449, 535; gloves, 140, 203, 211, 214, 365; janes (jeans), 125, 190-191, 247, 399-400, 414, 445-446; overcoat, 63, 211, 214, 416; pants, 125, 148, 151, 184, 188, 203, 211, 214, 247, 257-258, 285, 307, 344, 358, 360, 409, ; shirts, 125, 148, 203, 211, 214, 243, 259; shoes, 180, 185, 258, 442; socks, 126, 151, 203, 211, 214, 260, 358-360; underclothing, 151
Cobb, Howell, 94, 99-100, 117-118, 120, 140-141,147,149-152, 155-156, 161, 362, 474
Cobb, Thomas Reades Rootes, 107-108, 109, 110, 229-232
Cobb's Mill Pond, GA, 61
Coffeville, MS, 208
Coffeville, TX, 483-484
Cold Harbor, Battle of, 395-399, 401
Collins, E. O., 275
Collins, W.J. (or J.W), 144
Columbia, SC, 41, 445, 456, 461, 463-465
Commerce, GA, 466, 480, 542
Comer, Alice (Allie) Thurmond, 463-465, 534
Comer, George, 539
Comer, Henry, 535-536
Comer, Margie. *See* Margie Alexander
Comer, James T., 477, 533-534, 535-536, 539-540
Comer, Ralph, 534
Comer, William Jinkins, 533
Comersville (Comer), GA, 44, 539, 540
Confederate Cavalry, 201, 204, 208-209, 217, 248, 290, 323, 333, 335, 336, 346, 353, 356, 366, 389, 423, 425-428, 437, 458, 465, 467, 469, 474
Confederate Congress, 213, 242, 257, 409-410

Confederate Government, 109, 140, 141, 369, 435, 451-452, 472
Confederate Infantry Regiments, *See* individual states
Confederate Invalid Corps, 451
Confederate Legislation, Act to allow commissioned officers to draw rations and purchase clothes from Quartermaster, 410; laws establishing the Provisional Army of the Confederate States, 409-410; Conscription Act, 216-218, 452; Exemption Act, 213, 241-242
Confederate Money, 213, 241, 358, 470
Confederate Peace negotiations, 438, 459-460, 469
Confederate Veterans Reunion, 540-541
Conn, Charles A., Capt., 331,
Constitutional Union Party, 106, 112
Cornerstone Speech, 111
Covington, GA, 414-416, 433
Covington, KY, 205, 212
Cowan, J. P., 8
Cowan family, 38-39
Cowpens, SC, 473
Cox, H. J., Lt., 249- 250, 363
Crab Orchard, KY, 208
Crampton's Gap, Battle of, 152-156, 169, 210, 250, 275
Crater, Battle of, 421-422
Crittenden family, 174-176
Crocket, Mrs. (Widow), xvi
Crooked Run, Battle of. *See* Guard Hill, Battle of
Crooked Run, VA, 425-428
Crumpton, Mrs., 291
Culpepper, Ansel M., Pvt, 185-187, 191, 409-410
Culpepper, Caleb C., 191
Culpepper, William H., 191
Culpepper County, VA, 171
Culpepper Road, 174
Culpepper, VA, 422, 423, 424, 428
Cumberland Gap, TN, 197-199, 201-202, 204, 205-206, 208-209, 212
Cumberland Mountains, 197, 202

INDEX

Cumming, GA, 59-60, 62, 64, 67, 68, 112, 118, 234, 328, 407
Custer, George Armstrong, Gen. (Union), 426-228
Dahlonega, GA, 4, 17, 60, 474
Dailey, Jasper, 256
Daingerfield, TX, 497
Dallas, GA, 378
Dallas, TX, 482, 487, 493
Dalton, GA, 196, 344, 347, 349, 351, 354-357, 362, 408-413
Dam No. 1, Battle of, 146-147, 190
Dave. *See* African Americans, enslaved
David family, farm, 12; genealogical chart, 9
David, Daisy Lee (daughter of HJD), 505, 509-510, 541
David, Frances Harris (Fannie, Fanny) (wife of SBD), x, 27-29, 56-58, 120-122, 225, 232, 234-235, 369-370, 377, 400, marriage to Simeon, 34-36; trip with Thirza during war, 404-407, 423, 517-518; marriage to Van Davis, 546; *Letters*: January 23, 1861, 105-106; February 25, 1865, 448-450; May 8, 1873, 544-548
David, George Thomas (Tommie) (son of HJD), 505, 519-520, 525
David, Henry (father of JHD), xviii
David, Henry Franklin (brother of JHD), 46
David, Horatio Bowen (son of HJD), 505, 519-520, 525
David, Horatio James (Ratio, Rashe) (HJD, son of JHD and TBD), xi, xxi, xxii, 21, 39, 186, 292-293, 481, 505-506, 509, 524; attends Simeon's school, 38; enlists in Centre Hill Guards, 138; hospital in Richmond sick, 148-149; visited by mother while in hospital in Richmond wounded, 274-292; sent home wounded, 428-429, 441-445, 448, 450, 455, 463-464, 468; paroled, 473-474; works in Grange Store, 507-509, eye operation, 507, 508; pension file, 521-523; obituary, 524-525; *Battles participated in: See*: Dam No. 1, Seven Days, Fredericksburg, Chancellorsville, Overland Campaign, Petersburg, First Deep Bottom, Guard Hill; *Letters*: February 22, 1862, 145-146; May 1862 148-149; September 6, 1862 151-156; September 24, 1862 152-156, 168, 210; March 12, 1863 249-250; March 18 or 29, 1863, 250-251; March 25, 1863, 251-252; April 3, 1863, 253-254; April 7, 1863, 255-256; April 13, 1863, 256-257; April 17, 1863 257-159; April 22, 1863, 259-260; May 1863, 274; May 20, 1863, 275-276; February 2, 1864, 363-364; February 18, 1864, 365-367; May 25, 1864, 378-395; June 5, 1864, 395-399; June 28, 1864, 400-403; July 10, 1864, 418-419; August 2, 1864, 419-422; August 10, 1864, 422-423; August 15, 1864, 404, 423-425; August 27, 1900, 523-524
David, Isaac (grandfather of JHD), xvii-xix,
David, Isaac M. (brother of JHD), 24-25, 29, 63, 65, 105, 111, 127, 129
David, James M. (nephew of JHD)
David, James Horatio (JHD, father of the main family): x-xi, xiv, xviii-xx, xxii, 4, 3, 7, 12, 16, 20, 22, 30, 32-33, 37-39, 44, 46, 48, 50, 58, 66, 75, 77, 82, 83, 103, 111, 121, 123, 125, 129, 140, 141, 153, 180, 217, 221, 222, 251, 273, 288, 291, 295, 296, 302, 339, 341, 359, 403, 406, 466, 491, 502, 506, 512, 513; marriage, xix; fire at home, 240-248; obituary, 514
David, James Simeon (Simmie) (son of HJD), 505, 519-520, 525
David, Lena, *See* Thirza Lena David
David, Lois M (Mrs. Carson) (niece of JHD), 248
David, Mary (wife of Henry Franklin David), 46

587

David, Mary David McDonald (daughter of HJD), 525
David, Mary Elenora (Ellen) (Mrs. Hagen) (daughter of SBD), xi, 58, 60, 64, 85, 235. 450. 545-547
David, Mary Juliette (daughter of JHD and TBD). *See* Mary David Neal
David, Morrisett (distant cousin), 245-246

David, Owen Thomas (Tom, Toma, Tommy) (OTD, son of JHD and TBD), xi, xiii, xxi, 7, 21, 26, 27, 29, 30-32, 35, 37-38, 44, 46-48, 49-51, 54, 58-61,63, 65, 66, 86-87, 100, 117-120, 121, 124, 125, 127, 129, 143, 146; April Fool's joke, 52, marriage, 53, dentist, 54, address to ladies of Centre Hill, 136-138, obituary, 141-143, funeral, 143-144; *Letters*: August 30, 1855, 51-52; March 12, 1859, 53-55; August 23, 1861, 139 -141
David, Pillina Charity (daughter of JHD and TBD). *See* Pillina David Bell
David, Pillina White (mother of JHD), xvii, xviii, 7, 10, 17, 19, 23, 35, 57-58
David, Pillona White (Lona) (daughter of JHD and TBD). *See* Pillona (Lona) David Alexander
David, Sarah B. (Sallie) (daughter of SBD), xi, 255, 257, 450, 545-547
David, Sarah Elizabeth (distant cousin), 244-246
David, Sarah H. (niece of JHD), 27-29
David, Simeon Bowen (Sim) (SBD, son of JHD and TBD), xi, xiii, xx, xxiii, 124, 125, 126, 127, 129, 159, 186, 196, 200, 203, 254, 285, 287-288, 514; Hall County boys, 8; school teaching, 2, 5-6, 10, 12, 17, 22, 25, 27, 30, 31; poem, 8-9; education, 6; ambition, 25; militia: 29, 35-36, 69; rejects invitation to be candidate of Temperance Party, 58; church, civic, and early political offices, 22, 23, 59, 60, 62, 93: daguerreotype made, 27, 29; marriage, 34-36, 50; birth of first daughter, 58-59; birth of second daughter, 67, 68; election to Georgia legislature, 69; service in Georgia legislature, 1859, 70-71, 1860, 94, 105-111; view on secession, 93-102; enlists in Confederate army, 118; in West Virginia,117-123; in Yorktown, 146; maybe in Second Manassas, 152; at Manassas Junction, 157-158; promoted captain, 179; recorder of court of inquiry, 232-234; births of other children, 232, 235; judge advocate, 236-239; death, 369-377. 381. 399. 406. 448-449; Fannie's letter about children, 544-548

Places lived, pre-Civil War: Woodstock, Cherokee County, 2-7, 9-20; Jackson County, 21; Freemansville, Cherokee County, 21-32, 34-36, 56-57; Vickery's Creek, Forsyth County, 58-71, 105; *Battles, participated in*: *See* Battles of, Seven Pines, Seven Days, Cedar Mountain, Harper's Ferry, Fredericksburg, Chancellorsville, Gettysburg, Wilderness; *Letters*: March 2, 1847, 2-7; February 18, 1850, 9-11; August 19-20, 1850, 12-15; November 6, 1850, 16-18; May 19, 1853, 21-24; July 8, 1853, 24-26; September 22, 1853, 26-29; December 1, 1853, 29-30; July 20, 1854, 30-32; February 8, 1855, 34-36; April 5, 1855, 56-58; April 29, 1856, 58-56; October 16, 1856, 61-63; November 25, 1856, 63-65; January 10, 1858, 66-68; June 14, 1860, 93-102; January 23, 1861, 105-113; August 9, 1861, 117-120; September 2, 1861, 120-123; December 24, 1861, 158-160; July, 1862, 149-151, 160-171; August 15, 1862, 171-178; December 5, 1862, 224-232; January 21, 1863, 234-235; March 12, 1863, 235-239; March 31, 1863, 246-247, 253; May 9, 1863, 261-273; May 25,

INDEX

1863, 276-278, 327; March 21, 1864, 367-369
David, Susan Moon (wife of OTD), xi, 86, 87, 125, 139, 140, 141, 158, 225, 234, 235; married O. T David, 53, married J. W. Collins, 144; *Letters*, March 12, 1859, 53-55; March 12, 1862, 143-144
David, Teressa Ann Amanda Ellison (wife of HJD), 506, 510, 525
David, Thirza Bowen (TBD, mother of main family), x, xi, xiii, xiv, xv-xvii, xviii, xix, xx-xxiii, 4, 6, 16, 19, 34, 37, 39, 44, 50, 55, 82, 83, 93, 123, 128, 129, 143, 145, 156, 178, 190, 216, 244, 255, 259-260, 268, 285, 293-295, 339, 341, 344, 369, 378, 386, 449-450, 510-511, 516, 523, 545; marriage, xi; children, xi; home fire, 240-247; trip to Horatio in hospital in Richmond, 278-292; learns of Simeon's death, 369; trip with Fannie, 404-407; biographical sketch, 405-407, 424, 516-518; obituary, 512; *Letters*: May 7, 1852, 20-21; September 1861, 125-127; May 4, 1862 190-192; May 28, 1863, 278-280; June 2, 1863, 281-282; June 4, 1863, 282-284; June 4 or 5, 1863, 284-285; June 6, 1863, 285-287; June 9, 1863, 287-288; June 16, 1863 (1), 288-290; June 16, 1863 (2), 290-291; June 17, 1863, 291-292; June 18, 1863, 292; June 1, 1864, 369-378
David, Thirza Ann (Annie) (daughter of JHD and TBD), xi, xxi, 3, 7, 17-18, 21-22, 25, 26-28, 32, 38-39, 44, 45, 49-50, 53-54, 66, 67-68, 84-85, 86, 125, 183, 244, 259-260, 338-339, 502, 511, 513, 514-516
David, Thirza Lena (daughter of SBD), 67-68, 235, 295, 450, 545-547
David, Virginia Frances (Jennie) (daughter of SBD), 232, 235, 450, 545-547
David, William (brother of JHD), 12, 66, 245-246

David, William H. (nephew of JHD), 129
Davis, Alice Doris, 547
Davis, Billy, 545
Davis, Bob, 545
Davis, Fannie Harris David. *See* Frances Harris David
Davis, J. B. S., 478
Davis, Jefferson, President, CSA, 325-326, 438, 446, 460, 473-474
Davis, Joseph R., Gen., 382
Davis, Mr. (from Polk County), 67-68
Davis, Van William (Fannie David's 2nd husband), 68, 544-548
Deadwyler, George E., 535-536
Decatur, GA, 342, 345, 415-416
Deep Bottom, First Battle of, 365, 420-422
Deer Creek Expedition, 304-305
Delany, Landrum, 67
DeLay, Russel, V., Lt., 408
Democratic Party, 62, 69-70, 94-102, 106, 107, 438, 481, 506
Demopolis, AL, 325-326, 342
Detroit, MI, 533
Deverel, Ann, 260
Deverel, John H., 249-250, 251, 363-365
Dial, Cyrus, 10-11, 16-20
Dial, William, 16-20
Dinsmore, Bill, 67
Dorsey, Todd, xxiii
Douglas, Stephen A., Sen., 93, 95-96, 98, 99, 101, 106
Dred Scott decision, 94, 97, 101-102
Drewry's Bluff, VA, 149, 160, 162
Dubose, Dudley M. Col., 421
Duncan, Dr., 78
Dunlap, Commissioner, 526-527
Durham Station, NC, 469
Dyer, Lt., 363
Dyse, Dyer, Dire, or Dise. *See* African Americans, enslaved
Early, Jubal A., Gen., 174-175, 368, 422-423, 425
East Tennessee Campaign, 343-347
Eaton, William, Dr., 52-53
Eaves, Jesse, Lt., 225

Eclectic Medical Institute of Cincinnati, 75-91
Editorial method, xxiii
Edwards, Margaret, *Letter*, 1879, 502-504
Edwards, Mrs., 74, 77-78
Edwards, William, 503-504
Elk Run Valley, VA, 194
Ellison, Arnold (William A.), 183, 185, 255-256
Ellison, (Ellersons), James, 44, 182, 185, 255-256, 505
Ellison, James, Jr., 504
Ellison, Teresa Ann Amanda. *See* Teresa David
Ellsworth, Annie, 226
Ellsworth, Nancy Goodrich, 226
Emancipation Proclamation, 156
Emanda. *See* African Americans, enslaved
Emmett, Daniel DeCatur, 90
Emory, Bold, 529
Enforcement Act of 1870, 529
Enslaved, *See* African Americans, enslaved
Enterprise, MS, 326
Epperson, John Ira, 502, 511
Epperson, Mary Juliette David Neal. *See* Mary David Neal
Epperson, William J., 515
Euger, Benjamin, Gen., 161, 167,
Ewell, Richard S., Gen., 173-174, 194, 372-375, 378, 380, 422
Execution, Confederate, 365-367
Fair Oaks, Battle of. *See* Seven Pines, Battle of
Fairfax Station, VA, 128, 130
Fairview, GA, 81
Falkner, SC, 132
Falling Waters, MD, 336
Falls, R. I., Major (Union), 171-172, 177-178
Fame's Temple, 224, 226
Farmer's Bank of Virginia, 160
Farmville, VA, 153
Faulkner, Peter, 459-460
Few, DeLaFayette, 17

Field, Charles W., Gen., 380-381, 398, 421
Field, Lawson, Capt., 22, 24, 27, 31
Field, Louisa (Lou), 27, 29, 30-31
Field, Richard Jackson (Jack), 30-31
Field schools, 6, 490
Fielder, James M., Lt. Col., 179
First Deep Bottom, Battle of. *See* Deep Bottom, First Battle of
Fischer, David Hackett, iv
Fisher's Gap, VA, 226
Fisher's Hill, VA, 423
Fitzpatrick, Benjamin, 101
Flat Lick, KY, 209
Florida, state of, 24, 42, 52, 106, 351, 515
Floyd, John B., Gen, 123
Folsom, Robert W., Lt. Col., 171, 176-178, 179, 228-229, 237, 385 (footnote)
Foote, Shelby, 298
Ford, Lewis D., Dr., 290-291
Forrest, Nathan Bedford, Gen., 298, 314
Fort Gaines, GA, 28-29, 49-50, 102-104, 292
Forts: Fisher, 456; McAllister, 230, Sumter, 119
Fowler, William A., 313
Fran (horse), 23
Frankfort, KY, 206-207, 213
Frayser's Farm Battle, *See* Glendale, Battle of
Fredericksburg, Battle of, 108, 221-222, 224-232, 233, 243, 255
Freeman. *See* Arican American, enslaved
Freeman, Edwin, Dr, 79-81.
Freeman, Henry, Dr., 38
Freemanville, GA, xx, 21, 29, 34, 244-245
Frog Town (Hightower), GA, 23, 64-65
Front Royal, VA, 423-425, 428, 507
Fry, Birkett D. Gen., 450-451, 463, 472
Fugitive Slave Law, 110
Fullilove, Henry M., 280
Furgurson, Hamp, 341
Gadsden, AL, 314, 444, 519
Gaines Farm, VA, 395-396

INDEX

Gaines, Jack and Lewis, 43
Gaines Mill, Battle of, 162, 164-166, 168-169, 220-221, 396, 401, 479
Gainesville, GA, 8, 11, 69, 132, 190, 198, 406-407, 526-527, 533, 535, 540
Gaither, Allie Comer, 314-315
Gaither, James C., 473
Galloway, Nathan L., Dr., 409
Galveston, TX, 128, 493
Gardner, W.M., Gen., 342
Garrard, Kenner D., Gen. (Union), 415
Garrison, N, Cpt., 178
Garrison, Herod Daily, Prof., 78-79, 81
George, Elizabeth Poole, 41
George, Ezekiel, 41
George, Mary Jane (Mrs. Tolly), *Letter*: April 17, 1853, 39-41
Georgia Artillery units: Montgomery, 547, Troup, 118
Georgia Cavalry units: 11th Cavalry, 465; 16th Battalion, 248
Georgia Confederate Pensions, 521-523, 547
Georgia Counties: Banks, 105, 111, 132, 181, 345, 480, 485, 506, 508, 512, 514, 517, 521, 527, 530-532, 533; Barrow, 138, 144, 437; Bartow (Cass), 19-20, 72-73, 225, 546; Bibb, 547; Campbell, 294; Carroll, 13, 15, 43; Cherokee, xiii, xx, 2, 4-5, 6, 7, 9, 11, 12, 14, 1618, 21, 24, 26, 29, 32, 36-37, 44, 46, 51, 57, 58, 60, 66, 69, 113, 182, 245, 406, 497, 499; Clarke, 278-280; Clay (Early), 29, 50,103; Cobb, 22, 27, 113. 189; Catoosa, 59; Floyd, 73, 123, 503-504; Forsyth, 14. 22. 24. 34. 36, 52, 58, 60, 61, 63, 65, 69-70, 94, 111-113, 118, 157, 225, 234, 247, 268, 300,, 370, 405, 407, 408, 450, 516-517; Franklin, xv-xvii, xix, xxi, 4, 36, 37-38, 40, 42, 46, 48, 65, 66, 193-194, 214, 219, 282, 354, 358, 483, 487, 490, 493, 497-498, 542, 549; Fulton, 14, 21, 113, 245, 378; Gordon, 31; Gwinnett 197, 422, 521; Habersham, 25, 72, 92; Hall, 8, 11, 60, 126, 131-135, 146, 181-182, 183, 184, 188, 189, 190, 198, 210, 214, 253, 314, 340, 341, 358, 405, 435, 460, 517, 542; Hancock, 445-446; Jackson, xiv-xv, xvii, xix-xx, xxii, 2, 11, 14, 16-17, 19, 21, 24, 29, 32, 33, 35-36, 38, 48, 54, 58, 61, 131, 134-136, 138, 141, 144, 181, 183, 185, 189, 196, 212, 250, 256, 262, 274, 282, 284, 294-295, 305. 357. 364. 402. 409, 410, 432, 437, 441, 448, 470, 478, 480, 481, 485, 500, 501, 505-506, 509, 513, 514, 516, 527, 528, 529, 530, 532, 533, 542; Jones, 128, 130; Lumpkin 17, 19; Milton, 105, 113, 244-245; Newton, 41-41; Oglethorpe, 131; Paulding, 544; Polk, 67-68, 73, 546-548; Pulaski, 537; Thomas, 52, 128, 216; Walton, 54-55; Washington, 445-446; Wayne, 134; White, 92, 344, 506
Georgia Infantry regiments and other infantry units: 9th Battalion 194, 199, 210, 221; 9th (state guards), 280; 11th, 429-430; 15th, 225; 18th, 161, 168-169, 391-392; 21st, 194, 220, 480; 24th, 129, 155, 277, 282, 365-367, 391-392, 400, 426-428; 25th, 199; 29th, 194, 220, 354, 417, 419, 456; 35th, 164, 172, 232-234; 38th, 123, 126, 153-154, 168, 191, 198-199, 235, 242, 245, 377-378, 390-392, 422; 39th, 192-193; 40th, 296, 311 (footnote); 41st, 296; 42nd, 296, 326, 352-353, 409; 45th, 253, 331-332; 52[nd,] 296, 362, 456, 462, 471; 1st Partisan Rangers, 248; *David Family regiments*: 14th Georgia (Simeon), 28-29, 118, 119-120, 123, 126, 152, 157, 159-156, 159-160, 179, 237-239, 367-369, 403, *See also*: Battles of: Crampton's Gap, Seven Pines, Seven Days, Cedar Mountain, Fredericksburg, Chancellorsville, Wilderness; 16th Georgia (Horatio), 100, 120, 136-138, 139-142, 149, 151-

152, 169, 186, 236, 249-252, 253-254, 255-260, 337, 363-365, 516, 521-522; *See also*: Battles of: Dam No. 1, Malvern Hill, Crampton's Gap, Fredericksburg, Wilderness, Spotsylvania, North Anna, Cold Harbor, Petersburg, First Deep Bottom, Guard Hill; 43rd Georgia (Manning Alexander), 181-183, 213, 214, 215, 218, 221-222, 256, 329, 342-345, 362, 408-413; *See also*: Kentucky Campaign, Vicksburg Campaign, Chattanooga Campaign

Georgia Legions: Cobb's, 221, 348, 426; Phillip's, 458, 468-469; Wright's, 196

Georgia legislature: 1859 Session, xx, 69-71, 94, 105; 1860 Session, xx, 70, 71, 94, 105, 106-111

Georgia Military Institute, 182

Georgia Militia, xv, xvii, 29, 35-36, 36, 69, 132-133, 172, 178, 236, 362, 440-441

Georgia, Ordinance of Secession, 104-105, 111-113

Georgia State troops, 134-135

Gettysburg, Battle of: 288, 327-333, 337

Gettysburg, retreat of wounded from: 333-337

Gillespie, Jame L. 345

Gillsville (Stonethrow), GA, 181

Girardy, Victor J. B., Gen., 439

Glasgow, KY. 206,

Glendale, Battle of: 162, 167

Gober, Frances, 56-57

Gober, Robert H., 13, 24, 27-28, 56-57

Gold fields and mines, 4, 14, 16-18, 20, 59, 60, 111, 297

Goldsboro, NC. 186

Goodno, William G., 321

Gordon, A. C., Capt., 127

Gordon, John B., Gen. and Gov., 422, 521

Gordonsville, VA, 171-172, 226, 371-372, 379, 428

Graining Mill explosion, 439

Grand Gulf, MS, 307

Grand Junction, TN, 297

Grange, the, 507-509

Grant, Ulysses S., Gen. (Union), 185-186, 278, 366, 418-419, 439-441, 469, *See also*: Vicksburg Campaign, Chattanooga Campaign, Overland Campaign, Battle of Petersburg, Battle of First Deep Bottom

Gray, R.H., Lt. Col., 232

Grayson County, TX, 487

Green, E. H., 529, 532

Greencastle, PA, 335

Greeneville, TN, 366

Greensboro, GA, xv, 414-415, 417, 450-451, 460-463

Greenville, MS, 304

Greenville, SC, 41

Gresham, Rev. Joseph, 22

Grierson, Benjamin H., Col. (Union), 301-303

Gronto, Lydia Ella Epperson, 515

Guard Hill, Battle of: 422-429, 441

Guinea's Station, VA, 276, 327

Gunning or Gunion, William T., 366-367

Hagen, Billy, 544-546

Hagen, Newton, 544

Hagerstown, MD, 155

Hale, Hope Hull, 533

Hall County boys: *Letter*: November 1848, 8

Hall, George Washington, Pvt., 329-332

Halleck, Henry Wager, Gen. (Union), 173

Hamburg, SC, 280

Hamilton's Crossing, VA, 254-255, 261-262

Hammond, Mrs., 22

Hampton, Wade, Gen., 169, 467

Hanover Junction, 394

Harben, T. B., Rev., 131, 134-135

Hardee, William J., Gen., 355-356, 441, 458

Hardigree, D. G., 365

Hardman, L. G, Dr., 507

Hargrett Library, University of Georgia, xxii, 405, 422

INDEX

Harkinson's Ferry, MS, 307
Harkrep, Molly, 44
Harmony Grove, GA, 466, 480, 496
Harp, William, 128
Harper's Ferry, Battle of, 154-155, 179, 210, 225
Harper's Ferry, John Brown and, 70-71
Harral, Ansel, 68
Harral, Newton, 67
Harriet. *See* African Americans, enslaved
Harris, Archibald (Fannie's uncle), 35
Harris, Ezekiel (Fannie's uncle), 449
Harris, Francis (Fannie), *See* Fannie Harris David
Harris, Gilford (Fannie's cousin), 449
Harris, James (Fannie's uncle), , 35, 67-68
Harris, James Alpheus Skidmore, Col., 195, 196, 198, 311
Harris, Leroy ("old sot"), 22
Harris, Lorenzo Dow (Fannie's father), 27, 29, 35-36, 58, 121, 405-406, 423
Harris, Mary E. (Fannie's sister), 35-36, 62
Harris, Mat (Fannie's cousin), 449
Harris, Willson (Fannie's brother), 67068
Harrisburg, PA, 154
Harrison, George P., Gen., 134
Harrisonburg, VA, 367-368
Harrodsburg, KY, 207-208, 213
Hart, Charles Thomas, Prof., 78, 80, 88, 89
Harwell, Columbus, 281-282
Hawall, E. and his son, 16
Hawkins, Frederick Marshall, Rev., 36
Hellen (supposed correspondent with James Neal), 253
Henderson, John, 213
Henderson, Minta, 153
Henderson, Robert J., Col., 352-353
Henderson, Tom, 145, 152, 185, 196
Hendrix, Mr., 354, 355
Henry. *See* African Americans, enslaved
Henry City, AL, 127, 142
Henshall, J. G., Dr., 75, 81
Henshall, Duncan, Dr, 78, 81
Hero, 148-149

Heth, Henry, Gen., 201-212, 264-265, 329, 373-376
Hickory Flat, GA, 5, 12, 14, 242, 244-245
Higgins, E. A., Capt., 276-277
High Shoals, GA, 544
Highsmith, Nancy O., 341
Highsmith, Sarah, 339-341; *Letter*: January 17, 1864. 340
Hightower Baptist Association, 23
Hightower, GA, 23, 65
Hilburn, John, 545
Hill, Ambrose Powell, Jr. (A.P.), Gen., 162-168, 171-178. 226, 232, 233, 261, 264, 267-268, 288, 328-329, 330, 372-377, 380, 385 (footnote)
Hill, Daniel Harvey (D.H.), Gen., 163, 165-166, 261, 267, 457-458
Hitchcock, Jo, 546
Hogan, Manda, 240
Hoke, Robert F., General, 396-399
Holland, D. D., 543
Hollingsworth, Miss, 361
Holly Springs, MS, 298, 303
Homer, GA, 480, 506, 542
Hood, John Bell, Gen., 168, 416, 439-441, 444, 459
Hook, David, 28
Hook, Jacob Dr., 28-29, 56-57
Hook, Lewis, 244
Hook, Sarah, 28
Hooker, Joseph, Gen. (Union), 232, 261-269, 352-353
Hopkins County, TX, 482, 484
Horton, Hosea, 16-17, 20
Horton, Mrs. 184
Hoschton, GA, 138
Hospitals: Atlanta Receiving & Distribution, 359, Blackie (Augusta), 431-435, 444, 448, 451-461, 464-467, 470-472, 542; Blackie (Greensboro), 461-464, Blackie (Madison) 360-362, 410-414, 415, 417, 432, 443, 462; Blackie and Winship (Atlanta), 412-413; Chimborazo, 148, 282; General Hospital No. 4, 337, 425, 428; General Hospital No. 9, 377;

General Hospital No. 10, 274-276, 278-288; McLaw's Division's, 151-152; Stout, 414-415; Third Georgia, 453
Hot Springs, AK, 128
Howard, Nicholas F., Dr., 455-457, 462, 470
Howard, Wiley C., 500
Hoyt, H. F., Rev., 509, 540-541
Huguenots, xvii
Hunt County, TX, 489
Hunter, Henry: 499, *Letter*, November 15, 1871, 499

Hunter, S.G., 142
Huntersville, VA (now WV), 117-118, 120-121, 126, 157-158
Hurricane Shoals, GA, 13, 15
Hutchens, Drury, Rev., 59-60
Illinois, state of, 81-82, 200, 311
Imboden, John D., Gen., 333-336
Indiana, state of, 81, 538
Indians: general, xv-xvii, 3, 74, 77, 397, 487, 516, 536; Cherokees, xiv-xvi, xx, 4; Creeks xiv-xvi, 4-5; Red man, 3, Seminoles, 24
Inst, defined, 28
International Cotton Exposition, 531, 536
Iowa, state of, 78
Irwinville, GA, 474
Jackson, MS, 297, 302-303, 307-310
Jackson, Andrew, Pres., x, 24
Jackson, Lily Alexander, *See* Lily Alexander
Jackson, Thomas Jonathan ("Stonewall"), Gen., 152, 154-155, 163-168, 171-178, 193-194, 197, 226-229, 238, 261-264, 267, 268, 320, 398-399
Janis. *See* African Americans, enslaved
Jarrett, D. L., Capt, 169.
Jefferson, GA, 47-48, 58, 59, 61, 284, 481, 482
Jefferson, TX, 483, 486
Jenkins, Shepherd, 64
John. *See* African Americans, enslaved
Johnson, Andrew, Pres., 469

Johnson County, TX, 485, 487, 492-493
Johnson, Herschel Vespasian, Sen. and Gov., 98-99, 106
Johnson, Walter C., 429-430; *Letter*: November 19, 1864, 429
Johnston, John Cpt., 455-456
Johnston, Joseph Eggleston, Gen., 159, 162, 163, 308, 321-322, 326, 356, 411, 416, 439-441, 444, 469, 472
Johnston, Joseph W., 31
Jones, Amanda Bowen, x, 13, 15, 29, 33-34, 49-51, 103, 294-295, 523-524; *Letters*: April 22, 1855, 49-51; June 21, 1863, 292-293
Jones, James, 44
Jones, John H., 15, 29, 49-51, 102-104, 129, 142-143, 292-295, 523-524; *Letters*: April 22, 1856, 49-51; November 15, 1860, 102-104; June 21, 1863, 292-295
Jones, John ("Pony"), 103-104, 294-295
Jones, Lorenzo Elbridge, 80
Jones, Malachi III, xv
Jones, Malachi IV, xvi, xviii
Jones, S. H., 51-52
Jones, Thirza Linna, 295
Joshua. *See* African Americans, enslaved
Juddy. *See* African Americans, enslaved
Kane, Francis, Mr., 59-60
Kane, Mrs., 59-60
Kansas-Nebraska Act, 97
Kansas Territory, 97
Keit, Lawrence M., General, 396
Kellogg, Freeman, 236
Kellogg, George, 236
Kellogg, Henry C., Maj., 196-198
Kelly, George, 265
Kelly, James C., xiv
Kelly, Pastor, 143
Kelogg, Misses, 27
Kennesaw, GA. *See* Big Shanty
Kentucky campaign, 195-213
Kilpatrick, Judson, Gen. (Union), 467
Kilpatrick, William H., 113
Kimsey, J. J., Rev., 540
Kindrie, Rev. Mr. 413
King, R. M., 428

INDEX

Kingsville, SC, 279-280
Kirtland, OH, 26
Knights Templar, 512
Knoxville, TN, 41, 185-186, 196-198, 200, 203-204, 209, 211-212, 277, 344, 346-348, 350, 351, 355-356, 363-364, 366, 533
Ku Klux Klan, 526-532
La Grange, TN, 302
Lake Altoona, GA, 499
Lancaster, KY, 208
Landerman, Stacy, 529
Lane, James Henry, Gen., 261
Latner, Mr., family of, 188
Latter Day Saints, 26
Lattne, 213
Lattner, Joseph Travis, Dr, 81.
Law, Evander, General, 398-399
Lawrenceburg, KY, 207-208
Lawton, A. R., Gen., 168
Leadbetter, Danville, Gen., 192
Lee's Mill, Battle of, *See* Dam No. 1, Battle of
Lee, Robert E., Gen., 159, 172, 173, 182, 233 236-238, 255, 263, 277-278, 283, 288, 293, 327-328, 333-338, 368, 371. 401-402, 415, 441, 459-460, 465, 467, 469; *See also*, Battles of: Seven Days, South Mountain, Fredericksburg, Chancellorsville, Gettysburg, Overland Campaign, Petersburg, First Deep Bottom
Leesburg, TX, 486-497
Lenoir Station (Lenoir City), TN, 209-214
Lester, Mrs, 27, 28-29
Lester, Richard Paul, 28, 118, 179, 236-239, 385 (footnote)
Lester Volunteers, 29, 118; *See also* 14th Georgia Volunteer Infantry Regiment
Letters, general, vii-viii
Levy County, FL, 515
Lewis, Elisha Berry, 219, 221
Lewis, James W., 219, 221, 344, 347
Lewis, Martha Poole (Manning's aunt), 221, 347

Lewis, Sam, 344, 347
Lexington, GA, 131
Lexington, KY, 202, 204-206, 211
Lexington, VA, 423
Lightfoot (horse), 23
Lincoln, Abraham, Pres., 71, 104, 106, 107, 110, 119, 156, 173, 200, 360, 386, 438, 469
Linderman, Stacy, 526
Lindsey, John Green, 2, 7, 128, 130, 216-217
Little (Litle), F. W., Dr,, 188-189
Logan, J. P., Dr., 431, 457-459, 462
Loggans (Loggins), Amanda M., Mrs., 199
Loggans (Loggins), Samuel T., 199
London, KY, 208-209
Longstreet, James, Gen., 163-167, 227, 229-230, 330, 332, 347-348, 349-350, 355-356, 363-364, 366, 371, 379-388, 423
Lookout Mountain, TN, 346, 349-350, 352
Looney, George C., 43, 487; *Letter:* December 8, 1854, 42-43
Looney, Morgan H., 42, 43, 487
Loring, William, Gen., 408-409
Loudon, TN, 346-347
Louisiana, state of: 129, 303, 305, 324, 498
Louisiana, Battalion, 163-164, 167
Louisville, KY, 89, 206-207, 533
Lucky, T.S., 33-34
Lumpkin, Judge's sons, 118
Lyle, Dilmus Reid, 401-402, 403
Lyle, D.R., Mrs, 136
Lyle, J.E., 275
Lyle, James M., 502, 514
Lynchburg, VA, 117
Lyon, Nathan, Gen. (Union), 129
Macon Committee, 93, 96-102, 120
Macon, GA, 96, 104, 283, 432, 433, 439-440, 515, 541
Madison, GA, 25, 358-362, 408, 411-417, 432-434, 442-443, 455-456, 463, 490
Madison, VA, 226

595

Magruder, John Bankhead, Gen., 146-147, 150, 161, 167
Mahone, William, Gen., 382, 387
Malvern Hill, Battle of: 149-151, 162, 167-168, 365
Manassas, Battles of: First Manassas, 127, 129, 131; Second Manassas 129, 151-152, 169, 179, 225, 238, 398-399
Manassas Junction, VA, 157-160, 179, 236
Manchester, TN, 214-215, 296
Marietta, GA, 60, 182, 243, 245, 354
Marlin Bottom, VA (now WV), 120
Marlin, Lloyd G., 14
Marthasville, GA. *See* Atlanta
Martin (Simeon's hired man), 105
Martinsburg, WV, 336
Marye's Heights, 229-231, 398-399
Mashburn, Mrs., 196
Mashburn, Rev., 196, 197
Masons, 58, 138, 338
Massanutten Mountains, 226, 425
Mayfield, Thomas W., 59
Maysville, GA, xiv, xxiii, 4, 14-15, 21, 23, 28, 37, 39, 43-48, 51-52, 82-83, 85-87, 92, 125-127, 138, 181, 405-406, 429, 466, 479-480, 504, 506-510, 516-518, 522-525, 526, 527, 528, 530, 532-540, 542-543
McAfee, Joseph John Miller, 6
McAfee, Joseph M., Sgt., 337, 369-371, 377
McAfee, Julia, 2, 6
McAfee, Mrs, 2, 6
McClellan, George Brinton, Gen. (Union), 122. 145-146, 149-150, 154-156, 162-165, 173, 227, 438
McClernand, John Alexander, Gen. (Union), 307
McClintic, John, 124,
McClosky, Capt., 161, 168
McCulloch, Levi, 161, 168
McCullough, Ben, Gen. (Union), 129
McDonald, David L., Adm, 525.
McDonald, Mary David. *See* Mary David
McDonald, William Benjamin, Rev, 524.

McGlauglin, 121
McKennally, Palmer, Capt., 258
McLaws, Lafayette, Gen., 151, 152, 155, 229-231, 236, 263-264, 268, 271, 274-275, 387
McMillan Station, TN, 195-197
McMinn County, TN, 92
McRae, J.H.D., Capt. 273, 364
McRae, William, Lt. Col., 156
Meade, George, General (Union), 371
Mechanicsville (Beaver Dam Creek), Battle of: 162-164, 379
Memphis, TN, 297-298, 303
Mercer University, 537
Meridian, MS, 297, 302-303, 325-326
Millboro, VA, 158
Milledgeville, GA, 93-94, 104, 106, 132-133, 134, 229
Miller, Ange, 44
Miller, John D., 204, 210
Miller, Mr. 44
Millican, John, 256
Millican, William T., Maj., 35
Millwee, John, 73, 343, 345, 348, 357
Millwee, Mary, 73, 345
Minie Ball (bullet), 319, 369, 377
Mintz, Mrs., 82
Mintz, Michael M., Capt., 134-135
Missionary Ridge, Battle of, 346, 350-353, 362
Mississippi, state of, 92, 106, 200, 278, 294, 296-326, 392, 417, 459, 460, 474, 498; *See also*: Vicksburg Campaign
Missouri, state of, 101, 129, 200
Missouri Compromise, 97
Mitchell's Station, VA, 423
Mobile, AL, 18, 297, 313, 326, 466-467, 481, 483
Monroe, GA, 53-55. 89-91, 138
Monterey, VA, 117
Montgomery, AL, 18, 297, 483, 493
Moon, George M. (SMD's brother), 144
Moon, Robert (SMD's father), 54
Moon Robert B. (Bob, "Tobe,") (SMD's brother), 54, 144

INDEX

Moon, Susan (SMD). *See* Susan Moon David
Moore, Andrew P., 313
Moore, Samuel Preston, Dr., 464
Morgan, Blake, 284
Morgan, George Washington, Gen. (Union), 204
Morgan, Mrs. William, 283-285
Morris, 213
Morris, John F., Lt. (subject of court of inquiry) 232-234
Morris, Lt. (quartermaster of 43rd GA), 362
Morse, Samuel F. B., 226
Mount Sterling, KY, 206
Mount Vernon, KY, 208
Mulberry, GA, 143-144, 437-438
Murfreesboro (Stones River), Battle of, 222-223
Nashville, TN, 89, 215, 296
Neal, Ann Olivia (daughter of MDN): xi, 221, 26, 30-31, 58, 64, 242-245, 250-252, 378, 502, 511, 513, 514, 515; *Letter*: March 24, 1863, 244-245
Neal, Hiram Rienza (son of MDN), 511
Neal, J. M., 526
Neal, James (son of MDN), xi 30-31, 57, 65, 93, 125-126, 152, 153, 161, 168, 190-191, 196, 198-199, 217-218, 221-222, 225, 234-235, 243, 245 250, 262, 276, 281, 285, 370, 377-378, 390, 419, 422, 424, 460, 516; joined army, 125-126, wounded, 377-378; *Letters*: March 28, 1863, 252-253; April 6, 1863, 254-255
Neal, Jesse Horatio (son of MDN), xi, 15, 57, 93, 191, 244-245, 370, 378
Neal, John W (son of MDN), xi, 26, 30-31, 57, 121, 123, 125-126, 132, 181, 183, 241, 241, 242, 244-245, 370, 378, 448-449, 515, 516
Neal, Mary David (MDN), xi, xiii, xx, 2, 6, 10, 13, 15, 21, 23-24, 25-28, 31-32, 57-58, 61-62, 64, 93, 105, 125-126, 132, 140, 180, 183, 191, 234, 235, 251, 281, 370, 377, 378, 400, 449-450, 469, 501-502, 519-520, 546; death of first husband, 20-21, married second husband, John Ira Epperson, 502; *Letters*: April 6, 1857, 65-66; March 22, 25, 27, 1863, 242-244, 244-246; August 27, 1876, 501-502; October 31, 1882, 514-515; August 1883, 510-511; December 10, 1884, 515-516
Neal, Richard (first husband of MDN), xi, xx, 6, 15, 21, 23, 24, 28, 57, 511; death, 20-21,
Negroes: *See* African Americans, enslaved; African Americans, free
New Hope Church, GA, 378
New Market, VA, 226
New Market Heights, VA, 42-421
New Orleans, LA, 278, 297, 483
New York, NY, 85, 100, 166, 386, 394, 532, 533
Newton, Elizur, Col., 64
Newton, John H., 118, 292, 409
Newton, John H.'s son, 118, 292,
Newton, Robert Stafford, Prof., 78, 80
Nicholas County, VA (now WV), 123
Nightriders. *See* Klu Klux Klan
North Anna, Battle of: 378-379, 388, 394-395, 396
North Carolina, state of, xxii, 147, 156, 186, 230, 233, 261, 264, 267, 351, 368, 417, 446, 456, 463, 465, 466-477, 469, 474
North Georgia, xiv, xvi, 345, 500, 529
Nyle, Mrs., 442
O'Kelly, Mamie. *See* Mamie Alexander
O'Kelly, Thomas Washington, Rev., 537
Oak Grove, Battle of, 162
Oath of Allegiance, 447
Oath, Reconstruction, 478-479, 505
Oconee County Fair, 506
Ohio, state of, 26, 55, 75-76, 206, 407, 542
Olson, Elizabeth, 477
Opelika, AL, 18
Orange Courthouse, VA, 173, 225, 367
Oregon, state of, 99

597

Orphans' Home of the North Georgia Conference of the Methodist Episcopal Church, South, 500
Orr, Esq., 65
Ould, R.O., 342
Overby, Basil H., 57, 58
Overland Campaign, *See* Battles of, Wilderness, Spotsylvania, North Anna, Cold Harbor
Oxford, AL, 217, 218, 519, 520
Palmer, W. J., Gen. (Union), 473-474
Palmetto Academy, 43
Palmetto, GA, 43
Panama, 18-19
Panola County, TX, 128
Parks, Maison, 445
Parks, W. Fletcher, Capt., 282
Parks, William, Rev., 282
Patman, M.A., 142
Patterson, Josiah Blair, 112, 157, 158, 159, 179, 237-239, 247; *Letter*: December 12, 1861, 157
Paxton, H., Lt., 157
Peek, Soloman, 61
Peeler, William, 321
Pemberton, John Clifford, Gen., 296, 298, 392, 307-309, 312, 314, 315-316, 321-326
Pender, William Dorsey, Gen., 261, 264, 267-268, 328-330, 333, 334, 373
Pennsylvania, 1st Pennsylvania Cavalry, 177-178
Pentecost, Matthew, Sgt., 428
Perryville, Battle of, 207-208
Petersburg, Battle of, 400-403, 418-423, 435, 440-441, 465
Petersburg, VA,, 279-280, 400-403, 418, 420-423, 435, 440, 441, 465
Pfanz, Donald, xxii, 379
Phidelta, GA, 44
Philadelphia, PA, 154
Philadelphia, TN, 346
Pickett's Charge, 333
Pickett's Mill, GA, 378
Pine Hill, TX, 128
Pitchford, Henry P., Rev., 59
Pitchford, Lewis, 341

Pleasant Hill, GA, 45
Pocahontas County, VA (now WV), 117-118
Pocotaligo, SC, 254
Poems: "Forget me not," 44-45; Simeon's own, 8-9; "Soldier's Dream" 161, 169-171; "The Temple of Fame: A Vision," 225-226
Polksville, GA, 131, 210, 340, 341
Poole, Adam (brother of Mannng's mother), 184, 186, 196, 197
Poole, Manning (Manning's grandfather), 40
Poole, Mary (Manning's grandmother), 41
Poole, William H. (Uncle Billy) (Manning's mother's brother), 40, 41
Poorhouse, Battle of, 433
Pope, Alexander, 226
Pope, John, Gen. (Union), 171, 172-173
Poplar Spring Church, VA, 440, 441
Port Gibson, MS, 307-308
Port Hudson, LA, 278, 297
Port Royal Sound, SC, 129
Porter, R.L., Rev., 525
Prater, Josiah, Lt., 434, 435
Presbyterian, xv, 40, 197, 453-454. 496, 509, 540
Price, Felix, Col., 176 (footnote), 179
Price, Sterling, Gen. (Union), 129
Provisional Army of the Confederate States, 179, 195, 435, 451-452, 472
Pulliam family, farm of, 387
Pulliam, Helen Comer, xxii
Pulliam, Joseph, 497-498
Pulliam, Thomas, 497-498
Pulliam, William, 497-498
Raccoon Creek, GA, 544
Randolph County, AL, 219
Randolph, George Wythe, Sec. of War, CSA, 195
Randolph, Sue, 47
Raymond, MS, 308
Reavis, John Posey, 22, 24, 25, 27, 28, 56, 57, 67
Reconstruction Act, First, 479
Reconstruction Act, Second, 479

INDEX

Reconstruction Oath, 478-479, 505
Red House Ford, GA, 353
Redbone Church, MS, 307
Red River, 481-483, 498
Reed, Mr., 9-10
Reid (Reed), William P., Rev., 38, 48, 143, 181,183
Reilly Springs, TX, 484
Republican Party, Georgia, 530
Republican Party, national, 107, 136, 386, 530
Resaca, GA, 354
Reynolds, A. W., Col. (Union), 197, 201-202, 205
Reynolds, Abner M., Capt., 138, 155, 169, 250, 275
Rich, William Wofford, Lt. Col., 458
Richard, Sue, Miss, 424-425
Richmond, KY, Battle of, 204-205
Richmond, VA, convention in 95-96, letter writer in, 117, 120, 126, 127, 139-142, 146, 148-149, 161, 169, 171, 210, 235, 273, 274-288, 328, 336-337, 377, 422, 424, 425, 428, 429-430, 517
Rieves (Rives), John F., Cpt., 196, 214-215, 435
Ringgold, GA, 349, 351, 353, 449, 450
Roach, E.J. Dr, 471-472
Robertson, James A., Jr., 166
Robertsville, SC, 459
Robinson, A.N., 402-403,
Robinson, N. A., 401-402
Rockingham County, VA, 368
Rockmart, GA, 544-547
Rodes, Robert E., Gen., 267
Rogers Gap, 199, 202
Rogers, Mr., 340
Rogers, M. Louise, 170
Rogers, William, 59, 62, 63
Rogers, William Edward, 179
Rogersville, TN, 364, 366
Rome, GA, 63, 73, 307, 314, 503, 544
Rosecranz, William S., Gen. (Union), 121-123
Rossville Gap, 352-353
Roswell, GA, 13, 243, 245, 406-407

Rusk County, TX, 128
Russelville, TN, 363
Sacred Heart, The, 142
Sanders, Berry. *See* African Americans, free
Sanders, C.C., Lt. Col., 155
Sanders, Elizabeth (Lizzie), 184, 185
Sanders, Jerry, 184, 185
Sandersville, GA, 445, 446
Sandy Creek, GA, 453, 466
Savage's Station, Battle of, 162, 167
Savall, Emma (Emma Henderson). *See* African Americans, free
Savall (Savale), Isaiah, 468, 470
Savall, Mary A., 501
Savall, Rhoda. *See* African Americans, free
Savall (Savale), William, 468, 470, 501
Savanah, GA, 111, 127, 129, 134-135, 190-191, 236, 239, 354, 454, 458, 459, 460, 467, 542
Screven, GA, 134
Secessionists, 96, 105, 106, 111, 112, 157
Seidel, Charles B., Col. (Union), 407
Selman, Lt. *See* Lt. Sillman
Seminary Ridge, 329-333
Seven Days, Battles of, 149, 150-151, 162-164, 169, 173, 198-199, 218, 220, 270, 396, *See also*: Battles of, Oak Grove, Mechanicsville, Gaines Mill, Savage's Station, Glendale, Malvern Hill
Seven Pines (Fair Oaks), Battle of, 162, 169, 287, 288, 293
Seward, William H., 469
Sewell, Lou E. *See* Lou Sewell Alexander
Shanghai (Cochin) chickens, 46, 47
Shankle, Thomas S., Lt., 410
Sharpsburg, Battle of. *See* Antietam, Battle of
Shenandoah Valley, VA, 122-123, 163, 172-173, 194, 327, 337, 368-369, 373, 394, 421, 423, 424, 425-428
Shepherdstown Battle, *See* Antietam, Battle of
Sherman, William Tecumseh, Gen. (Union), 297-299, 303, 378, 415, 422,

437-441, 442-443, 445-446, 453-454, 458-461, 463-465, 466-467, 469, 472, 542
Shiloh, Battle of, 185
Shoals Creek, GA, xvii
Shreveport, LA, 483
Sillman, J. B. (Selman), Lt., 168-169
Simmons, Lavinia Bowen, x
Simon. *See* African Americans, enslaved
Simpson, Cornelia, 546
Simpson County, MS, 325
Sisson, Adaline, 10, 12, 18
Sisson, Elizabeth, 189
Sisson, John, 189-190
Sisson, Pillona, 17, 18
Sister's Ferry, GA, 460
Skyline Drive, VA, 226
Slaughter's Mountain, Battle of, *See* Cedar Run, Battle of
Slaves. *See* African Americans, enslaved
Slocum, Henry, Gen. (Union), 460
Smith County, MS, 324-325
Smith, Edmund Kirby, Gen., 182, 197, 199, 201-209, 296
Smith, Gustavus W., Gen., 169
Smith, Joseph, 26
Smith County, MS, 324-325
Social Circle, GA, 88-91
Songs, hymns, and other music: "Bonny Blue Flag," 392; "Dance Boatman Dance" ("Sailing Down the River on the Ohio"), 89-90; "Dixie," 90, 392; "Home Sweet Home," 392; "How sweet it will be in the beautiful land," 541; "I'm a Pilgrim" ("I can tarry but a night"), 67-68; "Nearer My God to Thee," 392; "New Harmony" ("I want to live a Christian here"), 142; "Star Spangled Banner," 392; "The Dead March," 392; "When shall we meet again," 187-188
South Carolina regiments: 6th Infantry Regiment (Revolutionary War), xv; 1st Regiment of Rifles, 220; Palmetto Regiment of Sharpshooters, 348
South Mountain, Battle of, 154-156, *See also* Crampton's Gap, Battle of
Sparta, GA, 445-446
Spartanburg, SC, xv-xvi
Spears & Hight, Druggists, 213

Speedwell, TN, 202
Speer, Emory, 529-530
Spencer, Col. (Union), 467
Spotsylvania, Battle of, 268, 378-379, 388-394, 395, 422,
Spotsylvania County, VA, 257
Springfield, MO, Battle of, 128-129
Stafford's Pond, FL, 501
Stark, Washington Franklin, 512
Starrsville Academy, 41-42
Starrsville, GA, 41-42
Staunton, VA, 117-118, 194, 224, 336-337, 423
Steele, H. L., 72; *Letter*, April 19, 1858, 72
Stephens, Alexander Hamilton, Vice Pres., CSA, 42, 97-98, 109-111, 487
Stevenson, AL. 192-193
Stevenson, Carter Littlepage, Gen., 197-198, 199, 201-202, 204, 206, 208, 210, 296, 309, 312, 314, 316, 324-326, 342, 346-347, 351
Stewart, Alexander P., Gen., 351
Stiles, B. Edward, Lt. Col., 364, 385, 427
Stokes, Sylvanus, 92
Stone, John M., Col., 382
Stoneman, George, Jr., Gen. (Union), 433, 437
Story, Joseph M., Capt., 180, 182, 197
Stout, Samuel H., Medical Director, 411, 412, 415
Stovall, Lewis, Pvt. 321
Stovall, Marcellus Augustus, Gen., 351-352, 362
Strasburg, VA, 423
Strawberry Plains, TN, 365-366
Strawberry Plains, VA, 365-366
Street family, George S. (Father), Mary (Mother), Metilda (Daughter), Mary (Daughter), Benjamin F. (Son), 22, 24
Streetman, Lovel, 529
Strickland, Hardy, Jr., 105, 111-113
Strickland, Madison, 50
Stuart, J.E.B., Gen., 264-266, 268, 458
Sulphur Springs, TX, 484-484
Sweetwater, TN, 347-348
Taliaferro, William B., Gen., 174-176
Talladega County, AL, 520
Tax in Kind, 368, 369
Taylorsville, GA, 546, 547
Tazewell, TN, Battle of, 201-202

INDEX

Temperance movement: 6-7, 22, 24, 509, 512
Temperance, Order of the Sons of, 15
Temperance Party, 57, 58
Tennessee, state of, 81, 98, 197-198, 203, 206, 208-209, 210, 248, 278, 296-298, 300, 302-303, 324, 325, 347, 363-364, 365, 371, 440, 444, 473
Tensaw Wharf, AL, 297
Texas, state of, 6, 32, 42, 81, 128-129, 168, 480-499, 504
Thomas, E. B., Capt., 277
Thomas, Edward L., Gen., 152, 171-172, 175, 178, 227-229, 232, 263-264, 328-332, 368-369, 373-377, 386
Thomas, Henry P., Lt. Col., 277, 364
Thomasville, GA, 52
Thompson, Cpt., 15
Thompson, Clark, 8
Thompson, H. J., 8
Thompson (Tomson), James R., Corp., 377, 448-449, 450
Thompson (Thomson, Thomas), Jo, 180, 258
Thompson, Obe, 8
Thompson, W. R.
Thrasher, Early W., 361, 413-414
Tillman County, OK, 547
Tolly, George Frederick, 41
Tompkinsville, KY, 205-206
Toombs, Robert Augustus, 97, 100-102, 108-109
Tories, 34-341
Trower, Joshua, 17
Tucker, Lewis, 61
Tunnel Hill, GA, 349, 351
Tunnel Hill, SC, 72
Turk, Billy Mrs., 188
Underwood, Joseph, Dr., 25-26, 32
Underwood, Mary Lou, 30, 32
Underwood, M.C., 31
Union Cavalry Regiments: 3rd Ohio,, 407; 15th Pennsylvania, 473
Union County, TN, 198
Union Mills, VA, 128
Union Point, GA, 90-91, 289-290, 358, 360, 415, 417, 463
United Confederate Veterans, 541, 542-543
United Daughters of the Confederacy, 405, 516-518

United States Congress, 481, 530
United States Constitution, 97, 98, 99, 100-102, 104-105, 106-111, 478
Upshur County, TX, 483, 486-487
Upton, Emory, Gen. (Union), 472
Van Dyke, Henry Merinus, Dr., 300. 304, 310, 312-313, 317
Van Dorn, Earl, Gen., 298
Venable, John Moreman, Capt., 249-250, 257, 259, 275, 365, *Letter:* May 18, 1863, 275
Versailles, KY, 207
Vickery's Creek (Vickery's Crossing), GA, 59, 63-64, 105, 234, 406-407
Vicksburg Campaign, 215, 222, 254-255, 286-287, 293, 296-297, 300-303; early Union attempts, 297-305; Union movements toward Vicksburg from the south, 305-308, siege, 278, 286-287, 314–322; surrender, 322-324, 334; march from, 324-326; *See also*: Battles of: Chickasaw Bayou, 297-300, 303, Deer Creek Expedition, 304-305, Champion Hill, 306-314
Virginia infantry regiments: 12th Virginia, 387
Virginia, Restored Government of, 122
Waco, TX, 487
Wadsworth, James S., Gen. (Union), 376, 379, 380-381, 384, 386-388
Walker, David, 118
Wall Street, GA. *See* Maysville, GA
Waller, Maitron (Madison Wallis), 363-364
Wallis (Wallace?), Bolin D., 183-184, 185
Walnut Hills, MS, 298-299
War of 1812, 178
Warren County, VA, 424
Warrenton, MS, 307
Warwick River, 146-147
Washaw County, TX. *See* Upshur County, TX
Washington, D.C., 122, 130, 136, 154, 157, 173, 174, 226-227, 341, 381, 423, 507
Waters, John E., 132
Watts, Morgan, 428
Wayne, Henry C., 131-132
Waynesboro, GA, 464, 465
Webster, Daniel, 26

601

Wedowee, AL, 124, 217, 219
Weems, Johnson, 492, 493
Weldon, NC, 279-280
Wells, Sallie, 44
Welsh, xv
West Point (U.S. Military Academy), 152
West Point, GA, 297, 481, 483
West, G. C., 473
West, William H,, 324
Westbrook, Sampson, 489, 490
West Virginia, state of, 117-123
Western Academy of Natural Sciences (Museum of Natural History and Science), 82
Wheeler, Joseph, Gen., 355, 356, 474
Wheeling, VA (now WV), 122
White family (related to Davids), xviii
White, Billy, 302, 408
White, H.C. (signed O. T. David's obituary), 142
White, Mr. (father of men in Manning's regiment), 211-212
White, Mrs. (mother of Robert), 196
White, Robert, (man in Manning's regiment), 196
White, Samuel S. (manufacturer of dental material), 481
White, William J., Sgt. (man in Manning's regiment), 356-357, 408
White, William P. (man in Manning's regiment), 408
Whitehead, Elridge, 283-284
Whitehead, John C., 284
Whitehead, Marcus J., 284
Whitehurst, Amanda A., 49
Whiting, W.H.C., Gen., 169
Wilcox, Cadmus M., Gen. 373-376
Wilderness, Battle of: 369-388, 393, 405, 449, 517
Williams, A.S.C., 274; *Letter:* May 7, 1863, 273
Williams, William, 225
Williamsburg, VA, 145, 149
Williamson, Adam, 262
Williamsport, MD, 336
Wills, John, Dr., Surgeon, 190, 196, 198, 289, 300
Willson, Mike, 172
Willson, neighbor, 25

Wilmington, NC, 279, 280, 446, 456, 458, 466
Wilson, Mrs., 245
Wilson, Woodrow, 453-454
Winchester, VA, 334, 336-337, 424, 425
Winder, C. S., Gen., 173-174
Winder, GA, 138, 144
Winnsboro, SC, 463
Winnsboro, TX, 482
Winters, Helen, 148
Wise, Henry A., Gov, 71
Wofford, Jake, 341
Wofford, William T., Gen., 234, 263, 264, 268, 271, 274-275, 337, 396-399, 402, 420-421, 425-429, 521
Wood County, TX, 481, 482, 484, 487
Woodstock, GA, 5, 6, 11, 12, 14, 32
World's Fair and Great International Cotton Exposition, 531
Yarborough, Caleb, 526
Yarbro (Yarbrough) (shoemaker, bootmaker), 140, 141, 180, 185,
Yarbrough, Dilmus, 529, 532
Yarbrough, James, 529
Yarbrough, Jasper, 529
Yarbrough, Nancy, x, 141, 183
Yarbrough, Neal, 529
Yorktown, VA, 120, 139, 145-146, 162, 190
Young, Bennett H., Gen., 542